THE EU CHARTER OF FUNDAMENTAL RIGHTS AS A BINDING INSTRUMENT

The entry into force of the Treaty of Lisbon in 2009 caused the EU's Charter of Fundamental Rights to be granted binding effect. This raised a host of intriguing questions. Would this transform the EU's commitment to fundamental rights? Should it transform that commitment? How, if at all, can we balance competing rights and principles? (The interaction of the social and the economic spheres offers a particular challenge.) How deeply does the EU conception of fundamental rights reach into and bind national law and practice? How deeply does it affect private parties? How much flexibility has been left to the Court in making these interpretative choices? What is the likely effect of another of the reforms achieved by the Lisbon Treaty, the commitment of the EU to accede to the ECHR? This book addresses all of these questions in the light of five years of practice under the Charter as a binding instrument.

Volume 20 Studies of the Oxford Institute of European and Comparative Law

Studies of the Oxford Institute of European and Comparative Law

Recent titles in this Series

Volume 12: Article 82 EC: Reflections on its Recent Evolution
Edited by Ariel Ezrachi

Volume 13: Prohibition of Abuse of Law: A New General Principle of EU Law?
Edited by Rita de la Feria and Stefan Vogenauer

Volume 14: Constitutional Pluralism in the European Union and Beyond
Edited by Matej Avbelj and Jan Komárek

Volume 15: The Protection of Fundamental Rights in the EU After Lisbon
Edited by Sybe de Vries, Ulf Bernitz and Stephen Weatherill

Volume 16: The Involvement of EU Law in Private Law Relationships
Edited by Dorota Leczykiewicz and Stephen Weatherill

Volume 17: Current Problems in the Protection of Human Rights: Perspectives from Germany and the UK
Edited by Katja S Ziegler and Peter M Huber

Volume 18: Legal Challenges in the Global Financial Crisis: Bail-outs, the Euro and Regulation
Edited by Wolf-Georg Ringe and Peter M Huber

Volume 19: The Unitary EU Patent System
Edited by Justine Pila and Christopher Wadlow

The EU Charter of Fundamental Rights as a Binding Instrument

Five Years Old and Growing

Edited by
Sybe de Vries
Ulf Bernitz
and
Stephen Weatherill

·HART·
PUBLISHING
OXFORD AND PORTLAND, OREGON
2018

Hart Publishing
An imprint of Bloomsbury Publishing Plc

Hart Publishing Ltd
Kemp House
Chawley Park
Cumnor Hill
Oxford OX2 9PH
UK

Bloomsbury Publishing Plc
50 Bedford Square
London
WC1B 3DP
UK

www.hartpub.co.uk
www.bloomsbury.com

Published in North America (US and Canada) by
Hart Publishing
c/o International Specialized Book Services
920 NE 58th Avenue, Suite 300
Portland, OR 97213-3786
USA

www.isbs.com

HART PUBLISHING, the Hart/Stag logo, BLOOMSBURY and the Diana logo are trademarks of Bloomsbury Publishing Plc

First published in hardback, 2015
Paperback edition, 2018

British Library Cataloguing-in-Publication Data
A catalogue record for this book is available from the British Library.

ISBN: PB: 978-1-50992-108-9
HB: 978-1-78225-825-4

Library of Congress Cataloging-in-Publication Data

The EU Charter of Fundamental Rights as a binding instrument : five years old and growing / edited by Sybe de Vries, Ulf Bernitz and Stephen Weatherill.
pages cm
Includes bibliographical references and index.
ISBN 978-1-78225-825-4 (hardcover : alk. paper) 1. Charter of Fundamental Rights of the European Union (2000 December 7) 2. Civil rights—European Union countries. I . Vries, Sybe Alexander de, 1970– editor. II . Bernitz, Ulf, editor. III. Weatherill, Stephen, 1961– editor.
KJE5132.A432E9 2015 341.4'8094–dc23
2015032033

Typeset by Compuscript Ltd, Shannon

Preface

This book is a follow-up to *The Protection of Fundamental Rights in the EU after Lisbon*, published in 2013 under the same editorial team. That 2013 volume was the product of a conference (held in Oxford in 2011): the same is true of this book. A follow-up conference under the title 'Five years legally binding EU Charter of Fundamental Rights—What is the state of play in the protection of fundamental rights in the EU?' was held in Oxford on 9 May 2014. It was organised by Sybe de Vries, Ulf Bernitz and Stephen Weatherill under the auspices of the Institute of European and Comparative Law in the Oxford University Law Faculty. At the conference, our speakers were Allan Rosas (European Court of Justice and Utrecht), Sionaidh Douglas-Scott (Oxford), Janneke Gerards (Nijmegen), Jan Komarek (LSE, London), Gunnar Thor Pétursson (Reykjavik), Ulf Bernitz (Stockholm and Oxford), Catherine Barnard (Cambridge), Jaan Paju (Stockholm), Stephen Weatherill (Oxford), Sybe de Vries (Utrecht), Peter Oliver (Brussels), Helene Andersson (Stockholm) and John Temple Lang (Trinity College Dublin).

This conference reflected on five years of life under the Charter, which reveals five years of remarkable activity. Some of the questions about the Charter's role that we addressed in our first book, published in 2013, have been answered, although in the main only in part and not always with compelling logic. Some have not been answered. And some new ones have emerged. Meanwhile, the legislative institutions of the EU have been engaged in trying to weave the Charter into their practice, while the Court too has been active. It has, for example, dealt with search engines and created an EU 'right to be forgotten' via the Charter's promise of privacy (Case C-131/12 *Google* judgment of 13 May 2014); it has annulled the data retention Directive as an unduly deep and broad interference with private life (Joined Cases C-293/12 & C-594/12 *Digital Rights Ireland* judgment of 8 April 2014); it has grappled with the notion of 'implementation' for the purposes of subjecting Member States to the reach of the Charter (Case C-206/13 *Cruciano Siragusa* judgment of 6 March 2014, Case C-198/13 *Hernández et al* judgment of 10 July 2014); and it has maintained its insistence on the 'supremacy' of EU law over national law even though the Charter seemed to subvert that (Case C-399/11 *Stefano Melloni* judgment of 26 February 2013).

The active role of the Court in applying the EU Charter in a number of cases seems to be in sharp contrast with the Court's recent Opinion on the Draft Accession Agreement concerning the EU's accession to the ECHR (Opinion 2/13). Opinion 2/13 may put into question the Court's role as human rights court and it asks whether fundamental rights are the first point on the agenda at the Court of Justice of the EU. Yet, at the same time, the approach of the CJEU to the ECHR reinforces the importance of the Charter as the document that 'enshrines the key political, social and economic rights of EU citizens and residents in EU law'.[1]

In this second book we discuss these and other issues in light of the rapid development of the Charter as arguably the very centrepiece of the EU legal order, reinforced by the growing distance between the EU and the ECHR.

Without the help and support of several people neither the conference nor the book would have become a reality. The conference was generously supported by the Wallenberg Foundation, Stockholm, for which we would like to express our gratitude. Jenny Dix helped very much in the organisation of this conference and we would like to thank her. Thom Wetzer wrote the conference report and assisted us in preparing the publication of this book for which we are very grateful. As ever, Hart Publishing have offered an exemplary service.

Sybe de Vries,
Ulf Bernitz and
Stephen Weatherill

[1] S Peers, T Hervey, J Kenner and A Ward (eds), *The EU Charter of Fundamental Rights—A Commentary* (Oxford, Hart Publishing, 2014).

Table of Contents

List of Contributors

Helene Andersson is a doctoral candidate at Stockholm University with a background in private practice. In her research, she focuses on EU competition law enforcement from a fundamental rights perspective. Alongside her research, she is a lecturer at Stockholm University, where she teaches general EU law and EU competition law. Over the years, she has published numerous articles in journals such as *Concurrences* and the *European Competition Law Review*.

Catherine Barnard MA (Cantab), LLM (EUI), PhD (Cantab) is Professor in European Union Law and Employment Law at the University of Cambridge, and Senior Tutor and Fellow of Trinity College. She specialises in EU law, employment law and discrimination law. She is author of *EU Employment Law* (4th edn, Oxford, Oxford University Press, 2012), *The Substantive Law of the EU: The Four Freedoms* (5th edn, Oxford, Oxford University Press, 2013) and is co-editor (with Steve Peers) of *European Union Law* (Oxford, Oxford University Press, 2014). She is also editor of various collections of essays, including *The Fundamentals of EU Law Revisited* (Oxford, Oxford University Press, 2007) and (with Okeoghene Odudu) *The Outer Limits of EU Law* (Oxford, Hart Publishing, 2009).

Ulf Bernitz is Professor of European Law at Stockholm University, as well as Senior Research Fellow at St Hilda's College, University of Oxford. He is also Director for the Söderberg Foundation Oxford/Stockholm Venture in European Law, based at the Institute of European and Comparative Law, University of Oxford. His research interests are in the fields of European law and private law (especially competition and marketing law, intellectual property law and consumer law). He is President for the Swedish FIDE Association for European Law.

Sionaidh Douglas-Scott is Anniversary Chair in Law and co-director at the Centre for Law and Society in a Global Context at Queen Mary, University of London. She works primarily within the field of EU and public law, human rights and legal and social theory. She is particularly interested in questions of justice and human rights in the EU and Europe more generally. She is the author of the monograph *Constitutional Law of the European Union* and her current projects include a monograph on European human rights law and a co-edited volume on the EU and human rights. She has also published a monograph, *Law after Modernity*, which explores at a more abstract level many of the issues of pluralism, justice and human rights that are also to be found in her work on the EU and, unusually for a work of legal theory, is illustrated with various images and artistic works.

Federico Fabbrini holds a PhD in Law from the European University Institute and is Associate Professor of European & International Law at iCourts (Center of Excellence on International Courts), Faculty of Law, University of Copenhagen. He is the author of *Fundamental Rights in Europe* (Oxford, Oxford University Press, 2014) and the coordinator of the Research Group on 'Constitutional Responses to Terrorism within the International Association of Constitutional Law'.

Janneke Gerards is Professor of European Law at the Faculty of Law of the Radboud University, Nijmegen, the Netherlands. Her research concentrates on fundamental rights and judicial review in the European, multilayered context. In particular, she examines legal methods of argumentation and interpretation that national and European courts (European Court of Justice, European Court of Human Rights) have developed in fundamental rights cases.

Xavier Groussot is Professor of EU Law at Lund University and Vice Dean of the Faculty of Law. He is also a guest professor at the European College of Paris (Université Paris 2, Panthéon-Assas) and at the University of Reykjavik. His fields of research are related to EU constitutional law, free movement and procedural law.

Jan Komárek is an Assistant Professor in EU law at the LSE. He studied law at the Charles University in Prague (Mgr 2001, JUDr 2002), Stockholm University (LLM 2004) and the University of Oxford (MSt 2007, DPhil 2011). He worked with the Czech Government Agent before the European Court of Justice at the Ministry of Foreign Affairs (2004–06) and was a legal secretary to the President of the Czech Constitutional Court (2009–10).

Peter Oliver was, until 2014, a Legal Advisor in the European Commission. He is a visiting professor at the Université Libre de Bruxelles and the author of over 70 publications on EU law, including *Free Movement of Goods in the European Union* (5th edn, Oxford, Hart Publishing, 2010). His forthcoming book is entitled *The Fundamental Rights of Companies—European and US Law Compared* (Oxford, Hart Publishing). He is also a barrister at Monckton Chambers.

Jaan Paju is Doctor of Laws at Stockholm University. He defended the thesis 'Suveränitetserosion?' ('Sovereignty Erosion?') on the impact of EU law on national social security models in late spring 2015. He has been the editor of the *Nordic Journal on European Law* (*Europarättslig Tidskrift*) since 1998. He is currently Research Fellow of Christ Church, University of Oxford (2015–16).

Gunnar Thor Petursson is Associate Professor at the School of Law, Reykjavik University. He graduated as a Cand juris from the Faculty of Law, University of Iceland in 1997 and with a LLM degree (1998) and Dr juris degree (2014) in European Law from the Faculty of Law, University of Lund, Sweden. He was a Deputy Director at the EFTA Surveillance Authority (1999–2004), Attorney-at-Law at Logos Legal Service (2004–05) and Head of Legal, Actavis Group (2005–08). He is also a guest lecturer at the Faculty of Law, Panthéon-Assas (Paris II), France and at the Faculty of Law, University of Lund, Sweden.

Clara Rauchegger, Mag iur Mag phil (Innsbruck), LLM (Cantab), is a PhD candidate at the University of Cambridge (Trinity Hall) and a doctoral scholar of the Austrian Academy of Sciences and the UK Arts & Humanities Research Council. Her research project examines the interaction between European and national fundamental rights from a perspective of EU and comparative constitutional law. She is also Managing Editor of the *Cambridge Journal of International and Comparative Law*. Before coming to Cambridge, she worked at the Court of Justice of the European Union, the European Parliament and the University of Innsbruck in Austria.

Allan Rosas, Dr Jur, Dr Jur hc, Dr Pol Sc hc, has been a Judge at the European Court of Justice since 2002. He is also a Senior Fellow of the University of Turku and a visiting Professor of the College of Europe and the University of Helsinki. He was a former Professor of Public Law of the University of Turku (1978–81) and Armfelt Professor of Law of the Åbo Akademi University (1981–95). Furthermore, he was a former Principal Legal Adviser at the Legal Service of the European Commission (1995–2001) and a Deputy Director-General of the said Legal Service (2001–02). His main publications concern the fields of EU law, international law, and Finnish and comparative constitutional and administrative law.

John Temple Lang has been with Cleary Gottlieb Steen & Hamilton in Brussels since 2000. He was a Director in the Competition Directorate General of the European Commission from 1988 to 2000. From 1974 to 1988, he was in the Legal Service of the European Commission. He is now Senior Visiting Research Fellow at the University of Oxford and a visiting professor at Trinity College, Dublin. He has published a book on European Community law and more than 300 articles, mostly concerned with European law.

Sybe de Vries is Professor of EU Single Market Law and Fundamental Rights and the Jean Monnet Chair at the Europa Institute of Utrecht University. In 2010, he was a visiting researcher at the Oxford Institute of European and Comparative Law. He is also the coordinator of the FP7 research project 'bEUcitizenship' on European citizenship. He is a member of the editorial boards of the *Journal for European and Economic Law* (*SEW*) and

The Netherlands Journal for Human Rights (*NTM/NJCM-Bulletin*). Since 2015, he has been an Honorary Judge in the Court of Rotterdam dealing with competition and consumer law cases.

Stephen Weatherill is Jacques Delors Professor of European Law at the University of Oxford, a Fellow of Somerville College and Deputy Director for European Law in the Oxford Law Faculty's Institute of European and Comparative Law.

Table of Cases

European Union

European Court of Human Rights

International Court of Justice

Domestic

Austria

Belgium

Bularia

Cyprus

Czech Republic

Germany

United States

Table of Legislation

International

European

EU Secondary Legislation

Regulations

Directives

Germany

Netherlands

Portugal

Romania

Spain

Sweden

United States

Introduction

Five Years Old and Growing: The EU Charter of Fundamental Rights as a Binding Instrument

SYBE DE VRIES, ULF BERNITZ AND STEPHEN WEATHERILL

I. INTRODUCTION[1]

A. Background of the Book

WHEN THE TREATY of Lisbon entered into force in 2009, it was generally agreed that the protection of fundamental rights at the EU level had reached a new and loftier summit. The respect for human rights more deeply inscribed as a foundational value of the EU, the Charter of Fundamental Rights elevated to formally binding status and the EU's intention to accede to the European Convention on Human Rights (ECHR) are all important changes that suggest that the EU entered a new stage in shaping its commitment to human rights protection. The binding effect of the Charter in particular raised a host of new and intriguing questions. Would this transform the EU's commitment to fundamental rights? Should it transform that commitment? How, if at all, can we balance competing rights and principles? The interaction of the social and the economic spheres offers a particular challenge. How deeply does the EU conception of fundamental rights reach into and bind national law and practice? How deeply does it affect private parties? How much flexibility has been left to the European Court of Justice in making these interpretative choices? What is the likely effect of another of the reforms achieved by the Lisbon Treaty: the commitment of the EU to accede to the ECHR?

Our first book, *The Protection of Fundamental Rights in the EU after Lisbon*, which was published in 2013 and was the result of a conference on the Charter held in Oxford in 2011, examines these themes. Meanwhile, the Charter's prominence today is undisputed. Article 2 of the Treaty on European Union (TEU) is foundational—'The Union is founded on the values

[1] We would like to especially thank Thom Wetzer, who as a research assistent at the Europa Institute of Utrecht University wrote the conference report and assisted us in preparing the publication of this book.

of respect for human dignity, freedom, democracy, equality, the rule of law and respect for human rights'—and the EU's institutions are busy making good this vision across the wide sweep of EU activity. As the Court boldly put it in its landmark ruling in *Fransson* in February 2013: 'The applicability of EU law entails applicability of the fundamental rights guaranteed by the Charter.' The Charter looms large over everything the EU does—and over what the Member States do too, insofar as they are 'implementing' EU law.

Some of the questions about the Charter's role that we addressed in our first book have been answered, although in the main only in part and not always with compelling logic. Some have not been answered and some new ones have emerged. Meanwhile, the legislative institutions of the EU have been engaged in trying to weave the Charter into their practice, while the Court too has been active. It has, for example, dealt with search engines and created an EU 'right to be forgotten' via the Charter's promise of privacy (Case C-131/12 *Google*, judgment of 13 May 2014); it has annulled the Data Retention Directive as an unduly deep and broad interference with private life (Joined Cases C-293/12 and C-594/12 *Digital Rights Ireland*, judgment of 8 April 2014); it has grappled with the notion of 'implementation' for the purposes of subjecting Member States to the reach of the Charter (Case C-206/13 *Cruciano Siragusa*, judgment of 6 March 2014; Case C-198/13 *Hernández et al*, judgment of 10 July 2014); and it has maintained its insistence on the 'supremacy' of EU law over national law, even though the Charter seemed to subvert that (Case C-399/11 *Stefano Melloni*, judgment of 26 February 2013).

The active role of the Court in applying the EU Charter at least in a number of cases seems to be in sharp contrast with the Court's recent Opinion on the Draft Accession Agreement concerning the EU's accession to the ECHR (Opinion 2/13), according to which the Agreement is contrary to EU law. The special and autonomous legal order that the EU has created is the running theme throughout the Opinion, which the Draft Accession Agreement, according to the Court of Justice of the European Union (CJEU), threatens to jeopardise. Opinion 2/13 may question the Court's role as a human rights court and whether fundamental rights are at the first point of the Court's agenda. Yet, at the same time, the approach of the CJEU to the ECHR reinforces the importance of the Charter as the document that 'enshrines the key political, social and economic rights of EU citizens and residents in EU law'.[2]

In this second book we discuss these and other issues in the light of the rapid development of the Charter as arguably the very centrepiece of the EU legal order, reinforced by the growing distance between the EU and the ECHR.

[2] S Peers, T Hervey, J Kenner and A Ward (eds), *The EU Charter of Fundamental Rights—A Commentary* (Oxford, Hart Publishing, 2014).

This book is the result of a follow-up conference held in Oxford in May 2014 under the auspices of the Institute of European and Comparative Law and reflects on five years of life under the Charter—five years of remarkable activity.

B. The Structure of the Book

The book consists of three parts. First, the constitutional dimension, in particular the relationship between the EU Charter, the ECHR and national constitutions, is addressed. Second, the scope of application of EU fundamental rights is considered. Third, the safeguarding of fundamental rights in Europe's internal market is covered.

In chapter one, Allan Rosas makes a number of observations on the trends in the case law of the ECJ since the Charter acquired binding force. He touches upon the important role that the Charter has gained in the Court's case law, the application of other sources of fundamental rights than the Charter, the application of the Charter at the national level and the relationship between the Charter and national constitutions. According to Rosas, the Court's case law has contributed to the construction of the constitutional structure of the EU. Furthermore, the status of the Charter as a binding part of primary EU law further underlines the existence of the EU's constitutional and 'federative' order.

In chapter two, Sionaidh Douglas-Scott turns to the relationship between the EU and the ECHR. She extensively reflects on the Court's Opinion on the Draft Accession Agreement, in which the CJEU holds that the agreement is contrary to EU law. She also argues that Opinion 2/13 is a 'robust declaration of the autonomy of EU law'. Furthermore, she observes that the Charter rather than the ECHR has become, at least in an increasing number of cases, the main document of reference to human rights for the ECJ.

In chapter three, Janneke Gerards more specifically focuses on the roles of the CJEU, the European Court of Human Rights (ECtHR) and the national courts in deciding on fundamental rights in Europe and how these roles can be coordinated. These courts seem equally capable of dealing with fundamental rights. Although courts have limited possibilities in choosing whether to address certain fundamental rights issues or not, they have a choice, which makes it possible to determine which of the courts should take the lead in deciding on fundamental rights issues. She suggests to use the specific tasks or functions of the courts—the 'raison d'etre'—as a criterion to guide the courts in choosing which fundamental rights cases they should take up.

Chapter four bears the intriguing title 'Why National Courts Should Not Embrace EU Fundamental Rights'. In this chapter Jan Komárek looks at the role of the national constitutional courts in protecting fundamental rights and comes to the conclusion that they should not decide on EU fundamental rights. The arguments he brings forward relate to the theory of law and democracy, the separation of constitutional and ordinary adjudication, and the fundamental difference between national and EU fundamental rights.

Chapter five, the last chapter of Part I, then addresses the interplay between the Charter and the national constitutions after the cases of *Åkeberg Fransson* and *Melloni*. In this chapter Clara Rauchegger argues that there are two major challenges for the protection of fundamental rights in Europe, which is first to ensure that the various fundamental rights catalogues interact in a way that guarantees a complete and coherent system of protection and, second, that the marginalisation of the national fundamental rights by the Charter should be avoided. Among other things, she calls for a greater role for Article 4(2) TEU to safeguard the national constitutional identity of the Member States and a constructive dialogue between the CJEU and the national constitutional courts.

Part II of this book focuses on the scope of application of fundamental rights, both from a more general perspective (in relation to Member States) and from a specific perspective (in relation to fundamental social rights). Chapter six, the first chapter in this part, by Xavier Groussot and Gunnar Thor Petursson addresses the question whether fundamental rights subsequent to the EU Charter are having an impact on the scope and nature of EU law and thus are bringing about a new constitutional framework. Their chapter focuses on Article 52(1) of the Charter and whether it constitutes a new analytical framework for assessing both EU and national measures in the light of the Charter. Furthermore, they look at the scope of application of the Charter and at an increasing number of cases where the Charter is not or hardly mentioned, but, according to them, should be mentioned. All these questions relate to an emerging constitutional framework in EU law.

Chapter seven specifically focuses on the implications of the *Åkerberg Fransson* case in Sweden and beyond. In this chapter Ulf Bernitz explains how the Court took a relatively broad, if not yet precisely defined, approach to the circumstances in which the Charter exercises control over national practices. He also reveals that the Court's apparent concern in *Åkerberg Fransson* to avoid connecting its interpretation of the Charter with the relevant case law of the ECtHR is not in reality the full story. In fact, Charter rules reinforce ECHR rules where EU law is in play. This is likely to prove a dynamic process. In the end, Bernitz also draws attention to the subsequent national application of the judgment and highlights the far-reaching effects on the case law of the Swedish Supreme Court.

In chapter eight, Catherine Barnard turns to the scope of application of the Charter with regard to social rights. The captivating title of the chapter, 'The Silence of the Charter', relates to three contrasting situations in the case law of the CJEU, which Barnard further elaborates upon in her chapter and which reveal the ambivalent attitude of the CJEU towards social rights.

She distinguishes between the situations where the CJEU does not but should have dealt with the Charter, situations where it does not and should not have dealt with the Charter and finally situations where it does but should not have dealt with the Charter. She refers to these situations as a vow of silence, a welcome silence and a plea for silence.

In chapter nine, the last chapter that relates to the scope of the Charter, Jaan Paju focuses on national social security systems and how the EU Charter challenges prevailing notions of territorial rights and solidarity. He argues that it is not so much the Charter in itself that informs national social security systems, but rather the internal market through which competences at the EU level are gradually expanded. In addition, it is questionable whether the Charter will lead to a substantial expansion of a right to social security.

The third and last part of this book deals with the relationship between fundamental rights and the EU single market. Various themes are discussed, such as the interaction between free movement and fundamental rights, and competition and fundamental rights. But also the interaction between EU (internal market) legislation and fundamental rights is analysed. Chapter ten, the first chapter in this part, by Stephen Weatherill is on 'protecting the internal market from fundamental rights'. Weatherill claims that the Charter's softening effects on internal market law are very limited, as internal market law itself has already long provided for sufficient safeguards for the protection of public interests and national values. He furthermore submits that the Charter should not be used to upset the existing balance between the internal market and public interests; so, for example, he opposes the use of the economic rights of the Charter as a means to strengthen the market dimension at the cost of social protection.

In chapter eleven, Sybe de Vries further embroiders on the interaction between free movement and the Charter. To provide for a deeper understanding of this relationship, two tracks are followed: first, how fundamental rights may affect the internal market freedoms in the context of free movement and EU legislation; and, second, how the internal market freedoms may affect fundamental rights in the context of free movement and EU legislation. The discussion in this chapter is first approached from a more general angle and then turns to the fields of data protection and privacy, which offer an interesting example of how fundamental rights may become entangled with EU single market law, as a case study.

In chapter twelve, Federico Fabbrini then focuses on the right to data privacy and how the CJEU in this field has taken up the role as a human rights court. Fabbrini shows how in the field of data privacy in particular, the Charter has contributed to the constitutionalisation of the CJEU. But there are also challenges for the Court, which specifically relate to the relationship between the right to data privacy and other fundamental rights like the freedom of speech, the right to information or the freedom to conduct a business.

Whereas the foregoing chapter more generally discusses data privacy and the role of the CJEU, chapter thirteen by Peter Oliver analyses the rights of economic actors in the fields of privacy and data protection. It is generally assumed that there exists an ambivalent relationship between fundamental rights and companies: companies tend to enjoy more limited fundamental rights than natural persons or non-profit entities. Meanwhile, there is a wealth of case law on the fundamental rights of economic actors, also in the fields of privacy and data protection. This case law clarifies the extent to which natural persons acting in a professional or economic capacity and legal persons enjoy more or limited protection under the rights to privacy and data protection as enshrined in Articles 7 and 8 of the Charter.

The book is concluded by two chapters on fundamental rights and competition law written by Helene Andersson and John Temple Lang, respectively. In chapter fourteen, Andersson focuses on the European Commission's practices in relation to dawn raids and the judicial review of such practices. She analyses whether the procedural safeguards surrounding the Commission's dawn raid procedures meet the Charter standards. There are an increasing number of competition cases where the Charter has been applied, particularly in relation to Article 7 on the right to privacy and Article 47 on the right to effective judicial protection. Andersson is rather critical as the EU competition system in place today does not even seem to meet the minimum standard of the ECHR, which means that a revision is required in order for the system to meet the Charter standards.

In chapter fifteen, John Temple Lang then addresses the question of how the Charter must be applied in EU state aid cases. The fact that the rights of companies and of interested parties in the field of EU state aid procedure are so limited means that there cannot be an effective remedy in the light of the Charter and particularly Article 47. Although the state aid procedure has been reformed, a process that according to Temple Lang has taken too long a time, there are still many issues that, from the perspective of the Charter, require close attention.

C. Fundamental Rights *Still* at the Heart of EU Law?

In the introduction of our first book, it was written that EU fundamental rights protection does not end with this book. The first book was just the beginning.

In this book, the quest for the position and role of fundamental rights in the EU's constitutional fabric continues. Again, the authors come up with interesting ideas about how EU law can more fully embrace fundamental rights and again they raise new and captivating questions relating to the three main themes of the book.

After five years of a legally binding Charter more well-founded conclusions can be drawn. For instance, in at least quite a few cases, the Charter has become the main document of reference for EU fundamental rights protection; it has not been used so far to undermine the existing division of competences between the EU and the Member States, and the Court, as shown by Opinion 2/13, is still very (too?) much concerned with the EU's special and autonomous legal order, which should be preserved at all costs and must not be undermined by the EU acceding to the ECHR without taking adequate account of the need to preserve the special characteristics of the EU legal order.

The EU's constitutional framework still has its limits. The five years of binding EU Charter has not changed that. But human rights feature more and more prominently in the constitutional self-understanding of the EU. For a number of fundamental rights, we see that the Court increasingly takes up the role of a human rights court, particularly in the fields of privacy and data protection. For other fundamental rights, most notably social rights, we see that the Court takes a much more restrained approach, hampered by the limited constitutional framework—the limited competences of the EU in this field—and the politically sensitive nature of social policy.

Opinion 2/13 implies that the claim of the EU as a human rights organisation may be more untenable than ever before,[3] but it makes clear that the EU is now thrown back to its own human rights agenda, which will only strengthen the already dominant role of the EU Charter. The story of the Charter that began five years ago has certainly not come to an end …

[3] P Craig and G de Búrca (eds), *The Evolution of EU Law* (2nd edn, Oxford, Oxford University Press, 2011) 495. See also S Peers, 'The EU's Acession to the ECHR: The Dream Becomes a Nightmare' (2015) 16 *German Law Journal* 213.

Part I

The Constitutional Dimension of Fundamental Rights

1

Five Years of Charter Case Law: Some Observations

ALLAN ROSAS

I. FROM GENERAL PRINCIPLES OF EU LAW TO THE CHARTER

BEGINNING WITH *STAUDER*, *Internationale Handelsgesellschaft* and *Nold*,[1] the European Court of Justice (ECJ) relied in its fundamental rights case law on a combination of two types of sources: 1) the 'general principles of Community law' as a directly binding source of law; and 2) some secondary sources as 'guidelines' or 'sources of inspiration'. To use the *Nold* formula, the latter consisted of the constitutional traditions common to the Member States as well as international human rights treaties 'on which the Member States have collaborated or of which they are signatories'. Gradually, the focus shifted away from the constitutional traditions common to the Member States towards the use of international human rights instruments and, more specifically since *Rutili*,[2] a stronger reliance on the European Convention on Human Rights (ECHR), which was given 'special relevance'.[3]

The reasons for this emphasis on the ECHR are not difficult to gather. First of all, it is a European instrument to which, since 1974, all EU Member States were Contracting Parties.[4] Second, it is a well-known whilst not too cumbersome instrument, distilling in one single document, as supplemented by the Protocols, most of the human rights considered as essential at least from a European perspective.

[1] Case 29/69 *Stauder* EU:C:1969:57; Case 11/70 *Internationale Handelsgesellschaft* EU:C:1970:114; Case 4/73 *Nold* EU:C: EU:C:1974:51.

[2] Case 36/75 *Rutili* EU:C:1975:137.

[3] Cases 46/87 and 227/88 *Hoechst* EU:C:1989:337. On these developments, see, eg, A Rosas, 'Fundamental Rights in the Luxembourg and Strasbourg Courts' in C Baudenbacher et al (eds), *The EFTA Court: Ten Years On* (Oxford, Hart Publishing, 2005) 163; A Rosas and L Armati, *EU Constitutional Law: An Introduction* (2nd revised edn, Oxford, Hart Publishing, 2012) 160 et seq.

[4] In *Rutili* (n 2) [32], the Court—in a judgment given after France had adhered to the ECHR—observed that the Convention had now been 'ratified by all the Member States'.

On the other hand, the efforts to make the EU itself becoming a Contracting Party to the Convention failed and in 1996 the ECJ held that, as Community law stood at the time, the Community lacked competence to accede.[5] At the same time, the EU legal order became increasingly to be seen as a *constitutional* order, which required its own bill of rights, a set of *fundamental* rights to be articulated by the EU itself rather than being expressed in an international instrument drawn up in the framework of an international organisation (by the Council of Europe with respect to the ECHR) comprising third states as well.

The constitutional character of the endeavour was further underlined by the composition and name of the body that prepared the draft text for the EU Charter. The Convention that produced the first draft leading to the 'solemn proclamation', on 7 December 2000, of the Charter as a formally non-binding instrument[6] was composed of representatives of not only the governments of Member States but also the European Parliament, national parliaments and the Commission. This format was also followed with respect to the European Convention which prepared the abortive Treaty establishing a Constitution for Europe.[7] While this Treaty, which was signed but never entered into force, incorporated the Charter as its Part II, the amendments to the Treaty on European Union (TEU) brought about by the Lisbon Treaty implied a comparable result as Article 6(1) TEU now refers to the Charter ('as adapted at Strasbourg, on 12 December 2007') and declares it to have 'the same legal value as the Treaties'.[8]

In view of this background, it should have come as no surprise that the ECJ, confronted with a new constitutional and legal reality (Article 6(1) TEU and the Charter itself, including its drafting history), took the 2007 version of the Charter and the entry into force of the Treaty of Lisbon, quite seriously and began to take the Charter as a starting point when approaching fundamental rights issues raised before it. It is to this general trend that I will now turn. Subsequently, I will make some observations on more specific problem areas which have been addressed in ECJ case law, notably the application of other sources than the Charter in the fundamental rights case law of the Court, the application of the Charter at the national level and the relationship between the Charter and national constitutions.

[5] Opinion 2/94 *Accession to the European Convention for the Protection of Human Rights and Fundamental Freedoms* EU:C:1996:140.

[6] [2000] OJ C364/1.

[7] Draft Treaty establishing a Constitution for Europe, adopted by consensus by the European Convention on 13 June and 10 July 2003 (Luxembourg, Office for Official Publications of the European Communities, 2003).

[8] On the preparatory work for the Charter, see, eg, G de Búrca, 'The Drafting of the European Union Charter of Fundamental Rights' (2001) 26(2) *European Law Review* 126.

II. THE CHARTER IN ECJ CASE LAW: GENERAL CONSIDERATIONS

Whilst Article 6 TEU even in its post-Lisbon version continues to refer to the general principles of EU law as a source of fundamental rights (paragraph 3), it is the Charter, as put into effect by the first paragraph of Article 6, that has become the main point of reference in post-Lisbon case law. It is true that first the General Court and the Advocates General of the ECJ and then, since June 2006, the ECJ itself[9] began to refer to the Charter as a soft law instrument well before it became a binding part of EU primary law.[10] Such references were rather sporadic, however, and in most cases simply served to back up a reasoning which was based primarily on other sources. In the post-Lisbon era, the ECJ has cited the Charter in more than 200 judgments or orders.[11] This estimation does not include the case law of the General Court or that of the EU Civil Service Tribunal.

That said, the role and importance that the Charter plays in a given case may vary to a great deal. The Charter, or fundamental rights more generally, are often invoked as one of many arguments and this may, in principle, occur across the wholespectrum of EU law. In some cases, fundamental rights become *the* issue, in some others, an interpretation of a Charter provision is a relevant although perhaps not predominant element in a judgment, while in yet others, a Charter provision is referred to simply to corroborate a reasoning mainly centred elsewhere or even in a purely descriptive manner. As will be developed in a separate subsection below, there is also a string of cases where the Court has held that the Charter is *not* applicable because of a missing link between it and EU law more generally.

The most striking category of the cases decided so far consists of the cases in which the Court has invalidated an EU legislative act as being in violation of one or more provisions of the Charter. In *Schecke*, several provisions of EU legislation relating to the financing of the common agricultural policy were invalidated as being contrary to Articles 7 (respect for private and family life) and 8 (protection of personal data) of the Charter to the extent that they imposed an obligation to publish personal data relating to beneficiaries without drawing a distinction between relevant criteria concerning the nature of aid received.[12] In *Test-Achats*, the Court struck down a provision of a Directive relating to the principle of equal treatment between men and

[9] Case C-540/03 *Parliament v Council* EU:C:2006:429 [38].

[10] A Rosas and H Kaila, 'L'application de la charte des droits fondamentaux de l'Union européenne par la Cour de justice: Un premier bilan' (2011) XVI(1) *Il diritto dell'Unione europea* 1 at 5–8.

[11] E Levits, 'The Court's Evolving Case Law on the Charter of Fundamental Rights: Some Aspects of the Application of the Charter', paper presented for the Court's visit to London on 6 October 2014 (unpublished) 1.

[12] Cases C-92/09 and C-93/09 *Volker and Markus Schecke* and *Eifert* EU:C:2010:662.

women as being incompatible with Articles 21 (non-discrimination) and 23 (equality between women and men).[13] The provision which was held to be invalid enabled Member States to maintain without temporal limitation an exemption from the rule of unisex insurance premiums and benefits provided for by the same Directive. And, most importantly, in *Digital Rights Ireland*, the entirety of Directive 2006/24 on data retention relating to the fight against serious crime was found to be invalid in light of Articles 7, 8 and 52(1) (the latter concerning limitations on the exercise of rights).[14]

III. THE USE OF SOURCES OTHER THAN THE CHARTER

As the Charter has become the main focus of proceedings and judgments, the use of other human rights or fundamental rights sources has become less frequent, at least from a relative perspective.[15] However, the ECHR still enjoys 'special relevance'. Whilst the ECHR 'does not constitute, as long as the European Union has not acceded to it, a legal instrument which has been formally incorporated into [EU] law',[16] Article 52(3) of the Charter establishes a close link between the ECHR and the Charter in providing that Charter rights which 'correspond to' rights guaranteed by the Convention should be given the same meaning and scope as the relevant Convention rights. The Explanations relating to the Charter, which according to Article 6(1) TEU shall be taken into account ('with due regard') in the interpretation of the Charter,[17] tell us that the meaning and scope of the relevant ECHR rights are to be determined not only by the text of the Convention but also by the case law of the European Court of Human Rights and by the Court of Justice of the European Union.[18] The ECHR is also mentioned in the Preamble to the Charter and in Article 6(3) TEU, which in reaffirming

[13] Case C-236/09 *Association belge des Consommateurs Test-Achats* EU:C-2011:100; Council Directive 2004/113/EC of 13 December 2004 implementing the principle of equal treatment between men and women in the access to and supply of goods and services [2004] OJ L373/37.

[14] Cases C-293/12 and C-594/12 *Digital Rights Ireland* and *Seitlinger* EU:C.2014:238; Directive 2006/24/EC of the European Parliament and of the Council of 15 March 2006 on the retention of data generated or processed in connection with the provision of publicly available electronic communications services or of public communications networks and amending Directive 2002/58/EC [2006] OJ L105/54.

[15] See also A Rosas, 'The Charter and Universal Human Rights Instruments' in S Peers et al (eds), *The EU Charter of Fundamental Rights: A Commentary* (Oxford, Hart Publishing, 2014) 1685 at 1697–701.

[16] Case C-617/10 *Åkerberg Fransson* EU:C:2013:105 [44].

[17] See also Art 52(7) of the Charter.

[18] The text of the Explanations has been published in [2007] OJ C303/17. They were prepared under the authority of the Praesidiums of the two Conventions involved in the drafting of the Charter (see at nn 6–7 above).

the relevance of the general principles of EU law for EU fundamental rights refers to the constitutional traditions common to the Member States as well as the ECHR.

The case law of the ECJ thus continues to cite both provisions of the ECHR and Strasbourg case law.[19] It may be that at least in a relative sense, this happens less frequently than was the case before the entry into force of the post-Lisbon Charter. It is my impression that the way in which the case is argued before the Court plays an important role in this regard: if the parties are invoking the Charter only and there are no particular grounds for considering that an envisaged interpretation of a Charter right would fall short of the minimum arguably required by the ECHR, the Court's decision will probably be based on the Charter alone. On the other hand, in some cases, the relationship between the Charter and the ECHR has become an issue and some judgments have also made explicit reference to Article 52(3).[20] Many judgments cite ECHR provisions, usually combined with references to Strasbourg case law as well, without specifically mentioning Article 52(3) of the Charter.[21]

Before the entry into force of the post-Lisbon Charter, the ECJ, whilst giving pride of place to the ECHR, referred now and then to international human rights instruments other than the ECHR and sometimes also to the constitutional traditions common to the Member States in support of reliance on a fundamental right as a general principle of Community law.[22] After 2009, such references have become quite rare.[23] A certain exception is provided for by the Geneva Convention relating to the Status of Refugees of 1951, which has been cited more often, no doubt due to the fact that the need to respect this Convention is brought out in Article 78(1) of the Treaty on the Functioning of the European Union (TFEU), Article 18 of the Charter and in the EU legislation concerning asylum seekers and refugees.[24]

[19] See Commentary on Art 52(3) prepared by S Peers in Peers et al (n 15) 1490–503.

[20] Judgments citing Art 52(3) include Case C-400/10 PPU *McBee* EU:C.2010:582 [53]; *Schecke* (n 12) [51]; Case C-279/09 *DEB* EU:C:2010:777 [35]. The judgment in *DEB* at [32] and [35] also refers to the Explanations relating to the Charter (n 18 above). See also Peers et al (n 15) 1493–98.

[21] See, eg, Cases C-411/10 and C-493/11 *NS* and *ME and others* EU:C:2011:865 [88]–[90], [111]–[112]; *Digital Rights Ireland* (n 14) [35], [54] and [55].

[22] A Rosas, 'The European Union and International Human Rights Instruments' in V Kronenberger (ed), *The European Union and the International Legal Order: Discord or Harmony* (The Hague, Asser Press, 2001) 53; Rosas (n 15) 1691–94.

[23] See Case C-271/08 *Commission v Germany* EU:C:2010:426 [37] (the European Social Charter); Case C-73/08 *Bressol and others* EU:C:2010:181 [83]–[88] (International Covenant on Economic, Social and Cultural Rights). Article 6(3) TEU relating to fundamental rights as general principles of EU law does not seem to have been cited in the post-Lisbon case law.

[24] Rosas (n 15) 1698, note 69, with references to case law.

IV. WHICH RIGHTS HAVE BEEN AT ISSUE?

Some words should be said about the main tendencies to which parts of the Charter have been at the forefront of during the close to five years of post-Lisbon Charter case law. In this respect, it is evident that most of this case law concerns what is often referred to as civil and political rights rather than the provisions of the Charter relating to so-called economic, social and cultural rights. However, it should be added that the distinction between these categories of rights is far from neat, as illustrated by the principle of equality, the prohibition of discrimination and the principle of cultural, religious and linguistic diversity (see Articles 20–23 of the Charter).[25] It is perhaps more pertinent to compare the six substantive Titles of the Charter.[26] In that respect, Title VI on Justice, and its Article 47 on the right to an effective remedy and to a fair trial in particular, stand out as the most frequently cited substantive part of the Charter.[27] Rights of an economic and social nature appear less frequently in the arguments presented by parties and interested persons or in the judgments.[28]

In this context, it should also be mentioned that the ECJ is often faced with the invocation of not one but two or more fundamental rights guaranteed under the Charter, or such a fundamental right and one of the economic freedoms enshrined in the TFEU, or a fundamental right and a general principle of EU law which is not a fundamental right in the strict sense.[29] In these cases, it falls to the Court to establish a fair balance between the different rights and principles in question. The *Schecke* judgment referred to above is a case in point.[30]

[25] On the relativity of the difference between these two main categories of human rights, see, eg, A Eide, C Krause and A Rosas (eds), *Economic, Social and Cultural Rights: A Textbook* (2nd revised edn, Dordrecht, Martinus Nijhoff Publishers, 2001).

[26] Title I: Dignity, Title II Freedoms, Title III: Equality, Title IV: Solidarity, Title V: Citizens' Rights and Title VI: Justice.

[27] A survey conducted by the author in August 2013 (for the purposes of a public presentation) gave 58 ECJ, 45 General Court and 12 Civil Service Tribunal judgments or orders citing Article 47. In July 2015, it can thus be estimated that the overall number of such judgments and orders is well beyond 150.

[28] To mention a few examples, in Cases C-159/10 and C-160/10 *Fuchs and Köhler* EU:C:2011:508 [62] and Case C-141/11 *Hörnfelt* EU:C:2012:421 [37], the Court observed that the prohibition of discrimination on grounds of age should be read in the light of Art 15(1) of the Charter, which provides for the right to engage in work. Article 31(2) on paid annual leave has been cited in some judgments, eg, Case C-78/2011 *Anged* EU:C:2012:372 [17]; Case C-579/12 RX-II *Commission v Strack* EU:C:2013:570 [36], [40], [45]–[46], [52], [58]. For an example citing Art 34 on social security and social assistance, see Case C-571/10 *Kamberaj* EU:C:2012:233 [92]. See also N Jääskinen, 'Fundamental Social Rights in the Charter—Are They Rights? Are They Fundamental?' in Peers et al (n 15) 1703, and on Arts 15, 31 and 34 of the Charter, respectively, ibid 423–35, 833–68, 927–49.

[29] See, eg, A Rosas, 'Balancing Fundamental Rights in EU Law' (2013–14) 16 *Cambridge Yearbook of European Legal Studies*, forthcoming.

[30] *Schecke* (n 12).

V. THE APPLICABILITY OF THE CHARTER AT THE NATIONAL LEVEL

Among the general provisions governing the interpretation and application of the Charter contained in Title VII, the most commonly cited provision is without doubt Article 51, which relates to the Charter's field of application. While the applicability of the Charter at the EU level (the functioning of the EU institutions and other bodies) does not pose any particular problem, the applicability of the Charter in the Member States has become a hotly debated issue. According to Article 51(1), the provisions of the Charter are addressed 'to the Member States only when they are implementing Union law'. Perhaps the main difficulty with this provision has been the interpretation of the word 'implementing', and the relation between this notion and other notions used in the ECJ' case law, such as the 'scope' or 'field' of application of EU law.

It is not possible here to do justice to the fairly extensive case law and legal doctrine that already exists on this subject.[31] The conclusions to be drawn from the post-Lisbon case law of the ECJ, including its by now well-known judgment in *Åkerberg Fransson*,[32] can be summarised as follows:

- A provision of the Charter can never be applied on a stand-alone basis; its applicability presupposes the existence of at least one relevant rule of EU law other than a Charter provision.[33]
- Article 51 has not brought about any noticeable change to the previous case law of the ECJ.[34]
- Thus, 'implementing' and 'scope of application' mean essentially the same thing.[35]
- 'Implementation' includes not only the interpretation but also the application of an EU legal norm other than a provision of the Charter.[36]
- There can be no gap in fundamental rights protection depending on whether the applicability of the Charter is determined at the EU or the national level.[37]

[31] See, eg, H Kaila, 'The Scope of Application of the Charter of Fundamental Rights' in P Cardonnel, A Rosas and N Wahl (eds), *The Constitutionalisation of the EU Judicial System* (Oxford, Hart Publishing, 2012) 291; A Rosas, 'The Applicability of the EU Charter of Fundamental Rights at National Level' (2013) 13 *European Yearbook on Human Rights* 97; A Ward, 'Article 51' in Peers et al (n 15) 1413.

[32] Case C-617/10 *Åkerberg Fransson* EU:C:2013:105.

[33] See, eg, Case 265/13 *Torralbo Marcos* EU:C:2014:187 [33]; Rosas (n 31) 105.

[34] *Åkerberg Fransson* (n 32) [18]–[19].

[35] See, ibid [20], where it is observed that the Explanations to the Charter (n 18) refer not only to the implementation of EU law but also to situations where the Member States 'act in the scope of Union law'.

[36] The application, without interpretation in the strict sense of the word, of a rule of EU law may be relevant with respect to regulations; in particular, see Joined Cases C-411/10 and C-493/10 *NS and ME* EU:C:2011:865 [64]–[69]. Interpretation here refers to situations of the validity of an EU norm as well.

[37] *Åkerberg Fransson* (n 32) [21]: 'situations cannot exist which are covered ... by European Union law without those fundamental rights being applicable. The applicability of European Union law entails applicability of the fundamental rights guaranteed by the Charter'.

— The determination of the applicability of an EU norm other than a provision of the Charter should take place *in concreto* rather *in abstracto*, considering the relevance of the norm for the litigation at hand.[38]

There are, in fact, tens of judgments or orders of the ECJ in which the Court has held that it lacks competence to answer a question put by a national court as the situation fell outside the scope of application of EU law.[39] Whilst this already by now fairly extensive case law contributes to a clarification of the meaning of Article 51, there is no denying that there is a certain grey area between applicability and non-applicability and that, in view of the often complex and multifarious nature of EU law, difficult problems of delimitation may present themselves in the future as well.

VI. THE CHARTER AND NATIONAL CONSTITUTIONS

As part of EU binding primary law, the Charter, of course, has primacy over the law of Member States.[40] The principle of primacy means that EU law, to cite the seminal judgment in *Costa v Enel*,[41] 'cannot be overridden by domestic legal provisions, however framed'. On the other hand, this promacy may apply only in situations covered by EU law and does not, in any case, require the setting aside of provisions of national law outside the realm of EU law.

The principle of primacy also applies to the relationship between EU law, including the Charter, and the national constitution.[42] That said, the question has arisen as to whether there is something in the Charter itself which could change the situation. In *Melloni*, the Spanish Constitutional Court asked, inter alia, if it could afford rights guaranteed under the Charter 'a greater level of protection than that deriving from European Union law,

[38] In many judgments or orders in which the Court has concluded that it lacks competence to answer questions on the interpretation of Charter provisions, it is observed that the order of reference submitted by the national court does not permit the ECJ to conclude that the legal situation at issue in the main proceedings comes within the scope of EU law. See, eg, *Torralbo Marcos* (n 33) [38]; Case C-483/12 *Pelckmans Turnhaut* EU:C:2014:304 [22]; and Rosas (n 31) 108.

[39] Most of the decisions are reasoned orders which do not exist in other languages than French (the Court's working language) and the language of procedure. Of other judgments than those already referred to above, mention may be made of Case C-40/11 *Iida* EU:C:2012:691; and Case C-206/13 *Siragusa* EU:C:2014:126.

[40] See, eg, Rosas and Armati (n 3) 66–71; and Declaration No 17 concerning primacy, annexed to the Final Act of the Intergovernmental Conference which adopted the Treaty of Lisbon, signed on 13 December 2007.

[41] Case 6/64 *Costa v ENEL* EU:C:1964:66. See also Case 106/77 *Simmenthal* EU:C:1978:49 [17].

[42] See, eg, *Internationale Handelsgesellschaft* (n 1) [3]; Case C-409/06 *Winner Wetten* EU:C:2010:503 [60]–[61]; and Rosas and Armati (n 3) 68.

in order to avoid an interpretation which restricts or adversely affects a fundamental right recognized by the [Spanish] constitution' (right of review of a conviction *in absentia*), even in a situation where affording that greater level of protection would run counter to a secondary act of EU law (in this case, the Council Framework Decision on the European arrest warrant).[43,44] The Spanish Court cited in this regard Article 53 of the Charter, 'interpreted schematically in conjunction with the rights recognized under Articles 47 and 48 of the Charter'. Article 53 provides that nothing in the Charter 'shall be interpreted as restricting or adversely affecting human rights and fundamental freedoms as recognized, in their respective fields of application ... by the Member States' constitutions'.

The ECJ first ruled that the Framework Decision precluded the executing judicial authorities from making the execution of a European arrest warrant conditional upon the conviction rendered *in absentia* being open to review in the issuing Member State (in this case Italy) and then held that the Framework Decision was in this regard compatible with Articles 47 and 48 of the Charter. Under these circumstances, Article 53 of the Charter did not give a Member State a right to disapply EU legal rules that are in compliance with the Charter. By virtue of the principle of primacy, 'which is an essential feature of the EU legal order', rules of national law, 'even of a constitutional order, cannot be allowed to undermine the effectiveness of EU law on the territory of that State'.

Article 53 would come into play, that is, Member States could apply national constitutional standards only in situations where 'the level of protection provided for by the Charter, as interpreted by the Court, and the primacy, unity and effectiveness of EU law are not thereby compromised'.[45] The Court added that allowing a Member State to have its own constitutional standards prevail over the Framework Decision would 'cast doubt on the uniformity of the standard of protection of fundamental rights as defined in that framework decision' and 'would undermine the principles of mutual trust and recognition which that decision purports to uphold and would therefore compromise the efficacy of that framework decision'.[46]

The *Melloni* judgment should be seen in the broader context of the status and role of the national constitutions in general. Since *Internationale Handelsgesellschaft*, it has been clear that EU law, and EU fundamental rights in particular, whilst drawing upon national constitutions, does not admit the direct applicability in EU law of a given national constitution and does

[43] Council Framework Decision 2002/584/JHA of 13 June 2002 on the European arrest warrant and the surrender procedures between Member States [2002] OJ L190/1, as amended by Council Framework Decision 2009/299/JHA of 26 February 2009 [2009] OJ L81/24.

[44] Case C-399/11 *Melloni* EU:C:2013:107 [26].

[45] ibid [58]–[60]. See also *Åkerberg Fransson* (n 32) [29].

[46] *Melloni* (n 44) [63].

not permit the application at the national level of the national constitution which would run counter to the provisions of EU law and the principle of primacy.[47] That is also why both the case law of the ECJ as well as Article 6(3) TEU and Article 52(4) of the Charter refer to the 'constitutional traditions common to the Member States' instead of referring to their constitutions as such. To be sure, Article 4 (2) TEU instructs the EU to respect the national identities of the Member States 'inherent in their fundamental structures, political and constitutional, inclusive of regional and local self-government', and Article 52(4) of the Charter provides that insofar as the Charter recognises fundamental rights as they result from the constitutional traditions common to the Member States, 'those rights shall be interpreted in harmony with those traditions'.

However, these provisions, whilst laying down a general obligation for the EU to respect the constitutional identities of Member States and to avoid discrepancies between interpretations of Charter provisions and the constitutional traditions common to the Member States, stop short of requiring the direct application of national constitutions in EU law or allowing for national constitutional provisions to trump the application of conflicting provisions of EU law (apart from a situation where an EU legal act would be held invalid to the extent that it does not respect the Member States' national identity).[48]

According to late Advocate General Mancini, writing in 1989, 'reading an unwritten bill of rights into Community law is indeed the most striking contribution the Court has made to the development of a constitution for Europe'.[49] Be that as it may, it is obvious that the Court's case law has contributed to the construction of a constitutional edifice for the EU. The status of the post-Lisbon Charter as a binding part of EU primary law and the implications of the Charter for the national constitutional orders of the Member States can only serve to further underline the existence of an EU constitutional and 'federative' order.[50] There is nothing in the five years of ECJ case law that we can already witness today that would cast into doubt that conclusion.

[47] See A Rosas, 'The European Court of Justice and Fundamental Rights: Yet Another Case of Judicial Activism?' in C Baudenbacher and H Bull (eds), *European Integration through Interaction of Legal Regimes* (Oslo, Universitetsforlaget, 2007) 34 at 37, 43–44.

[48] In Case C-156/13 *Digibet* EU:C:2014:1756 [34], the Court, as part of its reasoning for accepting, in principle, that gambling legislation may, at least temporarily, vary from one German *Land* to another, observed that 'the division of competences between the German *Länder* cannot be called into question, since it benefits from the protection conferred by Article 4(2) TEU, according to which the Union must respect national identities, inherent in their fundamental structures, political and constitutional, including regional and local self-government'.

[49] F Mancini, 'The Making of a Constitution for Europe' (1989) 26 *Common Market Law Review* 595 at 611.

[50] Rosas and Armati (n 3) 1–19.

2

The Relationship Between the EU and the ECHR Five Years on from the Treaty of Lisbon

SIONAIDH DOUGLAS-SCOTT

ADVOCATE GENERAL (AG) Cruz Villalon has described the current protection of human rights in Europe as 'a crowded house'.[1] Although the EU may have other more pressing problems, there is some agreement that the human rights framework in Europe is complex and unsatisfactory. One of the elements rendering it so is the current relationship between the EU and the European Convention on Human Rights (ECHR). This chapter focuses on this relationship,[2] concentrating on the following topics:

— Accession of the EU to the ECHR.
— With or without accession, what EU cases might we expect to see litigated in Strasbourg?
— A comparison of existing different case law approaches of the Court of Justice of the European Union (CJEU) and the European Court of Human Rights (ECtHR).
— The growth of a body of autonomous EU fundamental rights law (including discussion of the fact that the CJEU does not always take ECtHR case law into account despite Article 52(3) of the Charter).

[1] Pedro Cruz Villalón, 'Rights in Europe: The Crowded House', KCL Working Paper in European Law, 01/2012.

[2] This chapter, while being a free-standing contribution in its own right, also continues and updates the discussion in my earlier chapter, 'The European Court of Justice and the ECHR after Lisbon' in S Weatherill, S de Vries and U Bernitz (eds), *The Protection of Fundamental Rights in the EU after Lisbon* (Oxford, Hart Publishing, 2013). I have written further about the relationship between the EU and the ECHR—for example: 'A Tale of Two Courts: Luxembourg, Strasbourg and the Growing European Human Rights Acquis' (2006) 423 *Common Market Law Review* 619; 'Human Rights in the European Legal Space' in J Shaw, S Tierney and N Walker (eds), *Europe's Constitutional Mosaic* (Oxford, Hart Publishing, 2011); 'The European Union and Human Rights after the Treaty of Lisbon' (2011) 11(4) *Human Rights Law Review* 645–82.

I. ACCESSION

It has been suggested that the current relationship between the EU and Strasbourg is imperfect. Two features in particular contribute to this. The first factor is that although *EU institutions* currently observe the ECHR, there is no possibility of a direct action against the EU in the ECtHR should anyone wish to contest the EU's application or interpretation of the Convention. This means that EU institutions are the only public authorities in a Council of Europe of 47 Member States, whose acts are not amenable to challenge at the Strasbourg Court on human rights grounds.

The second factor is that although applicants may currently (under Article 34 ECHR, following the exhaustion of national remedies) bring an action against an EU Member State at the ECtHR, alleging an ECHR violation where the state's acts derive from domestic implementation of EU law, there exists at present no direct EU involvement in the action before the Strasbourg Court. This can create all sorts of problems at the enforcement stage, as the UK found in the *Matthews* case,[3] which is discussed further below.

For quite some time, there has been agreement that the accession of the EU to the ECHR would be the optimum way to resolve these issues. The 2009 Treaty of Lisbon and 2010 Protocol 14 ECHR provided the EU and the ECHR with the necessary legal competences to enable accession to take place. More specifically, Article 6(2) of the Treaty on European Union (TEU) provides a legal basis for EU accession and reads as follows:

> 2. The Union shall accede to the European Convention for the Protection of Human Rights and Fundamental Freedoms. Such accession shall not affect the Union's competences as defined in the Treaties.

Accession must follow the complex and cumbersome mandatory procedure that governs all EU agreements with third countries and international organisations set out in Article 218 TFEU. For such an agreement to be concluded, Article 218 requires unanimity in the Council, the consent of the European Parliament (by a two-thirds majority) and its ratification in all EU and Council of Europe Member States. Nonetheless, in April 2013, a draft (revised) agreement on accession was agreed between the Council of Europe and the European Commission.[4] Given that a number of Member States[5]—both from within and outside the EU—initially had reservations about the terms of EU participation in the Convention system, it is some achievement that agreement between them was reached, albeit in a regrettably secretive

[3] *Matthews v UK* [1999] 28 EHRR 361.

[4] This draft agreement is available at: www.coe.int/t/dghl/standardsetting/hrpolicy/Accession/Meeting_reports/47_1(2013)008rev2_EN.pdf.

[5] For example, France was worried about giving the ECtHR jurisdiction in relation to acts adopted by the EU under the common foreign and security policy.

process on the EU side, as the action brought by Leonard Besselink for access to accession documents revealed.[6]

However, the CJEU was also asked to provide an Opinion under Article 218(11) of the Treaty on the Functioning of the European Union (TFEU), which provides for a special procedure whereby a Member State or a major EU institution may obtain the Opinion of the CJEU as to whether any agreement envisaged by the EU is compatible with the Treaties. Notably, despite the fact that the three major EU institutions, as well as the EU's 28 Member States, submitted at the Court hearing that the Draft Accession Agreement was compatible with the EU Treaties, the Court held that it was not.[7] (Advocate General Kokott, in an Opinion delivered on 13 June 2014, had in contrast found the agreement compatible with EU law, albeit in highly qualified terms.)[8] Given the CJEU's adverse holding, the agreement may not enter into force unless it (or the EU Treaties) is revised.

A. The Court's Reasoning in Opinion 2/13

This chapter will now briefly consider, in order, each of the arguments made by the Court as to why, in its mind, accession would be incompatible with EU law.

First, the Court was quick to point out that, to date, only states had become members of the ECHR. The Court criticised the approach adopted in the draft agreement for treating the EU as a state, and thus ignoring its innovative nature, which the CJEU has characterised as 'a new legal order'. Furthermore, in Opinion 2/13, the CJEU asserted that, under international law, the EU is precluded by its very nature from being considered a state—a statement that may mollify those who fear the growth of the EU into a superstate. However, what followed in the Opinion amounts to a robust declaration of the autonomy of EU law, which has some troubling consequences, and ultimately led the CJEU to find the draft agreement incompatible with EU law. The Court structured the remainder of its arguments under the following headings.

i. The Specific Characteristics and the Autonomy of EU Law

The autonomy of EU law, and its specific, *sui generis* nature, has been a running theme throughout its legal history. On this basis, EU accession to the ECHR should therefore not disturb EU competences or the interpretive monopoly of the CJEU in the interpretation of EU law, and Protocol 8 of

[6] On which, see further below.
[7] *Opinion 2/13* [2014] ECR 0000.
[8] ibid.

the Lisbon Treaty was drafted with this in mind, specifically stating that the accession agreement must 'make provision for preserving the specific characteristics of the Union and Union law'. However, the CJEU found that the draft agreement failed to do this. It observed that, while after accession, the Strasbourg Court's interpretation of the ECHR would bind the EU, including the CJEU, nonetheless it would be unacceptable for the ECtHR to call into question the CJEU's findings in relation to the scope of EU law. The Court cited three specific ways in which the draft agreement failed to take account of the specific characteristics of EU law.

First, the CJEU was concerned that Article 53 ECHR, which gives Contracting Parties the power to lay down higher standards of protection than those guaranteed by the ECHR, should not compromise EU law. Although Article 53 of the EU Charter of Fundamental Rights[9] appears to state something very similar to Article 53 ECHR, in the 2013 *Melloni* judgment,[10] the CJEU held that Member States could not have higher standards than the EU Charter in cases where the EU has fully harmonised the relevant law. Thus, the CJEU asserted that the ECHR should be coordinated with (the CJEU's interpretation of) the Charter and found that there was no provision in the draft agreement to ensure such coordination.

Second, the CJEU was concerned that the principle of mutual trust under EU law, highly relevant in the context of the EU's Area of Freedom, Security and Justice (AFSJ), could be undermined. Much EU legal cooperation within the AFSJ (for example, the execution of European Arrest Warrants (EAWs)) is based on the presumption of human rights compliance throughout the EU. In contrast, the ECHR would require each Member State to check that other Member States had actually observed fundamental rights, even though EU law imposes an obligation of mutual trust between those Member States. The accession agreement contains no provision to prevent such a development. In those circumstances, the CJEU believed that accession was liable to upset the underlying balance of the EU and undermine the autonomy of EU law.

Third, the Court noted that Protocol 16 ECHR (only signed on 2 October 2013) allows ECHR states' highest courts to seek advisory opinions from the ECtHR regarding the interpretation and/or application of rights in the ECHR. Although the EU will not accede to this Protocol, the CJEU nonetheless perceived it as a threat to the autonomy of EU law because ECHR states' highest courts might prefer to make a preliminary

[9] Article 53 of the Charter reads as follows: 'Nothing in this Charter shall be interpreted as restricting or adversely affecting human rights and fundamental freedoms as recognised, in their respective fields of application, by Union law and international law and by international agreements to which the Union or all the Member States are party, including the European Convention for the Protection of Human Rights and Fundamental Freedoms, and by the Member States' constitutions.'

[10] Case C-399/11 *Stefano Melloni v Ministerio Fiscal* [2013] ECR I-000.

reference to Strasbourg on the compatibility of EU law with ECHR rights rather than to Luxembourg.

ii. Article 344 TFEU

The CJEU has consistently held that an international agreement cannot affect the allocation of powers fixed by the Treaties and, consequently, the autonomy of the EU legal system. This principle is enshrined in Article 344 TFEU, which provides that EU Member States may not to submit a dispute concerning the interpretation or application of the Treaties to any method of settlement other than those provided for by the Treaties. Given that the draft agreement did not exclude the possible use of the ECtHR to settle such disputes, the CJEU found that this undermined EU law.

iii. The Co-Respondent Mechanism

A large part of EU law is implemented by its Member States and therefore it will seem logical for the applicant to proceed against the Member State. Yet, Member States often have no discretion as to whether or how, an action emanating from the EU is implemented. In such cases, the root of the problem lies with the EU measure rather than the Member State. Therefore, the prospect of EU accession prompts tricky questions as to how responsibility between the Member States and the EU should be split because, post-accession, a novel situation would arise for the ECHR whereby the Contracting Party *enacting* a legal act (the EU) and the Contracting Party *implementing* that act (an EU Member State) may be different legal entities. A co-respondent mechanism was therefore provided in the draft accession agreement to solve these problems.

Not every case in which a Member State implements EU law in some way would be appropriate for application of the co-respondent mechanism. Most likely, the mechanism would come into play in cases where an EU measure has provided no discretion to a Member State as to its implementation at the national level—for example, in cases concerning the application of regulations, which are directly applicable, rather than those concerning many directives, which often leave scope for a Member State to apply its own discretion. For example, had the co-respondent mechanism then existed, it would probably have been applied in cases such as *Matthews*, *Bosphorus* and *Kokkelvisserij v The Netherlands*.[11] These are cases in which single EU Member States, as the only respondents, would not have been legally able to execute any Strasbourg Court judgment finding a rights

[11] *Bosphorus Hava Yollari Ve Ticaret Anonim Sirketi v Ireland* [2006] 42 EHRR 1; *Matthews v UK* [1999] EHRR 361; *Nederlandse Kokkelvisserij UA v The Netherlands* (2009) 48 EHRR 18.

violation originating in EU law, because this required the amendment of EU legislation, which requires the involvement of all Member States.

Article 3 of the draft accession agreement provided that a Contracting Party could become a co-respondent either by accepting an invitation from the ECtHR or following a decision of the ECtHR upon the request of that Contracting Party. However, carrying out such a review would require the ECtHR to assess the rules of EU law governing the division of powers between the EU and its Member States. The CJEU held that to permit the ECtHR to make such an assessment would risk adversely affecting the division of powers between the EU and its Member States, and thus found this to be another way in which the accession agreement was incompatible with EU law.

iv. The Procedure for the Prior Involvement of the CJEU

Regard for autonomy of EU law requires that the CJEU must have had the chance to interpret and rule on an issue of EU law before it reaches the ECtHR. The real problem emerges with indirect actions concerning EU law brought in the courts of the Member States and it is possible that in such a case, a national court might not refer to the CJEU for a preliminary ruling—in which case, the CJEU would be denied the ability to provide authoritative guidance on the treaties. This would place the CJEU's interpretive monopoly under *Foto Frost* and Article 19(1) TEU[12] at risk.

A solution to this problem was offered by Presidents Costa and Skouris in a joint communication,[13] which suggested that as part of the accession agreement, an internal procedure for indirect actions should be introduced, so that the CJEU should have a chance to make a ruling in such cases. This idea was adopted by the draft accession agreement (Article 3(6)).

However, the CJEU found fault with the draft agreement's terms because, first, it did not reserve to the CJEU only (ie, it did not exclude the ECtHR) the power to rule on whether the CJEU had already dealt with an issue and, second, it did not permit the CJEU to rule on the interpretation, but only on the validity, of EU law. Therefore, it was incompatible with EU law.

v. The Specific Characteristics of EU Law as Regards Judicial Review in CFSP Matters

Lastly, the Court analysed the specific characteristics of EU law as regards judicial review in matters of the common foreign and security policy (CFSP).

[12] Case 314/85 *Foto Frost* [1987] ECR 1129. Article 19(1) TEU states: 'The Court of Justice of the European Union shall ... ensure that in the interpretation and application of the Treaties the law is observed.'

[13] 'Joint Communication from Presidents Costa and Skouris', press release no 75, issued by the Registrar of the ECtHR on 27 January 2011, www.echr.coe.int.

The CJEU has limited jurisdiction over CFSP acts,[14] and so it is possible that it would have no chance to interpret the EU law at issue prior to an ECtHR ruling in a case concerning the human rights compatibility of a CFSP measure in Strasbourg. In such a situation, the ECtHR would itself interpret EU law without the aid of the CJEU. This might jeopardise the autonomy of EU law and also the CJEU's interpretative monopoly under Article 344 TFEU. For example, if as a consequence of an EU military action a human rights violation were pleaded, it would appear that, post-accession, an action against the EU in the Strasbourg Court would be feasible.[15] Such a situation would effectively entrust the exclusive judicial review as regards compliance with the rights guaranteed by the ECHR on the part of the EU to a non-EU body. Indeed, an amendment was proposed to exclude CFSP acts from the ECtHR's jurisdiction altogether. However, this was rejected by non-EU contracting parties to the ECHR, who insisted that no aspects of EU law be excluded from the EU accession process.[16] Therefore, the CJEU held that the draft agreement failed to have regard to the specific characteristics[17] of EU law in relation to the judicial review of acts in the area of the CFSP.

B. Reflections on the Opinion

This Opinion undoubtedly makes it difficult for the EU to proceed with accession. The draft agreement was only achieved after tortuous negotiations and redrafts, mainly—but not only—due to objections within the EU itself. The Court's Opinion sets out so many objections to accession (some requiring treaty change) that one is prompted to think that the Court wished to make accession as difficult as possible. And this is so, even given the Court's somewhat privileged position as a member of the Council Committee[18] that negotiated accession and the fact that its suggestions, in both

[14] The exceptions are so-called 'restrictive measures' under Art 275(2) TFEU, normally interpreted as referring to sanctions.

[15] See, for example, the joined cases of *Behrami v France* and *Saramati v France, Germany and Norway* (2007) 45 EHRR SE10, which concerned whether the ECtHR was competent to scrutinise the participation of ECHR Member States in the international civil and security presences in Kosovo.

[16] For more on this, see Friends Of Presidency (FREMP) (Brussels, 4 November 2011), 'Accession of the EU to the ECHR', Working Document from the Presidency, at Point 9: www.statewatch.org/news/2011/nov/eu-council-echr-accession-fop-ds-1675-11.pdf.

[17] Although paras 23–25 of Appendix V to the Accession Agreement (Draft explanatory report to the Agreement on the Accession of the EU to the ECHR) raise some of the above points.

[18] General Secretariat of the Council, 'Request for the Participation of a Delegate of the Court of Justice of the European Union as an Observer', Brussels, 17 September 2010, 13714/10, JAI 747 INST 333: http://register.consilium.europa.eu/doc/srv?l=EN&f=ST%20 13714%202010%20INIT.

a discussion document and a joint communication[19] from the presidents of the ECtHR and the CJEU, appear to have been accommodated.

The EU is required by the terms of its own treaty (Article 6(2) TEU) to accede to the ECHR, and the Commission is open to an infringement action if it fails to do so. The history of EU integration provides many illustrations of ad hoc, pragmatic actions in the face of seemingly impossible practical difficulties. So accession may still be achieved. Nonetheless, the CJEU's Opinion makes it highly problematic for the Commission to proceed. There may indeed be little prospect that non-EU ECHR states will acquiesce in renegotiating the agreement to suit the terms of the CJEU's Opinion. In such a situation, the Commission could not be blamed if non-EU action made it impossible to fulfil the obligation in Article 6(2).

What should our conclusions be if we value human rights? Peers characterises the Court's Opinion as 'a clear and present danger to human rights protection'[20] and I believe he is right. The Court's Opinion is shot through with statements on the autonomy and special position of EU law, and most particularly with concern for its own prerogatives as the ultimate determinant of the EU legal order, rather than any abiding concern with human rights. Thus, the old critique that the CJEU does not take rights seriously springs back to mind. As Leonard Besselink reminds us, instead we must take seriously the CJEU President's announcement at the FIDE Conference 2014: 'The Court is not a human rights court: it is the Supreme Court of the Union.'[21] Indeed, there is something highly ironic in Opinion 2/13, in that the CJEU appears to be opposing ECHR accession for fear that this might result in a loss of its sovereignty—a position uncannily similar to that taken by UK eurosceptics, who desire ECHR membership only on their own terms.

This is indeed doubly ironic, for the Court expresses these concerns about its constitutional position and autonomy of EU law just at a time when, with the expansion of EU criminal powers through the AFSJ, human rights control over the EU has never been needed more. The ECHR has an important role to play in underlining that the EU principles of mutual trust and

[19] 'Discussion Document of the Court of Justice of the European Union on Certain Aspects of the Accession of the European Union to the European Convention for the Protection of Human Rights and Fundamental Freedoms', http://curia.europa.eu/jcms/upload/docs/application/pdf/2010-05/convention_en.pdf; 'Joint Communication from Presidents Costa and Skouris', http://curia.europa.eu/jcms/upload/docs/application/pdf/2011-02/cedh_cjue_english.pdf.

[20] S Peers, 'The CJEU and the EU's Accession to the ECHR: A Clear and Present Danger to Human Rights Protection', http://eulawanalysis.blogspot.co.uk/2014/12/the-cjeu-and-eus-accession-to-echr.html.

[21] L Besselink, 'Acceding to the ECHR Notwithstanding the Court of Justice Opinion 2/13', VerfBlog, 23 December 2014, www.verfassungsblog.de/en/acceding-echr-notwithstanding-court-justice-opinion-213.

recognition, although lynchpins of European integration, must not threaten fundamental rights and subvert the very values of the EU.

Yet, were the EU to accede to the ECHR, in full compliance with the Court's requirements in Opinion 2/13, human rights protection in the EU would not be enhanced, for the EU would be shielded from many human rights claims, including many, if not most, in the highly controversial CFSP and AFSJ areas. Given all of the difficulties thrown out by the Court's Opinion, Besselink has suggested[22] that the treaties should now be amended to insert the following 'notwithstanding protocol' to read as follows:

> The Union shall accede to the European Convention for the Protection of Human Rights and Fundamental Freedoms, notwithstanding Article 6(2) Treaty on European Union, Protocol (No 8) relating to Article 6(2) of the Treaty on European Union and Opinion 2/13 of the Court of Justice of 18 December 2014.

This is a dramatic suggestion indeed. But would all EU Member States agree to such a protocol? The UK's present administration is unlikely to be very accommodating. Therefore, I reluctantly conclude that, in the light of the CJEU's Opinion, those who value human rights no longer have any reason to pursue EU accession to the ECHR. Accession in compliance with the CJEU's judgment would not provide effective external control of the EU's actions. This is a pessimistic conclusion,[23] but it is hard to conclude otherwise than that Opinion 2/13 does not take rights seriously.

C. Access to Accession Documents—The *Besselink* Case

However, there are other aspects to EU accession not raised in Opinion 2/13 that merit consideration. For example, the general public might be expected to have an interest in the terms which the EU negotiates for ECHR membership, given that such terms may ultimately have an impact on individual rights that may be vindicated in Strasbourg. There is also surely a public interest in the restraints that may be applied to the public conduct of the EU through scrutiny in the external forum of the ECHR. The EU is committed to transparency. Article 15 TFEU states that citizens and residents of the EU have a right of access to European Parliament, Council and Commission documents. Therefore, the Council's reluctance to disclose documents

[22] ibid.

[23] For two less pessimistic reflections on Opinion 2/13, see C Barnard, 'Opinion 2/13 on EU Accession to the ECHR: Looking for the Silver Lining', EU Law Analysis, 16 February 2015; D Halberstam, 'It's the Autonomy, Stupid!' A Modest Defense of Opinion 2/13 on EU Accession to the ECHR, and the Way Forward' (2015) University of Michigan Public Law Research Paper No 439; see also my response to Halberstam: S Douglas-Scott, 'Opinion 2/13 and the "Elephant in the Room": A Response to Daniel Halberstam', VerfBlog, 13 March 2015, www.verfassungsblog.de/opinion-213-and-the-elephant-in-the-room-a-response-to-daniel-halberstam/#.VX62ao3bLIU.

relating to the EU's accession to the ECHR has been somewhat puzzling. This occurred in the context of a request made by Leonard Besselink, then Professor of Constitutional Law at Utrecht University, to access documents relating to the EU's ECHR accession negotiations. In these documents, the Council discussed its instructions to the Commission, which negotiated the ECHR accession on behalf of the EU. However, the Council refused access, on the basis of Article 4(1) of Regulation 1049/2001 on public access to EU documents, which states that access must be refused where disclosure would undermine the public interest with regard to international relations. Besselink challenged this refusal in the General Court.[24]

One of Besselink's main arguments to the Court concerned the public interest in a broad societal debate about EU accession to the ECHR. He argued that accession was of a constitutional nature, which rendered disclosure of the relevant documents of exceptional societal relevance. He further argued that the right to freedom of information and expression in Article 11 of the EU Charter also supported his arguments.

The General Court, however, rejected this constitutional reading, refuting Besselink's claim of the exceptional, constitutionally weighty nature of the requested documents.[25] The General Court also took a rather narrow reading of Article 11 Charter, interpreting it in substance as a *negative right*, which imposed an obligation on the Council to refrain from interfering with the freedom of expression and information. This is regrettable, because a reading of Article 11 as entailing some positive actions could have suggested an obligation on the Council to enable debate on questions of great constitutional and political significance through the dissemination of relevant information on the issue.

However, the Court found that even if arguments regarding the constitutional nature of the document were approved, this would be irrelevant, since the focus of the Council decision was not whether the EU would accede to the ECHR, but the applicable procedure and strategic objectives. On this basis, the Court felt that the document fell within the public interest exception as regards international relations. Therefore, the General Court preferred to apply a procedural review of the access request, which required it to assess whether the Council correctly applied the relevant procedural requirements. The Court concluded that it had done so only for *some of* the requested documents.

The General Court found that the Council had interpreted the exception to disclosure too broadly, although it did not mention that the Council of

[24] Case T-331/11 *Leonard Besselink v Council* [2013] ECR I-000.

[25] The Court complained that 'the extremely laconic and summary nature of the way in which the complaint in question is presented does not enable the alleged infringement to be identified in such a way as to allow the Court to exercise its power of review' (ibid [39]).

Europe, with whom the EU negotiates accession, had placed all of its own negotiating directives online, which surely must have had an impact on EU confidentiality. However, the Court did find that provisions in directives merely referring to principles governing negotiations should have been disclosed, and left their identification up to the Council. Following reconsideration, the Council concluded that the applicant could have access to the entire document.

The EU's accession to the ECHR, although formally a matter of international relations, is surely an area in which there is a great public interest in transparency, especially as the Council of Europe had already made public its own negotiating positions. In this case it is hard to see what harm could be caused to mutual trust, or indeed more generally, and therefore it should not be assumed that just because a matter is in principle one of international relations, a blanket exception to disclosure should apply. It is also disappointing to see that the Charter should have been given so little consideration in this case.

II. WITH OR WITHOUT ACCESSION, WHAT KINDS OF EU CASES MAY BE LITIGATED IN STRASBOURG?

The CJEU's Opinion 2/13 clearly sets back the timetable for EU accession some considerable way, prompting speculation as to whether it may take place at all. However, regardless of accession, the following predictions might be made. Only case four (section II.D) is dependent on the actual accession of the EU to the ECHR.

A. The ECtHR will Continue to Determine Cases Brought Against EU Member States Relating to their Application of EU Law

Such cases have always been determinable in Strasbourg, as the ECtHR has taken the position that they fall within its jurisdiction under Article 1 ECHR. However, the nature of the litigation may vary, depending on the level of discretion accorded to the state in its implementation of EU secondary law.

So, for example, in the 1996 case of *Cantoni v France*,[26] an action was brought against France concerning a French law that implemented the EU Medicines Directive. Directives are binding only as to the results to be achieved, and often leave a wide margin of discretion to the state as to how

[26] *Cantoni v France* ECHR [1996] Reports 1996-V. In fact, *Cantoni* is notable for the fact that the ECtHR found the case admissible notwithstanding the fact that France had implemented the relevant directive almost word for word into national law.

it implements them in their domestic legal order, so the ECtHR has taken the position that in cases where states have a wide margin of discretion, they have responsibility for their acts. In such cases, the ECtHR has declared applications admissible.

B. The *Bosphorus* Presumption of Equivalent Human Rights Protection will not be Applied in Every Case

The *Bosphorus* case[27] arose from the fact that, in 1993, Ireland impounded an aircraft as obligated by an EC regulation, which was itself required by a UN Security Council Resolution imposing sanctions on the former Yugoslavia. Because the aircraft was impounded by Irish authorities on Irish territory, the ECtHR found that the applicant was within Ireland's jurisdiction according to Article 1 ECHR. However, in this case (which had already been extensively litigated in the Irish courts and in the CJEU),[28] the ECtHR found no violation of human rights to have taken place. It held that if equivalent protection of human rights to that under the ECHR existed in the EU legal order, then it could be presumed that an EU Member State had complied with the ECHR when it did no more than directly implement legal obligations flowing from its EU membership in cases where it had no discretion in the form of implementation. The ECtHR held that this presumption could, however, be rebutted where the human rights protection in the particular case was regarded as 'manifestly deficient'. However, the protection in the *Bosphorus* case was not found to have been manifestly deficient.

The *Bosphorus* doctrine has been criticised as shielding the application of EU law from ECtHR scrutiny. This presumption of equivalence, rebuttable only by a 'manifestly deficient' protection of rights, produces a minimal, abstract standard of human rights review rather than one based on the concrete circumstances of the case. In *Bosphorus*, there was no separate review on the facts of the case, leading to very harsh results.[29] As the concurring judges pointed out in *Bosphorus*, this was 'in marked contrast to the supervision generally carried out by the ECHR'.[30]

[27] Case 84/95 *Bosphorus* [1996] ECR I-3953 for CJEU proceedings and *Bosphorus Hava Yollari Ve Ticaret Anonim Sirketi v Ireland* [2006] 42 EHRR 1 in the ECtHR.

[28] Which had already found there to have been no human rights violation.

[29] Namely, Bosphorus was unable to run its airline, and lost three years out of a four-year aircraft lease. As it stated in argument, this was the only aircraft that had been impounded under the sanctions regulations.

[30] Joint concurring opinion of Judges Rozakis, Tulkens, Traja, Botoucharova, Zagrebelsky and Garlicki in *Bosphorus Hava Yollari Ve Ticaret Anonim Sirketi v Ireland* [2006] 42 EHRR 1 at [4]. Judge Ress, in a separate concurrence, warned that the concept of Convention compliance by international organisations should not be seen as a step towards the creation of a double standard. Nor did he believe that the presumption of compliance should prevent a case-by-case review.

It is arguable that accession of the EU to the ECHR would alter the relationship between the two courts, reserving the last word for the ECtHR rather than continuing the existing situation of cooperation and comity. As such, perhaps, post-accession, Strasbourg should apply a more rigorous, concrete review to EU acts rather than the abstract test of equivalence of *Bosphorus*. However, it could also be argued that the presumption reflects the specific *sui generis* situation of the EU legal order, as maintained and acknowledged in Protocol No 8 of the Lisbon Treaty, and that accession should change neither this nor the *Bosphorus* presumption. Whatever the arguments, there was no codification of the *Bosphorus* presumption in the draft accession agreement. Apparently, EU Member States agreed with the Commission not to request codification of *Bosphorus*, in spite of early calls to do so. Thus, the matter has been left up to the ECtHR to decide.[31]

Therefore, it is interesting to observe that in several post-*Bosphorus* cases, the ECtHR has *failed* to apply the presumption. In *MSS v Belgium and Greece*,[32] an asylum case, the ECtHR held that Belgium could not rely on the presumption of equivalence because it had acted wrongly in the context of EU asylum law in returning an asylum seeker to Greece, although inadequacies in the Greek asylum system were obvious. The 2012 case of *Michaud v France*[33] went even further. *Michaud* concerned France's implementation of EU money laundering Directives and the compatibility with Article 8 ECHR of reporting requirements placed on lawyers in respect of their clients. However, we might interpret *Michaud* as an example of a *Cantoni*-type case in which a Member State is exercising discretion in the implementation of EU law. Nonetheless, it is interesting that (and in the words of the ECtHR) 'above all', the Strasbourg Court found that *Michaud* should be distinguished from *Bosphorus* because the French Conseil d'Etat had not made a preliminary ruling to the CJEU, and there had been no opportunity for the CJEU to examine the issue. Therefore, according to the ECtHR, the Conseil d'Etat had delivered its opinion without the benefit of EU mechanisms for fundamental rights supervision—in principle equivalent to the ECHR—having been mobilised. In such a case, the presumption of equivalent protection did not apply. These cases indicate that the ECtHR is not willing to apply *Bosphorus* in a blanket fashion.

[31] Ladenburger, 'FIDE 2012—Session on 'Protection of Fundamental Rights Post-Lisbon—The Interaction between the Charter of Fundamental Rights, the European Convention of Human Rights and National Constitutions', Institutional Report, www.fide2012.eu/index.php?doc_id=88 at 45 (under point 5.1).

[32] *MSS v Belgium and Greece* (2011) 53 EHRR 2.

[33] Application 12323/11 *Michaud v France*, not yet reported, 6 December 2012.

C. There will be More Litigation Relating to the EU's AFSJ in Strasbourg

The EU's AFSJ concerns matters such as criminal, family, succession and procedural law. As such, it comprises many measures that were previously close to the heart of state sovereignty and considered national preserves. These are liable to be controversial and raise human rights issues. However, much EU legal cooperation within the AFSJ, for example, the execution of EAWs, is based on the presumption of human rights compliance throughout the EU. This is problematic because, in fact, human rights protection is not equivalent throughout EU Member States. Yet many EU measures in the field of cross-border criminal justice, asylum, immigration and matrimonial matters require recognition of judicial decisions of other Member States, or a quasi-automatic transfer of individuals, without any human rights scrutiny of the decision or situation in the requesting state. This is because of an underlying assumption that all EU Member States similarly ensure a comprehensive respect for human rights. For example, the CJEU stated in the *NS* case in respect of the Dublin II Regulation (which sets mechanisms for determining the applicable Member State for an asylum application):

> At issue here is the raison d'etre of the European Union and the creation of an area of freedom, security and justice and, in particular, the Common European Asylum System, based on mutual confidence and a presumption of compliance, by other Member States, with European Union law and, in particular, fundamental rights.[34]

However, EU Member States do not all provide comprehensive protection of human rights. We may note, for example, that a considerable number of EU states continue to violate even core human rights such as Article 3 ECHR, the prohibition on torture.[35] In these circumstances, EU AFSJ measures are liable to be contested in Strasbourg and this was clearly a factor contributing to the CJEU's negative finding in Opinion 2/13.

For example, the ECtHR Grand Chamber judgment in *MSS v Belgium and Greece* has already been mentioned in the last section. This case concerned the compatibility, with Articles 3 and 13 of the ECHR, of the return of asylum seekers to Greece under the Dublin II Regulation in circumstances in which Greece was experiencing severe problems in complying with human rights obligations to asylum seekers. The Grand Chamber held that

[34] Joined Cases C-411/10 *N.S. v Secretary of State for the Home Department* and C-493/10 *ME and others v Minister for Justice, Equality and Law Reform* [2011] ECR I-13905.

[35] For a small sample of recent cases in which states have been found to breach the prohibition in Art 3 ECHR, see, eg: *RR v Poland* (App No 27617), judgment of 26 May 2011; *Hellig v Germany* (App No 20999/05), judgment of 7 July 2011; *VC v Slovakia* (App No 18968/07), judgment of 8 November 2011; *Yoh-Ekale Mwange v Belgium* (App No 10486/10), judgment of 20 December 2011; *El Shennawy v France* (App No 51246/08), judgment of 20 January 2011.

Belgium was in violation for returning an Afghan asylum seeker to Greece. This case establishes that, according to the ECtHR, EU Member States may not simply rely on any presumption of equal protection.

To be sure, the CJEU has sought to ensure that EU law is coherent with the ECHR, such as in the joined cases *NS* and *ME* in 2011. In *NS*, the CJEU made it clear that precedence should be given to fundamental rights over Member State obligations under the Dublin II Regulation. The CJEU referenced the *MSS* case, holding that Member States must not transfer asylum seekers if systemic deficiencies in the receiving state result in a real risk of inhuman or degrading treatment under Article 4 of the EU Charter.

However, even though the ECtHR and the CJEU achieved, in substance, the same result in these cases, we can notice differences in their approach. For example, the ECtHR examines every case for breaches of the ECHR, whereas the CJEU has ruled that only systemic deficiencies in the asylum system in the responsible state will be a reason to refuse transfer of asylum seekers. As such, quasi-automatic transfers may continue in the EU in the absence of systemic violations.

Similar problems are likely to arise in the context of execution of EAWs, which are likely to face challenge in Strasbourg. The CJEU has underlined that the EAW is based on the principle of mutual recognition, requiring Member States to act upon them.[36] Furthermore, in the *Melloni* and *Radu* cases,[37] the CJEU gave little hope that surrender under an EAW might be refused on human rights grounds, or indeed on any grounds other than those in to be found in the EAW framework decision itself. *Melloni* is particularly noteworthy for its rejection of specific human rights grounds for refusal located in the Spanish constitution. The EAW is likely to face Strasbourg challenges because EAWs have too often been issued for minor offences and without due determination being given to whether surrender is proportionate, in spite of serious human and financial costs occasioned by surrender. Domestic courts are increasingly inclined to accept human rights-based refusal grounds to EAWs.[38]

Therefore, the Strasbourg Court has an important role to play in underlining that the EU principle of mutual recognition, although a lynchpin of European integration, must not threaten fundamental rights and subvert the very values of the EU. Accession may therefore place a strain on the AFSJ. Whereas the CJEU usually balances mutual trust and fundamental

[36] See, eg, Case C-42/11 *Lopes Da Silva Jorge* [2012] ECR I-000 [29]; Case C-388/08 PPU *Leymann and Pustovarov* [2008] ECR I-8983 [51]; Case C-261/09 *Mantello* [2010] ECR I-11477 [36] and [37].

[37] *Melloni* (n 10); Case C-396/11 *Ministerul Public—Parchetul de pe lângă Curtea de Apel Constanța v Radu* [2013] ECR 000. But also note Case C-168/13 PPU *Jeremy F* [2013] ECR 000, in which the CJEU appeared to leave more room for national constitutional diversity.

[38] For example, the UK Supreme Court held that surrender under an EAW may be refused if it constitutes a disproportionate interference with mother and child rights under Art 8 ECHR (*F-K v Polish Judicial Authority* [2012] UKSC 25).

rights by presuming human rights compliance by its Member States, rebuttable only in severe cases of systemic violation, the ECtHR applies no such presumption and, as we have seen, has even refused to apply the *Bosphorus* presumption in some of its case law. In this context we might wonder how far the ECtHR will acknowledge mutual recognition and mutual trust as applicable principles. There is little evidence so far that it will do so, and this no doubt prompted some of the CJEU's findings in Opinion 2/13.[39]

i. Disconnection Clause

In these circumstances, it has been suggested that the mechanism of a disconnection clause might be used to safeguard the coherence of the AFSJ in the event of the accession of the EU to the ECHR. Such disconnection clauses have been used in previous multilateral conventions, including those adopted within the Council of Europe framework, with the aim of protecting the autonomy of the EU legal order. With this in mind, these disconnection clauses provide that, *as between* the EU Member State parties to the international agreement at issue, the relevant provisions of EU law apply rather than the provisions of the international agreement.[40]

Judge Allan Rosas of the CJEU has suggested that such a clause could be included in the EU accession agreement.[41] His argument was that, in certain contexts, the EU should be taken as a whole entity in order that a clear distinction could be made between internal EU relations, and relations between the EU and third countries. However, such a general disconnection clause could be problematic, giving the impression that the EU was attempting to reduce the impact of the accession of the EU to the ECHR, or even seeking to make a special case for the EU, as in the case of the *Bosphorus* presumption. For that reason, it appears unlikely to take place.

D. Post-accession, Strasbourg Could Decide Cases that have Already been Determined in the EU Legal Order

This would mean that a case in which the CJEU had already given a ruling would be further litigated in Strasbourg. *Bosphorus* provides such a previous

[39] Namely, those evidencing the CJEU's concerns as to the application of the mutual trust principle from paras 191–95 of Opinion 2/13.

[40] For example, the disconnection clause included in the Council of Europe Convention on the Prevention of Terrorism 2005, CETS No 196 (Art 26(3)) is worded as follows: 'Parties which are members of the European Union shall, in their mutual relations, apply Community and European Union rules is as far as there are Community or European Union rules governing the particular subject concerned and applicable to the specific case, without prejudice to the object and purpose of the present Convention and without prejudice to its full application with other Parties.'

[41] A Rosas, 'Balancing Fundamental Rights in European Union Law' (2012) III *Evropeiski praven pregled* 9, 22.

past example, but at that time, the EU was not yet a member of the ECHR, and the ECtHR's somewhat diplomatic solution was the introduction of the presumption of equivalent protection (already discussed above). Post-accession, the ECtHR would be in a position to directly review all EU acts for compatibility with EU law. Cases such as *Connolly*[42] would become admissible. In *Connolly*, the applicant challenged a decision of the Luxembourg court in the ECtHR. Being unable to challenge an EU institution directly, he instead proceeded against all then EU Member States of the ECHR, claiming a violation of Article 6 ECHR. However, the Strasbourg Court rejected his complaint as inadmissible, holding that EU Member States could only be held responsible where there was an act of some sort on their territory (as was the case in *Bosphorus*, but not in *Connolly*). As such, Connolly was unable to bring an action in Strasbourg.

It would be somewhat uncomfortable for the EU if the ECtHR were to find EU law in breach of the ECHR, especially if the Strasbourg Court were to find that the CJEU had misinterpreted the ECHR. But what is the likelihood of this happening? An oft-cited fear is that of diverging standards between the ECtHR and the CJEU. There are indeed some differences in the case law of the two transnational courts, which will be discussed in the next section. However, it is worth noting that the ECHR has been recognised by the CJEU as an integral part of EU law for over 40 years and there has not been a case in which the CJEU has *deliberately* gone against Strasbourg's interpretation of the ECHR. The usually cited cases of conflict—eg, *Hoechst* and *Orkem*—are not evidence for this, but rather are examples of instances where there was either no, or no clear authority, from Strasbourg on the issue. Notably, in *Roquette*, the CJEU took trouble to reverse its earlier decision in *Hoechst* in the light of subsequent Strasbourg case law.[43]

Since 1998, the judges and court officials of the CJEU and the ECtHR have met up on a regular but not formally institutionalised basis. In the *Declaration on Article 6 § 2 TEU* appended to the Lisbon Treaty, the Conference noted the existence of a regular dialogue between the two courts and stated that such dialogue could be reinforced when the Union accedes to the Convention.[44] Therefore, the Courts are under a political obligation to continue with that dialogue and even intensify it. And, in the words of

[42] *Connolly v 15 Member States of the European Union* (App No 73274/01), 9 December 2008. The earlier action of Case T-163/96 *Connolly v Commission* [1999] ECR II-463 had concerned Connolly's employment dispute with the European Commission over his dismissal for the publication of his book, *The Rotten Heart of Europe*, which had criticised the Economic and Monetary Union (EMU) project. He alleged, inter alia, that his freedom of expression had been violated.

[43] Joined Cases 46/87 and 227/88 *Hoechst v Commission* [1989] ECR 2859, modified in Case C-88/99 *Roquette* [2000] ECR I-10465 at [23] and [29].

[44] See the Declaration on Article 6(2) of the Treaty on European Union: 'The Conference … notes the existence of a regular dialogue between the Court of Justice of the European Union and the European Court of Human Rights; such dialogue could be reinforced when the Union accedes to that Convention.'

a judge of the CJEU: 'The influence the one exerts on the other is mutual and real.'[45]

Nonetheless, there is still scope for difference between the courts. The future (or lack of it) of the *Bosphorus* presumption has already been discussed. The risks to the EU's AFSJ (and CFSP) of a vigorous ECtHR human rights review are also apparent and were clearly in the mind of the CJEU in Opinion 2/13. So we should not dismiss the possibility of the ECtHR finding that EU law breaches the ECHR. The next section further examines where some areas of friction might possibly arise.

III. EXAMPLES OF THE DISTINCT APPROACHES OF THE CJEU AND THE ECtHR

The discussion in this last section brings us nicely to the question of the extent to which the CJEU takes a different approach from that of the ECtHR. For reasons of space, this discussion will focus only on Article 6 ECHR, in which we may observe some groupings of cases in which there exists an observable difference of approach between Strasbourg and Luxembourg. Notably, these are not situations of direct conflict between the two courts, but rather are indications that the two courts might take a different view were the same legal issue to come before both courts in future. The discussion will centre on the four areas below.

A. The 'Right to Silence'

There is no explicit right to silence in EU law. Indeed, EU law accords a narrow scope to the right against self-incrimination, failing to recognise a general right not to testify against oneself, as illustrated by the *Orkem*[46] case, while recognising that a company may refuse to answer questions of a self-incriminating nature.

In contrast, while there is no specific provision on the right to silence in the ECHR, the ECtHR has held that a general right to silence exists. In *Funke v France*,[47] the ECtHR boldly read into Article 6 ECHR a full right to silence. It is likely, therefore, that the CJEU *Orkem* principle will be challenged in Strasbourg, as concerns the scope of the right against self-incrimination.

[45] C Timmermans, 'The Relationship between the European Court of Justice and the European Court of Human Rights' in A Arnull, C Barnard, M Dougan and E Spaventa (eds), *A Constitutional Order of States: Essays in Honour of Alan Dashwood* (Oxford, Hart Publishing, 2011) 153. Note also the Joint Communication of Judges Costa and Skouris regarding the accession of the EU to the ECHR.

[46] Case 374/87 *Orkem v Commission* [1989] ECR 3283.

[47] *Jean-Gustave Funke v France* [1993] 1 CMLR 897 ECHR.

B. The Equality of Arms Principle

In cases such as *Kress*,[48] the ECtHR has developed a 'theory of appearances' approach, advising that a violation of equality of arms can arise from *mere suspicion of bias*, even if there has been no actual harm to any party. However, the CJEU has not fully accepted this approach. So, for example, in *Otis*,[49] a case in which the Commission had imposed fines on companies involved in a lift sector cartel, the fact that the Commission was both claimant against the parties in domestic proceedings and imposed the fine in EU proceedings might have been thought to give rise to a suspicion of bias. However, this point was not addressed by the CJEU. Yet one may speculate on whether the CJEU would have altered its ruling if the EU acceded to the ECHR. At the very least, given that the case might have been further litigated in Strasbourg, it would have been prudent for the CJEU to expand on the issue of why there was no bias on the part of the Commission and thus that the equality of arms principle was satisfied.

C. The Right to a Public Hearing

Article 6(1) ECHR provides that everyone 'is entitled to a fair and public hearing' as one of the elements of a fair trial. Until quite recently, this could be taken for granted in EU courts, where applicants were entitled to a hearing. However, due to recent amendments[50] to the procedural rules in EU courts, this is no longer the case. Applicants must now adduce specific reasons as to why there should be an oral hearing, and there is no guarantee that it will be granted. Given the prominence of the right to a fair and public hearing in the ECHR, this change to the Luxembourg Court rules might well be challenged in Strasbourg, post-accession.

D. Lawyer–Client Privilege and In-House Counsel

The extent of legal-professional privilege has been litigated in the EU Courts. In the *AM & S* case,[51] the CJEU held that lawyer–client privilege applied to a lawyer's correspondence so long as it concerned the client's rights of defence, and that the correspondence was that of an 'independent lawyer', namely a lawyer who was not in a relationship of employment with the client.

[48] *Kress v France* (App No 39594/98) 2001 European Court of Human Rights 1.

[49] Case C-199/11 *Otis* [2012] ECR I-000.

[50] Article 76 of the new Rules of Procedure of the European Court of Justice adopted on 25 September 2012.

[51] Case 155/79 *AM & S Europe Ltd* [1982] ECR I-1575.

So far, it would appear that the ECtHR has not addressed the specific issue of whether legal privilege can apply to the correspondence of in-house counsel. However, neither has the Strasbourg Court excluded its applicability, so this is another potential cause of action in Strasbourg.

Sometimes, members of the CJEU have specifically suggested that the differing circumstances of the EU and the ECHR might explain the need for distinct approaches in the case law. For example, in the 2006 case of *SGL Carbon*,[52] Advocate General Geelhoed suggested that 'It is not possible simply to transpose the findings of the European Court of Human Rights without more to undertakings', also noting that case law from other jurisdictions, such as that under the US Fifth Amendment right against self-incrimination, could not be invoked by companies. The different contexts of these two courts, with Strasbourg acting as freestanding human rights court and Luxembourg possessing a much wider jurisdiction comprising a very large number of (sometimes competing) policies, should not be overlooked as a factor constraining and sometimes shaping human rights interpretations.

IV. THE CJEU DOES NOT ALWAYS TAKE ECHR CASE LAW INTO ACCOUNT DESPITE ARTICLE 52(3) OF THE CHARTER

Nonetheless, the special status of the ECHR has long been recognised in EU law. Indeed, even pre-Lisbon, the CJEU explicitly recognised its 'special significance', as interpreted by the ECtHR, in many of its cases.[53] The Charter has borrowed about half of its rights from the ECHR. One of its general provisions, Article 52(3), states that, to the extent that rights in the Charter are borrowed from the Convention, they are to be given the same meaning and content as they have in the European Convention.[54] This was underlined by the Joint Communication of Judges Costa and Skouris, which suggested a 'parallel interpretation' of such rights.[55] So the Charter itself establishes a strong link between its own fundamental rights and the Convention, and Article 52(3) aims to maintain consistency between the rights of the Charter and the ECHR. This provides a good reason for the CJEU, when applying the Charter, to maintain contact with the Strasbourg Court and its jurisprudence.

[52] Case C-308/04P *SGL Carbon v Commission* [2006] ECR I-5977.

[53] For example, in Case C-305/05, *Ordre des barreaux francophones et germanophone and others* [2007] ECR I-5305 [29].

[54] Article 52(3): 'In so far as this Charter contains rights which correspond to rights guaranteed by the Convention for the Protection of Human Rights and Fundamental Freedoms, the meaning and scope of those rights shall be the same as those laid down by the said Convention. This provision shall not prevent Union law providing more extensive protection.'

[55] *Joint Communication* at para 1.

However, it is not completely clear which rights of the ECHR are at issue. The wording of the Charter is not identical to that of the ECHR, nor are the rights protected therein identical. For example, Article 6 of the Charter—the right to liberty and security of the person—is expressed in one clause, whereas in Article 5 ECHR, it is expressed in five. However, a list of corresponding rights can be found in the Official Explanations[56] relating to the Charter, which, although they do not have the status of law, according to Article 52(7) of the Charter, 'shall be given due regard by the Courts of the Union and the Member States' when interpreting the Charter. But there is still room for uncertainty.

It should also be highlighted that the wording of Article 52(3) of the Charter does not make express reference to the ECtHR's case law. Only the ECHR itself is mentioned. On the one hand, it would seem unlikely that the drafters of Article 52(3) intended merely to refer to the then 50-year-old text of the ECHR, and not the ECtHR ongoing jurisprudence, particularly given the Strasbourg Court's dynamic interpretation of the ECHR as a 'living instrument'.[57] The Official Explanations regarding Article 52(3) explicitly mention the case law.[58] On the other hand, Article 52(7) of the Charter only postulates a duty to *duly regard* the Charter's Official Explanations and thus merely a duty to 'duly regard' the ECtHR's case law. Therefore, it might seem that there is little case for arguing that CJEU interpretations of the EU Charter must strictly follow the case law of the ECtHR.[59] Indeed, if the ECtHR's case law were to bind the CJEU, this might threaten the autonomy of the CJEU's interpretations of EU law. The Strasbourg Court is not bound by its own judgments, nor does the ECHR provide that the national courts of its Contracting Parties be bound by its decisions. Article 46 ECHR states that Court judgments are only binding *inter partes*.

However, in *J McB v LE*, the CJEU appeared to suggest that where Charter rights are derived from ECHR rights, the CJEU should follow the clear judgments of the ECtHR.[60] So, at the very least, a close link between the case law is established. In these and certain other cases, we may see the CJEU exercising some deference to the ECHR and to the ECtHR as a specialised human rights court. For example, in *DEB*, where the point at issue was access to a court, the CJEU held that Article 47(3) of the Charter 'must

[56] *Explanations relating to the Charter of Fundamental Rights* [2007] OJ C303/17.

[57] eg, *Tyrer v UK* [1978] Series A no 26 at 15–16, para 31.

[58] They state that: 'The meaning and scope of the guaranteed rights are determined not only by the text of those instruments, but also by the case law of the European Court of Human Rights and by the Court of Justice of the European Union.' Further, the Preamble to the EU Charter is phrased in a similar manner and also refers to the case law of the ECtHR and the CJEU.

[59] Further, it should be noted that there were various unsuccessful attempts to include an explicit reference to the ECtHR's case law during the Convention that drafted the Charter of Fundamental Rights.

[60] Case C-400/10 PPU *J McB v LE* [2010] ECR I-000.

be interpreted ... in the light of ... the case-law of the ECtHR'.[61] Likewise, we have already seen how the CJEU aimed for overall coherence between the Charter and the ECtHR case law in *NS* and *ME*, even though, as discussed, we have seen that there was some difference in their approach.

A. Recent CJEU Case Law: Towards a Merely Residual Role of the ECHR?

However, the CJEU's treatment of the ECHR, as illustrated by *DEB* and *J McB,* is only one approach that can be discerned in the CJEU's case law. For it is notable that, since the Lisbon Treaty came into force, the Luxembourg Courts have increasingly come to refer to the Charter to the detriment of the ECHR. The *Joint Communication from Presidents Costa and Skouris*[62] observed that the Charter has rapidly become of primary importance in the recent case law of the CJEU. The Charter has now become the departure point text for the CJEU's assessment of fundamental rights, and it would seem that where the ECHR and Strasbourg case law are employed, this will only be in cases where there is no existing authority from the CJEU on a particular issue. For example, in *Schecke and Eifert*,[63] the CJEU assessed the validity of the regulations at issue in the light of the provisions of the Charter[64] as the primary basis for judicial review. The *Otis* case further illustrates this trend. In its consideration of the principle of effective judicial protection, the CJEU held that: 'Article 47 of the Charter secures in EU law the protection afforded by Article 6(1) of the ECHR. It is necessary, therefore, to refer only to Article 47.'[65] (Indeed, as already discussed, in the context of the principle of equality of arms, the CJEU distinguished and disregarded relevant ECHR case law argued on behalf of the defendants.)

This recent trend is backed up by Gráinne de Búrca's[66] analysis (of all cases in which the Luxembourg courts referred to the EU Charter since it became binding to the end of 2012) in which she found that of 122 cases in which the Charter was mentioned, the CJEU referred to the ECHR in only

[61] Case C-279/09 *DEB v Bundesrepublik Deutschland* [2010] ECR I-13849.

[62] Joint Communication from Presidents Costa and Skouris, issued 27 January 2011.

[63] Joined Cases C-92/09 and C-93/09 *Volker und Markus Schecke GbR and Hartmut Eifert* [2010] ECR I-11063.

[64] And in which, notably, the CJEU did not discuss the temporal applicability of the Charter, despite the fact that the disputes at issue had occurred before the entry into force of the Treaty of Lisbon.

[65] *Otis* (n 49).

[66] G De Búrca 'After the EU Charter of Fundamental Rights: The Court of Justice as a Human Rights Adjudicator?' (2013) 20 *Maastricht Journal of European and Comparative Law* 168. Further, by the end of 2013, the Luxembourg courts had referred to the Charter in 275 cases following its entry into force and in seven per cent of the total number of decisions in 2013 ('Fundamental Rights: Challenges and Achievements in 2013', European Union Agency for Fundamental Rights, Annual Report, June 2014, 21).

18 of them. This illustrates a growing insistence in Luxembourg case law on the autonomy and separateness of the EU human rights system from other human rights instruments, confirming what the CJEU held in its *Kadi* ruling:

> [T]he review by the Court of the validity of any Community measure in the light of fundamental rights must be considered to be the expression, in a community based on the rule of law, of a constitutional guarantee stemming from the EC Treaty as an autonomous legal system which is not to be prejudiced by an international agreement.[67]

Indeed, on occasion, the CJEU has refused to engage with arguments drawn from the ECHR and ECtHR case law, as in *Akerberg Fransson*, where the CJEU stated that the ECHR:

> [D]oes not constitute, as long as the European Union has not acceded to it, a legal instrument which has been formally incorporated into European Union law. Consequently, European Union law does not govern the relations between the ECHR and the legal systems of the Member States, nor does it determine the conclusions to be drawn by a national court in the event of conflict between the rights guaranteed by that convention and a rule of national law.[68]

What then explains these variations in the CJEU's approach to the ECHR as authority? The following factors may all be relevant.

First, the Charter contains many more rights, and a far more up-to-date catalogue, than the ECHR, and according to Article 52(3) of the Charter, it may also offer more extensive protection than the ECHR. It is a document crafted with EU needs in mind rather than one borrowed from another international organisation. There is also the possibility of applying fundamental rights as general principles of law under Article 6(3) TEU, in new and potentially radical ways, as the principle of non-discrimination on grounds of age, applied in the *Mangold* case,[69] illustrates. Furthermore, truncating or excluding discussion of the ECHR also may aid the CJEU in avoiding tricky questions concerning the compatibility of EU law with the ECHR, for example, whether it is possible to dispense with the right to a hearing before EU courts. These factors may explain why the EU may consider its human rights protection to have developed a certain level of autonomy. This might even suggest an exciting, expansionist new era for human rights protection in the EU. Furthermore, if EU competences continue to grow, there is a possibility that the ECHR could be overshadowed and disregarded, at least as far as its EU members are concerned.[70] Strasbourg is currently overloaded and suffering from a very large backlog of applications, particularly from its

[67] Case C-402/05 *Kadi* v *Council and Commission* [2008] ECR I-6351 [298]–[299].

[68] Case C-617/10 *Åklagaren v Åkerberg Fransson* [2013] ECR I-000 [44]; Case C-571/10 *Kamberaj* [2012] ECR I-000 [62].

[69] Case C-144/04 *Mangold v Helm* [2005] ECR I-09981; see also Case C-555/07 *Seda Kücükdeveci* [2010] ECR I-365.

[70] For the suggestion that EU Member States should withdraw from the ECHR, see A Toth, 'The European Union and Human Rights: The Way Forward' (1997) 34 *CMLR* 491. See also

newer Member States. Indeed, in the past, friction has been noted between the EU and the Council of Europe (COE), evidence of a fear that the EU might seek to usurp or marginalise[71] the COE's role in the human rights field—a fear which was specifically addressed in the Juncker Report.[72]

On the other hand, there have also been warnings that the CJEU must resist any 'federal temptation', namely a self-empowerment of the CJEU, in which fundamental rights are used as tools of European integration.[73] The EU Charter does not permit the CJEU to emulate the US Supreme Court,[74] or the ECtHR, and identify a 'federal' or EU standard of fundamental rights against which all national laws may be assessed and even invalidated. We should not expect the CJEU to become a fully fledged fundamental rights court. A temptation to do so would provoke strong reactions in some states and their national courts.[75]

The important role played by the CJEU in the development of EU fundamental rights law is well known, but this role is ambivalent. The EU's current design reveals its limited capability as a human rights organisation. The Charter of Fundamental Rights does not declare a freestanding fundamental rights competence for the EU, but only applies to EU institutions and to the Member States in certain circumstances. The deliberate decision not to incorporate the Charter into the treaties by the Lisbon Treaty amendments also underlines a conscious choice not to endow it with a constitutional status. Moreover, the terse style of CJEU judgments, originally modelled on those of the French Conseil d'Etat, is not particularly productive of

H Schermers' early fear expressed in 'The European Communities under the ECHR' (1978) *Legal Issues of European Integration* 1. See also Andrew Williams 'Burying, Not Praising the European Convention on Human Rights: A Provocation' in Shaw, Tierney and Walker (n 2).

[71] Elsewhere the fear that the EU is becoming an 'Empire' has been expressed, partly due to an aggressive application of its rules to its neighbours, evidencing imperial politics—see J Zielonka, *Europa as Empire* (Oxford, Oxford University Press, 2007).

[72] Then Prime Minister Jean-Claude Juncker proposed a working rule, according to which 'the decisions, reports, conclusions, recommendations and opinions of [the Council of Europe] ... will be systematically taken as the first Europe-wide reference source for human rights'. See Jean-Claude Junker, Council of Europe/ European Union, 'A Sole Ambition for the European Continent', Report to the Heads of State and Government of the Member States of the Council of Europe (11 April 2006). See also Memorandum of Understanding between the Council of Europe and the European Union, CM (2007) 74 (10 May 2007).

[73] For more on this, see Pedro Cruz Villalón, 'Rights in Europe: The Crowded House', KCL Working Paper in European Law, 01/2012.

[74] See, for example, the 1925 case of *Gitlow v New York*, in which the US Supreme Court held that the First Amendment of the US Bill of Rights could also apply to the states through the operation of the 14th Amendment (which specifically applies to the states). Since then, the US Supreme Court has applied the Bill of Rights to state laws even when the states are acting within their own sphere of competence. In this way, the US Supreme Court has created a unified constitutional order of fundamental rights.

[75] For more on this, see S Douglas-Scott, 'Fundamental Rights Not Euroscepticism: Why the UK Should Embrace the EU Charter', at 21, available at: http://papers.ssrn.com/sol3/papers.cfm?abstract_id=2528768.

substantive discussion of human rights case law. The EU's main concern has been with market building and regulation. In this, it differs from traditional state constitutions and human rights regimes. Part of the problem is that most litigation brought by individuals comes to the CJEU by way of a preliminary reference from the national courts, in which the CJEU is only seized with certain aspects of a case, and fundamental rights are often pleaded in a collateral or tangential manner. This can be contrasted to the approaches of human rights courts, such as the ECtHR, in which fundamental rights themselves are the basis for an application. Given this, it is likely that the CJEU will continue to determine issues of fundamental rights on a case-by-case basis, with a particular focus on the proportionality of any infringement of rights rather than with an eye to the development of a coherent, substantive fundamental rights law.

Therefore, all sorts of possible consequences for the two institutions follow from the now binding nature of the Charter. At time of writing, shortly after Opinion 2/13, it is hard to predict if the EU will in fact accede to the ECHR. However, the attitude of the CJEU, whether in its stress on EU special characteristics of EU law in Opinion 2/13 or in its preference for the Charter as the first human rights point of reference, illustrates a strong focus on the autonomy of EU law. If that is to be the case, it is to be hoped that the EU, and particularly the CJEU, will show itself as equal to the task of a protector of rights.

V. CONCLUSION

In conclusion, the binding legal status of the Charter and its growing case law, as well as the requirement that the EU accede to the ECHR, have undoubtedly had an impact on the relationship between the EU and the ECtHR. The key question will be whether these further changes will do anything to improve fundamental rights protection in Europe or, by adding further layers of complexity, will obscure and problematise human rights in the European legal space.

For some time, there have been some reservations about the EU's capacity to function as a human rights organisation. One hopes that the Lisbon Treaty reforms will have improved this capacity. The Scottish philosopher and political economist Adam Smith is famously supposed to have said: 'On the road from the City of Skepticism, I had to pass through the Valley of Ambiguity.'[76] Since Lisbon, perhaps scepticism as to the EU's commitment to human rights has diminished a little. However, we are still in the valley of ambiguity.

[76] The statement may in fact be apocryphal. This author could not trace the source of the quotation.

3

Who Decides on Fundamental Rights Issues in Europe?

Towards a Mechanism to Coordinate the Roles of the National Courts, the ECJ and the ECtHR

JANNEKE GERARDS

I. INTRODUCTION

FOR A LONG time, the European Court of Justice (ECJ or Court) has been a relatively unimportant player in the field of European fundamental rights. Of course, it should not be ignored that it has achieved important results by recognising fundamental rights as general principles of EU law and by assessing national and European measures and decisions for their compatibility with such principles. Nevertheless, as a result of the lack of a binding fundamental rights catalogue and because of the limited competences of the EU institutions, the ECJ's role in developing European fundamental rights has long remained a modest one.[1] Often the ECJ has adopted a limited definition of fundamental rights[2] and it has hardly contributed to the development of a doctrine of fundamental rights law—although there are notable exceptions in the field of non-discrimination and equal treatment law.[3] Obviously the Court preferred applying existing concepts

[1] See, eg, B de Witte, 'The Past and Future Role of the European Court of Justice in the Protection of Human Rights' in P Alston et al (eds), *The EU and Human Rights* (Oxford, Oxford University Press, 1999) 859 at 869–70; G de Búrca, 'The Evolution of EU Human Rights Law' in P Craig and G de Búrca, *The Evolution of EU Law*, 2nd edn (Oxford, Oxford University Press, 2011) 465.

[2] eg, de Witte (n 1) 880.

[3] *cf*, eg, de Witte (n 1) 878–79; S Douglas-Scott, 'The European Union and Human Rights after the Treaty of Lisbon' (2011) 11 *Human Rights Law Review* 645, 649. As regards the exception of non-discrimination law, one may consider, for example, that the ECJ already developed notions such as that of indirect discrimination in the 1980s (Case 170/84 *Bilka Kaufhaus*

and notions, which it derived from a variety of national and European fundamental rights sources.[4] Moreover, it has often been remarked that the ECJ was not very 'fundamental rights minded' in the sense that in many cases about conflicts between fundamental rights and general interests, it favoured the general interests without giving much weight to fundamental rights issues.[5]

For the European Court of Human Rights (ECtHR), all this has been very different. The ECtHR has always been a specialised human rights court, which from the very beginning had the task of deciding on individual complaints about alleged breaches of the European Convention of Human Rights (ECHR).[6] Although it took some time for individuals to discover the possibility to seek redress at the European level, they started doing so ever more actively from the 1970s onwards.[7] This offered much opportunity to the ECtHR to develop an important European human rights *acquis*. The relative quiet in which it could do its work seems to have been favourable to the development of a number of greatly influential fundamental rights doctrines and methodologies, such as positive obligations, the margin of appreciation, proportionality, evolutive interpretation and common ground reasoning.[8] Over time, these have become deeply embedded in national law and they are ingrained in the fundamental rights language used throughout

[1986] ECR 1607), while the ECtHR recognised the concept only in its 2007 judgment in *DH and others v Czech Republic* ECHR 2007-IV). On the development of EU non-discrimination law, see, eg, M Bell, 'The Principle of Equal Treatment: Widening and Deepening' in Craig and de Búrca (n 1) 611–39; and D Schiek, 'Fundamental Rights Jurisprudence between Member States' Prerogatives and Citizens' Autonomy' in H-W Micklitz and B de Witte (eds), *The European Court of Justice and the Autonomy of the Member States* (Antwerp, Intersentia, 2012) 231ff; on the development of ECHR non-discrimination law, see, eg, JH Gerards, 'The Discrimination Grounds of Article 14 ECHR' (2013) 13 *Human Rights Law Review* 99.

[4] *cf*, eg, D Spielmann, 'Human Rights Case Law in the Strasbourg and Luxembourg Courts: Conflicts, Inconsistencies, and Complementarities' in Alston et al (n 1) 757, 764ff.

[5] eg, J Coppel and A O'Neill, 'The European Court of Justice: Taking Rights Seriously?' (1992) 29 *Common Market Law Review* (1992) 669; de Witte (n 1) 880–81; FMJ den Houdijker, *Afweging van grondrechten in een veellagig rechtssysteem. De toepassing van het proportionaliteitsbeginsel in strikte zin door het EHRM en het HvJ EU* [*Balancing Fundamental Rights: The Application of the Principle of Proportionality in the Strict Sense by the ECtHR and the CJEU*] (Nijmegen, WLP, 2012).

[6] See in detail E Bates, *The Evolution of the European Convention on Human Rights—From its Inception to the Creation of a Permanent Court of Human Rights* (Oxford, Oxford University Press, 2010).

[7] See, eg, ibid; MR Madsen, 'The Protracted Institutionalization of the Strasbourg Court: From Legal Diplomacy to Integrationist Jurisprudence' in J Christoffersen and MR Madsen (eds), *The European Court of Human Rights between Law and Politics* (Oxford, Oxford University Press, 2011) 43. For the increasing interest taken since the 1970s, see also A Lester, 'The European Court of Human Rights after 50 Years' in J Christoffersen and MR Madsen (eds), *The European Court of Human Rights between Law and Politics* (Oxford, Oxford University Press, 2011) 98, 100–01.

[8] An abundance of literature is available on all of these concepts; for a brief overview, see eg DJ Harris, M O'Boyle, EP Bates and CM Buckley, *Harris, O'Boyle & Warbrick's Law of the European Convention on Human Rights* (Oxford, Oxford University Press, 2014).

Europe.[9] Where the interpretation of fundamental rights is concerned, the ECJ has acquired such great authority that it has been termed a constitutional court for Europe.[10]

Over the past few years, however, in particular since the EU Charter of Fundamental Rights has become a binding document,[11] the fundamental rights landscape in Europe has started to change. The ECJ is increasingly dealing with fundamental rights issues and it is handing down an increasing number of judgments directly quoting Charter rights.[12] On the one hand, this seems due to the increase in the exercise of EU competences in areas where fundamental rights issues are particularly likely to arise, such as migration and asylum law, employment, protection of personal data, and sanction mechanisms in relation to international terrorism.[13] The greater activity of

[9] In more detail, see, eg, JH Gerards, 'The European Court of Human Rights and the National Courts—Giving Shape to the Notion of "Shared Responsibility"' in JH Gerards and JWA Fleuren (eds), *Implementation of the ECHR and of the Judgments of the ECtHR in National Case Law: A Comparative Analysis* (Antwerp, Intersentia, 2014); H Keller and A Stone Sweet (eds), *A Europe of Rights: The Impact of the ECHR on National Legal Systems* (Oxford, Oxford University Press, 2008); G Martinico and O Pollicino (eds), *The National Judicial Treatment of the ECHR and EU Laws: A Comparative Constitutional Perspective* (Groningen, European Law Publishing, 2010); LR Helfer, 'Redesigning the European Court of Human Rights: Embeddedness as a Deep Structural Principle of the European Human Rights Regime' (2008) 19 *European Journal of International Law* 125.

[10] See, eg, S Greer and L Wildhaber, 'Revisiting the Debate about "Constitutionalising" the European Court of Human Rights' (2012) 12 *Human Rights Law Review* 655; EA Alkema, 'The European Convention as a Constitution and its Court as a Constitutional Court' in P Mahoney et al (eds), *Protecting Human Rights: The European Perspective* (Cologne, Carl Heymans, 2000) 41.

[11] This is different from saying that these changes are a direct result of the Charter's becoming binding—it would seem that the 'bindingness' as such would have little impact, since the ECJ could equally have developed its fundamental case law based on the non-binding Charter, in particular through its general principles or by applying the Convention rights (*cf* S Weatherill, 'From Economic Rights to Fundamental Rights' in S de Vries et al (eds), *The Protection of Fundamental Rights in the EU after Lisbon* (Oxford, Hart Publishing, 2013) 11, 30. Opinions on the effect of the Charter's becoming binding differ, however; see, eg, in the same volume, SA de Vries, 'The Protection of Fundamental Rights within Europe's Internal Market after Lisbon—An Endeavour for More Harmony' at 74. See further D Sarmiento, 'Who's Afraid of the Charter? The Court of Justice, National Courts and the New Framework of Fundamental Rights Protection in Europe' (2013) 50 *CML Rev* 1267, 1270; S Iglesias Sánchez, 'The Court and the Charter: The Impact of the Entry into Force of the Lisbon Treaty on the ECJ's Approach to Fundamental Rights' (2012) 49 *Common Market Law Review CML Rev* 1565, 1568.

[12] Within three years, the number of preliminary rulings in which the Court directly quoted the Charter has tripled, from 43 cases in 2011 to 114 in 2013—see the Commission staff working document accompanying the European Commission's *2013 Report on the Application of the EU Charter of Fundamental Rights*, Brussels, 14 April 2014, COM(2014) 224 final, SWD(2014) 141 final, 7. See also C Ladenburger, 'European Union Institutional Report' in J Laffranque (ed), *The Protection of Fundamental Rights Post-Lisbon: The Interaction between the Charter of Fundamental Rights of the European Union, the European Convention on Human Rights and National Constitutions*, Reports of the XXV FIDE Congress Tallinn 2012, Vol 1 (Tallinn, Tartu University Press, 2012) 141, 149–51; and M Cartabia, 'Europe and Rights: Taking Dialogue Seriously' (2009) 5 *European Constitutional Law Review* 5.

[13] G De Búrca, 'After the EU Charter of Fundamental Rights: The Court of Justice as a Human Rights Adjudicator?' (2013) 20 *Maastricht Journal of European and Comparative Law* 168; Douglas-Scott (n 3) 646–47.

the EU in these areas seems to have alerted litigants not only to the risks thereby created for fundamental rights, but also to the possibilities offered by the EU Charter of Fundamental Rights to provide additional protection.[14]

On the other hand, the increased popularity of EU fundamental rights law seems due to the fact that the EU Charter protects a number of rights which are not mentioned in the ECHR, such as the right to conduct a business, the right to good administration, and a variety of socio-economic rights and principles.[15] The discovery by litigants of the possibilities offered by the Charter has the result that it is ever more frequently invoked before the national courts, and the national courts have not hesitated to forward these cases to the ECJ to learn its views on how the relevant fundamental rights provisions should be understood and applied.[16] In response to this, the ECJ has been able to confirm its autonomous and primary role in interpreting the Charter and in determining the appropriate level of protection.[17] Most recently and in a particularly pronounced fashion, it has done so in its Opinion 2/13, in which it declared the Draft Agreement on the Accession of the European Union to the ECHR to be incompatible with EU law.[18]

Finally, an important factor contributing to change seems to be the predicament that the ECtHR currently finds itself in. The Strasbourg Court's popularity together with the increased number of States Parties to the Convention and the poor human rights situation in many of the newly acceded States have resulted in an ever-growing caseload for this Court.[19]

[14] *cf* Ladenburger (n 12) 150; and, more implicitly, Iglesias Sánchez (n 11) 1577.

[15] For a statistical overview of the provisions of the Charter most often mentioned in preliminary references (the right to a fair trial, the right to good administration, the right to property and, amongst others, the freedom to conduct a business), see the Commission staff working document accompanying the European Commission's *2013 Report* (n 12) 9.

[16] A recent empirical and statistical analysis of cases in which the Charter was invoked before the Dutch courts has shown, for example, that in particular the right to a fair trial of Art 47 of the EU Charter is often invoked (which can be explained by the fact that the Dutch Constitution does not expressly protect this right and Art 6 ECHR is not applicable in migration cases), as well as Art 24 (rights of the child—a right which is not contained in the ECHR, but is often important in migration cases) and Art 41 (the right to good governance, which is also not protected by the ECHR); see H van Harten and H Grootelaar, 'Doorwerking van het Handvest van de Grondrechten van de Europese Unie in de Nederlandse rechtspraak: een kwantitatieve stand van zaken' [Effects of the EU Charter of Fundamental Rights in Dutch Case Law: A Quantitative State of Affairs] (2014) 39 *Nederlands Tijdschrift voor Mensenrechten/NJCM-Bulletin* 182, 194. The Dutch situation in this regard appears to be in line with the general European situation; see the statistics in the Commission staff working document accompanying the European Commission's *2013 Report* (n 12) 10.

[17] See in particular Case C-617/10 *Åkerberg Fransson* (ECJ, 26 February 2013); and Case C-399/11 *Melloni* (ECJ, 26 February 2013); on this, see further Sarmiento (n 11) 1287ff, who, however, also stresses that even where the EU Charter is said to play a primary role, the ECJ in turn is always bound to take the ECHR and the ECtHR's judgments into account (at 1292).

[18] See Opinion 2/13 (ECJ, 18 December 2014).

[19] See in more detail, with references, eg, JH Gerards and AB Terlouw, 'Solutions for the European Court of Human Rights: The *Amicus Curiae* Project' in S Flogaitis, T Zwart and J Fraser (eds), *The European Court of Human Rights and its Discontents: Turning Criticism into Strength* (Cheltenham, Edward Elgar, 2013) 158–60.

The increased influx of cases, in combination with limited resources, has made it ever more difficult for the ECtHR to deal with all its cases within a reasonable amount of time.[20] Perhaps it is not surprising, therefore, that individual victims of breaches of fundamental rights have started to look for redress elsewhere.[21] Perhaps this may also explain why litigants in the Member States of the EU increasingly base their claims on the EU Charter of Fundamental Rights. They may well hope that national courts are willing to refer a question to the ECJ in their case and that, by this means, they can obtain clarity and redress more quickly, that is, without needing to exhaust all domestic remedies and only then start the lengthy proceedings in Strasbourg.[22]

The result of these developments is that the ECJ is offered increasing possibilities to grow into a fundamental rights court in its own right. It has used these possibilities over the past five years by rather autonomously developing a set of fundamental rights standards and doctrines. It has recognised, for example, that large companies just as much as government authorities may have an obligation to respect fundamental rights,[23] it has started to develop its own doctrine regarding the justiciability of social rights[24] and it has set its own standards for limitation of fundamental rights.[25] The ECJ is thereby clearly building its own fundamental rights *acquis* on a par with that of the ECtHR, and its reluctance regarding the EU's accession to the ECHR seems to confirm that it values this development highly.[26]

[20] Although much improvement has been made as a result of a number of procedural amendments and efficiency-enhancing measures (see in particular CDDH, *Report Containing Elements to Contribute to the Evaluation of the Effects of Protocol No 14 to the Convention and the Implementation of the Interlaken and Izmir Declarations on the Court's Situation*, Strasbourg, 30 November 2012, CDDH(2012)R76 Addendum II). By 28 February 2015, 68,000 cases were pending before one of the judicial formations of the Court (http://echr.coe.int > statistics).

[21] *cf* Douglas-Scott (n 3) 658.

[22] *cf* also S Douglas-Scott, 'The Court of Justice of the European Union and the European Court of Human Rights after Lisbon' in de Vries et al (n 11) 153, 163.

[23] Case C-131/12 *Google Spain* (ECJ, 13 May 2014).

[24] eg, Case C-356/12 *Glatzel* (ECJ, 22 May 2014).

[25] eg, Joined Cases C-293/12 and C-594/12, *Digital Rights Ireland* (ECJ, 8 April 2014) (with a strong accent on core rights, suitability and necessity rather than on balancing, as would be more usual for the ECtHR). For a further analysis of the Court's approach to limitations of Charter rights, see K Lenaerts, 'Exploring the Limits of the EU Charter of Fundamental Rights' (2012) 6 *European Constitutional Law Review* 375; and G Anagnostaras, 'Balancing Conflicting Fundamental Rights: The *Sky Österreich* Paradigm' (2014) 39 *EL Rev* 111; *cf* Iglesias Sánchez (n 11) 1578.

[26] Indeed, several commentators to Opinion 2/13 (n 18) have indicated that the ECJ by means of its opinion strives to protect its own position and prerogatives as the highest court in the EU in the field of fundamental rights. See critically about this, eg, S Peers, 'The CJEU and the EU's Accession to the ECHR: A Clear and Present Danger to Human Rights Protection', *EU Law Analysis Blog* (18 December 2014), http://eulawanalysis.blogspot.co.uk/2014/12/the-cjeu-and-eus-accession-to-echr.html; W Michl, 'Thou Shalt Have No Other Courts before Me', *Verfassungsblog on Matters Constitutional* (23 December 2014), www.verfassungsblog.de/en/thou-shalt-no-courts; S Douglas-Scott, 'Opinion 2/13 on EU Accession

Thus, although the ECtHR continues to be regarded as the main standard-setting body in the field of human rights and it is common ground that its jurisprudence needs to be respected and applied by both the national courts and the ECJ, it is obvious that panels are shifting. Possibly as a corollary, the relationship between the European courts is becoming ever more strained and complicated,[27] as is illustrated by the ECJ's apparent power play of blocking the EU's accession to the Convention. The ECJ's Opinion has been characterised here as expressive of a certain degree of 'jealousy' and 'vanity', and even defenders of the Opinion have characterised its tone as making clear that 'Strasbourg is not welcome in Luxembourg'.[28] In turn, the President of the ECtHR voiced his disappointment at not being accepted as the apex court for fundamental rights matters, but he also clearly regarded it as an invitation to strengthen the Court's own role.[29] 'More than ever before', he stated, 'the onus will be on the Strasbourg Court to do what it can in cases before it to protect citizens from the negative effects of this situation'.[30] Hence, the present relationship between the two courts can be characterised as one of pluralism and heterarchy, and one of competition and tension, rather than one of comity.[31]

All this means that the fifth anniversary of the binding Charter is celebrated at a time of changing relationships between the courts competent to deal with fundamental rights issues.[32] Fundamental rights adjudication in Europe has thereby become increasingly complex and confusing for all involved. National litigants may wonder whether and when they should prefer basing their claims on the EU Charter over founding their pleas on

to the ECHR: A Christmas Bombshell from the European Court of Justice', *UK Constitutional Law Association Blog* (24 December 2014), http://ukconstitutionallaw.org/2014/12/24/sionaidh-douglas-scott-opinion-213-on-eu-accession-to-the-echr-a-christmas-bombshell-from-the-european-court-of-justice. Others have sought to nuance this image of 'judicial vanity' and jealousy; see, eg, C Barnard, 'Opinion 2/13 on EU Accession to the ECHR: Looking for the Silver Lining', *EU Law Analysis Blog* (16 February 2015), http://eulawanalysis.blogspot.co.uk/2015/02/opinion-213-on-eu-accession-to-echr.html; and D Halberstam, '"It's the Autonomy, Stupid!", A Modest Defense of Opinion 2/13 on EU Accession to the ECHR, and the Way Forward' (2015) *German Law Journal*, available at: http://ssrn.com/abstract=2567591.

[27] *cf* de Búrca (n 1) 489.

[28] Halberstam (n 26); see also Barnard (n 26) and see P Gragl, 'The Reasonableness of Jealousy: Opinion 2/13 and EU Accession to the ECHR' in W Benedek, WK Benoit-Rohmer and M Nowak (eds), *European Yearbook on Human Rights 2015* (Vienna, Neuer Wissenschaftlicher Verlag, 2015).

[29] D Spielmann, 'Foreword' in European Court of Human Rights, *Annual Report 2014* (Strasbourg, February 2015) 6.

[30] ibid.

[31] *cf*, eg, N Krisch, 'The Open Architecture of European Human Rights Law' (2008) 71 *MLR* 183, with many references to relevant literature on pluralism. See also G Di Federico, 'Fundamental Rights in the EU: Legal Pluralism and Multi-level Protection after the Lisbon Treaty' in G Di Federico (ed), *The EU Charter of Fundamental Rights. From Declaration to Binding Instrument* (Dordrecht, Springer, 2011) 15, 53.

[32] On this, see already I Cameron, 'Competing Rights?' in de Vries et al (n 11) 181.

national constitutional law or on principles and standards derived from the Strasbourg case law. National courts may ask themselves what role they can still play in the tripartite relationship with the Strasbourg and Luxembourg Courts, and to what degree they can continue to use their own constitutional standards to deal with fundamental rights cases.[33] The European courts, too, may wonder how to go about. Formerly, it seemed clear that in all fundamental rights cases, the ECJ should follow the lead of the ECtHR and apply the standards and doctrines defined in the Strasbourg case law, while, in turn, the ECtHR should respect the particularities of the EU legal system in cases related to EU law.[34] But now that the ECJ has started to develop its own doctrines and has to answer many questions before the ECtHR is able to deal with them, and now that it has very strongly voiced the autonomy of the EU system of fundamental rights protection, this natural division of roles no longer seems to work.[35]

These changes in the European fundamental rights landscape raise important theoretical and practical questions as to how the three 'levels' of courts competent to decide in fundamental rights cases should interrelate, and which of them should take the lead in answering novel fundamental rights questions.[36] A straightforward answer to these questions has not yet been offered and perhaps it is indeed impossible to find a conclusive coordinating mechanism that could help to decide which judicial level should have a certain responsibility. However, in order to reduce the existing confusion as to the competences of the different courts and their interrelationship, it is worth exploring the possibilities of finding such a coordinating mechanism. The aim of the current chapter is to take up this challenge.[37]

[33] This question has become particularly relevant after the ECJ's judgment in the *Melloni* case, which appears to leave little room for national fundamental rights application in the sphere of EU law, yet also appears to be limited to the particular situation in which there is full harmonisation of a certain fundamental rights issue; see *Melloni* (n 17); and see further on this Sarmiento (n 11) 1289ff.

[34] *cf* Krisch (n 31).

[35] Polakiewicz even has stated that 'the emerging pattern may suggest a division of labour, with the ECHR having only residual application where EU law applies'—J Polakiewicz, 'EU Law and the ECHR: Will EU Accession to the European Convention on Human Rights Square the Circle?', www.coe.int/t/dghl/standardsetting/hrpolicy/Accession/Accession_documents/Oxford_18_January_2013_versionWeb.pdf, 7.

[36] See L Wildhaber, 'About Co-existence of Three Different Legal Systems and Three Jurisdictions' (2005) 60 *Zeitschrift für öffentliches Recht* 313; Krisch (n 31); G Luebbe-Wolf, 'Who Has the Last Word? National and Transnational Courts—Conflict and Cooperation' (2011) 30 *Yearbook of European Law* 86, 96; Di Federico (n 31) 23; see also, in more depth, C van de Heyning, *Fundamental Rights Lost in Complexity: The Protection of Fundamental Rights against Violations by the Rulemaker in Converging National and European Legal Systems* (PhD thesis, Antwerp University, 2011).

[37] For another such effort, which is geared towards a notion of 'democratic subsidiarity', see S Besson, 'European Human Rights, Supranational Judicial Review and Democracy: Thinking Outside the Judicial Box' in P Popelier, C Van de Heyning and P Van Nuffel (eds), *Human Rights Protection in the European Legal Order: The Interaction between the European and the National Courts* (Antwerp, Intersentia, 2011) 97. The focus on the institutional

To be able to explain a number of possible coordinating factors and criteria, it is necessary to address the preliminary question of the extent to which courts actually do have a choice, that is, whether they have sufficient instruments available to decide to deal with certain human rights issues and leave other matters for the other courts to decide. This issue is addressed in section II. Section III then discusses a possible criterion that can be used to give direction to a division of tasks, which is related to the main tasks or raison d'etre of the different courts. Section IV aims to clarify the possibilities for use of this principle by applying it to two practical examples in order to see if it can help determine which court level would be best positioned to take the lead and set the standards in these cases. Since it will be concluded in this section that the raison d'etre criterion alone does not suffice as a coordinating device, section V explores some additional factors that may be of help. Section VI cautiously concludes that the criteria and factors set out in this chapter may indeed be useful in finding a way out of the quandary created by the existence of three levels of courts competent to deal with similar issues.

II. DO THE COURTS HAVE A CHOICE?

On first thoughts, one may easily consider that courts do not have any choice as to whether they will take on a certain fundamental rights case. With the exception of constitutional courts that have some discretion to select cases, national courts are usually simply presented with certain cases and they have to give judgment in all of them. Likewise, the ECJ cannot avoid having to give an answer to preliminary questions that concentrate on fundamental rights issues. The ECtHR also just has to deal with all applications that meet the admissibility criteria of the Convention, even if they are controversial and even if they originate from delicate national policy choices. Thus, it would seem illusory to state that the different courts could have a say in which of them should take the lead in dealing with fundamental rights cases and it would seem equally fanciful to start looking for some coordination mechanism.

However, saying that courts have no choice is plainly incorrect.[38] In reality, all courts, national courts as much as European courts, have a variety of

interrelationship between the courts chosen in this chapter is different from one related to setting the appropriate standard of protection; this chapter does not deal with that issue, for which mainly Art 53 of the EU Charter and Art 53 of the ECHR are relevant. On that topic, see, eg, Cameron (n 32) (with references to relevant sources); C Van de Heyning, 'No Place Like Home: Discretionary Space for the Domestic Protection of Fundamental Rights' in Popelier, Van de Heyning and Van Nuffel (n 37) 65.

[38] See also A Stone Sweet, 'The European Court of Justice' in Craig and de Búrca (n 1) 121, 128.

tools at their disposal which enable them to avoid or, by contrast, choose to expressly address certain issues. For example, they can find that a case does not really pertain to a fundamental rights matter or can be solved without having to deal with the fundamental rights questions raised by the litigants, or they can use techniques of deference to help them avoid having to take a substantive stance on a fundamental rights matter. In suitable cases, national courts may further decide to refer a fundamental rights related question to the ECJ, thereby 'outsourcing' or delegating the substance of the matter.[39] In the future, the highest national courts may even decide to direct a request to the ECtHR on the interpretation of the Convention.[40]

Likewise, the ECJ and the ECtHR can relatively easily decide not to decide. First, they can use procedural admissibility requirements to dismiss certain cases. The ECJ can, for example, hold that an issue is hypothetical in nature,[41] while the ECtHR can find that a case is manifestly ill-founded or that it does not meet the *de minimis* standard laid down in Article 35(3)(c) ECHR. Second, just like the national courts, the European courts can avail themselves of instruments that create a certain flexibility as to how deeply they will enter into the substance of fundamental rights issues. They can avoid having to take a substantive view on difficult cases, for example, by leaving a wide margin of discretion to the national authorities or to the EU institutions, by using incrementalist and minimalist approaches or by taking a 'procedural' turn.[42] Many instances of the use of such tools can be found

[39] For the circumstances in which the ECJ has obliged the Member States to do so, see in particular *Åkerberg Fransson* (n 17); and *Melloni* (n 17).

[40] That is, if Protocol No 16 enters into force for the relevant state. For an analysis of the advisory opinions procedure provided by that Protocol, see, eg, P Gragl, '(Judicial) Love is Not a One-Way Street: The EU Preliminary Reference Procedure as a Model for ECtHR Advisory Opinions under Draft Protocol No 16' (2013) 38 *EL Rev* 229; K Dzehtsariou, 'Interaction between the European Court of Human Rights and Member States: European Consensus, Advisory Opinions and the Question of Legitimacy' in S Flogaitis et al (eds), *The European Court of Human Rights and its Discontents: Turning Criticism into Strength* (Cheltenham, Edward Elgar, 2013) 116; JH Gerards, 'The Advisory Opinions Procedure of Protocol No. 16 to the European Convention of Human Rights—A Critical Appraisal' (2014) 21 *Maastricht Journal of European and Comparative Law* 630.

[41] The basis for this can be found mainly in Case 244/80 *Foglia (No 2)* [1981] ECR I-3045 [18]; see further, eg, P Craig and G de Búrca, *EU Law. Text, Cases and Materials*, 5th edn (Oxford, Oxford University Press, 2011) 467ff; T de la Mare and C Donnelly, 'Preliminary Rulings and EU Legal Integration: Evolution and Stasis' in Craig and de Búrca (n 1) 363, 371; T Tridimas, 'Constitutional Review of Member State Action: The Virtues and Vices of an Incomplete Jurisdiction' (2011) 9 *International Journal of Constitutional Law* 737, 739.

[42] On these tools, for the ECtHR, see in more detail Gerards (n 9); Van de Heyning (n 36) 190ff; for the EU, see, eg, K Lenaerts, 'How the ECJ Thinks: A Study on Judicial Legitimacy' (2013) 36 *Fordham International Law Journal* 1302, 1326ff; P Craig, 'Judicial Review, Intensity and Deference in EU Law' in D Dyzenhaus (ed), *The Unity of Public Law* (Oxford, Hart Publishing, 2004); JH Gerards, 'Pluralism, Deference and the Margin of Appreciation Doctrine' (2011) 17 *European Law Journal* 80; JH Gerards, 'Judicial Argumentation in Fundamental Rights Cases—The EU Courts' Challenge' in U Neergaard and R Nielsen (eds), *European Legal Method in a Multi-level EU Legal Order* (Copenhagen, DJØF Publishing, 2012) 27, 59ff. See also Cameron (n 32) 199.

in the doctrine of both courts. In recent years, for example, the ECtHR has often held that it will primarily investigate whether a certain fundamental rights matter has been dealt with by the national authorities in a procedurally careful manner.[43] If the legislative process has passed off well and meets all the standards of participation, transparency, deliberation and accountability, the ECtHR will not be much inclined to intervene.[44] The same is true if the ECtHR finds that the national courts have looked carefully at a fundamental rights issue and have applied a fair and reasonable set of standards to decide on the reasonableness of an interference.[45] This approach allows the ECtHR to leave the substance of the matter to be assessed at the national level, which helps it avoid having to take a decision of its own. Another convenient tool is that employed by the ECJ of answering preliminary questions only very minimally by restricting the interpretation to the facts of the case and thereby steering clear of a head-on confrontation with the wider fundamental rights issues concerned.[46] The ECJ also may opt for defining a relatively general and abstract interpretation while leaving it up to the national courts to apply these to the facts of the case.[47]

By using such techniques, the courts may make important choices as to leaving certain matters to be decided on another level of adjudication. Of course, such methods can also be used to the contrary effect, ie, to decide to deal with certain cases in great depth and detail, with priority or urgency, or in a particularly principled manner.[48] The ECtHR can choose, for example, to provide for early guidance in certain fundamental rights cases by using its 'priority policy', which means that it may give priority to cases in which important and new questions of interpretation are being raised.[49] Likewise, the ECJ can consciously decide to answer certain preliminary questions by

[43] Gerards (n 9) 52–62; Van de Heyning (n 36) 209–11.

[44] ibid; see, eg, *Maurice v France*, App No 11810/03 (ECtHR (GC), 6 October 2005) [124].

[45] ibid; see, eg, *Von Hannover No 2 v Germany*, App Nos 40660/08 and 60641/08 (ECtHR (GC), 7 February 2012) [107].

[46] An example of this may be found in *Melloni* (n 17); on the role of minimalism and incrementalism in the fundamental rights case law of the ECJ, see also, eg, Lenaerts (n 42) 1344ff and 1356ff; Stone Sweet (n 38) 129; de Búrca (n 13); on the role of this in the case law of the ECtHR, see Gerards (n 9) 62–71.

[47] See in more detail, eg, D Sarmiento, 'The Silent Lamb and the Deaf Wolves' in M Avbelj and J Komárek (eds), *Constitutional Pluralism in the European Union and Beyond* (Oxford, Oxford University Press, 2012) 285; Cameron (n 32).

[48] *cf* Tridimas (n 41).

[49] The policy is based on rule 41 of the Rules of Court; for the policy, see www.echr.coe.int/Documents/Priority%20policy_ENG.pdf. According to that policy, 'Applications raising questions capable of having an impact on the effectiveness of the Convention system (in particular a structural or endemic situation that the Court has not yet examined, pilot-judgment procedure) or applications raising an important question of general interest (in particular a serious question capable of having major implications for domestic legal systems or for the European system), inter-State cases' can be given priority level 2 of the seven levels distinguished, priority level 1 being reserved for urgent applications, which in particular would include a risk to life or health of the applicant.

setting uniform and general standards to be applied throughout the EU or at the least by providing for detailed guidance in the interpretation of the relevant norms.[50]

III. THE RAISON D'ETRE OF THE COURTS AS COORDINATING CRITERION

A. Introduction

The question this chapter will turn to now is how the various courts can use the tools described in section II in determining which of them should take the lead in deciding fundamental rights matters. National courts may consider, for example, whether they would need to answer a fundamental rights question themselves, or rather should direct a preliminary reference to the ECJ or, when the advisory opinions procedure of Protocol No 16 eventually enters into force, send a request for interpretation of the Convention to the ECtHR.[51] To make this choice, they need to know and understand at which level the best guidance for their decision making can be found. In turn, the ECtHR and the ECJ will need to know when it is reasonable or desirable to employ techniques such as those described above in order to leave certain matters to be decided by the national courts. And finally, the ECtHR may need to decide to what extent it should defer to the ECJ, and the ECJ, too, would need to know if it would be preferable to await guidance to be given by the ECtHR or whether it should take the lead itself.

B. The Raison d'Etre of the ECJ and the ECtHR

It is submitted here that an important criterion to guide the various courts in deciding which of them should have priority in dealing with fundamental

[50] Stone Sweet (n 38) 131; Tridimas (n 41) 740ff.

[51] As mentioned above, however, sometimes the national courts do not have a choice, since they may be obliged under EU law to refer a question (see n 39). Moreover, Voßkuhle has argued, from a strictly legal perspective, that such choices really cannot occur, since the starting point is exclusiveness of jurisdiction. From that perspective, the ECJ is competent for ensuring compliance with the Treaties, while the ECtHR ensures compliance with the ECHR, and their respective judgments are relevant only within their own judicial sphere (A Voßkuhle, 'The Cooperation between European Courts: The *Verbund* of European Courts and its Legal Toolbox' in Court of Justice of the European Union, *The Court of Justice and the Construction of Europe: Analyses and Perspectives on Sixty Years of Case-Law* (The Hague, TMC Asser Press, 2013) 81, 85. In reality, however, the questions arising may be of a similar nature and the courts are interpreting substantially comparable norms, which unavoidably implies some competition between the two European courts as to which would have the final say on their interpretation. Indeed, Voßkuhle seems to admit as much (ibid, 85).

rights issues is closely connected to their specific tasks and functions, or, in other words, to their raison d'etre. In particular, this criterion could be helpful in determining whether one of the two European courts should take the lead and, if so, which of them should do so. It is relatively clear, after all, that the raison d'etre of the ECJ is different from that of the ECtHR.[52] The main task of the ECJ is to guarantee, as the Court formulated it in its famous *Melloni* case, the 'primacy, unity and effectiveness of European Union law'.[53] Indeed, the ECJ has always been the champion of the *effet utile* of EU law, which of itself is closely related to achieving the ideals of economic and political integration.[54] Much of the Court's case law is based on principles directly related to such *effet utile* and to the Member States' duties in upholding it.[55] Important principles in this regard are those of direct effect and supremacy, harmony and uniformity in the interpretation of internal market and competition law, mutual respect and mutual recognition, effectiveness and equivalence of national procedural mechanisms to enforce EU law and, more recently, EU citizenship and the notion of autonomy. These principles clearly may be seen to reflect on the judicial strategies that the ECJ follows and the legal-political choices it makes.[56]

[52] See also Cameron (n 32) 197.

[53] *Melloni* (n 17) [60]. On the 'raison d'etre' of the EU as such, see, eg, G de Búrca, 'Europe's Raison d'Etre', NYU Public Law and Legal Theory Research Paper No 13-09, http://ssrn.com/abstract=2224310.

[54] See in particular Arts 2 and 3 TEU; and *cf* de Búrca (n 53) section 5; Schiek (n 3) 223. In fact, the ideals, values and objectives underlying the EU (as expressed in Arts 2 and 3 TEU) are not very different from those underlying the European Convention, but in practice the accent has become a different one—while the EU has long focused on economic integration (and more recently integration in many other arenas), the ECHR system has always focused on human rights. On this, see in particular G Quinn, 'The European Union and the Council of Europe on Human Rights Issues: Twins Separated at Birth?' (2001) 46 *McGill Law Journal* 849.

[55] *cf* JL da Cruz Vilaça, 'Le principe de l'effet utile du droit de l'Union dans la Jurisprudence de la Cour' in Court of Justice of the European Union (n 51) 279; S Morano-Foadi and S Andreadikis, 'Reflections on the Architecture of the EU after the Treaty of Lisbon: The European Judicial Approach to Fundamental Rights' (2011) 17 *European Law Journal* 595, 596; Van de Heyning (n 36) 84ff; J Temple Lang, 'The Development by the Court of Justice of the Duties of Cooperation of National Authorities and Community Institutions under Article 10 EC' (2008) 31 *Fordham International Law Journal* 1483; M Poiares Maduro, *We, the Court: The European Court of Justice and the European Economic Constitution* (Oxford, Hart Publishing, 1998); see further Lenaerts (n 42) 1308, who also points to other important objectives served by the Court, in particular respecting human rights and upholding checks and balances.

[56] eg, M Poiares Maduro, 'Interpreting European Law: Judicial Adjudication in a Context of Constitutional Pluralism' (2007) 1 *European Journal of Legal Studies* 2, 5; M Lasser, *Judicial Deliberations: A Comparative Analysis of Judicial Transparency and Legitimacy* (Oxford, Oxford University Press, 2004) 232–33; Stone Sweet (n 38) 131–40. The relevance of the principle is clear, in particular in relation to the protection of fundamental rights, where the ECJ for example has stated that the Member States remain free to exercise their discretion in implementing EU law in conformity with their own constitutional rights provisions, 'provided that the level of protection provided for by the Charter, as interpreted by the Court, and the primacy, unity and effectiveness of EU law are not thereby compromised' (*Melloni* (n 17) [60]; see also Sarmiento (n 11) 1295. The autonomy principle is particularly clearly expressed in the ECJ's Opinion on the accession of the EU to the ECHR (Opinion 2/13 (n 18)).

The raison d'etre of the ECtHR is a different one.[57] Originally created as an external mechanism of control to safeguard the States Parties' respect for the most important of rights, the Court's aim has always been to guarantee respect for fundamental rights and to offer redress to individual victims of violations.[58] The central principles and tenets underlying the ECtHR's case law clearly reflect this focus. Time and again, the Court has referred to the need to provide for 'practical and effective' protection of fundamental rights, 'in the light of present day conditions' and to the need to respect a number of 'meta-principles' underlying the Convention as a whole, such as human dignity, personal autonomy, pluralism and democracy.[59] Almost all of the Court's interpretations and applications can be connected to these 'meta-principles', which also inform the choices it makes to provide for a new interpretation, to leave a margin of appreciation or to give priority to certain cases.[60]

C. Core Rights Issues and the Primary Role of the ECtHR

Thus, each of the European courts has not only its own raison d'etre, but, following from this, also its own set of guiding principles. It is precisely the difference between these principles which may help to ensure a kind of division of tasks and a degree of coordination between the various levels of adjudication. In particular, it can be argued that, in the light of its raison d'etre, it is evident that the ECtHR should play a primary role with regard to cases raising core fundamental rights issues. In other words, if a case really concerns the interpretation of Convention rights, it should be up to the Strasbourg Court to decide on it, and the other courts should defer to its interpretations. Alternatively, if individual interests are at stake that are less clearly 'fundamental' in nature, ie, that do not really belong to the very core of the rights protected by the Convention, clearly there is less reason why a specialised human rights court should have the exclusive competence to deal with them.[61] Such issues then could just as well be decided upon by national courts or by the ECJ.

[57] *cf* Douglas-Scott (n 3) 646, who states that the EU cannot be primarily defined as a human rights organisation.

[58] See, eg, Gerards (n 7); T Hammarberg, 'The Court of Human Rights versus the "*Court of Public Opinion*"' in European Court of Human Rights, *How Can We Ensure Greater Involvement of National Courts in the Convention System?* (Strasbourg, Council of Europe, 2012) 30, 31; A Stone Sweet, 'The European Convention on Human Rights and National Constitutional Reordering' (2012) 33 *Cardozo Law Review* 1859; B Çalı, 'The Purposes of the European Human Rights System: One or Many?' (2008) 3 *European Human Rights Law Review* 299.

[59] See, in more detail and with references to case law, Gerards (n 7).

[60] ibid.

[61] JH Gerards, 'The Prism of Fundamental Rights' (2012) 8 *European Constitutional Law Review* 17; see also JH Gerards, 'The Scope of ECHR Rights and Institutional Concerns—The

Surely this criterion raises many questions, such as what, then, should be regarded as 'core fundamental rights issues'. It would be important for the Strasbourg Court to address that matter expressly in its case law. The Court thereby bears the task of setting standards to distinguish 'core' Convention rights matters from other individual interests and of demarcating the lines between rights belonging to the very core of the Convention rights and interests which are still clearly covered by the Convention, but which instead belong to their periphery.[62] The Strasbourg Court could do so by deploying core rights strategies such as determining the closeness of a certain rights aspect to the central values underlying the Convention, taking account of trends and developments in European views on the matter, and comparing a claim to cases it has decided before.[63]

D. Coordination in Cases Dealing with Core Convention Rights Matters

Once the ECtHR has given more shape to the core of the Convention rights, it should be allowed to take the lead in dealing with all novel matters of interpretation and application that pertain to such core rights. For the national courts, this would mean that they have to apply Convention

Relationship between Proliferation of Rights and the Caseload of the ECtHR' in E Brems and JH Gerards (eds), *Shaping Rights in the ECHR: The Role of the European Court of Human Rights in Determining the Scope of Human Rights* (Cambridge, Cambridge University Press, 2014) 84.

[62] ibid. See also, from a somewhat different perspective, AEM Leijten, 'The German Right to an *Existenzminimum*, Human Dignity, and the Possibility of Minimum Core Socio-economic Rights Protection' (2015) *German Law Journal* (forthcoming).

[63] ibid. The Court could also find inspiration in the minimum core obligations strategy as defined by the International Committee for Social and Economic Rights and accepted, albeit in a revised form, by national courts such as the German Federal Constitutional Court and the South African Constitutional Court. See, eg, UN Committee for Economic, Social and Cultural Rights, *General Comment No 3—The Nature of States Parties Obligations*, 5th Session (1990), UN Doc E/1991/23, annex III at 86 (1991), reprinted in Compilation of General Comments and General Recommendations Adopted by Human Rights Treaty Bodies, UN Doc HRI/GEN/1/Rev 6 at 14 (2003) para 10. For Germany, see Bundesverfassungsgericht [German Constitutional Court], judgment of 9 February 2010, 1 BvL 1/09 (*Hartz IV*) and Bundesverfassungsgericht, judgment of 18 July 2012, 1 BvL 10/10 (*Asylum Seekers Benefits*); see further, eg, IT Winkler and C Mahler, 'Interpreting the Right to a Dignified Minimum Existence: A New Era in German Socio-economic Rights Jurisprudence?' (2013) 13 *Human Rights Law Review* 388. For South Africa, see in particular *Soobramoney v Minister of Health, KwaZulu-Natal*, 1998 (1) SA 765 (CC); *Government of the Republic of South Africa v Grootboom*, 2001 (1) SA 46 (CC); *Minister of Health v Treatment Action Campaign (TAC)*, 2002 (5) SA 721 (CC); see further, eg, D Bilchitz, 'Towards a Reasonable Approach to the Minimum Core: Laying the Foundations for Future Socio-economic Rights Jurisprudence' (2003) 19 *South African Journal on Human Rights* 1; D Bilchitz, *Poverty and Fundamental Rights: The Justification and Enforcement of Socio-economic Rights* (Oxford, Oxford University Press, 2007). See more generally KG Young, 'The Minimum Core of Economic and Social Rights: A Concept in Search of Content' (2008) 33 *Yale Journal of International Law* 113; and P O'Connell, *Vindicating Socio-economic Rights: International Standards and Comparative Experiences* (London, Routledge, 2012) 186ff.

principles to the case and they should carefully follow the Court's standards and interpretation rather than relying on national constitutional principles. Eventually, if Protocol No 16 ECHR would enter into force, the courts of the ratifying States may even request advice from the ECtHR.

Of course, the ECJ could also be confronted with questions pertaining to core Convention rights. This may occur especially when a national court has referred a preliminary question in a case which is clearly about EU law, but which also contains a core ECHR rights issue. In addition, there may be an infringement procedure or a direct appeal against a decision by one of the EU institutions that raises core fundamental rights questions. In these cases, the ECJ should use its strategic and argumentative judicial instruments to answer the relevant fundamental rights questions in line with the approach taken by the ECtHR as much as possible. Not only does this mean that the ECJ should strive for a harmonious and non-divergent interpretation and it should refer to relevant case law of the ECtHR, but also, if need be, it should defer to the ECtHR. Whenever possible, it even ought to await a judgment by the ECtHR in a case in which similar questions have arisen. The use of informal mechanisms for attuning the case law may be of great relevance here, in the sense that, for example, the ECJ may informally invite the ECtHR to give priority to cases on its docket where comparable questions have arisen.

E. Dealing with Cases *not* Concerning Core Convention Rights Matters

If a fundamental rights issue does not pertain to core Convention rights issues, matters are different. It is then not necessary to have the ECtHR take the lead and give guidance based on its particular experience and functions. However, it still remains to be decided whether the issue primarily should be addressed and solved on the national level by the ECJ, or rather, still, by the ECtHR. Here, too, the raison d'etre of the courts could possibly offer some guidance. It is well arguable in this light that the more a case is related to central EU principles and values, such as uniformity, free movement or mutual trust, the more reason there is for the ECJ to take the lead and set the relevant interpretative standards.[64] In fundamental rights cases where such central EU values are at stake, the national courts would have good reason (and often even an obligation) to refer a preliminary question to the ECJ.[65] The ECJ then would then need to deal with the matter substantively, which means that it should provide for a transparent interpretation and a

[64] *cf*, rather implicitly, Schiek (n 3) 230.

[65] *cf Åkerberg Fransson* (n 17) [29]–[30]. For the question of when the national courts would have an obligation to refer and when it is desirable for them to do so, see in detail M Broberg and N Fenger, *Preliminary References to the European Court of Justice* (Oxford, Oxford University Press, 2010).

practicable set of standards, preferably without overreliance on strategies of judicial minimalism, incrementalism and 'silence'.[66]

It cannot be ruled out that the ECtHR is also sometimes confronted with such a case. It may be that the national courts have omitted to refer a preliminary question to the Luxembourg Court, but it may also be the case that the individual applicant resorts to the ECtHR after the ECJ has answered preliminary questions.[67] In both situations, the ECtHR should avail itself of the tools available to it to defer to the ECJ.[68] In particular, it should base its decisions on precedents, strategies and principles as developed in the ECJ's case law and, if possible, it should use its priority policy to await preliminary rulings of the ECJ in which it answers important EU related questions relevant to the case pending before the ECtHR.

F. Dealing with Cases Concerning Core Convention Issues *and* Central EU Values

Occasionally the situation may occur that a case clearly relates to core Convention rights, but is also closely related to the central values and principles of EU law. Here, too, the raison d'etre criterion may be of some help in determining who should take the lead in dealing with such a case. The

[66] For the use of such tools, see s II; see also de Búrca (n 13).

[67] The Draft Accession Agreement envisaged a solution for the first situation (no preliminary questions have been raised) in terms of a 'prior involvement procedure', which would enable the ECHR to suspend the proceedings and ask the ECJ to pronounce itself on the matter (see CDDH Ad Hoc Negotiation Group and the European Commission, 'Final Report to the CDDH', 47+1(2013)008rev2, 10 June 2013). For a further explanation of the prior involvement procedure, see, eg, P Craig, 'EU Accession to the ECHR: Competence, Procedure and Substance' (2013) 36 *Fordham International Law Journal* 1114; and X Groussot, T Lock and L Pech, 'EU Accession to the European Convention on Human Rights: A Legal Assessment of the Draft Accession Agreement of 14th October 2011', *Fondation Robert Schuman, European Issues No 218* (7 November 2011).

[68] In relevant cases, that is, where there is no discretion for the Member State to act, the ECtHR could also apply its *Bosphorus* doctrine (*Bosphorus Airways v Ireland* ECHR 2005-VI); *cf*, eg, S Douglas-Scott, 'A Tale of Two Courts: Luxembourg, Strasbourg and the Growing European Human Rights *Acquis*' (2006) 43 *CML Rev* 629; C Costello, 'The *Bosphorus* Ruling of the European Court of Human Rights: Fundamental Rights and Blurred Boundaries in Europe' (2006) 6 *Human Rights Law Review* 87; T Lock, 'Beyond *Bosphorus*: The European Court of Human Rights' Case Law on the Responsibility of Member States of International Organisations under the European Convention on Human Rights' (2010) 10 *Human Rights Law Review* 529. In many cases, however, there will be at least some degree of discretion; in that case, other coordination mechanisms will be needed. On this, see also G Harpaz, 'The European Court of Justice and its Relations with the European Court of Human Rights: The Quest for Enhanced Reliance, Coherence and Legitimacy' (2009) 46 *CML Rev* 105; and C Van de Heyning and R Lawson, 'The EU as a Party to the European Convention of Human Rights: EU Law and the European Court of Justice Case Law as Inspiration and Challenge to the European Court of Human Rights Jurisprudence' in Popelier, Van de Heyning and Van Nuffel (n 37) 35.

function of the criterion then is mainly to determine the intensity of the courts' review and the degree of deference they pay to the other courts. If a case of this nature would be presented to the ECtHR, it would not have to hesitate about taking the lead in setting standards and providing an interpretation of the relevant fundamental rights issues. After all, any case pertaining to core Convention rights is inevitably closely related to the fundamental values underlying the Convention system of protection, and the ECtHR's very raison d'etre would be to guide the national courts in determining how to respect these values. Nevertheless, it could be argued that the more the case is also related to central EU principles, the more the ECtHR would need to defer to the ECJ and take its precedents into account as far as the respect for these principles is concerned. Conversely, if a case would be presented to the ECJ first, there is good reason for the Court to take the lead and provide for an interpretation and a number of standards to solve the fundamental rights issues at stake. For this Court, too, however, the presence of core Convention rights issues would mean that it would need to defer to the ECtHR by following its case law as closely as possible.

IV. CAN IT BE MADE TO WORK? TWO EXAMPLES

A. Introduction

In theory, the raison d'etre criterion might seem helpful in determining in concrete cases which of the three court levels in Europe is the best placed to deal with a certain fundamental rights issue first. Nevertheless, it may be difficult to envisage how this can be made to work in practice. To illustrate its employability, this section therefore presents two examples of fundamental rights issues which, theoretically, could be decided on all three levels, ie, by the national courts, the ECJ and the ECtHR. After the two examples have been presented in section B, section C explains how and to what extent the raison d'etre criterion could help the courts decide whether they can take on the issue themselves or rather should use the instruments at their disposal to refer the substance of the case to be decided on a different level.

B. The Examples

The first example is related to the protection of intellectual property rights of producers of music, TV series, e-books and films. Currently a veritable battle is fought between rights owners and Internet pirates who want to make such music, films and other media freely available to all. In this battle, Internet service providers and organisations representing the rights and interests of artists also play an important role.[69] The battle thereby concerns typical fundamental rights matters, as the intellectual property rights of producers and artists are covered by the right to protection of property (which is laid down in many national constitutions, as well as in Article 17 of the EU Charter and Article 1 of Protocol No 1 to the ECHR), whilst Internet pirates and users make a claim to the right to receive and impart information (Article 11 of the EU Charter; Article 10 ECHR) and Internet service providers may invoke the right to conduct a business (Article 16 of the EU Charter). A variety of cases brought about by this conflict of rights have been brought to courts on the three different levels. National courts have been asked to impose blockades on torrent sites such as the Pirate Bay or compel Internet service providers to do so.[70] Some of these questions have been referred to the CJEU.[71] Also, Internet pirates have sometimes been criminally prosecuted and convicted, and the ECtHR has been asked to decide on the compatibility of such convictions with the freedom of expression.[72] Thus, this is clearly one of the issues where the problems and questions of coordination may easily occur.

The second example is that of access to genetic data by insurance companies. Genetic tests may provide important information about health risks. With increasing precision, they can help determine, for example, the chance that someone will fall victim to breast cancer or to certain kinds of arterial diseases, or whether there is a serious risk that someone's health will be affected by working with certain chemicals.[73] For health and life insurance companies, such information is highly relevant, as it can assist them in the process of risk calculation and premium setting.[74] Individuals who are genetically predisposed to high blood pressure or diabetes, for example,

[69] For an overview of relevant issues, see, eg, S Wolk, 'Filtering and Blocking of Copyright Infringement Works—A European Perspective' (2012), available at: http://ssrn.com/abstract=2186751; AR Lodder and NS van der Meulen, 'Evaluation of the Role of Access Providers Discussion of Dutch Pirate Bay Case Law and Introducing Principles on Directness, Effectiveness, Costs, Relevance, and Time' (2012) 4 *Journal of Intellectual Property, Information Technology and E-Commerce Law* 130.

[70] See, amongst many other cases, UK High Court of Justice, judgment of 28 July 2011, *Twentieth Century Fox Film Corp v British Telecommunications plc* [2011] EWHC 1981; UK High Court of Justice, judgment of 26 October 2011, *Twentieth Century Fox Film Corp v British Telecommunications plc* [2011] EWHC 2714; Court of Appeal Antwerp, Belgium, judgment of 26 September 2011, *BAF v Telenet and Belgacom*, 2011/8314; Trade Court Vienna, Austria, judgment of 13 May 2011, *Constantin and Wega v UPC Telekabel ('Kino.to')*, 22 CG 120/10; Administrative Court Cologne, Germany, judgment of 15 December 2011, 6 K 5404/10; Court of Appeal of The Hague, the Netherlands, judgment of 28 January 2014, *Ziggo and XS4ALL v BREIN*, ECLI:NL:GHDHA:2014:88.

[71] eg, Case C-314/12 *UPC Telekabel Wien* (ECJ, 27 March 2014); Case C-557/07 *LSG/Tele2* [2009] ECR I-1227; Case C-70/10 *Scarlet Extended* [2011] ECR I-11959.

[72] *Neij and Sunde Kolmisoppi v Sweden*, App No 40397/12 (ECtHR, 19 February 2013 (decision)).

[73] See, eg, R Drmanac, 'The Ultimate Genetic Test' (2012) 336(6085) *Science* 1110.

[74] eg, Y Joly et al, 'Life Insurance: Genomic Stratification and Risk Classification' (2014) 22 *European Journal of Human Genetics* 575.

could be placed in a different risk group from individuals whose risk profile is more favourable, and the insurer could set premiums accordingly.[75] Given the obvious economic advantages related to this, it is not surprising that insurance companies increasingly seek to have access to such data, at least insofar as it is relevant for actuarial calculations.[76] Sometimes this may be advantageous for individuals. If it can be shown that someone finds himself in a low-risk group for genetically determined diseases, for example, this can be very favourable in terms of the rate of the premiums he has to pay.[77] At the same time, access to genetic information by insurance companies may bring serious disadvantages. Those placed in a high-risk group can be confronted with sky-rocketing premiums as well as with concomitant difficulties in obtaining mortgages or access to health care.[78] Moreover, the access by insurers to genetic data clearly affects fundamental rights, such as the right to informational privacy, the right to data protection and the right to non-discrimination.[79] It may be considered unfair and discriminatory, for example, that individuals have to pay higher premiums because of genetic predispositions they are unable to influence or change.[80] Insurance companies' requirements may further compel them to learn about genetic risks they do not want to know about at all.[81] In addition, there is a chance that the information obtained by insurance companies is incorrect, as well as a risk that it is (consciously or inadvertently) shared with other interested parties, such as employers.[82] Although cases related to these fundamental rights issues are still only rarely brought before the courts,[83] this is likely to change, either because insurers complain about overly limiting legislation or because individuals complain about a lack of protection of their fundamental rights. In such cases, it will be up the courts to decide on a variety

[75] For the economic principles explaining why it is so important for insurers to be able to set risk groups as precisely as possible, see, eg, JH Gerards, 'General Issues Concerning Genetic Information' in JH Gerards, AW Heringa and HL Janssen, *Genetic Discrimination and Genetic Privacy in a Comparative Perspective* (Antwerp, Intersentia, 2005) 5, 14–17; Y Thiery, *Discriminatie en verzekering* [*Discrimination and Insurance*] (Antwerp, Intersentia, 2011) 202ff.

[76] ibid; see also more recently Joly et al (n 74).

[77] See, eg, DE Palmer, 'Insurance, Risk Assessment and Fairness: An Ethical Analysis' in P Flanagan, P Primaux and W Ferguson (eds), *Insurance Ethics for a More Ethical World* (Oxford, Elsevier, 2007); Gerards (n 75) 17; Thiery (n 75) 208.

[78] *cf* Gerards (n 75) 17–18.

[79] For the privacy risks related to the availability of genetic data, see, eg, Y Erlich and A Naranayan, 'Routes for Breaching and Protecting Genetic Privacy' (2014) 15 *Nature Reviews Genetics* 409; see also Gerards (n 75); and Thiery (n 75).

[80] See further, eg, Gerards (n 75) 6–10.

[81] See, eg, S McLean and P Gannon, 'Genetics and Insurance' in T Sorell (ed), *Health Care, Ethics and Insurance* (London, Routledge, 1998) 91; GT Laurie, 'In Defence of Ignorance: Genetic Information and the Right Not to Know' (1999) 6 *European Journal of Health Law* 122.

[82] See further Gerards (n 75) 8; and, more recently, Erlich and Naranayan (n 79).

[83] Y Joly, I Ngueng Feze and J Simard, 'Genetic Discrimination and Life Insurance: A Systematic Review of the Evidence' (2013) 11 *BMC Medicine* 11.

of questions related to access to genetic information, genetic privacy and genetic discrimination.[84]

C. Can the Raison d'Etre Criterion Help?

It is evident that the genetic information example and the Internet piracy example both relate to rights protected by the ECHR, such as the prohibition of discrimination, the right to privacy, property rights and the freedom of expression. Nevertheless, the question arises as to whether it is therefore the ECtHR that should make the most important choices in these cases, or rather the ECJ, or even the national courts? The raison d'etre criterion suggests answering this question by looking at the extent to which the issues clearly relate to core fundamental rights issues as well as to the central values of EU law.

It seems rather obvious that in the Internet piracy example, there is a very strong relationship with EU principles and EU law. There are many cross-border elements related to the provision of Internet services, as well as with the production and distribution of music and films. If a blockade is imposed in one Member State, it is just as easy for Internet pirates to move their activities to another Member State and provide access to Internet users from there, which means that only a harmonised European approach could help to protect intellectual property rights in an effective manner. Indeed, these matters have been regulated on the EU level by means of the E-commerce Directive,[85] the Copyright Directive[86] and the Intellectual Property Enforcement Directive.[87] Clearly, such regulation is closely related to central EU principles such as free movement of services, and the need for effective legal protection and effective sanctions to enforce the relevant regulations. Applying the raison d'etre factor, this implies that the ECJ would be particularly well-placed to deal with these kinds of cases, especially where the assessment of necessity and proportionality of restrictive measures are concerned. There would be the more reason for doing so because no core aspects of fundamental rights appear to be at stake. The ECtHR has conceded as much in its decision in *Neij and Sunde Kolmisoppi*, in which

[84] On this, see also elaborately Thiery (n 75).

[85] Directive 2000/31/EC of the European Parliament and of the Council of 8 June 2000 on certain legal aspects of information society services, in particular electronic commerce, in the internal market [2000] OJ L187/1 (E-Commerce Directive).

[86] Directive 2001/29/EC of the European Parliament and of the Council of 22 May 2001 on the harmonisation of certain aspects of copyright and related rights in the information society [2001] OJ L167/10 (Copyright Directive).

[87] Directive 2004/48/EC of the European Parliament and of the Council of 29 April 2004 on the enforcement of intellectual property rights [2004] OJ L157/45 (Intellectual Property Enforcement Directive).

it considered that: 'In the present case, although protected by Article 10, the safeguards afforded to the distributed material in respect of which the applicants were convicted cannot reach the same level as that afforded to political expression and debate.'[88] For that reason, there would not be any reason to require the ECtHR to provide for guidance and for an authoritative interpretation of the Convention, rather than the ECJ.

The combination of these circumstances makes it reasonable to allow the ECJ to play a primary role in Internet piracy cases with a fundamental rights aspect. This means that both the national courts and the Strasbourg Court would need to respect the standards set by the ECJ. Moreover, whenever possible, they should opt for a judicial strategy which would allow the ECJ to take the lead. For the national courts, this would imply that they are quick to refer preliminary questions on fundamental rights matters to the ECJ. The ECtHR could defer to the ECJ by consciously applying its priority policy so as to await a leading judgment from the Luxembourg Court. Subsequently, the principles and standards established by the ECJ could inform the ECtHR's and the national courts' review of the necessity and proportionality of restrictions of Convention rights.

Of course, this division of tasks also means that the ECJ should really take the lead and provide guidance to the national courts and the ECtHR by setting clear standards and providing authoritative interpretations of the relevant Charter provisions. Interestingly, it appears from the case law thus far that the ECJ is indeed willing to take up this role. Over the past few years, it has handed down a number of important preliminary rulings in which it carefully (though incrementally) has established a fundamental rights-based legal framework for deciding in cases related to Internet piracy.[89]

In the example of the insurers' use of genetic data, it seems relatively clear that the ECJ has not a very important role to play. Health and life insurance are topics which are mostly regulated by national law, and the regulation and organisation of health care and health insurance are heavily influenced by a variety of cultural and historical factors.[90] Although there is a growing degree of European coordination and regulation in this area, in particular insofar as the protection of personal data is concerned,[91] EU competences in

[88] *Neij and Sunde Kolmisoppi v Sweden*, App No 40397/12 (ECtHR, 19 February 2013 (decision)).

[89] See examples mentioned above, n 71.

[90] *cf*, eg, CI Velicu, 'Health Policy Governance in the EU: Composing a Jigsaw Puzzle?' (2011) *Eurolimes* 171.

[91] Particularly relevant in this respect is the Data Protection Directive (Directive 95/46/EC of the European Parliament and of the Council of 24 October 1995 on the protection of individuals with regard to the processing of personal data and on the free movement of such data [1995] OJ L281), of which Art 8 states that Member States shall prohibit the processing of data concerning health, which could be seen to include data about one's genetic predispositions or genotype. The new proposal for a Data Protection Directive even states expressly that Member

relation to the organisation of life and health insurance and the regulation of genetic discrimination have remained rather limited.[92] Therefore, it would hardly be in line with the raison d'etre criterion if the ECJ would pronounce itself clearly and authoritatively on fundamental rights matters related to genetic discrimination or the 'right not to know'.[93] In this area, it would be more appropriate for it to leave such matters to the ECtHR or, alternatively, to the national courts. At this very point, however, it appears that the raison d'etre factor would leave the courts in a state of indecision. Possibly a case could be made for having cases on genetic discrimination and genetic privacy decided primarily by the ECtHR, since these are typically fundamental rights issues and the Court is therefore well-placed to deal with them. But it could also be argued that, just like the Internet piracy cases, many of these cases do not pertain to the very *core* of the Convention rights, if only because the right to health care or access to life insurance is not protected by

States shall prohibit the processing of genetic data (Proposal for a Directive of the European Parliament and of the Council on the protection of individuals with regard to the processing of personal data by competent authorities for the purposes of prevention, investigation, detection or prosecution of criminal offences or the execution of criminal penalties, and the free movement of such data (COM/2012/010 final), Art 8, para 1); see also Art 9, para 1 of the proposal for a Regulation of the European Parliament and of the Council on the protection of individuals with regard to the processing of personal data and on the free movement of such data (General Data Protection Regulation) (COM/2012/011 final–2012/0011 (COD)).

[92] JH Gerards and HL Janssen, 'Regulation of Genetic and Other Health Information in a Comparative Perspective' (2006) 13 *European Journal of Health Law* 339, 367; more recently, with the Lisbon Treaty, EU competences in field of health care and health policy have grown and the ECJ is increasingly dealing with health insurance matters in relation to the freedom to provide services. On the changes, see, in particular, U Neergaard, 'EU Health Care Law in a Constitutional Light: Distribution of Competences, Notions of "Solidarity", and "Social Europe" in JW van de Gronden et al (eds), *Health Care and EU Law* (The Hague, TMC Asser Press, 2011) 19, 21. The non-discrimination competence clause of Art 19 TFEU does not expressly refer to genetic information as a ground on which the EU legislature could act, although the general notion of 'disability', which is contained in the provision, might provide some basis for legislation. However, in the proposal for a Directive relating to non-discrimination in the provision of services, the genetic data are not expressly mentioned, not even as part of a definition of 'disability' (Proposal for a Council Directive on implementing the principle of equal treatment between persons irrespective of religion or belief, disability, age or sexual orientation (COM/2008/0426 final—CNS 2008/0140)). Moreover, it is mentioned in the Preamble to this Directive that 'Actuarial and risk factors related to disability and to age are used in the provision of insurance, banking and other financial services' and that 'These should not be regarded as constituting discrimination where the factors are shown to be key factors for the assessment of risk', which makes clear that genetic predisposition will not easily be regarded as a prohibited ground in risk calculation in insurance, and which also bears witness to the unwillingness to regulate insurance matters on the EU level. Indeed, the presently existing Directives which relate to, for example, life insurance (Directive 2002/83/EC of the European Parliament and of the Council of 5 November 2002 concerning life assurance [2002] OJ L345/1) particularly respect the insurers' freedom to set premiums (see Art 34).

[93] This is not to say, of course, that the ECJ is not competent to pronounce itself on, for example, health insurance matters related to the freedom to provide services, but only that it would be wise to defer to the ECtHR as far as core rights questions are involved in such cases.

the Convention.[94] If that argument is followed, the cases could just as well be solved by national standards. The raison d'etre factor in some of these cases would therefore not appear to be of any great assistance in that it does not offer a decisive criterion to favour a certain level of judicial decision making over another.

V. ADDITIONAL FACTORS: THE ROLE OF DEFERENCE

The application of the raison d'etre criterion to the two examples of Internet piracy and genetic discrimination in insurance has shown that additional standards may sometimes be necessary to help the courts decide which of them should take the lead. It is suggested here that such a standard can be found in the classic doctrine of the margin of appreciation as it is developed by the ECtHR.[95] At least in theory, this doctrine implies that the Court

[94] Moreover, arguments have been made against treating 'genetic data' as a suspect ground, or at least as a ground that is not as suspect as grounds such as race or gender; according to that argument, genetic discrimination cases do not pertain to the very core of fundamental rights. For a further discussion, see Gerards (n 75). Moreover, most of these cases will relate to fundamental rights not expressly protected by the Convention, such as access to health care and access to life insurance, the possibility of obtaining a mortgage and so on. Except for the situation in which a case clearly affects the 'right not to know' or where genetic data have been unwarrantedly disclosed or shared, it is therefore arguable that most genetic privacy and genetic non-discrimination cases are not 'core' Convention cases.

[95] The doctrine and its effect have been analysed and discussed extensively; for a few of the most important contributions, see TA O'Donnell, 'The Margin of Appreciation Doctrine: Standards in the Jurisprudence of the European Court of Human Rights' (1982) 4 *Human Rights Quarterly* 474; R St J Macdonald, 'The Margin of Appreciation' in R St J Macdonald et al (eds), *The European System for the Protection of Human Rights* (Dordrecht, Martinus Nijhoff, 1993) 83; E Brems, 'The Margin of Appreciation Doctrine in the Case Law of the European Court of Human Rights' (1996) *Zeitschrift für ausländisches öffentliches Recht und Völkerrecht* 240; N Lavender, 'The Problem of the Margin of Appreciation' (1997) 4 *European Human Rights Law Review* 380; JGC Schokkenbroek, 'The Basis, Nature and Application of the Margin-of-Appreciation Doctrine in the Case Law of the European Court of Human Rights' (1998) 19 *Human Rights Law Journal* 30; E Benvenisti, 'Margin of Appreciation, Consensus, and Universal Standards' (1999) 31 *New York University Journal of International Law and Politics* 843; MR Hutchinson, 'The Margin of Appreciation Doctrine in the European Court of Human Rights' (1999) 48 *ICLQ* 641; S Greer, *The Margin of Appreciation: Interpretation and Discretion under the European Convention on Human Rights*, Human Rights Files No 17(Strasbourg, Council of Europe Publishing, 2000); Y Arai-Takahashi, *The Margin of Appreciation Doctrine and the Principle of Proportionality in the Jurisprudence of the ECHR* (Antwerp, Intersentia, 2002); G Letsas, 'Two Concepts of the Margin of Appreciation' (2006) 26 *OJLS* 705; J Christoffersen, *Fair Balance: Proportionality, Subsidiarity and Primarity in the European Convention on Human Rights* (Leiden, Martinus Nijhoff, 2009); JH Gerards, 'Pluralism, Deference and the Margin of Appreciation Doctrine' (2011) 17 *European Law Journal* 80; J Kratochvíl, 'The Inflation of the Margin of Appreciation by the European Court of Human Rights' (2011) 29 *Netherlands Quarterly of Human Rights* 324; D Spielmann, 'Allowing the Right Margin: The European Court of Human Rights and the National Margin of Appreciation Doctrine: Waiver or Subsidiarity of European Review?', CELS Working Paper 2012; Y Arai-Takahashi, 'The Margin of Appreciation Doctrine: A Theoretical Analysis

varies the intensity of its review in accordance with the leeway that the national authorities reasonably should be allowed to regulate the exercise of fundamental rights. In determining the scope of this margin of appreciation, the ECtHR uses a relatively coherent and fixed set of factors that help to determine the scope of the margin of appreciation in a transparent and rather predictable fashion. If properly transposed, the various factors used in relation to the margin of appreciation doctrine could also be of help in deciding the appropriate 'level' for judicial decision making in fundamental rights cases.[96] This is all the more true as the ECJ relies on a similar notion of variable intensity of review as the ECtHR does.[97] Although the ECJ's variation in intensity of review cannot really be classified as a 'doctrine',[98] its de facto reliance on similar factors demonstrates that they can be regarded as a 'trait d'union' for the purposes of this chapter.

One first relevant factor in determining the intensity of the European courts' review is the so-called common ground factor, which is related to the degree of agreement on a certain matter in regulation, policy making and case law in the various European states. If a certain matter is still hugely controversial, the courts may consider it wise to leave it to the states and accord them a wide margin of discretion.[99] By contrast, if opinions on a certain matter seem to have converged or if, at least, there is a clear trend of convergence, the courts will find less occasion to defer to the states. The ECtHR in particular often finds support in such consensus and trends to support a novel interpretation of the Convention of its own.[100]

Further, both courts generally attach great value to the so-called better-placed argument.[101] This argument is based on the importance of having sufficient knowledge and understanding of local facts and circumstances in

of Strasbourg's Variable Geometry' in A Føllesdal, B Peters and G Ulfstein (eds), *Constituting Europe: The European Court of Human Rights in a National, European and Global Context* (Cambridge, Cambridge University Press, 2013) 61; JH Gerards, 'Diverging Fundamental Rights Standards and the Role of the European Court of Human Rights' in M Claes and M de Visser (eds), *Constructing European Constitutional Law* (Oxford, Hart Publishing, forthcoming).

[96] *cf* also Van de Heyning, who has indicated that the margin of appreciation could be useful as a 'conflict rule' in helping to decide on the appropriate level of judicial review ((n 37) 82–83).

[97] For an brief overview of these factors as they are used in the ECJ's case law, see Gerards (n 95). In more recent years, the ECJ has sometimes even expressly employed the 'margin of appreciation' wording—see, eg, Case T-331/11 *Leonard Besselink* (General Court, 12 September 2013).

[98] More recently, however, the ECJ seems to be inclined to follow the ECtHR's lead more clearly here; see in particular *Digital Rights Ireland* (n 25) [47].

[99] For the ECtHR, see classically *Handyside v UK* (1976) Series A No 24 [47]; and, more recently, *Dickson v UK* ECHR 2007-V [78]. For the ECJ, see classically Case C-36/02 *Omega Spielhallen* [2004] ECR I-9609.

[100] See, eg, *Christine Goodwin v UK* ECHR 2002-VI [85].

[101] See classically, eg, *James and others v UK* (1986) Series A No 98 [46]; and more recently *RSz v Hungary*, App No 41838/11 (ECtHR, 2 July 2013).

regulating the exercise of fundamental rights. Since the national authorities are generally more aware of such facts and circumstances than any European court can be, the ECtHR is reluctant to intervene if particular knowledge or insight is required to determine the necessity of certain measures.[102] Similarly, the ECJ will be wary of strictly reviewing measures and decisions involving political and social choices or specialised technical assessments.[103] The argument is also related to the courts' awareness that moral and ethical values may be very much 'national' in character and, accordingly, can only be appropriately understood and valued by the national authorities.[104] Accordingly, the clearer it is that a fundamental rights matter is related to such moral or ethical issues, the more inclined the courts will be to defer to the national authorities.

Finally, both courts have referred to the nature and importance of the rights at stake and the intensity or seriousness of the interference with these rights. They do so in a way that is clearly connected to their 'raison d'etre'. The ECtHR has held, for instance, that the more clearly a complaint relates to a core rights issue, the more difficult it will be to find a justification for an interference with such a right, and the more intensively the Court will scrutinise the arguments advanced by the defendant state.[105] In the same vein, but geared to its own particular 'raison d'etre', the ECJ has always applied very strict review to measures and decisions affecting central EU interests, such as national restrictions of free movement rights.[106] Logically, the intensity of both the ECtHR's and the ECJ's review will increase in accordance with the seriousness or irreversibility of the interference with the relevant right or interest.[107]

As mentioned above, these three sets of factors may have a certain role to play in determining which of the three levels of courts is best placed to

[102] eg, *Anne-Marie Andersson v Sweden*, App No 20022/92 (ECtHR, 27 August 1997) [36]; *Velikovi and others v Bulgaria*, App No 43278/98 (ECtHR, 15 March 2007) [179]–[180]; *Pla and Puncernau v Andorra* ECHR 2004-VIII [46]; *cf* Arai-Takahashi (2013) (n 95) 69.

[103] eg, Joined Cases C-154/04 and C-155/04 *Alliance for Natural Health* [2005] ECR I-6451 [52]; Case C-326/05P *Industrias Químicas del Vallés* [2007] ECR I-6557 [75]; Case C-448/06 *cp-Pharma* [2008] ECR I-5685 [28]–[30]; Case C-356/12 *Glatzel* (ECJ, 22 May 2014) [52]; Case T-614/13 *Romonta GmbH* (General Court, 26 September 2014) [63].

[104] See, eg, for the ECtHR, *Maurice v France* ECHR 2005-IX [116]–[117]; *A, B and C v Ireland* ECHR 2010, [232]–[241]; and for the ECJ, see, classically Case 34/79, *Henn and Darby* [1979] ECR I-3795 [15]; Case 121/85 *Conegate* [1986] ECR I-1007 [14]; Case C-36/02 *Omega Spielhallen* [2004] ECR I-9609.

[105] eg, *Evans v UK* ECHR 2007-I [77]; *Dickson v UK* ECHR 2007-V [78]; *S and Marper v UK* ECHR 2008 [102].

[106] eg, Case C-438/05 *Viking Line* [2007] ECR I-10779; Case C-341/05 *Laval* [2007] ECR I-11767. See further Gerards (n 95) 91; and P Craig, *EU Administrative Law*, 2nd edn (Oxford, Oxford University Press, 2012) 630–31.

[107] For the ECtHR, see, eg, *The Observer and the Guardian v UK* [1991] Series A No 216 [60]; *Refah Partisi and others v Turkey* ECHR 2003-II [86]. For the ECJ, see, eg, *Digital Rights Ireland* (n 25) [48].

give guidance in fundamental rights cases.[108] This can best be explained by returning to the example of genetic privacy and genetic discrimination in insurance. It was stated in section IV that these matters are closely connected with matters of national health care organisation and regulation. There is little convergence between national law and policy in this field, let alone European regulation, and there does not seem to be much consensus as to how the insurance business should be regulated. Moreover, the moral and ethical aspects related to the regulation of genetic data render this field prone to controversy and debate. So even if this matter may be said to relate to important fundamental rights matters and even where the Convention could be held to be applicable, these additional factors may justify the conclusion that the national authorities are best placed to decide on these issues.

Nevertheless, it should be stressed here that the resulting division of competences will not be an absolute one. The ECtHR always retains the power of supervision in fundamental rights cases, even if its supervision sometimes can be limited and deferential. In particular, it will be competent to provide for corrections in cases of excess or when clearly arbitrary decisions have been taken, either by the national courts or by the ECJ, even in fields where it should normally adopt a deferential attitude. The additional factors thus really only constitute a useful yet flexible indication as to how the instruments for coordination can be used rather than indicating an absolute division of powers.

VI. CONCLUSIONS

At the fifth anniversary of the binding EU Charter of Fundamental Rights, it is clear that there are three levels of courts in Europe which would seem to be equally capable of dealing with fundamental rights matters. Originally, the national courts were used to being competent to decide national fundamental rights cases based on their national constitutions and, depending on the national constitutional system, international treaty provisions or unwritten principles. The ECtHR's task was to provide redress to individual victims of violation of the rights protected by the Convention, as well as to give authoritative and general interpretations to the terms and notions of the Convention. Finally, the ECJ was competent to interpret and apply fundamental rights as general principles of EU law, as more recently codified in the Charter of Fundamental Rights, but it was used to closely tail the

[108] On this function, see in particular also Gerards (n 42); and Tridimas (n 41) 749ff. The latter also explains how factors such as those mentioned above might be reflected in the specificity of the ECJ's preliminary rulings.

ECtHR in doing so. Over the past five years, however, the 'bindingness' of the Charter has turned out to be an important incentive for the ECJ to start to develop its own doctrines in the field of fundamental rights. By doing so in a relatively autonomous manner, it has created a certain degree of competition in the field of fundamental rights, and this seems to have been exacerbated by its unwillingness to accept the accession of the EU to the ECHR. As a corollary, where the interrelationship between the different adjudicatory levels was already complicated before the ECJ 'entered the market', it has now become even more complex. Moreover, given the ECJ's objections to the accession of the EU to the ECHR, it is likely that this situation will continue to exist at the least for some time to come.

This chapter has argued that, for that reason, there is a need for a coordinating mechanism to help determine which fundamental rights issues can be decided best by which level of courts. It was explained that the courts at all three levels can dispose of a wide array of judicial strategies and instruments to either refer a fundamental rights issue to be decided at a different level or to take on the matter itself. National courts may make preliminary references or they may choose to apply typical Convention standards, but they may also choose to apply their own constitutional rights provisions and principles. The ECJ may defer to national courts and the ECtHR and align its own approach to theirs, but it may also decide to take the lead and engage in standard-setting of its own. Likewise, the ECtHR may use its priority policy to provide for quick and authoritative guidance on certain interpretation matters, but it also may decide to await the judgments of the ECJ before giving its own view. Moreover, the European courts in particular can use classical instruments of incrementalism, judicial minimalism and deference to leave certain matters to be decided at the national rather than the European level.

This chapter further submitted that to guarantee some kind of coordination between the three adjudicatory levels, the courts should consciously deploy such instruments in line with the 'raison d'etre' criterion. In particular, this criterion could help determine which matters should be preferably decided by the ECtHR—namely those cases where core issues of Convention rights are at stake—and which matters should be determined by the ECJ—namely those which are clearly related to the *effet utile* and the central values and objectives of EU law. Where the raison d'etre criterion itself cannot be decisive, for instance, because a case relates to core fundamental rights issues as well as to core EU principles, or because the case neither relates to central fundamental rights issues nor has an important EU aspect, the factors developed by the ECtHR to determine the scope of the margin of appreciation could be of help. The existence or lack of European consensus or the 'better-placed' argument could then play a role especially in deciding to what extent the European courts should defer to the national level.

Evidently, this 'coordinating mechanism' may not provide for a straightforward and determinative basis that will always provide clarity as to the appropriate level of judicial decision making. The various factors are very general in nature and their application will be strongly dependent on the circumstances of the case and the precise fundamental rights matters at stake. Nevertheless, it would seem to make sense for the various courts at the least to take account of the coordinating factors described in this chapter and express them in their case law.

4

Why National Constitutional Courts Should not Embrace EU Fundamental Rights

JAN KOMÁREK

I. INTRODUCTION

SINCE THE CHARTER of Fundamental Rights of the European Union (hereinafter 'the EU Charter') formally came into force on 1 December 2009, the place of national constitutional courts in law and politics has been significantly transformed.[1] The increasing number of constitutional courts' preliminary references to the ECJ is perhaps the most visible sign of this transformation. What in the 1990s was an exception—it was only the Austrian and Belgian constitutional courts that were semi-regularly sending references to Luxembourg—has become a general practice of many, if not most, national constitutional courts today.

The ECJ's understanding of the principle of primacy also allowed ordinary courts to challenge the superiority of constitutional courts and the finality of their decisions. The controversy between the Czech Supreme Administrative

[1] See Jan Komárek, 'The Place of Constitutional Courts in the EU' (2013) 9 *European Constitutional Law Review* 420. By 'constitutional courts', I mean judicial institutions specialised in constitutional adjudication, where judicial review of legislation is concentrated. For a recent overview of the powers of constitutional courts, see reports for the XVth Congress of the Conference of European Constitutional Courts, 23–25 May 2011, *Constitutional Justice: Functions and Relationship with the other Public Authorities*, available at: www.confcoconsteu.org/en/reports/reports-xv.html. The following EU Member States have constitutional courts: Austria, Belgium, Bulgaria, Croatia, the Czech Republic, France, Germany, Hungary, Italy, Latvia, Lithuania, Luxembourg, Poland, Portugal, Romania, Slovakia, Slovenia and Spain. In Estonia, although there is no separate institution called the 'constitutional court', constitutional review is exercised by a specialised chamber within the Supreme Court, whereas in Cyprus, the review is somewhat centralised at the Supreme Court, through the system of mandatory appeals and constitutional references (similarly, in Portugal, the ordinary courts can find a statute unconstitutional, but such a decision will be subject to mandatory appeal). In Malta, on the other hand, although there is a nominal constitutional court, it is not separate and forms part of the Maltese judiciary.

Court and the Constitutional Court, which resulted in the latter's finding of the ECJ's decision to be ultra vires,[2] was only the most extreme instance of conflicts and tensions that arose between constitutional and ordinary courts. Numerous examples show that when ordinary courts dislike constitutional courts' interpretation of the national constitution, including constitutionally protected fundamental rights, they can contest it through a preliminary reference to the ECJ. The power of ordinary courts vis-à-vis constitutional courts has been recently reinforced by the ECJ's rulings in *Melki and Abdeli*, *Križan* and *A*.[3] *Melki and Abdeli* and *A* undermine the priority of national constitutional courts' constitutional review, whereas *Križan* makes it possible for ordinary courts to ignore decisions of constitutional courts which they find contrary to EU law. The pressure from ordinary courts can in fact explain the present willingness of national constitutional courts to refer preliminary questions to the ECJ: rather than being challenged or circumvented by ordinary courts that use the ECJ and the preliminary reference procedure instrumentally in a domestic judicial conflict, constitutional courts choose to cooperate. 'If you can't beat them, join them!', one might say.

National constitutional courts' embrace of EU fundamental rights is another sign of this transformation. The Austrian Constitutional Court went perhaps the furthest when it ruled that the EU Charter forms part of its standard of constitutional review, albeit only in areas delimited by Article 51(1) of the EU Charter.[4] But EU fundamental rights have become part of national constitutionality by less obvious means too: some national constitutional courts use them as interpretive guidance when giving meaning to fundamental rights guaranteed formally by their respective constitutions.[5]

In this chapter I will raise some doubts as regards this last-mentioned development, which is, however, inextricably linked to the broader phenomenon described above. It builds on my previous work on constitutional courts' place in the EU, which sought to provide a theoretical basis for what is argued here with regard to the more specific issue concerning EU fundamental rights.[6] I will shortly present this background argument in the

[2] See Michal Bobek, '*Landtová*, *Holubec*, and the Problem of an Uncooperative Court: Implications for the Preliminary Rulings Procedure' (2014) 10 *European Constitutional Law Review* 54. For a less conflictual, but also significant case of a clash between the German Federal Constitutional Court and the Supreme Labour Court, see Alec Stone Sweet and Kathleen Stranz, 'Rights Adjudication and Constitutional Pluralism in Germany and Europe' (2012) 19 *Journal of European Public Policy* 92.

[3] Joined Cases C-188/10 and C-189/10 *Melki and Abdeli* [2010] ECR I-5667; Case C-416/10 *Križan* (not yet officially reported); and Case C-112/13 *A* (not yet officially reported).

[4] Austrian Constitutional Court, Judgment of 14 March 2012, U 466/11-18 and U 1836/11-13, English translation available at: www.vfgh.gv.at/cms/vfgh-site/attachments/9/6/0/CH0006/CMS1353421369433/ grundrechtecharta_english_u466-11.pdf.

[5] On the variety of possible approaches, see G Martinico and O Pollicino (eds), *The National Judicial Treatment of the ECHR and EU Laws* (Groningen, Europa Law Publishing, 2010).

[6] Jan Komárek, 'National Constitutional Courts and the European Constitutional Democracy' (2014) 12 *International Journal of Constitutional Law* 525.

following section. It is based on a discourse theory of law and democracy, which puts specialised constitutional courts at the centre of what it calls a 'communicative arrangement', which connects law and politics in constitutional democracies. I will then sketch the understanding of fundamental rights that builds on it. On that basis, I will then discuss national constitutional courts' engagement with EU fundamental rights.

II. CONSTITUTIONAL COURTS IN A CONSTITUTIONAL DEMOCRACY[7]

In this section I will defend the view of constitutional courts that is linked to the discourse (or deliberative) theory of law and democracy. As will become apparent, this theory favours the separation of constitutional and ordinary adjudication, which is undermined by the transformation of constitutional courts resulting from different doctrines of EU law and from constitutional courts' own embracing of EU fundamental rights.

A. Constitutional Democracy

All current EU Member States aspire to be constitutional democracies.[8] They respect and in their constitutions positively provide for (albeit in different forms) the principles of political morality which were traditionally understood as constraints on democracy: the rule of law, fundamental rights or, at a more general level, equality and human dignity. These principles are often associated with constitutionalism, which established itself as an important independent value after the Second World War.[9]

Democracy and constitutionalism, understood narrowly, are sometimes presented as being in opposition to each other. This opposition can be expressed with different concepts and at a different level of abstraction: as a tension between positive and negative liberty, between public and private autonomy, between political and individual self-determination or between liberalism and communitarianism.

In the narrow understanding of the term, democracy is to be achieved through the political process (or politicians), whereas constitutionalism is

[7] Part of this section reproduces, in a slightly amended form, Komárek (n 6) section 3.

[8] According to Art 49 of the Treaty on European Union (TEU), in order to become a member of the EU, European states must respect the values listed in Art 2 TEU. These are 'human dignity, freedom, democracy, equality, the rule of law and respect for human rights, including the rights of persons belonging to minorities' and 'are common to the Member States in a society in which pluralism (non-discrimination, tolerance, justice, solidarity and equality between women and men) prevail'.

[9] See J-W Müller, *Contesting Democracy: Political Ideas in Twentieth-Century Europe* (New Haven, Yale University Press, 2011) 146–50.

the domain of courts and lawyers and constrains democracy or political will. The achievement of constitutional democracy is thus seen as a balancing act: fundamental rights and the rule of law apply *at the expense* of democracy and vice versa. This is justified with reference to the need to control democracy's undesirable outcomes, such as the oppression of minorities, and/or to make the democratic process work properly. The precise contours of this balancing act differ according to the understanding of democracy and constitutionalism, respectively, but the central point is that the two are seen as being in an irreconcilable tension with each other.[10]

Habermas' conception of constitutional democracy seeks to reconcile the two through the 'co-originality thesis': citizens can act as members of a political community (and thus decide democratically in the narrow sense) only if their individual rights (associated with the narrow understanding of constitutionalism) are guaranteed. In the 'post-metaphysical world', however, where no pre-established truth exists, the content of such individual rights can be determined only in common with others through the discursive process of opinion- and will- formation. The discursive process can 'lead to convincing positions to which all individuals can agree without coercion'[11] and is able to produce decisions with legitimacy. Individual and public autonomy is thus intertwined in a constitutional democracy.

The focus on discourse makes Habermas' account of constitutional democracy particularly helpful and distinguishes it from other attempts to reconcile constitutionalism and democracy into a unitary concept. The emphasis shifts from either side of the supposed opposition to the *process between them* through which they mutually interact and reinforce the legitimacy of the whole. In the real world, this discourse process is implemented through a communicative arrangement: the set of institutions and practices that are primarily constituted by and structured through the medium of law. Law is therefore put into a hierarchically superior position to other discourses: moral, aiming at universality; ethical, concerning individual and collective identities; and pragmatic, which establishes relations between means and ends, and ranks priorities between certain collective goods.

Although Habermas contends that this superior position of the legal discourse to others leaves other discourse's inner logic intact, the legal form nevertheless imposes important constraints: temporal, social and also substantive.[12] Habermas implicitly envisions a 'deliberative division of powers':[13] 'the distribution of the possibilities for access to different reasons

[10] For an overview, see CF Zurn, *Deliberative Democracy and the Institutions of Judicial Review* (Cambridge, Cambridge University Press, 2007) ch 2.

[11] J Habermas (W Rehg trans), *Between Facts and Norms* (Cambridge, Polity Press, 1996) 103.

[12] ibid.

[13] The term was not used by Habermas himself, but by Conrado H Mendes, 'Neither Dialogue nor Last Word: Deliberative Separation of Powers III' (2011) 5 *Legisprudence* 1.

and to the corresponding forms of communication that determine how these reasons are dealt with'.[14] He does not further develop what kind of institutionalisation is required (although his reconstruction draws on the practice of the Federal Republic of Germany and its Constitutional Court). As I will argue below, what is required is precisely the separation of constitutional courts (and constitutional legality) from ordinary ones, especially since the creative role of courts in the sphere of constitutional adjudication concerns the fundamental principles embodied in the Constitution. The transformation of constitutional courts, briefly described in the introductory part of this chapter, threatens this separation of national constitutional courts from the rest of the judiciary and their superior authority necessary for maintaining the communicative arrangement.

B. Deliberative Separation of Powers

The superior position of legal discourse has been criticised from many sides.[15] Gunther Teubner observed that Habermas' account 'underestimates the single-mindedness of legal dynamics which does far more than just filtering out arguments'.[16] Teubner further questions the ability of law 'to decide between economic, political and moral rationality and claim to be binding for all society'.[17]

The response to this objection can be twofold: first, by further distinguishing between ordinary and constitutional legality, law becomes much more open to rationalities other than those that Teubner acknowledges. Coherence, which in Teubner's view dominates law's internal logic, can be achieved to differing degrees and at different levels. That is also why Habermas distinguishes two opposing paradigms of law: bourgeois formal law, related to the nineteenth-century idea of a free-market economy, and welfare-state materialised law, which appeared in reaction to the injustices of the former after the First World War.[18] The bourgeois paradigm highlights formal justice and legal certainty, whereas the welfare paradigm places emphasis on substantive justice in the individual case. The discourse theory of law and democracy envisioned by Habermas in *Between Facts and*

[14] Habermas (n 11) 192.

[15] I do not consider the various critiques of Habermas' theory of constitutional democracy as such, since they are not central to the issue at heart here: the separation of constitutional courts from the ordinary judiciary.

[16] Gunther Teubner, 'Altera Pars Audiatur: Law in the Collision of Discourses' in R Rawlings (ed), *Law, Society and Economy: Centenary Essays for the London School of Economics and Political Science 1895–1995* (Oxford, Clarendon Press, 1997) 163.

[17] ibid, emphasis added.

[18] Habermas (n 11) 195 and ch 9.

Norms is realised through a third, procedural paradigm, which is able to arbitrate between the other two.[19]

Habermas envisions another separation of discourses: that between discourses of justification and application.[20] In the first, the validity of norms is established, whereas the second examines the appropriateness of their application to concrete situations. Habermas does not deny the creative role for courts. On the contrary: 'To the extent that legal programs are in need of further specification by the courts because decisions in the gray area between legislation and adjudication tend to devolve on the judiciary, all provisos notwithstanding juristic discourses of application must be visibly supplemented by elements taken from discourses of justification.'[21] In other words, the creative role of courts requires 'another kind of legitimation than does adjudication proper'.[22] It must, in Habermas' view, entail 'additional obligations for courts to justify opinions before an enlarged critical forum specific to the judiciary. This requires the institutionalization of a legal public sphere that goes beyond the existing culture of experts and is sufficiently sensitive to make important court decisions the focus of public controversies'.[23]

The second response to Teubner concerns revisability. Legal decisions, which arbitrate between different systems, can possibly claim binding force—or finality—from their own perspective only. The socio-political reality is different and the 'final word' has at least two temporal dimensions: one concerning the concrete case at hand and the other oriented beyond it. There are many possible ways in which 'the finitude of a procedural round' can be turned into 'the permanently possible continuity of political mobilization'. The last word is therefore always 'provisional'.[24] The question is therefore how to balance the desire for finality with that of revisability and change, while acknowledging that one can be achieved only at the expense of the other.

C. Constitutional Courts

The dual separation of ordinary and constitutional legality and the discourses of application and justification, together with the desire for revisability,

[19] ibid.

[20] ibid 217–18. This distinction has been criticised in the literature: see particularly Robert Alexy, 'Justification and Application of Norms' (1993) 6 *Ratio Juris* 157, who nevertheless recognises the distinction between the two contexts and its importance for adjudication, which is central for the argument made here.

[21] ibid 439.

[22] ibid 440.

[23] ibid.

[24] Mendes (n 13) 22.

are best realised through the institutional separation of constitutional adjudication in concentrated constitutional courts.[25] They form an important part of the communicative arrangement of constitutional democracies. This is for the following reasons. First, judges of concentrated courts have more time and resources to engage in constitutional/justificatory discourses which place specific demands on their competence. Second, the process before concentrated courts can be structured so that other institutions have a proper voice and representation. Third, cases before concentrated courts can also obtain proper attention from the general public, and concentrated courts cannot easily avoid hard cases through 'legalistic' tactics. Altogether, these factors establish a more effective communicative arrangement than disperse constitutional review. Fourth, concentrated constitutional courts can also be constituted with a view to greater professional diversity, so that they include members with different backgrounds, not just lawyers or even career judges, as is still usual in continental Europe. Fifth, a shorter term of office can also secure the greater responsiveness of constitutional adjudication.

The separation of constitutional and ordinary courts does not concern 'democratic legitimacy', which we usually relate to political institutions, especially not in terms of what Robert Alexy calls 'decisional' or 'volitional' representativeness centred around the concepts of election and majority rule.[26] The point is not to make constitutional courts democratically legitimate in terms of majoritarian democracy, but to employ them in the communicative arrangement, which legitimates decisions, adopted in the given constitutional democracy. For that aim, it is therefore not so important that elected officials mostly appoint the judges of constitutional courts, but rather that the appointment is somewhat responsive to the communicative power generated in society.

Whether concentrated constitutional courts are better than other institutional alternatives and whether the above reasons for their superiority are valid in reality depends on their specific powers and the overall design of a given political system. These differ greatly from country to country, which makes it difficult to present a truly universalisable argument. Yet, the analysis provided here offers a more general theoretical framework which can be used to justify the more specific institutional settings of individual Member States. Thus, the separation of constitutional and ordinary legality does not preclude the involvement of other actors in constitutional review.

[25] The following draws on V Ferreres Comella, *Constitutional Courts and Democratic Values: A European Perspective* (New Haven, Yale University Press, 2009) ch 4, who also considers the 'classical' justification for concentrated constitutional courts, based on the separation of powers and legal certainty, presented by the father of the idea, Hans Kelsen.

[26] See Robert Alexy, 'Balancing, Constitutional Review, and Representation' (2005) 3 *International Journal of Constitutional Law* 572, 579.

On the contrary, this is what deliberative theories of democracy explicitly envision.[27] That is also why I consider many of the arguments presented here as directly relevant for the defence of such other arrangements, if threatened by the requirements of European integration.

There seem to be two kinds of reactions to the transformation of constitutional courts and their loss of exclusivity in constitutional adjudication. One is principled, offering different kinds of normative theories that justify the transformation. The other is pragmatic, suggesting that it can simply be the only viable strategy for constitutional courts if they want to remain influential actors in constitutional law and politics. Both need to find justification in (positive) law in order to be usable in the actual practice of European courts. In this section I will argue that the competing normative theories justifying the greater involvement of national constitutional courts in EU fundamental rights adjudication are problematic. In section IV I will then argue that the pragmatic strategies do not really deliver on what they promise and that some doctrinal legal arguments made by the proponents of both approaches are problematic.

III. THE NATURE OF FUNDAMENTAL RIGHTS IN EUROPE

The authors who welcome the greater involvement of national constitutional courts in EU fundamental rights adjudication share one important assumption: that *the nature* of fundamental rights is the same whatever their formal legal source (be it a national constitution, the European Convention on Human Rights (ECHR) or the EU Charter). Instances of possibly different (or even conflictual) *application* of the rights in concrete cases do not undermine their essential identity. On this point, see sections III.A and III.B below.

Some authors then add that if this different application leads to a 'greater' protection of rights (while the greater protection is usually given by European courts), we should understand this as an enhancement of fundamental rights in Europe (section III.C). This should also be the case when there is a 'gap' in the protection of fundamental rights, usually because a particular right cannot be effectively enforced at the national level, and a supranational court (either in Strasburg or in Luxembourg) fills this gap (section III.D). I think that all three assumptions are problematic. In this section I will explain why.

[27] These can, for example, be self-review panels with legislatures and regulatory agencies, mechanisms for interbranch debate and decisional dispersal, making it easier to amend constitutions and, finally, the establishment of civic constitutional fora. See Zurn (n 10) ch 9.

A. The Duality of Fundamental Rights

The supposed identity of fundamental rights in Europe seems to follow from the universality of fundamental rights. The most well-known fundamental rights documents in the Western political tradition claim to be 'universal': the Universal Declaration of Human Rights adopted by the United Nations in 1948 or its archetypes from the eighteenth-century revolutions in America and France. The state or another public authority can at best guarantee or declare such rights, but their true source comes from somewhere else and is not amendable to will. The liberal idea that fundamental rights protect individuals from the excessive encroachments by the state and the individual lies at the centre of any political project both contribute to this understanding.

Whereas in the eighteenth century the ultimate source of fundamental rights could be the intentions of a divine creator,[28] in our secular or, as some call it, post-metaphysical world, this is no longer possible. Morality therefore became the alternative source of fundamental rights, providing them with universal validity.[29] This, for Habermas, would however overlook their structure and content, which are quite different from moral norms.[30] Habermas explains that while it is true that like moral norms, fundamental rights 'are equipped with a universal validity claim because they can be justified exclusively from the moral point of view … this form of justification by no means robs the [fundamental] rights of their juridical character'.[31] This is because fundamental rights are 'actionable individual rights whose meaning at least in part is to free legal persons in a carefully circumscribed manner *from the binding force of moral commands* by creating domains of legal conduct in which actors can act in accordance with their own preferences'.[32] In other words, Habermas sees law and morality as separate and this separation is one of the points of positive law.

Fundamental rights are a modern phenomenon, tied to a 'new form of political rule', which privileges the rights of the individual over the duties elaborated from a religious or metaphysical perspective.[33] This 'new form of

[28] As Martin Loughlin points out, this was precisely what Thomas Jefferson did when drafting the American Declaration. See M Loughlin, *Sword and Scales: An Examination of the Relationship between Law and Politics* (Oxford, Hart Publishing, 2000), 201.

[29] This of course assumes that moral norms are universal. I will not enter the debate on whether this is the case here.

[30] For Habermas' conception of fundamental rights, see Habermas (n 11) ch 3. See also his essay 'Kant's Idea of Perpetual Peace: At Two Hundred Years' Historical Remove' in C Cronin and P De Greiff (eds), *The Inclusion of the Other* (Cambridge, Polity Press, 1999), particularly at 188–93. For a concise introduction that also considers Habermas' main critics, see Jeffrey Flynn, 'Habermas on Human Rights: Law, Morality, and Intercultural Dialogue' (2003) 29 *Social Theory and Practice* 431.

[31] Habermas (n 30) 191.

[32] ibid, emphasis added.

[33] See Loughlin (n 28) 198.

political rule' was established through positive law—hence the conceptual affinity of fundamental rights and positive law. The fact that many political liberals have been adherents of what we would call today 'legal positivism' (from Jeremy Bentham to Joseph Raz) reflects this conceptual affinity. It is important to understand that this claim about fundamental rights is conceptual rather than simply practical: fundamental rights are *inherently* tied to a *particular* legal system. They are not merely 'universal in abstraction but national in application', as a senior British judge observed.[34] Their very establishment (their creation 'in abstract') is 'particularistic', that is, tied to a particular legal and political system: not only a national one, but also those of the ECHR and the EU. Legal systems, in turn, are formed by norms and institutions: there are those created by states as the most institutionalised (and comprehensive) type, but there is also the ECHR containing a system of norms implemented by its own institutional structure (the Strasbourg Court in particular), and then of course the EU.[35] They are distinctive, whatever the level of the mutual interlocking or the 'fusion' of them.[36]

B. Implicit Social Theory as the Basic Distinction Between EU and National Fundamental Rights

The distinctive character and separation of various fundamental rights legal systems in Europe manifests itself at different levels. Analytical jurisprudence would look at 'the existence and practices of certain kinds of institutions as providing the key to questions regarding the identity of legal systems'.[37] Scholars working in this tradition would look at either law-creating or law-applying institutions in order to find answers. As Julie Dickson shows, the identification and separation of particular legal systems in Europe can be quite difficult if such an approach is used.[38]

Critical legal positivism developed by Kaarlo Tuori thus adds to this kind of examination a deeper one, looking at legal-cultural elements. For Tuori, these are general legal concepts and principles, legal theories or doctrines, and patterns of argumentation that lie at the 'sub-surface level' of the legal

[34] Lord Hoffmann, 'The Universality of Human Rights' (2009) 125 *LQR* 416.

[35] For a sketch of the approach to law as an 'institutional normative order', see N MacCormick, *Questioning Sovereignty: Law, State, and Nation in the European Commonwealth* (Oxford, Oxford University Press, 1999) ch 1.

[36] For an analysis, see Julie Dickson, 'Towards a Theory of European Union Legal Systems' in J Dickson and P Eleftheriadis (eds), *Philosophical Foundations of European Union Law* (Oxford, Oxford University Press, 2012). See also K Tuori, *European Constitutionalism: Towards a Constitutional Theory of the EU* (Cambridge, Cambridge University Press, forthcoming, manuscript on file with the author).

[37] Dickson (n 36) 40.

[38] Dickson (n 36).

order.[39] This sub-surface level also contains an 'implicit [or 'hidden'] social theory': 'a particular view of the respective social field' regulated by the legal order as a whole or its component part under examination.[40] This implicit social theory helps to distinguish legal systems where the analytical approach of analytical legal positivists gets into difficulties. As I explain below, constitutional and political systems of Western European states were established after the Second World War on different foundations (different 'implicit social theory') than the European integration project. The transformation of national constitutional courts and the 'nationalisation' of European rights is part of a larger process whereby this distinction disappears.

What the implicit social theory of law in post-war Europe is (or should one rather say 'was'?) depends on the discipline one takes when articulating the view. Political and constitutional theorists would probably observe that constitutions in Western Europe established regimes of 'constrained democracies', where popular sovereignty was explicitly (and quite strongly) limited by fundamental rights and protected by specialised constitutional courts.[41] Constitutional courts mediated claims based on individual rights and those referring to democracy and popular sovereignty, and became central to the maintenance of constrained democracies. This is what Peter Lindseth calls the 'post-war constitutional settlement'.[42] Political economists and historians speak of the era of constrained or coordinated capitalism, which recognised a strong role for the state, committed to providing for the welfare of its citizens while at the same time respecting the market.[43] The success of coordinated capitalism depended heavily on the organisation of labour and the ability of trade unions to commit the labour force to agreements achieved with the government and employers.[44] Importantly, neither political and constitutional theory nor political economy saw the market as the dominant social sphere or organisational principle—quite the contrary. The former simply ignored the market (and economy) for most of the time, whereas the latter recognised the need to regulate it in order to constrain it. It is plausible to interpret the post-war constitutional settlement as a project of emancipation from economic insecurity and dependence on the market, which were perceived after the war as its root causes.[45]

[39] See K Tuori, *Critical Legal Positivism* (Aldershot, Ashgate, 2002) chs 5–7. For a summary, see Tuori (n 36) Prologue.

[40] Tuori (n 36).

[41] See Müller (n 9) 146–50.

[42] P Lindseth, *Power and Legitimacy: Reconciling Europe and the Nation-State* (Oxford, Oxford University Press, 2010) 17.

[43] See Christopher J Bickerton, *European Integration: From Nation-States to Member States* (Oxford, Oxford University Press, 2012) 76–90.

[44] See particularly B Eichengreen, *The European Economy since 1945: Coordinated Capitalism and Beyond* (Princeton, Princeton University Press, 2007).

[45] See Alexander Somek, *The Cosmopolitan Constitution* (Oxford, Oxford University Press, 2014) 10–11.

This relates to the role of constitutional adjudication in the mediation of social conflicts in the post-war constitutional settlement. By this I do not mean merely express provision for social rights (which did not, for example, appear explicitly in the German Basic Law),[46] but rather the structure of rights which presupposed the express balancing of classical liberal rights, including the right to property, with certain public goods and policies.[47] Europeans thus have always had many weak rights, which are not 'trumps', but rather tickets to deliberative forums: constitutional courts.[48] Therefore, such a conception of rights fits very well with the notion of constitutional democracy sketched above, presupposing mediation between private and public autonomy. It allows constitutional courts to form part of the communicative arrangement established by post-war European constitutions. This explains why the controversy concerning constitutional review in Germany was always limited to the proper method of interpretation of constitutional rights rather than the very existence of the institution, whose legitimacy was undisputed from the very beginning.[49] The new method of constitutional interpretation, defended by the advocates of the Federal Constitutional Court, stressed 'the community-embedded and community-bound nature of persons without however diminishing their inherent independent value'.[50]

However, the place of the market changed dramatically with the rise of what we used to call neoliberalism, for which the market is of paramount importance as 'the universal law governing our social existence'.[51]

[46] See Christian Bommarius, 'Germany's *Sozialstaat* Principle and the Founding Period' (2011) 12 *German Law Journal* 1879.

[47] For an excellent account of the history of the idea of balancing in the European and American legal thinking in the twentieth century, see J Bomhoff, *Balancing Constitutional Rights: The Origins and Meanings of Post-war Legal Discourse* (Cambridge, Cambridge University Press, 2013).

[48] See, eg, Mattias Kumm, 'Institutionalising Socratic Contestation: The Rationalist Human Rights Paradigm, Legitimate Authority and the Point of Judicial Review' (2007) 1(2) *European Journal of Legal Studies* 1.

[49] Christoph Möllers, 'The Scope and Legitimacy of Judicial Review in German Constitutional Law—The Court versus the Political Process' in H Punder and C Waldhoff (eds), *Debates in German Public Law* (Oxford, Hart Publishing, 2014).

[50] German Federal Constitutional Court, Judgment of 20 July 1954, 1 BvR 459, 484, 548, 555, 623, 651, 748, 783, 801/52, 5, 9/53, 96, 114/5, BVerfGE 4, 7 at 15, as translated and quoted by Bomhoff (n 47).

[51] Alexander Somek, *Engineering Equality: An Essay on European Anti-discrimination Law* (Oxford, Oxford University Press, 2011) 85. The term 'neoliberalism' is now used in ideological battles much like 'communism' used to be and, as Somek (at 84) notes, it has become 'the battle cry of last resort used by those who bemoan the demise of economic alternatives to global capitalism'. In this chapter, I essentially mean 'a theory of political economic practices that proposes that human well-being can best be advanced by liberating individual entrepreneurial freedoms and skills within an institutional framework characterized by strong property rights, free markets, and free trade'. The role of the state is minimal. See David Harvey, *A Brief History of Neoliberalism* (Oxford, Oxford University Press, 2005) 2.

We do not need to decide at this point whether the 'original' implicit social theory of the European Communities was that of constrained democracy and capitalism or whether it already contained the seeds of neoliberalism, which started to flourish with the help of the integration structures after the 1970s.[52] Nevertheless, it is clear that EU fundamental rights rest firmly on the foundations of a market integration project and not the emancipatory project of post-war liberal constitutionalism that underlies national constitutions.

This has been argued by many people with reference to the priority of market freedoms over classical liberal freedoms as exemplified by the *Schmidberger* case,[53] or pointing to the shift from 'the traditionally labour-friendly thrust of horizontal direct effect' to 'an instrument that can be used even against internationally concerted trade union action, such as combating the reflagging practice at issue in *Viking*'.[54] At the deepest level, however, the major difference consists in the fact that while national systems of fundamental rights are tied to a functional political system, this is not the case of EU rights.[55] Yet this coupling is necessary for their legitimacy, since rights simply 'do not come from heaven', to paraphrase one ECJ Advocate General,[56] but are always formulated in the context of a political system and the community of citizens who occupy it. This also explains why we should worry about the ECJ adjudicating classical liberal rights in the context of the EU security constitution (especially in the context of the Area of Freedom, Security and Justice),[57] which are not concerned with the emancipation from the market.

This can help us to understand why national constitutions seem to be resistant to the complete neoliberal transformation. This is due, I believe, to the embeddedness of national fundamental rights in the communicative arrangement of a constitutional democracy described above in section II.A.[58] No such mechanisms exist at the EU level, despite the recent efforts to

[52] See Bickerton (n 43) 125–40.

[53] ECJ, Judgment of 12 March 2003 in Case C-112/00 *Schmidberger* [2003] ECR I-5659. See in general Daniel Augenstein, 'Engaging the Fundamentals: On the Autonomous Substance of EU Fundamental Rights Law' (2013) 14 *German Law Journal* 1917.

[54] Somek (n 51) 49; Case C-438/05 *The International Transport Workers' Federation and The Finnish Seamen's Union ('Viking')* [2007] ECR I-10779.

[55] Speaking comparatively, at least, since national democracies were also considerably hollowed out in the course of the neoliberal transformation and it would be a mistake to present them as an ideal. See, eg, Wendy Brown, 'Neoliberalism and the End of Liberal Democracy' in *Edgework: Critical Essay on Knowledge and Politics* (Princeton, Princeton University Press, 2005).

[56] Opinion of AG J Mazák in Case C-411/05 *Palacios de la Villa* [2007] ECR I-8531 [86].

[57] On the EU security constitution, see Tuori (n 36) ch 7.

[58] Post-communist constitutions can be different in this respect, since the post-1989 transformation was based on—and helped to reinforce—neoliberalism as the implicit social theory. See my 'Waiting for the Existential Revolution in Europe' (2014) 12 *International Journal of Constitutional Law* 190–212.

'politicize' it. In this sense, the legitimacy of EU fundamental rights depends on the legitimacy of the EU political process—which is very contested, to say the least.

At this point, one can object to my analysis that this is just another biased leftist critique of the EU and market integration project. However, the point is to realise the fundamental difference between the post-war logic of constrained democracy and capitalism, which informed the formation of national constitutions of that era (including their bills of rights), and the shift to neoliberalism, which exerts pressure on that settlement. It is of course possible to argue that neoliberalism is what Europeans truly want, but this should be done openly and not under the guise of the protection of fundamental rights, which are said to be 'universal' or at least 'the same' in the EU and its Member States.

C. Fundamental Rights and Fundamental Boundaries

This relates to the question of whether we should always welcome the fact that the rights of individuals are 'better' protected with the greater involvement of national constitutional courts and their opening to EU fundamental rights. Quarrels concerning the (im)possibility of comparing the level of protection aside,[59] Aida Torres Pérez suggested that 'preserving a role for constitutional courts under a mutual checks and balances rationale might foster better protection for individuals, since they will seek to bring their cases before the courts that better protect them'.[60] However, this amounts to individuals seeking a forum that, disembedded from the claimant's own political system and its internal communicative arrangement, will give them the highest amount of individual autonomy at the expense of public autonomy of the relevant polity (and, ultimately, the individual), which is uncoupled in the context of the supranational adjudication.

Joseph Weiler addressed the problem of the priority of rights and the individual over a community and its collective choices as the problem of boundaries: as much as individuals have their right to autonomy and self-determination, the same applies to communities. The different line drawn in different polities between these two competing rights reflects a social choice, which is an expression of the core values of the given polity.[61] Yet it is

[59] Leonard FM Besselink, 'Entrapped by the Maximum Standard: On Fundamental Rights, Pluralism and Subsidiarity in the European Union' (1998) 35 *CML Rev* 629.

[60] Aida Torres Pérez, 'The Challenge for Constitutional Courts as Guardians of Fundamental Rights in the European Union' in P Popelier, A Mazmanyan and W Vandenbruwaene (eds), *The Role of Constitutional Courts in Multilevel Governance* (Cambridge, Intersentia, 2012) 62.

[61] Joseph HH Weiler, 'Fundamental Rights and Fundamental Boundaries: On the Conflict of Standards and Values in the Protection of Human Rights in the European Legal Space' in *The Constitution of Europe* (Cambridge, Cambridge University Press, 1999).

remarkable how little space Weiler actually leaves for national autonomy and differentiation. First of all, he considers the ECHR to represent the '"universal", which transcend[s] any legitimate cultural and political difference among different societies in, at least, the universe of Europe'.[62] As argued above, the claim of universality is based on wrongful assumptions (Weiler ultimately seems to ground his understanding of fundamental rights on the tomistic theory of natural law).[63]

Second, Weiler praises the ECJ's creation of EU fundamental rights 'as a call to acknowledge the Community and Union as a polity with its own separate identity and constitutional sensibilities which has to define its own fundamental balances'.[64] However, the problem is that it is a call to acknowledge something that hardly exists, at least not in the sense of a thick identity able to back up a true political system, which would underpin the legal side of fundamental rights, presupposed by their inherent duality discussed above in section III.A.

D. The Institutional Dimension

Finally, there are arguments that welcome the greater involvement of EU fundamental rights (and correspondingly national ordinary courts acting in cooperation with the ECJ) as a way to fill the gaps in judicial protections of such rights. In some countries, fundamental rights are protected by different mechanisms than a strong judicial review, most remarkably the UK. Weiler comments on this as follows: 'One can, of course, take the view that UK constitutional arrangements and the denial of power to UK courts to apply the ECHR are matters which should be left to the UK. But in anybody's book that would hardly qualify as a position which takes human rights seriously.'[65] I suppose it was due to such statements that the rich scholarship on non-judicial protection of fundamental rights has emerged in the last 20 years and I do not have the space to dwell into this debate here.[66] In relation to the argument from the duality of fundamental rights, I want to stress something else: part of the 'fundamental choice' Weiler seeks to protect is the institutional structure for the implementation of rights and communal goods. To say that those who do not think that a strong judicial review is the best way to protect fundamental rights in fact means to say that the choice is not to be taken seriously at all. It is not only about abstract norms, but also

[62] ibid 105.
[63] See ibid 103.
[64] ibid 117.
[65] ibid 124.
[66] Most famously perhaps, see Jeremy Waldron, 'The Core of the Case against Judicial Review' (2006) 115 *Yale Law Journal* 1346.

institutions that implement them and the deliberative separation of powers thus achieved.

Weiler makes another assumption that is often shared by the supporters of the greater fundamental rights involvement or, as he puts it, 'confess[es] to a bias'. It is rebuttable, he admits, but it favours 'human rights judicial review by courts not directly part of the polity the measures of which come under review'.[67] He then gives rather horrendous examples of defending discrimination against blacks in the South of the US or female mutilation and corporal punishments in other countries as examples of defences that make a mockery of the transcendental notion of human dignity. In his 'impressionistic view, local courts, close to local culture, are over-susceptible to this type of argument'.[68] Crucially, he adds:

> I prefer, in this respect, the bias of the transnational forum to that of the national one, tempered as it is by the doctrine of margin of appreciation and mindful that the transnational forum is, as noted, often a second bite at the apple, the national jurisdiction having already had its say.[69]

However, due to the doctrine of primacy (and the overall ambition of the ECJ to create a uniform legal order), there is little room for a doctrine of the margin of appreciation to emerge, contrary to the ECHR. And due to the current structure of the preliminary ruling procedure, the ECJ actually gets 'the first bite at the apple', while national constitutional courts remain often excluded.

IV. 'IF YOU CAN'T BEAT THEM, JOIN THEM!'

For a self-proclaimed 'realist', the normative question about the fundamental difference between national and EU fundamental rights, discussed in the previous section, does not seem to arise: 'focus[ing] on aspects of control and power',[70] it will always depend on the vantage point from which one assesses the role of national constitutional courts in the EU. From the point of view of national constitutions, it is a matter of course to demand that constitutional courts' special position remains protected, so as they keep their superior position in domestic legal orders. And it is equally legitimate (or perhaps 'rational', in the language of such 'realist' analysis) to displace constitutional courts and put the ECJ in control, if one looks at the matter

[67] Weiler (n 61) 126.
[68] ibid 128.
[69] ibid.
[70] Michal Bobek, 'The Impact of the European Mandate of Ordinary Courts on the Position of Constitutional Courts' in M de Visser and C Van de Heyning (eds), *Constitutional Conversations in Europe* (Cambridge, Intersentia, 2012).

from the Plateau de Kirchberg in Luxembourg. Michal Bobek thus suggests a kind of trade, or a '"give and take" compromise':[71] national constitutional courts would have 'to come out of their national constitutional splendid isolation'[72] and accept 'the Charter as a part of national constitutionality ... using it either directly or indirectly for the purpose of constitutional review'.[73] This, in Bobek's view, will lead to their 'regaining the power of review of national implementing measures they have previously abdicated to ordinary courts in cooperation with the Court of Justice'.[74]

There are several problems with this suggestion—even if we ignore its normative dimension, discussed in the previous section of this chapter. If the argument covers the area where constitutional courts decide on questions referred to them by ordinary courts, then constitutional courts gain precisely nothing by embracing EU fundamental rights as their standard of review. This is so because it is still the ordinary courts that have the first say in cases where issues concerning the compatibility of national legislation with EU fundamental rights arise. National constitutional courts cannot change this by making EU fundamental rights part of the national constitutional standard since, according to *Simmenthal II*,[75] ordinary courts must decide *immediately* on the basis of EU law, including the Charter, *without referring the matter* to another national institution, including national constitutional courts.[76]

The true change could come from the ECJ's recognition of the desirability of having the national measure (which possibly implements EU rules) reviewed first in the light of the national constitution. However, this has little to do with constitutional courts' embrace of EU fundamental rights—and one can hardly find a reason in EU law that would support this. The possible invocation of judicial subsidiarity makes little sense here, since what is at stake under this reading is the review by national courts of a national measure in the light of the national constitution, whereas subsidiarity is based on an idea of a shared normative area.

Therefore, change could only come if national constitutional courts started to use the Charter to review national legislation in the abstract review, which is independent from ordinary courts and can take place before a dispute concerning the Charter ever arises before ordinary courts. This would be true especially for those systems that allow for ex ante review. Here, however, it is a question of whether recognising the Charter as part of the standard of review really enhances the power of the constitutional court in

[71] ibid 308.
[72] ibid 305.
[73] ibid.
[74] ibid.
[75] Case 106/77 *Amministrazione delle Finanze dello Stato v Simmenthal* [1978] ECR 629.
[76] This is precisely what the ECJ stresses in *Melki and Abdeli* and later in *A* (see n 3).

question, since it at the same time means that the court must refer questions of interpretation of the Charter to the ECJ—and obey its rulings or face a direct conflict. It seems questionable whether this, even from a 'realist' point of view, increases the autonomy of national constitutional courts.

V. CONCLUSION: NOWHERE TO GO?

If my diagnosis is correct, the change cannot come from either the ECJ or national constitutional courts. The former would have to give up its most cherished doctrines of primacy and effective judicial protection of EU rights, whereas the latter would have much lesser room for manoeuvre than is usually assumed. In my view, therefore, the change must come from within the ordinary judiciary, which should realise that constitutional courts were established with a special purpose and philosophy in mind, and that their too assertive approach may undermine the very foundations of constitutional democracy they also operate within. However, this would require a sort of existential revolution, changing minds of the judges from those of rational actors to virtuous individuals, whose work has a purpose that goes beyond their institutional self-interest. There are many reasons to be sceptical of such 'existential revolution'.[77]

[77] See Komárek (n 58).

5

The Interplay Between the Charter and National Constitutions after Åkerberg Fransson *and* Melloni

Has the CJEU Embraced the Challenges of Multilevel Fundamental Rights Protection?

CLARA RAUCHEGGER*

I. INTRODUCTION

THE EU CHARTER of Fundamental Rights (hereinafter 'the Charter' or 'CFR') has been legally binding for more than five years. It has enhanced the status and visibility of EU fundamental rights. A significant and rapidly increasing number of judgments of the Court of Justice of the European Union (CJEU) and of references for a preliminary ruling refer to the Charter.[1] According to its Article 51(1), the Charter is binding not only on the EU, but also on its Member States when they are implementing EU law. As implementation by the Member States is the standard mode of delivering EU law, EU fundamental rights have an increasingly important impact at the national level.

In addition to the Charter, national measures are subject to fundamental rights as protected in particular by national constitutional law and they have to respect the minimum standard of the European Convention on Human Rights (ECHR).[2] The highest national courts of each Member State and the European Court of Human Rights (ECtHR) ensure that national authorities

* I am grateful to Kenneth A Armstrong, Alicia Hinarejos, David Feldman and Sybe de Vries for their helpful comments. All views and errors remain my own.

1 European Commission, 'Commission Staff Working Document Accompanying the Document 2013 Report on the Application of the EU Charter of Fundamental Rights' SWD(2014) 141 final, 6–7.

2 Convention for the Protection of Human Rights and Fundamental Freedoms (4 November 1950) 213 UNTS 222 (ECHR).

respect those commitments. There is thus no lack of fundamental rights sources or adjudicators in the EU constitutional space.

The coexistence of EU, ECHR and domestic fundamental rights has not arisen with the conferral of binding force on the Charter. EU fundamental rights were already developed by the CJEU as 'parameters of national law' in the period between 1989 and 1991.[3] Since the seminal *Wachauf* judgment, Member States are bound to respect EU fundamental rights as general principles of law when they implement EU law.[4] In *ERT*, the CJEU famously clarified that the obligation to respect fundamental rights as general principles applies even when Member States are derogating from fundamental market freedoms.[5] However, the challenges of this coexistence become considerably more acute post-Lisbon in light of the impact of the Charter and the gradually expanding scope of EU law.

The plurality of sources and actors of fundamental rights protection in the EU raises two major challenges. The first challenge is to ensure that the various fundamental rights catalogues interact in a way that guarantees a complete and coherent system of protection. There should neither be gaps in the system of protection nor should legal certainty be diminished by making it too difficult for the person concerned to know on what standard of protection she or he can rely on. This challenge is typical for the protection of fundamental rights in a multilevel system.[6]

The second challenge is to avoid the marginalisation of national fundamental rights by the Charter.[7] It is linked to the supranational character of the EU legal order and is therefore specific to the interaction between EU and domestic fundamental rights. While the ECHR only offers a minimum standard of protection which diminishes the risk of conflicts with national constitutions,[8] the relationship between EU and national law is traditionally shaped by the primacy principle. Under this principle, EU norms take precedence even over national constitutional law.[9] Domestic fundamental rights therefore risk being displaced by the standard of the Charter.

[3] P Cruz Villalón, '"All the Guidance", ERT and Wachauf' in MP Maduro and L Azoulai (eds), *The Past and Future of EU Law: The Classics of EU Law Revisited on the 50th Anniversary of the Rome Treaty* (Oxford, Hart Publishing, 2010) 163. See also X Groussot, L Pech and GT Petursson, 'The Reach of EU Fundamental Rights on Member State Action after Lisbon' in S de Vries, U Bernitz and S Weatherill (eds), *The Protection of Fundamental Rights in the EU after Lisbon* (Oxford, Hart Publishing, 2013) 98.

[4] Case 5/88 *Wachauf* [1989] ECR 2609.

[5] Case C-260/89 *ERT* [1991] ECR I-2925.

[6] See also F Fabbrini, *Fundamental Rights in Europe: Challenges and Transformations in Comparative Perspective* (Oxford, Oxford University Press, 2014) 46, who argues that a 'challenge of inconsistency' exists every time transnational law acts as a floor.

[7] This corresponds to the general 'challenge of ineffectiveness' identified by Fabbrini (ibid).

[8] Article 53 ECHR.

[9] See especially Case 11/70 *Internationale Handelsgesellschaft* [1970] ECR 1125.

The displacement of national constitutional rights is problematic for various reasons. First, there is a danger of a race to the bottom of fundamental rights standards if fundamental rights scrutiny at the national level is more favourable for the individual than protection under the Charter as interpreted by the CJEU. Second, national differences representing various constitutional traditions could be lost through judicial harmonisation. Linked to this is, third, an institutional concern. As national constitutional courts are the ultimate guardians of domestic fundamental rights, their role is endangered by the increasing impact of the Charter, while the central adjudicator, the CJEU, and ordinary national courts become more powerful.

This chapter examines how these two challenges are addressed by the CJEU. Several recent CJEU judgments, including the landmark rulings in *Åkerberg Fransson*[10] and *Melloni*,[11] shed light on the interplay between EU and national fundamental rights from an EU law perspective. The chapter will start by exploring the scope of application of the Charter as identified by the CJEU. It will then turn to the relationship between EU and national fundamental rights within this scope.

II. THE SCOPE OF APPLICATION OF THE CHARTER

The scope of application of domestic fundamental rights generally extends to all acts of national authority. The Charter, however, is only applicable when the Member States are implementing EU law (Article 51(1) CFR). The zone in which the interplay of EU and national fundamental rights takes place is therefore determined by the scope of the Charter. That is why this section of the chapter critically examines the boundaries of the applicability of the Charter as interpreted by the CJEU case law.

By assessing the delimitation of the scope of the Charter by the CJEU, this section attempts to find out to what extent the Court contributes to a complete and coherent multilevel system of fundamental rights protection and thus whether it successfully addresses the first challenge identified in the introduction to this chapter. However, it cannot be answered at this stage of the inquiry whether the CJEU lives up to the second challenge of not marginalising domestic fundamental rights. That the Charter is applicable in a given situation does not necessarily mean that domestic rights are displaced. The effect on national fundamental rights rather depends on their relationship with the Charter within this scope, which will be discussed in the next section of this chapter.

[10] Case C-617/10 *Åkerberg Fransson* (CJEU, 26 February 2013).
[11] Case C-399/11 *Melloni* (CJEU, 26 February 2013).

This section starts by appraising some principled statements of the CJEU on the scope of the Charter and by putting them into the broader context of the case law before and after Lisbon (section II.A). It concludes that while the general statements of the CJEU on the scope of the Charter are coherent on a conceptual level, the Court should explain more transparently why the Charter is applicable or not in a case at issue. Two types of situations which trigger the applicability of the Charter are then identified. It is argued that the applicability of the Charter in both situations is coherent. First, the Charter is applicable when a Member State fulfils an EU law obligation—including an obligation to ensure the effectiveness of EU law—because the Member State functionally acts as an agent of the EU (section II.B). Second, when a Member State acts pursuant to an option granted by EU law, the exercise of this option is determined by EU law and the applicability of the Charter is thus justified (section II.C).

A. General Characteristics

i. Same Scope as the General Principles of EU Law

Post-Lisbon, the CJEU applies the Charter only where this is justified *ratione temporis*. At the same time, it refers to the general principles abundantly to underline the consistency of its interpretation of the Charter with its pre-Lisbon case law.[12] It results from the CJEU's seminal ruling in *Åkerberg Fransson*[13] and subsequent case law[14] that the scope of the Charter in the sense of Article 51(1) CFR with regard to the Member States corresponds to the scope of fundamental rights as general principles as developed by the Court pre-Lisbon.[15] Just like the general principles, the Charter therefore

[12] See also W Obwexer, 'Der Schutz der Grundrechte durch den Gerichtshof der EU nach Lissabon: Auslegung und Anwendung der Grundrechte-Charta gegenüber den EU-Organen, den Mitgliedstaaten und dem allgemeinen Völkerrecht' (2013) 68 *Zeitschrift für öffentliches Recht* 487.

[13] *Åkerberg Fransson* (n 10) [17]–[19].

[14] See, eg, Case C-258/13 *Sociedade Agrícola* (CJEU, 28 November 2013) [18]–[19]; Case C-265/13 *Torralbo Marcos* (CJEU, 27 March 2014) [28]–[29]; Case C-390/12 *Pfleger* (CJEU, 30 April 2014) [31]–[32]; Case C-483/12 *Pelckmans Turnhout* (CJEU, 8 May 2014) [17]–[18]; Case C-198/13 *Hernández* (CJEU, 10 July 2014) [33]; Case C-354/13 *FAO* (CJEU, 18 December 2014) [31]–[39].

[15] For an overview of the arguments for and against a more limited scope of the Charter in comparison with the general principles, see D von Arnim, *Der Standort der EU-Grundrechtecharta in der Grundrechtsarchitektur Europas* (Frankfurt am Main, Peter Lang, 2006) 259–65. See also J Nusser, *Die Bindung der Mitgliedstaaten an die Unionsgrundrechte: Vorgaben für die Auslegung von Art. 51 Abs. 1 S. 1 EuGrCh* (Tübingen, Mohr Siebeck, 2011) 52–56. The scope of application of the Charter with regard to private parties remains somewhat unclear, however. See N Lazzerini, '(Some of) the Fundamental Rights Granted by the Charter May Be a Source of Obligations for Private Parties: AMS' (2014) 51 *CML Rev* 907.

applies to an *ERT*-type situation, ie, when Member States are derogating from the fundamental freedoms.[16]

ii. The Charter as the Shadow of EU Law

In *Åkerberg Fransson*, the CJEU has furthermore clarified that 'applicability of European Union law entails applicability of the fundamental rights guaranteed by the Charter'.[17] The CJEU underlines the importance it accords to this holding by repeating it in various formulations.[18] Moreover, the Court saw a need to clarify the basis for its reliance on the Charter in several recent cases in which it usually cited *Åkerberg Fransson* to recall that the Charter applies only where national legislation falls within the scope of EU law.[19] The CJEU declares itself incompetent to answer a preliminary question if a case is only governed by a Charter provision with no connection to any other provision of EU law.[20] The Charter is thus only applicable if a national measure is determined by a provision of primary or secondary EU law other than a Charter provision. This means, to use the words of Lenaerts and Gutiérrez-Fons, that the Charter is the 'shadow' of EU law.[21]

Consequently, the scope of application of the Charter is not the same as the EU's legislative competences.[22] The CJEU has recently confirmed this by stating that 'the mere fact that a national measure comes within an area in which the European Union has powers cannot bring it within the scope of EU law'.[23]

EU law can completely determine the national action in the case at issue,[24] but it can also leave the Member States a degree of discretion. If they are left

[16] *ERT* (n 5).

[17] *Åkerberg Fransson* (n 10) [21].

[18] ibid [21]–[22].

[19] See, eg, Case C-45/12 *Hadj Ahmed* (CJEU, 13 June 2013) [56]–[57]; Case C-418/11 *Texdata* (CJEU, 26 September 2013) [71]–[75]; *Sociedade Agrícola* (n 14) [18]–[21]; Case C-176/12 *Association de médiation sociale* (CJEU, 15 January 2014) [42]; Case C-206/13 *Siragusa* (CJEU, 6 March 2014) [21]; *Torralbo Marcos* (n 14) [28]–[31]; *Pfleger* (n 14) [31]–[34]; *Hernández* (n 14) [34]–[49].

[20] See eg Case C-555/12 *Loreti and others* (CJEU, 14 March 2013) [17]; Case C-499/12 *Gentile* (CJEU, 7 February 2013) [13]–[14]; Case C-106/13 *Fierro and Marmorale* (CJEU, 30 May 2013); Case C-117/14 *Grima* (CJEU, 5 February 2015).

[21] K Lenaerts and JA Gutiérrez-Fons, 'The Place of the Charter in the EU Constitutional Edifice' in S Peers et al (eds), *The EU Charter of Fundamental Rights: A Commentary* (Oxford, Hart Publishing, 2014) 1567–68.

[22] See generally S Prechal, S de Vries and H van Eijken, 'The Principle of Attributed Powers and the "Scope of EU Law"' in LFM Besselink, F Pennings and S Prechal (eds), *The Eclipse of the Legality Principle in the European Union* (Alphen aan den Rijn, Kluwer Law International, 2011).

[23] *Hernández* (n 14) [36]. For a suggestion *de lege ferenda* to extend the scope of EU law so that it corresponds to the legislative competences, see Case C-34/09 *Ruiz Zambrano* [2010] ECR I-1177, Opinion of AG Sharpston [163]–[170].

[24] See, eg, Joined Cases C-293/12 and C-594/12 *Digital Rights Ireland* (CJEU, 8 April 2014); *Melloni* (n 11).

such a degree of discretion, the Member States have to make use of it in a way that is compatible with fundamental rights. The degree of determination of the national measure does not affect the applicability of the Charter, but it has an impact on the role which national fundamental rights can play within the scope of the Charter, as will be shown in the next section of this chapter.

A degree of discretion has to be distinguished from the adoption of a stricter national standard which goes beyond what is required by EU law. Stronger protection clauses which allow the Member States to go beyond minimum harmonisation should be seen only as a declaratory reminder that Member States are free to act as long as they do not come into contradiction with EU law.[25] Pre-Lisbon, the CJEU has held that national regulatory standards adopted within the field of application of an EU measure providing for only minimum harmonisation fall outside the scope of the general principles.[26] This approach was recently confirmed by the Court.[27] Article 11 of Directive 2008/94 stated that the Directive 'shall not affect the option of Member States to apply or introduce laws, regulations or administrative provisions which are more favourable to employees'.[28] The Court made clear that this provision merely 'recognises the power which the Member States enjoy under national law to provide for such more favourable provisions outside the framework of the regime established by that directive' and therefore did not trigger the applicability of the Charter.[29] It can, however, be difficult in practice to distinguish whether a provision of EU law refers to the freedom which Member States enjoy outside a regime of secondary EU law or to an area of discretion left within such a regime.

iii. Intention of the National Legislator is not Decisive

The CJEU has repeatedly mentioned obiter that to find out whether the Charter is triggered, it had to be taken into account among other criteria whether the national legislation at issue is intended to implement a provision

[25] J Kokott and C Sobotta, 'The Charter of Fundamental Rights of the European Union after Lisbon' (2010) EUI Working Paper AEL 6, http://cadmus.eui.eu/bitstream/handle/1814/15208/AEL_WP_2010_06.pdf?sequence=%203. See also EM Frenzel, 'Die Charta der Grundrechte als Maßstab für mitgliedstaatliches Handeln zwischen Effektivierung und Hyperintegration' (2014) 53 *Der Staat* 1, 10.

[26] Editorial Comments, 'The Scope of Application of the General Principles of Union law: An Ever Expanding Union?' (2010) 47 *CML Rev* 1589, 1591. The Editoral Comments referred to Case C-2/97 *Borsana* [1998] ECR I-8597; Case C-6/03 *Deponiezweckverband Eiterköpfe* [2005] ECR I-2753; Case C-82/09 *Dimos Agiou Nikolaou Kritis* [2010] ECR I-3649.

[27] *Hernández* (n 14) [44].

[28] Directive 2008/94/EC of the European Parliament and of the Council of 22 October 2008 on the protection of employees in the event of the insolvency of their employer [2008] OJ L283/37.

[29] *Hernández* (n 14) [44].

of EU law.[30] To emphasise that the scope of the Charter corresponds to the scope of the general principles in this regard, the Court referred to its pre-Lisbon judgment in *Annibaldi*.[31] However, in these judgments, the CJEU never actually applied this criterion when determining whether the Charter is triggered or not.[32] Moreover, in *Åkerberg Fransson*, the Grand Chamber of the CJEU expressly declared that it is not a decisive condition for the applicability of the Charter that the national legislation is adopted to transpose the provision of secondary EU law in question.[33] As a result, the Charter was applicable in this case.

These apparently conflicting statements can only be reconciled if one assumes that it is not an essential precondition for the applicability of the Charter that the national legislation in question was intended to implement EU law. However, that a Member State adopted national legislation to transpose EU law can suggest that it is likely implementing EU law. This interpretation of the case law is convincing if one takes into account the flexibility with which Member States can implement Directives, 'including by reference to pre-existing legislation, or to judicial interpretation, or by various combinations of old and new legislative and judicial measures'.[34] Besides, Member States can also regulate national matters not mandated by EU law in legislation intended to transpose secondary EU law.[35] The obligation to cite the Directive in question can indicate that the Member State is effectively implementing EU law.[36]

iv. Appraisal of the Court's Approach

It is to be welcomed that the Charter and the general principles are held to have the same scope. Sarmiento rightly argues that 'if the Charter's aim was to overrule the [Court's] pre-2009 case law on the scope of application of fundamental rights, it would have done so in unambiguous terms'.[37] However, as the CJEU points out, the wording of the Charter Explanations,[38]

[30] Case C-40/11 *Iida* (CJEU, 8 November 2012) [79]; Case C-87/12 *Ymeraga* (CJEU, 8 May 2013) [41]; *Siragusa* (n 19) [25]; *Hernández* (n 14) [37].

[31] Case C-309/96 *Annibaldi* [1997] ECR I-7493 [21]; *Iida* (n 30) [79]; *Ymeraga* (n 30) [41]; *Siragusa* (n 19) [25].

[32] See, eg, *Hernández* (n 14).

[33] *Åkerberg Fransson* (n 10) [27].

[34] See Editorial Comments (n 26) 1593.

[35] See HD Jarass, 'Die Bindung der Mitgliedstaaten an die EU-Grundrechte' [2012] *Neue Zeitschrift für Verwaltungsrecht* 457, 459.

[36] Frenzel (n 25) 10.

[37] D Sarmiento, 'Who's Afraid of the Charter? The Court of Justice, National Courts and the New Framework of Fundamental Rights Protection in Europe' (2013) 50 *CML Rev* 1267, 1277.

[38] Explanation on Art 51, Explanations Relating to the Charter of Fundamental Rights [2007] OJ C303/17 (Charter Explanations).

which have to be given due account,[39] and the case law cited therein suggest that the criteria of applicability of fundamental rights have not changed.[40] Moreover, a restrictive interpretation of Article 51(1) CFR would only limit the scope of application of the Charter. The general principles would still apply to the same extent as before the Lisbon Treaty under Article 6(3) of the Treaty on European Union (TEU). A differentiation between the scope of the Charter and the scope of the general principles would have risked leading to confusion and legal uncertainty.[41] The Court's approach is therefore not only a convincing interpretation of Article 51(1) CFR, but also contributes to the coherence of EU fundamental rights protection.

To find out whether it also contributes to the coherence of fundamental rights protection in Europe that the Charter applies to all national measures determined by EU law, the raison d'etre of EU fundamental rights protection has to be explored. Is it legitimate that the Charter applies to all situations determined by EU law?

One view, to which the CJEU seems to adhere, is that fundamental rights protection at the EU level is necessary to ensure the effective implementation of EU law. It is well known that the CJEU developed EU fundamental rights as a corollary to the primacy principle. EU fundamental rights as general principles closed the gap that arose because national constitutional law could be set aside under the primacy principle. More recently, the CJEU expressed that EU fundamental rights protection is justified because of 'the need to avoid a situation in which the level of protection of fundamental rights varies according to the national law involved in such a way as to undermine the unity, primacy and effectiveness of EU law'.[42]

There is no doubt that the application of an EU standard of fundamental rights protection instead of a national one to acts determined by EU law contributes to its uniform and effective implementation. However, the goal of a fundamental rights catalogue such as the Charter cannot be to ensure that EU law is applied effectively and in the same way in all Member States. After all, the purpose of fundamental rights protection is not to guarantee the effectiveness of legislation or regulation, but rather to impose limits on the power of public authorities.[43] It is first and foremost the protection of

[39] Article 52(7) CFR.

[40] *Åkerberg Fransson* (n 10) [20]. See also D Leczykiewicz, 'The Charter of Fundamental Rights and Member States' Derogations from Internal Market Obligations' in PM Huber (ed), *The EU and National Constitutional Law* (Stuttgart, Boorberg, 2012) 82; Frenzel (n 25) 9–10.

[41] A Rosas, 'When is the EU Charter of Fundamental Rights Applicable at National Level?' (2012) 19 *Jurisprudence* 1269, 1282. See also Case C-108/10 *Scattolon* [2011] ECR I-7491, Opinion of AG Bot [120]; M Safjan, 'Areas of Application of the Charter of Fundamental Rights of the European Union' (2012) EUI Working Paper Law 22, 5, http://cadmus.eui.eu/bitstream/handle/1814/17597/LAW_2011_08.pdf?sequence=1.

[42] *Siragusa* (n 19) [32]; *Hernández* (n 14) [47].

[43] Nusser (n 15) 68–71.

the rights of individuals which has to lie behind the Charter. It results from the rule of law principle enshrined in Article 2 TEU that every EU measure has to be scrutinised for its compliance with EU fundamental rights.[44]

One might argue that every national measure is already subject to domestic fundamental rights protection and that there is thus no need for the Charter to apply. Some commentators place emphasis on the 'universal, deductive and natural law-like character of human rights, as values and rights common to all human beings'.[45] According to this conception, there can be no difference between EU and national fundamental rights.

However, in a seminal contribution, Weiler has convincingly argued that beyond a certain core, protected in Europe by the ECHR, the definition of fundamental rights can differ from polity to polity. The level of protection of a fundamental right is the 'expression of a compromise between competing social goods in the polity'.[46] Similarly, Cartabia has successfully shown that while the idea of human rights 'necessarily contains a universal dimension rooted in human dignity', they are linked to historical and cultural traditions.[47] As Advocate General Bot expressed it:

> The fundamental rights to be protected and the level of protection to be afforded to them reflect the choices of a society as regards the proper balance to be achieved between the interests of individuals and those of the community to which they belong. That determination is closely linked to assessments which are specific to the legal order concerned, relating particularly to the social, cultural and historical context of that order, and cannot therefore be transposed automatically to other contexts.[48]

It is thus coherent that the Charter acts as the shadow of EU law.[49] If an action is determined by EU law, the balancing exercise inherent to fundamental rights protection needs to be undertaken at the EU level to guarantee that countervailing interests arising in an EU context can be taken into account. While the effectiveness of EU law cannot be the objective of EU fundamental rights protection, it has an important role to play in this balancing exercise. Under Article 52(1) CFR, limitations to fundamental

[44] ibid 71.

[45] J Reestman and LFM Besselink, 'After *Åkerberg Fransson* and *Melloni*' (2013) 9 *European Constitutional Law Review* 169, 170.

[46] JHH Weiler, 'Fundamental Rights and Fundamental Boundaries: On Standards and Values in the Protection of Human Rights' in N Neuwahl and A Rosas (eds), *The European Union and Human Rights* (The Hague, Kluwer Law International, 1995) 55.

[47] M Cartabia, 'Europe and Rights: Taking Dialogue Seriously' (2009) 5 *European Constitutional Law Review* 5, 20.

[48] Case C-399/11 *Melloni* (CJEU, 2 October 2012), Opinion of AG Bot [109].

[49] This is not to say that what falls under 'EU law' for the purposes of triggering the Charter in the view of the CJEU is always convincing. See in particular Barnard's contribution in ch 8 of this volume. See also C Kilpatrick, 'Are the Bailouts Immune to EU Social Challenge Because They are Not EU Law?' (2014) 10 *European Constitutional Law Review* 393.

rights enshrined in the Charter 'may be made only if they are necessary and genuinely meet objectives of general interest recognised by the Union or the need to protect the rights and freedoms of others'. The example of the *Melloni* case discussed in the next section of this chapter will illustrate that the effective implementation of EU law can meet objectives of general interests or the need to protect the rights and freedoms of others, and therefore has to be taken into account in the balancing exercise.[50]

Even if Member States are left a degree of discretion, their action is still partially determined by EU law. It is thus justified to extend the applicability of the Charter to national actions which are not completely determined by EU law. In effect, the compliance of Member States with the Charter is of particular relevance where the rule of EU law leaves the Member States with a degree of autonomy.[51]

That the applicability of the Charter is justified when a national measure is determined by EU law means that it cannot be a decisive factor whether the Member State intended to transpose EU law or not. As a result, even without regard to the difficulty of identifying the Member State's intention to transpose, it is warranted to look at the function of the national measure and not at its intention. If it was correctly assumed above that the CJEU does not see the intentional transposition by the legislation as an essential precondition for the applicability of the Charter, the Court's approach is therefore convincing.

While the definition of the general characteristics of the scope of the Charter by the CJEU is coherent, the Court's approach cannot be described as fully transparent. It is certainly a positive development that the Court discusses the applicability of the Charter explicitly in many cases, something it did not do before Lisbon. Furthermore, it is to be welcomed that the Court has recently started deciding cases in which the Charter does not apply in the form of judgments instead of Court orders that were often not translated into all official languages. However, with the recent *Hérnandez* case as a notable exception, the reasoning of the Court is usually short and cursory, and leaves many details open.[52] Instead of specifying in which situations the Charter applies, the Court keeps repeating the general formula that the scope of the Charter corresponds to the scope of EU law. Sometimes, for example regarding the intentional transposition, the Court's reasoning is even contradictory. The Court should give clear reasons to substantiate why the Charter applies or does not apply in a given case and it should not

[50] See text to n 123 below.

[51] Prechal, de Vries and Eijken (n 22) 216–17; H Sauer, 'Grundrechtskollisionsrecht für das europäische Mehrebenensystem: Konkurrenzbestimmung–Kollisionsvermeidung–Kohärenzsicherung' in N Matz-Lück and M Hong (eds), *Grundrechte und Grundfreiheiten im Mehrebenensystem: Konkurrenzen und Interferenzen* (New York, Springer, 2011).

[52] *Hernández* (n 14).

hesitate to engage in a more thorough and convincing discussion on the objective of EU fundamental rights protection.[53]

B. Trigger 1: Obligation Imposed by EU Law

We have seen that the Court's definition of the general characteristics of the scope of the Charter contributes to a coherent and complete system of fundamental rights protection. The question remains as to what 'determined by EU law' really means. An analysis of the recent fundamental rights case law of the CJEU shows that a national measure falls within the scope of the Charter if it fulfils an EU law obligation.[54] According to the type of EU law obligation, two implementing situations can be distinguished. Not only a directly relevant substantive provision of EU law, but also an explicit EU law mandate to ensure the effectiveness of a rule of EU law triggers the applicability of the Charter.

i. Relevant Substantive EU Law Provision

That the scope of the Charter corresponds to the scope of EU law must mean that the existence of a substantive rule of EU law governing the facts of the case triggers the applicability of the Charter.[55] There was, for instance, no doubt that an administrative decree refusing to grant asylum fell within the scope of a Directive on minimum standards for the qualification and status of third-country nationals or stateless persons as refugees.[56] To find out whether a provision of EU law is relevant, the Court examines inter alia whether the national legislation pursues the same objectives as a rule of EU law.[57] That it is sometimes not easy to decide whether a norm is sufficiently relevant to the case is an old problem that may also arise in situations where fundamental rights are not at issue.[58]

The German Federal Constitutional Court, as a reaction to the *Åkerberg Fransson* judgment, emphasised that it would not accept an application of

[53] For an in-depth and critical analysis of the minimalist methodology which the CJEU uses in its case law, see D Sarmiento, 'Half a Case at a Time: Dealing with Judicial Minimalism at the European Court of Justice' in M Claes et al (eds), *Constitutional Conversations in Europe: Actors, Topics and Procedures* (Cambridge, Intersentia, 2012).

[54] This category of implementing situations corresponds to some extent to Sarmiento's 'mandating rules'. However, in contrast to Sarmiento's classifcation, it also includes the obligation to ensure the effectiveness of EU law. See Sarmiento (n 37).

[55] ibid 1279–80.

[56] Joined Cases C-199–201/12 *X and others* (CJEU, 7 November 2013).

[57] *Iida* (n 30) [79]; *Hernández* (n 14) [38]–[41].

[58] Rosas (n 41) 1278.

the Charter based on a tenuous link to national legislation.[59] However, the recent fundamental rights case law of the CJEU shows that a simple overlap of subject matter between measures of secondary EU law and the exercise of national regulatory competence is not sufficient to bring a matter within the scope of EU law. The CJEU held that to find out whether a Member State is implementing EU law, it had to be determined 'whether there are specific rules of European Union law on the matter or capable of affecting it'.[60] Conversely, the Charter could not be applied where 'the provisions of EU law in the area concerned did not impose any specific obligation on Member States'.[61] Where a substantive provision of EU law somehow affected the national action, but did not determine it in the form of a specific obligation, the Court held that the Charter was not applicable.[62]

ii. Obligation to Ensure the Effectiveness of EU Law

The Charter also applies when Member States are under an obligation to guarantee the effectiveness of a rule of EU law. Two conditions need to be fulfilled: first, a national measure has to have an impact on the effectiveness of specific provisions of secondary EU law; and, second, the effective implementation has to be clearly mandated by EU law.

The first condition is that the national measure affects the effectiveness of specific provisions of secondary EU law.[63] This typically applies to national criminal and administrative sanctions.[64] In *Åkerberg Fransson*, correct tax collection as guaranteed by provisions of domestic law allowed for the effective application of the Sixth VAT Directive.[65] Similarly, in *Texdata*, it was emphasised that the Austrian legislation in question penalised infringements of disclosure obligations laid down in several VAT directives.[66]

[59] 1 BvR 1215/07 (German Federal Constitutional Court, 24 April 2013) para 91. For a detailed analysis of the judgment, see D Thym, 'Separation versus Fusion: How to Accomodate National Automy and the Charter? Diverging Visions of the German Constitutional Court and the European Court of Justice' (2013) 9 *European Constitutional Law Review* 391.

[60] *Siragusa* (n 19) [25]; *Hernández* (n 14) [37]. See also *Annibaldi* (n 31) [23]; *Iida* (n 30) [79]; *Ymeraga* (n 30) [41].

[61] *Hernández* (n 14) [35].

[62] See, eg, *Siragusa* (n 19) [24]–[30]; *Ymeraga* (n 30) [42]; *Iida* (n 30) [80]; *Hernández* (n 14) [34].

[63] See J Akandji-Kombé, 'Arrêt "Åkerberg Fransson": L'application juridictionnelle de la Charte européenne des droits fondamentaux' (2013) 21 *Journal de droit européen* 184, 185.

[64] See Sarmiento (n 37) 1281; J Schmoll, 'Unionsgrundrechte, innerstaatliche Grundrechte und die nationalen Höchstgerichte' (2011) 66 *Zeitschrift für öffentliches Recht* 461, 466.

[65] Sixth Council Directive 77/388/EEC of 17 May 1977 on the harmonisation of the laws of the Member States relating to turnover taxes–Common system of value added tax: uniform basis of assessment [1977] OJ L145/1 (Sixth VAT Directive); *Åkerberg Fransson* (n 10) [24].

[66] *Texdata* (n 19) [74]; Case C-418/11 *Texdata* (CJEU, 31 January 2013), Opinion of AG Mengozzi [69]. For a recent confirmation that the Charter is triggered by an obligation to ensure the effectiveness of EU law, see Case C-662/13 *Surgicare* (CJEU, 12 February 2015) [33]; Case C-510/13 *E.ON* (CJEU, 19 March 2015) [50].

This approach of the Court does not defer from its pre-Lisbon case law. Domestic law penalisation of violations of EU law was already subject to the test of compliance with fundamental rights as general principles.[67]

Not only domestic sanctions but also procedural law can have an impact on the effectiveness of provisions of EU law. In *DEB*, a national procedural rule was likely to hinder legal entities of introducing an action for infringement of provisions of EU law in national courts.[68] The Vice President of the CJEU has (extra-judicially) interpreted *DEB* to mean that the Charter applies to national procedural law which has an impact on the effectiveness of EU law, even if it does not directly transpose it.[69]

The second condition is that the effective implementation is clearly mandated by EU law. A specific obligation to guarantee the effectiveness of secondary EU law can take the form of a rule of EU law granting an individual a right vis-a-vis the Member States.[70] The right would be devoid of its meaning if it were not effectively guaranteed at the national level. Likewise, where directives contain explicit provisions obliging the Member States to ensure the effective implementation of its provisions, a mandate can be easily identified.[71] In *Texdata*, the Charter was applied because domestic penalties were based directly on EU law.[72] The Court and Advocate General Mengozzi referred to a provision of secondary law which obliged the Member States to put in place appropriate penalties for the failure to respect the disclosure obligations imposed by the VAT Directives.[73]

Advocate General Mengozzi distinguished the *Texdata* case from *Åkerberg Fransson*. He argued that the latter case was more problematic because the Sixth VAT Directive did not contain an explicit requirement to lay down appropriate penalties for breach of the obligations it imposed.[74] For this reason, Judge Rosas had expressed, extra-judicially and before the judgment was delivered, that no provision of secondary EU law was directly relevant to the outcome of the case.[75] Under a strict interpretation of Article 51(1)

[67] Case C-276/01 *Steffensen* [2003] ECR I-03735; C Ranacher, 'Die Bindung der Mitgliedstaaten an die Gemeinschaftsgrundrechte: Reichweite–Konsequenzen–Perspektiven' (2003) 58 *Zeitschrift für öffentliches Recht* 21; Schmoll (n 64) 466. See also (regarding the general principle of proportionality) P Eeckhout, 'The EU Charter of Fundamental Rights and the Federal Question' (2002) 39 *CML Rev* 945, 963.

[68] Case C-279/09 *DEB* [2010] ECR I-13849.

[69] K Lenaerts, 'Die EU-Grundrechtecharta: Anwendbarkeit und Auslegung' (2012) 47 *Europarecht* 3, 5. See also V Kronenberger, 'Quand "mise en œuvre" rime avec "champ d'application": La Cour précise les situations qui relèvent de la Charte des droits fondamentaux de l'Union européenne dans le contexte de l'application du ne bis in idem' (2013) 20 *Revue des Affaires Européennes* 147, 153.

[70] See Sarmiento (n 37) 1280–81.

[71] See Kronenberger (n 69) 152.

[72] *Texdata* (n 19) [71]–[75]; *Texdata*, Opinion of AG Mengozzi (n 66) [69]–[71].

[73] *Texdata* (n 19) [74]; *Texdata*, Opinion of AG Mengozzi (n 66) [69].

[74] *Texdata*, Opinion of AG Mengozzi (n 66) [70].

[75] Rosas (n 41) 1280.

CFR, the case at issue in *Åkerberg Fransson* could therefore have been interpreted as falling outside the scope of the Charter.[76]

However, the Grand Chamber of the CJEU (to which Judge Rosas did not belong) found that the national law imposing tax penalties fell within the scope of the Charter. It first repeated its case law according to which it results from a combination of the provisions of the Sixth VAT Directive and the principle of loyal cooperation that Member States are obliged 'to take all legislative and administrative measures appropriate for ensuring collection of all the VAT due on its territory and for preventing evasion'.[77] The CJEU also based its reasoning on Article 325 of the Treaty on the Functioning of the European Union (TFEU), which imposes a clear obligation on the Member States to protect the financial interests of the EU. This suggests that where an act of secondary law does not explicitly require the adoption of sanctions to ensure its effective application, an obligation of this kind has to clearly result from another provision of EU law.[78]

It has been argued that to invoke the general obligation of Article 325 TFEU would have been sufficient for the national measures to constitute an implementation.[79] Even taking into account that *Åkerberg Fransson* concerns the EU's own financial resources which are fundamental to EU membership and clearly defined in primary law,[80] such an interpretation would have far-reaching consequences. It would ultimately mean that every general EU law requirement to attain specific goals would entail the applicability of the Charter, even in the absence of secondary law concretising this obligation. *Åkerberg Fransson* is surely not an indicator of such a future expansive trend, as it is based on both the obligations flowing from the Sixth VAT Directive and from the more general Treaty provision of Article 325 TFEU. Under the current state of EU law, implementing therefore requires that a Member State acts under an express mandate 'to attain goals *through specific means*'.[81]

iii. Appraisal of the Court's Approach

In both types of implementing situations described above, it is a specific EU law obligation that triggers the applicability of the Charter. In the first category identified, the obligation consists in a directly relevant substantive

[76] Case C-617/10 *Åkerberg Fransson* (CJEU, 12 June 2012), Opinion of AG Cruz Villalón [40]. See also Akandji-Kombé (n 63) 184.

[77] *Åkerberg Fransson*, Opinion of AG Cruz Villalón (n 76) [25].

[78] Kronenberger (n 69) 153.

[79] E Hancox, 'The Meaning of "Implementing" EU Law under Article 51(1) of the Charter: Åkerberg Fransson' (2013) 50 *CML Rev* 1411, 1419.

[80] J Morijn, 'Åkerberg and Melloni' (2013) Eutopia Blog, http://eutopialaw.com/2013/03/14/akerberg-and-melloni-what-the-ecj-said-did-and-may-have-left/#more-1826.

[81] See Sarmiento (n 37) 1280.

provision of EU law. In the second category, it is the combination of a substantive provision of EU law and the concrete mandate to implement it effectively that constitutes the EU law obligation. This approach is justified. If a Member State fulfils obligations imposed by EU law, the application of EU fundamental rights is justified on the ground that it functionally acts as the EU's decentralised executive branch.[82] Acting as agent, the Member State 'does something required by EU law by means conflicting with EU fundamental rights'.[83] The EU should not escape the binding nature of EU fundamental rights by acting through the Member States.[84]

The *Åkerberg Fransson* judgment has attracted a lot of attention and criticism. This criticism, however, generally relates to the fact that the Sixth VAT Directive did not explicitly impose an obligation on Member States to effectively sanction a breach of its obligations. It is usually not contested that a specific obligation to guarantee the effectiveness of EU law triggers the Charter. If one interprets the judgment, as has been done above, to mean that it was the combination of the obligations flowing from the Sixth VAT Directive and the more general Treaty obligation of Article 325 TFEU which triggered the Charter,[85] applying the EU fundamental rights in this situation seems justified.[86]

C. Trigger 2: Option Granted by EU Law

Member States are not only implementing EU law when they act pursuant to an EU law obligation, but also when they are given the possibility to make a choice by virtue of EU law.[87] Two types of situations in which the Charter is triggered by an option granted by EU law can be identified in the case law. In one type of situation, the Member State is allowed discretion to opt into the regime provided by EU secondary law. In another type of situation, the Member State is granted the possibility to derogate from EU law.

[82] Weiler (n 46) 68.

[83] Z Kühn, 'Wachauf and ERT: On the Road from the Centralised to the Decentralised System of Judicial Review' in Maduro and Azoulai (n 3) 156.

[84] R Schütze, 'European Fundamental Rights and the Member States: From "Selective" to "Total" Incorporation?' (2011–12) 14 *Cambridge Yearbook of European Legal Studies* 337, 337.

[85] See text to n 81 above.

[86] See also J Kühling, 'Kernelemente einer kohärenten EU-Grundrechtsdogmatik in der Post-Lissabon-Ära' (2013) 68 *Zeitschrift für öffentliches Recht* 469, 475, who argues that the judgment in *Åkerberg Fransson* is sensible and convincing as it constitutes a variant of the agency situation.

[87] This category of implementing situations corresponds to Sarmiento's 'optioning rules', but goes beyond this classification by also including derogation situations under this heading. See Sarmiento (n 37) 1281.

i. NS-*Type Discretions*

Member States are bound by the Charter if they make use of an option granted by EU law within the framework of a regime of secondary law. The Grand Chamber judgment in the *NS* case made clear that although a Member State was free to decide whether it examined an asylum application for which it is in principle not responsible under the regulation in question, once it decided to make use of this 'discretionary power which forms part of the Common European Asylum System' and is thus confined by the provisions of the Regulation, it was implementing EU law.[88]

The more recent Grand Chamber judgment in the *Sabou* case is another illustration of this approach.[89] The Directive in question established that the tax authorities of one Member State may request the authorities of another Member State for information enabling correct taxation. The Grand Chamber held that 'the fact that the requesting Member State is not bound to submit a request for assistance to another Member State' does not mean this request falls outside the scope of EU law.[90] Once a Member State decides to make use of this assistance procedure, it is bound by the provisions of the Directive.[91]

ii. Derogation Situations

The choice granted to the Member States can also take the form of an allowed derogation from EU law. Ever since the seminal ruling in the *ERT* case,[92] the CJEU has imposed fundamental rights-based requirements on the Member States when derogating from the fundamental freedoms (the so-called *Schranken-Schranken*).[93] In an *ERT*-type situation, a Member State relies on a public policy justification or even a competing fundamental right to derogate from a market freedom. Although it could have been argued that the narrow wording of 'implementing' in Article 51(1) CFR does not cover derogation situations,[94] the CJEU has clarified in *Åkerberg Fransson* that the scope of the general principles is the same as the scope of the Charter.[95]

[88] Joined Cases C-411/10 and C-493/10 *NS* [2011] ECR I-13905 [65]–[68]. See also K Lenaerts, 'Exploring the Limits of the EU Charter of Fundamental Rights' (2012) 8 *European Constitutional Law Review* 375, 379.

[89] Case C-276/12 *Sabou* (CJEU, 22 October 2013). This judgment concerned the application of fundamental rights as general principles because the Charter was not applicable *ratione temporis*.

[90] ibid [26].

[91] ibid.

[92] *ERT* (n 5).

[93] For an overview of the case law, see Prechal, de Vries and Eijken (n 22) 217.

[94] See Frenzel (n 25) 3.

[95] See text to n 13 above.

The recent judgment in the *Pfleger* case was the first opportunity for the CJEU to apply the Charter to an *ERT*-type situation.[96] It concerned national restrictions on gambling and thus the freedom to provide services. When discussing the applicability of the Charter, the CJEU (interestingly, not the Grand Chamber) referred to *Åkerberg Fransson* to reassert that the scope of EU law for the purposes of the general principles and the implementation of EU law in the sense of the Charter are the same.[97] It then cited *ERT* and stated that it had already held that where a Member State relied on a public policy derogation 'provided for by European Union law' in order to justify an exception to a fundamental freedom, the derogation had to be 'interpreted in the light of' EU fundamental rights.[98]

iii. Appraisal of the Court's Approach

It has been argued that if derogation is permissible under the Treaties, the Court should not address the further question of whether the derogation is applied with respect of fundamental rights.[99] This is not convincing. Respect of fundamental rights in *NS*-type and derogation situations can be seen as an instance of the principle that secondary law needs to be interpreted in light of primary EU law.[100] Although the Member State is given a choice, the exercise of this choice is determined by EU law. Once a Member State decides to make use of the option granted by EU law, it is subject to specific obligations imposed by EU law. As the scope and contours of the national measure are determined at the EU level, the balancing of fundamental rights and competing interests has to be undertaken at this level as well.[101] The 'crucial factor' is therefore, as highlighted by Advocate General Kokott, not 'whether European Union law imposes obligations on a Member State or confers rights on the Member State', but 'whether or not a Member State's action is based on European Union law'.[102]

[96] *Pfleger* (n 14).

[97] ibid [30]–[34].

[98] ibid [35].

[99] PM Huber, 'Unitarisierung durch Gemeinschaftsgrundrechte: Zur Überprüfungsbedürftigkeit der ERT-Rechtsprechung' (2008) 43 *Europarecht* 190, 191; FG Jacobs, 'Wachauf and the Protection of Fundamental Rights in EC Law' in Maduro and Azoulai (n 3) 137.

[100] See (regarding derogations situations) Eeckhout (n 67) 978; Ranacher (n 67) 54; Frenzel (n 25) 8–10.

[101] See (regarding derogation situations) Kokott and Sobotta (n 25) 10; T von Danwitz and K Paraschas, 'A Fresh Start for the Charter: Fundamental Questions on the Application of the European Charter of Fundamental Rights' (2012) 35 *Fordham International Law Journal* 1396, 1406.

[102] *Sabou* (n 89) [43].

III. THE RELATIONSHIP BETWEEN THE CHARTER AND NATIONAL FUNDAMENTAL RIGHTS

When the applicability of the Charter is triggered, EU and national fundamental rights apply concurrently. Whether national fundamental rights are marginalised depends on the role they can play within the scope of the Charter. The relationship between the Charter and national rights within the scope of the Charter therefore determines to what extent the CJEU lives up to the second challenge identified above.

EU and national fundamental rights standards within the scope of the Charter can clash, but they can also converge or coexist.[103] This section considers each of these possible interactions of EU and national fundamental rights in turn. It starts by critically analysing the CJEU's solution to a direct conflict (section III.A). It is argued that the Court rightly gives priority to the Charter over a higher domestic standard of protection if the national measure in question is completely determined by EU law. However, an exception to the priority of the EU standard should be made if the protection of a conflicting domestic right expresses the constitutional identity of a Member State.

As far as the coexistence of EU and national standards is concerned, it is convincing that the Charter acts as a minimum standard only where Member States are left a margin of discretion in their implementation (section III.B). If the national action is not completely determined by EU law, it is functionally both an EU and a national measure. The CJEU is called to allow for the application of domestic fundamental rights standards to areas of discretion as long as the effectiveness of EU law is not thereby completely frustrated. Finally, a convergence of the standards of protection takes place if the CJEU meets its obligation to interpret Charter rights in harmony with the common constitutional traditions of the Member States (section III.C). The CJEU should make more transparent the extent to which it lives up to this requirement.

A. Conflict: Divergent Standards of Protection

i. Mr Melloni and the Problem of Conflicting Standards

A conflict between the Charter and national fundamental rights arises when a national implementing act complies with the Charter, but not with the national standard of fundamental rights protection. These conflicts take

[103] See Sauer (n 51) 4–5.

place above the floor of the ECHR and will therefore not be solved by the EU's accession to the Convention mandated by Article 6(2) TEU.[104]

The problem of conflicting standards is best illustrated by the *Melloni* case.[105] Mr Melloni was convicted in his absence for bankruptcy fraud by an Italian court. He had failed to make an appearance before the national court, although the forthcoming trial had been notified to the two lawyers he had appointed. When he was arrested by the Spanish police after he had fled to Spain, Mr Melloni opposed his surrender to the Italian authorities under the European Arrest Warrant (EAW) that had been issued, ultimately before the Spanish Constitutional Court. According to the previous case law of the Spanish Constitutional Court, the execution of an EAW had to be made conditional on the conviction for very serious offences *in absentia* being open to review.[106] As this was not guaranteed in Italy, Mr Melloni could not have been surrendered under Spanish constitutional law.[107] However, a provision of EU law, Article 4(1)(a) of the EAW Framework Decision,[108] seemed to impose the execution of an EAW in a situation such as Mr Melloni's. It was never questioned that Article 4(1)(a) of the EAW Framework Decision was compatible with the ECHR as interpreted by the ECtHR.[109] There was thus a potential conflict between the Charter and the Spanish Constitution. The Spanish Constitutional Court decided to make its first ever preliminary reference to the CJEU to ask it for guidance.

As far as the validity of the contested provision of secondary law was concerned, the CJEU held that Article 4(1)(a) of the EAW Framework Decision was compatible with the Charter.[110] Regarding the conflict between the standard of the Charter and the standard of domestic constitutional law, the Court held that it results from the well-established principle of primacy that national constitutional rights cannot be given priority over secondary EU law which is compliant with the Charter.[111] Mr Melloni's surrender could

[104] A Torres Pérez, 'Dialogue on the European Arrest Warrant: The Spanish Constitutional Court Knocking on Luxembourg's Door' (2012) 8 *European Constitutional Law Review* 105, 114.

[105] *Melloni* (n 11) [13]–[19].

[106] *Melloni* (n 11) [20]; Torres Pérez (n 104) 108.

[107] The execution and implementation of the EAW has led to constitutional concerns in many Member States. See, eg, J Komárek, 'European Constitutionalism and the European Arrest Warrant: In Search of the Limits of the "Contrapunctual Principles"' (2007) 44 *CML Rev* 9.

[108] Council Framework Decision 2009/299/JHA amending Framework Decisions 2002/584/JHA, 2005/214/JHA, 2006/783/JHA, 2008/909/JHA and 2008/947/JHA, thereby enhancing the procedural rights of persons and fostering the application of the principle of mutual recognition to decisions rendered in the absence of the person concerned at the trial [2009] OJ L81/24 (EAW Framework Decision).

[109] *Melloni* (n 11) [35]–[46].

[110] ibid [47]–[54].

[111] ibid [58]–[59].

thus not be made dependent on the conviction being open to review in Italy, as required by Spanish constitutional law.

ii. Appraisal of the Court's Approach

In *Melloni*, the Spanish Constitutional Court asked the CJEU whether, in order to avoid restricting the national constitutional right, it could give priority to the domestic standard of fundamental rights protection over that of the Charter. It suggested that Article 53 CFR, a provision newly added to primary EU law by the Charter, could possibly require it to opt for this solution.[112]

Advocate General Bot argued that Article 53 CFR was not applicable because it did not regulate conflicts between a provision of secondary law interpreted in the light of the Charter and a national constitutional right. His reasoning relied on the wording 'in their respective fields of application'.[113] Yet Article 51(1) CFR already stipulates that the Charter only applies when Member States are implementing EU law.[114] Article 53 CFR would thus merely serve the political aim of ensuring that the Charter does not replace national constitutional standards outside the scope of the Charter. The problem with this reading is not only that it leaves no independent meaning to Article 53 CFR, but that it also represents the fields of application of EU and national fundamental rights protection as discrete and separate, although they overlap significantly.[115]

A stronger argument advanced by the Advocate General is the one on which the CJEU's judgment is solely based: Article 53 CFR has to be interpreted in accordance with the primacy principle.[116] The Court rightly presented primacy as a well-established and essential feature of the EU legal order.[117] Since *Internationale Handelsgesellschaft*, the Court has continuously held that 'rules of national law, even of constitutional nature, cannot

[112] For an overview of the possible interpretations of Art 53, see M Almhofer and J Hartlieb, 'Article 53 of the Charter of Fundamental Rights of the EU: Recent Developments' [2014] *European Yearbook on Human Rights* 149, 151.

[113] *Melloni*, Opinion of AG Bot (n 48) [99]–[100].

[114] JB Liisberg, 'Does the EU Charter of Fundamental Rights Threaten the Supremacy of Community Law' (2001) 38 CML Rev 1171, 1192.

[115] ibid. See also LFM Besselink, 'General Report' in J Laffranque (ed), *The Protection of Fundamental Rights Post-Lisbon: The Interaction between the Charter of Fundamental Rights of the European Union, the European Convention on Human Rights and National Constitutions: Reports of the XXV Fide Congress Tallinn 2012* (Tallinn, Tartu University Press, 2012) 134.

[116] N de Boer, 'Addressing Rights Divergences under the Charter: Melloni: Case C-399/11, *Stefano Melloni v Ministerio Fiscal*, Judgment of the Court (Grand Chamber) of 26 February 2013, nyr' (2013) 50 *CML Rev* 1083, 1093.

[117] *Melloni* (n 11) [59]; *Melloni*, Opinion of AG Bot (n 48) [98]–[99]; A Levade, 'Mandat d'arrêt européen: Quand confiance et reconnaissance mutuelle font obstacle au "sauf si"' [2013] *Constitutions* 184, 187.

be allowed to undermine the effectiveness of EU law on the territory of that state'.[118] Although it is hard to determine the exact meaning of Article 53 CFR, this provision cannot be interpreted to have explicitly departed from this settled case law.[119]

Although the CJEU's approach seems compatible with Article 53 CFR, it can be argued that the Court's ruling cannot be reconciled with the aim of providing the highest possible level of fundamental rights protection.[120] Opting for the highest standard of protection in case of a conflict would certainly have the advantage of being the most protective of fundamental rights. Mr Melloni could not be surrendered if it was not ensured that his conviction would be subject to review in Italy. Moreover, there would be no risk of conflict with national constitutional courts.[121] The Spanish Constitutional Court could stick to its case law even though it did not comply with EU law.

However, the application of the primacy principle by the CJEU to address the divergent standards of protection is not only compatible with primary EU law, but is also justified on a broader conceptual level. The reason for this is that the balance of competing interests which characterises fundamental rights adjudication is specific to a legal order.[122] The balance between the right to a fair trial and the effectiveness of the EAW framework in the *Melloni* case is unique to the EU legal order and should therefore be undertaken at this level. A stronger protection of the right to a fair trial would adversely affect the uniform application of the EAW, which is based on the principles of mutual recognition and mutual trust in the Member States.[123] Moreover, as the Advocate General pointed out, offenders might be encouraged 'to take refuge in the Member State whose constitutional rules offer better protection than the others, thus undermining the effectiveness of the Framework Decision'.[124] Only a proportionality analysis undertaken at the EU level would make it possible to take into account the interests of individuals in the entire EU in a functioning system of mutual recognition of arrest warrants.

In a situation such as that in *Melloni*, the balancing exercise needs to be undertaken at the EU level alone because the national measure is completely

[118] *Internationale Handelsgesellschaft* (n 9) [3]; *Melloni* (n 11) [59].

[119] De Boer (n 116) 1093–94; Sauer (n 51) 43. Liisberg comes to the same conclusion based on the drafting history of Art 53 CFR: Liisberg (n 114) 1193. But see F Vecchio, 'I casi Melloni e Akerberg: Il sistema multilivello di protezione dei diritti fondamentali' [2013] *Quaderni Costitutionali* 454, 456.

[120] N Lavranos, 'The ECJ's Judgments in *Melloni* and *Åkerberg Fransson:* Un ménage à trois difficulté' [2013] *European Law Reporter* 133, 140.

[121] See Weiler (n 46) 58.

[122] See text to n 46 above.

[123] *Melloni* (n 11) [63].

[124] *Melloni*, Opinion of AG Bot (n 48) [103].

determined by EU law.[125] Article 4(1)(a) of the EAW Framework Decision imposed a surrender of Mr Melloni and did not leave the Spanish authorities with a degree of discretion in this regard. If EU law does not give the Member States a choice on how to implement a specific EU law obligation, national authorities functionally act as EU authorities or agents of the EU only; not even a part of their action is based on national law.

However, the fact that the primacy of the standard of the Charter over the national constitutional standard in cases of complete determination is convincing on a conceptual level does not mean that the effectiveness of EU law should always prevail in the balancing exercise; it only means that countervailing interests arising at the EU level should be taken into account in this analysis. Moreover, the standard of the Charter should never fall below the standard of the ECHR as the latter corresponds to the common core of fundamental rights protection in Europe. Whether the proportionality analysis applied by the CJEU in *Melloni* in particular or in its fundamental rights case law more generally lives up to that undertaken at the national level or by the ECtHR is a different question that, however important, goes beyond the scope of this chapter, focusing on the interplay of EU and national fundamental rights.[126] If the passages on Article 53 ECHR and on the principle of mutual recognition in the recent Opinion 2/13 of the CJEU meant that the Charter can fall below the standard of the ECHR in the view of the CJEU, this would be highly problematic.[127]

Although giving priority to the EU standard of protection was justified in the *Melloni* case, the CJEU was wrong not to engage with the conceptual justification of this approach or the arguments brought forward by the domestic constitutional court.[128] The judgment would probably have been more readily accepted if it had done so. The reasoning of the CJEU, however, is short and cursory and exclusively self-referential.[129] In a way which has been called brutal by one commentator, the Court reintroduces the primacy principle to the discussion.[130]

[125] See *e contrario Åkerberg Fransson* (n 10) [29]; *Melloni* (n 11) [60].

[126] For a critique of the Court's low level of review in fundamental rights cases, see, eg, A Albi, 'An Essay on How the Discourse on Sovereignty and on the Cooperativeness of National Courts Has Diverted Attention from the Erosion of Classic Constitutional Rights in the EU' in Claes et al (n 53).

[127] Opinion 2/13 (CJEU, 18 December 2014). For a critical analysis of the relationship of the Charter and the ECHR in the light of Opinion 2/13 of the CJEU, see Douglas-Scott's contribution in ch 2 of this volume. See also M Berger and C Rauchegger, 'Opinion 2/13: Multiple Obstacles to the Accession of the EU to the ECHR' [2015] *European Yearbook on Human Rights* 61.

[128] See also A Torres Pérez, 'Melloni in Three Acts: From Dialogue to Monologue' (2014) 10 *European Constitutional Law Review* 308, 317; de Boer (n 116) 1100.

[129] Vecchio (n 119) 456.

[130] Levade (n 117) 187.

Nevertheless, conflicts with national constitutional courts should in principle not arise in areas of complete determination, provided that the standard of protection at the EU level is not generally low. To give priority to the EU standard of protection if the national measure is completely determined by EU law has for a long time been accepted, for instance, by the German Federal Constitutional Court, as long as the EU generally ensures an effective protection of fundamental rights comparable to the national standard of protection.[131] As a reaction to the CJEU's judgment, the Spanish Constitutional Court lowered its standard of protection in the case at issue and allowed the surrender of Mr Melloni.[132]

iii. Constitutional Identity as a Safeguard

Although it is justified that the exercise of balancing fundamental rights and competing interests is undertaken at the EU level if a situation is completely determined by EU law, there is a danger that national differences corresponding to national constitutional identity may be lost in this process. Arguing that the balance of fundamental rights and competing interests is specific to a legal order is a 'double-edged sword'.[133] Fundamental rights protection is the result of a compromise in a given society not only at the EU but also at the national level. Even when they act as agents of the EU only, national authorities remain national authorities bound by domestic constitutional law.

The CJEU should therefore show respect to national constitutional identity when deciding whether to give priority to an act of secondary EU law over national constitutions. Several constitutional courts have only accepted the primacy of EU law over national constitutional law as long as their constitutional identity is not affected.[134] Moreover, since the entry into force of the Treaty of Lisbon, Article 4(2) TEU states more clearly than ever that the EU has to respect national identity.[135] This provision could be used to justify an exception to the primacy principle when the reliance on a particular national fundamental rights standard forms part of domestic constitutional identity.[136]

[131] German Federal Constitutional Court, 2 BvR 197/83 *Solange II* [1986] BVerfGE 73, 339.

[132] Spanish Constitutional Court, STC 26/2014 *Melloni* [2014] BOE 60, 85. For an analysis in English, see Torres Pérez (n 128) 319–23.

[133] Reestman and Besselink (n 45) 170.

[134] See, eg, M Wendel, 'Lisbon before the Courts: Comparative Perspectives' (2011) 7 *European Constitutional Law Review* 96, 131; M Claes, 'Negotiating Constitutional Identity or Whose Identity is it Anyway?' in Claes et al (n 53) 222–26.

[135] Besselink (n 115) 135.

[136] De Boer (n 116) 1083.

National constitutional courts are the guardians of the constitution at the national level. That is why they should be given the opportunity to explain in front of the CJEU why an EU measure compromises national constitutional identity. If the case at issue arises in front of a national constitutional court, this court should make a preliminary reference to the CJEU.[137] More and more constitutional courts already use this formal avenue of dialogue with the CJEU.[138] Admittedly, domestic courts could simply hold a national implementing measure to be incompatible with national constitutional identity without consulting the CJEU. However, giving preference to national constitutional identity over primacy in a preliminary ruling of the CJEU is preferable to the mere non-application of EU law by national courts. A decision taken at the EU level enhances transparency and allows for an EU-wide debate based on a judgment translated into the 24 official languages of the EU. Furthermore, the trust of the national constitutional courts in the CJEU could be enhanced if the Court shows that it is willing to protect national constitutional identity. It has also been argued that Article 4(2) TEU cannot be interpreted as intending to allow national courts to unilaterally refuse to apply EU law.[139]

How can the interpretation of the national constitution by the domestic constitutional court be taken into account if the case arises in front of an ordinary court? The CJEU has recently confirmed its case law according to which an ordinary court that considers that a national act is not only unconstitutional but also contrary to EU law cannot be prevented from directly referring a preliminary question to the CJEU.[140] As the identification and protection of national constitutional identity is the role of the domestic constitutional courts, it is highly problematic that they are circumvented in this way.[141] One way to address this concern *de lege ferenda* would be to allow the assessment of national constitutional courts to be presented in front of the CJEU even if the reference stems from an ordinary court.[142] Currently, third-party interventions are limited under Article 23 of the Statute of the Court.[143]

[137] See also Claes (n 134) 232.

[138] See eg Spanish Constitutional Court in *Melloni* (n 11); Austrian Constitutional Court in *Digital Rights Ireland* (n 24); German Federal Constitutional Court in C-62/14 *Gauweiler* (pending).

[139] Claes (n 134) 221.

[140] C-112/13 *A* (CJEU, 11 September 2014), [28]–[46].

[141] On the displacement of national constitutional courts post-Lisbon see J Komárek, 'The Place of Constitutional Courts in the EU' (2013) 9 European Constitutional Law Review 420, 427; M Bobek, 'The Impact of the European Mandate of Ordinary Courts on the Position of Constitutional Courts' in Claes et al (n 53).

[142] See M de Visser, 'National Constitutional Courts, the Court of Justice and the Protection of Fundamental Rights in a Post-Charter Landscape' (2014) 15 *Human Rights Review* 39, 48.

[143] G de Búrca, 'After the EU Charter of Fundamental Rights: The Court of Justice as a Human Rights Adjudicator?' (2013) 20 *Maastricht Journal of European and Comparative Law* 168, 178.

That the assessment of constitutional courts should be taken into account is not to say that the CJEU should be the last guardian of national constitutional identity. The Court should rather be under an obligation to follow the interpretation of the constitutional court if the latter's claim is not completely unreasonable. The role of EU law in the national legal orders is by now already established. Moreover, many powerful constitutional courts have shown their commitment to European integration.[144] The CJEU should show trust in them. In a smiliar fashion to the ultra vires review developed by the German Constitutional Court in its Maastricht judgment,[145] the CJEU could step in if a national court seems to rely on a manifest misconception to shield national law from EU influences.

In an obiter statement in *Melloni*, the Advocate General left open the possibility that a Member State could challenge a provision of EU law on the basis of a constitutional provision if the latter is part of the national constitutional identity.[146] However, this avenue of challenge cannot replace the dialogue with national constitutional courts, which remain the ultimate guardians of the domestic constitutions. As fundamental rights protection imposes restrictions on the government, the executive cannot be expected to defend a strict protection of domestic fundamental rights. For the same reason, it is not a valid argument that the EU legislature has already balanced national constitutional law against the demands of the EU legal order in the legislative process.[147]

So far, the CJEU has not been confronted with a case in which national authorities argued that a provision of secondary law was incompatible with national constitutional identity.[148] Neither the Spanish government nor the Spanish Constitutional Court in *Melloni* indicated that the constitutional court's interpretation of the right to a fair trial was part of Spanish constitutional identity.

B. Coexistence: The Charter as a Minimum Standard

We have seen that the primacy of the Charter is justified if a national measure is completely determined by EU law. An exception to the primacy principle should only be made if giving priority to the EU standard of protection

144 See Wendel (n 134).

145 See, eg, Thym (n 59) 398–401.

146 *Melloni*, Opinion of AG Bot (n 48) [137]–[141].

147 But see de Boer (n 116) 1099.

148 On the role of Art 4(2) TEU in the CJEU's case law when derogations from fundamental freedoms are concerned, see T Konstadinides, 'Constitutional Identity as a Shield and as a Sword: The European Legal Order within the Framework of National Constitutional Settlement' (2010–11) 13 *Cambridge Yearbook of European Legal Studies* 195, 200.

would endanger the constitutional identity of the Member States. However, conflicts between the EU and the national level of fundamental rights protection do not arise in the first place if the standards of protection can coexist. Co-applicability is made possible when one legal order provides only for a minimum standard, permitting a different and higher standard of protection for the other.

i. Primacy, Not Pre-Emption

In *Melloni* and *Åkerberg Fransson*, the CJEU held that where national measures implement EU law but are 'not entirely determined' by it, 'national authorities and courts remain free to apply national standards of protection'.[149] With this statement, the Court clarified for the first time what role national fundamental rights can play within the scope of applicability of EU fundamental rights.[150] The Court has recently confirmed that the notion of 'determination' is the equivalent of the concept of discretion.[151]

Two additional conditions have to be fulfilled. The minimum level of protection of the Charter has to be respected and the 'supremacy, unity and effectiveness' of EU law cannot be compromised.[152] That the minimum level of the Charter is respected has to mean that national fundamental rights have to be 'more advantageous *pro individuo*'.[153] Within the scope of the Charter, national fundamental rights therefore apply under three conditions: first, national measures need to be only partially determined by EU law; second, they have to offer a higher level of protection corresponding at least to that offered by the Charter; and, third, the 'supremacy, unity and effectiveness' of EU law cannot be compromised.

In all types of situations in which the Charter is triggered, the Member States can be granted a scope of discretion. When Member States fulfil an EU law obligation, they often have the freedom to achieve the specific goal set by EU law in various ways. When Member States are granted a discretionary power within the framework of a regime of secondary law in an *NS*-type scenario, they have the choice to make use of this option or not. EU law also quite evidently allows for diversity when establishing possible derogations from fundamental market freedoms. The same applies to public policy exceptions granted by secondary law which can be invoked to refuse the recognition of a judgment.[154]

[149] *Åkerberg Fransson* (n 10) [29]; *Melloni* (n 11) [60].
[150] Almhofer and Hartlieb (n 112) 153.
[151] *A* (n 140) [44].
[152] *Åkerberg Fransson* (n 10) [29]; *Melloni* (n 11) [60].
[153] Almhofer and Hartlieb (n 112) 156.
[154] LFM Besselink, 'Case Comment: The Parameters of Constitutional Conflict after *Melloni*' (2014) 39 *European Law Review* 531, 546.

ii. Appraisal of the Court's Approach

It is convincing that the Charter applies in situations where the Member States enjoy a degree of discretion. It has already been shown in the preceding section of this chapter that Member States are implementing EU law even if the latter does not regulate all details of the national action.[155] Moreover, it is warranted that if a national measure is not completely determined by EU law, the Charter acts only as a minimum standard and therefore does not displace national fundamental rights standards. When making use of a degree of discretion, Member States, although constrained by the limits which EU law imposes on their discretion, are acting autonomously. The implementing measure is therefore functionally both an EU and a national measure.

According to the third criterion identified above, national fundamental rights can only be applied within the scope of EU law if the 'supremacy, unity and effectiveness' of EU law are not thereby compromised. The supremacy of EU law is not a goal in itself. As the CJEU has argued, the principle rather serves the uniform and effective application of EU law.[156]

By granting a degree of discretion to the Member States, the EU legislator accepts that EU law is not implemented in the same way across the entire EU. EU law explicitly allows for diversity. The interest of a uniform application of EU law is therefore not a criterion to be taken into account for the purpose of fundamental rights scrutiny in areas of national discretion. That is why it makes sense that the CJEU does not require that the *uniformity* of EU law is upheld as part of its third criterion. The two concepts are semantically different; the unity of EU law is not necessarily endangered if there is no uniformity.[157] It remains unclear, however, how the unity of EU law can be compromised.

While the uniform application of EU law is not required when Member States are granted a degree of discretion, there is still a need to ensure the effective implementation of EU law.[158] However, if domestic fundamental rights could only be invoked if their application does not adversely affect the effective application of EU law, they would have no role to play within the scope of EU law. A domestic constitutional right which cannot impose any limits to the effective application of EU law is devoid of its meaning. The distinction between completely and partially determined situations would be futile because domestic fundamental rights would always be displaced. The third criterion stated by the CJEU can therefore only be understood

[155] See text to n 51 above.
[156] Case 6/64 *Costa/ENEL* [1964] ECR 585.
[157] Besselink (n 154) 547.
[158] But see ibid 546.

as meaning that domestic fundamental rights are displaced if they would completely frustrate, ie, annul, all effects of the provisions of EU law in question.[159]

Two cases which were decided after *Åkerberg Fransson* and *Melloni* illustrate that the CJEU leaves at least some leeway to national authorities and does not defend the full effect of EU law at all costs. The *Jeremy F* case was referred by the French Constitutional Council, the very first preliminary reference of this court.[160] Like the *Melloni* case, it concerned the EAW. The EAW Framework Decision did not expressly provide for the possibility of bringing an appeal with suspensive effect against the decision of the requested authority to execute the EAW. According to the CJEU, this was compatible with the Charter.[161] However, the Court stated that as the Framework Decision leaves the national authorities with 'a discretion' in relation to the possibility of providing for an appeal with suspensive effect, they were not prevented from applying their own 'constitutional rules' under the condition that the Framework Decision was not frustrated.[162] The execution of the EAW was not frustrated, the CJEU went on to hold, if the general time limit which the Framework Decision imposed was respected.[163] The judgment therefore confirms that the requirement that the 'primacy, unity and effectiveness' cannot be compromised means that domestic standards can be applied as long as the obligation imposed by EU law is not frustrated.

This approach is not limited to rulings reacting to references from the highest national jurisdictions. The *Sabou* case was referred by the Prague City Tax Directorate.[164] The Grand Chamber held that EU rights of defence did not require that a taxpayer is heard in the phase of the mutual assistance in tax proceedings before the requested Member State sends information necessary for the correct evaluation of income tax to the requesting Member State.[165] However, the Court then went on to state that Member States were not prevented from extending the right to be heard to this phase of the tax proceedings.[166]

Both cases suggest that the CJEU accepts certain restrictions to the effectiveness of EU law. It has been argued that the result in *Jeremy F* gives 'the impression that human rights rank high on the ECJ's agenda' and that it helps to 'lure' national constitutional courts which remain reluctant to

[159] But see Almhofer and Hartlieb (n 112) 156, who interpret this statement by the Court to mean that even in areas of discretions, primacy will generally prevail.
[160] Case C-168/13 PPU *Jeremy F* (CJEU, 30 May 2013).
[161] ibid [47].
[162] ibid [52]–[53].
[163] ibid [75].
[164] *Sabou* (n 89).
[165] ibid [44].
[166] ibid [45].

engage in a dialogue with the CJEU.[167] However, there is a danger that the Court sees the effectiveness of EU law frustrated too easily. In *Jeremy F*, national constitutional rights could only be applied by the French Constitutional Council under the condition that very stringent time limits were respected, which, in practice, makes it very difficult to enforce the right to appeal.[168] The national constitutional standard should only be displaced if the effectiveness of EU law is actually frustrated, but not if it is merely adversely affected.

C. Convergence: The Common Constitutional Traditions of the Member States

We have seen that conflicts between EU and national fundamental rights do not arise when both standards can coexist. Moreover, divergent standards of fundamental rights protection do not lead to conflicts if either the European standard is adjusted to the domestic standard or vice versa.

The ECHR plays a crucial role in the harmonisation of the core of European fundamental rights protection. Every Member State is also a Contracting Party of the Convention. At the same time, Article 52(3) CFR expressly obliges the CJEU to give 'the same meaning and scope' as the ECHR to Charter rights derived from the Convention.[169] It is crucial for the effectiveness and consistency of fundamental rights protection in Europe that this obligation is respected by the EU courts. It can therefore be seen as highly problematic that the recent Opinion 2/13 of the CJEU has made a prompt accession of the EU to the ECHR highly unlikely.[170] However, as this chapter focuses on the interaction between the Charter and national fundamental rights, a different relationship is of interest for our purposes: to what extent does the standard of protection of the Charter converge with domestic constitutional standards?

i. National Constitutional Standards in the CJEU Case Law

The common constitutional traditions of the Member States are not only a source of EU fundamental rights as Article 6(3) CFR stipulates—they also

[167] F Millet, 'How Much Lenience for How Much Cooperation? On the First Preliminary Reference of the French Constitutional Council to the Court of Justice' (2014) 51 *CML Rev* 195, 212.

[168] Torres Pérez (n 128) 326.

[169] For an analysis of the role of the ECHR in the CJEU case law, see, eg, B de Witte, 'The Use of the ECHR and Convention Case Law by the European Court of Justice' in P Popelier, C van de Heyning and P van Nuffel (eds), *Human Rights Protection in the European Legal Order: The Interaction Between the European and the National Courts* (Cambridge, Intersentia, 2011).

[170] Opinion 2/13 (n 127). See Douglas-Scott's contribution in ch 2 of this volume.

guide the interpretation of Charter rights according to Article 52(4) CFR. In addition, Article 53 CFR can be interpreted to complement Article 52(4) CFR by also imposing a high standard of protection at the EU level.[171] Despite the requirement to take into account the common constitutional principles of the Member States when interpreting the Charter, the Court's assessment of potential fundamental rights violations seems to be based on the Charter alone in the vast majority of cases. Just like pre-Lisbon,[172] the Court has only referred to national constitutional traditions in a small number of isolated cases since October 2009. While the Court recognises for some fundamental right that they stem from common constitutional traditions,[173] Article 52(4) CFR does not play any explicit role in its reasoning.[174] This observation also applies to the seminal judgments in *Åkerberg Fransson*[175] and *Melloni*.[176]

Several Advocate Generals have attempted substantive comparative analyses in their opinions.[177] In the *Akzo Nobel* case, for instance, Advocate General Kokott came to the conclusion that in-house lawyers do not enjoy the protection of communications with their clients based on the results of a comparative analysis showing that only three Member States recognise such professional privileges.[178] Nevertheless, the CJEU referred to the comparative analysis of its Advocate General in only one case. In *DEB*, it acknowledged that in the practice of the Member States 'there is a relatively widespread distinction between profit-making and non-profit-making legal persons'.[179]

However, the fact that the CJEU does not explicitly refer to constitutional traditions of the Member States does not mean that they play no role in the case law. The recent judgment in *Digital Rights Ireland* could be considered

[171] Von Danwitz and Paraschas (n 101) 1419–20; W Obwexer, 'Funktionalität und Bedeutung der Rechtsvergleichung in der Rechtsprechung des EuGH' in A Gamper and B Verschraegen (eds), *Rechtsvergleichung als juristische Auslegungsmethode* (Vienna, Jan Sramek, 2013) 125.

[172] See S Seyr, 'Verfassungsgerichte und Verfassungsvergleichung: Der EuGH' (2010) 18 *Journal für Rechtspolitik* 230, 236; I Pernice and FC Mayer, 'Grundrechtsschutz und rechtsstaatliche Grundsätze' in E Grabitz et al (eds), *Das Recht der Europäischen Union: Kommentar* (Munich, Beck, 2010) para 13.

[173] For the principle of retroactive application of the more lenient penalty, see Case C-61/11 PPU *El Dridi* (CJEU, 28 April 2011) [62]; Case C-17/10 *Toshiba Corporation* (CJEU, 14 February 2012) [64]. For Art 47 CFR, see Case C-93/12 *Agrokonsulting* (CJEU, 27 June 2013) [55]; Case C-619/10 *Trade Agency* (CJEU, 6 September 2012) [52]. For Art 48 CFR, see Case C-72–77/10 *Costa* (CJEU, 16 February 2012) [86].

[174] See also Obwexer (n 171) 116.

[175] *Åkerberg Fransson* (n 10).

[176] *Melloni* (n 11).

[177] C McCrudden, 'Using Comparative Reasoning in Human Rights Adjudication: The Court of Justice of the European Union and the European Court of Human Rights Compared' (2012–13) 15 *Cambridge Yearbook of European Legal Studies* 383, 403.

[178] Case C-550/07 P *Akzo Nobel* ECR I-8301, Opinion of AG Kokott. See also Kokott and Sobotta (n 25) 3–4.

[179] *DEB* (n 68) [44].

as an example of a case in which the Court takes into account a high level of fundamental rights protection offered by domestic constitutions.[180] Two preliminary references by the Austrian Constitutional Court and the Irish High Court had asked the CJEU to rule, inter alia, on the validity of the Data Retention Directive[181] in light of the Charter.

In its preliminary reference, the Austrian Constitutional Court interpreted Articles 52(4) and 53 CFR to mean that if a comparative study of domestic constitutions revealed a high level of protection at the national level, EU courts are compelled to choose an interpretation of the Charter right which guarantees that the EU standard of protection is not lower.[182] According to the Constitutional Court, Austrian constitutional law as interpreted by this court demands for a strict proportionality review of restrictions to the right to data protection, going beyond what is required under Article 8 ECHR.[183] The Constitutional Court then listed various concerns raising doubts on the proportionality of the Data Retention Directive.[184] Finally, it argued that the right to data protection is part of the common constitutional traditions by referring generally to the case law of the constitutional courts of the Member States and more specifically to the German and Polish Constitutions.[185]

The judgment and the preliminary reference of the Irish High Court, on the other hand, do not contain any statements on the national standard of protection going beyond the recognition of the existence of a right to privacy.[186] However, prior to the judgment of the CJEU, several highest national courts had questioned the compatibility of national provisions implementing the Data Retention Directive with domestic fundamental rights, mainly data protection and the right to privacy.[187] Although all these

[180] *Digital Rights Ireland* (n 24).

[181] Directive 2002/58/EC of the European Parliament and of the Council of 12 July 2002 concerning the processing of personal data and the protection of privacy in the electronic communications sector (Directive on privacy and electronic communications), as amended by Directive 2009/136/EC of the European Parliament and of the Council of 25 November 2009 [2009] OJ L337/11 (Data Retention Directive).

[182] G 47/12-11, G 59/12-10, G 62, 70, 71/12-11 (Austrian Constitutional Court, 28 November 2012), paras 50–51.

[183] ibid paras 32–34.

[184] ibid paras 39–46.

[185] ibid paras 50–51.

[186] Irish High Court 2006 3785 P [2010] IEHC 221, para 53; 2006 3785 P (Irish High Court, 31 May 2012).

[187] 13627 (Bulgarian Supreme Administrative Court, 11 December 2008); 1258 (Romanian Constitutional Court, 8 October 2009); 1 BvR 256/08, 1 BvR 263/08, 1 BvR 586/08 (German Federal Constitutional Court, 2 March 2010); 65/2009, 78/2009, 82/2009, 15/2010 (Cypriot Supreme Court, 1 February 2011); Pl ÚS 24/10 (Czech Constitutional Court, 22 March 2011). For an overview of the main findings, see E Kosta, 'The Way to Luxemburg: National Court Decisions on the Compatibility of the Data Retention Directive with the Rights to Privacy and Data Protection' (2013) 10 *SCRIPTed* 339; C Jones, 'National Legal Challenges to the Data Retention Directive' EU Law Analysis Blog, http://eulawanalysis.blogspot.co.uk/2014/04/national-legal-challenges-to-data.html.

judgments scrutinise the implementing legislation only and avoid discussing the proportionality of the Directive itself, they illustrate the domestic standard of review. The Romanian Constitutional Court generally stated that the blanket retention of data of all users of electronic communication services without adequate and sufficient safeguards is not compatible with the Romanian Constitution and the ECHR.[188] The German Federal Constitutional Court undertook a strict proportionality review and concluded that the domestic implementation provisions violated the standards of the German Constitution on purpose limitation, data security, transparency and legal remedies.[189] The Czech Constitutional Court raised similar concerns.[190]

In its preliminary ruling in *Digital Rights Ireland*, the CJEU did not mention any national judgment or refer to the level of protection of data protection and privacy in the Member States. In the light of its answers to the questions on the validity of the Data Retention Directive, it also did not find it necessary to provide guidance on the correct interpretation of Articles 52(4) and 53 CFR, something the Austrian court had explicitly asked for.[191] What is interesting for our purposes, however, is the approach to the proportionality analysis adopted by the Court.

The CJEU first clarified that it applied a traditional proportionality review as developed in its own case law which it cited extensively.[192] It then referred to the ECtHR case law as a basis for the claim that it had to adopt a strict review of the legislator's discretion in view of the 'important role' played by data protection for the right to privacy and the 'extent and seriousness of the interferences with that right' by the Directive.[193] This clearly shows that the Court intentionally opts for a strict proportionality review. The Court could in addition have referred to the strict standard of review adopted in various Member States, such as Austria, Romania or Germany.

Similarly, the CJEU's arguments with regard to the necessity of the interference are evocative of the arguments voiced by the national constitutional

[188] Kosta (n 187) 348; C Murphy, 'Romanian Constitutional Court, Decision No 1258 of 8 October 2009: Regarding the Unconstitutionality Exception of the Provisions of Law No 298/2008' (2010) 47 *CML Rev* 933, 938.

[189] German Federal Constitutional Court (n 187); A Kaiser, 'German Federal Constitutional Court: Decision of 2 March 2010, NJW 2010, p 833: German Data Retention Provisions Unconstitutional in Their Present Form' (2010) 6 *European Constitutional Law Review* 503, 509.

[190] Czech Constitutional Court (n 187); P Molek, 'Czech Constitutional Court Decision of 22 March 2011, Pl. ÚS 24/10: Unconstitutionality of the Czech Implementation of the Data Retention Directive' (2012) 8 *European Constitutional Law Review* 338, 346.

[191] *Digital Rights Ireland* (n 24) [72]. See also Joined Cases C-293/12 and C-594/12 *Digital Rights Ireland* (CJEU, 12 December 2013), Opinion of AG Cruz Villalón [29].

[192] *Digital Rights Ireland* (n 24) [46].

[193] ibid [47]–[48]. For a discussion of this 'strict scrutiny test', see M Granger and K Irion, 'The Court of Justice and the Data Retention Directive in *Digital Rights Ireland:* Telling Off the EU Legislator and Teaching a Lesson in Privacy and Data Protection' [2014] *European Law Review* 835, 845.

courts. The CJEU criticised the fact that the Directive covers 'in a generalised manner, all persons and all means of electronic communication as well as all traffic data without any differentiation, limitation or exception being made in the light of the objective of fighting against serious crime'.[194] Just like many national courts, the CJEU was also concerned about the unlimited access of the national authorities to the data, in particular that there was no purpose limitation.[195] Ultimately, it concluded that the Directive contained serious interferences with fundamental rights which were not strictly necessary and was therefore invalid.[196] A more recent judgment is a further indication that the CJEU takes data protection and privacy seriously.[197]

The CJEU's reasoning and the end result suggest that it, at least to a certain extent, took into account the high standard of data protection offered by various national constitutions. Regrettably, it is impossible to know for sure which factors influenced the Court. It did not refer to Article 52(4) CFR or any domestic case law. The decision in *Digital Rights Ireland* could thus also simply reflect the increasing awareness of the dangers of public surveillance in the aftermath of the Snowden revelations without being based on the high standards of national constitutional law.

ii. Appraisal of the Court's Approach

According to the Charter Explanations, the aim of Article 52(4) CFR is to ensure that the Charter is interpreted 'in a way offering a high standard of protection' instead of following 'a rigid approach of a "lowest common denominator"'.[198] Insofar as Article 52(4) CFR contains a mandate to opt for a high level of protection, it has the potential to pre-empt conflicts with national constitutional standards of protection[199] and more generally a race to the bottom of European fundamental rights standards. Indeed, the strict review applied by the Court in *Digital Rights Ireland* ensures a high standard of data protection and contributes to the coherence of the protection of this right in Europe. Besides, the interpretative rule of Article 52(4) CFR prevents the 'petrifying effect' the codification of fundamental rights could have.[200]

194 *Digital Rights Ireland* (n 24) [57].
195 ibid [60]–[62].
196 ibid [71].
197 Case C-131/12 *Google Spain* (CJEU, 13 May 2014).
198 Explanation on Art 52, Charter Explanations.
199 De Boer (n 116) 1097; M Safjan, 'Areas of Application of the Charter of Fundamental Rights of the European Union' (2012) EUI Working Paper Law 22 5, http://cadmus.eui.eu/bitstream/handle/1814/17597/LAW_2011_08.pdf?sequence=1.
200 S Iglesias Sánchez, 'The Court and the Charter: The Impact of the Entry into Force of the Lisbon Treaty on the ECJ's Approach to Fundamental Rights' (2012) 49 *CML Rev* 1565, 1606.

The use of the verb 'shall' in Article 52(4) CFR leaves no doubt that EU courts are under an obligation to take into account high standards of national constitutional traditions. The fact that an interpretation 'in harmony' with the constitutional traditions is required as opposed to an interpretation which gives the 'same meaning and scope' to Charter rights as to the ECHR does not mean that the obligation of Article 52(4) CFR is less imperative than the obligation of Article 52(3) CFR.[201] The wording instead takes into account that the constitutional traditions derive from the standards of various Member States, whereas the ECHR offers one single standard of protection. Although there is no list of Charter articles subject to Article 52(4) CFR, it can be assumed that many Charter rights are derived from national constitutional traditions, including some or even all rights corresponding to ECHR rights.[202] Article 52(4) CFR is therefore not a mere political statement reassuring the Member States that their competences will not be limited by the Charter, but an obligation.[203] An interpretation in harmony with national constitutional traditions also has to take the case law of the national constitutional courts into account.[204]

The standard of protection not only has to be high in consistency with the common constitutional traditions, but also has to be 'adequate for the law of the Union'.[205] Thus, Article 52(4) CFR does not impose the adoption of highest possible standard of protection around, but the adoption of the highest possible standard adequate for the EU legal order. The maximalist approach is rejected for a good reason. Again, this argument relates to the idea that fundamental rights are the result of a balance of social goods specific to a particular polity.[206] Weiler has rightly argued that to adopt the highest possible standard of protection would mean that the entire EU would be 'subject to the constitutional dictate of an individual Member State', even though this standard is not necessarily suitable for the EU legal order.[207] The *Melloni* case is a very good example of this.[208] For the same reason that the local maximum standard approach cannot be applied as a rule of conflict, the adoption of the Spanish standard across the entire EU in general cannot be justified.

[201] But see T Kingreen, 'Grundrechtecharta: Artikel 52' in C Calliess and M Ruffert (eds), *EUV, AEUV Kommentar: Das Verfassungsrecht der Europäischen Union mit Europäischer Grundrechtecharta* (4th edn, Munich, Beck, 2011) para 40.

[202] S Peers, 'The Rebirth of the EU's Charter of Fundamental Rights' (2010–11) 13 *Cambridge Yearbook of European Legal Studies* 283, 303.

[203] Against Kingreen (n 201) para 41.

[204] Obwexer (n 171) 123.

[205] Explanation on Art 52, Charter Explanations. See also A Gamper, 'Methodische Problemstellungen der Rechtsvergleichung als Auslegungsmethode des Verfassungsrechts' in A Gamper and B Verschraegen (eds), *Rechtsvergleichung als juristische Auslegungsmethode* (Vienna, Jan Sramek, 2013) 170–71.

[206] See text to n 46 above.

[207] Weiler (n 46) 59.

[208] *Melloni* (n 11).

The highest appropriate standard approach suggested by the Explanations is supposed to reflect the pre-Lisbon case law of the Court.[209] When developing fundamental rights on the basis of national constitutional traditions, the CJEU has rejected not only a minimalist but also a maximalist approach.[210] The *Hauer* case, cited by the Explanations, is one of the few explicit illustrations of this approach.[211] The CJEU compares national constitutional standards in order to identify the appropriate standard for the EU.[212] A constitutional tradition does not have to be common to the majority of the Member States;[213] rather, it is the best solution identified through a critical comparison of all national solutions.[214] This approach is known as *wertende Rechtsvergleichung* in German (evaluative comparison). Admittedly, it is not very predictable and leaves a lot of freedom to the interpreter.[215]

The CJEU's approach fails to live up to the requirement to adopt the highest appropriate standard in harmony with the common constitutional traditions of the Member States. Even the very few cases in which the Court explicitly refers to the common constitutional traditions do not include a real comparison. In all other fundamental rights cases, the lack of transparency makes it impossible to ascertain whether the Court even attempted to take into account national constitutional law. This makes the Charter interpretation of the Court unpredictable and arbitrary, which is unacceptable.[216]

The CJEU is not only under an obligation to engage in an evaluative comparison, it is also appropriately equipped for such an exercise. Comparing national constitutional standards is certainly challenging in an EU of 28 Member States.[217] However, the CJEU is predestined for undertaking comparative law analyses.[218] Not only is it composed by one judge per Member State supported by a number of legal assistants with different national backgrounds (*référendaires*),[219] but it also benefits from a well-staffed research unit, including experts on all 28 domestic legal systems and from a translation unit consisting of trained lawyers from all jurisdictions.[220]

[209] European Convention, 'Final Report of Working Group II' (22 October 2002) CONV 354/02, 7.

[210] See von Arnim (n 15) 352.

[211] Case 44/79 *Hauer* [1979] ECR 3727 [17]–[22].

[212] Seyr (n 172) 233.

[213] See, eg, S Schumann, 'Grenzenlose Freiheit für den EuGH? Zur legitimierenden und bindenden Kraft wertender Rechtsvergleichung' (2010) 18 *Journal für Rechtspolitik* 240, 244; Obwexer (n 171) 130.

[214] See K Zweigert, 'Der Einfluss des europäischen Gemeinschaftsrechts auf die Rechtsordnungen der Mitgliedstaaten' (1964) 28 *Rabel Journal of Comparative and International Private Law* 601, 611.

[215] Pernice and Mayer (n 172) para 14.

[216] Gamper (n 205) 187.

[217] See Kokott and Sobotta (n 25) 2.

[218] Obwexer (n 171) 136–38.

[219] Seyr (n 172) 232.

[220] ibid.

Admittedly, a thorough and methodologically sound constitutional comparison remains challenging and time-consuming.[221] There is thus a considerable role to play for academics. To build on substantive academic comparative constitutional research on fundamental rights can make it even more manageable for the Court to comply with the obligations of the horizontal Charter provisions.

Why then are the references to common constitutional traditions in the CJEU's post-Lisbon case law so limited? Gráinne De Búrca has recently suggested various convincing reasons for the Court's practice not to explicitly draw on international and comparative law when deciding cases.[222] One reason is the generally 'formalistic, impersonal and fairly minimalist style of judicial reasoning' of the CJEU.[223] Further, comparative and international law sources have rarely been cited to the Court.[224] Another important argument is that the CJEU does not cite judgments of national courts in order to avoid the impression of 'cherry-picking' or privileging of some Member States over others.[225]

iii. Enhanced Constitutional Dialogue as Opportunity

By declaring the Data Retention Directive invalid with immediate effect in *Digital Rights Ireland*, going beyond what the Advocate General had suggested, the CJEU has signalled that it is committed to a high level of fundamental rights protection.[226] However, the Court should in general make more transparent to what extent its reasoning is influenced by the level of protection offered by the Member States. A 'better-informed and fuller style of judicial ruling' would provide the judgments of the Court with more legitimacy.[227]

Making it explicit that the CJEU complies with the interpretative guidelines of the Charter could also considerably increase the trust of domestic courts in the CJEU. Constitutional courts are not only guardians of national constitutional identity—they also play a specific role for the protection of fundamental rights at the national level. The decision of a national constitutional court not to refer a preliminary question to the CJEU cannot simply be dismissed as anti-European;[228] it can also be considered pro-fundamental rights.[229] After all, the CJEU was reluctant in the past to

[221] Gamper (n 205) 188.
[222] De Búrca (n 143) 176–78.
[223] ibid 176.
[224] ibid 177.
[225] ibid 178.
[226] *Digital Rights Ireland* (n 24).
[227] De Búrca (n 143) 181.
[228] See, eg, 1 BvR 1215/07 (German Federal Constitutional Court, 24 April 2013).
[229] See generally Albi (n 126).

declare EU legislation invalid.[230] If a high level of protection in consistency with national constitutional traditions is guaranteed by the CJEU and this is clearly communicated, it is likely that more national constitutional courts would refer preliminary questions to the Court.[231]

If a high standard of protection by the CJEU is guaranteed, preliminary references would be the ideal place for constitutional courts to voice their concerns regarding the compatibility of EU legislation with fundamental rights, as the Austrian Constitutional Court did. The Austrian and Irish references provided the CJEU with the opportunity to put an end to conflicting standards of data protection at the EU level and the national level by declaring the Data Retention Directive invalid. Individuals in all Member States would have benefited from an earlier setting aside of a Directive violating their fundamental rights, had the national courts confronted with the challenges of data retention before the Austrian and Irish courts not hesitated to engage the CJEU.

Preliminary references can only be made by the court in front of which the dispute arises. However, the identification of common constitutional traditions by the CJEU would benefit from presentations by national constitutional courts of the various constitutional traditions of each Member State. Although the CJEU is well placed for comparative legal analyses, national constitutional courts remain the experts on the interpretation of domestic constitutional law. It can certainly not be expected that national governments present the same picture of the national fundamental rights situation as the courts because their own actions are restricted by the domestic constitution. It would therefore be sensible, as argued above, that the possibility of intervening as a third party in front of the CJEU is extended to the highest national courts.[232]

IV. CONCLUSION

This chapter has examined the recent CJEU case law on the interaction between EU and national fundamental rights. Its goal was to determine to what extent the Court has successfully tackled the two main challenges of multilevel fundamental rights protection: to guarantee a complete and coherent system of protection and to avoid national fundamental rights being marginalised.

[230] The only two cases where this has happened so far were decided post-Lisbon. See Cases C-92/09 and 93/09 *Schecke and Eiffert* [2010] ECR I-11063; Case C-236/09 *Test-Achats* [2011] ECR I-773. See also Granger and Irion (n 193) 844–45.

[231] For a detailed analysis of judicial dialogue as a source of legitimacy for supranational adjudication, see A Torres Pérez, *Conflicts of Rights in the European Union: A Theory of Supranational Adjudication* (Oxford, Oxford University Press, 2009) 98.

[232] See text to n 142 above.

In section II of this chapter, the claim was made that the post-Lisbon case law which determines the scope of the Charter lives up to the challenge of ensuring a complete and coherent protection of fundamental rights in the EU. Notably, the general characteristics of the scope of the Charter are convincing. First, it is in line with the Explanations to Article 51(1) CFR that the Charter has the same scope of application with regard to the Member States as the general principles. Moreover, this clarification by the CJEU increases legal certainty as it prevents difficult distinctions between the applicability of the Charter and of the general principles. Second, the equivalence of the scope of the Charter and of the scope of EU law is conceptually justified. If an action is determined by EU law, the balancing exercise inherent to fundamental rights adjudication needs to be undertaken at the EU level to ensure that countervailing interests arising (only) in an EU context can be taken into account. Consequently, third, it cannot be a decisive factor for the applicability of the Charter whether the Member State intended to transpose EU law or not.

The applicability of the Charter is triggered in two types of situation. The Charter applies, first, if national measures respond to a specific EU law obligation, including when there is a clear mandate to guarantee the effectiveness of EU law in a domestic context such as in the seminal *Åkerberg Fransson* case.[233] Second, Member States are also bound by the Charter if they make use of an option granted by EU law. The applicability of the Charter is justified in both situations because their autonomy is defined, constrained or structured by the presence of binding EU norms. Even if Member States enjoy a degree of discretion, the exercise of this discretion is determined by EU law.

Section III explored the threat of the potential marginalisation of national fundamental rights by the CJEU's case law on the relationship between the Charter and national constitutional rights. It was argued that the Court was right in solving a conflict between divergent standards of protection by giving priority to the Charter over the higher domestic standard in the seminal *Melloni* case.[234] If a national measure is completely determined by EU law, it is attributable to the EU only. The primacy of the EU standard ensures that the examination of the proportionality of restrictions of Charter rights takes into account the particular features of the EU legal order. However, in order to safeguard the constitutional identity of the Member States and thus to avoid a power struggle with the highest domestic courts, exceptions to the primacy principle should be allowed on the basis of Article 4(2) TEU.

Moreover, it is warranted that in situations which are not completely determined by EU law, the Charter and national fundamental rights standards

[233] *Åkerberg Fransson* (n 10).
[234] *Melloni* (n 11).

can coexist as long as the effectiveness of EU law is not thereby completely frustrated. When Member States are granted a degree of discretion on how to implement provisions of EU law, their action is determined by both EU and domestic law. The respect of EU law thus needs to be reconciled with the respect of domestic fundamental rights. Primacy serves the uniform and effective implementation of EU law. The uniform implementation of EU law is not required where EU law itself allows for a degree of diversity by granting a degree of discretion. The effectiveness of EU law, on the other hand, can only be accommodated with the effectiveness of domestic fundamental rights protection if national fundamental rights are applied as long as the EU rule is not completely frustrated.

In any event, many conflicts could be avoided if the CJEU took more seriously the obligation of Articles 52(4) and 53 CFR to interpret Charter rights harmony with the common constitutional traditions of the Member States. The judgment of the Court in *Digital Rights Ireland* seems to go in the right direction.[235] However, the legitimacy of the fundamental rights judgments of the CJEU would be greatly enhanced if the Court made it more explicit to what extent it meets the requirement to adopt the highest standard of protection appropriate for the EU legal order, taking into account the constitutional traditions of the Member States.

In general, the dialogue between the CJEU and domestic courts could be much improved. The Court needs to give clearer reasons to substantiate why the Charter applies or does not apply in a given case or why a specific level of protection is adopted. Its reasoning should include a thorough and convincing engagement with the justification for EU fundamental rights protection. A more transparent judicial reasoning in fundamental rights cases would not only enhance the CJEU's legitimacy, but also increase the trust of the domestic constitutional courts in the Court. As constitutional courts are responsible for upholding the constitution at the domestic level, their involvement is crucial when the interpretation of domestic fundamental rights law needs to be taken into account by the CJEU. National constitutional courts should voice their understanding of a particular national fundamental right or of national constitutional identity in a preliminary reference. In addition, the Statute of the Court should be changed to allow for third-party interventions by the highest national judges.

As the interaction between EU and national fundamental rights is not determined by EU law and the CJEU alone, a complete picture can only be gained by taking into account the reactions of the national courts to the Court's approach. This, however, is beyond the scope of this chapter and needs to be addressed in a large-scale comparative study.

[235] *Digital Rights Ireland* (n 24).

Part II

The Scope of Fundamental Rights in EU Law

6

The EU Charter of Fundamental Rights Five Years on

The Emergence of a New Constitutional Framework?

XAVIER GROUSSOT AND GUNNAR THOR PETURSSON

I. INTRODUCTION

THE SCOPE AND impact of fundamental rights in EU law is a fascinating topic. Part of the fascination lies in their somewhat unclear role and ambit, and the force with which these rights may be charged when and if applicable. The entry into force of the EU Charter of Fundamental Rights (hereinafter 'the EU Charter' or 'the Charter') has certainly given a new impetus in the academic discussion of the status of fundamental rights in EU law. Irrespective of that discussion, the fundamental rights are now increasingly being invoked in cases before the Court of Justice of the European Union (hereinafter 'the Court of Justice' or 'the Court'). An intriguing question in this context is whether fundamental rights, post the EU Charter, are having an impact on the scope and nature of EU law, and thus are bringing about a new constitutional framework.

As stipulated by the work of ancient Greek philosophers like Aristotle, the beginning of thinking is classification. Therefore, it was appropriate in our contribution published three years ago to deal with the classification of types of cases in which fundamental rights play a prominent role in EU law.[1]

We pointed out that the classical first type of review is vis-a-vis the EU institutions, and their (legislative) actions, first laid down in *Stauder* and *Internationale Handelsgesellschaft*.[2] In this category, we have certainly seen

[1] X Groussot, L Pech and GT Petursson, 'The Reach of Fundamental Rights of Member State Action' in Sybe de Vries, Ulf Bernitz and Stephen Weatherill (eds), *The Protection of Fundamental Rights in the EU after Lisbon* (Oxford, Hart Publishing, 2013).

[2] Case 29/69 *Erich Stauder v City of Ulm* [1969] ECR 419; and Case 11/70 *Internationale Handelsgesellschaft* [1970] ECR 1125.

an interesting development post the EU Charter, with three recent cases, *Volker*, *Test-Achats* and *Digital Rights* (further discussed below), where the Court of Justice has annulled EU law for the first time on the basis of reference to fundamental rights—more specifically with a reference to the EU Charter. Apart from the traditional fundamental rights review of the EU institutions and their (legislative) actions, two main types of case categories were identified. These concerned a judicial review of Member States' measures, based on the Court's ruling in the *Wachauf* and *ERT* cases.[3] A broader reading of this line of cases was offered, where in terms of the *Wachauf* line of cases, it was established that the EU Member States, as agents of EU law, are obliged to comply with fundamental rights both when *implementing* and *applying* EU secondary law at the national level.[4] Similarly concerning the *ERT* line of cases, it was established that fundamental rights may serve both as an 'additional hurdle' and as a 'per se' derogation ground when it comes to the review of national measures restricting the fundamental freedoms, or in fact any fundamental right under the EU Treaties subject to limitation. Importantly, it was stipulated that this categorisation is deemed to exist both in terms of vertical and horizontal legal relationships (*Wachauf* and *ERT* 'à l'horizontale').

According to our more recent analysis, this classification still holds post the EU Charter, and adds to clarity and coherence in both the practical application and academic discussion of a fundamental human rights review under EU law. However, other issues involving the EU Charter and a fundamental rights review in EU law seem not to be as clear and foreseeable, specifically the analytical framework under which the Court of Justice is operating in this context. Will the Charter offer a solution in this respect, with its framework for functioning and limitation of the EU Charter rights in its horizontal provisions in Title VII? In particular, it would be interesting if the review of EU instruments, as seen in the recent above-mentioned cases, on the basis of Article 52(1) of the EU Charter is the key to a new analytical framework. Linked to that is the question of whether there will be a spillover from these *types of cases* into the (current) *methodology* applied by the Court of Justice when reviewing Member States' measures. These questions will be dealt with in section II.

The questions concerning Article 52(1) of the EU Charter and its breadth will form the core of the discussion in this chapter, where the more recent case law of the Court involving the EU Charter is analysed. Furthermore, in sections III–V, three related issues will also be discussed that all may be related to an emerging constitutional framework. *First*, there is the question

[3] Case 5/88 *Wachauf* [1989] ECR 2609; and Case C-260/89 *ERT* [1991] ECR I-2925.

[4] See, eg, Case C-465/00 *Österreichischer Rundfunk* [2003] ECR I-4989; Case C-101/01 *Lindqvist* [2003] ECR I-12971; Cases C-20/00 and C-64/00 *Booker Aquaculture* [2003] ECR I-7411; and Case C-276/01 *Steffensen* [2003] ECR I-3735.

of the circumstances under which the EU Charter is brought into the picture *ex officio* in cases before the Court of Justice and, *second*, there is the question of whether the Charter is impacting the intensity of the review of EU institutions' measures (a judicial review of EU acts). *Third* and finally, there is the question of the hiding nature of the Charter, which concerns the situation whereby the Charter is, for unclear reasons, not invoked or the scope of EU law is narrowly construed in order to avoid its application.

II. REQUIREMENTS OF ARTICLE 52(1) OF THE EU CHARTER: THE NEW ANALYTICAL FRAMEWORK?

A. Introduction

When examining the Court's analytical framework, Article 52(1) of the EU Charter is of vital importance and reads as follows:

> Any limitation on the exercise of the rights and freedoms recognised by this Charter must be provided for by law and respect the essence of those rights and freedoms. Subject to the principle of proportionality, limitations may be made only if they are necessary and genuinely meet objectives of general interest recognised by the Union or the need to protect the rights and freedoms of others.

The EU Charter has neither a traditional limitation clause along with each right nor a principle, as found inter alia in the European Convention on Human Rights (ECHR).[5] In this context, the specific reference to the principle of proportionality is important, since this principle, although applied both by the Court of Justice and the European Court on Human Rights (ECtHR), has not been explicitly laid down in the respective treaties in the context of limitation of fundamental (human) rights. Article 52(1) of the EU Charter is a specific limitation clause, which is to be applied 'horizontally' throughout the EU Charter. It is an analytical framework that bears a resemblance to the Strasbourg framework of limitation of ECHR rights. However, it has to be kept in mind that the Strasbourg framework of limitation of ECHR rights is not contained in a single provision, but is found along with each right and has been developed through application of the Strasbourg Court through an extensive line of cases.

Interestingly, Article 52(1) of the EU Charter is the first limitation clause on fundamental rights at the EU (Treaty) level. According to the explanations to the EU Charter,[6] the purpose of Article 52 is to set the scope of

[5] Apart from Arts 17 and 32 of the EU Charter, which contain such wording.

[6] Hereinafter referred to as the 'explanations'. Explanations Relating to the Charter of Fundamental Rights [2007] OJ C303/17.

the rights and principles of the Charter, and to lay down rules for their interpretation. The first time that the Court relied upon the Article 52(1) framework was in the *Volker* case.[7] This ruling concerned the validity of EU secondary law, reviewed in the light of the EU Charter, in which the Court went through the 'analytical stages' much as Advocate General Sharpston had suggested. The 'analytical stages' laid down in Article 52(1) include that limitations 'must be provided for by law', must be 'subject to the principle of proportionality' and 'must be made only if they are necessary and genuinely meet objectives of general interest recognised by the Union or the need to protect the rights and freedoms of others'.

Unfortunately, reference to Article 52 of the EU Charter has not been made consistently by the Court of Justice and is, for example, not found in the recent *Test Achats* or *Deutsches Weintor* cases,[8] which were otherwise similar to the *Volker* case. But what does this entail? Is the Article 52(1) framework materially different from the analytical framework otherwise applied by the Court of Justice, ie, when reviewing national measures—or even EU measures? In the *explanations* to the Charter, it is stated that the wording of Article 52 of the EU Charter is based on the case law of the Court of Justice. Is that entirely true? Two issues in particular deserve a closer scrutiny in this context: the first concerns the reference to the 'provided for by law' requirement and the second the requirement to 'respect the essence' of the rights and freedoms limited.

B. Provided for by Law

When adjudicating fundamental rights in EU law, this requirement has until the entry into the force of the EU Charter not been part of the Court's standard approach, although a reference has been made to that condition in the context of direct reference to the ECHR regime or provisions.[9]

In fact, the condition is well known and honed in application by the Strasbourg Court. This requirement is found in Article 8(2) of the ECHR, Articles 2(3) and (4) of Protocol 4 to the ECHR and Article 1(1) of Protocol 7 to the ECHR. The condition is worded 'prescribed by law' in the second paragraph of Article 9 of the ECHR and in Article 2(2) of Protocol 7 to the ECHR. In the French text, which is equally as authentic, the condition is

[7] Cases C-92/09 and 93/09 *Volker und Markus Schecke and Eifert* [2010] ECR I-11063.

[8] Case C-236/09 *Test Achats* [2011] ECR I-773; and Case C-544/10 *Deutsches Weintor*, judgment of 6 September 2012.

[9] S Peers and S Prechal, 'Article 52: Scope and Interpretation of Rights and Principles' in S Peers, A Ward, T Hervey and J Kenner (eds), *The EU Charter of Fundamental Rights: A Commentary* (Oxford, Hart Publishing, 2013) 1470.

worded 'prévue(s) par la loi' in the second paragraphs of Articles 8–11 of the ECHR, and in Article 2(3) of Protocol 4 to the ECHR.

According to the Strasbourg case law, it is not mandatory that the law is a statutory law, as it can also be an unwritten law. What matters here is not only the literal conformity with national law, but also, importantly, the 'quality of the law'.[10] In that respect, the Strasbourg Court has stated that the law must be 'adequately accessible and foreseeable, that is, formulated with sufficient precision to enable the individual—if need be with appropriate advice—to regulate his conduct', to 'foresee its consequences for him'[11] and 'to foresee, to a degree that is reasonable in the circumstances, the consequences which a given action may entail'.[12]

There is of course a difference between verifying whether or not a restriction or limitation has a legal basis in national or EU law compared to a detailed assessment of the quality of the law in itself. But how has the Court of Justice dealt with this in the post-EU Charter case law? Interestingly, the Court made an infrequent reference to this requirement and an even less detailed in application in its case law. The *Scarlet Extended* case[13] is a good example. In this case, Advocate General Cruz Villalón discussed this condition in detail, linking it to 'rule of law' requirements. In his opinion, the national legal provisions at issue did not meet 'these requirements'.[14] The Court, however, made no reference to this condition, even though it applied Article 17(2) of the Charter in the case. However, in other cases that concern the validity of EU measures, the Court has verified whether or not the requirement is fulfilled, but in a 'thin' manner, not testing the quality of the law as such. In fact, in the *Volker* case, 'provided for by law' was the first analytical stage which the Court went through when it verified that the measures at stake were in fact laid down by the EU secondary norm at issue.[15] This was similarly done in *Schwartz*,[16] whereas in the otherwise detailed analysis under Article 52(1) in the *Digital Rights Ireland* case, there was no specific application of this criterion.[17]

[10] FG Jacobs and RCA White, *The European Convention on Human Rights* (Oxford, Oxford University Press, 1996) 303 and 336.

[11] European Court of Human Rights, judgment in *Leander v Sweden* [1987] no 9248/81, Series A no 116, § 50.

[12] European Court of Human Rights, judgment in *Margareta and Roger Andersson v Sweden* [1992] no 12963/87, Series A no 226-A, p 25, § 75.

[13] Case C-70/10 *Scarlet Extended SA* [2011] ECR I-11959.

[14] ibid [67] of the Advocate General's opinion. The Court, however, did not make any reference to Art 52(1) of the EU Charter in its decision.

[15] *Volker* (n 7) [66].

[16] Case C-291/12 *Schwartz*, judgment of 17 October 2013 [35].

[17] Joined Cases C-293/12 and C-594/12 *Digital Rights Ireland and Seitlinger and others*, judgment of 8 April 2014. Again, AG Cruz Villalón had suggested an approach similar 'to that adopted by the European Court of Human Rights' ([109]) and which would therefore analyse 'the quality of the law' involved—much as the Advocate General had done in the *Scarlet* opinion.

Interestingly, apart from still not engaging in testing the 'quality of the law' following the EU Charter,[18] the Court has not, as demonstrated by *Scarlet Extended*, made a reference to this requirement in the cases falling in the case category of *review of Member States' measures*, ie, both when implementing and applying EU law and when derogating from fundamental principles laid down in the EU Treaties (ie the TFEU). There might be no real reason behind the non-systemic application of the 'provided for by law' requirement, but it could have something to do with the distinction between a review of EU measures and national measures in the light of fundamental rights, where the nature of the measures reviewed may be of a different character.

Restrictions to the fundamental freedoms laid down in the Treaty on the Functioning of the European Union (TFEU), for which there might be a justification (which may as of *Schmidberger*[19] be a fundamental right in itself), are not necessarily based on statutory law and may in fact be based on 'actions' or even 'inactions' where law, even if a broad notion is applied, does not play a decisive role. Furthermore, even if the horizontal application of fundamental rights has traditionally been contested, the same does not hold true for all of the fundamental free movement provisions in the TFEU. In fact, the horizontal application of the fundamental provisions of EU law, including the free movement principles, has already been accepted in the case law of the Court of Justice. Even the Court of Justice has laid down in its case law that the fundamental free movement provisions may apply in pure horizontal situations.[20] Furthermore, as demonstrated by the well-known *Viking* and *Laval* cases, a conflict between fundamental freedoms and fundamental rights may very well arise in private (or semi-private) situations, such as between undertakings and trade unions.[21]

In her opinion in the *Dominguez* case, Advocate General Trstenjak relied on the 'provided for by law' condition in order to argue for a limitation of the horizontal application of fundamental rights. In her opinion, individuals failed at fulfilling the 'legislative proviso contained in Article 52(1) of the Charter', since this 'rule of law' requirement could 'naturally be directed only at the European Union and its Member States as agencies of the State'.[22] These reasons might explain why it could be 'technically' difficult to really apply the 'provided for by law' condition in cases which

[18] The Court has, however, engaged in such analysis in a limited number of cases decided prior to the entry into force of the EU Charter, as seen from *Österreichischer Rundfunk* (n 4) [76] and [77] and *Lindqvist* (n 4) [84]. See also [53] of the opinion of AG Kokott in *Promusicae* (Case C-275/06 *Promusicae* [2008] ECR I-271), which undertook an analysis of the foreseeability of the EU measure, although this was not followed up by the Court of Justice in its ruling of the case.

[19] Case C-112/00 *Eugen Schmidberger* [2003] ECR I-5659.

[20] See Case C-281/98 *Angonese* [2000] ECR I-4139

[21] Case C-438/05 *Viking Line* [2007] ECR I-10779; and Case C-341/05 *Laval* [2007] ECR I-11767.

[22] Case C-282/10 *Dominguez*, judgment of 24 January 2012, AG's Opinion at [83]. The Court did not rely on the EU Charter in its decision in this case.

concern a review of Member States' measures. Part of this 'problem' might be solved by the Court relying on Article 52(2) of the EU Charter. In fact, in the recent *Gardella* (2013)[23] and *Sokoll* (2014) cases,[24] the Court seemingly did not wish to use Article 52(1) of the EU Charter in issues that concern the fundamental free movement provisions. In *Gardella*, the Court stated that since, in that case, Article 15(2) of the EU Charter 'reiterates' rights laid down in Article 45 TFEU (free movement of workers), in the light of Article 52(2) of the Charter, the case was to be analysed on the basis of Articles 45 and 48 TFEU. This would seem to suggest that a dual framework exists, at least prima facie, but at this stage it is not clear how the Article 52(1) framework will develop in the future and to what extent its character will be really distinct from the limitation methodology applied by the Court hitherto. However, it is difficult to see how the operation of two methodologically distinct frameworks will be helpful in terms of consistency and coherence. Particularly it could be confusing in this context to have one type which requires limitations to fundamental rights to be 'provided for by law' and another type that does not.

Finally, it is suggested that the condition of 'provided for by law' could be dealt with through the ordinary, although detailed, application of the proportionality principle, particularly in terms of an assessment of the quality of the law.[25] In fact, according to Stone Sweet and Mathews, this condition is one of the steps of the proportionality assessment, the first out of four.[26] Therefore the 'four-step approach' would be the 'fully developed' form of proportionality analysis, where the judge confirms that the government is 'constitutionally' authorised to take the restrictive measure. However, again, here 'horizontality' is neither anticipated nor excluded.

C. The Essence Test

Article 52(1) of the EU Charter stipulates that any limitation on the exercise of the rights and freedoms recognised by this Charter must, apart from being 'provided for by law', 'respect the essence' of those rights and freedoms. This 'essence requirement' has its roots in German constitutional law,

[23] Case C-233/12 *Gardella v Istituto nazionale della previdenza sociale (INPS)*, judgment of 4 July 2013 [39]–[41].

[24] Case C-367/12 *Sokoll*, judgment of 13 February 2014. In this case, contrary to *Gardella*, there is no explicit reference to Art 52(2) of the EU Charter, since the Court chose not to solve the case on the basis of the national court's reference to Art 16 of the Charter, but, instead, solely on the basis of Art 49 TFEU, since the reference to EU law in the provisions of Art 16 was to be 'understood as meaning that Article 16 of the Charter refers, inter alia, to Article 49 TFEU' (at [22]).

[25] In fact, this seems to have been the case in the Court's ruling in *Scarlet* (n 13).

[26] A Stone Sweet and J Mathews, 'Proportionality Balancing and Global Constitutionalism' (2008) 47 *Columbia Journal of Transnational Laws* 72, 76.

and in his book *A Theory of Constitutional Rights*, Robert Alexy relates this to the requirements found in Article 19(2) of the German Basic Law. In Alexy's view, requirements of guaranteeing 'the essential core' laid down in Article 19(2) of the Basic Law do not lay down any additional requirements on the limitability of constitutional rights beyond what is already contained in the principle of proportionality. In his view, limitations that correspond to the principle of proportionality do not infringe the principle of proportionality, even if in the end there is nothing left of the constitutional right in a given case.[27] The question here is whether Article 52(1) of the Charter is meant to bring about any material change, ie, making an 'essence test' a self-standing condition.

In the *Sky Österreich* case,[28] the Court did not follow the 'analytical stages' as thoroughly as seen in *Volker* (discussed above). However, it acknowledged that Article 16 of the Charter, which was being used to review the EU Directive at stake, could be limited and was subject to a 'broad range of interventions on the part of public authorities which may limit the exercise of economic activity in the public interest'.[29] Thereafter, the Court made a direct reference to Article 52(1) of the Charter. Before conducting a detailed proportionality assessment, it noted that the EU Directive at stake did not 'affect *the core content* of the freedom to conduct business'.[30] In *Digital Rights Ireland*, an essence test of a kind is made separately from the proportionality analysis undertaken in the case, and the Court verified that the interference at issue did not adversely affect the essence of the fundamental rights at stake (Articles 7 and 8 of the EU Charter). However, this was a rather case-specific exercise and did not seemingly exclude or impact the following comprehensive analysis, which included a detailed proportionality analysis.

The approach to the 'essence test' is, however, different in the *Alemo-Herron* case,[31] in which the Court discussed the core of the right to conduct business and maintained that Directive 2001/23/EC, concerning safeguards of employees' rights in the case of a transfer of undertakings, may not be interpreted in such a way that it entitles the Member States 'to take measures which, while being more favourable to employees, are liable to adversely affect the very essence of the transferee's freedom to conduct a business'.[32] In the view of the Court, the Directive could not be interpreted in such a way that it would reduce a transferee's contractual freedom to the

[27] R Alexy, *A Theory of Constitutional Rights* (Julian Rivers trans) (Oxford, Oxford University Press, 2002) 193 and 196.

[28] Case C-283/11 *Sky Österreich*, judgment of 22 January 2013.

[29] ibid [46].

[30] ibid [49], emphasis added.

[31] Case C-426/11 *Mark Alemo-Herron*, judgment of 18 July 2013.

[32] ibid [36]. In this case, no reference was made by the Court to Art 52(1) of the EU Charter.

point that the limitation would be liable to adversely affect 'the very essence of its freedom to conduct business'.[33] Therefore, the UK's 'more favourable' national measures were deemed by the Court to be in conflict with EU law.

As stipulated above, Article 52(1) of the EU Charter states that the limitation of the Charter's rights must 'respect the essence of those rights and freedoms'. Therefore, and in the light of the above-mentioned cases, it is understandable if the question is raised as to whether there should be a detailed 'essence test' that is separate from the proportionality analysis required by Article 52(1) of the Charter. Even if the *Alemo-Herron* case might indicate this, we are not convinced that this should be the case.[34]

The 'respect for the essence' part of Article 52(1) of the EU Charter has to be looked upon in the context of the non-absolute nature of those fundamental rights in the Charter that are subject to limitations based on Article 52(1) of the Charter. In fact, *the explanations* to the Charter cite, in the context of Article 52(1), the *Karlsson* case. The *Karlsson* case is in fact citing paragraph 18 of the *Wachauf* case,[35] which may be looked upon as the more appropriate founding for Article 52(1) of the Charter. The paragraph reads as follows:

> The fundamental rights recognized by the Court are not absolute, however, but must be considered in relation to their social function. Consequently, restrictions may be imposed on the exercise of those rights … provided that those restrictions in fact correspond to objectives of general interest pursued by the Community and do not constitute, with regard to the aim pursued, a disproportionate and intolerable interference, impairing the very substance of those rights.

As seen from this, the focus here is on the non-absolute nature of the fundamental rights and the fact that the limitation to the rights is not disproportionate and intolerable interference to the very substance (or the essence) of the right at stake. Similar reference is found in other important cases, such as *Nold*[36] and perhaps most importantly in *Schmidberger*, which demonstrates the relevance of a method of limitation of fundamental rights that might, in particular circumstances, lead to *stricto sensu* balancing.

In this light, we would like to suggest that the 'essence of the right' requirement should not be viewed separately, as a per se condition, but rather in the context of the proportionality analysis—and thus could impact the

[33] ibid [35].

[34] In fact, the *Alemo-Herron* case has been heavily criticised as being out of line with the Court's normal (more balanced) approach; see J Prassl, 'Freedom of Contract as a General Principle of EU Law? Transfers of Undertakings and the Protection of Employer Rights in EU Labour Law' (2013) 42(4) *Industrial Law Journal* 434; and S Weatherill, 'Use and Abuse of the EU's Charter of Fundamental Rights: On the Improper Veneration of "Freedom of Contract". judgment of the Court of 18 July 2013: Case C–426/11, *Mark Alemo-Herron and Others v Parkwood Leisure Ltd*' (2014) 10(1) *European Review of Contract Law* 167.

[35] Case C-292/97 *Karlsson* [2000] ECR I-2737; *Wachauf* (n 3).

[36] Case 4/73 *Nold* [1974] ECR 419.

depth or the intensity of the review.[37] The *Mark Alemo-Herron* approach, should not, however, be the model case, since here the Court was applying a limitation methodology outside its proper context. In fact, the approach of the Court appears as a manipulation of the 'essence of the right' condition, since it was playing Article 16 of the Charter out as an *absolute* fundamental right, which it is not. Thereby, in this case, the Court failed seriously in not viewing the fundamental rights 'in relation to their social function'. This absence of balancing amounts to a hierarchical approach where social rights are being subsumed or forgotten. This also defeats the very nature and purpose of Article 16 of the Charter, as explained so well in *Sky Österreich*, where the Court's Grand Chamber emphasised the strong links between Article 16 of the Charter and the social rights found in Title IV of the EU Charter.[38]

III. *EX OFFICIO* APPLICATION OF THE EU CHARTER

In their Joint Declaration of January 2011, the Presidents of the Strasbourg and Luxembourg Courts stated that: 'the Charter has become the reference text and the starting point for the CJEU's assessment of the fundamental rights which that legal instrument recognises'. Similar views have been endorsed by the CJEU's Advocate Generals, which may be seen in the view of Advocate General Bot in the *Ivana Skattolon* case, who stated that: 'Since the Charter now occupies a central place in the system of protection of fundamental rights in the Union, it must ... constitute the reference legislation each time the Court is called upon to rule on the compliance with an EU measure or a national provision with the fundamental rights protected by the Charter.'[39]

Now, the EU Charter does not form a part of an EU constitution, as was initially the plan. However, it is arguably an important part of the constitutional framework of EU law, even if this only exists in substance

[37] This is in fact how the Strasbourg court most often applies the essence test (See eg J Christoffersen, *Fair Balance: Proportionality, Subsidiarity and Primarity in the European Convention on Human Rights* (Martinus Nijhoff Publishers 2009) 135-163). *Gerards* also maintains that in the Strasbourg case law, the 'core' test is used to adjust the scope of the margin (depth of the review) (J Gerards 'Pluralism, Deference and the Margin of Appreciation Doctrine' (2011) 17(1) European Law Journal, 80–120, at 112-113). *Peers & Prechal* also argue that it would be difficult in EU law to conduct a separate essence test, in isolation from other condition referred to in Article 52(1), *Peers & Prechal, above* n 9, at 1480.

[38] *Sky Österreich, above* n 28, para 46, goes as follows: 'On the basis of that case law and in the light of the wording of Article 16 of the Charter, which differs from the wording of the other fundamental freedoms laid down in Title II thereof, yet is similar to that of certain provisions of Title IV of the Charter, the freedom to conduct a business may be subject to a broad range of interventions on the part of public authorities which may limit the exercise of economic activity in the public interest'. Similarly, in *Deutches Weintor, above* n 8 the Court is embracing balancing which favours social protection (see in particular paras 54-58 of the case).

[39] Case C-108/10 *Ivana Skattolon* [2011] ECR I-7491, AG Bot's opinion at [108].

rather than in form.[40] As seen from the pre-Charter case law, such as that found in the *Kadi* case, the Court of Justice has emphasised that respect for fundamental rights is part of 'the constitutional principles of the EC Treaty'.[41] Does this mean that the EU Charter, including its rights and principles, should be raised in any proceedings before the Court of Justice—even *ex officio*, that is by the Court itself, if necessary? Interestingly, looking back at some of the founding cases concerning review of Member States' measures in light of fundamental rights, we see for example both in *Wachauf*[42] and *Familiapress*[43] that the fundamental rights issues were not raised by the referring court, but were raised effectively by the Court of Justice itself (although raised in the proceedings before the Court in *Familiapress* and by the Advocate General in *Wachauf*).[44]

In *Test-Achats*, a preliminary ruling from the Belgian Constitutional Court on the validity of Article 5(2) of Directive 2004/113, it appears clear from its reasoning that the starting point of the Court of Justice's inquiry is the Charter,[45] more precisely Articles 21 and 23 of the Charter, which state that any discrimination based on sex is prohibited and that equality between men and women must be ensured in all areas. Since recital 4 to Directive 2004/113 expressly refers to Articles 21 and 23 of the Charter, however, it is not unreasonable that the validity of Article 5(2) of that Directive was assessed in the light of those provisions.[46] It is also worth noting that the facts of *Test-Achats* were prior to the entry into force of the Charter (the reference was lodged on 29 June 2009) and the national court in its question does not mention the Charter. Yet giving the Charter a retroactive effect confirms its status as *leitnormen*.[47] Furthermore, the reasoning in *Digital*

[40] K Tuori, *Ratio and Voluntas—The Tension Between Reason and Will in Law* (Aldershot, Ashgate, 2011) 309–10.

[41] Joined Cases C-402/05/P and C-415/05/P *Kadi and Al Barakaat International Foundation v Council and Commission* [2008] ECR I-635 [285].

[42] *Wachauf* (n 3).

[43] Case C-368/95 *Familiapress* [1997] ECR I-3689.

[44] Interestingly, in *Mark Alemo-Herron* (n 31), the referring national UK court asked about the applicability of Art 11 of the ECHR in the case, which is equivalent to Art 12 of the EU Charter, but made no reference to Art 16 of the EU Charter, on the basis of which the Court of Justice finally solved the case.

[45] *Test-Achats* (n 8) [16] and [32]. One should highlight here that the question put by the national court was formulated in light of Art 6(2) EU. As put by the Court: 'Article 6(2) EU, to which the national court refers in its questions and which is mentioned in recital 1 to Directive 2004/113, provides that the European Union is to respect fundamental rights as guaranteed by the European Convention for the Protection of Human Rights and Fundamental Freedoms and as they result from the constitutional traditions common to the Member States, as general principles of Community law. Those fundamental rights are incorporated in the Charter, which, with effect from 1 December 2009, has the same legal status as the Treaties.'

[46] ibid [17]. See also, to that effect, Joined Cases C–92/09 and C–93/09 *Volker und Markus Schecke and Eifert* [2010] ECR I–11063 [46].

[47] See also the opinion of AG Wathelet in Case C–170/13 *Huawei Technologies*, delivered on 20 November 2014, in a competition law case decided under Art 102 TFEU, which the Advocate General in fact argued was about balancing the right to intellectual property with freedom to conduct business (see [59]).

Rights Ireland is relevant in this context. Indeed, the Court relied on the Charter as the *leitnormen* to assess the validity of the Data Retention Directive and also referred to the ECHR case law related to the right to privacy.[48]

However, the procedural nature of cases before the Court of Justice varies. Therefore, it is questionable whether Charter rights should be brought into the picture in cases that are purely *inter partes*, such as in infringement proceedings, based on Article 258 TFEU. In the *KME* case, which concerned an appeal of a Commission fine for concerted practices, the Court stated that 'proceedings before the court are *inter partes*'.[49] Now that sounds like a sweeping statement and it is questionable whether preliminary reference procedures should be regarded as purely *inter partes* proceedings. However, it is interesting that the Court then went on and held that the courts are required to raise of their own motion matters of public policy such as the failure to state reasons for a contested decision, which is of course a question of procedural guarantees.[50]

That brings us to Article 47 of the EU Charter—which has in fact, in a few recent cases, been raised by the Court, *ex officio*, such as in *Penarroja*, but here is used in order to secure compliance with certain procedural guarantees.[51] In addition, in *DEB*, the Court applied Article 47 of the EU Charter as entailing the 'principle of effective judicial protection'.[52] In *ZZ*, the Court also made reference to and relied upon Article 47 of the Charter in relation to procedural requirements for an administrative decision refusing entry into the State taken under Article 27(1) of the Citizenship Directive.[53] Indeed, at least since the *German Beer* case,[54] the Court has placed compliance with minimum procedural guarantees, such as an obligation to state reasons and effective judicial protection, as a part of the proportionality principle. However, since *International Handelsgesellschaft*,[55] compliance with the proportionality principles has been closely associated with a fundamental rights review in EU law, a fact also emphasised in *Wachauf*. Applying Article 47 of the Charter under the umbrella of the proportionality principle does of course open up the possibility of *ex officio* application of the EU Charter in many circumstances. Nonetheless, this does not necessarily mean that Article 47 of the Charter may only be applied in the context and under the wings of the proportionality principle.

[48] *Digital Rights Ireland* (n 17) [35]. See, as regards Art 8 of the ECHR, European Court of Human Rights, *Leander v Sweden*, 26 March 1987, § 48, Series A no 116; *Rotaru v Romania* [GC], no 28341/95, § 46, ECHR 2000-V; and *Weber and Saravia v Germany* (dec), no 54934/00, § 79, ECHR 2006-XI.

[49] Case C-389/10 P *KME v Commission* [2011] ECR I–13125 [131].

[50] ibid.

[51] Case C-373/09 *Peñarroja Fa* [2011] ECR I-1785.

[52] Case C-279/09 *DEB* [2010] ECR I-13849 [59].

[53] Case C-300/11 *ZZ*, judgment of 4 June 2013.

[54] Case 178/84 *Commission v Germany* [1987] ECR 1227.

[55] Case 11/70 *Internationale Handelsgesellschaft* [1970] ECR 1125.

Of course, the EU Charter should be the Court's *leitnormen*, and brought up *ex officio*, as appropriate. However, this does not mean that all the EU Charter provisions should be treated equally in that respect or that the *inter partes* nature of certain proceedings should be overruled. The EU Charter is not an indivisible piece and there is, for example, a distinction between absolute rights, such as those found in Article 1, and other rights that are non-absolute and subject to limitation, as appropriate. Furthermore, procedural guarantees, such as those found in Article 47 of the EU Charter, should enjoy a special status and it should be the responsibility of the Court to make sure that they are respected *ex officio*, irrespective of the nature of the proceedings.

IV. MANIFEST TEST

How about the depth or the intensity of the review undertaken by the Court when analysing EU or Member States' measures in the light of fundamental rights, particularly Charter rights? The Court's long-lasting standard approach when it comes to a review of EU measures may be summarised as follows:

> In reviewing the exercise of [the EU's legislative] power the Court must confine itself to examining whether it contains a manifest error or constitutes a misuse of power or whether the authority in question did not clearly exceed the bounds of its discretion.[56]

Advocate General Kokott has given an outstanding summary of the manifest test in her opinion in the *SPCM* case,[57] where she referred to this test as entailing 'in principle a presumption of the lawfulness of Community law' and that the EU legislature 'enjoys a wide margin of assessment and action ("discretion") when it makes complex technical and/or political choices'.[58] She stated that 'the Court may not substitute its own assessment for that of the Community legislature, and must confine itself to examining whether the legislature's assessment contains a manifest error or constitutes a misuse of powers or whether the legislature clearly exceeded the bounds of its discretion'.[59] However, she warned that the proportionality principle is not entirely without purpose or meaning and stated that: 'If there are clearly less

[56] Case 138/79 *SA Roquette Frères v Council of the European Communities* [1980] ECR 3333 [25]. An even more extreme version seems to be suggested by AG Jääskinen in Case C-249/0 *Novo Nordisk* [2011] ECR I-3155, where he refused to engage in a balancing exercise in the case and awarded a wide and unrestricted margin of discretion to the EU legislature, which in fact will not be reviewed—see, eg, his opinion at [49]–[50].

[57] Case C-558/07 *SPCM and others* [2009] ECR I-5783.

[58] ibid [70]–[71].

[59] ibid [72].

oppressive measures available which are equally effective, or if the measures adopted are obviously out of proportion to the aims pursued, the persons affected must be given judicial protection. Otherwise the principle of proportionality, which is part of primary law, would be deprived of its practical effect.'[60]

A valid point which should not be overlooked is that the EU institutions are subject to Article 5 of the Treaty on European Union (TEU) as a 'part of primary law'. The message of Advocate General Kokott seems to be that even if a manifest test is warranted in certain situations, it may never become the rule. Interestingly, in the above-mentioned cases (*Volker*, *Test Achats*, *Sky Österreich* and *Deutches Weintor*) where EU secondary norms are reviewed in the light of EU Charter rights, there is no mention of a 'manifest test'. Furthermore, in *Digital Rights Ireland*, the Court even signified that the review of the EU legislature's discretion should be 'strict'—which must be the real opposite to a 'manifest test'. Whether that approach will signify a lasting change in approach, at least in certain type of cases, is too early to say, but certainly it is an indication that a review in light of certain Charter rights may make a 'manifest test' inappropriate.[61] It should, however, be highlighted that in the recent case of *Schaible* (17 October 2013), the Court referred to the 'manifest test' again, even if EU Charter rights (Article 16) are involved, and stated:

> In the area of agriculture, the European Union legislature enjoys, inter alia, such a broad discretion, corresponding to the political responsibilities given to it by Articles 40 TFEU to 43 TFEU. Consequently, review by the Court is limited to verifying whether that legislature has manifestly exceeded the limits of its discretion.[62]

Therefore, the manifest test is still present, but it remains an open question as to exactly what weight is to be attached to the Court's wording 'In the area of agriculture'.[63] Nevertheless, the manifest test is by no means a test that should necessarily disappear—although arguably it will not always be appropriate, particularly when a review in light of fundamental rights is taking place. In addition, there are no good grounds to limit this test to a

[60] ibid [74].

[61] In that context, it is relevant to refer to the case of the EFTA Court in E-15/10 *Posten Norge*, judgment of 18 April 2012, where the EFTA Court argued that it is not bound by 'manifest' review only in competition law cases entailing 'complex economic assessment'. Seemingly this is based on the fact that the EFTA Court regards Art 6 ECHR as being applicable as a standard to be complied with in the case, arguably resulting in 'manifest test' not being sufficient—see, eg, [101]–[102] and [285]–[286].

[62] Case C-101/12 *Schaible*, judgment of 17 October 2013 [48]. It should, however, be pointed out that the Court largely followed the Art 52(1) of the Charter framework in this case and also seems to have 'reviewed' to an extent the balancing that the EU institutions needed to make in adopting the EU legislation at stake, as discussed below.

[63] In the opinion of AG Trstenjak in Case C-365/08 *Agrana Zucker* [2010] ECR I-4341, the Advocate General argued for a 'manifest test' being applied at each of the levels of the proportionality assessment, including the *stricto sensu* level in cases dealing with EU's Common Agricultural Policy—see [63] and [70].

review of EU norms only. A 'manifest review' may also be appropriate when the measures originate in the Member States, not least if it is demonstrated that the legislature has conducted its own proportionality assessment prior to enacting the legislation and the field concerns deep national interests.[64]

V. THE HIDING EFFECT OF THE EU CHARTER

But after five years of application by the Court of Justice, can we really say that the Charter holds the status of a true guiding norm? Is there an 'increased tendency', if we may use the *Keck* wording, in referring to the EU Charter, which calls for a limitation of its scope, or applicability in general? It is difficult to leave this topic without reflecting upon various recent cases where the Charter has not been mentioned, but should or could have been mentioned. Another related issue is where the scope of EU law has surprisingly been narrowly construed—in contrast to previous case law. That would be a surprising effect of the EU Charter, ie, in limiting the scope of EU law and thus also the scope of rights, which individuals should be able to realise irrespective of the EU Charter.

A rapid look at the Court's case law allows us to conclude that reference to fundamental rights standards is not systematic in EU litigation. Often the Court follows an orthodox approach of the *ultra petita* principle in action in a judicial review under Article 263 TFEU, whereas it could view EU fundamental rights as *moyen d'ordre public*. This lack of systematic use of EU fundamental rights is also detectable in preliminary rulings. In that sense, three Grand Chamber cases—ie *Römer*,[65] *Ruiz-Zambrano*[66] and *Dominguez*[67]—offer an excellent illustration. In *Römer* and *Dominguez*, the Court of Justice failed to refer to Articles 21(1) and 31(2) of the EU Charter, respectively, in cases concerning the recognition of general principles of EU law. In *Ruiz-Zambrano*, the Court of Justice in a cryptic reasoning focused merely on a citizenship provision (Article 20 TFEU) and failed to give guidelines on the right to family protection under Article 7 of the EU Charter. These cases reflect judicial minimalism in the context of EU fundamental rights.[68] Moreover, in the recent *Google* case from 2014, the

[64] This has been suggested, for example, by AG Bot in his opinion in Case C-42/07 *Liga Portuguesa* [2009] ECR I-763 [258], where he suggested this type of a review in the field of gambling.

[65] Case C-147/08 *Römer* [2011] ECR I-3591.

[66] Case C-34/09 *Ruiz Zambrano* [2011] ECR I-1177.

[67] *Dominguez* (n 22).

[68] D Sarmiento, 'Half a Case at a Time: Dealing with Judicial Minimalism at the European Court of Justice' in P Popelier, C Van de Heyning and P Van Nuffel (eds), *Human Rights Protection in the European Legal Order: The Interaction between the European and the National Courts* (Antwerp, Intersentia, 2011) 65. See also L Pech, 'Between Judicial Minimalism and Avoidance Strategy: On the Court of Justice's Sidestepping of the Fundamental Constitutional Issues in the Cases of *Römer* and *Dominguez*' (2012) 49 *CML Rev* 1.

Court of Justice should have, in our view, referred to Article 11 of the EU Charter on freedom to expression, but failed to do so in making merely a reference to Articles 7 and 8 of the Charter.[69]

Sometimes the Court of Justice has the possibility to solve cases either from the angle of EU fundamental rights or in another manner.[70] For instance, *Ruiz Zambrano* was a judgment that could have been dealt with merely in terms of citizenship or free movement of persons, or on the grounds of the fundamental right to family life. In *Google*, it was enough for the Court to rely heavily on secondary legislation to show the 'level of protection' of fundamental rights and it did not use Article 11 of the EU Charter in a balancing of interest with Articles 7 and 8 of the EU Charter.[71] As underlined by Sarmiento: 'Minimalism plays an important role here, for it is the means through which the ECJ refrains from acting as a Court that *promotes* (and not only *guarantees*) the protection of fundamental rights, affecting, at the same time, the way in which the ECHR reacts to cases under the scope of application of EU Law'.[72]

Moreover, if the EU Charter is the Court's true guiding (written) norm, the reference to (unwritten) general principles of EU law in the Court's case law should cease. Looking at the text of Article 6 TWU, this situation is seen as perhaps the most coherent solution and the general principles could perform a more modest role, lying dormant in most situations. This is obviously not the situation when looking at the recent jurisprudence of the Court of Justice.[73] In *Kokopelli*, the Court could have mentioned the relevant provisions of the Charter in relation to the principle of non-discrimination and the freedom to pursue an economic activity, but preferred to rely instead

[69] Case C-131/12 *Google Spain*, judgment of 13 May 2014.

[70] See Sarmiento (n 68).

[71] *Google Spain* (n 69).

[72] See Sarmiento (n 68).

[73] See Joined Cases C-29/13 and 30/13 *Global Trans Lodzhistik*, judgment of 13 March 2014 [57]. According to the Court, it must be noted that observance of the rights of the defence is a general principle of EU law that applies where the authorities are minded to adopt a measure which will adversely affect an individual. See also Case C-206/13 *Siragusa*, judgment of 6 March 2014 [33–34]. According to the Court: 'It follows from all the foregoing that it has not been established that the Court has jurisdiction to interpret Article 17 of the Charter (see, to that effect, Case C–245/09 *Omalet* [2010] ECR I–13771, paragraph 18; see also the Orders in Case C–457/09 *Chartry* [2011] ECR I–819, paragraphs 25 and 26; Case C–134/12 *Corpul Național al Polițiștilor* [2012] ECR, paragraph 15; Case C–498/12 *Pedone* [2013] ECR, paragraph 15; and Case C–371/13 *SC Schuster & Co Ecologic* [2013] ECR, paragraph 18). .... 34 As for the principle of proportionality, that is one of the general principles of EU law which must be observed by any national legislation which falls within the scope of EU law or which implements that law (see, to that effect, Case 77/81 *Zuckerfabrik Franken* [1982] ECR 681, paragraph 22; Case 382/87 *Buet and EBS* [1989] ECR 1235, paragraph 11; Case C–2/93 *Exportslachterijen van Oordegem* [1994] ECR I–2283, paragraph 20; and Joined Cases C–422/09, C–425/09 and C–426/09 *Vandorou and Others* [2010] ECR I–12411, paragraph 65)'.

on the case law on general principles of EU law.[74] In the recent *Fag og Arbejde (FOA)* case, the Court had to answer the Danish national court as to whether there is in EU law a general principle against discrimination based on obesity.[75] It is worth noting that the starting point of the inquiry as to the existence of such a principle was not the EU Charter, but Article 19 TFEU and EU secondary legislation. The EU Charter was not used as a source of inspiration.

Notably, the general principles of EU law are still quite present in the Court's case law. It seems that the Court has had some problems in getting rid of its general principles' arsenal.[76] This reluctance is perhaps not so surprising given the flexibility of such unwritten norms. In that respect, *Wimmer* provides two main reasons for which such a situation can be explained; first, general principles are part of the 'argumentative budget' of the legal professions and enable an autonomous legal discourse; and, second, the general principles serve as cement between various sources of law and are a factor of increasing coherence within the system. In other words, the main reason for keeping the general principles is to allow a sound balance between consistency and flexibility in the case law of the Court.[77] Problematically, the very existence of multiple norms of fundamental rights protection may lead to a divergent standard of protection. However, such a risk is in our view quite limited given the ruling in the *Åkerberg* case, which arguably unifies the personal scope of protection of general principles and rights enshrined within the EU Charter.[78]

The hiding effects of the EU Charter are also confirmed by the Court's case law in relation to its lack of reference to the horizontal provisions of the EU Charter. For instance, in *Association Médiation Sociale*, the Court was asked by the national court to clarify its interpretation of 'rights' and 'principles' as mentioned in Article 52(5) of the Charter.[79] In its ruling delivered in February 2014, the Grand Chamber of the Court of Justice failed to mention and explain this provision. This is worrying in particular when the national court explicitly asked for an interpretation of a key provision of the EU Charter. In addition, the Court of Justice should have explicitly mentioned Article 52(3) of the Charter in *Åkerberg*.[80] In this high-profile case, though the Court of Justice impliedly followed the ECHR standard as to the interpretation of *ne bis in idem*, it failed to mention the key horizontal

[74] Case C-59/11 *Association Kokopelli*, judgment of 12 July 2012.
[75] Case C-354/13 *Fag og Arbejde (FOA)*, judgment of 18 December 2014.
[76] See P Cruz-Villalón, 'Rights in Europe: The Crowded House', King's College Working Paper 01/2012.
[77] M Wimmer, 'The Dinghy's Rudder: General Principles of European Union Law through the Lens of Proportionality' (2014) 20 *European Public Law* 331, 342.
[78] Case C-617/10 *Åkerberg*, judgment of 26 February 2013.
[79] Case C-176/12 *Association de médiation sociale (AMS)*, judgment of 15 January 2014.
[80] *Åkerberg* (n 78).

provision of the EU Charter that established an obligation to respect the ECHR case law when the rights are corresponding, namely Article 52(3). Once again, the Luxembourg judges refused to engage in the interpretation of one of the most essential provisions of the EU bill of rights. This attitude is particularly worrying when taking the recent Opinion 2/13 of the Court, of 18 December 2014 on the impossibility for the EU to accede to the ECHR into consideration. Due to this negative Opinion, in our view there is now a heightened duty to refer to the obligation to respect the ECHR case law.

In addition, the case law on Article 52(2) of the EU Charter is also problematic. Indeed, according to the *Gardella* case[81] discussed above, Article 52(2) provides that rights recognised by the Charter for which provision is made in the treaties are to be exercised under the conditions and within the limits defined therein. In that vein and for the Court, Article 15(2) of the EU Charter reiterates inter alia the free movement of workers guaranteed by Article 45 TFEU, as confirmed by the explanations relating to that provision. However, in the *Pfleger* case, the Court, in failing to refer to Article 52(2) of the EU Charter, considered that Articles 15–17 of the EU Charter are fully assimilated with the freedom to provide services, so it seems, and 'that separate examination [under the Charter] is not necessary'.[82] In contrast, in the *Sokoll-Seebacher* case, the Court relied on its *Gardella* reasoning by prioritising the freedom of establishment (Article 49 TFEU) over Article 16 of the Charter.[83] But like *Pfleger*, the Court failed to refer to Article 52(2) of the EU Charter.

Finally, the Court of Justice may hide the EU Charter by considering that the matter submitted to its interpretation does not fall within the scope of EU law. For instance, in *Pelckmans*, the Court eluded the application of Article 16 of the EU Charter by considering that the Sunday trading rules did not fall within the scope of EU law.[84] Would the same have been applied if only the fundamental freedoms of the TFEU had been relied on by the parties? In a similar vein, the Grand Chamber in *Dano* refused to rely on the EU Charter when it considered that the national measures providing for social benefits constitute a purely internal situation and therefore did not constitute implementing measures falling within the scope of EU law as defined by Article 51 of the Charter.[85] But was it not the case that Elizabeta Dano had exercised her right to free movement?

Perhaps even more problematic when it comes to hiding the EU Charter is the recent case law of the Court of Justice on austerity measures. In these

[81] *Gardella* (n 23).
[82] Case C-390/12 *Pfleger*, judgment of 30 April 2014 [60].
[83] Case C-367/12 *Sokoll-Seebacher*, judgment of 13 February 2014.
[84] Case C-483/12 *Pelckmans*, judgment of 8 May 2014.
[85] Case C-333/13 *Dano*, judgment of 11 November 2014.

cases, the Court of Justice was asked by national courts to decide on the application of the Charter in relation to measures taken in the wake of the economic crisis. In two orders issued in the summer of 2013 and the summer of 2014 (*Sindicato dos bancarios* and *Sindicato nacional*),[86] the Court rejected as inadmissible questions put by the Portuguese labour courts as to the application of the EU Charter to national legislation implementing the austerity measures of the European Stability Mechanism (reduction of wages in the public sector). These decisions are sadly marked by an absolute lack of reasoning as to why the EU Charter is not applicable to the circumstances of the case.[87]

VI. CONCLUSIONS

As can be seen from the above discussion, the EU Charter is having a strong impact in bringing about a new era of EU law where fundamental rights are playing a key role. However, even if the fundamental rights recognised by the EU Charter are 'at the heart' of EU's legal structure, as the Court held in paragraph 169 of its Opinion 2/13, and are therefore an essential part of the (wider) constitutional framework of the EU, the (narrower) analytical framework lacks certain consistency in its application. In addition, as stipulated above and perhaps due to the same incoherence and lack of foreseeability in application, there are a growing number of cases where the EU Charter is not referred to by the Court of Justice, even if logically it should be, or where the scope of EU law is narrowly construed in the presence of the EU Charter. Is that to willingly avoid the EU Charter? In fact, as demonstrated above, the EU Charter should be the Court's *leitnormen* and should not be shied away from. The EU Charter's own instruments, found in its horizontal provisions, offer sufficient flexibility in defining its scope of application, both in terms of its material scope and on the basis of an analytical framework of limitations. Therefore, the presence of the EU Charter itself should keep no court awake at nights.

[86] Case C-128/12 *Sindicatos dos Bancários do Norte*, order of the Court of 7 March 2013; and Case C-264/12 *Sindicato Nacional*, order of the Court of 26 June 2014.

[87] For more developments, see C Kilpatrick and B de Witte, 'A Comparative Framing of Fundamental Rights Challenges to Social Crisis Measures in the Eurozone' (2014) 7 *European Policy Analysis* 1–12.

7

The Scope of the Charter and its Impact on the Application of the ECHR

The *Åkerberg Fransson* Case on *Ne Bis in Idem* in Perspective

ULF BERNITZ

I. INTRODUCTION

THE GRAND CHAMBER judgment in 2013 by the European Court of Justice (CJEU) in the *Åkerberg Fransson* case[1] is a seminal case on the scope and importance of the EU Charter of Fundamental Rights (hereinafter 'the Charter') and its impact on the application of the European Convention on Human Rights (ECHR). This chapter will discuss the Court's preliminary ruling in the case as well as its scope, effects and repercussions.[2] The emphasis lies on providing an account and analysis of the considerations of the Court in the case and the conclusions to be drawn with regard to the scope and strength of EU law protection of human and fundamental rights, in particular in relation to ECHR law. The right at stake is the *ne bis in idem* principle, ie, the right not to be tried or punished twice for the same offence, as expressed in Article 50 of the Charter and in Article 4 of Protocol No 7 to the ECHR. Mr Åkerberg Fransson was a Swedish self-employed fisherman who was charged in criminal court proceedings with

[1] Case C-617/10 *Prosecutor v Hans Åkerberg Fransson* EU:C:2013:105, decided 26 February 2013.

[2] The literature on the subject is becoming comprehensive. See in English case comment on *Åkerberg Fransson* by E Hancox in (2013) 50 *CML Rev* 1411 ff; D Sarmiento, 'Who's Afraid of the Charter?' (2013) 50 *CML Rev* 1267 ff; S Peers, T Hervey, J Kenner and A Ward (eds), *The EU Charter of Fundamental Rights: A Commentary* (Oxford, Hart Publishing, 2014) 1385 ff, 1419 ff; C Brokelind, Case Note on Åkerberg Fransson (Case C-617/10) (2013) 53(6) *European Taxation*; on the general background, see B Van Bockel, *The Ne Bis in Idem Principle in EU Law* (Dordrecht, Kluwer Law 2010); A-I Kargopoulos, '*Ne Bis in Idem* in

tax offences, despite the fact that he had already paid a tax surcharge for undeclared tax, inter alia, undeclared VAT. Sweden applied a policy of double sanctions and duplication of proceedings in the area.

There are in particular three problem areas that will be covered. The first one is the scope of the Charter where the CJEU decided in favour of a fairly broad interpretation, while simultaneously in the *Melloni* judgment[3] curtailing the scope of national constitutional human rights protection in matters covered by EU law.

The second problem area deals with the way in which the CJEU defined the scope of the *ne bis in idem* principle and, in particular, how the Court applied the ECHR law as developed by the European Court of Human Rights (ECtHR) only indirectly in order to define the scope of the principle.

The third problem area deals with the relation between the Charter and the ECHR law in a wider sense, making use of the *Åkerberg Fransson* case as a basis for the discussion. The problems are related to the two courts' different positions in the norm hierarchy and differences in their procedural structure.

In European law, it is rare to know how national law has reacted to preliminary rulings by the CJEU and what has been the ultimate result in subsequent national application of the judgment. In fact, the *Åkerberg Fransson* judgment has had far-reaching effects and caused the Swedish Supreme Court to radically change its case law in a plenary ruling, certainly a rare occasion. This chapter will also highlight these effects.

II. THE *ÅKERBERG FRANSSON* CASE AND ITS BACKGROUND

The origins of the case were that the Swedish Tax Agency scrutinised the tax returns and the book-keeping of Mr Åkerberg Fransson, who was fishing vendace roe which he sold directly to first-class restaurants.[4] He did not have a limited company; instead, he ran his financial activities as a sole trader. He was therefore personally responsible for paying tax on his income and paying VAT on that income. His business operations almost entirely lacked any cross-border aspects.

Criminal Proceedings', Swedish Studies in European Law, Vol 5 (Oxford, Hart Publishing, 2014) 85 ff; M Gulliksson, 'Effective Sanctions as the One-Dimensional Limit to the Ne Bis in Idem Principle in EU Law', Swedish Studies in European Law, Vol 6 (Oxford, Hart Publishing, 2015) 141 ff. See in Swedish, inter alia, K Fast, 'Dubbelbestraffningsförbudet i EU:s rättighetsstadga och det svenska systemet med skattetillägg och skattebrott' (2013) *Svensk Skattetidning* 138 ff; M Gulliksson, 'Klart till halvklart—om ne bis in idem och skattetilläggen' (2013) *Svensk Juristtidning (SvJT)* 645 ff; D Ritleng, 'Lärdomar av EU-domstolens parallella domar i målen Åkerberg Fransson och Melloni' (2014) *Svensk Juristtidning (SvJT)* 36 ff.

[3] Case C-399/11 *Stefano Melloni v Ministerio Fiscal* EU:C:2013:107.

[4] As a side remark, he was fishing in the Gulf of Bothnia, primarily far north in Sweden at the mouth of the Kalix River. Vendace (*coregonus albula*) from that area is full of valuable roe, Kalix vendace roe, which is an expensive delicacy and also enjoys a protected designation of origin in the EU.

The Tax Agency made the assessment that there were substantial deficiencies in the book-keeping when it came to the sale of roe and decided, based on a discretionary assessment, to increase Mr Åkerberg Fransson's declared income and declared VAT for 2004 and 2005.[5] The Tax Agency also decided to charge a tax surcharge as the tax returns were found to be unsatisfactory. For the income part, the surcharge was 40 per cent and for the VAT part 15 per cent. Mr Åkerberg Fransson did not appeal the Tax Agency's decision. When the case was being considered by the CJEU, the tax surcharge had been paid and gained legal force.

Despite the fact that Mr Åkerberg Fransson had been ordered to pay a tax surcharge, he was prosecuted by the public prosecutor and summoned to appear before Haparanda *tingsrätt* (Haparanda District Court) in 2009 on charges of serious tax offences. Given the circumstances, he was facing the risk of an imprisonment sentence of approximately six to eight months. Sweden has a system of parallel jurisdictions. Tax surcharges are decided by the tax authority and can be appealed to the administrative courts while tax offences are handled as criminal cases by the ordinary courts of law. In the criminal case before the District Court, the counsel for the defence pleaded that the case should be rejected with reference to the *ne bis in idem* principle. In December 2010, the District Court decided to stay the proceedings and request a preliminary ruling from the CJEU with regard to whether the Swedish policy of double procedures and double sanctions could be regarded as being compatible with the prohibition against *ne bis in idem* in Article 50 of the Charter. In its request to the CJEU, the District Court stressed in particular that the tax surcharge partly concerned VAT.

By requesting a preliminary ruling, the District Court displayed its independence and knowledge of the Charter. As will be discussed in section VI below, by referring the case to the CJEU, the District Court questioned the legality of the case law established by the Swedish Supreme Court.[6]

III. THE SCOPE OF ARTICLE 51 OF THE CHARTER

The *Åkerberg Fransson* case proved to be a touchstone of the scope of the Charter and the jurisdiction of the CJEU. According to Article 51(1) of the Charter, it is only applicable to the legal systems of the Member States when they 'are implementing Union law'. In Article 51(2), it is stated that 'the

[5] The Tax Agency decided to increase his taxable income by approximately SEK 500,000 (*c* €55,000) and VAT payable by approximately SEK 150,000 (*c* €17,000).

[6] In an effort to 'silence' the District Court, the Prosecutor appealed to the Court of Appeals the decision to stay the proceedings while waiting for the decision by the CJEU. However, that court rejected the request and referred to Case 210/06 *Cartesio Oktató és Szolgáltató bt* EU:C:2008:723. According to the *Cartesio* principle, a court of the higher instances may not prevent a court of the lower instance from requesting a preliminary ruling from the Court of Justice.

Charter does not extend the field of application of Union law beyond the powers of the Union or establish any new power or task for the Union, or modify powers and tasks as defined in the Treaties'. The text of the Charter shall be read in conjunction with Article 6(1) in the Treaty on European Union (TEU), which states in similar language that the Charter 'shall not extend in any way the competences of the Union as defined in the Treaties'. According to the Explanations to the Charter, the requirement to respect fundamental rights defined in the context of the Union is only binding on the Member States 'when they act in the scope of Union law'.[7] As is well-known, these texts reflect fears among Member States during the negotiations leading to the Lisbon Treaty that the Charter would extend EU law competence in the human rights field beyond the treaty limits.

There has been legal uncertainty about the exact meaning of 'implementation' of EU law. The Court found the provisions mentioned meant that the applicability of the Charter is connected fully to the scope of EU law. As the Court phrased it: 'The applicability of Union law entails applicability of the fundamental rights guaranteed by the Charter'.[8]

On this point, one should observe that there is a certain ambiguity between language versions. While the English version talks in Article 51(1) of the Charter about 'implementing Union law', the French uses the expression 'mettent en oeuvre le droit de l'Union' and the German 'Durchführung des Rechts der Union'. The Swedish version uses the expression *tillämpa unionsrätt* which best translates as 'apply' EU law. The *Åkerberg Fransson* judgment seems to make clear that the CJEU understands implementation of EU law to mean application of EU law.[9] In the legal argumentation in the case before the CJEU, a narrow view of what was meant by 'implementation' of a directive was put forward by several intervening Member States, arguing that a specific article in a legal act of EU law actually had to be implemented in national law. However, the Court decided in favour of a broader understanding of the scope of the Charter. Thus, all situations that the Court finds to be governed by EU law are covered by the protection of fundamental rights guaranteed by the Charter, but not situations lying outside the scope of EU law. The Charter does not establish any new powers or tasks for the EU.[10]

[7] Article 52(7) of the Charter states: 'The explanations drawn up as a way of providing guidance in the interpretation of this Charter shall be given due regard by the courts of the Union and of the Member States.' Similar text in Art 6(1) third subparagraph TEU.

[8] *Åkerberg Fransson* (n 1) [21].

[9] S Peers, T Hervey, J Kenner and A Ward (eds), *The EU Charter of Fundamental Rights* (Oxford, Hart Publishing, 2014) 1385.

[10] *Åkerberg Fransson* (n 1) [19] and [21]. The Court took a distinctly different view on the scope of the Charter than did AG Cruz Villalón in his comprehensive opinion; see, inter alia, his opinion at [57].

The CJEU has referred to its statements on the scope of Article 51(1) of the Charter in *Åkerberg Fransson* in a substantial number of later cases; today the Court's pronouncements in that case constitute well-settled EU law.[11] However, the exact scope of what is 'governed' by Article 51(1) in the Charter is still not fully clear. In *Cruciano Siragusa*,[12] decided in 2014, the Court has stated that the concept of 'implementing Union law' as referred to in that Article requires a certain degree of connection above and beyond the matters covered, being closely related or one of those matters having an indirect impact on the other.[13] Such connection was not found to exist in the *Siragusa* case, which was about landscape conservation. In *Hernández*, the Court has given some more guidance. It is necessary, inter alia, to determine whether the national legislation is intended to implement a provision of EU law, the nature of the legislation at issue and whether it pursues objectives other than those covered by EU law.[14] The Court's reasoning in *Åkerberg Fransson* about the connection between the VAT Directive and national legislation will be discussed in section IV below.

As the Court stated in *Åkerberg Fransson*, situations cannot exist which are covered by EU law without the fundamental rights guaranteed by the Charter being applicable.[15] However, suppose the constitutional law of a Member States goes further than EU law in its protection of fundamental rights. This situation came to the fore in the judgment in the *Melloni* case,[16] which was decided on the same day as *Åkerberg Fransson*.[17] In this high-profile judgment, the CJEU established that the European Arrest Warrant Regulations regarding extradition to another Member State for criminal prosecution would take precedence over the conflicting rules adopted in the Spanish Constitution. Citing inter alia the *Internationale Handelsgesellschaft* case of 1970,[18] the Court stated that rules of national law, even of a constitutional order, cannot be allowed to undermine the effectiveness of EU law on the territory of that state.[19] The primacy of EU law could not have been demonstrated more clearly. Thus, the Charter is not only an instrument for the improvement of human rights protection, but it is also within its scope to limit the Member States' fundamental rights protection if this is found to conflict with EU law requirements. To mention another example,

[11] See, eg, Case C-390/12 *Pfleger et al* EU:C:2014:281 [31]–[34]; and Case C-117/14 *Poclava v Toledano*, EU:C:2015:60 [29].

[12] Case C-206/13 *Cruciano Siragusa v Regione Sicilia et al* EU:C:2014:126.

[13] ibid [24]. The Court has repeated this statement in Case C-198/13 *Hernández et al v Reino de Espana et al* EU:C:2014:2055 [34].

[14] *Hernández* (n 13) [36].

[15] *Åkerberg Fransson* (n 1) [21].

[16] *Melloni* (n 3).

[17] Judge Safjan was rapporteur in both cases.

[18] Case 11/70 *Internationale Handelsgesellschaft v Einfuhr- und Vorratsstelle für Getreide und Futtermittel* EU:C:1970:114.

[19] *Melloni* (n 3) [59].

Sweden has a detailed Freedom of the Press Act with constitutional status. Conflicts between specific rules of EU law and the Swedish Act can easily occur. According to the *Melloni* principle, EU law would prevail in such situations. Whether 'respect for national identity' (Article 4(2) TEU) could be pleaded with any chance of success is at least doubtful.

However, the Court made an important distinction between *Melloni* and *Åkerberg Fransson*. While it found the situation in *Melloni* to be entirely determined by EU law, it noted that this was not the case with regard to *Åkerberg Fransson*, as much of the implementation was left to the national level. It stressed that in such situations, national authorities and courts remain free to apply national standards of protection of fundamental rights, provided that the level of protection provided for by the Charter as interpreted by the CJEU and the primacy, unity and effectiveness of EU law is observed and not compromised.[20] In other words, the Member States would normally be free to apply more advanced fundamental rights standards in relation to the enforcement of, for example, tax law.

The distinction is important from the viewpoint of constitutional law principles. In the *Melloni* type of situation, EU fundamental rights protection constitutes the ceiling, while in the *Åkerberg Fransson* type of situation, it constitutes the floor.

IV. THE SCOPE OF THE CHARTER AS APPLICABLE TO THE VAT DIRECTIVE

The outcome in *Åkerberg Fransson* was far from given. First, it should be observed that the CJEU only examined the *ne bis in idem* issue with regard to the VAT aspects of the case, not the income tax aspects, which seem to be a matter for national law outside the scope of the Charter. I will come back to that aspect in section VI. But in what way were the sanctions attached to undeclared VAT considered to be within the scope of the Charter?

On the one hand, VAT legislation in the Member States, Sweden included, is based primarily on the comprehensive VAT Directive.[21] On the other hand, the VAT Directive does not contain any detailed provisions about what sanctions will be applied in the Member States when VAT is not declared correctly.

The Member States took a restrictive view in their written observations in *Åkerberg Fransson* and at the oral hearing in the case based on the idea of tax sovereignty. Seven Member States supported the position of the Swedish

[20] *Åkerberg Fransson* (n 1) [29]; a similar statement appears in *Melloni* (n 3) [60]. In *Melloni*, the Court referred to Art 53 of the Charter. See Sarmiento (n 2) 1294 ff; Peers et al (n 2) 1419.

[21] Council Directive 2006/112/EC on the common system of value added tax of 28 November 2006.

government that the Charter was not applicable as the case was about the application of tax law. More concretely, it was added that the sanctions for failing to declare VAT correctly should be regarded as lying outside the remit of EU law since the VAT Directive lacks detailed rules regarding how these sanctions should be designed. Only one Member State, Austria, took a different position and stressed that the *ne bis in idem* principle should be observed. Counsel for Mr Åkerberg Fransson particularly stressed that the main freedom of Member States to determine sanctions with regard to upholding the system for paying VAT could not be allowed to include the freedom to disregard the *ne bis in idem* principle as stipulated in the Charter and instead must be kept within its framework.

The Court noted in particular that the VAT Directive contains provisions stating that every Member State is under an obligation to take all legislative and administrative measures appropriate for ensuring collection of all the VAT due on its territory and for preventing evasion.[22] The Court also emphasised that efficient VAT collection is important for the EU's own financial interests given that VAT revenue forms part of the EU's own resources.[23] It found that penalties such as tax surcharges and prosecution for a tax offence constitute implementation of the VAT Directive and therefore of EU law. Hence, the Court found the provisions of the Charter to be applicable to the design of the VAT sanction systems in the Member States. Member States must therefore abide by the Charter when they design sanctions to implement material provisions that have been established in a directive adopted by the EU. On this point, a very significant legal principle has been clarified as a result of the *Åkerberg Fransson* judgment.

The CJEU has undoubtedly settled on a relatively extensive interpretation of what constitutes 'implementation of Union law' by a Member State, but it does not lack support in previous case law.[24] It is worth mentioning that the VAT Directive explicitly stipulates an obligation on business operators to declare and pay VAT correctly. Member States have a certain amount of room for manoeuvre as regards the design of procedures and penalties to ensure the collection of VAT, but they also have an obligation to observe the legal principles of EU law. These include, inter alia, the principle of effectiveness, the principle of cooperation and the proportionality principle. In earlier case law, we can refer to three cases in particular, *Louloudakis*[25] regarding punitive import provisions, *Commission v Italy*[26] regarding a 'VAT amnesty' and *Profaktor Kulesza* [27] regarding a reduction of the extent

[22] *Åkerberg Fransson* (n 1) [25] with further references.
[23] In my view, this was a supporting argument that was not needed to reach the conclusion.
[24] *Åkerberg Fransson* (n 1) [25] and [26].
[25] Case C-262/99 *Paraskevas Louloudakis v Ellinko Dimosio* EU:C:2001:407.
[26] Case C-132/06 *Commission v Italy* EU:C:2008:412.
[27] Case C-188/09 *Dyrektor et al v Profaktor Kulesza et al* EU:C:2010:454.

of the right to deduct VAT. In *Commission v Italy*, the Court found every Member State to be under an obligation to take all legislative and administrative measures appropriate for ensuring collection of all the VAT due on its territory and for preventing evasion.[28] In *Profaktor Kulesza*, the Court pointed out that Member States are empowered to choose the sanctions which seem to them to be appropriate, but must, however, exercise that power in accordance with EU law and its general principles, and consequently in accordance with the principle of proportionality.[29]

In my opinion, the outcome in *Åkerberg Fransson* should not be regarded as surprising or particularly far-reaching. The Charter builds to a large extent on general principles already established in EU law. It has been a well-settled principle that Member States when shaping the sanctions to support the effective implementation of EU directives should observe the general principles of EU law. *Ne bis in idem* is such a principle, as will be discussed in section V below. There is no reason why the concept 'implementing Union law' should be understood more narrowly in the Charter than in the application of the EU Treaties. A different outcome in *Åkerberg Fransson*, finding the national system of double procedures and double sanctions to be outside the scope of EU law, would have been deplorable, as it would have severely weakened the fundamental rights protection in relation to Member States' implementation of directives.

V. THE *NE BIS IN IDEM* PRINCIPLE IN LIGHT OF ECHR LAW

Ne bis in idem was, moreover, a well-established general principle in EU law even before the Charter entered into force, applied inter alia in a number of judgments regarding the Schengen Agreement.[30] The first case in which the principle was applied seems to be the *Gutmann* case from the mid-1960s, which concerned double disciplinary procedures for the same offence.[31] However, like several other general principles of EU law, it was laid down for the first time in writing in the Charter. Article 50 of the Charter on the *ne bis in idem* principle has the title 'Right not to be tried or punished twice in criminal proceedings for the same criminal offence' and reads:

> No one shall be liable to be tried or punished again in criminal proceedings for an offence for which he or she has already been finally acquitted or convicted within the Union in accordance with the law.

[28] *Commission v Italy* (n 28) [37] and [46].
[29] *Profaktor Kulesza* (n 27) [29].
[30] See Van Bockel (n 2). See also W Devroe, 'How General Should General Principles Be? *Ne Bis in Idem* in EU Competition Law' in U Bernitz, X Groussot and F Schulyok (eds), *General Principles of EU Law and European Private Law* (Dordrecht, Kluwer Law, 2013) 401 ff, discussing in particular Case C-17/10 *Toshiba Corp* EU:C:2012:72.
[31] Joined Cases 18 and 35/65 *Max Gutmann v Commission of the EAEC* EU:C:1967:6.

When drafting the Charter, it was decided to connect Article 50 of the Charter closely to the very similar provision on *ne bis in idem* in Article 4 in Protocol No 7 to the ECHR, which also prohibits a person from being tried or punished twice in criminal proceedings for the same crime.[32] The guaranteed right has the same meaning in the Charter as the corresponding right in the ECHR. Article 50 of the Charter is intended to be interpreted in the same way as the ECHR article according to what has been stated in the Explanations regarding the Charter of Fundamental Rights,[33] which will be considered for guidance when courts apply the Charter.[34] *Ne bis in idem* is a good example of an area where we have two parallel European instruments for the protection of fundamental/human rights.

However, there are two important differences between the Charter and the ECHR provisions. The first one is of principal importance even if it did not come into question in *Åkerberg Fransson*. While the article in the ECHR applies to a prohibition against charging a person again for the same offence 'in the same state', Article 50 of the Charter has a much broader geographical scope as it is applicable 'in the Union'; in other words, it also prohibits charging a person again in another EU Member State, which is of importance not least in relation to the application of the Schengen system. The second more pertinent difference relates to the actual scope. While the ECHR is always applicable in relation to any person who is in a country that is a signatory to the Convention, the Charter as discussed in section IV above is applicable to the legal systems of the Member States 'only when they are implementing Union law' (Article 51(1) of the Charter).

The *ne bis in idem* principle not only applies to the right not to be convicted twice for the same breach of law, but also applies to the right not to be tried twice in different proceedings for the same offence. To take an example, for a person who has been charged with a tax surcharge which is criminal in nature, the *ne bis in idem* principle includes the right not to be tried twice for the same offence and not just the right not to be punished twice for the offence. Thus, the protection of rights foreseen by the *ne bis in idem* principle is not sufficiently met if, for example, a court, when determining the severity of a penalty in a subsequent judgment on a tax offence, applies proportionality-infused thinking and takes certain consideration of the fact that the person in question has already been ordered to pay a surcharge by the tax authorities or by an administrative court related to the same offence. Yet the *ne bis in idem* principle does not constitute an obstacle for applying a combination of a sanction fee (for example, a tax surcharge)

[32] The ECHR text reads: 'No one shall be liable to be tried or punished again in criminal proceedings under the jurisdiction of the same State for an offence for which he has already been finally acquitted or convicted in accordance with the law and penal procedure of that State.'

[33] EUT 2007/C 303/02, 14 December 2007.

[34] Article 52(7) of the Charter.

and a personal criminal sanction of the usual kind (for example, a fine or prison sentence) when determining the sanction within the framework of one and the same procedure.[35]

The ECtHR gave the right of a person not to be tried or punished twice for the same offence an amended and more exact content in its seminal *Zolotukhin v Russia* judgment of 2009.[36] In this Grand Chamber decision, the ECtHR reconsidered its case law in the field. In earlier case law, although not fully consistent, the ECtHR had held that the *ne bis in idem* rule does not forbid two convictions for offences possessing different essential elements.[37] However, in *Zolotukhin*, which concerned disciplinary punishment in the armed forces, it clarified that the *ne bis in idem* principle 'must be understood as prohibiting a new prosecution or trial of a second offence in so far as it arises from identical facts or facts which are substantially the same'.[38] In other words, it is the identity of the offence that is the decisive factor.

The judgment in *Zolotukhin* has been followed by several subsequent judgments where the ECtHR has expressed the same position. One of these cases is *Ruotsalainen v Finland*.[39] That case dealt with a situation where a person who had filled his vehicle with a banned type of fuel was first ordered to pay a fine and was subsequently charged an administrative sanction fee for the same offence; in other words, a situation with evident similarities to the combination penalty for a tax offence and a tax surcharge.

The CJEU found in *Åkerberg Fransson* that the VAT Directive, as a part of EU law, also had an impact on the design of the VAT sanction systems in the Member States. It established that the *ne bis in idem* principle, as stipulated in Article 50 of the Charter, prohibits a Member State from applying two separate procedures for tax surcharges and penalties, provided that the tax surcharge is criminal in nature.[40] Whether that was so in the actual case was, according to the Court, for the national court to determine based on the legal principles that the Court had expressed.

In this regard, one observes in particular that the CJEU was not willing to connect to the case law developed by the ECtHR based on the very similar *ne bis in idem provision* in the ECHR. On the contrary, the Court stated explicitly in the judgment that the ECHR is a legal instrument not formally incorporated into EU law as long as the EU has not acceded to it. Thus, the Court continued, EU law does not govern the relations between the ECHR

[35] *cf Åkerberg Fransson* (n 1) [34].

[36] *Sergey Zolotukhin v Russia*, App No 14939/03, judgment of 10 February 2009.

[37] On this basis, the ECtHR had accepted the Swedish parallel systems of tax surcharges and criminal sanctions in the earlier case of *Rosenquist v Sweden*, App No 60619/00, 14 September 2004.

[38] *Zolotukhin* (n 36) [82].

[39] *Ruotsalainen v Finland*, App No 13079/03.

[40] *Åkerberg Fransson* (n 1) [37].

and the legal systems of the Member States, and does not determine the conclusions to be drawn by a national court in the event of conflict between the rights guaranteed by the ECHR and a rule of national law.[41] Actually, the Court cited no decision taken by the ECtHR in the *Åkerberg Fransson* judgment, not even *Zolotukhin*. In addition, it did not mention that the ECtHR had in 2002 already found the Swedish tax surcharge to be of a criminal nature.[42] However, the Court found a way to link indirectly to the case law of the ECtHR by referring in *Åkerberg Fransson* to its own ruling in the *Bonda* case[43] to determine whether a tax surcharge is criminal in nature or not. *Bonda* referred in its turn to the three well-known 'Engel criteria' established by the ECtHR[44] to assess whether administrative penalties are to be criminal in nature and thus affected by the *Zolotukhin* ruling.[45] So, in reality, the CJEU linked the assessment as to whether a tax surcharge is criminal in nature to the case law of the ECtHR, albeit in a rather indirect fashion. In effect, the Court found the Swedish system to be incompatible with the *ne bis in idem* principle when applied to VAT.

The conclusion to be drawn seems to be that the CJEU deliberately maintains a certain arm's-length distance in relation to the case law built up on the basis of the ECHR, even when deciding very parallel cases. Other aspects of the relation between the Charter and the ECHR will be discussed in the next section.

VI. THE IMPACT ON ECHR LAW IN LIGHT OF THE NATIONAL AFTERMATH

A very important aspect of *Åkerberg Fransson* is its substantial impact on the ECHR law and its application in national jurisdictions. Before dealing with these issues, it is necessary to give a brief orientation about the national aftermath of the decision of the CJEU.

The ruling of the CJEU in *Åkerberg Fransson* had dramatic effects in Sweden. It caused the Swedish Supreme Court to act very swiftly, using two pending cases similar to *Åkerberg Fransson* as pilot cases. In two rulings in June and July 2013 based on the *ne bis in idem* principle, the Supreme

41 ibid [44], referring to Case C-571/10 *Servet Kamberaj v IPES et al* EU:C:2012:233 [62].

42 *Janosevic v Sweden*, App No 34619/97; and *Västberga Taxi and Vulk v Sweden* App No 36985/97.

43 Case C-489/10 *Criminal Proceedings against Lukasz M Bonda* EU:C:2012:319; *Åkerberg Fransson* (n 1) [35]. See also A Andreangeli, 'Ne Bis in Idem and Administrative Sanctions: Bonda' (2013) 50 *CML Rev* 1827 ff.

44 *Engel and others v The Netherlands* App Nos 5100/71, 5101/71, 5102/71, 5354/72, 5370/72.

45 The three criteria are the legal classification of the offence under national law, the very nature of the offence and the nature and degree of severity of the penalty that the person concerned is liable to incur: *Bonda* (n 43) 37.

Court made a U-turn as regards the approach to imposing a tax surcharge on a person and prosecuting the same person for a tax offence in different legal proceedings. In the first ruling, a unanimous plenary ruling in June 2013,[46] the Supreme Court found the double proceedings and double sanction system incompatible with the *ne bis in idem* principle. Thereafter, in a follow-up ruling in July 2013,[47] the Supreme Court established that as a consequence of the change in the law, a person has the right to a new trial if he or she has paid a tax surcharge and has in addition been sentenced in a criminal procedure for tax offence. The Court set the break-off point for the right to use this extraordinary legal remedy to 10 February 2009, which was the date when the ECtHR delivered its judgment in the *Zolotukhin* case.[48]

The two rulings by the Supreme Court proved very quickly to have great practical importance and far-reaching effects in order to rectify the previous legal treatment.[49] In the following months, a substantial number of individuals were released from prison, where they were serving sentences for tax offences, and many ongoing tax offence prosecutions were terminated. In all these cases, the individuals had had to pay a tax surcharge. A large number of cases dealing with the right of a new trial or awarding of damages are still pending.

How is this extraordinary development to be explained? Basically, the explanation is found in the different legal status of the Charter and the ECHR. There are fundamental differences regarding the constitutional position of the two European human rights instruments in Sweden, as is also the case in most other Member States. While the Charter enjoys primacy over Swedish national law, the ECHR has been incorporated into Swedish law as a statute enacted by Parliament. However, according to a special provision in the Constitution, legislation must not be enacted which is contrary to Sweden's obligations under the ECHR.[50] This provision gives the ECHR a kind of quasi-constitutional position of a somewhat unclear character, but

46 NJA (Nytt Juridiskt Arkiv) 2013, 502 (the Supreme Court's publication of decisions).

47 ibid 746.

48 See section V above.

49 The final outcome in *Åkerberg Fransson* is now known. When the proceedings in the case continued in the Haparanda District Court based on the preliminary ruling of the CJEU, the public prosecutor dropped the tax offence charges. However, Mr Åkerberg Fransson was also charged for book-keeping offences. The charges for book-keeping offences had not been included in the preliminary reference. Although there was a close relationship between the inadequate book-keeping and the undeclared tax, he was convicted for book-keeping offences to six months' imprisonment on probation. The judgment was appealed to the Court of Appeal, but was upheld, decision by the Hovrätten för Övre Norrland in case B 192-14, 12 September 2014 (final). The appeal court did not find the *ne bis in idem* principle to comprise the inadequate book-keeping, but regarded the inadequate book-keeping and the information submitted to the tax authorities as two different offences. This is in line with the position taken a few months later by the ECtHR in *Lucky Dev v Sweden* (see below).

50 Chapter 2, para 19 of the Constitution (called *The Instrument of Government*).

not of the same status as the Charter. This is largely similar to the situation in many other Member States. It should be recalled that the Charter does not interfere with the relationship between the ECHR and national law in the Member States.[51]

The issue of whether it was legally possible under the law of the ECHR on *ne bis in idem* to apply separate legal proceedings for tax surcharge orders and prosecution for tax offence based on the same incorrect information in a tax return had been much debated in legal and political circles in Sweden for a long time without change of position. As mentioned in section V above, the ECtHR had concluded in two cases in 2002 that the Swedish system with tax surcharges was criminal in nature.[52] However, the decisions by the ECtHR did not cause the Swedish legislator to alter the legislation, nor did the courts change their practice. Obviously, the legislator wanted the taxation system to be enforced by sharp sanctions, Sweden being a country with high taxes. As was described in section V, in 2009, the ECtHR sharpened its definition of what constitutes *ne bis in idem* in the *Zolotukhin* judgment by clarifying that this legal rule prohibits double punishment and duplication of proceedings for the same offence. The *Zolotukhin* judgment made the Swedish legal situation acute. However, in two new judgments in 2010 and 2011,[53] the majority of the Swedish Supreme Court justices took the view that the *Zolotukhin* judgment did not give 'clear support' to the need to change Swedish practice.[54] In the 2011 case, where the factual circumstances were quite similar to *Åkerberg Fransson*, the Court even found by a 3:2 vote that there was no reason to ask the CJEU for a preliminary ruling as the Charter was not applicable in the opinion of these judges.[55]

In Sweden, decisions taken by the Supreme Court are not formally binding on judges in lower courts, but are in practice always observed and followed. However, the Supreme Court judgments of 2010 and 2011 caused a kind of revolt among judges in the lower courts. In several parts of the country, different judges declined to follow the Supreme Court's position, referring to the *Zolotukhin* judgment, and refused to hear cases about tax offences brought by prosecutors in which the person to be prosecuted had

[51] In *Servet Kamberaj* (n 41), the Court stated explicitly in [63] that Art 6(3) TEU does not govern the relationship between the ECHR and the legal systems of the Member States, nor does it lay down the consequences to be drawn by a national court in the event of conflict between the rights guaranteed by that convention and a provision of national law.

[52] See n 41 above.

[53] NJA 2010, 168, NJA 2011, 444.

[54] The Supreme Administrative Court took the same position in another case, *RÅ (Regeringsrättens Årsbok)* 2009 ref 94 (the Supreme Administrative Court's publication of decisions).

[55] In *Åkerberg Fransson* (n 1) 47, the CJEU found it necessary to include a reminder—obviously addressed to the Swedish Supreme Court—about the duty to observe Art 267 TFEU as interpreted in Case 283/81 *CILFIT and others* EU:C:1982:335.

already been charged a tax surcharge.[56] However, it was only the District Court in the small town of Haparanda that seems to have been aware that the Charter offered the solution.

In its request for a preliminary ruling in *Åkerberg Fransson*, the District Court brought up the issue whether the requirement of 'clear support', which the Supreme Court had applied in relation to the ECHR, has an equivalent in the Charter. The CJEU recalled the *Simmenthal* case[57] and gave a firm negative reply.[58] Fully in line with established EU law, the Court explained that the national court is under a duty to give full effect to the EU provisions, if necessary refusing by its own motion to apply any conflicting provision of national legislation, even if adopted subsequently, and it is not necessary for the court to request or await the prior setting aside of such a national provision. By expressly dissociating itself from a restrictive requirement of 'clear support', the CJEU essentially gave the previous practice of the Swedish Supreme Court the kiss of death. In its seminal decision in June 2013 mentioned above, the Supreme Court changed its position on the interpretation of the *ne bis in idem* provision in ECHR law and stated that it should not be interpreted as giving a person a less comprehensive protection than that awarded by Article 50 of the Charter. The Supreme Court referred to fundamental principles of foreseeability and equal treatment.[59] Thus, the Charter reinforced the impact of the ECHR.

This is certainly an effect that is not limited to this particular case. In most EU Member States, the ECHR has a weaker constitutional position than the Charter, which might open the way for a certain amount of leniency and discretion in the national application of the ECHR rules. The decisions taken by the Swedish Supreme Court provide an example. The Charter's constitutional status combined with the duty to give full effect to EU law makes it impossible to apply Charter provisions in a similar way. This means that to the extent that Charter provisions are overlapping with ECHR rules, the former reinforce the latter, provided that the matter falls within the scope of EU law.

However, the influence of the Charter can indirectly stretch beyond the limits of EU law. Also in this regard, the aftermath of the *Åkerberg Fransson* case provides a good example.

The questions referred to the CJEU by the Swedish court in *Åkerberg Fransson* dealt with both income tax and VAT. However, the CJEU only dealt with VAT, as mentioned above. Mr Åkerberg Fransson's business operations

[56] O Zetterquist, 'Ne bis in idem and the European Legal Tsunami of 2013: A Vision from the Bench, Human Rights in Contemporary European Law' in *Swedish Studies in European Law*, Vol 6 (Oxford, Hart Publishing, 2015) 131 ff.

[57] Case 106/77 *Simmenthal* EU:C:1978:49.

[58] *Åkerberg Fransson* (n 1) [45].

[59] NJA 2013, 502, para 59.

almost entirely lacked cross-border aspects. This caused the Swedish Prosecutor-General to argue that the previous Swedish case law should be maintained with regard to income tax. The Swedish Supreme Court chose to see the legal issues differently, however. It ascertained that the collective Swedish system of tax surcharges and prosecution for tax offences had essentially been undermined by the CJEU's judgment in *Åkerberg Fransson*. Only upholding certain parts of a system that is intended to be connected would result in a perplexing set of rules and in certain cases discrepancies in the reaction to similar breaches of the rules that were difficult to explain.[60] The Supreme Court's conclusion was that the same rules should be applied to income tax and similar taxes as to VAT. The result was thus that the CJEU's ruling, as understood and applied by the Swedish Supreme Court, resulted in a full-scale rejection of the combination of tax surcharge/prosecution for a tax offence.

The conclusion reached by the Swedish Supreme Court can probably be generalised. If a certain legal rule or practice in the law of a Member State is found to be contrary to the protection of fundamental rights under EU law as far as EU law is applicable, it would at least be very difficult for the Member State to defend and continue to apply the same legal rule or practice in purely internal situations. In reality, EU law has effects in the fundamental rights area which go beyond the scope of EU law.

From this perspective, there is reason to consider the value of reservations made by Member States to provisions in the ECHR and its Protocols in areas of overlap between EU law and ECHR human rights law, in particular with regard to the *ne bis in idem* principle. As mentioned in section V above, the principle is included in the Convention as Article 4 of Protocol No 7. Some of the Member States of the EU have not ratified this Protocol or have, in conjunction with ratification, issued a reservation with regard to the application of Article 4 in Protocol No 7.[61] This does not, however, apply to Sweden, which has ratified Protocol No 7 without reservations.[62] The EU Charter, on the other hand, has been ratified in its entirety by all Member States, where it has been included as part of the Member States' ratification of the Lisbon Treaty. In this process, there was no room for Member State reservations or declarations related to specific articles.[63] This means that the Member States are bound to observe the *ne bis in idem*

[60] ibid, para 58.

[61] Protocol No 7 has not been ratified by Germany, the Netherlands and the UK. There are reservations from four EU Member States; see Peers et al (n 2) 1381. The reservations were observed by AG Cruz Villalón in his opinion in *Åkerberg Fransson* (n 1) [70]–[74].

[62] Government Bill to Parliament 1984/85:123. The Bill stated that Swedish legislation was in full conformity with Art 4 on *the ne bis in idem* (at 10), a somewhat questionable statement.

[63] Sweden has ratified the Lisbon Treaty including the Charter based on Government Bill 2007/08:168. The Bill does not include any more detailed analysis of the Charter. As is well-known, a Protocol has been appended to the Lisbon Treaty where two Member States, the UK

principle as expressed in Article 50 in the Charter when they implement EU law irrespective of their position in relation to Article 4 in Protocol No 7 to the ECHR. So what is the value today of the reservations made by some EU Member States in relation to the *ne bis in idem* provision in the ECHR? In reality, the reservations seem to have lost most of their importance.

There is still another aspect where the Charter has established itself as a stronger legal instrument than the ECHR, namely in relation to the procedure and length of litigation time. In *Åkerberg Fransson*, a district court which was not convinced that the case law of its own Supreme Court was in conformity with EU law referred the case to the CJEU for a preliminary ruling in December 2010. The Luxembourg Court delivered its Grand Chamber judgment in February 2013, which caused the Swedish Supreme Court to reverse its case law in a seminal judgment in June 2013. This should be compared with the lengthy procedure in Strasbourg. As is well-known, an application cannot be made to the ECtHR until all domestic remedies have been exhausted. Actually, several cases on the *ne bis in idem* issue in relation to tax offence/tax surcharge, in which persons had exhausted their domestic remedies, were pending against Sweden in the ECtHR at the time when the Supreme Court decided in 2010 and 2011 to uphold its earlier case law, despite the *Zolotukhin* judgment. Owing to the lengthy litigation and waiting time in Strasbourg, it was not until November 2014 that the ECtHR could deliver judgment. At that time, the ECtHR did not find it necessary to decide most of these cases, as the June 2013 Swedish Supreme Court decision based on *Åkerberg Fransson* had made it possible to re-open the proceedings. However, the ECtHR found one case in which the facts made it possible for it to state the ECHR law.

This case is *Lucky Dev v Sweden*.[64] The ECtHR upheld its position that proceedings involving tax surcharges are to be considered 'criminal' for the purposes of the *ne bis in idem* provision in the ECHR.[65] Ms Dev had been tried in court for tax offence, but was finally acquitted before the *Zolotukhin* case was decided. However, the separate tax proceedings had not been terminated, but continued, and she had been imposed a tax surcharge. Relying on the interpretation of the provision in *Zolotukhin*, the ECtHR found that there had been a violation of Article 4 of Protocol No 7.

The Strasbourg decision in *Lucky Dev* is a welcome confirmation of the state of the law on *ne bis in idem* and confirms that the Swedish Supreme

and Poland, have issued a special statement on how the Charter is to be applied in these two Member States. This Protocol does not contain any specific text on *ne bis in idem* and will not be discussed here.

[64] *Lucky Dev v Sweden*, App No 7356/10, judgment 27 November 2014. Swedish court proceedings against Ms Dev had started in 2005, nearly a decade before final judgment in the ECtHR.

[65] See section V above.

Court took the right decision when it reversed its case law. However, the developments just described illustrate very clearly that in areas where the EU fundamental rights law and ECHR law are overlapping, the EU Charter offers the most forceful protection as it is much faster and offers lower courts the opportunity to ask for preliminary references in pending cases. Possibly, the new Protocol No 16 to the ECHR, giving the highest national courts a new option to request the ECtHR to give advisory opinion on questions of principle, might partially change the balance.[66] It is now subject to ratification procedures.

VII. CONCLUDING REMARKS

Åkerberg Fransson has become a seminal case in recent EU law. Like quite a few other cases of that sort over the years, its background is a reference from a local court and the matters at stake in the individual case were of limited economic significance. However, the effects and repercussions of the decision taken by the CJEU in the case are far-reaching and establish the Charter as a legal instrument of particular strength. We now know that the Member States have to observe the Charter provisions not only when they implement legal acts of the EU in a strict sense, but also as soon as the situation at hand is considered to be governed by EU law, although the exact boundaries are still somewhat diffuse. We also know that the Member States are free to apply national standards of fundamental rights protection as a complement only in cases where the action of Member States is not entirely determined by EU law.

Much can be learnt from *Åkerberg Fransson* when it comes to the relationship between the Charter and the ECHR. In its judgment in the case, the CJEU was cautious to safeguard its independent application of the Charter. Although the provisions on *ne bis in idem* are identical in substance in the Charter and the ECHR, the CJEU avoided making any direct references in *Åkerberg Fransson* to the rich case law of the ECHR and, in particular, avoided any mention of the seminal *Zolotukhin* case. In my opinion, this was to go too far, in particular as it is necessary for the courts in the Member States to consider both the Charter and the ECHR, and to evaluate how they interrelate in a given situation.

As has been illustrated, the Charter enjoys a stronger constitutional status in the Member States than the ECHR normally does. The requirement to give full effect to the provisions in the Charter offers no room for a certain

[66] Protocol No 16 to the ECHR, Strasbourg 2.X.2013, Council of Europe Treaty Series No 214, critically assessed by the CJEU in its Opinion 2/13 on the Draft Agreement for the Accession of the EU to the ECHR EU:C:2014:2454 [196]–[199].

amount of leniency and discretion in the national application. Thus, to the extent that Charter and ECHR rules are overlapping, the former can reinforce the latter, provided that EU law is applicable. However, as illustrated by the aftermath of *Åkerberg Fransson*, the influence of the Charter can go beyond the reach of EU law. When, in essence, the CJEU had found the Swedish system of double proceedings and sanctions in tax law to be incompatible with the Charter in relation to an incorrect declaration of VAT, it was no longer possible for the national supreme court to uphold the same system in relation to an incorrect declaration of income tax. This is hardly an isolated case. It will not be easy to uphold practices in purely national law which cannot be applied when EU law is applicable, as they are contrary to Charter provisions.

Finally, as the developments leading up to *Åkerberg Fransson* clearly illustrate, the possibilities for lower courts in the Member States to refer cases to the CJEU for a preliminary ruling and the fairly speedy proceedings in that court add substantially to the particular strength of the Charter as an efficient instrument, in particular in comparison with the system for enforcement of the ECHR as it is presently working. In sum, the conditions for a fast-growing impact of the Charter seem to be present.

8

The Silence of the Charter: Social Rights and the Court of Justice

CATHERINE BARNARD

I. INTRODUCTION*

THE INCORPORATION OF the EU Charter of Fundamental Rights into the EU Treaties was rightly heralded as one of the major constitutional moments in the development of the EU. Although the Court of Justice of the European Union has long recognised the position of fundamental rights as general principles of law, their precise content, status, scope and use was somewhat uncertain. The incorporation of the Charter (may have) changed this. Article 51(1) made clear that the Charter applied to the EU institutions and to the Member States when 'implementing' EU law. The Court of Justice may have taken this even further: in *AMS*,[1] it hinted that certain Charter rights could apply to private parties, particularly Article 21 on non-discrimination, but not Article 27 on information and consultation and possibly the other provisions in the Solidarity Title of the Charter.

The uncertainty generated by *AMS* in respect of the rights in the Solidarity Title reflects a broader ambivalence to social rights. Although the Charter was praised as one of the first documents which placed economic and social rights on the same footing as civil and political rights, in fact that equality is more apparent than real. First, the Charter draws a distinction between rights and principles, with principles being judicially cognisable only in considering any implementing acts. In the UK government's eyes at least, the provisions in the Solidarity Title of the Charter are in fact principles, not rights. Second, Article 1(2) of Protocol 30 suggests that if, contrary to the UK's views, the Solidarity Title of the Charter is found to contain

* Various versions of this chapter have been presented at the seminars on Five Years after the Charter in Oxford, May 2014, the bEUcitizen annual seminar in Istanbul in June 2014 and the Norwegian Labour Law Conference in Brussels in September 2014. I am grateful to the participants for their comments. I am also grateful to Ana Julía Mauricio for her observations on the section concerning Portugal.

[1] Case C-176/12 *AMS* EU:C:2014:2, [2014] ECR I-000.

rights, not principles, then these rights will not apply to the UK and Poland (although this does not prevent the Court ruling that the specific rights are general principles of law which apply to all Member States on the basis of Article 6(3) of the Treaty on European Union (TEU)).[2]

Discussions about all aspects of the Charter have generated a lot of noise; I want to talk about silence. More specifically, I want to examine three contrasting situations of silence in the case law of the Court of Justice in the social field. The first is where the Charter has been raised by the parties, but the Court has refused to hear the arguments. This is a case where, in my view, the silence of the Court is unacceptable. The Court's failure to engage with the Charter issues serves merely to delegitimise the Court and the constitutional guarantees of rights in the eyes of EU citizens. The second situation is where the Court has not raised the Charter in its judgment and I think the Court's silence on the Charter may well be justified. The third case is where the Charter is very much in evidence, but reference to the Charter has, in fact, clouded, not clarified the analysis. In this situation I think the Court should be (more) silent about the Charter.

I will refer to these three situations respectively as:

(i) a vow of silence;
(ii) a welcome silence; and
(iii) a plea for silence.

I will examine these three situations in turn.

II. A VOW OF SILENCE

A. Introduction

There have already been a number of references to the Court of Justice on the question of whether reforms to national labour law (introduced by states as part of the agreement with the EU/International Monetary Fund (IMF)/European Central Bank (ECB) troika to receive 'bailout' funds) are

[2] This assumes that Protocol 30 is not a general opt-out for the UK and Poland from the Charter, as was claimed at the time. The UK Coalition government has since conceded that the Protocol is not an opt-out, a fact recorded by Lord Neuberger in *Saeedi* [2010] EWCA Civ 1990: '8. Contrary to the Judge's holding, the Secretary of State accepts, in principle, that fundamental rights set out in the Charter can be relied on as against the United Kingdom, and submits that the Judge erred in holding otherwise (judgment, paragraphs 155 and 157, first sentence).' The Court of Justice has confirmed that Art 1(1) of Protocol 30 is not an opt-out: Case C-411/10 *NS v Secretary of State for the Home Department* EU:C:2011:865. See also House of Commons, European Scrutiny Committee report, *The Application of the EU Charter of Fundamental Rights in the UK: A State of Confusion*, 2013–14, 11.

compatible with the Charter.[3] In all such cases, the Court has found the reference inadmissible. The Court's reluctance to hear such cases is, in some ways, understandable. The stakes are high. On the one hand, huge sums of money are involved— possibly the future of the Economic and Monetary Union (EMU) project as we know it—were the Court to find a breach of the Charter. On the other hand, national labour standards are at issue, matters which, as part of the original settlement of the Treaty of Rome, were to be delivered at Member State level.[4]

I seek to argue that these considerations point to discretion on the part of the Court, but not total silence. I would argue that the curt dismissal of the claims challenging the troika-backed reforms to national labour standards in the 'bailout' countries (and other countries in receipt of financial assistance), on the grounds that this is not a matter for EU law, overlooks the EU origins of the reforms and thus the EU law element of the case. If this view is correct, then the question is what approach might the Court take to deal with Charter-based challenges to troika reforms. I will examine these two issues by looking at the litigation brought challenging the Portuguese labour law reforms.

B. The Case of Portugal

When Portugal received its 'bailout' (ie, loan) from the troika in May 2011,[5] it committed itself to a range of measures in the Memorandum of Understanding (MoU),[6] including reforms to large tracts of its labour law, including its dismissal rules. Up to €26 billion was to come to Portugal from the European Financial Stabilisation Mechanism (EFSM). The EFSM was adopted under Regulation 407/2010.[7] Article 3(3) of Regulation 407/2010 requires not only that the decision to grant a loan should contain details

[3] See, eg, Case C-434/11 *Corpul Național al Polițiștilor v Ministerul Administrației și Internelor (MAI) and others* EU:C:2011:830, [2011] ECR I-196*; Case C-134/12 *Ministerul Administrației și Internelor (MAI), Inspectoratul General al Poliției Române (IGPR) and Inspectoratul de Poliție al Județului Tulcea (IPJ) v Corpul Național al Polițiștilor—Biroul Executiv Central* EU:C:2012:288, [2012] ECR I-000 More generally, the Court has refused to hear references on the compatibilty with the Charter of reforms to national labour law: Order in Case C-361/07 *Polier* EU:C:2008;16.[13], even where there were some links with, eg, EU funding: Case C-117/14 *Poclava v Ariza Toeldano* (2015), judgment of 5 February.

[4] See, eg, C Barnard, *EU Employment Law*, 4th edn (Oxford, Oxford University Press, 2012) ch 5; J Kenner, *EU Employment Law: From Rome to Amsterdam and Beyond* (Oxford, Hart Publishing, 2003).

[5] http://ec.europa.eu/economy_finance/assistance_eu_ms/portugal/index_en.htm.

[6] http://ec.europa.eu/economy_finance/eu_borrower/mou/2011-05-18-mou-portugal_en.pdf.

[7] [2010] OJ L118/1. Since 2013 the ESM Treaty has applied. This is an agreement between Member States which raises more complex issues for the application of the Charter.

about the amount and average maturity of the loan, but also that the decision must contain provisions on conditionality, namely:

> [T]he general economic policy conditions which are attached to the Union financial assistance with a view to re-establishing a sound economic or financial situation in the beneficiary Member State and to restoring its capacity to finance itself on the financial markets; these conditions will be defined by the Commission, in consultation with the ECB; and
>
> an approval of the adjustment programme prepared by the beneficiary Member State to meet the economic conditions attached to the Union financial assistance.

Article 3(5) of the Regulation requires the Commission and the beneficiary Member State to conclude an MoU detailing the general economic policy conditions laid down by the Council. Portugal's MoU[8] contained a number of commitments. These included ensuring that 'the aggregate public sector wage bill as a share of GDP decreases in 2012 and 2013'. This was to be done by, inter alia, 'Freez[ing] wages in the government sector in nominal terms in 2012 and 2013 and constrain[ing] promotions' and reducing 'pensions above EUR 1,500 according to the progressive rates applied to the wages of the public sector *as of January 2011*, with the aim of yielding savings of at least EUR 445 million'.[9] This reference to the rates applied to public sector wages concerns the Lei do Orçamento do Estado para 2011 (the budget law which pre-dated the bailout),[10] Chapter III of which made special provision for public sector workers. Article 19 was headed 'pay reduction'. Article 19(1) provided for a 3.5 per cent pay cut for monthly salaries of between €1,500 and €2,000 and a 10 per cent cut on salaries above €4,165.[11] These pay cuts were unsuccessfully challenged before the Portuguese Constitutional Court.[12]

The Council adopted Implementing Decision 2011/344/EU granting EU financial assistance to Portugal. The MoU is expressly referred to in Article 1(4) of the Decision:

> The first instalment shall be released subject to the entry into force of the Loan Facility Agreement and the Memorandum of Understanding. Any subsequent loan releases shall be conditional upon a favourable review by the Commission, in consultation with the ECB, of Portugal's compliance with the general economic policy conditions as defined by this Decision and the Memorandum of Understanding.

[8] http://ec.europa.eu/economy_finance/eu_borrower/mou/2011-05-18-mou-portugal_en.pdf.

[9] Paragraphs 1.9–1.12 (emphasis added).

[10] http://sifide.adi.pt/arq/fich/Lei_n.__55-A_2010.pdf.

[11] Those receiving between €2,000 and €4,165 were subject to proportional cuts of between 3.5% and 10%.

[12] Acórdão nº 396/2011, *Diário da República, 2.ª série—Nº 199—17 de Outubro de 2011*, http://dre.pt/pdf2sdip/2011/10/199000000/4109641106.pdf.

Article 3(5) of the Decision refers to the 2011 budget. It provides that:

> Portugal shall implement fully the fiscal consolidation measures foreseen in the 2011 budget amounting to around EUR 9 billion and additional measures introduced before May 2011 worth more than EUR 400 million.

In Case C-128/12 *Sindicatos dos Bancários do Norte*,[13] the pay cuts envisaged by the 2011 budget were challenged in the Portuguese court, which referred various questions to the Court of Justice, including:

> 2. Is the salary cut made by the State, by means of the Lei do Orçamento do Estado para 2011, applicable only to persons employed in the public sector or by a public undertaking, contrary to the principle of prohibition of discrimination in that it discriminates on the basis of the public nature of the employment relationship?
> 3. Must the right to working conditions that respect dignity, laid down in Article 31(1) of the Charter of Fundamental Rights of the European Union, be interpreted as meaning that it is unlawful to make salary cuts without the employee's consent, if the contract of employment is not first altered to that effect?

The Court of Justice, however, refused to answer any of the questions referred. It began by noting the limits to the application of the Charter laid down by Article 51(1), namely that it applied only when Member States were implementing EU law and that the Charter did not create any new competences. It then said:

> 12. Or, malgré les doutes exprimés par la juridiction de renvoi quant à la conformité de la loi de finances pour 2011 avec les principes et les objectifs consacrés par les traités, la décision de renvoi ne contient aucun élément concret permettant de considérer que ladite loi vise à mettre en œuvre le droit de l'Union.[14]

Thus, given that the reference contained no indication as to why the national law was implementing EU law, the Court said it had no competence to respond to the question referred.

If the Court had wanted to hear the case, it could have followed *Akerberg Fransson*,[15] where it said: 'Since the fundamental rights guaranteed by the Charter must therefore be complied with where national legislation falls within the scope of European Union law, situations cannot exist which are covered in that way by European Union law without those fundamental rights being applicable.' The Court could therefore have found that, given the link between the EFSM Regulation, the MOU, Decision 2011/344/EU

[13] Case C-128/12 *Sindicatos dos Bancários do Norte* EU:C:2013:149, order of the Court of 7 March 2013.

[14] The Order is available only in French and Portuguese.

[15] Case C-617/10 *Åklagaren v Hans Åkerberg Fransson* EU:C:2013:105.

and the Lei do Orçamento do Estado para 2011, Portugal was acting within the scope of EU law and so the Charter should apply.

Yet, the Court refused to follow this reasoning.[16] This may have been because it thought that the links between the EU measures and the budget law had not been sufficiently articulated (for example, were pay cuts actually required?). Or it may have been because the budget law pre-dated the bailout. Or it may have been that it simply did not want to hear the case.

Following Case C-264/12 *Sindicato Nacional dos Profissionais de Seguros e Afins*,[17] the view that the Court does not want to hear the case looks increasingly likely. This case concerned the 2012 budget,[18] the first budget adopted by the new government (now composed of the Social-Democratic Party and the Popular Party, replacing the Socialist Party) after the bailout programme had been agreed to. This budget went further than its 2011 predecessor and required, in Article 21, the suspension of the thirteenth and fourteenth month salary as an 'exceptional measure of budgetary stability' for three years.[19] In this case, a question was referred to the Court of Justice on the compatibility of this measure with the Charter.[20] Once again, the Court refused to hear the case on the ground that it was 'manifestement incompétente' to respond to the question referred.

Meanwhile, various Portuguese MPs challenged the 2012 budget, including Article 21, before the Portuguese Constitutional Court. On 5 July 2012 the Constitutional Court delivered its decision,[21] finding that Article 21 (and Article 25, which imposed similar rules on pensioners) violated the principle of equal treatment under the Portuguese Constitution. Controversially, however, it suspended its decision since the budget had already been in force for more than six months and the decision risked jeopardising continued troika financing.[22]

The budget for 2013 maintained most of the cuts.[23] Once again, the Portuguese Constitutional Court declared the budget unconstitutional for

[16] For potential criticism and an indication that a future court might decide differently, see K Lenaerts, 'EMU and the European Union's Constitutional Framework' (2014) 39 *EL Rev* 753.

[17] EU:C:2014:2036.

[18] Diário da República, 1ª série—N.º 250—30 de Dezembro de 2011, www.dre.pt/pdf1s/2011/12/25001/0004800244.pdf.

[19] Article 21.

[20] The relevant question referred asked: is the non-payment by the state of previously due holiday and Christmas allowances, by means of the Lei do Orçamento do Estado para 2012, applicable only to persons employed in the public sector or by a public undertaking, contrary to the principle of prohibition of discrimination in that it discriminates on the basis of the public nature of the employment relationship?

[21] Acordão 353/2012, Diário da República, 1ª série—Nº 140—20 de julho de 2012, https://dre.pt/pdf1sdip/2012/07/14000/0384603863.pdf.

[22] The Court said that meeting the deficit targets for 2012 was an exceptionally important public interest, which is one of the constitutional reasons for the Court to restrict the scope of the effects of a declaration of unconstitutionality. See Art 282(4) of the Constitution. See further www.mjilonline.org/wordpress/wp-content/uploads/2013/07/Pires.pdf.

[23] Diário da República, 1ª série—Nº 252—31 de dezembro de 2012, http://dre.pt/pdf1s/2012/12/25201/0004200240.pdf. Articles 28 and 29 of the Budget Law (2013) no longer suspended

breaches of the principle of equality. This time, however, it did not suspend the effect of its judgment.[24] The same happened in 2014[25] in respect of the 2014 budget, albeit that the focus of this decision was on different measures.[26] The decisions of the Portuguese Constitional Court have left EU officials expressing their frustration with judicial interference with the Portuguese reform programme.[27]

Yet, from the perspective of the protection of human rights and the rule of law, it is surely right that there should be some review of troika-inspired reforms. As we have seen, so far the Portuguese Court has been doing the constitutional legwork, not the Court of Justice. The Greek Constitutional Court has been doing the same.[28] In the short term, this has the benefit of subsidiarity—national courts striking down provisions of national law. However, it overlooks the European context in which these decisions are taken.[29] Eventually, the Court of Justice will have to recognise this when it is finally faced with a better-worded question which more effectively makes the link between the national reforms and EU law—and when it develops an appetite for hearing these difficult cases.

A revolution in the Court's attitude may be some time in coming if the views of the Commission, expressed in the somewhat different context of Greece, are in any way representative of the thinking of the EU institutions. The UN Special Rapporteur Cephas Lumina said that the austerity measures being taken by the Greek government as part of the fiscal adjustment programme were undermining the protection of the fundamental rights enshrined in international UN Conventions and the EU Charter.[30] In its

the payment of the Christmas subsidy (thirteenth salary), but still suspended the payment of the holiday subsidy and other similar ones (fourteenth salary).

[24] Acórdão do Tribunal Constitucional n° 187/2013, Diário da República, 1ª série—N° 78—22 de abril de 2013, http://dre.pt/pdf1sdip/2013/04/07800/0232802423.pdf.

[25] Acórdão do Tribunal Constitucional n° 413/2014, www.tribunalconstitucional.pt/tc/acordaos/20140413.html.

[26] Lei n° 83-C/2013, de 31 de dezembro de 2013, que aprova o Orçamento do Estado para 2014. Article 33(1): cuts for those earning more than €675: progressive tax between 2.5% and 12% for salaries between €675 and €2,000; and 12% for salaries above €2,000, https://dre.pt/pdf1s/2013/12/25301/0005800295.pdf. Article 33 was one of the Articles that was declared unconstitutional by the Constitutional Court because it violated the principle of equality.

[27] www.theportugalnews.com/news/head-of-constitutional-court-dismisses-insinuations-of-bias/31770; P Wise and S Gordon, 'Legal Roadblocks on Lisbon's Fiscal Path', *Financial Times* (16 June 2014) 8.

[28] Portugal is not alone; see, eg, 'Court Cases Threaten Greek Overhaul' *International New York Times* (13 June 2014) 1.

[29] Martinho Lucas Pires, 'Private versus Public or State versus Europe? A Portuguese Constitutional Tale', www.mjilonline.org/wordpress/wp-content/uploads/2013/07/Pires.pdf.

[30] Report on the effects of foreign debt and other related international financial obligations of states on the full enjoyment of all human rights, particularly economic, social and cultural rights, Addendum, Mission to Greece, UN A/HRC/25/50/Add.1.

response to a parliamentary question about Cephas Lumina's criticism,[31] the Commission said that it was:

> [C]ommitted to ensuring that, when EU law applies, CFREU rights will be respected. However, as regards [adjustment] programme documents [such as the MoUs], we are not dealing with EU law but with instruments that have been agreed between Greece and its creditors: consequently, the Charter cannot be invoked.

The Commission continued that it was up to Greece to ensure its international obligations regarding fundamental rights are upheld. That said the ECtHR has declared that the specific measures taken by the Greek authorities are not in breach of the ECHR.[32]

C. How Might the Court Decide Such Cases?

It seems that we may be waiting some time for a question about the compatibility of bailout conditionality with the Charter to be considered in detail by the Court of Justice. But if (and when) it does come, how might the Court decide any such case? There are various approaches it might take. The first is to conduct a substantive review of the national implementing measure. This seems both unlikely and undesirable. The Court lacks the contextual knowledge enjoyed by the national court of how national social systems work. It also risks exceeding its judicial function by making assessments of how budget cuts could be better made. So, if the Court has the appetite for a substantive review, it might be better to do so only where, using the language of Article 52(1) of the Charter, the 'essence of the right' has been infringed.[33] This would be the exception rather than the norm.[34] More likely, and in my view more feasibly, would be the Court insisting that certain procedural safeguards be put in place.[35] For example, it might insist that the measures have gone through national parliamentary processes;[36] that, where relevant, the social partners have been consulted/involved in the process (they were in the case of Portugal and one main trade union did agree); and that a social

[31] www.europarl.europa.eu/sides/getDoc.do?pubRef=-//EP//TEXT+WQ+E-2014-005633+0+DOC+XML+V0//EN.

[32] I am grateful to Fotis Vergis for the translation of this document from the Greek.

[33] See also Case C-544/10 *Deutsche Weintour v Land Rheinland-Pfalz* [2012] ECR I-000 [54]; Case C-426/11 *Alemo-Herron v Parkwood Leisure Ltd* [2013] ECR I-000 [36].

[34] See, by way of analogy, the European Court of Human Rights' approach in *Valkov and others v Bulgaria* App Nos 2033/04 et al, judgment of 25 October 2011 [91].

[35] Cases C-92/09 and C-93/09 *Volker and Schecke v Land Hessen* [2010] ECR I-000 [81]; Case C-269/90 *Hauptzollamt Muenchen-Mitte v Hauptzollamt München-Mitte* [1991] ECR I-5469 [13]–[14] and [20]–[22].

[36] *Koufaki and Adedy v Greece* App Nos 57665/12 and 57657/12, decision of 7 May 2013 [31].

impact assessment has been made of the measures (this would be a way of ensuring the realisation of the social mainstreaming provisions in Article 9 of the Treaty on the Functioning of the European Union (TFEU)).[37] In this way, the Court might square the circle of ensuring a degree of EU judicial control over what is being done, in the name of the EU, while respecting the discretionary and largely political nature of the policy choices being made.

III. A WELCOME SILENCE

So far we have listened to the sounds of silence: the situation where, in my view, the Court's silence on the matter of the Charter is unjustifiable. Its self-restraint has effectively left EU citizens without any access to review at EU level. I want now to turn to the second situation, where the Court has not raised the Charter in the particular area and where I think the Court's silence on the Charter is justified. This is the case of the Posted Workers Directive (PWD) 96/71, as interpreted by the Court in the leading cases of *Laval*, *Rüffert* and *Luxembourg*.[38] In essence, the PWD requires *host* states to apply a 'nucleus of mandatory rules for minimum protection' in the areas listed in Article 3(1)(a)–(g) PWD (eg, restrictions on working time, minimum rates of pay, conditions on the hiring-out of workers, health and safety, protection of pregnant workers and those who have recently given birth and equality legislation) to posted workers, that is, to workers temporarily posted to another Member State to work under Article 56 TFEU on the free movement of services. The application of any host state rule to posted workers appears to go against the grain of both Article 8(2) of the Rome I Regulation and Article 56 TFEU, which advocate home, not host, state control. There was thus a risk that Article 3(1) PWD was ultra vires Article 56 TFEU.

In the *Laval* line of case law, the Court avoided finding the Directive incompatible with Article 56 TFEU, but at the price of ensuring a strict application of the rules and conditions in the PWD. So we now know that Article 3(1)(a)–(g) PWD contains an exhaustive list of rules which the host state must apply to posted workers, provided: (1) those rules exist in its state; (2) there is transparent information about the host state's requirements; and (3) the provisions of Article 3(1) and 3(8) PWD are satisfied to the letter. The Court has also interpreted the two exceptions to Article 3(1)

[37] See further European Commission President Juncker, 'A New Start for Europe: My Agenda for Jobs, Growth, Fairness and Democratic Change', http://ec.europa.eu/priorities/docs/pg_en.pdf, 20.

[38] Case C-341/05 *Laval un Partneri Ltd v Svenska Byggnadsarbetareförbundet* [2007] ECR I-11767; Case C-346/06 *Rechtsanwalt Dr Dirk Rüffert v Land Niedersachsen* [2008] ECR I–1989; Case C-319/06 *Commission v Luxembourg* [2008] ECR I-4323.

(namely Article 3(7) and 3(10) PWD) restrictively (in essence viewing them as exceptions to the exceptions in Article 3(1)).

The decisions in the *Laval* line of case law were deeply unpopular, particularly with Northern European trade unions. However, I think the Court's approach to the interpretation of the PWD can be justified. It delicately upheld the balance struck by the legislature between the competing interests of: (1) home and host states; and (2) posted workers (and their employers) and host state workers.[39]

The Charter was not mentioned in any of the cases on the interpretation of Article 3(1)(a)–(g) PWD. Would reference to the Charter have made any difference? I think not—and nor should it. If the Charter had been cited, the relevant provisions would presumably have been Article 16 on the freedom to conduct a business, which would have to be balanced against Article 31 on fair and just working conditions. Yet, the (democratically elected) legislature has already conducted that balance when negotiating and adopting the PWD: it decided that posted workers would enjoy equal treatment with host state workers in respect of terms and conditions in the areas listed in Article 3(1)(a)–(g) PWD (Article 31 prevails); however, posting employers could enjoy the competitive advantage derived from being established in an economy with lower labour costs in respect of other terms and conditions (Aticle 16 prevails). The legislative compromise encapsulated in the PWD might not be the one that the Court (nor the Northern European trade unions) like, but it is the compromise that the legislature came to. And it would ill behove the Court to second guess the legislature, using the rhetoric of balancing under the Charter, to produce a different outcome.

The Court has not done so—and, in my view, rightly so. Indeed, there are signs that it is reluctant to allow Article 16 of the Charter to be invoked separately from Article 56 TFEU. For example, in the freedom of establishment case *Sokoll-Seebacher*,[40] the Court said:

> 22. That reference to European Union law must be understood as meaning that Article 16 of the Charter refers, inter alia, to Article 49 TFEU, which guarantees the fundamental freedom of establishment.
> 23. In those circumstances and given that the questions referred concern the freedom of establishment only, the national legislation at issue in the main proceedings should be assessed with regard to Article 49 TFEU alone.

This suggests that there is no role for Article 16 of the Charter where the Treaty is already in play, as it is in the case of posting where there is a strong Treaty presumption in favour of home state control.

[39] C Barnard, 'The protection of fundamental social right after Lisbon: A Question of Conflicts of Interests' in S de Vries, U Bernitz and S Weatherill (eds), *The Protection of Fundamental Rights in the EU After Lisbon* (Oxford, Hart Publishing, 2013).

[40] Case C–367/12 *Sokoll-Seebacher* [2014] ECR I-000.

There is a further, less benevolent reason why the Court should stay silent about the Charter: it might get the balancing exercise wrong. In *Alemo-Herron*,[41] the Court did apply the Charter to a social policy case, but in an asymmetrical way, with the result that economic interests were prioritised over social interests. The case raised the question whether Article 3(3) of (what is now) Directive 2001/23 on transfer of undertakings[42] required a (private sector) transferee to apply the revised terms of a (public sector) collective agreement whose negotiation it had not been—and could not be—involved with. The Court said that the interpretation of the Directive had to 'comply with Article 16 of the Charter, laying down the freedom to conduct a business'.[43] It continued: 'That fundamental right covers, inter alia, freedom of contract.' No reference was made to any of the social provisions in the Solidarity Title—such as Article 31 on fair and just working conditions, as a counterweight. It then said that, by reason of the freedom to conduct a business, the transferee had to be able to assert its interests effectively in a contractual process to which it was party.[44] Because the transferee was unable to participate in the relevant collective bargaining body, it could neither assert its interests effectively in a contractual process nor negotiate the aspects determining changes in working conditions for its employees with a view to its future economic activity.[45] The Court concluded:

> In those circumstances, the transferee's contractual freedom is seriously reduced to the point that such a limitation is liable to adversely affect the very essence of its freedom to conduct a business.

While the outcome of the case was not surprising at a European level[46] given the earlier decision of *Werhof*,[47] the fact is that the asymmetrical application of the Charter resulted in an entirely pro-employer reading of one of the EU's earliest 'pure' social policy measures without any consideration of the countervailing social interests.[48] It thus turned upside down the interpretation of Directive 2001/23. It is for this reason that I welcome the Court's silence on the Charter in respect of the balancing under Article 3(1)(a)–(g) PWD.[49]

[41] Case C-426/11 Alemo-Heron EU:C:2013:521.
[42] [2001] OJ L82/16.
[43] ibid [31].
[44] ibid [33].
[45] ibid [34].
[46] Although *cf* the Supreme Court's view in *Parkwood v Alemo-Herron* [2011] UKSC 26 [47]: 'The matter depends entirely on the domestic law of contract, under which parties are at liberty to agree to abide by agreements arrived at by a process in which they do not, and are not required to, participate.'
[47] Case C-499/04 *Werhof* EU:C:2006:168, [2006] ECR I-2397.
[48] S Weatherill (2014) 10 *European Review of Contract Law* 167.
[49] In Case C-396/13 *Sähköalojen ammattiliitto v Elektrobdowa* [2015] ECR I-000 [26], a case about the PWD, the Charter was considered by the Court, but only in the context of the locus standi of trade unions and not on the key points about Art 3(1)(a)–(g) PWD.

IV. A PLEA FOR SILENCE

So far we have considered: (1) the situation where the Court has been silent about the Charter, but where I think it should not have been; and (2) the opposite situation, where the Court has been silent about the Charter and where I think this is justifiable. I want now to consider my third and final situation: where the Court has been been anything but silent about the Charter, but I think it should have been. This is because I think a rights analysis obscures the main issues. This is my most controversial category. The situation I have in mind is mandatory retirement and age discrimination.

A. Retirement and Age Discrimination: The Legal Position

The principle of equality has long been regarded as a fundamental right by the Court of Justice.[50] This has now been confirmed by Article 21 of the Charter. However, discrimination on the grounds of age has always been considered as somewhat different. The concrete legislative manifestation of this difference is the fact that, unlike the other protected categories, both direct and indirect age discrimination can be objectively justified. Article 6 of Directive 2000/78 provides:

> Notwithstanding Article 2(2), Member States may provide that differences of treatment on grounds of age shall not constitute discrimination, if, *within the context of national law*, they are *objectively and reasonably* justified by a legitimate aim, including legitimate *employment policy, labour market and vocational training* objectives, and if the means of achieving that aim are appropriate and necessary. (Emphasis added)

Such differences of treatment may include '(a) the setting of special conditions on access to employment and vocational training, employment and occupation, including dismissal and remuneration conditions, for young people, older workers and persons with caring responsibilities in order to promote their vocational integration or ensure their protection'.

The majority of cases that have gone to the Court of Justice have concerned mandatory retirement schemes. The general tenor of the Court's case law has been that the schemes are directly discriminatory, but that: (1) they can be objectively justified; and (2) they are probably proportionate.

As far as the *justifications* are concerned, the Court has variously recognised that employers need to:

- strike a balance between political, social, economic, demographic and/or budgetary considerations (*Rosenbladt*);[51]

[50] See, eg, Case 149/77 *Defrenne v Sabena (No 3)* [1978] ECR I-1365 [27].
[51] Case C–45/09 *Rosenbladt v Oellerking Gebäudereinigungsges mbH* [2010] ECR I–9391.

— engage in workforce planning *(Georgiev)*;[52]
— ensure intergenerational fairness (essentially the prevention of 'job blocking' by older workers, thereby providing opportunities for the recruitment and retention of younger workers (*Palacios*[53] and *Rosenbladt, Fuchs*));[54]
— protect dignity at work, avoiding the need to performance manage long-serving employees, avoiding disputes over fitness to work (*Fuchs*) and
— ensuring a high quality of service and continued competence (*Petersen*[55] and *Fuchs*).

As far as *proportionality* is concerned, the Court has tended to find the retirement age proportionate provided:

— it is set at a reasonably high level (in *Petersen* the age was set at 68);
— the retiree will receive a pension (*Palacios* and *Rosenbladt*); and
— the employer gives specific consideration to individual cases (*Andersen*[56]).

While most Member States have retained (justified) retirement ages in some form, the UK abolished the so-called default retirement age (DRA) for all workers in 2011.[57] For some employers, this has posed considerable problems and a few, notably the Universities of Oxford and Cambridge, have introduced an Employer Justified Retirement Age (EJRA). The EJRA is essentially a mandatory retirement age which operates like the DRA, justified on the grounds of Article 6 of Directive 2000/78 as interpreted by the Court.[58]

I am broadly supportive of the Court's approach to justification and proportionality. I would like to see more flexibilty applied in respect of the proportionality review, creating space for employers, in negotiation with their staff and the trade unions, to come up with a solution best suited to their needs. But generally I think the Court has got the balance about right. My concern is that the application of the Charter may upset this carefully balanced apple cart.

[52] Joined Cases C-250/09 and C-268/09 *Georgiev v Tehnicheski universitet—Sofia, filial Plovdiv* [2010] ECR I-11869.

[53] Case C-411/05 *Palacios de la Villa v Cortefiel Servicios SA* [2007] ECR I–8531.

[54] Joined Cases C-159/10 and C-160/10 *Fuchs and Köhler v Land Hessen* [2011] ECR I-6919.

[55] Case C-341/08 *Domnica Petersen v Berufungsausschuss für Zahnärzte für den Bezirk Westfalen-Lippe Zahnärzte* [2010] ECR I-47.

[56] Case C-499/08 *Ingeniørforeningen i Danmark, acting on behalf of Ole Andersen v Region Syddanmark* [2010] ECR I-09343.

[57] It is thought that employers can still have their own DRA provided it is justified and proportionate, a test whose vagueness is such that it has deterred all but a very few (including the Universities of Oxford and Cambridge) from using it.

[58] See C Barnard and S Deakin, 'Age Discrimination and Labour Law in the UK: Managing Ageing' in M Rönnmar and A Numhauser-Henning (eds), *Age Discrimination and Labour Law*, forthcoming.

B. The Problem with a Rights-Based Analysis

Retirement is a sensitive issue. In many high-skilled, high-paid professional jobs, people do not want to retire. Yet, if they carry on working in a closed system with a limited number of posts, they may be depriving younger workers of a job or a promotion. In some sectors, notably universities, retirement is thus an important way of creating opportunities for younger—and often more diverse—staff. Yes, the retirement of senior professors can be facilitated with financial incentives, but this may be an unattractive option in straitened times. Alternatively, individuals can be performance-managed out, although this can be time-consuming for those involved and degrading to the individual (and probably unlawful if performance management is applied only to older workers). Mandatory retirement—subject to the provisos that the age is set at a sufficiently high level, individual circumstances are taken into account and the individual has an adequate pension to fall back on—may still be the best solution.

But what if older workers do not want to retire? There is a range of Charter rights on which they may wish to rely:

- the right to engage in work (Article 15);
- the right to be treated with dignity (Article 1);
- the right not to be discriminated against on the ground of age (Article 21).

Yet, these are the very same rights that younger workers would also rely on to justify having access to employment. And the Court has encouraged the use of such arguments. In *Kücükdeveci*,[59] the first post-Lisbon case after the Charter came into force, the Court said:

> It should also be noted that Article 6(1) TEU provides that the Charter of Fundamental Rights of the European Union is to have the same legal value as the Treaties. Under Article 21(1) of the Charter, '[a]ny discrimination based on ... age ... shall be prohibited'.

And, as we saw above, the importance of Article 21—and its potential application even in a horizontal situaiton—was emphasised by the Court in *AMS*.

In subsequent age discriminaiton cases, the Court has focused more on the Article 15 right to work. So, for example, in *Hörnfeldt*,[60] it said:

> The prohibition of discrimination on grounds of age set out in Directive 2000/78 must be read in the light of the right to engage in work recognised in Article 15(1) of the Charter of Fundamental Rights of the European Union. It follows that

[59] Case C-555/07 *Seda Kücükdeveci v Swedex GmbH & Co KG* [2010] ECR I-365.

[60] Case C-141/11 *Hörnfeldt v Posten Meddelande AB* EU:C:2012:421. See also *Fuchs and Köhler* (n 54) [62] and [63].

> particular attention must be paid to the participation of older workers in the labour force, and thus in economic, cultural and social life. Keeping older workers in the labour force promotes diversity in the workforce, which is an aim recognised in recital 25 in the preamble to Directive 2000/78. Furthermore, it contributes to the realising of their potential and to the quality of life of the workers concerned, in accordance with the concerns of the European Union legislature set out in recitals 8, 9 and 11 in the preamble to that directive.

So whose right should prevail—those of the older or the younger worker? Traditional labour law principles do not help here. There is no obviously weaker party: this is not the case of pitting worker against employer (weak versus strong) but worker against worker (weak versus weak).[61] And since both younger and older workers wish to invoke the same rights, for me framing age discrimination in terms of human rights obfuscates rather than clarifies what are deeply difficult issues. For this reason, I would call for silence about the Charter and rights, and a rethinking of how the competing interests might be reconciled.

C. Resolving the Problem

In the context of retirement, I would argue that what is really at stake is not human rights (except in the broadest sense), but the question who has the greatest need of access to the labour market. In fact, Directive 2000/78 itself locates the discrimination issue in the wider labour market context. The Preamble to Directive 2000/78 provides:

> 8. The Employment Guidelines for 2000 agreed by the European Council at Helsinki on 10 and 11 December 1999 stress the need to foster a labour market favourable to social integration by formulating a coherent set of policies aimed at combating discrimination against groups such as persons with disability. They also emphasise the need to pay particular attention to supporting older workers, in order to increase their participation in the labour force.
> 9. Employment and occupation are key elements in guaranteeing equal opportunities for all and contribute strongly to the full participation of citizens in economic, cultural and social life and to realising their potential.

The 25th recital expresses similar sentiments: 'The prohibition of age discrimination is an essential part of meeting the aims set out in the Employment Guidelines and encouraging diversity in the workforce.' It goes on to recognise that 'differences in treatment in connection with age may be

[61] *cf* E Dewhurst, 'Intergenerational Balance, Mandatory Retirement and Age Discrimination in Europe: How Can the ECJ Better Support National Courts in Finding a Balance between the Generations?' (2013) 50 *CML Rev* 1333.

justified under certain circumstances and therefore require specific provisions which may vary in accordance with the situation in Member States. It is therefore essential to distinguish between differences in treatment which are justified, in particular by legitimate employment policy, labour market and vocational training objectives, and discrimination which must be prohibited'.

If the question is framed in terms of 'who has greater need for access to the labour market', the answer to the question how to balance the competing interests may become more obvious (ie the rights of the younger worker). Apart from at the highest level of generality and abstraction, human rights do not feed into this debate. For this reason, I am concerned about the increasing use of human rights language in the vexed context of retirement age. If reference to the Charter and human rights language serves as a bridge between age discrimination and the other protected characteristics, fine, but I do not think that human rights speak really illuminates the underlying policy issues. It is for this reason I am calling for silence in (the) Court about the Charter and rights.

V. CONCLUSIONS

The language of human rights serves an important legitimising function in the evolving EU legal order. I am not denying the significance of human rights: as my first situation shows (the potential to review conditionality provisions attached to 'bailout' loans), I think the Court should address the human rights questions raised. I am not advocating unnecessary garrulousness on the Charter, but a nuanced and careful reflection on how the Charter might apply. For this reason, I would argue that the Court's self-imposed vow of silence on the Charter needs to be broken.

The logical corollary to my first point is that human rights arguments should not serve as a make-weight or as general ornamentation in each case. Careful consideration needs to be given as to what added value human rights might offer. In my second situation (the case of the PWD), I think none at all. The legislature has done the balancing and the Court of Justice should not disturb that equilibrium through the use of the Charter. For this reason, I welcome the Court's continued silence on the Charter.

In my third situation, the case of mandatory retirement, I have argued that the rights language obfuscates the main issue. Like chilli powder in cooking, rights can be powerful when deployed effectively, but overwhelming and muddling when they are not. This, I have argued, is the case with applying human rights to the difficult question of retirement age. For this reason, I would plead for silence on the Charter in this case.

Silence can sometimes be golden—but not always.

9

Much Ado About Nothing?

How the EU Charter of Fundamental Rights Could Challenge Prevailing Notions of Territorial Rights and Solidarity as Regards National Social Security Systems

JAAN PAJU

I. THE SOCIAL RIGHTS SET OUT IN THE EU CHARTER OF FUNDAMENTAL RIGHTS

SOCIAL RIGHTS LIKE social security[1] and social assistance are characterised as positive rights in a fundamental right context. Positive rights—as opposed to negative rights where a state will refrain from infringing rights—assume that a state will guarantee certain foreseen freedoms and rights. Guaranteeing social rights 'costs', since the rights are based on a social policy and welfare models, which are funded via both taxes and social fees that are paid within a state by a group of entitled people (*ratione personae*) regulated in national legislation.

Unlike political freedoms and rights, which to a large extent are understood in the same way in all Member States, views diverge as regards the position and essence of social rights.[2] Moreover, the construction and scope of the welfare systems differ between Member States due to various parameters like social development, political outlook and financial resources.

[1] In the EU context, the material scope of the notion of social security is defined by Regulation 883/2004, which regulates eg family benefits, sickness and care benefits, and old-age benefits in cross-border situations. See further Regulation (EC) No 883/2004 of the European Parliament and of the Council of 29 April 2004 on the coordination of social security systems [2004] OJ L166, 1–123.

[2] The Member States' views on social security as a fundamental right differ; in some, social security is enshrined in the constitution, while in others, like Sweden, the view is taken that social security cannot be regarded as a fundamental right, but instead is determined by the political choices of a state, which may change over time.

Social rights have furthermore been regulated at different levels in the Member States depending on constitutional traditions and political views.[3]

In an EU legal context, social rights have been regarded as an internal matter for the Member States because of the costs involved and because social rights are regulated and perceived differently in the various Member States. Until the ratification of the EU Charter of Fundamental Rights (hereinafter 'the Charter'), social rights therefore have languished in the EU unless they have figured in an internal market context where they have been a complement to and have reinforced the free movement of workers.[4] A broader agenda as regards social rights has not been developed in the EU context since Member States have decided not to relinquish any general competence. Instead, the EU's social dimension has developed slowly and often in a roundabout way over time.[5]

The question that this chapter aims to answer is whether the Charter will change this relationship and whether an independent EU legal social right as regards social security will emerge. Are we talking about a social right which is a complement to *or* challenges the current EU legal coordination of the social security systems of the Member States?

The chapter gives a short discussion of the background to the coordination of the national social security systems in section II before asking, in section III, the essential question: when does a Member State implement EU law in coordination situations? Section IV analyses whether Article 34 of

[3] '[S]ocial rights are traditionally associated with a common history, homogeneity, and a common identity which goes hand in hand with a willingness to accept the redistribution of costs of social policies.' Y Borgmann-Prebil, and M Ross, 'Promoting European Solidarity: Between Rhetoric and Reality?' in M Ross and Y Borgmann-Prebil, *Promoting Solidarity in the European Union* (Oxford, Oxford University Press, 2010) 5; compare W Lamping, 'Mission Impossible? Limits and Perils of Institutionalizing Post-national Social Policy' in Ross and Borgmann-Prebil, *Promoting Solidarity in the European Union*. See also S Coppola, 'Social Rights in the European Union: The Possible Added Value of a Binding Charter of Fundamental Rights' in G Di Federico, *The EU Charter of Fundamental Rights, Ius Gentium: Comparative Perspectives on Law and Justice* (New York, Springer, 2011) 200 f.

[4] In these situations, Regulation 492/2011 and Regulation 883/2004 have included the welfare system of the state, where the activity is pursued for these groups of persons. Compare Coppola(n 3) 202. As regards migrant EU citizens, however, a certain independent social solidarity has emerged for the state of residence. See Case C-184/99 *Rudy Grzelczyk v Centre public d'aide sociale d'Ottignies-Louvain-la-Neuve* EU:C:2001:458; Case C-456/02 *Michel Trojani v Centre public d'aide sociale de Bruxelles (CPAS)* EU:C:2004:488; Case C-209/03, *The Queen, at the request of Dany Bidar v London Borough of Ealing and the Secretary of State for Education and Skills* EU:C:2005:169. This social solidarity has been codified as regards an EU citizen who legally resides in the state in Art 14(3) of Directive 2004/38 on the right to move and reside freely. This solidarity is however subject to change, see Case C-333/13 *Elisabeta Dano and Florin Dano v Jobcenter Leipzig* EU:C:2014:2358. See further D Thym, 'The elusive limits of solidarity: Residence rights of and social benefits for economically inactive Union Citizens' (2015) 52 *CMLR* 17, H Verschueren, 'Preventing "benefit tourism" in the EU: A narrow or broad interpretation of the possibilities offered by the ECJ in *Dano*?' (2015) 52 *CMLR* 363.

[5] P Watson, *EU Social and Employment Law*, 2nd edn (Oxford, Oxford University Press, 2014) ch 2.

the Charter gives any rights regarding social security. Section V supplements this analysis and discusses other fundamental rights as a way to extend the EU Charter rights vis-a-vis the Member States' Social Security. Finally, Section VI concludes the chapter.

II. THE COORDINATION OF THE NATIONAL SOCIAL SECURITY SYSTEMS

The EU does not have a direct competence as regards the regulation of social security. Instead, competence emanates from the free movement of persons, since the national social security systems can hinder cross-border movement. Regulation 883/2004 coordinates the social security systems of the Member States as regards the free movement of persons.

Coordination in this context refers to a legal construction where the social security systems of the parties to the agreement remain untouched and where the systems are interlocked so that an individual can be sure that he or she is covered by the security scheme of *a* state and that his or her earning periods and rights are not lost if he or she moves to other signatory states.[6] However, the coordination within the EU takes place in the context of the internal market and has therefore developed to a much greater degree than the corresponding international law agreements.

Since the end of the 1990s, the internal market context has been supplemented due to the case law of the Court of Justice of the European Union (hereinafter 'Court of Justice') on the EU citizenship and, as is raised in this chapter, issues regarding the possible impact of fundamental rights on the social security schemes of the Member States.

III. IMPLEMENTING EU LAW WHEN COORDINATING?

In the autumn of 2014, the Court of Justice had to consider 'the implementation of' EU law as follows from Article 51 in the Charter in relation to Regulation 883/2004 in its preliminary ruling in the *Dano* case.[7]

The German court had observed that *human dignity* and *equality before the law* could come into question in the *Dano* case. It was in this light that the German court, in its fourth and final question in its request for a preliminary ruling, put the question regarding Articles 1 and 20 of the EU Charter would allow the German special non-contributory cash benefits to be limited to the provision of the necessary funds for non-economically nationals to return to their home state.

[6] See F Pennings, *European Social Security Law*, 6th edn (Antwerp, Intersentia, 2015) 4 ff.

[7] Case C-333/13 *Dano* EU:C:2014:2358.

The Court of Justice did not, however, consider the concept of the implementation of EU law in *Dano*, as it established that the Member States do not in fact implement EU law when they lay down national conditions for the granting of special non-contributory cash benefits and the extent of such benefits. The Court referred to *Brey*,[8] where it established that the Regulation 883/2004 rule (Article 70) on the applicable legislation only points at the competent state without laying down the conditions that must be fulfilled to be entitled to the national benefit.[9] *Dano* (and *Brey*) is thus in line with the line of reasoning of the Court of Justice in *McB*[10] and the Charter can thus only be applicable in relation to Regulation 883/2004, but not in relation to the underlying national systems of social benefits which it is supposed to coordinate.

With *Brey* and *Dano*, however, the Court disregarded the statement regarding the division of competence between the Member States and the EU that was made by adding recital 17a in Regulation 988/2009:

> Once the legislation of a Member State becomes applicable to a person under Title II of this Regulation, the conditions for affiliation and entitlement to benefits should be defined by the legislation of the competent Member State while respecting Community law.[11]

Thus, regardless of the fact that it only has a coordinating role, Regulation 883/2004 is to be seen in a greater EU law context.[12] This point of departure is abundantly clear in *Dumont de Chassart*[13] (which strikingly forms the basis of the Court's ruling in *Brey*):

> In the absence of harmonisation at the European Union level, each Member State retains the power to determine in its legislation, *in compliance with European Union law*, the conditions pursuant to which benefits may be granted under a social security scheme.[14] (Emphasis added)

The wording in recital 17a is thus confirmed by the Court in *Dumont de Chassart*. In other words if the national rules prevent an EU citizen from exercising his or her right to free movement as is stipulated in the Treaty

[8] Case C-140/12, *Pensionsversicherungsanstalt v Peter Brey* EU:C:2013:565, 41.
[9] ibid 49; Case C-333/13 *Dano* EU:C:2014:2358, 89.
[10] Case C-400/10 PPU *J McB v LE* EU:C:2010:582, s I-8965.
[11] Regulation (EC) No 988/2009 of the European Parliament and of the Council of 16 September 2009 amending Regulation (EC) No 883/2004 on the coordination of social security systems, and determining the content of its Annexes, OJ L 284/43 30.10.2009.
[12] See also Case C-135/99 *Ursula Elsen and Bundesversicherungsanstalt für Angestellte* EU:C:2000:647; Case C-227/03 *AJ van Pommeren-Bourgondiën v Raad van bestuur van de Sociale verzekeringsbank* EU:C:2005:431; and Joint Cases C-225/02 and C-306/03 *Rosa García Blanco vs. Instituto Nacional de la Seguridad Social (INSS) and Tesorería General de la Seguridad Social (TGSS) and Cristalina Salgado Alonso vs. Instituto Nacional de la Seguridad Social (INSS) and Tesorería General de la Seguridad Social (TGSS)* EU:C:2005:34.
[13] Case C-619/11 *Patricia Dumont de Chassart v Office national d'allocations familiales pour travailleurs salariés (ONAFTS)* EU:C:2013:92.
[14] ibid 41.

and secondary legislation, it will not be possible to enforce the national legislation. Subsequently, the Court underlined in *Saleminck*[15] that Article 45 of the Treaty on the Functioning of the European Union (TFEU) does not allow for the introduction of a further national residence requirement after the rules in the Regulation on applicable legislation have designated the Member State as the competent state.

Even if Article 70 of Regulation 883/2004 regarding the applicable legislation is not akin to the direct implementation of EU law, it concerns at least a situation where the legislation of a Member State is covered by EU law in that its national qualification requirements may limit the freedom of movement of persons as stipulated by the Treaties. This view—that implementation should be understood in the broad sense of the word—has been confirmed by previous case law such as *Åkerberg Fransson*,[16] *AMS*[17] and *Pfleger*.[18]

The question is whether this view on the implementation of EU law in the Charter now needs to be revised in the light of the *Dano* case. The Court seems to be of the opinion that an implementation of EU law according to the meaning of the Charter requires more than just taking account of or respecting EU law when national entitlement rules regarding the social security systems are being drawn up. But how does this stand in relation to previous case law in the area of social security when it comes to the determination of applicable legislation? EU law has in *Salemink* been found, at least as regards supplementary residence requirements, to constitute an obstacle to too far-reaching entitlement rules for the Member States. Can such a situation be regarded as an implementation of EU law in the sense of the Charter? In my view, it should be possible to claim that such a situation constitutes an implementation of EU law since it is not possible to apply national entitlement rules: EU law requires the Member States to abstain from applying conflicting national law. The preliminary ruling in *ERT*[19] also points in the direction of a restriction in the national competence being regarded as an implementation.

However, had the Court of Justice applied this broad understanding of 'implementing Union Law' in *Dano*, it would have faced the dilemma opening up the issue of 'social tourism' to fundamental rights in relation to sensitive issues such as solidarity, sovereignty and the sustainability of welfare state systems. The outstanding issue is therefore whether *Brey* and *Dano*

[15] Case C-347/10 *A Salemink v Raad van bestuur van het Uitvoeringsinstituut werknemersverzekeringen* EU:C:2012:17.

[16] Case C-617/10 *Åklagaren v Hans Åkerberg Fransson* EU:C:2013:280, 21.

[17] Case C-176/12 *Association de médiation sociale v Union locale des syndicats CGT et al* EU:C:2014:2, 42.

[18] Case C-390/12 *Proceedings brought by Robert Pfleger and Others* EU:C:2014:281, 34.

[19] Case C-260/89 *Elliniki Radiophonia Tiléorassi AE and Panellinia Omospondia Syllogon Prossopikou v Dimotiki Etairia Pliroforissis and Sotirios Kouvelas and Nicolaos Avdellas et al* EU:C:1991:254.

can be seen as a shift in the general understanding of the 'implementation of Union law' or whether the shift will only apply with regard to special non-contributory cash benefits. Future case law should provide us with the answer.

IV. THE RIGHT TO SOCIAL SECURITY PURSUANT TO ARTICLE 34 OF THE CHARTER: A (DIRECTLY INVOKABLE) RIGHT?

A. Introduction

Article 34 of the Charter expressly stipulates that social security is a fundamental right:

> **Social security and social assistance**
>
> 1. The Union recognises and respects the entitlement to social security benefits and social services providing protection in cases such as maternity, illness, industrial accidents, dependency or old age, and in the case of loss of employment, in accordance with the rules laid down by Union law and national laws and practices.
> 2. Everyone residing and moving legally within the European Union is entitled to social security benefits and social advantages in accordance with Union law and national laws and practices.
> 3. In order to combat social exclusion and poverty, the Union recognises and respects the right to social and housing assistance so as to ensure a decent existence for all those who lack sufficient resources, in accordance with the rules laid down by Union law and national laws and practices.

Hence, the Charter regulates two different situations as regards social security: first, it recognises and respects the entitlement to social security in EU legal contexts; and, second, it confirms the entitlement to social security in free movement situations. Since the wording is general in nature, it is therefore of the utmost importance vis-a-vis the impact of the Article to decide whether it can be regarded as a *right* or whether it is a *principle* which is dependent on a more precise description in further legislation at the national or EU level.[20] If the Charter requires supplementary legislation when it comes to social security, its impact will only be in compliance with legislation and the case law. Thus, a leverage effect is not possible where Article 34 itself expands the fundamental rights vis-à-vis national social security. As regards the Member States, this means that 'Community law does not detract from the powers of the Member States to organise their social security systems',[21] both in situations where EU law is invoked on a general level and where there is only coordination.

[20] Compare Art 52(5) of the Charter.
[21] Case C-158/96 *Raymond Kohll v Union des caisses de maladie* EU:C:1998:171.

The most important cases as regards the question of Article 34 as a right or a principle are *Kamberaj*[22] and *AMS*.[23]

In *Kamberaj*, the issue was whether a regional housing benefit could be covered by Article 34(3) regarding the entitlement to social assistance. This case raised the issue if Italian legislation was in accordance with Directive 2003/109 concerning the status of third-country nationals who are long-term residents.[24] In its preamble, the Directive refers to the Charter where Recital 3 stipulates that the Directive respects the fundamental rights. Against this background, the Court of Justice ruled that a Member State in its application of EU law and Directive 2003/109 must take special consideration of Article 34(3), stating that a Member State must 'recognise and respect the right to social assistance'.

The Court of Justice's line of reasoning follows a logic where Article 34(3) of the Charter is dependent on the existence of a Directive. The Court bases its decision on the fact that Article 34(3) stipulates that social assistance shall be understood 'in accordance with the rules laid down by Union law and national laws and practices'. In this way, the Court of Justice emphasised that Member States have to ensure an appropriate effect of the Directive. On the other hand, the case indicates that national legislation on social assistance cannot come under attack merely by a referral to Article 34(3). The fact that the Court of Justice linked the Charter to a reference to the preamble of the Directive and did not explicitly make reference to Article 34(3) thus indicates that the right to social assistance in accordance with Article 34(3) should be seen as a principle and not a right.[25]

The subsequent preliminary ruling in *AMS* further confirms the Court of Justice's unwillingness to recognise the social rights in Article 34 as rights. It is true that the Court does rule on Article 27 in *AMS*, but the wording of Articles 27 and 34 are similar, and for that reason the ruling in *AMS* can also be said to have a bearing on whether Article 34 can be seen as a right.[26] The Court of Justice found in *AMS* that the wording in Article 27 of the Charter is not sufficiently precise to be understood as a right.[27] The Court

[22] Case C-571/10 *Servet Kamberaj v Istituto per l'Edilizia sociale della Provincia autonoma di Bolzano (IPES) and others* EU:C:2012:233.

[23] *AMS* (n 17).

[24] Council Directive 2003/109/EC of 25 November 2003 concerning the status of third-country nationals who are long-term residents, [2003], 23. 1. 2004, OJ L 16–44.

[25] According to Peers, the fact that the Court of Justice chose to refer to Art 34 in itself indicates how important the Charter is: S Peers, 'The Court of Justice Lays the Foundations for the Long-Term Residents Directive: *Kamberaj, Commission v Netherlands, Mangat Singh*' (2013) 50 *CMLR* 529, 542.

[26] Article 27 stipulates that a worker has the right to information and consultation 'in the cases and under the conditions provided for by Union law and national laws and practice'. This can be compared to the wording of Art 34(1) about the entitlement to social security being conditional by specifying the right 'in accordance with the rules *laid* down by Union law and national laws and practice'.

[27] *AMS* (n 17) 44–45. Compare the Advocate General's line of reasoning at 54. Advocate General Cruz Villalón's Opinion in Case 176/12 *AMS* EU:C:2013:491.

ruled that it is *clear* that Article 27 must be complemented by secondary law or national law to ensure its full impact.[28] This is, however, not applicable, since the Court of Justice ruled that the Directive in question could not be linked to Article 27. Thus, it was not possible to invoke the Charter in *AMS*.[29]

In the light of the above, my assessment is that the Court of Justice will not regard the entitlement to social security as a right, at least, in the near future. This, in particular, bearing in mind the fact that the social security systems are part of the inner core of what forms a state. Article 34 should in general therefore be seen as a *principle* dependent on supplementary legislation.

The Charter differentiates between the entitlement to social security (Article 34(1)) and the right to social security in free movement situations (Article 34(2)). These two situations differ and even the wording regarding references to EU law and national law differs to a certain extent too. These *principles* will thus be dealt with separately below in order to analyse what these principles entail.

B. Article 34(1): The Entitlement to Social Security Benefits—Outside the Scope *Ratione Materiae*?

Article 34(1) of the Charter can be divided into two parts as it stipulates that the EU 'recognises and respects the entitlement to social security benefits ... in accordance with the rules laid down by Union law and national laws and practices'.

The expression 'recognises and respects' in Article 34(1) is not very far-reaching textually and one might be tempted to draw the conclusion that Article 34(1) is merely a vague principle which is fully dependent on supplementary legislation on the part of a legislator. Nevertheless, the Court of Justice stated in *Kamberaj* that the entitlement to social benefits in accordance with Article 34(3)—here the wording is identical—could be used as a basis for interpretation and could in that way reinforce the substance of a Directive. Hence, if the Court of Justice has to rule on a situation where social security can be claimed in an EU legal context and there is relevant EU legislation that can be invoked, one could argue that Article 34(1) constitutes a lever in the same way as it does in *Kamberaj*. There is, however, a decisive difference that speaks against such an approach. Article 34(3) states

[28] *AMS* (n 17) 45. However, the wording 'fully effective' is an opening towards Art 27 having a certain impact, notwithstanding that it is a matter of a principle.

[29] The Court of Justice also took the opportunity to state that age discrimination can be regarded as an independent right by at 47 referring to the preliminary ruling in Case C-555/07 *Seda Kücükdeveci v Swedex GmbH & Co KG* EU:C:2010:21.

expressly that its aim is to combat social exclusion and poverty. This specific aim constituted the Court of Justice's lever in *Kamberaj*. However, such a corresponding lever is lacking in Article 34(1).

As regards the second part of Article 34(1), 'in accordance with the rules laid down by Union law and national laws and practices', the Court of Justice has, as far as social security is concerned, established in, for example, *Kohll*, that in 'the absence of harmonisation at Community level, it is therefore for the legislation of each Member State to determine, first, the condition concerning the right or duty to be insured with a social security scheme ... and second, the conditions for entitlement to benefits'.[30] The Member States are thus free to determine both the *rationae personae* that may be entitled to the benefits foreseen by the respective social security schemes as well as the *ratione materiae*.

Notwithstanding this fact, the Member States shall take account of EU law when exerting their national competence; the right to determine one's own system is therefore conditional in a broader EU legal context.[31] A related issue is therefore whether the Charter may have an impact on powers of the Member States to organise their social security systems in that it stipulates the benefits that the Member States shall provide the entitled *rationae personae*. As seen above it may certainly be difficult for Member States to claim that the national social security schemes are not at all within the scope of the EU law. However, the social security systems of the Member States were not set up to incorporate EU legislation, but to coordinate. Furthermore, Regulation 883/2004 in itself does not provide substantial rights or benefits. In *Annibaldi*[32] and *Dereci*,[33] the Court established that the legislation of a Member State, which does not stem from a Member State's EU law obligations, does not fall within the remit of the Charter. Moreover, the Court ruled in *McB*[34] that the Charter's application is limited in those cases where an EU legislative act does not aim to make any substantial changes to the powers or tasks of the EU. For such situations, 'the Charter should be taken into consideration solely for the purposes of interpreting [the] [r]egulation ... and should be no assessment of national law as such'.

The social security schemes of the Member States do not stem from EU legal obligations. However, the Member States have decided to coordinate

[30] *Kohll* (n 21) 18. Compare with the earlier Case 110/79 *Una Coonan v Insurance Officer* EU:C:1980:112, 12; Case C-349/87 *Elissavet Paraschi v Landesversicherungsanstalt Württemberg* EU:C:1991:372, 15. See also Case C-275/96 *Kuusijärvi v Riksförsäkringsverket* EU:C:1998:279 and subsequent case law summarised in Case C–388/09 *Da Silva Martins* EU:C:2011:439, 71; compare also with *Dumont de Chassart* (n 13) 40–41.

[31] See *Elsen* (n 12); Case C-227/03 *van Pommeren-Bourgondiën* (n 12); *Rosa García Blanco* (n 12).

[32] Case C-309/96 *Daniele Annibaldi v Sindaco del Comune di Guidonia and Presidente Regione Lazio* EU:C:1997:631.

[33] Case C-256/11 *Murat Dereci and others v Bundesministerium für Inneres* EU:C:2011:734.

[34] PPU *J McB v LE* (n 10).

the security systems in order to reinforce the free movement of persons, but the Charter could, in accordance with *McB*, only be asserted as regards Regulation 883/2004 itself and not the underlying national social security systems that it is coordinating. Furthermore from a purely textual point of view, Article 34(1) lists different social insurance benefits that the entitlement to social security *may* include as the Article states 'in such cases as' and not giving an exhaustive list.[35] Hence, as regards the wording, it should be a matter for the Member States to determine the scope of each respective national social security scheme even in the future.

In conclusion, due to the wording of Article 34(1) and case law as well as the division of competences between the Member States and the EU, it would be difficult to claim that Article 34(1) constitutes a right. Instead, it should be seen as a principle in accordance with Article 52(5) of the Charter.[36]

This principle needs to be supplemented by EU legislation within the Social Policy area, which requires unanimity amongst the Member States or a thorough amendment of Regulation 883/2004. It is therefore still up to the Member States to decide whether to supplement the Charter's social rights as regards entitlement to social security with more substance.

Regardless of the fact that Article 34(1) is to be seen as a principle and not a right in the sense of the Charter, it is interesting to examine, *if* Article 34(1) would be regarded as a right, what such a fundamental right might encompass in concrete terms.

Article 51(2) establishes that the Charter cannot entail an expansion of the EU's scope. It is thus rather a matter of a reinforcement of the impact on the existing scope. A material right which can certainly be asserted is a ban against gender discrimination in the context of social security, since the EU has competence in this area.[37] As regards other possible areas, it may be difficult to assert these since the Court, as mentioned above, has established in *Annibaldi*[38] and *Dereci*[39] that national legislation that does not stem from the EU legal obligations of a Member State cannot fall under the Charter. The above leads to the conclusion that *even if* Article 34(1) were to be found to be a right and not a principle, it will not be possible to assert the Charter to obtain any substantial rights above and beyond what is already included in the social security system of any particular Member State.

A final question is which *ratione personae* could invoke Article 34(1). Article 34(2), as stated above, covers situations where a person moves

[35] Compare other language versions: 'in cases such as' (English), 'die in Fällen wie' (German) and 'f.eks. i tilfælde af' (Danish).

[36] Compare R White, 'Article 34' in S Peers, T Hervey, J Kenner and A Ward (eds), *The EU Charter of Fundamental Rights* (Oxford, Hart Publishing, 2014) 938.

[37] P Watson, *EU Social and Employment Law*, 2nd edn (Oxford, Oxford University Press, 2014) ch 26.

[38] *Annibaldi* (n 32).

[39] *Dereci* (n 33).

between two or several Member States and where coordination in accordance with Regulation 883/2004 comes into force. These persons constitute the lion's share of the people who are able to assert an EU legal social security dimension. Situations where there is no free movement between Member States would therefore be covered by Article 34(1). However, the remaining *ratione personae* where EU law comes into question without any crossings of borders is normally already covered by the national social security system. Moreover, the Court of Justice, as mentioned above, has in *Kohll* established that it is for the Member States to determine the conditions for being insured in its social security schemes. Hence, the *ratione personae* that could claim rights under Article 34(1) would almost boil down to no one.

To summarise, the situation is thus that it is difficult to regard Article 34(1) of the Charter as a right according to the Charter. As a principle resulting from the Charter, it is instead fully dependent on the consensus of the Member States in favour of an expansion of the scope of social security at the EU level or of national legislative initiatives that expand the substantial social security of each respective state. If the Court of Justice was still to decide that Article 34(1) is a right, the scope would be very limited as the EU lacks legislative competence in the area. Finally, it has to be said that the *ratione personae* that would be able to invoke these limited rights is almost non-existent.

C. Article 34(2): The Charter in Cross-Border Situations

The second situation where the national social security systems of the Member States might come into question as a fundamental right is in cross-border situations (Article 34(2) of the Charter). The question, however, is whether any substantial rights can be introduced beyond the coordination and the equal treatment that already follows from Regulation 883/2004 and Regulation 492/2011. *White* is doubtful whether any rights can be added bearing this secondary law in mind.[40] I share these doubts.

The wording in Article 34(2) differs from that in Article 34(1) as there already exists a right to social security in cross-border situations compared to Article 34(1), which expresses it as a right being dependent on secondary or national law: 'in accordance with the rules laid down in Union law'. The question is, however, whether the different wording entails a substantial difference since primary law and the general legal principles can always be said to apply.

[40] *White* (n 36) 938.

To begin with, it can be pointed out that the same line of reasoning as above with regard to Article 34(1) and its standing as a principle or right in accordance with Article 52(5) of the Charter applies with regard to Article 34(2). The wording is certainly more direct as it stipulates a right to social security rather than the wording in Article 34(1), which states that the EU recognises and respects a right to social security. Nonetheless, this right is subject to EU law and, as such, is conditional and is not a right on its own.

Unlike the situation in Article 34(1), where the EU lacks legislative competence, the EU does have legislative competence in cross-border situations according to Article 48 TFEU. Thus, the principle is supplemented with secondary law and Article 34(2) of the Charter can therefore be invoked. Hence, there is a fundamental right to social security in cross-border situations. However, as follows from the preliminary ruling in *McB*, the Charter can only be invoked in relation to the Regulation and its rules, but not national laws.[41] If the rules of Regulation 883/2004 were to be found to hinder the underlying idea of the Regulation, which is to strengthen the free movement of persons, it would thus be possible for the Court of Justice to declare such articles as invalid by invoking Article 45 TFEU as well as the Charter. There would therefore be a dual order where Article 34(2) constitutes a lever in the same way as Article 27 was a lever in *Kamberaj* when the aim of the underlying Directive was being interpreted.[42] However, the Court of Justice has in a subsequent preliminary ruling, *Pfleger*,[43] established that a restriction of the freedom to provide services entailed a possible restriction in accordance with the Charter. There was thus no need for a special examination in the light of the Charter.[44] The freedom of movement of services according to the Court thus takes account of the rights that the Charter is set to guarantee. Hence, in the light of *Pfleger*, the Charter should not provide added value in the situations where Regulation 883/2004 is found to restrict the free movement of persons.

To sum up, Article 34(2) should not entail any added value to the right to social security in cross-border situations.

If the Court of Justice was still to undertake an expansion of competences 'in the light of' the Charter, the Member States would have the possibility of claiming subsidiarity as well as referring to Article 52(1) of the Charter as referring to Article 52(1) of the Charter and thereby limiting the rights as meeting objectives of overriding general interests.[45]

[41] See further the discussions as regards the possibility of the Charter expanding both the material and persona scope in the area of social security, above section VB.

[42] See above p 197.

[43] *Pfleger* (n 18).

[44] ibid 60.

[45] This does not apply to the fundamental rights that are classed as absolute rights.

D. Conclusions

During the negotiations leading up to the Convention and also in doctrine, it has been argued that the entitlement to social security runs a special risk with regard to an expansion of competences.[46] After five years with the Charter and in the absence of case law, it can be said that it remains unclear whether and how Article 34(1) of the Charter will affect the social security systems of the Member States. Similarly, it is unclear whether Article 34(2) means that Regulation 883/2004 may give rise to substantial rights or may come into question in other situations other than those currently covered by the Regulation. Instead, the development of the competences of the EU in the area of social security is more likely to continue through the development of case law in the area of the free movement of persons—a development that is governed by the principles of the internal market, which through the constitutionalisation of these principles in the Charter in retrospect legitimises an expansion of competences.[47]

V. SOCIAL SECURITY AND OTHER FUNDAMENTAL RIGHTS AS A WAY TO EXTEND COMPETENCES

A. Introduction

The EU Charter entails a comprehensive catalogue of fundamental rights stemming to a large extent of previous case law of the Court of Justice.[48] The catalogue of fundamental rights includes rights that have already indirectly affected the national social security systems.

As regards the fundamental rights, apart from Article 34, which may have an impact on national social security systems, these are primarily rights that are closely linked to the internal market, like the free movement of persons and the equal treatment principle, but also other rights such as the right to family life.

The principle of non-discrimination, which can be found in Article 21(1) in the Charter, is another right that in the context of age discrimination has been proved to be directly invokable and may have a potential impact on the national social security systems and in particular the pension schemes. In this volume, Barnard asks whether the present case law in the area of age discrimination threaten issues other than the functioning of the internal

[46] Coppola (n 3) 209. See also O Zetterquist, 'The Charter of Fundamental Rights and the European *Res Publica*' in Di Federico (n 3) 12.

[47] See p 207 ff. Compare also Weatherill, chapter 10, this volume.

[48] Compare D Sarmiento, Who's Afraid of the Charter? The Court of Justice, National Courts and the New Framework of Fundamental Rights Protection in Europe (2013) 50 *CMLR* 1267, 1269 f; see also Weatherill, ch 10, this volume.

market.[49] The relationship between the Charter and EU citizenship is another delicate issue, since EU citizenship challenges the ideas of national citizenship as well as solidarity.[50] A fundamental right that has proved to have an intricate impact on the national social security systems is the rights of the child, which is codified in Article 24 of the Charter.

B. The Rights of the Child

Children are obviously covered by applicable general fundamental rights in the Charter. Two Articles in the Charter, apart from these general rights, take a particular children's perspective: Article 24 on the rights of the child and the more specific Article 32, which bans child labour.

I am cautious as regards Article 24 being a right, compared to age discrimination, as in Article 21(1), where the Court of Justice points out in *AMS* that the preliminary ruling in *Kücükdeveci*[51] confirms that the Article constitutes a right even in horizontal situations.[52]

It may be difficult to draw any conclusions regarding whether rights of the child are designated as rights or principles based on a textual interpretation. Nor do the Explanations in the Charter comment on the status of Article 24 in any detail. Besselink, however, finds that certain rights beyond those mentioned in the Explanations might be regarded as enforcable rights, albeit not Article 24.[53] The wording of Article 24, however, has not been made dependent on further explanation via EU law or national laws. Therefore the rights of the child could potentially be regarded as rights and thus directly invokable. But what are the rights of the child?

The rights of the child entail at least a right to education as regulated in Regulation 492/2011. Through the Court of Justice case law, this right has had an impact on the national social security systems in an internal market context in a complex way, where derived family benefits can be claimed by parents to children who have an individual right to education in a Member State.

[49] Barnard, ch 8, this volume.

[50] The question of how EU citizenship can generate independent rights originating from the Charter were brought to the fore but not expressed in the groundbreaking preliminary ruling of the Court of Justice in Case C-34/09 *Gerardo Ruiz Zambrano v Office national de l'emploi (ONEm)* EU:C:2011:124.

[51] *Kücükdeveci* (n 29).

[52] E Muir, 'Of Ages in—and Edges of—EU Law' (2011) 48 *CMLR* 39; K LeVan Bergman, 'Going Horizontal? Four Possible Interpretations of the Kücükdeveci Case' (2011) *Europarättslig Tidskrift* 88,

[53] LFM Besselink, 'The Protection of Fundamental Rights post-Lisbon—The Interaction between the EU Charter of Fundamental Rights, the European Convention on Human Rights (ECHR) and National Constitutions', *Reports of the XXV FIDE Congress Tallinn 2012*, Vol 1, 63, 109–10.

The background is that when Directive 2004/38[54] was adopted, the parts of Regulation 1612/68 (currently Regulation 492/2011) that dealt with the right to take up residence in the country of work, the right to take up work for the family members and the right to equal treatment were incorporated into the Directive.[55] However, one right regarding the migrant workers' family members was not transferred; the right to education of the child of the migrant worker. Thus, a migrant worker's child is able to claim in parallel a right to education based on Regulation 492/2011 and Directive 2004/38. Nevertheless, these rights differ in a decisive way: the right to equal treatment in the Directive is conditional upon the carer of the child having residence, while the Court of Justice has found that the right to education in accordance with Regulation 1612/68 is a child's independent right.[56] This independent right leads to a right to residence for the child that is not connected with Directive 2004/38 and its requirements of an EU citizen not becoming a burden on the country of residence: it is an independent fundamental right for a young EU citizen to studies.[57]

In *Ibrahim*[58] and *Teixiera*,[59] this independent right of the child was confirmed, but was also put to the test.[60] These two preliminary rulings indicate how the welfare system of a state of residence may be burdened, regardless of the balance struck in Directive 2004/38 between the EU citizen and the state of residence.

The preliminary ruling in *Ibrahim* concerned four minor EU citizens where the two eldest siblings had just started school in the UK. The family was of Somali origin, but the father Yusuf and the children were Danish citizens. The father started working in the UK in the autumn of 2002 and the family followed him to the UK during the winter of 2003. After May 2003, the father did not work anymore, the family living instead on social benefits. In 2006 the parents separated and the children stayed in the UK with the mother, who was unemployed.

[54] European Parliament and Council Directive 2004/38/EC of 29 April 2004 on the right of citizens of the Union and their family members to move and reside freely within the territory of the Member States amending Regulation (EEC) No 1612/68 and repealing Directives 64/221/EEC, 68/360/EEC, 72/194/EEC, 73/148/EEC, 75/34/EEC, 75/35/EEC, 90/364/EEC, 90/365/EEC and 93/96/EEC [2004] OJ L158/77.

[55] Articles 10 and 11 of Regulation 1612/68 were repealed through Article 38(1), Directive 2004/38.

[56] Joint Cases C-389/87 and C-390/87 *Echternach and Moritz* EU:C:1989:130, 21, confirmed in Case C-413/99 *Baumbast and R v Secretary of State for the Home Department* EU:C:2002:493, 50–53.

[57] Compare J Schiratzki, *Children's Rights in the EU—A Tool for Autonomous Citizenship or Patriarchy Reborn?*, Europarättslig Tidskrift, 2011, 70, in particular 82.

[58] Case C-310/08 *London Borough of Harrow v Ibrahim* EU:C:2010:80.

[59] Case C-480/08 *Teixiera v London Borough of Lambeth* EU:C:2010:83.

[60] For an in-depth examination of these preliminary rulings and their ramifications concerning the British welfare system, see C O'Brien, 'Case C-310/08 *Ibrahim*, Case C-480/08 *Teixiera*' (2011) 48 *CMLR* 203. See also Schiratzki (n 56) 70.

In January 2007, the mother, Ibrahim, applied for housing benefit, but was denied this since the local administration was of the opinion that she as a third-country citizen no longer had a right of residence. The question arose as to whether Article 12 of Regulation 1612/68 on a child's right to education[61] could come to the fore and whether this independent right could lead to derived rights of the mother.

The same question was brought to the fore in *Teixiera*, where a Portuguese woman was found not to have a right of residence as she lacked sufficient resources in accordance with Directive 2004/38. Teixiera was however a mother to a daughter who went to school in the UK. The Court of Appeal requested therefore a preliminary ruling in order to decide whether this fact might have any bearing on Teixiera's situation.

The Court of Justice issued both preliminary rulings in the Grand Chamber on the same day with more or less the same line of reasoning. In both *Ibrahim* and *Teixiera*, the Court of Justice ruled that the right to education in accordance with Article 12 of Regulation 1612/68 was an independent right enjoyed by the children of migrant workers. However, it also established that the carer has a derived right of residence in the Member State in order to guarantee the child's independent right to education. Thus, the carer becomes the person who guarantees that the child is able to study regardless of whether the carer has a right of residence in accordance with Directive 2004/38 or not.[62]

Normally, as the Court of Justice observed, it is the carer who is authorised to apply for benefits for himself or herself as well as for his or her dependent children. Thus, through the child's independent right to education in accordance with Regulation 492/2011, the scheme of social benefits will be burdened; social assistance must be paid to the parent because otherwise it would mean that the child's independent right to education would be restricted.

As regards the impact of the perspective of the child on the national social security systems, it can be observed that national systems with residence-based elements in their security systems will in the light of *Ibrahim* and *Teixiera* need to grant benefits. According to *Brey*, residence-based benefits shall be granted when there is a matter of residence.[63] In this respect, an assessment should be made based on the residence of the child, not the carer, who if he or she is not an EU citizen cannot be regarded as having residence in accordance with Directive 2004/38.

Ibrahim and *Teixiera* are examples of how the rights of the child may have an impact on the social assistance and social security schemes of a

[61] Article 10 of Regulation 492/2011.

[62] Compare the reasoning of the Court of Justice in Case C-200/02 *Kunqian Catherine Zhu and Man Lavette Chen v Secretary of State for the Home Department* EU:C:2004:639; and *Zambrano* (n 48).

[63] *Brey* (n 8) 43.

Member State. The right to education should be covered by both the first sentence in Article 24(1)—'Children shall have the right to such protection and care as is necessary for their well-being'—as well as by Article 24(2), which stipulates that the best interests of the child shall be respected as regards 'all actions relating to children'.

The right to education is, however, not expressly established and therefore one could argue that if the Court of Justice is of the opinion that the Charter covers this right, it should have said so when the *Ibrahim* and *Teixiera* rulings were delivered, since the Charter had come into effect at that time. However, the British court requested a preliminary ruling only in order to obtain an answer to how the relationship between Article 12 of Regulation 1612/68 and Directive 2004/38 was to be understood. It is therefore possible to claim that the legal situation is still open as regards the scope of the rights of the child in accordance with Article 24 of the Charter, in particular bearing in mind that the rulings in *Ibrahim* and *Teixiera* were entirely based on an internal market perspective.

C. Age Discrimination

As regards age discrimination, Barnard analyses this in detail in her chapter in this volume. I have thus decided only to touch upon these rights very briefly.

Article 25 on the rights of the elderly should in all probability be regarded as a principle in the sense of Article 52(5), as Article 25 expresses that the EU *recognises and respects* the rights of the elderly. Furthermore, in the Explanations of the Charter, Article 25 is highlighted as an example of a principle.[64] Therefore Article 25 should not be possible to be relied upon to a larger extent for rights of the elderly.

To safeguard the rights of the elderly in accordance with the Charter, the understanding of the principle of non-discrimination in Article 21(1) is therefore decisive: 'Any discrimination based on any grounds such as … age … shall be prohibited.' In a number of preliminary rulings, of which in particular *Mangold*[65] and *Kücükdeveci*[66] stand out, the Court of Justice has established that age discrimination can be directly applicable even in horizontal contexts. In *AMS*,[67] the Court took it a step further and established that the right in Article 21(1) in the Charter 'is sufficient in itself to confer on individuals an individual right which they may invoke as such'.

64 Amendments to the Charter of Fundamental Rights [2007] OJ C 303/17.
65 Case C-144/04 *Werner Mangold v Rüdiger Helm* EU:C:2005:709.
66 Kücükdeveci (n 29).
67 *AMS* (n 17).

In *AMS*, the Court opted to connect existing case law and the corresponding Article 21(1) of the Charter to establish that age discrimination is a right in the sense of Article 52(5).

This means that in the future, the Charter could possibly be invoked by individuals in national courts by combining Articles 21(1) and 34(2), where issues regarding age and equal treatment in relation to Regulation 883/2004 could be asserted in parallel with the more specific articles of the Regulation and the general principle of equal treatment established in Article 18 TFEU.[68]

The question is however whether the combination of these two rights may constitute leverage in the same way as the principle of equal treatment constituted leverage for the EU citizen in *Martínez Sala*.[69] What speaks against this is that the situations covered by Article 34(1) are primarily domestic situations and that the competence of the EU only covers the internal market aspects as regards the social security schemes of the Member States.[70] Barnard also asks, based on a different perspective, whether the Court of Justice in its rulings in the area of age discrimination has started to threaten the delicate balance of overarching national priorities that does not stem from discriminatory measures, but rather from economic principles regarding the efficiency of the labour market.[71] According to Barnard, this constitutes a legitimate distinction that must be made without it being drowned in a flood of individual complaints.

This question is relevant since there is a tendency that the Charter individualises the fundamental rights at the cost of collective common needs that benefit all at the end of the day. By continuing to assert individual rights, individual rights will paradoxically be threatened since in the end it will not be possible to uphold a public and general system of welfare based on solidarity if there is no solidarity. The question that politicians in both the national and the EU contexts need answer is: who should foot the bill?

D. The Charter's Codification of the Free Movement of Persons

The competence of the EU in the area of social security stems from an indirect competence supporting the free movement of persons. The free movement of workers and other economically active persons has been constitutionalised

[68] Compare S O'Leary, 'The Charter and EU Social and Employment Law' in P Cardonnel, A Rosas and N Wahl (eds), *Constitutionalising the EU Judicial System—Essays in Honour of Pernilla Lindh* (Oxford, Hart Publishing, 2012) 317, especially at 331.

[69] Case C-85/96 *María Martínez Sala v Freistaat Bayern* EU:C:1998:217.

[70] However, compare Case C-212/06 *Gouvernement de la Communauté française and Gouvernement wallon v Gouvernement flamand* EU:C:2008:178, where the Court hinted at a broader interpretation of the concept of 'an EU legal dimension' (see 42–60).

[71] Barnard, ch 8, this volume.

and is guaranteed through Article 15(2) of the Charter, which stipulates: 'Every citizen of the Union has the freedom to seek employment, to work, to exercise the right of establishment and to provide services in any Member State.'

The question in the context at hand is whether Article 15(2) of the Charter might reinforce the free movement of persons and thus indirectly also affect the national social security systems.

To begin with, it can be said that Article 15(2) purely textually does not broaden the concept of the free movement of persons since it does not specify how this right can be ensured for the group of entitled persons. Article 15(2) seems rather to 'shadow' the Articles in the Treaty on the free movement for persons and services. In line with this, the Court of Justice noted in *Pfleger*[72] that Article 15(2) cannot be understood as independent from Article 56 TFEU on the free movement of services. It therefore decided to respond to the queries of national courts by noting that it was possible to deliver the preliminary ruling based on the principle of equal treatment resulting from the free movement of services.

In situations that are not as straightforward, however, Article 15(2) could possibly be used by the Court of Justice as a lever. In such a case, Article 15(2) could, together with Article 34(2) and its underlying idea of an *entitlement to* social security, reinforce an interpretation of Regulation 883/2004 in future rulings in the same way as the Court referred to Article 34(3) in its line of reasoning in *Kamberaj*.[73]

The Court of Justice already made similar market access interpretations in *van Munster*[74] and *Leyman*.[75] In those preliminary rulings, the national pieces of legislation in question were neutral and Regulation 883/2004 was applied correctly, but the effect was still to hamper the free movement of workers. With that situation, the Court of Justice ruled in *van Munster* and *Leyman* that the national laws must be overridden and instead the national courts and authorities must apply primary law to resolve the cases outside the national legislation in order to ensure the free movement.

A corresponding situation could be advantageously strengthened by referring to the fundamental right to free movement of persons in the Charter, since this link could lend further weight to the line of reasoning of the Court of Justice without the area being expanded.

An independent expansion of the free movement of persons against the background of Article 15(2) should, however, not come into question, since Article 6(1) of the Treaty on European Union (TEU) and Article 51(2) of

[72] *Pfleger* (n 18) 60.

[73] See above p 197.

[74] Case C-165/91 *Simon JM van Munster v Rijksdienst voor Pensioenen* EU:C:1994:359.

[75] Case C-3/08, *Ketty Leyman v Institut national d'assurance maladie-invalidité (INAMI)* EU:C:2009:595.

the Charter underline that the intention is not to expand the competences of the EU. But as *van Munster* and *Leyman* indicate, such an independent development is not actually necessary. The leverage can be seen in an internal market context where the Charter's corresponding right will be used as a strong argument to interpret a preliminary ruling in an expansive direction, but based on market access.

VI. REGULATION 883/2004 AND THE EUROPEAN CHARTER: ADDED VALUE OR DOES THE CHARTER STAND ON ITS OWN TWO FEET?

As of 2015, the Charter has been in force for six years and the question that still needs to be answered is whether it is possible to regard it simply as a codification of applicable law or whether it can lead to deeper integration.

Lenaerts, Vice-President of the Court of Justice, believes that the Charter fulfils three functions.[76] First, it can form the basis for interpretation when secondary law and national law are interpreted 'in the light of the Charter'. Second, it constitutes a legal act which, when applicable, can invalidate EU legislation and national law stemming from EU law obligations. Finally when the Court of Justice develops new general legal principles. Some like *Ward* believe that the Charter will lead to material changes,[77] while others like *Weatherill* are of the opinion that there has as yet been no material expansion and nor will there ever be.[78]

Five years of case law indicate that the Charter is applicable as soon as an EU law aspect can be asserted. As shown in *Åkerberg Fransson* and subsequently confirmed in *Pfleger*, EU law is applied even when the measures taken by the Member States are not fully determined by EU law.[79] However, *Dano* indicates a Court of Justice narrowing down the understanding of the notion in Article 51 *implementing EU law*. As discussed in section III, *Dano* focusses solely on the coordination of social security, so one could therefore argue that *Dano* should not have a general bearing.

As regards social security, section IV.B has indicated that it will not be possible to invoke Article 34(1) of the Charter to any greater extent, since the right to social security is a principle and is thus dependent on the legislative initiative of the Member States. Concerning Article 34(2), which regulates free movement of persons, the situation is slightly different, as shown in section IV.C, since this fundamental right, regardless being a principle or a right, can be asserted only when secondary legislation is present

[76] K Lenaerts, 'The Court of Justice of the European Union and the Protection of Fundamental Rights' (2011) XXXI *Polish Yearbook of International Law* 79, 81.

[77] A Ward, 'Article 51', in Peers et al (n 36) 1425; S O'Leary, 'The Charter and the Future Contours of EU Social and Employment Law', in Cardonnel et al (n 67).

[78] Weatherill, ch 10, this volume.

[79] *Åkerberg Fransson* (n 16), 21, 25 and 26.

as Regulation 883/2004. In the light of Article 6(1) TEU and Article 51(2) of the Charter, the Court of Justice could not expand the competences of the EU by referring to Article 34(2), since this would challenge the Member States in two ways: it would lead to an erosion of the sovereignty of the national social security systems alongside the introduction of a federal catalogue of rights.

Instead, legal evolution will continue in the area of the internal market and the Charter could, as discussed in section V, shadow this development just as has occurred in the area of the rights of the child and age discrimination.[80]

To sum up as regards coordination through Regulation 883/2004, the Court of Justice will be able to lean on the rights of the Charter when there is a need to strengthen a line of reasoning, as observed in section V.D regarding social rights in *Kamberaj*. Examples of situations where such a lever might be resorted to in the future which would legitimise a far-reaching impact of EU law on national social security systems could be possibly foreseen in situations akin to *van Munster* and *Leyman*. A substantial expansion of the right to social security purely on the basis of the Charter will, however, be long in coming, if it ever does.

[80] Compare S Weatherill, 'From Economic Rights to Fundamental Rights' in S de Vries, U Bernitz and S Weatherill (eds), *The Protection of Fundamental Rights in the EU after Lisbon* (Oxford, Hart Publishing, 2013) 30; S Weatherill, 'Protecting the Internal Market from the Charter' in S de Vries, U Bernitz and S Weatherill, ch 10, this volume.

Part III

Safeguarding Fundamental Rights in Europe's Internal Market

10

Protecting the Internal Market from the Charter

STEPHEN WEATHERILL

I. INTRODUCTION

IN A CHAPTER completed in 2011, a relatively short time after the entry into force of the Treaty of Lisbon in December 2009, I argued that, in short, the attribution of binding effect to the EU Charter of Fundamental Rights would not alter the structure or content of EU internal market law and that it should not alter it either.[1] In this companion chapter I argue, from the experience of almost five years during which the Charter has been in force, that the attribution of binding effect to the EU Charter of Fundamental Rights has not altered the structure or content of EU internal market law and that it should not alter it either. So the mainstream of my argument is that the Charter does not have and should not have a transformative effect on internal market law.

A claim that the attribution of binding status to the Charter is apt to soften the harsh deregulatory edge of the law of the EU's internal market misses the point that the interests found in the Charter were *already* loaded into the law of the internal market. So, although the Treaty of Lisbon forced concern for fundamental rights to the top of the EU's agenda, requiring that the protection of fundamental rights become part of the constitutional framework of the internal market and providing a constitutionally sturdy defence of social and political interests against the incisive deregulatory impetus of internal market law, the argument presented here holds that the key EU institutions—both the judicial and the legislative—have long embedded such wider concerns in internal market law. Internal market law was already 'fundamental rights compliant'. The Charter is confirmation, not transformation. But I have one exception to address, where I hope the

[1] S Weatherill, 'Economic Rights and Fundamental Rights' in S De Vries, U Bernitz and S Weatherill (eds), *The Protection of Fundamental Rights in the EU after Lisbon* (Oxford, Hart Publishing/Institute of European and Comparative Law, 2013).

Charter may be used to rescue an earlier grievous error. This is *Viking Line* and *Laval*.

The risk—and this is the intent behind this chapter's title—is that the Charter will be used to upset existing balances between EU market integration and the regulation of markets expressed through national choices, and that the Charter, especially its Articles 16 and 17, will be used to attack legitimate choices about market regulation (at the national and at the EU level). Is the Charter a deregulatory threat? So far, and gratifyingly, it has not been interpreted in this way by the Court of Justice. But here too I have one exception to address, where the Charter has been misguidedly used in a way apt to undermine existing commitments to social protection. This is *Alemo-Herron*.

II. EU FREE MOVEMENT LAW

Article 36 TFEU provides that: 'The provisions of Articles 34 and 35 shall not preclude prohibitions or restrictions on imports, exports or goods in transit justified on grounds of ... [inter alia] the protection of health and life of humans, animals or plants.' So the law governing the free movement of goods between Member States of the EU does not assert an absolute right to free trade, but rather leaves space for obstructive national rules to be shown to be justified. The law governing the free movement of persons and services adopts the same structure.

The Treaty rules are, however, only a starting point. The Court has a lengthy track record which reveals its thematic readiness to develop a much more flexible framework for assessing the possible justification of practices than is explicitly allowed by the Treaty. This is the sweet taste of *Cassis de Dijon*.[2]

A. Justification Writ Large

In *Cassis de Dijon*, that justifiably and enduringly famous landmark ruling, the Court considered the application of what is today Article 34 of the Treaty on the Functioning of the European Union (TFEU) to German rules requiring a minimum amount of alcohol in particular types of beverage. Having concluded that the matter fell within the scope of the Treaty due to the fact that a French-made blackcurrant liqueur could not be sold in Germany because the French rules (with which the product complied) were

[2] Case 120/78 *Rewe Zentrale v Bundesmonopolverwaltung fur Branntwein* [1979] ECR 649 (hereinafter '*Cassis de Dijon*').

different from those prevailing in Germany (with which the product did not comply), the Court then turned to the possibility of showing justification for the measure. What is now Article 36 TFEU contains a list of justifications that covers public health (one of the grounds on which Germany wished to rely), but it does not cover protection of the consumer (another of the German grounds). The Court did not feel constrained by the textual limitations of the Treaty. It ruled that 'the requirements relating to the minimum alcohol content of alcoholic beverages do not serve a purpose which is in the general interest and such as to take precedence over the requirements of the free movement of goods'.[3] Germany had no plausible justification on the facts, and in fact surrendered its pride to the pressures of local producer interests by raising absurd arguments to explain its regulatory choices. *Weak* alcohol was a more insidious threat to consumers than *strong* alcohol! German consumers would be left bemused by the appearance on the market of a novel product! The Court was more polite to such submissions than Germany deserved, but of course it rejected them. And, as is well known, it has been similarly unreceptive to feeble attempts to justify anachronistic and protectionist national measures across a wide sweep of the regulatory landscape, as the Court's interpretation of Article 34 TFEU pioneered in *Cassis de Dijon* has provoked litigation aimed at clearing away the accumulation of centuries of legislative and administrative deadwood in the Member States.[4] Crucially, however, the Court in *Cassis de Dijon* did not rule out *in principle* the possibility of invoking consumer protection as a justification for trade-restrictive measures.

The Court dealt with a classic case of 'over-regulation' in *Cassis de Dijon*, but the structural point of the judgment was to extend the reach of available justification beyond (what is now) Article 36 TFEU. The Court created a test involving balancing of the general interest pursued by the national rules and the interest in the free movement of goods which would be served by holding those national rules incompatible with EU law. The Court has maintained this approach. It regularly assesses measures of alleged consumer protection. Occasionally it agrees, unlike in *Cassis*, that the interest in national-level regulation is more important than the interest in integration expressed through setting aside the national rules.[5]

The important thematic point informing the Court's approach is that it opens up the defence of national measures that restrict trade to a far wider

[3] ibid [14].

[4] From among a huge catch, see as typical examples Case 261/81 *Walter Rau* [1982] ECR 3961; Case 286/86 *Deserbais* [1988] ECR 4907; Case C-166/03 *Commission v France* [2004] ECR I-6535; Case C-147/04 *De Groot* [2006] ECR I-245; Case C-254/05 *Commission v Belgium* [2007] ECR I-4269.

[5] eg, Case 53/80 *Eyssen* [1981] ECR 409; Case 382/87 *Buet* [1989] ECR 1235; Case C-441/04 *A-Punkt Schmuckhandels GmbH v Claudia Schmidt* [2006] ECR I-2093; and in the services sector Case C-265/12 *Citroën Belux*, judgment of 18 July 2013.

range of interests and sensitivities than Article 36 TFEU seems to promise. The calculatedly generous approach taken by the Court to the possibility in principle to justify national measures that impede cross-border trade is vividly illustrated by its ruling in *Dynamic Medien*.[6] This case concerned German rules dealing with the labelling of videos and related media products. It had much in common with *Cassis de Dijon*. Barriers to inter-state trade arose as a result of differences between German regulatory requirements and those applicable in other Member States. But were the rules, which inter alia aimed to protect children from unsuitable images, justified? The Court stated that:

> The protection of the child is also enshrined in instruments drawn up within the framework of the European Union, such as the Charter of fundamental rights of the European Union, proclaimed on 7 December 2000 in Nice (OJ 2000 C 364, p. 1), Article 24(1) of which provides that children have the right to such protection and care as is necessary for their well-being … Furthermore, the Member States' right to take the measures necessary for reasons relating to the protection of young persons is recognised by a number of Community-law instruments, such as Directive 2000/31.[7]

It is immediately evident that the Court was freely willing to range its inquiry across a plurality of sources remote from the key Treaty provisions dealing with the free movement of goods in determining whether Germany's restriction of inter-state trade was justified. The Charter was at the time not binding, but according to the Court's approach, it served to influence the availability and scope of the German justification for intervention in the product market concerned. The cited Directive 2000/31 is a harmonisation measure dealing with e-commerce which, admittedly, has some peripheral association with the protection of minors, but which is principally a measure designed to promote the development of information society services within the internal market. The Court is not in any sense wrong or mischievous to rely on it, but the Directive is a rather frail basis for finding that EU law recognises the value of protecting young persons. The Court, however, is visibly eager to interpret claims to free movement in a way that is sensitive to, and potentially limited by, the national regulatory concerns with which trade integration comes into contact.

The Court proceeded to accept that conceptions of the necessary level of protection vary from one Member State to another on the basis of moral or cultural views and that accordingly Member States 'must be recognised as having a definite margin of discretion'.[8] The German rules restricted trade, but they were treated as justified. The vital structural point therefore holds

[6] Case C-244/06 *Dynamic Medien* [2008] ECR I-505.
[7] ibid [41].
[8] ibid [44].

that free movement law does not force standards of regulatory protection down to the lowest common denominator to be found among the Member States. This is not a charter of remorseless deregulation.

Assessing justification demands a creative Court. The internal market as a legal concept, built on a shared competence to open up markets and to regulate them,[9] forces the Court to develop its own notion of what is proper and tolerable when pursued at the national level. The regulatory concern expressed through the national rule is absorbed by and reflected in the EU test of justification. The Court, nudged by the Treaty and sometimes by secondary legislation, has long ensured that EU economic law embraces more than economic concerns.[10]

B. Fundamental Rights in Free Movement Cases

Vivid as *Cassis de Dijon* and *Dynamic Medien* are as demonstrations of the Court's readiness to develop the law of trade integration with due respect for the virtues of national regulatory choices, the cases in which the—fundamental!—right to trade comes into collision with the exercise of—fundamental!—rights and freedoms of a social and political nature are still more colourful. These reveal just how porous EU free movement law under the Court's approach to justification has become.

ERT v Dimotiki stands as the first ruling in which the Court established a clear link between justification for trade barriers and compliance with fundamental rights.[11] It insisted on interpretation of the scope of the freedom to provide services in the light of the general principle of freedom of expression embodied in Article 10 of the European Convention on Human Rights. State restrictions on broadcasting which impeded trade in services had to be justified with reference to the Convention. No adequate justification for the restrictions was demonstrated. Certainly, today the Charter of Fundamental Rights would be part of this inquiry: its Article 11, on Freedom of Expression and Information, would buttress the sceptical attitude taken in relation to the possibility to justify state restrictions on broadcasting which impede trade in services. But the Court had already in 1991 shaped the structure of free movement law in such a way as to accommodate such social and political values.

[9] Articles 2(2) and 4(2)(a) TFEU.

[10] It would be possible to extend this analysis into EU competition law, which possesses a clutch of functionally similar devices apt to permit assessment of the objectives of practices that appear to constitute prohibited restrictions of competition: eg, Case C-67/96 *Albany International* [1999] ECR I-5751; Case C-309/99 *Wouters* [2002] ECR I-1577; Case C-519/04P *Meca-Medina & Majcen v Commission* [2006] ECR I-6991; Case C-136/12 *Consiglio nazionale dei geologi*, judgment of 18 July 2013.

[11] Case C-260/89 *ERT v Dimotiki* [1991] ECR I-2925.

Schmidberger v Austria is another of the Court's classics.[12] The Austrian authorities had permitted a protest to block the movement of transport through the Brenner Pass. The Austrian failure to intervene was in principle capable of falling within the scope of what is now Article 34 TFEU because it led to a temporary obstacle to trade in goods. But it was motivated by a concern to protect the freedom of assembly and freedom of expression of those wishing to draw attention to the environmental damage caused by such trade. This, then, was a perfect model of the problem: economic rights clashing with political rights. The Court declared that:

> [S]ince both the Community and its Member States are required to respect fundamental rights, the protection of those rights is a legitimate interest which, in principle, justifies a restriction of the obligations imposed by Community law, even under a fundamental freedom guaranteed by the Treaty such as the free movement of goods.[13]

Economic versus political! These are fundamental rights, but they are not absolute rights. The Court stated that 'the interests involved must be weighed having regard to all the circumstances of the case in order to determine whether a fair balance was struck between those interests' and added that the 'competent authorities enjoy a wide margin of discretion in that regard'.[14] Noting a range of factors,[15] the Court then made plain that the Austrian (lack of) action against those conducting the protests constituted no violation of EU law, despite the restrictive effect on cross-border trade in goods.

The more sensitive and the more remote from commercial considerations the matters advanced in the context of justification of trade barriers, the more generous the Court tends to be to the available scope for justification and also to the breadth of the margin of appreciation enjoyed by the regulator—sometimes too, but not always, the more sensitive it is to the authority of the national court to make the final judgement on whether the challenged practices are in fact justified.

A comparable result, but according to slightly different reasoning, may be identified in *Omega Spielhallen*.[16] This case concerned the suppression of games involving simulated killing in Germany on the basis that such practices offended against constitutionally protected standards of respect for human dignity. This restricted the importation of services from the UK. Was the German intervention justified? The Court was favourably inclined:

> [T]he Community legal order undeniably strives to ensure respect for human dignity as a general principle of law. There can therefore be no doubt that the

[12] Case C-112/00 *Schmidberger v Austria* [2003] ECR I-5659.
[13] ibid [74].
[14] ibid [81]–[82].
[15] ibid [81]–[94].
[16] Case C-36/02 *Omega Spielhallen* [2004] ECR I-9609.

> objective of protecting human dignity is compatible with Community law, it being immaterial in that respect that, in Germany, the principle of respect for human dignity has a particular status as an independent fundamental right.[17]

The structure of this approach is enticingly skilful. The Court did not construct this as EU free movement law versus German protection of human dignity, but instead as EU free movement law versus *EU* protection of human dignity. The justification was rooted not in German specificity, but in an EU embrace of a standard of protection comparable with that chosen in Germany (but not found to the same degree in other Member States). So EU law accommodates German anxieties: free movement law is about *much* more than free movement.[18]

C. The Charter will not and Should not Make and is not Making a Difference

The argument presented above holds that the Court deserves credit for sincere engagement with the shaping of a mature fundamental rights regime for the EU, here in the particular context of free movement law. If this is correct, one would expect to see the Charter play a presentational role in free movement cases, but one would not expect it to alter the structure of the legal analysis or the outcome. One would expect it merely to buttress the Court's existing inclination to embrace non-economic values in the development of free movement law.

The claim that the Charter is not apt to exert a transformative effect in free movement cases enjoys support from the (admittedly still limited) amount of case law decided since it acquired binding force in 2009.

Commission v Austria[19] is not a ruling which makes any connection with the wider range of social and political rights and freedoms considered above, but it is a ruling which shows how easy it is to fit the Charter into the existing *structure* of free movement law. Moreover, it also supports the argument that the Charter causes no likely change to the *result*. Austria had banned lorries over 7.5 tonnes from carrying certain goods—those with an 'affinity to rail'—from using a section of motorway in the Inn valley.

[17] ibid [34].

[18] For a similar conclusion, see J Schwarze, 'Die Abwägung von Zielen der europäischen Integration und mitgliedstaatlichen Interessen in der Rechtsprechung des EuGH' (2013) 3 *Europarecht* 253. See also, eg, N NicShuibhne, 'Margins of Appreciation: National Values, Fundamental Rights and EC Free Movement Law' (2009) 34 *European Law Review* 230; C Semmelmann, 'The European Union's Economic Constitution under the Lisbon Treaty: Soul-Searching Shifts the Focus to Procedure' (2010) 35 *European Law Review* 516; D Damjanovic, 'The EU Market Rules as Social Market Rules: Why the EU Can Be a Social Market Economy' (2013) 50 *CML Rev* 1685.

[19] Case C-28/09 *Commission v Austria*, judgment of 21 December 2011.

This was found to have a substantial effect on the free movement of goods between Northern Europe and Northern Italy. In assessing whether the intervention was justified, the Court referred to (what were then) Articles 2, 3, 6 and 152(1) EC and Articles 35 and 37 of the Charter as sources of respect for health and environmental protection. But it then found the 'radical' traffic ban to go too far.[20] Austria had not sufficiently considered alternative, less restrictive methods of achieving its ends, including applying a lower permanent speed limit in preference to the prevailing variable speed limit. The main structural point of the ruling is that the Court drew on, inter alia, the Charter as a basis for injecting concern for health and environmental protection into its application of the free movement rules, but it was doing nothing new. Health protection is and always has been recognised as a justification for national initiatives that obstruct inter-state trade. It is on the Article 36 TFEU list. Environmental protection is not on that list, but it has been embraced as an available justification by the Court's case law for almost 30 years.[21] The ruling demonstrates how the Charter fits easily into the familiar structure of free movement law as an amplification, but not an adjustment, of the relevant material relied on to assess whether a restriction is justified.

Essent Belgium, a case decided in September 2014, approaching five years since the entry into force of the Lisbon Treaty and the attribution of binding effect to the Charter, also raised questions about environmental protection in the context of the free movement of goods.[22] It concerned 'green certificates': such a certificate establishes the quantity of electricity which has been produced from renewable energy sources. Essent had been fined by the Flemish authorities for failure to provide appropriate certificates, but its complaint was that the Flemish authorities had refused to accept guarantees attesting to the production of 'green electricity' in the Netherlands and in Norway. This refusal, the Court found, had the potential to restrict electricity imports from other Member States. It fell foul of what is now Article 34, unless shown to be objectively justified. The Court noted that the use of renewable energy sources for the production of electricity 'is useful for the protection of the environment inasmuch as it contributes to the reduction in greenhouse gas emissions, which are amongst the main causes of climate change that the European Union and its Member States have pledged to combat'.[23] In addition to environmental concerns recognised by (what are

[20] ibid [140].
[21] Case 302/86 *Commission v Denmark* [1988] ECR 4607; Case C-2/90 *Commission v Belgium* [1992] ECR I-4431; Case C-379/98 *Preussen Elektra* [2001] ECR I-2099.
[22] Joined Cases C-204/12–C-208/12 *Essent Belgium*, judgment of 11 September 2014.
[23] ibid [91].

today) Articles 11 and 191(1) TFEU,[24] this too helps to protect the health and life of humans, animals and plants, as explicitly recognised by Article 36 TFEU.[25] The measures were justified and the Court found in addition that, given the absence of common rules governing national support schemes for green electricity, the territorial limitation on recognition of certificates was necessary in order to attain the legitimate objective pursued. This fell within the Member State's 'margin of discretion'.[26] The Charter is not mentioned *at all*. There was, presumably, no need to mention it, although its Articles 35 and 37 could have easily been fitted into the analysis. The job—balancing the objectives of environmental and health protection against the demands of trade integration—could be done perfectly well with the existing materials of free movement law. The Charter would change nothing.

In *Pfleger*, the Court provided further confirmation that it is disinclined to use the Charter to achieve a balance between competing interests that is different from that which it has crafted in and since *Cassis de Dijon*.[27] In *Pfleger*, the Court carefully examined the justification for restricting the freedom to provide gambling services within the scope of Article 56 TFEU, and agreed that there was room to justify such restrictions in the name of consumer protection and the prevention of both fraud and incitement to squander money on gambling, subject to compliance with the conventional dictates of proportionality and non-discrimination. It then added that the challenged national measures were restrictive not only from the point of view of Article 56 TFEU, but were also limitations from the perspective of Articles 15–17 of the Charter dealing with the freedom to choose an occupation, the freedom to conduct a business and the right to property. But it seems that this adds nothing and changes nothing. The Court simply declared that there was no need for any separate examination of the Charter-based claims. Analysis seems to run in perfect parallel with the well-established approach to assessing restrictions on gambling under Article 56, according to which the Court has typically been remarkably mild in the intensity of its review of national controls.[28] As Advocate General Sharpston remarked in her Opinion in the case, where a restriction fulfils the Court's criteria governing justification, 'it is not precluded by Articles 15, 16 or 17 of the Charter'.[29] The Charter has not changed free movement law.

[24] ibid [94].
[25] ibid [93].
[26] ibid [108].
[27] Case C-390/12 *Pfleger*, judgment of 30 April 2014.
[28] eg, Joined Cases C-338/04 et al *Massimiliano Placanica* [2007] ECR I-1891; Case C-258/08 *Ladbrokes* [2010] ECR I-4757; Cases C-316/07 et al *Markus Stoss* [2010] ECR I-8069; Cases C-186/11 and C-209/11 *Stanleybet*, judgment of 24 January 2013.
[29] *Pfleger* (n 27); see her Opinion at [71].

D. Nor is Article 4(2) a Force for Qualitative Change

The Charter is not the only element of the reforms introduced with effect from 2009 by the Lisbon Treaty that deserves assessment for its potential to effect a reshaping of the law of the internal market. According to Article 4(2) of the Treaty on European Union (TEU), the EU 'shall respect the equality of Member States before the Treaties as well as their national identities, inherent in their fundamental structures, political and constitutional, inclusive of regional and local self-government'. This is the more elaborate successor to a provision which pre-Lisbon simply provided that: 'The Union shall respect the national identities of its Member States.' The new version could be read as an invitation to show increased respect for national diversity, inter alia in connection with free movement law's application to national restrictions. Here too, however, this chapter defends the view that change is improbable because the relevant values were already inscribed in internal market law.

Omega Spielhallen and *Schmidberger* stand as strong challenges to a claim that justification of trade barriers has not previously been receptive to the possibility of showing how and why national constitutional sensitivities should be tolerated even where they impede cross-border trade. They fit comfortably within the steer found in Article 4(2) TEU: they show that it is nothing new. The Court's more recent case law dealing with Article 4(2) more or less confirms this. *Ilonka Sayn-Wittgenstein v Landeshauptmann von Wien* is a ruling with a colourful background.[30] At stake was an Austrian law from 1919 abolishing the nobility which inter alia did away with titles, whereas, by contrast, Germany had done away with privileges but allowed parts of the noble title to be retained in the surname. So here was the diversity in treatment that triggered a barrier to movement of the classic *Cassis de Dijon* type. The applicant was Ilonka Fürstin von Sayn-Wittgenstein in Germany. In Austria she was advised she must be registered instead as Ilonka Sayn-Wittgenstein. This constituted serious inconvenience to her commercial activity—which was selling castles. This was a restriction of the freedom envisaged by Article 21 TFEU. It was doubtless also a matter apt for examination pursuant to Article 56 TFEU, though the Court did not pursue this dimension. The key question in any event was whether the Austrian rule was justified. The Court noted that Austria was concerned to abolish titles in the service of equality of citizens before the law and added that this is also recognised under EU law in Article 20 of the Charter. The Court cited *Omega Spielhallen*:[31] these are sensitive issues, where national authorities are permitted a 'margin of discretion'.[32] It then observed that in

[30] Case C-208/09 *Ilonka Sayn-Wittgenstein v Landeshauptmann von Wien* [2010] ECR I-13693.
[31] *Omega Spielhallen* (n 16).
[32] ibid [87].

accordance with Article 4(2) TEU, the EU is to respect the national identities of its Member States and that it did not appear disproportionate for a Member State to seek to attain the objective of protecting equal treatment by prohibiting use of titles of nobility.[33]

In *Omega*, the Court converted a national constitutional concern into an EU constitutional concern. In *Sayn-Wittgenstein*, it used Article 4(2) TEU to show respect for a specifically *Austrian* concern. One might find a hint here that Article 4(2) TEU is a route to soften free movement law yet further. But in fact the Court's approaches in the two cases have far more similarities than differences. In *Sayn-Wittgenstein*, the Court used Article 4(2) to convert a particular substantive national concern, equality, into the EU concern to respect difference among legal regimes where it operates at a sufficiently elevated level, that is, where national identity is engaged. The outcome is in any event the same. Free movement law yields to justified national measures. In the background lies the Court's concern to take seriously *as a matter of EU law* sensitive matters of national identity which, as *Omega* and *Schmidberger* demonstrate, is by no means a post-Lisbon innovation.

E. But *Viking Line* and *Laval*

The mood of this chapter is sunny. It argues that free movement law has always been 'fundamental rights compliant': the rise of the Charter is not transformative, for the Court has always interpreted and applied the Treaty rules on free movement in a way that has ensured their receptivity to the values pursued by national measures that happen in some way to interfere with cross-border trade patterns. But two rulings of the Court lurk sullenly, challenging this relentlessly positive vision. *Viking Line* and *Laval* spoil the party.[34]

The Court's rulings in *Viking Line* and *Laval* were delivered in December 2007. They expose the Court to the allegation that its rhetoric of respect for (in short) non-economic values is contaminated by an economic bias in favour of harsh deregulation. The two cases had many similarities and some differences, but at heart they asked whether EU free movement law protected a firm wishing to move aspects of its business from one state to another from collective action by labour unions aimed at deterring such corporate strategies.

The cases ask what type of internal market is being built: freedom to trade? Freedom to act collectively to compete effectively against corporate

[33] ibid [92]–[93].

[34] Case C-438/05 *Viking Line* [2007] ECR I-10779; Case C-341/05 *Laval* [2007] ECR I-11767.

power? In concrete legal terms, what mattered was whether the restrictive effects of the collective labour action were *justified*. The Court had never before been invited to address the need to reconcile fundamental (but not absolute) rights in the context of labour disputes. It accepted in principle that the right to take collective action to protect workers is a legitimate interest which justifies a restriction of economic freedoms guaranteed by the Treaty. But the Court proceeded to hold that a national court must ascertain whether the objectives pursued by means of the collective action concern the protection of workers, and in *Viking Line* it ruled that:

> [E]ven if that action—aimed at protecting the jobs and conditions of employment of the members of that union liable to be adversely affected by the reflagging of the *Rosella*—could reasonably be considered to fall, at first sight, within the objective of protecting workers, such a view would no longer be tenable if it were established that the jobs or conditions of employment at issue were not jeopardised or under serious threat.[35]

So, it seems that *only* action aimed at protecting the jobs of union members is recognised as capable of being justified under EU law. The Court appears to have excluded the possibility of more long-term strategic action taken by unions insofar as it impedes cross-border economic activity. This constitutes a dramatic incursion into the scope of collective labour rights as they have been developed—and fought for—over time. The litigation in *Viking Line* itself was settled out of court shortly after the Court's judgment, but the consequence was deep unease that the Court, drawn into an area in which it possesses little expertise by an accident of litigation, had adopted a test which significantly favours corporate interests over worker protection.[36] The Court's judgment empowers actors at the national level seeking to propel reform of the 'social partnership' to the benefit of employer interests: it is likely to place a deterrent effect on collective labour action.

The judgments are marred still further by a failure explicitly to concede the margin of discretion which is required in cases that are as complex as this. In *Schmidberger*, the Court accepted that the competent authorities enjoyed a wide margin of discretion. Rightly so, given the difficulty involved in expecting an intensive *judicial* review of which interests should prevail in the particular circumstances. But in *Viking Line* and *Laval*, cases of at least equal and perhaps greater sensitivity, the Court missed out this nuanced restraint on judicial intervention.

[35] *Viking Line* (n 34) [81].

[36] *cf*, eg, L Azoulai, 'The Court of Justice and the Social Market Economy: The Emergence of an Ideal and the Conditions for its Realisation' (2008) 45 *CML Rev* 1335; A Davies, 'One Step Forward, Two Steps Back? The Viking and Laval Cases in the ECJ' (2008) 37 *Industrial Law Journal* 126.

This places the rulings out of line with internal market orthodoxy. In fact, *Viking Line* and *Laval* have an anachronistic feel to them. They are similar in tone to the cases of the early years—concerning French turkeys,[37] blackcurrant liqueur[38] and the fat content of cheese[39]—in which the Court rather brusquely swept aside thoroughly implausible claims to justification made on behalf of protectionist measures by public authorities, and deservedly so. But *Viking Line* and *Laval*, dealing with the place of collective labour action pursued by private parties in the face of aggressive corporate attempts to exploit the EU to cut costs, raised serious and delicate questions about priorities. These were evaded by the Court's refusal to take seriously what was at stake.

This is deeply unfortunate. The Court has unduly limited the scope for legitimate action by what the Treaty today terms 'social partners', whose autonomy is to be respected according to Article 152 TFEU. Troubling too is the fact that the Court's interference in the name of free movement law cannot be readily adjusted through the EU *legislative* process. In part, this is because of the constitutional limits placed by the Treaties on EU legislative action in these realms, but also because of the difficulty in finding a political consensus to act even within those permitted limits. And in fact the Commission Proposal for a Regulation on the exercise of the right to take collective action within the context of the freedom of establishment and the freedom to provide services, which was designed to clarify the rulings, proved too politically controversial, even though its intent was in fact rather modest.[40] Attacked by some Member States, influential groups within the European Parliament and some national Parliaments too, the proposal was dropped.[41]

The structural critique of EU law, which asserts its tendency to impose radical deregulatory pressures on national socio-economic choices, seems to me to carry real weight, yet to deserve some degree of challenge driven by concrete assessment of the case law. As argued above, many national measures which have been cut down fully deserve to have been cut down and where genuine and sincere justification for national practices that oppose free movement is advanced, then the Court is normally properly respectful

[37] Case 40/82 *Commission v UK* [1982] ECR 2793.

[38] *Cassis de Dijon* (n 2).

[39] *Deserbais* (n 3).

[40] COM (2012) 130 21 March 2012 ('Monti II').

[41] For the Commission's explanation, see Annual Report 2012 on Subsidiarity and Proportionality, COM (2013) 566, 6–8; see also F Fabbrini and K Granat, 'Yellow Card But No Foul: The Role of the National Parliaments under the Subsidiarity Protocol and the Commission Proposal for an EU Regulation on the Right to Strike' (2013) 50 *CML Rev* 115; M Goldoni, 'The Early Warning System and the Monti II Regulation: The Case for a Political Interpretation' (2014) 10 *European Constitutional Law Review* 90.

of such regulatory virtue. True, Luxembourg case-crunching cannot provide a complete refutation of the critique. Even if one is ready to praise the Court's skilful balancing in the cases that have reached its door, one would be complacent unless attempts were also made to take account of how many national measures have been withdrawn or not even proposed because of the 'pre-litigation' dissuasive effect of EU law. And one would need to inspect the supplementary deregulatory pressure introduced by EU legislative intervention. But, focusing on the Luxembourg case law alone, I think it is not insensitively deregulatory. That is why I cannot defend *Viking Line* and *Laval*. They are out of line.

The mistake made in *Viking Line* and *Laval* could be corrected by reliance on the reforms made by the Treaty of Lisbon. The commitment to undistorted competition in the Treaty was shifted out of the Treaty 'proper' and into a Protocol. This may readily be thought to adjust the constitutional balance in favour of socially motivated public regulation at the expense of market competition. Article 28 of the Charter provides, inter alia, that workers have the right to take collective action to defend their interests, including strike action—and this is now binding. Moreover, Article 3(3) TEU now commits the EU to, inter alia, a 'social market'. These do not amount to *definitive* changes to the heartland of internal market law, but were one seeking to defend the (trade-restrictive) expression of social and political freedom in circumstances such as those which arose in *Viking Line* and *Laval*, one would now argue that, post-Lisbon, the emphasis has shifted. Two Advocates General—Cruz Villalón in *Santos Palhota and others* and Trstenjak in *Commission v Germany*[42]—have already tried to push the Court in these directions, albeit so far without success. What is at stake is rebalancing priorities with consequences sympathetic to social protection.[43] The Court will ultimately have to make a choice.

One would certainly understand that if the Court does choose to repent, it will use the reforms made by the Lisbon Treaty as its excuse. That, indeed, is exactly how both Advocates General, especially Cruz Villalón, structured their Opinions. However, there was plenty of material available in the state of EU internal market law existing at the time of the judgments in *Viking Line* and *Laval* that was apt to justify such a rebalanced approach. In this sense, the entry into force of the Lisbon Treaty in 2009 could provide a convenient cover for the Court to resile from *Viking Line* and *Laval*, but to do

[42] Case C–515/08 *Santos Palhota and others* (5 May 2010); AG Trstenjak in Case C–271/08 *Commission v Germany* (14 April 2010).

[43] *cf*, eg, NicShuibhne (n 18); Semmelmann (n 18); D Schiek, 'The EU Constitution of Social Governance in an Economic Crisis: In Defence of a Transnational Dimension to Social Europe' (2013) 20 *Maastricht Journal of European and Comparative Law* 185; I Lianos, 'Competition Law in the European Union after the Treaty of Lisbon' in D Ashiagbor, N Countouris and I Lianos (eds), *The European Union after the Treaty of Lisbon* (Cambridge, Cambridge University Press, 2013).

so would be to bring the law back into line with what it should have been had those cases been decided with greater circumspection and in line with pre-existing orthodoxy. Advocate General Trstenjak's Opinion is very much in this vein, as she pressed (fruitlessly) for a rethinking in *Commission v Germany*:

> [C]onfirmation of this approach characterised by an equal ranking of fundamental rights and fundamental freedoms in which the principle of proportionality serves as the basis for the resolution of conflicts between the exercise of fundamental freedoms and the exercise of fundamental rights would not constitute a fundamental reorientation in the case-law. Instead, this analysis implies a return to the values already inherent in *Schmidberger*.[44]

Such rebalancing would serve to bring the intersection between labour law and EU internal market law into conformity with the general pattern whereby sensitive national practices and concerns are reviewed with care in the light of their impact on the internal market, under a model which also permits a margin of appreciation.

Therefore, the Charter can in this instance save the Court from itself. The flaws in *Viking Line* and *Laval* are not endemic to internal market law, but rather arise from the Court's own misguided, one-sided approach in those rulings, which even at the time of the rulings was sorely out of line with the orthodoxy of free movement law.

III. LEGISLATIVE HARMONISATION

For the purposes of this chapter, examination of the legislative contribution to making the EU's internal market involves an assessment of the extent to which (in short) non-economic values form part of the project. It has this in common with the exploration provided above of the judicial contribution. And, as with free movement law, so too with the EU's legislative activity: the question whether the internal market takes adequate account of fundamental rights—and, in particular, whether the Lisbon Treaty has changed or should change the groundrules—is dependent upon assessment of the long-term trajectory of EU internal market law.

A. Article 114 and Re-Regulation of the Internal Market

It is plain that, reaching back long before the Lisbon Treaty came into sight, legislative practice involved an embrace of a wide range of 're-regulatory concerns' and that, moreover, this regulatory breadth was approved by the

44 *Commission v Germany* (n 42) [193].

Court. The key provision on legislative harmonisation today is Article 114 TFEU. It provides for the adoption of measures 'for the approximation of the provisions laid down by law, regulation or administrative action in member states which have as their object the establishing and functioning of the internal market'. So such harmonisation is tied to the achievement of the objectives set out in Article 26 TFEU, which means the establishment of an internal market within the EU, defined in Article 26 as 'an area without internal frontiers in which the free movement of goods, persons, services and capital is ensured in accordance with the provisions of the Treaties'. The rationale for EU action holds that variation between national laws impedes market integration, prompting a need for harmonisation at the EU level. A viable internal market requires common rules. Free trade is facilitated because protection is achieved according to a common EU standard which irons out trade-restrictive differences between national systems. Once national laws are swept within the harmonisation net, the EU assumes the function of setting its own—common—rules in the relevant fields. EU laws come into existence in order to integrate the market, but their incidental effect is also to regulate it—or more pertinently to 're-regulate' it, in the sense that the EU is not acting as a de novo regulator, but rather is responding to the pre-existing diverse regulatory choices among the Member States.

Harmonisation therefore has a dual function: it sets common rules for the European market, but, against a background of diverse national sources of regulatory inspiration, it also involves a choice of the appropriate standard of re-regulatory protection that will apply in common throughout the EU.

So, provided Article 114 may be validly relied upon, the EU has a competence to reach deep and wide as a (re)-regulator. And although valid reliance on Article 114 depends on demonstrating that harmonisation will serve the interests of the internal market, this has proved to be a threshold that is remarkably easy to cross. In fact, the Court's famous ruling in *Tobacco Advertising*,[45] in which it found a measure of harmonisation to be invalid for want of adequate market-making capacity, is high profile precisely because it is so very rare. Normally the legislature is astute to draft measures in a way that will satisfy the Court, if challenged.[46] And consequently harmonisation has a wide scope.

Harmonisation of laws has long involved choices about the suppression of particular commercial practices in order to achieve protection of

[45] Case C-376/98 *Tobacco Advertising* [2000] ECR I-8419.

[46] eg, Case C-66/04 *UK v Parliament & Council* [2005] ECR I-10553; Case C-380/03 *Germany v Parliament and Council* [2006] ECR I-11573; Case C-58/08 *Vodafone, O2 et al v Secretary of State* [2010] ECR I-4999; Case C-270/12 *UK v Council and Parliament*, judgment of 22 January 2014. See S Weatherill, 'The Limits of Legislative Harmonisation Ten Years after *Tobacco Advertising:* How the Court's Case Law Has Become a "Drafting Guide"' (2011) 12 *German Law Journal* 827.

particular values. The Court has declared that provided that the conditions for recourse to Article 114 TFEU as a legal basis are fulfilled, the EU legislature 'cannot be prevented from relying on that legal basis on the ground that public health protection is a decisive factor in the choices to be made' and logically, in the light of the commitment of key provisions such as Articles 114(3) and 168 TFEU to public health concerns, the harmonised rule 'may consist in requiring all the Member States to authorise the marketing of the product or products concerned, subjecting such an obligation of authorisation to certain conditions, or even provisionally or definitively prohibiting the marketing of a product or products'.[47] There is plainly no objection in principle to a harmonised *ban* on goods—provided that the generally applicable criteria for reliance on Article 114 are met, which will typically mean that the ban must form part of a regime dealing with a wider category of products than simply those subjected to the harmonised ban.

So, to pick a simple example, a harmonised ban on unsafe products opens up the market for safe products, and the matter therefore falls within the permitted scope of legislative harmonisation.[48] In this vein, legislative practice has long shaped a distinctive form of consumer, public health and environmental protection at the EU level, and the Court has actively supported the notion that harmonisation in the service of the internal market inevitably involves a sensitive choice between a range of possible approaches and techniques. Harmonisation of national laws is an exercise in vertical allocation of regulatory responsibility. It locates at the EU level the need for an *EU* understanding of the nature and purpose of whatever is harmonised. Provisions such as Articles 11, 12, 114(3) and 168 TFEU, which have long been part of the Treaty, albeit over time in different form and under different numbering, are among those that lend constitutional support for such regulatory interlinkage.

One might choose to treat the Lisbon reforms, and in particular the grant of binding effect to the Charter, as apt to increase the profile of such protective concerns. But they do not mark a qualitative change in the texture of the law of the internal market. One could readily line up Charter provisions such as Articles 35, 37 and 38 alongside Articles 11, 12, 114(3) and 168 TFEU as expressions of concern for market regulation. But they would not dictate anything new.

So the Charter, in particular but not only in its Chapter IV entitled 'Solidarity', is apt to confirm the constitutional virtue of market regulation. But do other provisions of the Charter promote a deregulatory shove? Article 16 (freedom to conduct a business) and Article 17 (right to property)

[47] eg, Cases C-154/04 and C-155/04 *Alliance for Natural Health* [2005] ECR I-6451; *Germany v Parliament and Council* (n 46).

[48] Directive 2001/95 [2002] OJ L11/4.

might be deployed in order to attack the validity of interventions in the market. This is the Charter's threat—this is what the internal market needs to be protected against, as suggested by the title of this chapter. So far, the Court has—with one exception—been vigilant in resisting the threat.

Such attacks as have been launched by disgruntled traders against the exercise of legislative competence have not typically impressed the Court in the times when the Charter lacked binding status. The right to property, for example, is recognised by EU law, but it 'is not an absolute right and must be viewed in relation to its social function' and the Court has no objection to legislative restriction on its exercise 'provided that those restrictions in fact correspond to objectives of general interest … and do not constitute a disproportionate and intolerable interference, impairing the very substance of the rights guaranteed'.[49] *Alliance for Natural Health* offers an illustration of the Court's reluctance to allow legislative intervention in the market to be overturned.[50] The Court had pressed on it by the applicant the argument that it was disproportionately restrictive to allow the marketing only of nutrients that had received a favourable opinion from the competent scientific authorities. Instead, it was argued, nutrients that had not been shown to represent a risk to human health should also be allowed. The Court declined to intervene. The measures were 'appropriate for achieving the objective which they pursue and that, given the obligation of the … legislature to ensure a high level of protection of human health, they do not go beyond what is necessary to attain that objective'.[51] While accepting that the 'positive list' system was a more burdensome means of regulating the market than a 'negative list', the Court ruled that it was not a disproportionate burden.

A margin is allowed to the EU legislature. The Court attributes no absolute status to property rights or to the freedom to conduct a business, but rather accepts that in principle their exercise may be limited by market regulation in the general interest. It is, moreover, rare for measures based on the exercise of political judgment to be tripped up by non-compliance with the proportionality principle. The Court is astute to the proper limits of its institutional role—and in consequence EU internal market law allows space for market regulation as well as market deregulation. This vision has already been examined in relation to free movement law: this is now the version found in relation to the EU's legislative capacity.

As for free movement, so for legislative harmonisation: the trends pursued by the Treaty of Lisbon are trends that are already firmly part of EU internal

[49] Case C-491/01 *R v Secretary of State ex parte BAT and Imperial Tobacco* [2002] ECR I-11543 [149]. See also, eg, Case C-280/93 *Germany v Council* [1994] ECR I–4973 [78]; Cases C-184/02 and C-223/02 *Spain and Finland v Parliament and Council* [2004] ECR I-7789 [52].

[50] *Alliance for Natural Health* (n 47).

[51] ibid [111].

market law. The Court's ruling in the autumn of 2012 in *Deutsches Weintor eG v Land Rheinland-Pfalz* offers support for this argument.[52] Regulation 1924/2006 harmonises rules governing nutrition and health claims made about food. Pursuant to the Regulation, a German public authority prohibited use of the phrase 'easily digestible' in connection with wines. This was challenged by a wine growers' cooperative. The Court found that the matter concerned a 'health claim' within the scope of the Regulation and then turned to consider whether the restriction was compatible with EU law. On the one hand, Article 15(1) of the Charter grants the right to engage in work and to pursue a freely chosen or accepted occupation, and Article 16 guarantees the freedom to conduct a business. On the other hand, Article 35 of the Charter requires that a high level of human health protection be ensured in the definition and implementation of EU policies and activities. The Court was therefore required 'to reconcile the requirements of the protection of those various fundamental rights protected by the Union legal order' and to strike 'a fair balance between them'.[53] The Court emphasised that alcoholic beverages are typically subject to particularly strict regulation and cited existing case law in which *national* restrictions on the advertising of such products have been held to be compatible with EU law despite their hindrance to trade.[54] It added that it is essential that all claims in relation to such beverages are unambiguous so that consumers are in a position to regulate their consumption in an informed manner. The problem with the claim made, which highlighted *only* the easy digestion of the wine, was its likely encouragement of consumption with increased risks for consumers' health, and that consequently the prohibition of such claims was warranted.

This reliance on Article 35 of the Charter on public health therefore brought the Court to the conclusion that the legislative regime was based on a reconciliation of the several fundamental rights at stake, striking a fair balance between them. It was compatible with EU law. The Court could easily have fitted Article 38 of the Charter on consumer protection into its analysis, but chose not to. The crucial point, however, is that there is nothing in this analysis that is qualitatively different from the type of examination the Court would have conducted prior to the entry into force of the Lisbon Treaty. Articles 16 and 17 of the Charter are neither subversive nor revolutionary.[55] Reliance on the Charter as the formal basis for examination

[52] Case C-544/10 *Deutsches Weintor eG v Land Rheinland-Pfalz*, judgment of 6 September 2012.

[53] ibid [47]. *cf* Case C-283/11 *Sky Österreich GmbH*, judgment of 22 January 2013; Case C-101/12 *Herbert Schaible*, judgment of 17 October 2013.

[54] eg, Joined Cases C–1/90 and C–176/90 *Aragonesa de Publicidad Exterior* [1991] ECR I–4151; Case C–262/02 *Commission v France* [2004] ECR I–6569.

[55] *cf* P Oliver, 'What Purpose Does Article 16 of the Charter Serve?' in U Bernitz, X Groussot and F Schulyok (eds), *General Principles of EU law and European Private Law*

might be new, but the substance of the Court's approach in *Deutsches Weintor* has a great deal common with that in a case such as *Alliance for Natural Health*.

The Court does not aggressively defend commercial freedom from EU legislative intervention. It never has done. Post-Lisbon, 'balancing' is structurally nothing new compared with pre-existing practice. So, to make the point, in *Denise McDonough v Ryanair Ltd*,[56] the Court upheld provisions on compensation for air passengers in Regulation 261/2004 as striking a 'fair balance' between, on the one hand, Articles 16 and 17 of the Charter and, on the other, Article 38, and it cited both *Promusicae*[57] (a pre-Lisbon ruling) and *Deutsches Weintor*[58] (a post-Lisbon ruling) without suggesting that they carry the slightest difference in their substantive significance.

B. *Alemo-Herron*

In connection with free movement law, the narrative presented above of a Court normally attuned to the virtue of social protection was disrupted by *Viking Line* and *Laval*.[59] And the Court's treatment of the legislative context has a single nasty twist too. The awkward case here is *Alemo-Herron*.[60] This concerns employee protection on the transfer of undertakings. A reference from the UK's Supreme Court asked whether a particular judicial approach to (measures implementing) Directive 2001/23 was correct. This approach, which took a 'dynamic' view of the place of collective bargains in governing the rights of employees of transferred undertakings, was noticeably more generous to the employee than the alternative competing ('static') interpretation.

A starting point might have been that the proper requirements of EU law did not much matter to the resolution of the case itself, since Article 8 of Directive 2001/23 provides that the Directive 'shall not affect the right of Member States to apply or introduce laws, regulations or administrative provisions which are more favourable to employees or to promote or permit collective agreements or agreements between social partners more favourable to employees'. This seems to guarantee that that the UK is *permitted* to adopt a more generous system of employee protection, embracing

(Aalphen aan den Rijn, Kluwer, 2013: 'it seems clear that Article 16 is reserved for extreme cases' (at 299). See also M Everson and R Correia Gonçalves, 'Article 16' and F Wollenschläger, 'Article 17' in S Peers, T Hervey, J Kenner and A Ward (eds), *The EU Charter of Fundamental Rights: A Commentary* (Oxford, Hart Publishing, 2014).

[56] Case C-12/11 *Denise McDonough v Ryanair Ltd*, judgment of 31 January 2013.
[57] Case C-275/06 *Promusicae* [2008] ECR I-271.
[58] *Deutsches Weintor* (n 52).
[59] *Viking Line* (n 34); *Laval* (n 34).
[60] Case C-426/11 *Alemo-Herron*, judgment of 18 July 2013.

the 'dynamic' approach, even if it should be concluded that the Directive *requires* only the 'static' approach. Not so, however. The Third Chamber of the Court took the view that this proviso could not be interpreted 'as entitling the Member States to take measures which, while being more favourable to employees, are liable to adversely affect the very essence of the transferee's freedom to conduct a business'.[61] This is to write in a major limitation to the legislative grant of autonomy to Member States to adopt measures more favourable to employees. The Court appears to rest its interpretation on Article 16 of the Charter, but that is to stretch the wording of Article 16 a very long way, and in a direction that is favourable only to employers' interests.

The Court's ruling insists on the need for a 'fair balance' between the employer and the employee, and finds that the managerial flexibility of the company to which the transfer has been made would be improperly confined were the dynamic interpretation to prevail. So it chooses the 'static' interpretation. This is a balance of sorts—but one that is tilted towards the employer, not the employee, and it is hard to attach the adjective 'fair' to it with any conviction. Most alarming of all is the Court's heavy reliance on Article 16 of the Charter, which (it was said by the Court) covers freedom of contract within the freedom to conduct a business.[62] It is claimed in the judgment that were the English courts' interpretation to prevail, then the private firm, to which the business has been transferred, would find its contractual freedom seriously reduced to the point that there may be damage to the very essence of its freedom to conduct a business. This is a blatant exaggeration. The Court's aggressive protection of the constitutional value of freedom of contract goes too far when one assesses the factual background to this litigation. But more generally, and more seriously, it is an approach which is out of line with the scepticism about the reality of freedom of contract found in the EU's consumer legislation and case law, and in some of the older employee protection material as well. The Court's ruling in *Alemo-Herron* misses the thematic rationale of protecting weaker parties.[63] Moreover, *Alemo-Herron*, asserting this powerful and revolutionary new role to be played by Article 16 of the Charter, cites in support the Court's rulings in *Sky Osterreich* and *Deutsches Weintor*, while failing utterly to confess that these were rulings in which the Court authorised legislative *restrictions* on contractual and commercial freedom. This verges on judicial deception.

[61] ibid [36].

[62] ibid [31]–[32].

[63] *cf* S Weatherill, 'Use and Abuse of the EU's Charter of Fundamental Rights: On the Improper Veneration of Freedom of Contract' (2014) 10 *European Review of Contract Law* 157; J Prassl, 'Freedom of Contract as a General Principle of EU Law? Transfers of Undertakings and the Protection of Employer Rights in EU Labour Law' (2013) 42 *Industrial Law Journal* 434. See more generally on protection of the weaker party in EU law N Reich, *General Principles of EU Civil Law* (Antwerp, Intersentia, 2014) ch 2.

Alemo-Herron is a ruling to be resisted. Its reasoning is a threat to the established shape of internal market law and therefore internal market law needs to be protected from this (over-)reading of Article 16 of the Charter. Gratifyingly, in the first and so far only ruling in the area since the Third Chamber's misadventure in *Alemo-Herron*, the Fourth Chamber in *Österreichischer Gewerkschaftsbund* showed no inclination at all to adopt its reasoning.[64] It mentioned *Alemo-Herron*, but avoided the Charter altogether, found no hindrance to the transferee's ability to make adjustments to its operation and expressly embraced the longer-standing thematic concern for worker protection. True, the point at issue concerning transfer of undertakings was in detail not the same as that in *Alemo-Herron*, and the ruling in *Österreichischer Gewerkschaftsbund*, though distinctly different in tone, does not put a stake through the dark heart of *Alemo-Herron*. It suggests, however, that questions about how vigorously to push Article 16 of the Charter to upset regulatory protection are contested within the Court. So—thus far—*Alemo-Herron* is, like *Viking Line* and *Laval*, an aberrant ruling of the Court that is out of line with orthodoxy rather than a demonstration of any rising deregulatory whirlwind.

IV. CONCLUSION

EU internal market law has never been narrowly concerned with economic liberalisation alone. Even before the Charter was granted formally binding status, the Court was open to assessing justification of trade-restrictive national practices and the validity of EU measures of market regulation with reference to (in short) non-economic concerns. True, the narrative does not *fully* comply with this depiction of a cautious Court that is sensitive to the damage that may be done by over-emphasis on economic liberalisation at the expense of social protection. There is no defence here of *Viking Line* and *Laval*, or *Alemo-Herron*. These rulings are, however, aberrations, which are out of line with a developed law of the internal market which is porous to non-economic values and to the promotion of fundamental rights. The Lisbon Treaty in general and the Charter of Fundamental Rights in particular are not transformative: they do not make a qualitative change to the structure and scope of the law governing the internal market. Nor should they.

[64] Case C-328/13 *Österreichischer Gewerkschaftsbund*, judgment of 11 September 2014.

11

The EU Single Market as 'Normative Corridor' for the Protection of Fundamental Rights: The Example of Data Protection

SYBE DE VRIES

I. INTRODUCTION

JANUS WAS THE Roman god of gates and doors (ianua), beginnings and endings, and hence he was represented with a double-faced head: 'He was worshipped at the beginning of the harvest time, planting, marriage, birth, and other types of beginnings, especially the beginnings of important events in a person's life. Janus also represents the transition between primitive life and civilization, between the countryside and the city, peace and war, and the growing-up of young people.'[1]

The relationship between the EU single market and fundamental rights bears some resemblance with the double-headed Roman god Janus. On the one hand, the internal market constituted the very foundation for the development of EU fundamental rights. The European Court of Justice (hereinafter ECJ or 'the Court') has created within the slipstream of the internal market an autonomous fundamental rights regime, whereby fundamental rights were developed as general principles of EU law. In its judgment in the *Hauer* case, the ECJ formulated it as follows:

> The question of a possible infringement of fundamental rights by a measure of the Community institutions can only be judged in the light of Community law itself. The introduction of special criteria for assessment stemming from the legislation or constitutional law of a particular Member State would, by damaging the substantive unity and efficacy of Community law, lead inevitably to the destruction of the unity of the common market and the jeopardizing of the cohesion of the Community.[2]

[1] MF Lindemans, 'Janus', *Encyclopedia Mythica*, available at: www.pantheon.org/articles/j/janus.html?esc.

[2] Case 44/79 *Liselotte Hauer v Land Rheinland-Pfalz (Hauer)* [1979] ECR 3727 [14].

Yet, on the other hand, the EU single market puts serious constraints on the exercise of domestic fundamental rights. As Janus was the god of the beginnings and endings, representing the middle ground between barbarism and civilisation, the equation can also be used to describe the coming of age of fundamental rights of the EU: an EU based upon the rule of law, democracy and human rights, enriched with a binding Charter of Fundamental Rights, whilst embracing a more inclusive, holistic internal market.

The expansion of fundamental rights within the EU legal order offers numerous challenges and concerns, for instance, whether the EU legal framework, which is to a large extent designed with EU single market building blocks, is sufficiently apt to accommodate fundamental rights and the diversity that exists between the Member States in protecting national constitutional rights. In this chapter, these challenges and concerns will be further explored using the example of data protection. The central question is to examine how the internal market constitutes the 'normative corridor' for EU fundamental rights and internal market freedoms, which mutually affect each other and may be in conflict with each other.[3] With a view to examining the relationship between EU single market law and fundamental rights, the following two tracks will be followed: how fundamental rights may affect the internal market freedoms in the context of free movement and EU legislation; and, vice versa, how the internal market freedoms may affect fundamental rights in the context of free movement and EU legislation.

The discussion in this chapter will first be approached from a more general angle and will then turn to the fields of data protection and privacy, which offer an interesting example of how fundamental rights may become entangled with EU single market law, as a case study. It may, for instance, reveal that fundamental rights could be further harmonised at the EU level through the EU single market, possibly at the cost of existing diversity and different levels of protection of fundamental rights across the EU.

II. DATA PROTECTION AND PRIVACY AS AN ILLUSTRATION

Ongoing technological developments entail that the sound processing of data is becoming increasingly important. And the cross-border flow of information, particularly through the use of the Internet, calls for a transnational approach on how to protect data. Furthermore, the different approaches of

[3] The term 'normative corridor' is used here as a metaphor for the internal market, which with its common norms and standards entails a collectiveness and common normative approach also to fundamental rights. But, the 'corridor' should be large enough to accommodate internal conflicts and different approaches as standards of fundamental rights differ across Member States. See with regard to the concept of a 'normative corridor' C Kantner, 'What is a European Identity? The Emergence of a Shared Ethical Self-understanding in the European Union, EUI Working Papers (RSCAS No 2006/28) 13.

the states as to how to protect data might seriously hamper the economy and the functioning of the EU internal market.[4] At the same time, there is a need for adequate, harmonised rules at the EU level offering citizens a high level of protection of their personal data in accordance with the fundamental rights to protect personal data and privacy.

A. The Data Protection Directive and the Internal Market Link

The Data Protection Directive is based upon the internal market legal basis of Article 114 of the Treaty on the Functioning of the European Union (TFEU) and introduced an obligation for the Member States to protect citizens' rights to privacy, in particular to 'protect ... their right to privacy, with respect to the processing of personal data within their jurisdictions'. According to the (preamble of the) Directive, the establishment and functioning of the internal market will necessarily lead to a substantial increase in cross-border flows of personal data between all those involved in a private or public capacity in economic and social activity in the Member States. Furthermore, the exchange of personal data between undertakings in different Member States is set to increase. And as a justification for harmonisation, the EU legislature refers to the difference in levels of protection of the right to privacy with regard to the processing of personal data afforded in the Member States, which may prevent the transmission of such data from the territory of one Member State to that of another Member State. And, as a result of different national provisions, this difference may constitute an obstacle to the pursuit of a number of economic activities at the EU level, distort competition and impede authorities in the discharge of their responsibilities under EU law.

B. Privacy and Data Protection as Fundamental Rights

The right to protection of personal data and the right to protect family life (privacy) are strongly linked. If privacy, like freedom, is a kind of natural freedom of each human being, a broad definition of privacy could be 'the claim of individuals, groups or institutions to determine for themselves when, how and to what extent, information about them is communicated to others'.[5]

Compared to the European Convention on Human Rights (ECHR), it is noteworthy that the EU Charter of Fundamental Rights recognises the

[4] H Kranenborg, 'Commentary on Article 8' in S Peers et al (eds), *The EU Charter of Fundamental Rights—A Commentary* (Oxford, Hart Publishing, 2014) 265. See also the contribution by Fabbrini, Ch 12 in this volume.

[5] B Perninan, 'The Origin of Privacy as a Legal Value: A Reflection on Roman and English Law' (2012) 52 *American Journal of Legal History* 187.

protection of personal data as an *independent* right (Article 8), next to the right to privacy (Article 7), which can also be found in Article 8 ECHR. In addition, Article 16 TFEU, which was introduced by the Treaty of Lisbon, stresses the importance of data protection and empowers the EU to adopt specific harmonisation measures in this field. The proposed General Data Protection Regulation, which seeks to replace Directive 95/46 on the protection of personal data, is based upon this provision.[6]

The current EU Data Protection Directive defines personal data as any information relating to an identified or identifiable natural person ('data subject'); an identifiable person is one who can be identified, directly or indirectly, in particular by reference to an identification number or to one or more factors specific to his physical, physiological, mental, economic, cultural or social identity.[7] Generally the right to data protection is distinguished from the right to privacy by the fact that EU data protection rules look beyond consent only, which is a constitutive element of privacy—the concept of informational self-determination—and 'create a system of checks and balances which ensures lawful processing also without asking the consent of the person involved'.[8]

III. FUNDAMENTAL RIGHTS AFFECTING INTERNAL MARKET FREEDOMS

As a preliminary remark, it should be observed that according to its Article 52(2), the Charter does not establish any new power or task for the EU. Furthermore, Article 51(1) of the Charter sets limits to the scope of application. These jurisdictional boundaries imply that the Charter cannot in itself extend the reach of EU law or, more specifically, the scope of the internal market freedoms.[9]

Fundamental rights and the different ways in which they are (constitutionally) accommodated in the Member States and in the EU Charter may affect the internal market freedoms in roughly speaking two ways: (i) some fundamental (economic) rights could *strengthen* the internal market

[6] Commission, 'Proposal for a Regulation on the protection of individuals with regard to the processing of personal data and on the free movement of such data' COM (2012) 11 final (General Data Protection Regulation). See also latest information by the European Commission: http://europa.eu/rapid/press-release_MEMO-15-3802_en.htm.

[7] Directive 95/46/EC of the European Parliament and of the Council of 24 October 1995 on the protection of individuals with regard to the processing of personal data and on the free movement of such data [1995] OJ L281/31.

[8] H Kranenborg, 'Commentary on Article 8' in Peers et al (n 4) 229.

[9] In a similar vein, see D Augenstein, 'Engaging the Fundamentals: On the Autonomous Substance of EU Fundamental Rights Law' (2013) 14 *German Law Journal* 1919. But in the field of citizenship, the 'fifth freedom' there has been a lively debate as to whether EU fundamental rights in combination with the citizenship provisions should not also grant protection in internal situations.

freedoms; yet (ii) other fundamental rights could *soften* the application of the internal market freedoms, particularly in the context of the justification grounds, ie, the Treaty exceptions and mandatory requirements.

Within the legislative context, the EU legislature has the duty to take account of fundamental rights, particularly since the EU Charter acquired binding force. It is mainly in the areas of data protection and privacy where the ECJ has employed a rigorous standard of review for internal market legislation in the light of the Charter.

A. Fundamental Rights Affecting the Internal Market Freedoms in the Context of Free Movement

i. Strengthening the Internal Market Freedoms

Next to the inherently fundamental character of the internal market freedoms as highlighted by the Court in its case law,[10] in a number of cases the Court has also made clear that the economic Treaty freedoms could be seen as a specific amplification of the Charter.[11] Certain Charter provisions, most of all Article 15(2) on the freedom of every EU citizen to exercise the right of establishment and to provide services in any Member State, Article 16 on the freedom to conduct a business and Article 17 on the right to property, may reinforce the free movement rules and thus the market integration process. The question that arises in this context is whether the four internal market freedoms—reinforced by the economic rights contained in the Charter—have gained more importance at the expense of other fundamental rights enshrined in the Charter. This hierarchical shift is, however, disputable. Where the Charter provisions can be applied alongside the free movement rules, the Court will normally focus on the latter.[12] Otherwise, the traditional scheme under which restrictions on free movement are adjudicated will be upset.[13]

[10] P Oliver and W-H Roth, 'The Internal Market and the Four Freedoms' (2004) 41 *CML Rev* 407, 407–11. See, for instance, Case C-112/00 *Eugen Schmidberger, Internationale Transporte und Planzüge v Republik Österreich (Schmidberger)* [2003] ECR I-5659; Case C-281/98 *Roman Angonese v Cassa di Risparmio di Bolzano SpA (Angonese)* [2000] ECR I-4139 (workers); Case C-341/05 *Laval un Partneri Ltd v Svenska Byggnadsarbetareförbundet and others (Laval)* [2007] ECR I-11767 (services); and Case C-36/02 *Omega Spielhallen- und Automatenaufstellungs-GmbH v Oberbürgermeisterin der Bundesstadt Bonn* (*Omega*) [2004] ECR I-9609 (services).

[11] Case C-233/12 *Simone Gardella v Istituto Nazionale della Previdenza Sociale (INPS) (Gardella)* (ECJ, 4 July 2013) [39]: 'Article 12(2) of the Charter reiterates inter alia the free movement of workers guaranteed by Article 45 TFEU'; Case C-367/12 *Susanne Sokoll-Seebacher (Sokoll-Seebacher)* (ECJ, 13 February 2014) [22]: 'Article 16 of the Charter refers, inter alia, to Article 49 TFEU, which guarantees the fundamental freedom of establishment.'

[12] Case C-390/12 *Robert Pfleger and others (Pfleger)* (ECJ, 30 April 2014).

[13] See also the contribution by Weatherill, ch 10 in this volume.

ii. Softening the Internal Market Freedoms

Market integration is not pursued in isolation, but must be counterbalanced by social considerations and public interests, which is inter alia confirmed by the concept of social market economy introduced by the Lisbon Treaty.[14] In the case law of the ECJ, we see that EU free movement law is receptive to considerations of a non-economic nature and to fundamental rights.[15] Following the course set by the *Dassonville* and *Cassis de Dijon* judgments, the Court has accepted that Member States may rely on mandatory requirements—next to the Treaty exceptions—to justify national measures that restrict trade and free movement.[16] The four freedoms are not absolute, which is essential as this underlines their *relative* importance in the Treaty.[17] In respect of the fundamental rights and their relationship with the fundamental economic freedoms, this is reiterated by the Court in *Pfleger*:

> [A]n unjustified or disproportionate restriction of the freedom to provide services under Article 56 TFEU is also not permitted under Article 52(1) of the Charter in relation to Articles 15 to 17 of the Charter. It follows that ... an examination of the restriction represented by the national legislation at issue ... from the point of view of Article 56 TFEU covers also possible limitations of the exercise of the rights and freedoms provided for in Articles 15 to 17 of the Charter, so that a separate examination is not necessary.[18]

In cases like *Schmidberger* or *Omega*, the Court has shown its willingness to take fundamental rights seriously and put them on an equal footing with the EU rules on free movement.[19] Member States may take recourse to national constitutional provisions as long as sufficient account has been taken of the constitutional position of the four internal market freedoms.[20]

[14] This developed over time; see P Craig, 'The Evolution of the Single Market' in C Barnard and J Scott (eds), *The Law of the Single European Market—Unpacking the Premises* (Oxford, Hart Publishing, 2002) 32.

[15] Stephen Weatherill, 'From Economic Rights to Fundamental Rights' in Sybe de Vries, Ulf Bernitz and Stephen Weatherill (eds), *The Protection of Fundamental Rights in the EU after Lisbon* (Oxford, Hart Publishing, 2013) 12, 16–17; see also the contribution by Weatherill in ch 10 of this volume. SA de Vries, *Tensions within the Internal Market—The Functioning of the Internal Market and the Development of Horizontal and Flanking Policies* (Groningen, Europa Law Publishing, 2006).

[16] Case 8/74 *Procureur du Roi v Benoît and Gustave Dassonville (Dassonville)* [1974] ECR 837; Case 120/78 *Rewe-Zentral AG v Bundesmonopolverwaltung für Branntwein (Cassis de Dijon)* [1979] ECR 649.

[17] P Oliver and WH Roth, 'The Internal Market and the Four Freedoms' (2004) *CML Rev* 410.

[18] *Pfleger* (n 12) [59] and [60].

[19] *Schmidberger* (n 10); Case C-36/02 *Omega Spielhallen- und Automatenaufstellungs-GmbH v Oberbürgermeisterin der Bundesstadt Bonn (Omega)* [2004] ECR I-9609.

[20] D Sarmiento, 'Who's Afraid of the Charter? The Court of Justice, National Courts and the New Framework of Fundamental Rights Protection in Europe' (2013) 50 *CML Rev* 1267, 1297.

Although the Charter reinforces the fundamentality and universality of EU fundamental rights, which should steer the orientation and interpretation of free movement rules in this field, the exact added value in conflicts between fundamental rights and the internal market freedoms remains unclear. Two remarks can be made in this respect. First, the Charter may play a role in recognising a fundamental right as mandatory requirement, which may justify a restriction on free movement. This follows from the Court's judgment in *Dynamic Medien*, where it held that the protection of the right of the child as inter alia laid down in Article 24 of the Charter constitutes a legitimate ground to restrict the free movement of goods.[21] And, in addition, according to Article 52(1) of the Charter, the exercise of fundamental rights may be limited subject to the conditions, first, that the limitations are provided for by law and, second, that the limitations are necessary and proportionate. This entails that fundamental rights are—in principle—not absolute, which appears to embrace the Court's balancing approach as conducted in the context of the internal market freedoms. But in this balancing exercise, the Court must take into account the ECHR as well as typically national approaches to fundamental rights as referred to in Article 52(4) of the EU Charter and Article 4(2) of the Treaty on European Union (TEU). This is also reflected by inter alia the Court's judgment in *Omega*, where it took into account, within the context of the free movement of services, the particularly German conception of human dignity.[22] Crucially it also drew from the typically German approach an EU approach to human dignity, which became part of the assessment conducted in the name of free movement.

B. Fundamental Rights Affecting the Internal Market Freedoms in the Legislative Context

i. Strengthening the Internal Market Freedoms

Judgments like *Alemo Herron* or *Scarlet Extended* suggest that the Court is inclined to stress the importance of economic rights.[23] In these two cases the ECJ focused on Article 16 of the EU Charter on the freedom to conduct a business, thereby sidelining other rights. However, it is so far unclear whether this approach is structural.[24]

21 Case C-244/06 *Dynamic Medien* [2008] ECR I-505.

22 Case C-36/02 *Omega Spielhallen- und Automatenaufstellungs-GmbH* [2004] ECR I-9609. See also Augenstein (n 9).

23 Case C-438/05 *International Transport Workers' Federation and Finnish Seamen's Union v Viking Line ABP and OÜ Viking Line Eesti (Viking)* [2007] ECR I-10779 [42]; Case C-426/11 *Mark Alemo-Herron and others v Parkwood Leisure Ltd (Alemo Herro)* (ECJ, 18 July 2013); Case C-70/10 *Scarlet Extended SA v Société belge des auteurs, compositeurs et éditeurs SCRL (SABAM)(Scarlet Extended)* [2011] ECR I-11959.

24 See also the contribution of Weatherill in ch 10 in this volume.

In the case of *Scarlet Extended*, wherein the ECJ had to decide on the compatibility of the requirement for an Internet Service Provider (ISP) to install a filtering system in response to infringements of intellectual property rights and to combat piracy with EU fundamental rights, the E-Commerce Directive (Directive 2000/31) constituted one of the main reasons for the Court to put the freedom to conduct a business at the heart of its judgment, thereby outflanking other fundamental rights, such as the rights of Internet users to privacy and to the protection of personal data. The freedom to conduct a business as contained in Article 16 of the Charter in fact strengthens Article 15(1) of the E-Commerce Directive, prohibiting too severe a measure such as the requirement to install a filtering system. In the procedure before the Belgian court, Scarlet had argued that it could not possibly comply with the court order inter alia because the installation of a filtering or blocking system was faced with numerous practical obstacles.[25]

The *Alemo-Herron* case concerned the interpretation of the Directive on employees' rights in the event of transfers of undertakings.[26] The Court ruled that Article 16 precluded a national measure more generous to employees without considering whether fundamental social rights of the Charter, in this case Article 30 on the protection of workers' rights, could serve as a counterweight. These judgments give the impression that there is an inherent danger that economic freedoms and rights are overstretched with the help of the Charter. But, as will be seen below things are never as bad as they present themselves at first.

ii. Softening the Internal Market Freedoms

The EU Charter also constitutes an important counterweight to economic rights and freedoms expanded by EU legislation. Since the entering into force of the Treaty of Lisbon, EU (internal market) legislation will have to meet the specific (proportionality) requirements set by Article 52 of the Charter:

> [A]ny limitation on the exercise of the rights and freedoms recognized by this Charter must be provided for by law and respect the essence of those rights and freedoms. Subject to the principle of proportionality, limitations may be made only if they are necessary and genuinely meet objectives of general interest recognized by the Union or the need to protect the rights and freedoms of others.

The Court may employ different standards of proportionality review where conflicting fundamental rights are at issue. This inter alia appears from the Court's judgment in *Sky Österreich*[27] This case concerned the requirement

[25] *Scarlet Extended* (n 23) 24.

[26] Council Directive 2001/23/EC of 12 March 2001 on the approximation of the laws of the Member States relating to the safeguarding of employees' rights in the event of transfers of undertakings, businesses or parts of undertakings or businesses [2001] OJ L82, 16.

[27] ibid 1484.

of broadcasters holding exclusive broadcasting rights to produce short news reports without the possibility of obtaining additional compensation. The ECJ was asked to rule on the compatibility of the Audiovisual Media Services Directive (AMSD) with the EU Charter,[28] in particular the freedom to conduct a business and the right to property as contained in Articles 16 and 17 of the Charter.[29] The question was whether Article 15(6) AMSD, which requires the holder of exclusive broadcasting rights to authorise any other broadcaster to make short news reports without being able to seek compensation exceeding the additional costs directly incurred in providing access to the signal, infringes the fundamental rights of the holder of exclusive broadcasting rights. According to the ECJ, the Directive had been adopted in accordance with the Charter. In the light of the importance of safeguarding the fundamental freedom to receive information and the freedom and pluralism of the media guaranteed by Article 11 of the Charter and of the protection of the freedom to conduct a business as guaranteed by Article 16 of the Charter, the EU legislature was entitled to adopt rules which limit the freedom to conduct a business and to give priority, in the necessary balancing of the rights and interests at issue, to public access to information over contractual freedom.[30]

The Court extensively embroidered on Article 16 of the Charter and held the following:

> On the basis of that case–law and in the light of the wording of Article 16 of the Charter ... the freedom to conduct a business may be subject to a broad range of interventions on the part of public authorities which may limit the exercise of economic activity in the public interest. That circumstance is reflected, inter alia, in the way in which Article 52(1) of the Charter requires the principle of proportionality to be implemented.[31]

Article 52(1) does not expressly distinguish between different types of Charter rights and which of those rights should prevail in a specific case. And the Court did not elaborate further on this possible distinction in *Sky Österreich*, so the extent to which the Court will pursue a differentiated approach in the context of the proportionality test remains unclear. It will ultimately depend on the area concerned, the nature of the Charter right at issue, the nature and seriousness of the interference, and the objective pursued in determining

[28] Directive 2010/13/EU of the European Parliament and of the Council of 10 March 2010 on the coordination of certain provisions laid down by law, regulation or administrative action in Member States concerning the provision of audiovisual media services [2010] OJ L95/1 (Audiovisual Media Services Directive).

[29] Case C-283/11 *Sky Österreich GmbH v Österreichischer Rundfunk (Sky Österreich)* (ECJ, 22 January 2013).

[30] ibid [66].

[31] ibid [46]–[47]. See in particular S Peers and S Prechal, 'Article 52' in Peers et al (n 4) 1484–85.

how restrictions on fundamental rights are assessed.[32] When it comes to the rights to privacy and protection of personal data, as will be seen below, the ECJ takes a tough stance affording these rights a particular status, thereby suggesting some sort of hierarchy of rights in the Charter.[33]

iii. The Strong Impact of the Rights to Data Protection and Privacy

The Court's case law in the field of data protection shows that the standard of review on the basis of Article 52 of the Charter appears to be more in depth, structured and rigorous than in cases where no fundamental rights are at stake. This strict judicial review by the Court is clearly visible in the most recent and rather spectacular ruling in *Digital Rights Ireland* on the validity of the Data Retention Directive in the light of the Charter,[34] where the Court held that:

> [W]ith regard to judicial review of compliance with those conditions, where interferences with fundamental rights are at issue, the extent of the EU legislature's discretion may prove to be limited, depending on a number of factors, including, in particular, the area concerned, the nature of the right at issue guaranteed by the Charter, the nature and seriousness of the interference and the object pursued by the interference.[35]

In his Opinion in the *Digital Rights Ireland* case, Advocate General Cruz Villalón held that the requirement of proportionality 'acquires, in the context of the Charter, a particular force, which it does not have under Article 5(4) TEU'.[36] In the much earlier *Volker and Schecke* case, the Court had already had the opportunity to assess EU legislation in the light of the Charter and was forced to balance conflicting rights on the basis of Article 52. This case concerned the publication of information on beneficiaries of agricultural aid, which is provided for by an EU Regulation. The question was whether this requirement was contrary to the right to have one's private life respected (Article 7 of the Charter) and the right to the

[32] Joined Cases C-293/12 and C-594/12 *Digital Rights Ireland Ltd v Minister for Communications, Marine and Natural Resources and others and Kärntner Landesregierung and others (Digital Rights Ireland)* (ECJ, 4 April 2014) [47].

[33] See also MP Granger and K Irion, 'The Court of Justice and the Data Retention Directive in *Digital Rights Ireland*: Telling Off the EU Legislator and Teaching a Lesson in Privacy and Data Protection' (2014) 39 *EL Rev* 835, 846.

[34] Directive 2006/24/EC of the European Parliament and of the Council of 15 March 2006 on the retention of data generated or processed in connection with the provision of publicly available electronic communication services or of public communications networks and amending Directive 2002/58/EC [2006] OJ L105/54 (Data Retention Directive). See also O Lynskey, 'The Data Retention Directive is Incompatible with the Rights to Privacy and Data Protection and is Invalid in its Entirety: *Digital Rights Ireland*' (2014) 51 *CML Rev* 1789.

[35] *Digital Rights Ireland* (n 32) [47].

[36] ibid, Opinion of AG Cruz Villalón at [133].

protection of personal data (Article 8(1) of the Charter). In assessing the validity of these provisions of the Regulation, the Court had to balance the interests of the Community in increasing transparency with respect to the use of agricultural aid by revealing the names of the beneficiaries against the protection of the fundamental rights enshrined in Articles 7 and 8 of the Charter according to Article 52 of the Charter.[37] From this case, it was by now apparent that the Court would employ a rather stringent test when it comes to interference with fundamental rights by the EU legislature.[38]

Where in *Volker and Schecke*, the ECJ declared only a provision of a Regulation invalid, in *Digital Rights Ireland*, the entire Data Retention Directive was held to be incompatible with the Charter. According to the ECJ, the Directive 'affects in a comprehensive manner, all persons using electronic communications services, but without the persons whose data are retained being, even indirectly, in a situation which is liable to give rise to criminal prosecutions'.[39] The Court concluded that the Directive 'does not lay down clear and precise rules governing the extent of the interference with the fundamental rights enshrined in Articles 7 and 8 of the Charter'. It 'entails a wide-ranging and particularly serious interference with those fundamental rights in the legal order of the EU, without such an interference being precisely circumscribed by provisions to ensure that it is actually limited to what is strictly necessary'.[40]

Furthermore, the Court stated that in cases where fundamental rights like the right to protection of personal data and privacy are seriously impaired, the EU legislature's discretion is reduced and the review of that discretion should be strict.[41] Hence, the margin of discretion for the EU legislature in the field of fundamental rights has become (much) more limited compared to other policy fields, where the ECJ normally exercises only limited appraisal of EU harmonisation measures—also with a view to prevent putting itself in the place of the legislature.[42] The effects of the Charter for the EU legislature are thus clearly visible.

In *Digital Rights Ireland*, the ECJ focused on the public security aims of the Directive, which constituted, according to the Court, the material objective of the Directive.[43] In its judgment on the legal basis of the Data Retention Directive, the Court had emphasised the internal market

[37] Joined Cases C-92/09 and C-93/09 *Volker and Markus Schecke GbR and Hartmut Eifert v Land Hessen (Volker and Schecke)* [2010] ECR I-11036.

[38] ibid [86]; *Sky Österreich* (n 29).

[39] *Digital Rights Ireland* (n 32) [58].

[40] ibid [65].

[41] ibid [48].

[42] SA de Vries, *Tensions within the Internal Market—The Functioning of the Internal Market and the Development of Horizontal and Flanking Policies* (Groningen, Europa Law Publishing 2006) 388.

[43] *Digital Rights Ireland* (n 32) [41].

rationale underlying this Directive. One of the reasons for the Court to draw the attention to the security aims now could be its preference for a 'stricter human rights scrutiny of security policies'.[44] But a case like *Google Spain*, which will be discussed below, shows that also outside the field of security and within the context of the internal market, the Court gives considerable weight to privacy and data protection.[45]

In any event, *Digital Rights Ireland* makes clear that the EU legislature cannot simply subsume fundamental rights under EU free movement law. The Charter, at least according to the Court, requires more 'inclusive or holistic legislation',[46] which in turn means more detailed rules on standards of fundamental rights at the EU level. And the Court calls upon the EU legislature 'to assume greater responsibility for ensuring compliance with human rights standards'.[47]

C. Final Observations

The impact of EU fundamental rights on the internal market freedoms, both in the free movement context and in the legislative context, seems rather limited. Where both the rules on free movement and the economic rights in the Charter may be applicable, the Court prefers to apply the free movement rules. Furthermore, fundamental rights have not substantially affected the traditional scheme under which restrictions on free movement and their possible justification grounds are assessed. The principles that have been developed in the case law ever since *Cassis de Dijon* are still relevant. But the EU Charter (and the Lisbon Treaty) entails that sufficient room is given to national approaches to fundamental rights or constitutional diversity. In this sense, the Charter plays 'an important role on delimiting the CJEU's interpretative autonomy' in the field of free movement.[48]

The effects of the Charter are, however, most visible in the legislative context. Specifically regarding the requirement to comply with the rights to data protection and privacy, the Court is inclined to perform an in-depth proportionality review of EU measures. This approach deviates from the softer style that usually applies to EU legislation.

[44] Granger and Irion (n 33) 847. See also Case C-291/12 *Michael Schwarz v Stadt Bochum (Schwarz)* (ECJ, 17 October 2013), in which the ECJ provided for a strict interpretation of Regulation No 2252/2004 on standards for security features and biometrics in passports and travel documents for privacy reasons.

[45] Case C-131/12 *Google Spain SL and Google Inc v Agencia Española de Protección de Datos (AEPD) and Mario Costeja González (Google Spain)* (ECJ, 13 May 2013).

[46] Granger and Irion (n 33) 845.

[47] ibid.

[48] Augenstein (n 9).

IV. INTERNAL MARKET FREEDOMS AFFECTING FUNDAMENTAL RIGHTS

EU fundamental rights developed as an autonomous legal regime within the slipstream of the internal market and from the autonomous EU legal order. The emphasis on the autonomy and primacy of the EU fundamental rights regime is the running theme throughout the case law of the ECJ, of which the recent Opinion 2/13 regarding the EU's accession to the ECHR is probably the most prominent example.[49] The development of fundamental rights within the slipstream of the internal market has had a number of consequences. Principles like direct effect, supremacy or proportionality have been firmly incorporated into EU fundamental rights law, either in the EU Charter, for instance, through the inclusion of Article 52(1) in the Charter, or in the Court's case law on general principles.

Furthermore, there is a (growing) overlap in the substantive and personal scope of application of internal market freedoms and fundamental rights. One pressing issue is whether the Charter rights have, in a similar vein to the internal market freedoms, horizontal direct effect. And the internal market freedoms, as seen above, set limits on the exercise of fundamental rights. In a procedure before the Court, fundamental rights are considered within the context of the exceptions to the Treaty provisions on free movement.

In the legislative context, EU law accords a broad scope to the internal market legal bases, which allows for the regulation of fundamental rights at the EU level. And, as will be explained below, internal market legislation regulating fundamental rights may influence the Court's view on the extent to which fundamental rights that lie outside the regulatory framework or typically national approaches to fundamental rights can be considered.

A. Internal Market Freedoms Affecting Fundamental Rights in the Context of Free Movement

i. The Scope

a. Substantive Scope

As regards the relationship between the four fundamental economic freedoms and fundamental rights, there is a growing overlap of these two

[49] Opinion 2/13 of 18 December 2014; see also Joined Cases C-402/05 P and C-415/05 P *Yassin Abdullah Kadi and Al Barakaat International Foundation v Council and Commission (Kadi)* [2008] ECR I-6351; Joined Cases C-584/10 P, C-593/10 P and C-595/10 P *Commission, Council and UK v Yassin Abdullah Kadi (Kadi II)* [2013] ECR I-0000. See also the contribution by Douglas-Scott in ch 2 in this volume.

fundamentals in the Court's case law.[50] Looking at the *scope of application* of the Treaty provisions on free movement and EU fundamental rights, it can be observed that a widening of the scope of application of the four freedoms 'automatically results in an enlargement of the scope of the fundamental rights'.[51] The expansionist character of EU economic law because of the functional breadth of the Treaty rules on free movement and the Court's broad approach to EU free movement law explains the expansion of EU fundamental rights. As the outer reaches of EU (economic) law are ambiguous, exploited by 'ingenious and well-funded litigants' who are helped by the principle of direct effect (and of supremacy),[52] domestic fundamental rights became easily absorbed by EU economic law.

The ECJ held that EU fundamental rights have to be respected by Member States whenever they act within the scope of EU law.[53] In *ERT*,[54] the Greek television monopoly case, it held that in the process of justifying the monopoly on broadcasting services, Article 10 ECHR, the freedom of expression, had to be taken into account. It found that the public policy, public security and public health derogation must be interpreted and applied in such a way that they respect the general principle enshrined in Article 10 ECHR.[55] The *ERT* approach has now been confirmed by the ECJ in the above-mentioned case of *Pfleger*, wherein it held that the EU Charter also applies in so-called 'derogation-situations'.[56]

[50] V Trstenjak and E Beysen, 'The Growing Overlap of Fundamental Freedoms and Fundamental Rights in the Case-Law of the CJEU' (2013) 38 *EL Rev* 293.

[51] ibid 305.

[52] See Weatherill (n 15) 12, 16–17.

[53] This is roughly speaking the case in three situations: the provision of national law must implement EU law, it must invoke some derogation from EU law or some specific rule of EU law applies to the situation. Editorial Comments, 'The Scope of Application of General Principles of Union Law: An Ever Expanding Union?' (2010) 47 *CML Rev* 1589, 1590; here a slightly different but still similar classification of situations falling within the scope of the Treaties is made. See also S Prechal, S de Vries and H van Eijken, 'Ch 12: The Principle of Attributed Power and the Scope of EU Law' in L Besselink, F Pennings and S Prechal (eds), *The Eclipse of the Legality Principle in the European Union* (Alphen aan den Rijn, Kluwer Law International, 2011) 216–18.

[54] Case C-260/89 *Elliniki Radiophonia Tileorassi AE v Dimotiki Etairia Pliroforissis and Sotirios Kouvelas (ERT)* [1991] ECR I-2925.

[55] See for a discussion on the implications of this case law: JHH Weiler and NJS Lockhart, '"Taking Rights Seriously' Seriously: The European Court and its Fundamental Rights Jurisprudence—Part I' (1995) 32 *CML Rev* 77.

[56] *Pfleger* (n 12). With regard to the scope of application of the Charter in general, see Case C-617/10 *Åklagaren v Hans Åkerberg Fransson (Åkerberg Fransson)* (ECJ, 7 May 2013) [20]–[21]. In the more recent *Siragusa* judgment, the Court has further demarcated the scope of fundamental rights protection and it appears that a mere link with EU law does not suffice to trigger the application of the Charter: Case C-206/13 *Cruciano Siragusa v Regione Sicilia—Soprintendenza Beni Culturali e Ambientali di Palermo (Siragusa)* (ECJ, 6 March 2014).

b. Personal Scope: Widening the Circle of Parties to whom they are Addressed

Although it was thought that the EU provisions on free movement were primarily drafted for the Member States, 'the authorities',[57] it is now clear that they may also be directed at private individuals.[58] Regarding the Treaty provisions on the freedom of establishment and the free movement services, the Court has accepted a form of limited horizontal direct effect.[59] In the area of workers, the Court has recognised a broader form of horizontal direct effect, but only insofar as it concerns the principle of non-discrimination.[60] And, with respect to the free movement of goods, the situation remains undecided.[61]

Now, do fundamental rights bind private individuals in a similar fashion? Looking at the Charter, Article 51(1) only refers to EU institutions and Member States. According to Advocate General Trstenjak in the *Dominguez* case, which concerned the applicability—in a horizontal dispute—of the right to paid annual leave as contained in Article 31 of the Charter, Articles 51(1) and 52(2) of the Charter 'indicate an intentional restricting of

[57] For such private individuals, the drafters of the Treaty envisaged the provisions on competition: S Prechal and S de Vries, 'Seamless Web of Judicial Protection in the Internal Market?' (2009) 34 *EL Rev* 5.

[58] Case 36/74 *BNO Walrave and LJN Koch v Association Union cycliste internationale, Koninklijke Nederlandsche Wielren Unie and Federación Española Ciclismo (Walrave)* [1974] ECR 1405 [28] and [17].

[59] In one way, this seems close to a mere extension of vertical direct effect to non-governmental regulatory bodies. For the resemblance with the broad interpretation of a 'measure' within the meaning of Art 34 TFEU, see J Snell, 'And Then There were Two: Products and Citizens in Community Law' in T Tridimas and P Nebbia (eds), *EU Law for the Twenty-First Century: Rethinking the New Legal Order*, vol II (Oxford, Hart Publishing, 2004) 57. Noteworthy is the similar reluctance of the Court to acknowledge horizontal direct effect explicitly in the Court's case law on Directives: see, eg, Case C-188/89 *A Foster et al v British Gas* plc *(Foster)* [1990] ECR I-3313; Case C-106/89 *Marleasing SA v La Comercial Internacional de Alimentacion SA (Marleasing)* [1990] ECR I-4135; Case C-555/07 *Seda Kücükdeveci v Swedex GmbH & Co KG (Kücükdeveci)* [2010] ECR I-365. Interesting in this respect is the Opinion of Advocate General Maduro in the *Vodafone* case arguing in favour of, more generally, a horizontal application of the free movement rules, as a consequence of which the scope of Art 114 TFEU—the legal basis for internal market legislation—could be extended to the regulation of private behaviour as well: Case C-58/08 *The Queen, on the application of Vodafone Ltd and others v Secretary of State for Business, Enterprise and Regulatory Reform* [2010] ECR I-4999, Opinion of AG Maduro.

[60] A Dashwood, '*Viking and Laval*: Issues of '"Horizontal Direct Effect"' (2008) 10 *Cambridge Yearbook of European Legal Studies* 525, 525; S Prechal and S De Vries, 'Seamless Web of Judicial Protection in the Internal Market?' (2009) 34 *EL Rev* 5, 16.

[61] Case C-171/11 *Fra.bo SpA v Deutsche Vereinigung des Gas- und Wasserfaches eV (DVGW)—Technisch-Wissenschaftlicher Verein (Fra.bo)* [2012] ECR I-0000; S de Vries and R van Mastrigt, 'Chapter 11—The Horizontal Direct Effect of the Four Freedoms: From a Hodgepodge of Cases to a Seamless Web of Judicial Protection in the EU Single Market?' in U Bernitz, X Groussot and F Schulyok (eds), *General Principles of EU Law and European Private Law* (Alphen aan den Rijn, Kluwer Law International, 2013) 263.

the parties to whom fundamental rights are addressed'.[62] But the Court is not always impressed by restrictive textual interpretations. In a number of cases, it had already established that general principles of EU law could be horizontally applicable. In cases like *Mangold* and *Kucukdeveci*, 'the domain of constitutionally protected individual rights'[63] as a standard for review was extended.[64] Yet, the horizontal disputes at issue in these cases, where private parties were able to rely on the principle of non-discrimination on grounds of age, took place against the background of national law, which due to its close ties with EU legislation fell within the scope of EU law.[65]

Advocate General Cruz Villalon in his persuasive Opinion in the *AMS* case on a conflict between a trade union and the private body AMS noted that 'it would be paradoxical if the advent of the Charter changed this state of affairs in a negative sense' and held:[66]

> There is nothing in the wording of the article or, unless I am mistaken, in the preparatory works or the Explanations relating to the Charter, which suggests that there was any intention, through the language of that article, to address the very complex issue of the effectiveness of fundamental rights in relations between individuals.[67]

Furthermore, in *Defrenne II*, the Court made clear that private parties can rely on certain fundamental rights as general principles of EU law in horizontal disputes, in this case the principle of equal pay between men and women as laid down in Article 157 TFEU.[68] It now seems to pursue this line of thought in the *AMS* case in respect of the Charter, although very cautiously and without being explicit. It does at least not exclude the possibility of horizontal direct effect of Charter provisions per se.[69] In this case, the Charter provision at issue was Article 27 on workers' representation, which was not considered to be fully effective. It had to be given more specific expression in EU law or national law before it could be invoked. Whether Article 27 should accordingly be considered as a principle rather than a right within the meaning of Article 52(5) of the Charter was not addressed

[62] Case C-282/10 *Maribel Dominguez v Centre informatique du Centre Ouest Atlantique and Préfet de la region (Dominguez)* [2012] ECR I-0000, Opinion of AG Trstenjak at [80].

[63] E Muir, 'Fundamental Rights: An Unsettling EU Competence' (2014) 15 *Human Rights Review* 25, 29.

[64] S Prechal, 'Competence Creep and General Principles of Law' (2010) 3(1) *Review of European Administrative Law* 5, 19.

[65] X Groussot, L Pech and G Thor Petursson, 'The Reach of Fundamental Rights on Member State Action after Lisbon' in de Vries, Bernitz and Weatherill (n 15) 109.

[66] See A Ward, 'Article 51—Field of Application' in Peers and others (eds), *The EU Charter of Fundamental Rights: A Commentary* (Oxford, Hart Publishing, 2014) 1429.

[67] Case C-176/12 *Association de médiation sociale v Union locale des syndicats CGT (AMS)* [2014] ECR 0000, Opinion of AG Cruz Villalón, para 31.

[68] Case 43/75 *Gabrielle Defrenne v Société anonyme belge de navigation aérienne Sabena (Defrenne II)* [1976] ECR 455.

[69] Case C-176/12 *Association de médiation sociale v Union locale des syndicats CGT (AMS)* [2014] ECR 0000.

by the Court, nor was the question as to what extent Charter rights may have (full or limited) horizontal direct effect. In this respect, it is interesting to refer to a judgment by the English Court of Appeal in *Benkharbouche v Sudan and Janah v Libya*. The case involved two UK workers bringing employment law complaints against the embassies of Sudan and Libya. The question was whether invoking state immunity amounted to a breach of fundamental rights, in particular Article 6 ECHR and the corresponding provision in the EU Charter, Article 47, on effective judicial protection. One of the issues was whether Article 47 could have horizontal direct effect, as the Court assimilated the embassies of non-EU Member States to private parties.[70] The Court held:

> In our judgement, however, Article 47 must fall into the category of Charter provisions that can be the subject of horizontal direct effect. It follows from the approach in *Kücükdeveci* and *AMS* that EU Charter provisions which reflect general principles of EU law will do so.[71]

The approach of the Court of Appeal to horizontal direct effect of Charter provisions, which reflect general principles of EU law, fits with the more recent Opinion of Advocate General Mengozzi in the *Fenoll* case.[72]

In legal literature, suggestions have been put forward to adopt a similar approach to the horizontal application of the Charter as to the fundamental freedoms. Charter rights could be granted limited horizontal direct effect depending on the role of private parties in horizontal situations—do they act as regulators of future individual relationships or are they stronger vis-a-vis the other party in these relationships—and, in the case of individual contracts, depending on the regulatory context.[73] This brings us to the question of whether the rights to privacy and data protection can be applicable in horizontal fashion, which, considering the increasingly important role of private companies in the processing of personal data, is imminent.

c. Personal Scope: The Rights to Privacy and Protection of Personal Data

The cases decided by the ECJ that are related to the protection of intellectual property rights of producers of films, music or other protected works

[70] See S Peers, EU Law Analysis at: http://eulawanalysis.blogspot.nl/2015/02/rights-remedies-and-state-immunity.html (consulted at 21 March 2015).

[71] Case Benkharbouche/Janah v Sudan Embassy/Libya, [2015] EWCA Civ 3, para 78.

[72] Opinion of Advocate General Mengozzi in Case C-316/13 *Gérard Fenoll v Centre d'aide par le travail «La Jouvene» and Association de parents et d'amis de personnes handicapées mentales (APEI) d'Avignon (Fenoll)* at [59–60].

[73] D Leczykiewicz, 'Horizontal Application of the Charter of Fundamental Rights' (2013) 38 EL Rev 479–97. In respect of the four freedoms: S de Vries, '*Sport, TV and IP rights: Premier League* and *Karen Murphy:* Joined Cases C-403 & 429/08, *Football Association Premier League Ltd, NetMed Hellas SA, Multichoice Hellas SA (C-403/08)* v. *QC Leisure et al., and Karen Murphy* v. *Media Protection Services Ltd (C-429/08),* Judgment of the Court (Grand Chamber) of 4 October 2011, nyr.' (2013) 50 CML Rev 591–622, 611.

on the one hand and the rights of consumers and Internet pirates to privacy and protection of personal data on the other are typically set in a horizontal context.[74] In the *Scarlet Extended* case, for instance, there was a conflict between the owners of intellectual property rights and the fundamental rights of the ISP and its customers. The horizontal obligations of the owners of intellectual property rights towards other individuals' fundamental rights in this case rest upon the E-Commerce Directive. Although the Court's focus was on the freedom to conduct a business, the fundamental rights of ISP customers affected by an injunction, including the right to protection of personal data and the freedom to receive information, were also touched upon. The question of whether fundamental rights do have horizontal *direct* effect could be avoided as the legal context was to a large extent determined by EU Directives. Hence, it concerned an indirect rather than a direct obligation for private individuals to respect fundamental rights.[75] In a similar vein, *UPC Telekabel Wien* concerned a horizontal dispute between an ISP, UPC Telekabel Wien, on the one hand and Constantin Film Verleih and Wega Filmproduktionsgesellschaft on the other as to the availability of a wide range of films protected by copyright on a website.[76] The Court had to decide on an injunction ordering the blocking of a copyright-infringing website; the decision in the end depended on a balancing of fundamental rights between private parties.

In the well-known *Google Spain* case, the Court was more explicit on the prospect of horizontal direct effect of EU fundamental rights contained in the Charter.[77] The central question relates to Mr Costeja González's request to order Google Spain SL and Google Inc to withdraw personal data relating to Mr Costeja González from its index and to prevent access to the data in the future.[78] In particular, he wanted the links to two pages of the *La Vanguardia* newspaper on which an announcement mentioning his name appeared for a real-estate auction connected with attachment proceedings for the recovery of social security debts to be removed. Regarding the rights to privacy and protection of personal data, the ECJ considered that 'the data subject may … request that the information in question no longer be made available to the general public by its inclusion in such a list of results, it should be held … that those rights override, as a rule, not only the economic interest of the operator of the search engine but also the interest of

[74] See also the contribution of Gerards in ch 3 of this volume.

[75] See also X Groussot, L Pech and G Thor Petursson, 'The Reach of Fundamental Rights on Member State Action after Lisbon' in de Vries, Bernitz and Weatherill (n 15) 116.

[76] Case C-314/12 *UPC Telekabel Wien GmbH v Constantin Film Verleih GmbH and Wega Filmproduktionsgesellschaft mbH (UPC Telekabel Wien)* (ECJ, 24 March 2014).

[77] J Emaus, 'Rechten, beginselen & horizontale directe werking van de grondrechten in het EU-Handvest' (2015) *Nederlands Tijdschrift voor Burgerlijk Recht* (forthcoming).

[78] *Google Spain* (n 45).

the general public in finding that information upon a search relating to the data subject's name'.[79]

This consideration of the Court's judgment seems to suggest that the data subject has a self-standing right to request, on the basis of fundamental rights enshrined in Articles 7 and 8 of the Charter, that Google will no longer make the information available. This entails a truly horizontal application of EU Charter rights.

The rapid developments in the field of information technology whereby citizens' lives are increasingly also invaded by private companies undeniably calls for effective legal means to protect privacy as a legal value in horizontal situations. A form of (limited) horizontal direct effect is therefore desirable. For that matter, solutions for the protection of privacy in these situations could already be found in ancient Rome: 'The protection provided was the result of the existence of certain actions, mainly the *actio iniuriarum*, as the means to protect individual personality.'[80] Whereas the need to recognise some form of horizontal direct effect of the right to privacy arises from the protection of European citizens in present-day information society, the legal actions to protect Roman citizens' personality emerged from 'the development of the classical legal system … and the social requirement of protection of individuality as a legal value'.[81]

ii. *Assessment of Fundamental Rights Against the Background of Internal Market Freedoms*

The broad scope of application of the four freedoms entails that fundamental rights become part of their assessment.[82] The important consequence of this approach is a shift in the burden of proof. Where in *Strasbourg* the proponents of economic rights might have to justify a restriction on human rights, in *Luxembourg* the fundamental human rights proponents will have to justify their actions and establish that the restriction on free movement is justified on the basis of protecting the fundamental rights. As Brown observed, 'the language of prima facie breach of economic rights suggests that it remains something which is at the heart wrong, but tolerated, which sits rather uneasily with the State's paramount constitutional obligation to protect human rights'.[83]After all, the very fact that the protection of fundamental rights in cases where a conflict with fundamental freedoms arise must be *justified* in the light of the economic freedoms could jeopardise the

[79] ibid [97].
[80] Perninan (n 5)183.
[81] ibid 199.
[82] Weatherill (n 15) 12, 16–17.
[83] C Brown, 'Case C-112/00, *Eugen Schmidberger, Internationale Transporte und Planzüge v. Austria*. Judgment of 12 June 2003, Full Court' (2003) 40 *CML Rev* 1499, 1508.

equality or indivisibility of fundamental rights and economic freedoms. It will then be essential to establish: (i) under what type of ground of exception fundamental rights fall; and (ii) the conditions under which fundamental rights can deviate from the Treaty freedoms.

Regarding (i), the *Viking Line* case illustrates how a fundamental right, in this case the fundamental right to take collective action and to strike, which was considered to restrict the freedom of establishment, may be 'subsumed' under a rule of reason exception ground, ie, the protection of workers. The ECJ did not examine whether the fundamental right *as such* may justify a restriction on free movement.[84] Advocate General Trstenjak in the *Commission v Germany* case stated that such an approach 'sit[s] uncomfortably alongside the principle of equal ranking for fundamental rights and fundamental freedoms'.[85] *Viking Line* is, however, not a typical example of how the Court normally deals with fundamental rights under the scheme of free movement. As shown above, cases like *Schmidberger*, *Omega* and *Dynamic Medien* show that fundamental rights can constitute a self-standing exception ground.

Regarding (ii), the conditions under which fundamental rights can be justified in the light of the free movement rules depend on the context. The starting point is the proportionality test as normally applied by the ECJ in the framework of Treaty exceptions and mandatory requirements. Also here *Viking Line* highlights the inherent risk of applying the proportionality test, which may lead to the subordination of a fundamental right to an internal market freedom. According to the Court, collective action was just one of the ways that may serve workers' interests and account should be taken of less restrictive means before initiating a strike.

Although judgments like *Viking Line* may well constitute isolated incidents, they make clear that internal market freedoms may affect fundamental rights to a considerable extent. Furthermore, through the proportionality principle, the Court has to provide an interpretation of national fundamental rights invoked by the Member State. Potential disagreements about the meaning and scope of these fundamental rights 'are not resolved on the basis of perceived commonalities between the Member States', but against the background of the internal market freedoms.[86]

[84] See also T Novitz, 'A Human Rights Analysis of the Viking and Laval Judgments' (2007–08) 10 *Cambridge Yearbook of European Legal Studies* 541, 557; J Malmberg and T Sigeman, 'Industrial Actions and EU Economic Freedoms: The Autonomous Collective Bargaining Model Curtailed by the European Court of Justice' (2008) 45 *CML Rev* 1115, 1130. The Court has been criticised for prioritising economic rights over social rights: C Barnard, 'The Charter, the Court—and the Crisis', Legal Studies Research Paper Series, Paper No 18/2013, Cambridge.

[85] Case C-271/08 *Commission v Germany* (ECJ, 15 July 2010) Opinion of AG Trstenjak at [183].

[86] Augenstein (n 9).

B. Internal Market Freedoms Affecting Fundamental Rights in the Legislative Context

i. Broad Legislative Powers in the Field of the Internal Market

a. The Broad Scope of Article 114 TFEU

According to Articles 6 TEU and 51(2) of the EU Charter, the provisions of the Charter shall not extend the competences of the EU. And the Charter does not contain a specific provision constituting a legal basis for the 'harmonisation of fundamental rights'. True, the principle of conferral as laid down in Article 5(1) TEU should prevent the unbridled expansion of EU powers in areas where there is no competence for the EU to act. But there are various other avenues for the EU legislator to harmonise national fundamental rights standards at the EU level.

First and foremost, the potentially very wide scope of Article 114 TFEU, the internal market legal basis, allows for the harmonisation of national laws designed to protect public interests or fundamental rights, but constituting an obstacle to free movement, even when the Treaty limits or excludes legislative powers in certain policy fields. This follows from the *Tobacco Advertising* case law, which concerned the challenge to Article 114 TFEU as a proper legal basis for the Directive on advertising and sponsorship of tobacco products.[87] According to the Court, a Directive can be adopted on the basis of these provisions only if measures have as their object either the objective of removal of obstacles to the exercise of fundamental freedoms *or* the removal of appreciable distortions of competition. The ECJ added that the EU legislature cannot be prevented from relying on that legal basis on the ground that public health protection is a decisive factor in the choices to be made. The Court's judgment implies that once the threshold requirements have been met, the EU legislature has the power to intervene in practically any policy field regulated by the Member States.[88] This is particularly relevant in areas where the EU does not dispose of specific harmonisation powers, such as in the field of fundamental rights. Fundamental rights can then be regulated at the EU level by exploiting 'the broad and fuzzy contours of Article 114 TFEU' and bypassing Articles 6(1) TEU and 51(2) of the EU Charter.[89]

[87] Case C-376/98 *Federal Republic of Germany v European Parliament and Council Germany (Tobacco Advertising)* [2000] ECR I-8419; European Parliament and Council Directive 98/43/EC of 6 July 1998 on the approximation of the laws, regulations and administrative provisions of the Member States relating to the advertising and sponsorship of tobacco products [1998] OJ L213/9.

[88] This also follows from the follow-up case law on tobacco advertising: Case C-491/01 *The Queen v Secretary of State for Health ex parte British American Tobacco (Investments) Ltd and Imperial Tobacco Ltd. (BAT/Imperial Tobacco)* [2002] ECR I-11453; Case C-210/03 *Swedish Match AB and Swedish Match UK Ltd v Secretary of State for Health (Swedish Match)* [2004] ECR I-11893.

[89] S Weatherill, 'The Limits of Legislative Harmonization Ten Years after *Tobacco Advertising*: How the Court's Case Law Has Become a 'Drafting Guide'' (2011) 12 *German Law*

b. Article 16 TFEU and the Harmonisation of Data Protection Rules

Article 16 TFEU has been introduced by the Treaty of Lisbon and constitutes a self-standing legal basis for EU rules on data protection, as well as covering all areas of EU law. This means that a single instrument can be adopted replacing the current patchwork of EU rules thereby creating new possibilities for the EU legislator to harmonise in the field of data protection. It allows the EU legislature to advance legislation that is more ambitious and specifically aimed at offering a high level of protection of personal data.

Article 16 first states that 'everyone has the right to the protection of personal data concerning them'. Paragraph 2 of Article 16 includes two options for the regulation of right to the protection of personal data at the EU level: (1) rules protecting individuals with regard to the processing of personal data if Member States act within the scope of EU law; and (2) rules concerning the free movement of personal data. Article 16 thus seems to have a broader scope of application than Article 114 TFEU; however, as stated above, the broad interpretation given by the Court to the Data Protection Directive already meant that the requirement of free movement had become more or less superfluous. In that sense, Article 16 TFEU is not only related to the internal market legal basis of Article 114 TFEU but also constitutes a natural successor to Article 114 TFEU.

Article 16 TFEU is the legal basis for the current proposals for a General Regulation on Data Protection and a Directive on the processing of data by law enforcement authorities for law enforcement purposes.[90] The proposed Regulation inter alia includes a right to be forgotten or rather a right to erasure and the definition of the concept of 'consent', which the data controller will have to prove. The link between data protection and the internal market remains visible as the Commission in the explanations to the proposed Regulation notes that the Regulation contributes to the functioning of the internal market.[91]

Journal 848; SA de Vries, *Tensions within the Internal Market: The Functioning of the Internal Market and the Development of Horizontal and Flanking Policies* (Groningen, Europa Law Publishing, 2006) 339.

[90] Commission, 'Proposal for a Regulation of the European Parliament and of the Council on the protection of individuals with regard to the processing of personal data and on the free movement of such data' COM (2012) 011 final (General Data Protection Regulation); Commission, 'Proposal for a Directive of the European Parliament and of the Council on the protection of individuals with regard to the processing of personal data by competent authorities for the purposes of prevention, investigation, detection or prosecution of criminal offences or the execution of criminal penalties, and the free movement of such data' COM (2012) 010 final.

[91] S Peers, 'Basic Data Protection Principles in the Proposed Data Protection Regulation: Back to the Future?' *EU Law Analysis*, http://eulawanalysis.blogspot.nl/2015/03/basic-data-protection-principles-in.html.

c. *Digital Rights Ireland*: An Incentive to Regulate Data Protection at the EU Level in Detail?

The broad legislative powers in the field of the internal market and the requirement to comply with, for instance, the rights to privacy and data protection in rather close detail may provide an *incentive* for the EU legislature to pursue and protect fundamental rights at EU level more actively. According to Advocate General Cruz Villalon in his Opinion in *Digital Rights Ireland*, 'there was nothing to prevent the European Union legislature, in defining the obligation to collect and retain data, from accompanying that obligation with a series of guarantees at least in the form of principles, to be developed by the Member States, that were intended to regulate use of the data and, thereby, to define the exact extent and complete profile of the interference which that obligation entails'.[92] He admitted, though, that at the time, it may have been difficult to incorporate specific guarantees regarding access to the data retained in an internal market Directive.

If the EU legislature is called upon to regulate fundamental rights in more detail, the margin of discretion for the Member States to pursue fundamental rights at the national level but within the context of EU legislation will eventually be reduced. It follows from the well-known *Åkerberg Fransson* and *Melloni* cases of the Court that once the EU legislature has fully harmonised a field of EU law and thereby regulated EU fundamental rights, which is particularly possible within the context of the internal market, it is no longer possible for the Member State to take recourse to more stringent national constitutional standards.[93]

ii. *Interpretation of Fundamental Rights in the Light of the Regulatory Framework*

The single market regulatory framework in the field of data protection has induced the ECJ to provide for a broad scope of application of these rules and a more in-depth assessment and autonomous interpretation of the fundamental rights of data protection and privacy. In the *Österreichischer Rundfunk* case, the ECJ held that it is not necessary for the applicability of the Data Protection Directive to establish in each situation a link with free movement.[94] This led Advocate General Kokott to conclude in the *Satamedia* case that the broad scope of Data Protection Directive 'reaches almost beyond the establishment of the internal market'.[95] The establishment of

[92] *Digital Rights Ireland* (n 32) Opinion of AG Cruz Villalon at [124].

[93] *Åkerberg Fransson* (n 56); and Case C-399/11 *Melloni* (ECJ, 26 February 2013).

[94] Joined Cases C-465/00, C-138/01 and C-139/01 *Österreichischer Rundfunk and others (Österreichischer Rundfunk)* [2003] ECR I-4989.

[95] Case C-73/07 *Tietosuojavaltuutettu v Satakunnan Markkinapörssi Oy and Satamedia (Satamedia)* [2008] ECR I-9831, Opinion of AG Kokott at [53]. See also H Kranenborg, 'Commentary on Article 8' in Peers et al (n 4) 227.

a cross-border element is thus not always necessary. The proposed Data Protection Regulation, which is based on Article 16 TFEU, constituting a specific legal basis outside the frame of the internal market but containing a reference to the 'free movement of data', would have a similar broad scope of application.[96]

The Court in *Google Spain* interprets the Directive alongside Articles 7 and 8 of the Charter and holds that the rights to privacy and data protection override, 'as a rule, not only the economic interest of the operator of the search engine but also the interest of the general public in finding that information upon a search relating to the data subject's name'.[97]

The problem of removing search results from the Internet is thus (almost) exclusively viewed through the lens of the Data Protection Directive. In other words, the EU single market framework allows the ECJ to provide for a far-reaching right to protect personal data, which in principle deserves approval, although possibly at the cost of other fundamental rights, like the freedom of expression or the freedom to receive information.[98]

In a similar vein, but now possibly at the cost of privacy and data protection, in *Scarlet Extended* the E-Commerce Directive (Directive 2000/31) constituted one of the main reasons for the Court to put the freedom to conduct a business at the heart of its judgment, thereby outflanking other fundamental rights, such as the rights of Internet users to privacy and to the protection of personal data. As stated above, in this case, the ECJ had to decide on the compatibility of the requirement for an ISP to install a filtering system in response to infringements of intellectual property rights and to combat piracy with EU fundamental rights. The freedom to conduct a business as contained in Article 16 of the Charter in fact strengthens Article 15(1) of the E-Commerce Directive, prohibiting too severe a measure such as the requirement to install a filtering system.[99] According to the Court, an injunction by the court 'would result in a serious infringement of the freedom of the ISP concerned to conduct its business since it would require that ISP to install a complicated, costly, permanent computer system at its own expense'.[100]

The Court's preference for an autonomous standard of fundamental rights protection also appears in the above-mentioned *Sky Österreich* case. The requirements of various conflicting rights and interests were reconciled

[96] H Kranenborg, 'Commentary on Article 8' in Peers et al (n 4) 228.

[97] *Google Spain* (n 45) [97].

[98] See also S Kulk and F Borgesius, 'De implicaties van het Google Spain arrest voor de vrijheid van meningsuiting' (2015) *NTM/NJCM-Bulletin* (forthcoming); S Kulk, and FJ Zuiderveen Borgesius, '*Google Spain v González*: Did the Court Forget about Freedom of Expression?' (2014) 2 *European Journal of Risk Regulation* 389–98.

[99] *Scarlet Extended* (n 23) [24].

[100] ibid [48].

in accordance with an *EU standard* of fundamental rights[101] The Austrian 'federal communications senate' (Bundeskommunikationssenat), which had asked for the preliminary ruling, expressed serious doubts as to whether the provisions of the AMSD were compatible with the principle of proportionality, as the right to produce short news reports without compensation in her opinion constituted a serious interference with the right to property. Meanwhile, the Austrian and German Constitutional Courts had also found that the right to produce short news reports disproportionately infringed the right to property and professional freedom in the light of the Austrian and German Constitutions respectively. Although both the ECJ and the constitutional courts had to conduct a balancing approach, they reached diametrically opposite conclusions.

The ECJ did not take the decisions of the national constitutional courts into account. The fact that national standards of fundamental rights do not or hardly play a role in the case law of the Court or that the ECJ is not willing to draw on comparative law and sticks to its own style and method of legal reasoning has been criticised in legal literature.[102] But according to Advocate General Bot in his Opinion, the context in *Sky Österreich* is determined by the completion of the *internal market*, to which the Directive contributes. This dimension plays a role in balancing fundamental rights and calls for a different approach compared to the balancing of fundamental rights within a purely national context.[103]

C. Final Observations

The impact of the internal market freedoms on fundamental rights may be substantial. Within the context of free movement, the internal market freedoms determine the scope of application of EU fundamental rights and the conditions under which they can be safeguarded by the Member State. Although the Court leaves ample room for Member States to protect fundamental rights according to their own agenda, there are limits, which are mostly determined by the proportionality principle.

In the fields of data protection and privacy, the legislative context is particularly relevant and the case law of the Court reveals that the internal market legislative framework constitutes a rather solid basis for the

[101] Georgios Anagnostaras, 'Balancing Conflicting Fundamental Rights: The *Sky Österreich* Paradigm' (2014) *EL Rev* 123. Annotation by P-A Van Malleghem, (2013) *SEW, Tijdschrift voor Europees en economisch recht* 447–53.

[102] G de Búrca, 'After the EU Charter of Fundamental Rights: The Court of Justice as a Human Rights Adjudicator?' (2013) 20 *Maastricht Journal of European and Comparative Law* 168.

[103] *Sky Österreich* (n 29) Opinion of AG Bot at [52].

development of an autonomous EU fundamental rights regime. It also narrows the Court's view on fundamental rights, as rights that are not specifically regulated by EU legislation are not or are hardly taken on board.

V. CONCLUSION

The two tracks that have been followed in this chapter with a view to examining the relationship between EU single market law and fundamental rights reveal a somewhat blurred but not always worrying picture. The internal market freedoms and fundamental rights mutually affect each other, but the effect of the internal market freedoms on fundamental rights seems more substantial, particularly due to the (limited) scope of application of the rules on free movement, the assessment of fundamental rights within the context of the exception grounds and the broad legislative powers in the field of the internal market vis-a-vis the lack of powers in the field of EU fundamental rights. This may hamper the development of a full-fledged EU system of human rights. However, it does not (always) prevent the Court from having a mature conception of fundamental rights. The Court has managed to settle conflicts between the internal market freedoms and fundamental rights within the single market as a 'normative corridor' in a rather satisfactory manner. And the examples of privacy and data protection show that at least in these areas, certainly helped by the close nexus with the internal market, the Court has developed an impressive case law in strong support of these rights.

The main challenge for the Court will now be whether the traditional approach under the scheme of free movement will endure, in particular where conflicts between fundamental rights are at issue. The fact that the EU Charter has now been squeezed in between the universal declaration of human rights, the ECHR and the national constitutions means that more different rights have been recognised legally, producing at the EU level, in addition to the internal market freedoms, a new clash potential.

12

The EU Charter of Fundamental Rights and the Rights to Data Privacy: The EU Court of Justice as a Human Rights Court

FEDERICO FABBRINI*

I. INTRODUCTION

WITH THE RISE of digital technology, the need to protect data privacy has acquired greater importance. Since each of us increasingly interacts with the rest of the world through the medium of electronic communications—and because most of the actions we undertake leave a digital trace that makes a huge amount of personal information potentially available to others—growing concerns have been raised about the possibility to defend a sphere of individual autonomy in the digital age.[1] In this context, the protection of the rights to data privacy has emerged as one of the greatest challenges of our generation.[2] This chapter uses the notion of the rights to data privacy to define a number of entitlements that individuals shall enjoy when interacting in the digital world and concerning both a substantive core of protection as well as a set of procedural guarantees regulating the processing of personal data by third parties. The notion of rights to data privacy does not have an explicit recognition in binding legal text. Yet, arguably it can be framed as a helpful concept that condenses a set of entitlements associated with individual (inter)action in the digital world. In these terms, the notion of data privacy brings together traditional ideas of privacy and data protection into a new constitutional concept specifically

* I am grateful to Sybe de Vries, Tuomas Ojanen, and Oreste Pollicino for their helpful comments on earlier drafts.

[1] See generally D Cole, 'Can Privacy Be Saved?' *New York Review of Books* (6–19 March 2014) 23.

[2] See also Office of the United Nations High Commissioner for Human Rights, report, 'The Right to Privacy in the Digital Age', 30 June 2014, A/HRC/27/37.

tailored to the digital age.[3] As Lee A Bygrave has explained, data privacy 'has entered the discourse more recently than "privacy" and "data protection". It is gaining traction on both sides of the Atlantic. Its use can be seen as an attempt to signal more accurately than the other two terms the focus, thrust and rationale of relevant norms'.[4]

The aim of this chapter is to discuss the protection of the rights to data privacy in the legal system of the EU.[5] In particular, the goal is to examine the provisions of the EU Charter of Fundamental Rights—and of the EU Treaties—dealing with data privacy and to assess their implications on the case law of the EU Court of Justice (ECJ). The argument of this chapter is that since the entry into force of the Lisbon Treaty in 2009, and especially in the past year, the ECJ has dramatically expanded the protection of the rights data privacy, drawing on the Charter of Fundamental Rights to ensure a leading degree of protection in the field. As revealed by the analysis of several recent ECJ rulings reviewing compliance with data privacy rights by the EU Member States, the EU political branches of government as well as private corporations, the ECJ has vested with confidence the role of a human rights court in the area of data privacy, holding inter alia that data subjects have a fundamental right to be protected against systematic retention of personal data for law enforcement purposes and a right to request removal of data about them from online search engines. Nevertheless, as this chapter suggests, the jurisprudence of the ECJ, by being at the forefront of legal developments on digital technology, has also raised a number of challenges. While the ECJ has so far promoted an uncompromising view of the rights of data privacy, its case law has left open some key questions which will need to be addressed in the near future.

The chapter is structured as follows. Section II provides an overview of the original EU legislative framework on the protection of personal data and considers the effect of the adoption of the Charter of Fundamental Rights—first as a merely declaratory document and subsequently as a binding norm of EU primary law. Section III analyses several recent judgments of the ECJ concerning the application of EU data privacy law—including the provisions of the Charter of Fundamental Rights—to legislation by the Member States and the EU institutions, and to action by private parties. Section IV, then, seeks to draw insights from the analysis of the case law of the ECJ

[3] For an introduction to the concepts of privacy and data protection under EU and ECHR law, see also J Kokott and C Sobotta, 'The Distinction between Privacy and Data Protection in the Jurisprudence of the CJEU and the ECtHR' (2013) 3 *International Data Privacy Law* 222.

[4] LA Bygrave, *Data Privacy Law: An International Perspective* (Oxford, Oxford University Press, 2014) 26.

[5] On the protection of fundamental rights in Europe, see generally F Fabbrini, *Fundamental Rights in Europe: Challenges and Transformations in Comparative Perspective* (Oxford, Oxford University Press, 2014).

and emphasises its far-reaching implications in terms of the protection of data privacy rights. Here, I underline how the ECJ has taken the lead in protecting the rights to data privacy in a digital world, showing its willingness and ability to secure the protection of data privacy rights even in the face of rapid technological developments. However, I also shed light on some of the challenges that the case law of the ECJ raised—in particular by pointing out how the uncompromising approach of the ECJ has left open the question of how to balance data privacy with competing rights and interests. Finally, section V briefly concludes.

II. EU DATA PRIVACY LAW AND THE CHARTER OF FUNDAMENTAL RIGHTS

The EU has been endowed with a comprehensive legislative framework on data protection since the 1990s. However, with the adoption of the Charter of Fundamental Rights in 2000 and with the entry into force of the Lisbon Treaty in 2009, data privacy rights have been constitutionalised in EU primary law.

A. Legislative Framework

The EU is endowed with a complex legislative framework for the protection of privacy and personal data.[6] Since 1995, it has had a regulation on the processing of personal data in the context of commercial transactions.[7] Directive 95/46[8]—the so-called Data Protection Directive—was adopted as an internal market measure aimed at ensuring the free flow of data across the Member States. However, it introduced a far-reaching obligation for the Member States to 'protect the fundamental rights and freedoms of natural persons, and in particular their right to privacy, with respect to the processing of personal data'[9] within their jurisdictions.[10] The Data Protection Directive provides that personal data shall be processed only on the basis of "qualitative principles", including the requirement that data collection shall

[6] For a comprehensive survey of the legal instruments and mechanisms for data protection in the EU, see the report M Scheinin, T Ojanen, N Kyriakou, M Tzanou, and I prepared for the EU Fundamental Rights Agency, 'Data Protection in the European Union: The Role of National Data Protection Authorities' (2010), available at: http://fra.europa.eu/en/publication/2012/data-protection-european-union-role-national-data-protection-authorities.

[7] See S Simitis, 'From the Market to the Polis: The EU Directive on the Protection of Personal Data' (1995) 80 *Iowa Law Review* 445.

[8] Directive 95/46/EC [1995] OJ L281/31.

[9] ibid Art 1.

[10] ibid Art 4.

be proportionate to the purpose for which it is undertaken[11] and generally conditional on the consent of the data subject.[12] It prohibits the processing of sensitive data, such as those revealing 'racial or ethnic origin, political opinions, religious or philosophical beliefs, trade-union membership, and ... concerning health or sex life'.[13] And it requires that data subjects be informed about the collection of data.[14] Moreover, it empowers data subjects to obtain access to the data and demand rectification, blocking or erasure when necessary,[15] and imposed on the Member States an obligation to institute independent authorities charged to supervise that the processing of personal data at the national level conforms to EU data protection principles.[16]

The Data Protection Directive served as the template for data privacy protection in the EU.[17] Since the adoption in 2001 of the EU Regulation on the protection of individuals with regard to the processing of personal data by the Community institutions,[18] which also established the European Data Protection Supervisor (EDPS),[19] the principles codified in the Directive must also be respected by the EU institutions when processing personal

[11] ibid Art 6 (stating that 'Member States shall provide that personal data must be: (a) processed fairly and lawfully; (b) collected for specified, explicit and legitimate purposes and not further processed in a way incompatible with those purposes. Further processing of data for historical, statistical or scientific purposes shall not be considered as incompatible provided that Member States provide appropriate safeguards; (c) adequate, relevant and not excessive in relation to the purposes for which they are collected and/or further processed; (d) accurate and, where necessary, kept up to date; every reasonable step must be taken to ensure that data which are inaccurate or incomplete, having regard to the purposes for which they were collected or for which they are further processed, are erased or rectified; (e) kept in a form which permits identification of data subjects for no longer than is necessary for the purposes for which the data were collected or for which they are further processed. Member States shall lay down appropriate safeguards for personal data stored for longer periods for historical, statistical or scientific use').

[12] ibid Art 7 (stating that 'Member States shall provide that personal data may be processed only if: (a) the data subject has unambiguously given his consent; or (b) processing is necessary for the performance of a contract to which the data subject is party or in order to take steps at the request of the data subject prior to entering into a contract; or (c) processing is necessary for compliance with a legal obligation to which the controller is subject; or (d) processing is necessary in order to protect the vital interests of the data subject; or (e) processing is necessary for the performance of a task carried out in the public interest or in the exercise of official authority vested in the controller or in a third party to whom the data are disclosed; or (f) processing is necessary for the purposes of the legitimate interests pursued by the controller or by the third party or parties to whom the data are disclosed, except where such interests are overridden by the interests for fundamental rights and freedoms of the data subject which require protection under Article 1(1)').

[13] ibid Art 8(1).

[14] ibid Art 10.

[15] ibid Art 12.

[16] ibid Art 28.

[17] See J Fromholz, 'The European Union Data Privacy Directive' (2000) 15 *Berkeley Technology Law Journal* 461.

[18] Regulation 45/2001/EC [2001] OJ L8/1.

[19] See H Hijmans, 'The European Data Protection Supervisor: The Institutions of the EC Controlled by an Independent Authority' (2006) 43 *CML Rev* 1313.

data. Moreover, the principles of the Data Protection Directive, which was enacted before the spread of the Internet, were extended to the electronic communication sector by Directive 2002/58, which harmonised Member States' laws to ensure an equivalent level of protection of fundamental rights and freedoms, and in particular the right to privacy and confidentiality, with respect to the processing of personal data in the electronic communications sector.[20] At the same time, the ECJ interpreted the Data Protection Directive so as to ensure its effectiveness and to update its protection to new technological developments.[21] Hence, in *Österreichischer Rundfunk*, the ECJ held that provisions of the Directive are directly applicable, in that they may be relied on by an individual before the national courts to oust the application of rules of national law which are contrary to those provisions.[22] And in *Lindqvist*, it ruled that the placing of information on the Internet constituted processing of personal data wholly or partially by automated means, within the meaning of the Data Protection Directive.[23]

Nevertheless, the Data Protection Directive was subject to a number of limitations and exceptions. To begin with, EU general data protection law did not apply in the field of EU Common Foreign and Security Policy and in the EU Area of Freedom, Security and Justice—the former second and third pillars of the EU.[24] In the latter, a Council Framework Decision on the protection of personal data in the framework of police and judicial cooperation in criminal matters[25] was adopted in 2008: yet this piece of legislation only lightly replicated the data privacy protections enshrined in the Data Protection Directive.[26] Moreover, even in the first pillar, important exceptions constrained the effectiveness of data protection law.[27] Since 2006, in particular, the Data Retention Directive[28] introduced a permanent derogation to the principles of the Data Protection Directive with the aim of fighting terrorism and protecting national security.[29] Specifically, the Data Retention Directive required Member States to adopt legislation imposing on IT or

[20] Directive 2002/58/EC [2002] OJ L201/37.

[21] See P De Hert and S Gutwirth, 'Data Protection in the Case Law of Strasbourg and Luxembourg: Constitutionalization in Action' in P De Hert et al (eds), *Reinventing Data Protection* (Vienna, Springer, 2009) 3.

[22] Joined Cases C-465/00, C-138/01 and C-139/01 *Österreichischer Rundfunk* [2003] ECR I-4989.

[23] Case C-101/01 *Lindqvist* [2003] ECR I-12971.

[24] See generally E Sanfrutos Cano, 'The End of the Pillars? A Single EU Legal Order after Lisbon' in C Murphy and P Green (eds), *Law and Outsiders* (Oxford, Hart Publishing, 2011) 67.

[25] Council Framework Decision 2008/977/JHA [2008] OJ L350/60.

[26] See further K Lachmayer, 'Rethinking Privacy beyond Borders' (2015) 20 *Tilburg Law Review* 78.

[27] See F Bignami, 'Privacy and Law Enforcement in the European Union: The Data Retention Directive' (2008) 8 *Chicago Journal of International Law* 233.

[28] Directive 2006/24/EC [2006] OJ L105/54.

[29] ibid Art 3.

telephone companies a duty to store and retain the data relating to source, addressee, date, time, length and type of the communication[30]—although not the content of the communication itself.[31] Retention had to last for a period of not less than six months and not more than two years.[32] Pursuant to the Directive, Member States had to regulate in national laws conditions for access to these data in accordance with necessity and proportionality requirements, and consistent with EU and European Convention on Human Rights (ECHR) law.[33] Yet, Member States were left discretion in defining the conditions that justify access to the retained data.[34]

B. Constitutional Rights

Beyond the complex EU legislative framework for the protection of personal data, in recent years the rights to data privacy have raised to constitutional status in the EU. The ECHR, which has always been a source of inspiration for the protection of fundamental rights in the EU,[35] held in Article 8 that: 'Everyone has the right to respect for his private and family life, his home and his correspondence.' However, although the European Court of Human Rights (ECtHR) had taken steps to apply Article 8 ECHR to the protection of personal data,[36] the provision was not explicit in securing such a right. On the contrary, the EU Charter of Fundamental Rights adopted in 2000 introduced a constitutional recognition of the right to data protection in the EU legal order.[37] Whereas Article 7 of the Charter (entitled 'Respect for Private and Family Life') reaffirmed the content of Article 8 ECHR, proclaiming that 'Everyone has the right to respect for his or her private and

[30] ibid Art 5(1).

[31] ibid Art 5(2).

[32] ibid Art 6.

[33] ibid Art 4 (stating that 'Member States shall adopt measures to ensure that data retained in accordance with this Directive are provided only to the competent national authorities in specific cases and in accordance with national law. The procedures to be followed and the conditions to be fulfilled in order to gain access to retained data in accordance with necessity and proportionality requirements shall be defined by each Member State in its national law, subject to the relevant provisions of European Union law or public international law, and in particular the ECHR').

[34] See ibid Art 1.

[35] See Art 6 TEU (stating that 'Fundamental rights, as guaranteed by the [ECHR ...], shall constitute general principles of the Union's law'). But see also Case 4/73 *Nold* [1974] ECR 491 (stating that the ECJ will draw inspiration from the ECHR in developing its human rights jurisprudence).

[36] See, eg *MS v Sweden*, ECtHR judgment of 27 August 1997 (recognising that the protection of personal data is of a fundamental importance to a person's enjoyment of his or her right to respect for private life guaranteed by Art 8 ECHR); and *Rotaru v Romania*, ECtHR judgment of 4 May 2000 (stating that Art 8 ECHR should encompass the protection of personal data ensured by Council of Europe Convention 108).

[37] See M Tzanou, 'Data Protection as a Fundamental Rights Next to Privacy? "Reconstructing" a Not so New Right' (2013) 3 *International Data Privacy Law* 88.

family life, home and communications', Article 8 of the Charter (entitled 'Protection of Personal Data') introduced a new recognition of the rights to data privacy by stating that: 'Everyone has the right to the protection of personal data concerning him or her. Such data must be processed fairly for specified purposes and on the basis of the consent of the person concerned or some other legitimate basis laid down by law. Everyone has the right of access to data which has been collected concerning him or her, and the right to have it rectified. Compliance with these rules shall be subject to control by an independent authority.'

As is well known, the Charter of Fundamental Rights initially did not have a binding value:[38] it was only declared by the EU institutions and was subsequently included in the failed Constitutional Treaty. However, with the entry into force of the Lisbon Treaty in 2009, the Charter has eventually acquired full *valeur juridique*.[39] Pursuant to Article 6(1) of Treaty on the European Union (TEU): 'The Union recognises the rights, freedoms and principles set out in the Charter of Fundamental Rights … which shall have the same legal value as the Treaties.' Moreover, the Lisbon Treaty introduced another provision confirming the centrality that the rights to data privacy now play in the constitutional order of the EU.[40] Pursuant to Article 16 of the Treaty on the Functioning of the European Union (TFEU): 'Everyone has the right to the protection of personal data concerning them.' The same provision, empowers the EU legislature—the European Parliament jointly with the Council—to 'lay down the rules relating to the protection of individuals with regard to the processing of personal data by Union institutions, bodies, offices and agencies, and by the Member States when carrying out activities which fall within the scope of Union law, and the rules relating to the free movement of such data. Compliance with these rules shall be subject to the control of independent authorities'.

The constitutional effects of the Charter of Fundamental Rights had been a matter of discussion in the field of EU law.[41] Although—as formally stated in the Preamble—the Charter simply purported to 'reaffirm[], with due regard for the powers and tasks of the Union and for the principle of subsidiarity, the rights as they result, in particular, from the constitutional traditions and international obligations common to the Member States, the [ECHR …] and the case-law of the [ECJ] and of the [ECtHR]', several

[38] See generally K Lenaerts and E de Smijter, 'A "Bill of Rights" for the European Union' (2001) 38 *CML Rev* 273.

[39] S Douglas-Scott, 'The European Union and Human Rights after the Treaty of Lisbon' (2011) 11 *Human Rights Law Review* 645.

[40] See also S Rodotà, 'Data Protection as Fundamental Rights' in P de Her et al (eds), *Reinventing Data Protection* (Vienna, Springer, 2009) 77.

[41] See E Bribosia, 'L'avenir de la protection de droits fondamentaux dans l'Union Européenne' in G Amato et al (eds), *Genesis and Destiny of the European Constitution* (Brussels, Bruylant, 2007), 995; and R Lawson, 'Human Rights: The Best is Yet to Come' (2005) 1 *European Constitutional Law Review* 27.

scholars had emphasised the transformative effect that was connected to the codification of an EU bill of rights. As Marta Cartabia remarked, even if the original aim of the Charter's drafter was to 'provide a restatement of the law of fundamental rights already recognised by a plurality of legal sources, it was easily foreseeable that the effects of writing the Charter would go well beyond the original intent'.[42] On the one hand, the Charter constitutes one of the most innovative and updated human rights catalogues in the world—as is well evidenced by its provision on data privacy rights. On the other hand, it offers a clear reference text for the hermeneutical activity of the EU courts—that is, a principled document from which to draw inspiration to address new legal challenges. As a matter of fact, the case law of the ECJ in the field of data privacy rights has largely confirmed this prediction. The ECJ has built on the Charter of Fundamental Rights a new line of jurisprudence which significantly expanded the protection of the rights to data privacy of individuals interacting in the digital world. We shall now turn to the analysis of this recent case law.

III. THE POST-CHARTER CASE LAW OF THE ECJ

The ECJ has enforced a high standard of data privacy protections: vertically, ie, vis-à-vis the Member States; horizontally, ie, vis-à-vis the EU political branches; as well as diagonally, ie, vis-à-vis private companies which wield relevant power in the processing of personal data. Recent judgments by the ECJ shed light on each of these three dimensions.

A. The Vertical Dimension

In two recent cases delivered after the entry into force of the Lisbon Treaty, the ECJ held the Member States responsible for failing to secure a sufficiently high level of data privacy protection. In its judgments in *Commission v Germany*[43] and the follow-up case of *Commission v Austria*,[44] the ECJ ruled that the failure to ensure full independence to (some) national data protection authorities violated the Data Protection Directive, as well as Article 8 of the Charter of Fundamental Rights.[45] In the first case, the

[42] M Cartabia, 'L'ora dei diritti fondamentali nell'Unione Europea' in M Cartabia (ed), *I diritti in azione* (Bologna, Il Mulino, 2007) 32 (my translation).

[43] Case C–518/07 *Commission v Germany* [2010] ECR I-1885.

[44] Case C–614/10 *Commission v Austria*, judgment of 16 October 2012, nyr.

[45] For an analysis of the first judgment, see F Fabbrini, 'Il diritto dell'UE e l'indipendenza delle autorità nazionali garanti della protezione dei dati' (2010) 16 *Giornale di diritto amministrativo* 1028. On the second judgment, see instead M Pachinger, 'Datenschutzkommission quo vadis?' (2012) 100 *jusIT* 211.

Commission had brought proceedings against German regional legislation. Under German law, a relevant distinction existed with regard to the supervisory authorities empowered to monitor the processing of personal data by public bodies and by non-public bodies. Whereas both federal and regional legislation endowed authorities supervising processing of data by public bodies with full independence, the Länder government maintained a scrutiny of various sort over the authorities supervising processing of data by non-public bodies. In the second case, the Commission had brought proceedings against Austria. Pursuant to Austrian federal legislation, the data protection authority was structurally integrated within the departments of the federal Chancellery, subject to the day-to-day management of a federal official and information to the federal Chancellor. In both cases, the Grand Chamber of the ECJ ruled for the Commission, declaring that by making the authorities responsible for monitoring the processing of personal data subject to several forms of state oversight, Germany and Austria had incorrectly transposed the requirement of 'complete independence' of the supervisory authorities responsible for ensuring the protection of that data required by the Data Protection Directive, and thus had violated EU law.

In *Commission v Germany*, the ECJ began its judgment by underlining how the requirement of independence contained in the Data Protection Directive ought to be interpreted in light of 'the wording itself of that provision and the aims and scheme of Directive 95/46'.[46] First, with regard to the wording, the ECJ emphasised how 'the term "independence" normally means a status which ensures that the body concerned can act completely freely, without taking any instructions or being put under any pressure'.[47] Second, with regard to the aim of the Directive, the ECJ underlined how the EU legislation sought to achieve, together with the free flow of personal data, also 'a high level of protection of fundamental rights and freedoms with respect to the processing of personal data'[48] in the EU. Yet, supervisory authorities constituted in the design of the Directive 'an essential component of the protection of individuals with regard to the processing of personal data'[49]—and ensuring their independence was therefore paramount: the guarantee of the independence of national supervisory authorities in fact 'is intended to ensure the effectiveness and reliability of the supervision of compliance with the provisions on protection of individuals with regard to the processing of personal data and must be interpreted in the light of that aim'.[50] Third, with regard to the scheme of the Directive, the ECJ stressed that the requirement of independence imposed on national supervisory authorities by the Data Protection Directive was equivalent to that imposed

[46] *Commission v Germany* (n 43) § 17.
[47] ibid § 18.
[48] ibid § 22.
[49] ibid § 23.
[50] ibid § 25.

on the EDPS by Regulation 45/2001, and ought to be interpreted in the same terms.[51]

In light of the above, the ECJ stated that:

> Article 28(1) of Directive 95/46 is to be interpreted as meaning that the supervisory authorities responsible for supervising the processing of personal data outside the public sector must enjoy an independence allowing them to perform their duties free from external influence. That independence precludes not only any influence exercised by the supervised bodies, but also any directions or any other external influence, whether direct or indirect, which could call into question the performance by those authorities of their task consisting of establishing a fair balance between the protection of the right to private life and the free movement of personal data.[52]

Checked by these standards, the domestic legislation adopted by the German Länder on supervisory authorities empowered to monitor the processing of personal data by non-public bodies failed to pass the test. As the ECJ remarked, 'the government of the respective *Land* or an administrative body subject to that government [can] influence, directly or indirectly, the decisions of the supervisory authorities or, as the case may be, to cancel and replace those decisions'.[53] Admittedly, as the ECJ conceded, this state scrutiny 'seeks only to guarantee that acts of the supervisory authorities comply with the applicable national and [EU] provisions, and that it therefore does not aim to oblige those authorities potentially to pursue political objectives inconsistent with the protection of individuals with regard to the processing of personal data and with fundamental rights'.[54] Nevertheless, as the ECJ stressed, 'the mere risk that the scrutinising authorities could exercise a political influence over the decisions of the supervisory authorities is enough to hinder the latter authorities' independent performance of their tasks'.[55] As a result, the ECJ concluded 'that the State scrutiny exercised over the German supervisory authorities responsible for supervising the processing of personal data outside the public sector is not consistent with the requirement of independence'[56] demanded by the Data Protection Directive.

Having found that German Länder legislation failed to comply with EU law, the ECJ set aside a number of objections raised by the defendant state. To begin with, it discarded the argument by Germany that the principle of democracy precluded a broad interpretation of the requirement of independence. As the ECJ remarked, the principle of democracy:

> [D]oes not preclude the existence of public authorities outside the classic hierarchical administration and more or less independent of the government ... Such

[51] ibid § 28.
[52] ibid § 30.
[53] ibid § 33.
[54] ibid.
[55] ibid § 36.
[56] ibid § 37.

> independent administrative authorities, as exist moreover in the German judicial system, often have regulatory functions or carry out tasks which must be free from political influence, whilst still being required to comply with the law subject to the review of the competent courts. That is precisely the case with regard to the tasks of the supervisory authorities relating to the protection of data.[57]

Moreover, the ECJ rejected the argument that a broad interpretation of the requirement of independence conflicted with the principle of the attribution of powers.[58] And, finally, it forcefully denied that it would be inconsistent with the principles of subsidiarity and proportionality 'to oblige ... Germany to adopt a system which is foreign to its legal order and, thus, to give up an effective supervisory system established for almost 30 years and which has acted as a model for legislation on the protection of data, well beyond the national level'.[59] As the ECJ unequivocally ruled, 'by making the authorities responsible for monitoring the processing of personal data by non-public bodies and undertakings governed by public law which compete on the market in the different *Länder* subject to State scrutiny, and by thus incorrectly transposing the requirement that those authorities perform their functions "with complete independence" ... Germany failed to fulfil its obligations [under the Data Protection Directive]'.[60]

In *Commission v Austria*, the ECJ followed in the footsteps of its previous decisions and ruled that:

> [B]y failing to take all of the measures necessary to ensure that the legislation in force in Austria meets the requirement of independence with regard to the [Datenschutzkommission (DSK), the Austrian data protection agency], more specifically by laying down a regulatory framework under which; the managing member of the DSK is a federal official subject to supervision; the office of the DSK is integrated with the departments of the Federal Chancellery; and the Federal Chancellor has an unconditional right to information covering all aspects of the work of the DSK ... Austria has failed to fulfil its obligations under ... Directive 95/46.[61]

Moreover, whereas the judgment in *Commission v Germany*, which was rendered only four months after the entry into force of the Lisbon Treaty, referred just to the ECHR, the ECJ in *Commission v Austria*, decided in October 2012, cited explicitly Article 8 of the Charter of Fundamental Rights in support of its argument that a high degree of independence for supervisory authorities was instrumental to the protection of the rights to data privacy. As the ECJ stated, 'the requirement that compliance with [EU] rules on the protection of individuals with regard to the processing of personal data is subject to control by an independent authority derives

[57] ibid § 42.
[58] ibid § 51.
[59] ibid § 54.
[60] ibid § 56.
[61] *Commission v Austria* (n 44) § 66.

from the primary law of the [EU], inter alia Article 8(3) of the Charter of Fundamental Rights of the [EU] and Article 16(2) TFEU'.[62] Hence, the ECJ clearly drew legitimation from the Charter, as well as from the TFEU, to mandate a high level of data privacy protection on the Member States.

B. The Horizontal Dimension

While the ECJ has adopted a strict scrutiny when reviewing Member States' legislation affecting the right to data privacy, it has embraced the same standard when scrutinising the action of the EU political branches of government. In its April 2014 decision in *Digital Rights Ireland Ltd v Minister for Communication et al* and *Kärtner Landesregierung*[63] in particular, the ECJ took the unprecedented step of striking down an entire piece of EU legislation for violating the rights of privacy and data protection engraved in Articles 7 and 8 of the Charter of Fundamental Rights.[64] The cases, which had been raised through preliminary reference procedures by the Irish High Court and by the Austrian Verfassungsgerichtshof, concerned the legality of the Data Retention Directive, which imposed an obligation on Internet and telephone service providers to retain all the meta-data (but not the data) of emails, phone calls and text messages, and to make them available to law enforcement agencies when needed to fight serious crimes.[65] In its judgment, the Grand Chamber of the ECJ emphasised that the retention of personal data for a long period of time, and its potential subsequent use by police authorities, 'is likely to generate in the minds of the persons concerned the feeling that their private lives are the subject of constant surveillance'[66] and it therefore ruled that the Data Retention Directive fell short of the constitutional requirement of data privacy enshrined in EU law.

The ECJ began its analysis by underlying how the Data Retention Directive required the collection and storage of meta-data produced in the electronic communication and stated that: 'Those data, taken as a whole, may allow very precise conclusions to be drawn concerning the private lives of the persons whose data has been retained, such as the habits of everyday life,

[62] ibid § 36.

[63] Joined Cases C-293/12 and C-594/12 *Digital Rights Ireland Ltd v Minister for Communication et al* and *Kärtner Landesregierung et al*, judgment of 8 April 2014, nyr.

[64] For a more specific comment on this decision, see F Fabbrini, 'Human Rights in the Digital Age: The European Court of Justice Ruling in the Data Retention Case and its Lessons for Privacy and Surveillance in the US' (2015) 28 *Harvard Human Rights Journal* 65.

[65] The Data Retention Directive had already been challenged in Case C-301/06 *Ireland v European Parliament and Council* [2009] ECR I-593. However, the ruling of the ECJ in that case only focused on the legal basis of the Directive and did not address its compliance with human rights. See also MP Granger and K Irion, 'The Court of Justice and the Data Retention Directive in *Digital Rights Ireland*' (2014) 39 *European Law Review* 835.

[66] *Digital Rights Ireland* (n 63) § 37.

permanent or temporary places of residence, daily or other movements, the activities carried out, the social relationships of those persons and the social environments frequented by them.'[67] Hence, although Directive 2006/24 did 'not permit the retention of the content of the communication',[68] according to the ECJ, the retention 'directly and specifically affects private life and, consequently, the rights guaranteed by Article 7 of the Charter. Furthermore, such a retention of data also falls under Article 8 of the Charter because it constitutes the processing of personal data'.[69] Having clarified the constitutional framework applying in the case, the ECJ considered, following the approach customary also in the ECHR,[70] first, whether the Data Retention Directive constituted an interference with Articles 7 and 8 of the Charter of Fundamental Rights and, second, whether such interference was justified.[71] On the first point, the ECJ quickly settled the issue, holding that the obligation imposed by the Directive 2006/24 to retain the meta-data 'constitutes in itself an interference with the rights guaranteed by Article 7 of the Charter'[72] Furthermore, according to the ECJ, the fact that national authorities could access these data 'constitute[d] a further interference with that fundamental right'.[73] Likewise, the ECJ underlined how Article 8 of the Charter of Fundamental Rights was restricted by the Directive,[74] and it emphasised how the interference produced by Directive 2006/24 was 'wide-ranging' and 'particularly serious'.[75]

On the second question—whether the interference with the right guaranteed by Articles 7 and 8 of the Charter of Fundamental Rights was justified—the ECJ set aside the argument raised by the some of the parties that Directive 2006/24 violated the essence of the right to privacy, and acknowledged that the Data Retention Directive pursued a legitimate 'objective of general interest',[76] namely the 'fight against serious crime'[77] and the 'fight against international terrorism in order to maintain international peace and security'.[78] However, it ruled that the Data Retention Directive interfered with

[67] ibid § 27.
[68] ibid § 28.
[69] ibid § 29.
[70] *Klass v Germany*, ECtHR judgment of 6 September 1978, Series A no 28 (assessing, first, whether a law authorising the secret services to carry out secret monitoring of postal and telephone communications constitutes an interference with Art 8 ECHR and, second, whether such interference is justified).
[71] In light of its finding concerning Arts 7 and 8 of the Charter, the ECJ in the end did not find it necessary to rule whether the Data Retention Directive was also in violation of Art 11 of the Charter concerning freedom of speech. See *Digital Rights Ireland* (n 63) § 70.
[72] ibid § 34.
[73] ibid § 35.
[74] ibid § 36.
[75] ibid § 37.
[76] ibid § 44.
[77] ibid § 41.
[78] ibid § 42.

the right to privacy in a disproportionate way. The ECJ recalled that 'the principle of proportionality requires that acts of the EU institutions be appropriate for attaining the legitimate objectives pursued by the legislation at issue and do not exceed the limits of what is appropriate and necessary in order to achieve those objectives'.[79] At the same time, citing the ECtHR,[80] it clarified that the nature of its review would be stricter in this case 'in view of the important role played by the protection of personal data in the light of the fundamental right to respect for private life and the extent and seriousness of the interference with that right caused by Directive 2006/24'.[81]

According to the ECJ, the Data Retention Directive met the first tier of the proportionality analysis—the so-called 'suitability test': Directive 2006/24, in fact, was appropriate to the objective of expanding national authorities' 'opportunities to shed light on serious crime'.[82] Yet, according to the ECJ, the Data Retention Directive did not pass the second tier of the proportionality analysis—the so-called 'necessity test'. As the ECJ put it:

> The fight against serious crime, in particular against organised crime and terrorism, is indeed of the utmost importance in order to ensure public security and its effectiveness may depend to a great extent on the use of modern investigation techniques. However, such an objective of general interest, however fundamental it may be, does not, in itself, justify a retention measure such as that established by Directive 2006/24 being considered to be necessary for the purpose of that fight.[83]

In particular, the ECJ underlined that the Data Retention Directive set up a regime which failed to provide an interference with privacy right 'limited to what is strictly necessary'[84]—suggesting emphatically that, instead, the Data Retention Directive 'entail[ed] an interference with the fundamental rights of practically the entire European population'.[85]

In the ECJ's view, five major faults doomed the legality of Directive 2006/24. First, the Directive did not set any limit on the personal scope of application: it 'affects, in a comprehensive manner, all persons using electronic communications services ... It therefore applies even to persons for whom there is no evidence capable of suggesting that their conduct might have a link, even an indirect or remote one, with serious crime'[86] Second, the Directive did not set any limit on the possibility of national authorities to access the data retained by private companies—failing to specify conditions that justify the use of these data for law enforcement purposes: 'On the

[79] ibid § 46.
[80] See *Marper v UK*, ECtHR judgment of 4 December 2008 (finding the UK in violation of Art 8 ECHR).
[81] *Digital Rights Ireland* (n 63) § 48.
[82] ibid § 49.
[83] ibid § 51.
[84] ibid § 56.
[85] ibid.
[86] ibid § 58.

contrary, Directive 2006/24 simply refer[red], in Article 1(1), in a general manner to serious crime, as defined by each Member State in its national law'[87] and did not made access dependent 'on a prior review carried out by a court or by an independent administrative body whose decision seeks to limit access to the data and their use to what is strictly necessary for the purpose of attaining the objective pursued and which intervenes following a reasoned request of those authorities'.[88] Third, the Directive did not set a sufficiently restrictive timeframe for the retention of data: 'Article 6 of Directive 2006/24 required that those data be retained for a period of at least six months, without any distinction being made between the categories of data set out in Article 5 of that directive on the basis of their possible usefulness for the purposes of the objective pursued or according to the persons concerned.'[89] Fourth, the Directive did not provide for sufficient safeguards relating to the security and protection of data retained by private providers of electronic communications.[90] Finally, the Directive did 'not require the data in question to be retained within the [EU], with the result that it cannot be held that the control, explicitly required by Article 8(3) of the Charter, by an independent authority of compliance with the requirements of protection and security ... is fully ensured'.[91] In light of these serious flaws in the Data Retention Directive, the ECJ ruled that 'the EU legislature ha[d] exceeded the limits imposed by compliance with the principle of proportionality in the light of Articles 7, 8 and 52(1) of the Charter'[92] and struck down the Directive, removing the legislation adopted by the EU political branches of government from the EU legal order.[93]

C. The Diagonal Dimension

The ECJ, finally, has promoted the application of constitutional principles of privacy and data protection between private parties, requiring that private companies which wield substantial power in today's information society abide by the high data privacy standards set by EU law. Most strikingly, in the May 2014 ruling in *Google Spain SL v Agencia Española de Protección de Datos (AEPD)*,[94] the ECJ recognised a new right for data subjects to request the removal of online content and, correspondingly, an obligation for the operator of a search engine to remove from the list of results

[87] ibid § 60.
[88] ibid § 62.
[89] ibid § 64.
[90] ibid § 66.
[91] ibid § 68.
[92] ibid § 69.
[93] ibid § 71.
[94] Case C-131/12, *Google Spain v Agencia Española de Protección de Datos (AEPD)*, judgment of 14 May 2014, nyr.

displayed following a search made on the basis of a person's name links to webpages published by third parties and containing information relating to that person, also in a case where that name or information is not erased beforehand or simultaneously from those webpages, and even when its publication in itself on those pages is lawful.[95] The case had originated from a preliminary reference by the Spanish Audiencia Nacional and concerned the interpretation of a number of provisions of the Data Protection Directive, which were relevant in domestic proceedings between Google and the AEPD, the Spanish data protection agency. Pursuant to the application by a Spanish national, the AEPD had required Google to remove from its search engine links to information relating to the applicant, on the grounds that data privacy law applied to it. Google had challenged the administrative decision in the Spanish court, which decided to refer several questions to the ECJ. In its ruling, the Grand Chamber of the ECJ confirmed that Google was bound by data protection laws and took major steps forward in mandating respect of data privacy rights by private parties.

The first question that the ECJ was asked to address was whether the Data Protection Directive was 'to be interpreted as meaning that the activity of a search engine as a provider of content which consists in finding information published or placed on the internet by third parties ... must be classified as "processing of personal data" within the meaning of [the Directive]'.[96] After explaining the technical process of indexing provided by a search engine,[97] the ECJ emphasised how 'it is undisputed that that activity of search engines plays a decisive role in the overall dissemination of those data in that it renders the latter accessible to any internet user making a search on the basis of the data subject's name, including to internet users who otherwise would not have found the web page on which those data are published'[98] In light of this assessment, the ECJ held that, because the activity of a search engine is liable

> to affect significantly, and additionally compared with that of the publishers of websites, the fundamental rights to privacy and to the protection of personal data, the operator of the search engine as the person determining the purposes and means of that activity must ensure, within the framework of its responsibilities, powers and capabilities, that the activity meets the requirements of Directive 95/46 in order that the guarantees laid down by the directive may have full effect and that effective and complete protection of data subjects, in particular of their right to privacy, may actually be achieved.[99]

[95] For a first comment to the case, see D Streitfeld, 'European Court Lets Users Erase Records on Web' *New York Times* (13 May 2013).
[96] *Google Spain* (n 94) § 21.
[97] ibid § 28.
[98] ibid § 36.
[99] ibid § 38.

As a result, the ECJ ruled that a search engine like Google must be classified as a processor and controller of personal data within the meaning of the Data Protection Directive.[100]

The second question which the ECJ considered concerned instead the territorial scope of the Data Protection Directive and its applicability to the present case. As the referring court had explained, the search engine, Google Inc, is established in the United States, whereas Google Spain, a subsidiary of Google Inc registered in Spain, only operates in the promotion of the sale of advertising space generated by the search engine.[101] Yet, as the ECJ underlined, 'in the light of the objective of Directive 95/46 of ensuring effective and complete protection of the fundamental rights and freedoms of natural persons, and in particular their right to privacy, with respect to the processing of personal data, [the provision of the Directive defining the notion of establishment] cannot be interpreted restrictively'.[102] In fact, as the ECJ stressed, 'it is clear ... that the [EU] legislature sought to prevent individuals from being deprived of the protection guaranteed by the directive and that protection from being circumvented, by prescribing a particularly broad territorial scope'.[103] In light of this, the ECJ excluded that 'the processing of personal data carried out for the purposes of the operation of the search engine should escape the obligations and guarantees laid down by Directive 95/46, which would compromise the directive's effectiveness and the effective and complete protection of the fundamental rights and freedoms of natural persons which the directive seeks to ensure'[104] and ruled that an establishment such as Google Spain fell under the scope of application of EU data protection law.

The ECJ then moved to the third question raised by the national court, discussing the extent of the responsibility of the operator of a search engine to remove content upon the request of the data subject.[105] In this regard, it recalled once more how 'Directive 95/46 seeks to ensure a high level of protection of the fundamental rights and freedoms of natural persons, in particular their right to privacy, with respect to the processing of personal data'[106] and emphasised how its case law,[107] and now Articles 7 and 8 of the Charter,[108] attributed particular importance to this right. Considering that a name search through Google could provide a 'more or less detailed profile of [the data subject]'[109] and that this constituted an important interference

[100] ibid § 41.
[101] ibid § 43.
[102] ibid § 53.
[103] ibid § 54.
[104] ibid § 58.
[105] ibid § 62.
[106] ibid § 66.
[107] ibid § 68.
[108] ibid § 69.
[109] ibid § 80.

with its data privacy rights,[110] the ECJ ruled that 'the supervisory authority or judicial authority may order the operator of the search engine to remove from the list of results displayed following a search made on the basis of a person's name links to web pages published by third parties containing information relating to that person'.[111] Moreover, 'since the inclusion in the list of results, displayed following a search made on the basis of a person's name, of a web page ... makes access to that information appreciably easier for any internet user making a search in respect of the person concerned and ... is liable to constitute a more significant interference with the data subject's fundamental right to privacy than the publication on the web page',[112] the ECJ held that the operator of a search engine

> is obliged to remove from the list of results displayed following a search made on the basis of a person's name links to web pages, published by third parties ... also in a case where that name or information is not erased beforehand or simultaneously from those web pages, and even, as the case may be, when its publication in itself on those pages is lawful.[113]

Having recognised an obligation for a search engine to remove content, the ECJ as a final matter outlined a corresponding right for the data subject to require the removal of online content. In doing so, the ECJ recognised that the Data Protection Directive is to be interpreted as 'enabling the data subject to require the operator of a search engine to remove from the list of results displayed following a search made on the basis of his name links to web pages published lawfully by third parties and containing true information relating to him, on the ground that that information may be prejudicial to him or that he wishes it to be "forgotten" after a certain time'.[114] Moreover, in light of Articles 7 and 8 of the Charter, the ECJ stated that the data subject's right to request the removal of online content 'override[s], as a rule, not only the economic interest of the operator of the search engine but also the interest of the general public in finding that information upon a search relating to the data subject's name'.[115] It therefore ended up with a strong presumption in favour of the right to be forgotten—tempering this statement only with the qualification that this would not be the case 'if it appeared, for particular reasons, such as the role played by the data subject in public life, that the interference with his fundamental rights is justified by the preponderant interest of the general public in having, on account of inclusion in the list of results, access to the information in question'.[116]

[110] ibid § 81.
[111] ibid § 82.
[112] ibid § 87.
[113] ibid § 88.
[114] ibid § 89.
[115] ibid § 97.
[116] ibid.

Applying its balancing framework in the specific case pending before the national court, the ECJ thus concluded that the Spanish national who had started proceedings before the AEPD was entitled under the Data Protection Directive to require the removal from Google of the links which affected him,[117] 'without it being necessary in order to find such a right that the inclusion of the information in question in that list causes prejudice to the data subject'.[118]

IV. THE CASE LAW OF THE ECJ IN CONTEXT

The summary undertaken in the previous section has shed light on how the latest case law of the ECJ on Articles 7 and 8 of the Charter of Fundamental Rights has developed in multiple dimensions. This section will explain the achievements of the ECJ as a human rights court in the field of data privacy rights. However, it will also underline the challenges raised and the questions that remain open as a result of the line of jurisprudence followed by the ECJ.

A. Achievements

Since the entry into force of the EU Charter of Fundamental Rights, the ECJ has remarkably expanded the protection of the rights to data privacy in EU law. Although as explained in section II the EU has already been endowed with a complex framework of data protection since the 1990s, during the last five years the ECJ has drawn from the Charter to herald a new era in the protection of data privacy rights.[119] As section III has evidenced, in fact, the ECJ has extended the list of addressees who are required to respect the right to data privacy and has enriched its content. In *Commission v Germany* and, more explicitly, in *Commission v Austria*, the ECJ held that Article 8 of the Charter and Article 16 TFEU implied a need for data protection authorities to be fully independent and ruled against two Member States which had failed to secure this objective in their legislation. In *Digital Rights Ireland*, the ECJ found that Articles 7 and 8 of the Charter gave to data subjects a right to be protected from practices of systematic government surveillance and struck down the EU Data Retention Directive as in violation of primary EU law. And in *Google Spain*—although the ECJ did not make explicit

[117] ibid § 98.
[118] ibid § 99.
[119] For a discussion about the implication of the Charter on the latest case law of the ECJ on human rights, see generally S Iglesias, 'The Court and the Charter: The Impact of the Entry into Force of the Lisbon Treaty on the ECJ Approach to Fundamental Rights' (2012) 49 *CML Rev* 1565.

whether the Charter granted constitutional rights that private parties could directly invoke against other private parties[120]—it openly stated that 'the data subject may, in light of his fundamental rights under Articles 7 and 8 of the Charter, request that the information in question no longer be made available to the general public [through internet search engines]'.[121]

Moreover, the ECJ has elevated the status of data privacy, as revealed by its unwillingness to compromise the protection of the rights enshrined in Articles 7 and 8 of the Charter in the name of safeguarding alternative, or competing, rights or interests. Hence, in *Commission v Germany*, the ECJ rejected the argument advanced by Germany in its defence that securing the absolute independence of data protection authorities could compromise the democratic process. In *Digital Rights Ireland*, it ruled out that the need to fight terrorism and protect national security, which underpinned the Data Retention Directive, could trump the protection of privacy rights. And in *Google Spain*, it went as far as to state that the right to be forgotten empowered every data subject to request that online information concerning him be deleted by search engines and that this right override as a rule not only the economic interests of the operator of the search engine, but also the interest of the general public in having access to that information. Whereas the stand of the ECJ in *Digital Rights Ireland* appears consistent with its unwillingness to defer to the EU political branches in national security cases[122]—a trend epitomised by the *Kadi* saga[123]—the quasi-absolute defence of data privacy rights in *Google Spain*, albeit tempered by the possibility that these may give way to the right to freedom of information when the online data concerned public figures, suggests a strong commitment by the ECJ towards the protection of the right to data privacy in a digitalising world.[124]

It is the argument of this chapter that the innovative language of the Charter has emboldened the ECJ to push forward the protection of data privacy rights. However, it is plausible that the ECJ also benefited from the institutional system in which is embedded. It has become almost a cliché to emphasise in EU constitutional law and human rights scholarship the

[120] On the question whether EU primary law generally enjoys what German constitutional lawyers call *Drittwirkung*, that is, the direct application of constitutional rights between private parties, see A Hartkamp, 'The Effect of the EC Treaty in Private Law: On Direct and Indirect Horizontal Effects of Primary Community Law' (2010) 3 *European Review of Private Law* 5273. See also German Constitutional Court [BVerfG] 7, 198, *Lüth* (1955) (holding that the German Basic Law has horizontal effect among private parties).

[121] *Google Spain* (n 94) § 99.

[122] See generally F Fabbrini, 'The Role of the Judiciary in Times of Emergency: Judicial Review of Counter-terrorism Measures in the United States Supreme Court and the European Court of Justice' (2009) 28 *Yearbook of European Law* 664.

[123] See now Joined Cases C-584/10 P, C-593/10 P and C-595/10 P *Council, Commission and UK v Kadi*, judgment of 18 July 2013, nyr.

[124] See also F Fabbrini, 'Privacy and National Security in the Digital Age' (2015) 20 *Tilburg Law Review* 5.

importance of the judicial dialogue between the ECJ and national courts.[125] However, the interaction between judicial authorities across the EU multi-layered human rights architecture likely played a role in the evolution of the ECJ case law. This has happened not only through the official mechanism of the preliminary reference procedure[126]—as evidenced by the referral of the Spanish Audiencia Nacional in *Google Spain*, which put the ECJ in the condition to decide on the applicability of data protection law to internet search engines. It has also happened through indirect means.[127] As is well known, the transposition of the Data Retention Directive into the law of the EU Member States had raised a number of constitutional challenges in several countries—including Romania,[128] the Czech Republic[129] and Germany.[130] Although no national court had called into question the legality of the Data Retention Directive, they all had raised concerns about the 'feeling of surveillance' created by it and signalled their uneasiness with this piece of EU legislation.[131] In striking down the Data Retention Directive, the ECJ showed awareness for this case law and took an important step to remedy a situation perceived as highly problematic at the domestic level.[132]

On the other hand, the ECJ has not only been influenced by a *vertical* dialogue with national courts—it has also benefited from a *horizontal* dialogue with the other EU branches of government. The proceedings against Germany and Austria concerning the independence of national data protection authorities were brought by the European Commission in its capacity as guardian of EU law.[133] Moreover, while the Data Retention Directive had been voted for by the Council and the Parliament, in recent times the European Parliament had raised its voice against dragnet programmes of data surveillance by national intelligence agencies.[134] In response to the Snowden affair in particular, the European Parliament adopted a strongly

[125] See A Torres Pérez, *Conflicts of Rights in the European Union: A Theory of Supranational Adjudication* (Oxford, Oxford University Press, 2009). But see G de Vergottini, *Oltre il dialogo tra le corti. Giudici, diritto straniero, comparazione* (Bologna, Il Mulino 2010) (criticising over-emphasis on the idea of judicial dialogue).

[126] Art 267 TFEU.

[127] See generally F Fontanelli and G Martinico, 'Alla ricerca della coerenza: le tecniche del "dialogo nascosto" fra i giudici nell'ordinamento costituzionale multi-livello' [2008] *Rivista Trimestrale di Diritto Pubblico* 374 (emphasising informal techniques of judicial dialogue).

[128] Romanian Constitutional Court, Decision No 1258 of 8 October 2009.

[129] Czech Constitutional Court, judgment of 22 March 2011, Pl ÚS 24/10.

[130] German Constitutional Court [BVerfG], judgment of 3 March 2010, 1 BvR 256/08.

[131] See C De Simone, 'Pitting Karlsruhe against Luxembourg? German Data Protection and the Contested Implementation of the EU Data Retention Directive' (2010) 11 *German Law Journal* 291.

[132] See also A Vedaschi and V Lubello, 'Data Retention and its Implications for the Fundamental Right to Privacy' (2015) 20 *Tilburg Law Review* 14.

[133] See Art 258 TFEU.

[134] See also V Mitsilegas, 'Transatlantic Counter-terrorism Cooperation and European Values: Constitutional Accommodation or a Race to the Bottom?' (2015) 20 *Tilburg Law Review* 35.

worded report condemning the practice of data retention and calling for its termination[135]—a position of which the ECJ was certainly aware when deciding *Digital Rights Ireland*. Otherwise, while in *Google Spain* the ECJ took a major step forward in spelling out a right to be forgotten,[136] it is well known that the issue was at the heart of a new comprehensive package of legislative proposals advanced by the European Commission in 2012[137]—the General Data Protection Regulation, which would replace the Data Protection Directive,[138] and a Directive which would lay down a harmonised framework for all data processing activities by law enforcement authorities for law enforcement purposes[139]—and is currently subject to discussion by the Council and the Parliament.[140]

Be that as it may, the ECJ has certainly taken a leading position in the protection of data privacy rights. In fact, its recent case law has moved well beyond that of the ECtHR: although the ECtHR has played a crucial task in expanding the protections of Article 8 ECHR to the field of digital technology,[141] it has recognised a greater margin of appreciation to states' parties, especially when the predicament of data privacy conflicted with demands to protect national security.[142] The strong stand embraced by the ECJ in *Digital Rights Ireland* and its determination to render data privacy law effective also in inter-private relations suggest instead that in the field of digital rights the ECJ has worn with confidence the clothes of a human rights court. Despite the repeated criticisms that are moved to the ECJ for not taking fundamental rights seriously enough,[143] its case law on Articles 7 and 8 of the Charter proves that the ECJ has been willing and able to be a frontrunner in the protection of rights to data privacy in the digital age. Nevertheless, being at the forefront of a new legal development is not an easy task. In fact, the latest case law of the ECJ has raised challenges, advanced several controversial issues and left open a number of key questions on the protection

[135] European Parliament Resolution of 12 March 2014 on the US NSA surveillance programme, surveillance bodies in various Member States and their impact on EU citizens' fundamental rights and on transatlantic cooperation in Justice and Home Affairs, P7_TA(2014)0230.

[136] See on this J Rosen, 'The Right to Be Forgotten' (2012) 64 *Stanford Law Review Online* 88.

[137] See V Reding, 'Tomorrow's Privacy: The Upcoming Data Protection Reform for the European Union' (2011) 1 *International Data Privacy Law* 3.

[138] COM(2012)11 final, 25 January 2012.

[139] COM(2012)10 final, 25 January 2012.

[140] See European Parliament, LIBE Committee report, 22 November 2013, A7-0402/2013 (supporting the Commission proposals). But see Council of the EU, Press Release 7–8 October 2013, Doc 14149/13 (explaining that the Council has been unable to arrive at a general approach on the new data protection legislative package).

[141] See n 36 above.

[142] See further D Cole and F Fabbrini, 'Reciprocal Privacy: Towards a Transatlantic Agreement' in F Fabbrini and V Jackson (eds), *Constitutionalism across Borders in the Struggle against Terrorism* (Cheltenham, Edward Elgar, forthcoming, 2016).

[143] See already the famous piece by J Coppel and A O'Neill, 'The European Court of Justice: Taking Rights Seriously?' (1992) 29 *CML Rev* 669.

of data privacy rights, which will require further reflection and elaboration, both within the EU judicial process and elsewhere.

B. Challenges

In pushing very much forward the protection of data privacy rights, the ECJ has raised a number of challenges, and several important questions triggered by the case law of the ECJ remain open. In a nutshell, the core problem raised by the latest decisions of the ECJ has to do with the balancing between the rights to data privacy and competing rights and interests. The idea that fundamental rights are often conflicting with each other and that a strong protection of one right may result in the excessive limitation of another right is very familiar in comparative constitutional law.[144] The ECJ has recognised the same logic by embracing the principle of proportionality as a tool to reconcile conflicting rights and interests.[145] However, the uncompromising approach to the protection of data privacy that the ECJ has adopted in its latest case law seems to have abandoned the idea of a horizontal balancing between rights in favour of some form of hierarchical ordering of interests which sees as a rule the rights to data privacy prevail against any other right.[146] Whereas the issue surfaced in *Commission v Germany*, where the ECJ set aside the argument that the independence of data protection authorities necessitated by Article 8 of the Charter could be limited by the principle of democracy and public accountability, this point has emerged strikingly both in *Digital Rights Ireland* and *Google Spain*.

In *Digital Rights Ireland*, the ECJ ruled that national security could not trump data privacy, and although it acknowledged the legitimacy of fighting crime and terrorism, it used such sweeping language that it is uncertain whether any legislation allowing for some form of data retention would be acceptable to it.[147] However, it seems undeniable that national governments and supranational authorities have an obligation to provide security to their citizens, and that serious terrorist threats still exist, both globally and locally. Even if the judgment of the ECJ may be welcomed as a wake-up call against trends toward over-securitisation,[148] one is left wondering

[144] See L Zucca, *Constitutional Dilemmas. Conflicts of Fundamental Legal Rights in Europe and the USA* (Oxford, Oxford University Press, 2007); A Barak, *Proportionality: Constitutional Rights and their Limitations* (Cambridge, Cambridge University Press, 2012).

[145] See A Stone Sweet and J Mathews, 'Proportionality, Balancing and Global Constitutionalism' (2008) 47 *Columbia Journal of Transnational Law* 73.

[146] See text accompanying nn 122–24 above.

[147] But see Case C-291/12 *Schwarz*, judgment of 17 October 2013, nyr (holding that the storage of fingerprints data on EU citizens' biometric passports does not violate the right to data protection).

[148] See also T Ojanen, 'Privacy is More than Just a Seven-Letter Word: The Court of Justice of the European Union Sets Constitutional Limits on Mass Surveillance' (2014) 10 *European Constitutional Law Review* 528.

whether less systematic, and less intrusive, forms of surveillance would be unlawful—as the ECJ's ruling seems to suggest.[149] Similarly, in *Google Spain*, the ECJ embraced such a pervasive defence of the rights to data privacy, including the right to be forgotten, that it almost displaced tout court the freedom to undertake an economic activity and the freedom of expression and information. Whereas one may agree that data privacy shall prevail over the commercial interests of an Internet search engine, free speech ought to be treated with some caution. As it is well known, freedom of expression and information is not only enshrined in Article 11 of the Charter, but is also one of the most fundamental preconditions for the functioning of a democratic system.[150] Balancing data privacy and freedom of expression and information is therefore a very delicate task.

Yet, it cannot be argued that in *Google Spain* the ECJ has traded with the issue lightly.[151] By stating that the data subject's right to require the removal of online content (even when this is lawfully uploaded) always prevails over the freedom of expression and information of others, the ECJ has essentially reduced the scope of application of Article 11 of the Charter in a very significant way. But are we sure that in the abstract there may not be situations in which the right to know ought to prevail over the right to be forgotten, even when information concerns individuals who do not have a public profile? Directly connected to this point is another thorny question. If every individual has a right to request the removal of online content, who should make the ultimate decision on the claim and consider the possible free speech issue at stake? Should it be the Internet search engine directly? Or should it be the data protection authority? Or should it be a specialised court? The first option does not seem particularly attractive, as it would entirely delegate to private parties decisions of constitutional relevance and would possibly lead to forms of self-censorship.[152] However, while some countries have considered experimenting with the second or third options following the ECJ's ruling,[153] much uncertainty remains on the ground, and

[149] For a reading of the decision of the ECJ in *Digital Rights Ireland* which leaves open initiatives by the political branches in the retention of data, see, however F de Londras, 'CJEU Strikes Down Data Retention Directive' *Blog for Human Rights in Ireland*, 8 April 2014, available at: http://humanrights.ie/civil-liberties/cjeu-strikes-down-data-retention-directive.

[150] See also *Abrams v US*, 250 US 616, 621 (1919) (Justice Holmes dissenting, holding that freedom of speech protects the marketplace of ideas at the basis of a democratic system).

[151] See also E Frantziou, 'Further Developments in the Right to Be Forgotten' (2014) *Human Rights Law Review* 761.

[152] See also O Pollicino and M Bassini, 'Reconciling Right to Be Forgotten and Freedom of Information in the Digital Age' [2014] *Diritto pubblico comparato ed europeo* 641.

[153] See, eg F Milano, 'Privacy, La Germania avrà i "tribunali del web"', *Il Sole 24 Ore* (28 May 2014) (reporting that Germany debited the creation of specialised tribunals to handle request for removal of online content following the decision of the ECJ in *Google Spain*).

future action by the ECJ—or possibly by the political branches—will have to provide a satisfactory answer to these questions.[154]

In sum, by taking the lead in the protection of the rights to data privacy, the ECJ has opened a Pandora's box of problems which largely concern the interrelation between the innovative predicament of Article 8 of the Charter (combined with Article 7 of the Charter and Article 16 TFEU) with alternative interests such as democracy, freedom of speech, the protection of public security and the right to private economic initiative. Ironically, as much as the ECJ is being criticised when it allegedly does not take fundamental rights seriously enough, the latest case law of the ECJ on data privacy may be subject to criticism for taking fundamental right so seriously—elevating data privacy in a way that imperils the protection of other rights and liberties. But this is the price to be paid to be a human rights court and to stand at the forefront of a new legal development such as the one we are witnessing in the field of digital technology. By being one of the first—and certainly the most influential—judicial authority to step into the minefield of human rights in the digital age, the ECJ has inevitably shaken a delicate equilibrium, raising substantive questions about how to balance data privacy with conflicting rights and liberties, and institutional questions on who should effectively carry out such balancing, which will require future answers.[155] Nevertheless, it will not be exclusively up to the ECJ to settle these matters. The Member States, the EU institutions and ultimately the EU citizens at large all have a role to play in defining the constitutional formula through which the protection of the right to data privacy will be reconciled with other important legal interests in a rapidly developing technological world.

V. CONCLUSION

A legally binding EU Charter of Fundamental Rights has greatly contributed to the constitutionalisation of the ECJ. This chapter has tested the effects of the Charter on the protection of the rights to data privacy and has emphasised the important developments that have recently occurred in the case law of the ECJ. As the analysis of rulings such as *Commission v Austria*, *Digital Rights Ireland* and *Google Spain* have revealed, the ECJ has worn with confidence the role of a human rights court, setting a vanguard standard of protection for the right to data privacy and making sure that Member States, EU institutions and private companies operating in IT

154 See also Editorial, 'Europe's Expanding Right to Be Forgotten' *New York Times* (4 February 2015) (emphasising challenges posed by the ECJ ruling from the perspective of US tech companies).

155 For a comparative analysis of court pronouncements dealing with the balancing between data privacy and other fundamental rights, see O Pollicino et al (eds), *Internet: Regole e tutela dei diritti fondamentali* (Rome, Aracne, 2013).

technology comply with this standard. Although the EU was already characterised by a comprehensive legislation for data protection, the Charter of Fundamental Rights has offered to the ECJ a powerful and innovative tool to take the global lead in the protection of the rights to data privacy in the digital world. In the last few terms, the ECJ has recognised, among other things, that data privacy requires the full independence of data protection authorities, secures a right to be protected from systematic surveillance and empowers every data subject to require the removal of online content in order to be forgotten. However, the latest case law of the ECJ has also raised challenges, notably because uncertainty still surrounds the judicial balance between the rights to data privacy and conflicting or alternative rights or interests. In the near future, therefore, one must expect further actions in the courts and the political process to settle the status and scope of the rights to data privacy in the EU and beyond.

13

Privacy and Data Protection: The Rights of Economic Actors

PETER OLIVER*

I. INTRODUCTION

FOLLOWING THE JUDGMENTS of the Grand Chamber in *Schecke*,[1] *Digital Rights Ireland*[2] and *Google Spain*,[3] the complex and protracted negotiations on the Commission's proposals on data protection[4] and the scandal surrounding the US National Security Agency, privacy and data protection are very much in the limelight today. What is more, it is striking that the first two of these cases are amongst the very few in which provisions of EU acts have been struck down as being in breach of the EU Charter of Fundamental Rights.[5] Nevertheless, despite the judgment in *Schecke*, there is a dearth of literature on what privacy rights economic actors enjoy and should enjoy under the law as it stands at present. This chapter aims to go some way towards remedying that deficit.

This chapter is confined to the privacy of economic actors. In the modern world, the principal economic actors are of course companies,[6] but

* The author wishes to thank Thomas Bombois, Christopher Docksey, Herke Kranenborg and Wouter Wils for their comments on an earlier version of this paper, but responsibility for any errors is his alone.

1 Case C-92/09 *Schecke* [2010] ECR I-11063.

2 Joined Cases C-293/12 *Digital Rights Ireland* and C-594/12 *Seitlinger* (judgment of 8 April 2014).

3 Case C-131/12 *Google Spain* (judgment of 13 May 2014).

4 Proposal for a Regulation of the European Parliament and the Council on data processing (COM(2012) 11 final), based on Articles 16(2) and 114(1) TFEU (the General Data Protection Regulation) and a proposal for a Directive of the European Parliament and the Council on data protection in relation to judicial cooperation in criminal matters and police cooperation (COM(2012) 10 final). The proposed Regulation is set to repeal Directive 95/46, the Data Protection Directive (1995 OJ L281/31) as amended, and the proposed Directive will repeal Council Framework Decision 2008/977/JHA [2008] OJ L350/60.

5 Another is Case 236/09 *Test-Achats* [2011] ECR I-773. The current version of the Charter is published in [2007] OJ C303/1 and again in [2012] OJ C326/391.

6 The words 'company' and 'corporation' will be used here interchangeably to denote commercial entities unless otherwise indicated, and 'corporate' should be construed accordingly.

individuals may also be economic actors, and the same even applies to non-profit entities, which frequently supply goods or services. We shall therefore concentrate primarily on companies, while mentioning natural persons acting in a professional or economic capacity as well as non-profit entities, where relevant. As we shall see, in certain circumstances companies enjoy more limited rights than either of the other two categories of economic actors, and that is scarcely surprising.

When considering the fundamental rights of companies, it is as well to bear in mind the celebrated quip attributed to Lord Thurlow, a Lord Chancellor of the late eighteenth century, which runs: 'Did you ever expect a corporation to have a conscience, when it has no soul to be damned and no body to be kicked?'[7] Undeniably, there is considerable force in this rhetorical question. Companies differ from natural persons in a variety of ways: not only are companies immune from torture, but they can also live far longer than any human being, and no doubt their greatest advantage from the point of view of their shareholders is limited liability. For these reasons and because they exist solely to make money, companies tend to enjoy more limited fundamental rights than natural persons or non-profit entities.

After briefly considering the concept of corporate personality (section II), we shall examine the impact of the European Convention on Human Rights (ECHR) on economic matters and on the rights of companies (section III.A), before summarising the extent to which companies enjoy the benefits of the Charter (section III,B). Section IV will be devoted to Article 8 ECHR, while section V contains an introduction to Articles 7 and 8 of the Charter. We will discuss the highly important ruling in *Schecke* in section VI, and the four most relevant Directives together with the judgment in *Digital Rights Ireland* in section VII. The next three sections will be devoted to business secrets (section VIII), the right to a reputation (section IX), inspections (section X) and the freedom to pursue a trade or profession or to conduct a business (section XI), respectively. In section XII, we will consider the case law on companies acting to ensure the privacy and/or data protection of their stakeholders. A brief conclusion will be found in section XIII.

II. CORPORATE PERSONALITY: WHAT DOES IT MEAN?

Theories abound as to the nature of corporate personality,[8] but we cannot discuss them within the confines of this chapter. Suffice it to refer to

[7] John Poynder, *Literary Extracts* vol 1 (1844) 268 and quoted by AG Sharpston in Case C-58/12P *Groupe Gascogne* (judgment of 26 November 2013) [128].

[8] eg, Reuven Avi-Yonah, 'The Cyclical Transformations of the Corporate Form: A Historical Perspective on Corporate Social Responsibility' (2005) 30 *Delaware Journal of Corporate Law* 767 and '*Citizens United* and the Corporate Form' [2010] *Wisconsin Law Review* 999; Martin Petrin 'Reconceptualizing the Nature of the Firm—From Nature to Function' (2013) 118

the celebrated judgment in *Salomon v Salomon and Co Ltd*.[9] Salomon had formed a company to purchase his business; his wife and five children each owned one share as his nominees and he owned the remaining 20,001 shares. When the company ran into difficulties, the holders of the debentures forced the liquidation of the company, which then sought indemnification from him. In the absence of any evidence of fraud, the House of Lords dismissed the action unanimously. Its reasoning is neatly encapsulated in the splendid words of Lord Halsbury LC:

> Either the limited company was a legal entity or it was not. If it was, the business belonged to it and not to Mr. Salomon. If it was not, there was no person and no thing to be an agent at all; and it is impossible to say at the same time that there is a company and there is not.[10]

Only this down-to-earth view wholly recognises that companies have legal personality and does full justice to the fact that they enjoy limited liability and the potential to survive their founders by centuries. Accordingly, when we speak of a company's privacy, we mean the privacy of that entity itself, not that of its stakeholders.[11]

Of course, in some cases the courts are prepared to pierce the veil of incorporation, but they remain exceptional. For instance, it was recently held that in English law, 'the corporate veil may be pierced only to prevent the abuse of corporate legal personality'.[12] As is clear from this statement, piercing the veil usually works to the disadvantage of the stakeholders, as it renders them liable for acts of the corporation.[13] However, occasionally the veil is pierced for the benefit of stakeholders who are the victims of a breach of fundamental rights.[14] Thus, if a company is refused goods or services because it is owned, run or staffed largely by women (or men), then

Penn State Law Review 1; Beth Stephens 'Are Corporations People? Corporate Personhood under the Constitution and International Law' (2013) 44 *Rutgers Law Journal* 1, Anne Tucker 'Flawed Assumptions: A Corporate Law Analysis of Free Speech and Corporate Personhood in *Citizens United*' (2011) 61 *Case Western Reserve Law Review* 497.

[9] *Salomon v Salomon and Co Ltd* [1897] AC 22.

[10] ibid 31. See also *Lee v Lee's Air Farming Ltd* [1961] AC 12 (PC) and *Adams v Cape Industries plc* [1990] Ch 433 Scott J and Court of Appeal.

[11] The term 'stakeholders' will be used here to denote individuals involved in the company as shareholders, directors or (other) members of staff.

[12] Per Lord Sumption delivering the leading judgment in *Prest v Petrodel Resources Ltd* [2013] UKSC 34 [34]. See also Paul Davies, *Gower and Davies: The Principles of Modern Company Law*, 9th edn (London, Thomson Reuter, 2012) 214ff. That is also the position in international law: *Belgium v Spain (Barcelona Traction)* [1970] ICJ Rep 4; *Agrotexim v Greece* (judgment of ECtHR, 24 October 1995).

[13] In addition, courts have been known to find shareholders liable for acts of a company without piercing the veil by holding that the company has acted as the shareholders' agent. But this is highly exceptional. See *Adams* (n 10) 547–49; and Davies (n 12) 220–21.

[14] An analogous phenomenon is also recognised in international law: *Barcelona Traction* (n 12) [59ff]; and *US v Italy (ELSI)* [1989] ICJ Rep 15. However, these rulings would appear to have no bearing on municipal law.

that company and/or the relevant stakeholders would seem to have a cause of action under EU law.[15] The same will apply if a company suffers similar discrimination by reason of the race of its stakeholders.[16] Manifestly, companies are bereft of both gender and race, but anyone discriminating against a company by reason of the gender or race of its stakeholders is in reality targeting them and piercing the veil is consequently appropriate.[17]

A similar phenomenon seems unlikely to occur in relation to privacy. Indeed, both the European Court of Human Rights (ECtHR) and the Court of Justice of the European Union have encountered the converse situation: companies have brought actions purporting to protect the privacy of their stakeholders. As we shall see in section XII below, the ECtHR has treated such claims with more indulgence than the General Court.

III. FUNDAMENTAL RIGHTS OF COMPANIES GENERALLY

A. Under the ECHR

As the reader will be aware, the Court of Justice first alluded to the ECHR in *Nold*[18] back in 1974, just 11 days after it was ratified by the last Member State (namely France), and since then it has repeatedly held that the ECHR enjoys 'special significance' in the EU.[19] Moreover, Article 6(3) of the Treaty on European Union (TEU) provides: 'Fundamental rights, as guaranteed by the [ECHR] and as they result from the constitutional traditions common to the Member States, shall constitute general principles of the Union's law.' Accordingly, the ECHR must necessarily be the starting point for an examination of the rights of economic actors to privacy and data protection in EU law.

[15] Council Directive 2004/113 on Gender Equality in Goods and Services [2004] OJ L373/37; see Evelyn Ellis and Philippa Watson, *EU Anti-discrimination Law*, 2nd edn (Oxford, Oxford University Press, 2012) 366; and Philippa Watson, 'Equality between Europe's Citizens: Where Does the Union Now Stand?' (2012) 35 *Fordham International Law Journal* 1426.

[16] Council Directive 2000/43 on Race Equality [2000] OJ L180/22; see Ellis and Watson (n 15) 362.

[17] Moreover, where a company suffers discrimination in the award of a public procurement contract covered by the Public Procurement Directives, this will also be a breach of those Directives: Article 3 of Directive 2014/23 on the award of concessions [2014] OJ L94/1; Article 18 of Directive 2014/24 on public procurement [2014] OJ L94/65; and Article 36 of Directive 2014/25 on public procurement in utilities [2014] OJ L94/243. However, it would seem that the stakeholders have no cause of action; only the company hoped to secure the contract and it had no chance of doing so. On this view, the corporate veil is not pierced.

[18] Case 4/73 *Nold v Commission* [1974] ECR 491 [13].

[19] See, eg, Case C-274/99P *Connolly v Commission* [2001] ECR I-1611 [37] ; Case C-94/00 *Roquette Frères v Directeur général de la concurrence* [2002] ECR I-9011 [25]; Case C-20/00 and C-64/00 *Booker Aquaculture v Scottish Ministers* [2003] ECR I-7411 [65]; and Cases C-402/05P and C-415/05P *Kadi and Al Barakaat International Foundation v Council and Commission (Kadi I)* [2008] ECR I-6381 [283].

In *Airey v Ireland*, the ECtHR held that while the rights enshrined in the Convention are of an 'essentially civil and political' character, 'many of them have implications of a social or economic nature'.[20] Unsurprisingly, however, the Court has frequently asserted that economic rights are less deserving of protection than political and civil rights—regardless of whether the party concerned is a natural or a legal person. For instance, although it has held that Article 10 ECHR on the freedom of expression covers commercial expression (ie, advertising and promotion), it has repeatedly stated that political expression, including expression on matters of public interest and concern, qualifies for a higher level of protection.[21]

Furthermore, it is well established that companies may rely on the Convention.[22] The ECHR and the Protocols thereto contain three clear references to legal persons.[23] The very first case in which a company succeeded in an action before the ECtHR was *Sunday Times v UK*, where that Court found a breach of Article 10.[24] Amongst the numerous subsequent actions lodged by companies, *Comingersoll v Portugal* is especially illuminating: in a case where the defendant State was found to be in breach of Article 6 ECHR by virtue of an excessive delay in civil proceedings, the applicant company was awarded, in addition to damages for pecuniary loss, compensation for non-pecuniary damage on the basis, inter alia, of harm suffered to the company's reputation, uncertainty in decision planning and disruption in the management of the company.[25]

[20] *Airey v Ireland* (judgment of 9 October 1979) [26].

[21] *Hertel v Switzerland* (judgment of 25 August 1998) [47]; *Verein gegen Tierfabriken v Switzerland* (judgment of 28 June 2001) [66]; *Steel and Morris v UK* (judgment of 15 February 2005) [88]. See also *Niemietz v Germany* (judgment of 16 December 1992) [31], discussed in section IV.B below. This point was stressed by AG Geelhoed in his Opinion in Case C-301/04 P *Commission v SGL Carbon* [2006] ECR I-5915 at [64].

[22] For a thorough survey, see Marius Emberland, *The Human Rights of Companies: Exploring the Structure of ECHR Protection* (Oxford, Oxford University Press, 2006). Other studies include: Nicholas Bratza, 'The Implications of the Human Rights Act 1998 for Commercial Practice' [2000] *European Human Rights Law Review* 1; Olivier De Schutter, 'L'accès des personnes morales à la Cour européenne des droits de l'homme' in *Mélanges offerts à Silvio Marcus Helmons* (Brussels, Bruylant, 2003) 83; Elisabeth Fura-Sandström, 'Business and Human Rights—Who Cares?' in *Liber Amicorum Luzius Wildhaber: Human Rights—Strasbourg Views* (Kehl, Engel, 2007) 159; Michael Smyth, 'Business and the Human Rights Act 1998' (Bristol, Jordans, 2000); and also Peter Oliver, *The Fundamental Rights of Corporations* (Oxford, Hart Publishing, forthcoming).

[23] Article 1 of Protocol 1 (the right to property) begins: 'Every natural or *legal person* is entitled to the peaceful enjoyment of his possessions' (emphasis added). See *Lithgow v UK* (judgment of 8 July 1986); *Pye (Oxford) Ltd v UK* (judgment of 30 August 2007) (GC). In addition, Art 10 of the Convention contains a sentence stating: 'This Article shall not prevent States from requiring the licensing of broadcasting, television or cinema *enterprises*' (emphasis added). Third, Art 34 of the Convention, entitled 'Individual Applications', provides: 'The Court may receive applications from any person, non-governmental organisation or group of individuals.'

[24] Judgment of 26 April 1979 ('thalidomide'). It would be meaningless to grant that right to individuals while effectively allowing the corporations which employ them to be gagged. See also *Autronic AG v Switzerland* (1990) 12 EHRR 485 [47]. The celebrated judgment of the US Supreme Court in *New York Times v Sullivan* 376 US 254 (1964) proceeds on the same basis.

[25] *Comingersoll v Portugal* (judgment of 6 April 2000) [35].

On the other hand, in some instances, companies fare less well under the ECHR than individuals and non-profit entities. Thus, the ECtHR has held that Article 6 ECHR confers on natural persons[26] and non-profit entities[27] the right to legal aid in certain, relatively limited circumstances. In *VP Diffusion Sarl v France*,[28] the ECtHR upheld the rule of French law whereby legal persons were only eligible for legal aid if they were non-profit making, thus excluding commercial companies. This disparate treatment was held to be warranted in view of the different tax status of the two types of entity in France. Subsequently, in *Granos Organicos Nacionales v Germany*, the ECtHR held that it was lawful for Germany to grant legal aid only to companies based on its territory or on that of another Member State of the EU or the European Economic Area (EEA), except where a company was based in a third country prepared to grant legal aid to German companies.[29] Indeed, in that case, the Court appeared to take the view that the Contracting Parties were under no general obligation to provide legal aid to companies at all.

In a separate development, the ECtHR has held that a legal entity, unlike an individual taxpayer, can be expected to take legal advice[30] and that 'the level of diligence expected from an entity engaged in a commercial activity may be higher than that required from a natural person'.[31] The applicant company claimed that the court fees which it had been charged were in breach of Article 6(1) ECHR. The action was dismissed, inter alia because the applicant had failed to take the necessary steps to mitigate its fees.

B. Under the EU Charter of Fundamental Rights

As already mentioned, the ECHR, which was signed in 1950, contains two articles indicating that some of its provisions apply for the benefit of companies, and Article 1 of Protocol 1, which was signed the following year, clearly states that it applies in favour of legal persons. Moreover, the German Basic Law, which dates from 1949, contains a provision, Article 19(3), which reads: 'Fundamental rights also apply to domestic legal persons to the extent that their nature permits.'[32] In these circumstances, it is striking

[26] *Steel and Morris v UK* (judgment of 15 February 2005).

[27] *VP Diffusion Sarl v France* (decision of 26 August 2008); *Granos Organicos Nacionales v Germany* (judgment of 22 March 2012).

[28] ibid.

[29] ibid [46ff].

[30] *Spacek v Czech Republic* (judgment of 9 November 1999) [59].

[31] *Elcomp v Poland* (judgment of 19 April 2011) [41], confirmed in *Pietka v Poland* (judgment of 16 October 2012) [61]. The first case concerned a company and the second a partnership.

[32] See the commentaries by Hans Jarass, commentary on Article 19 GG in Jarass and Pieroth (eds), *Grundgesetz für die Bundesrepublik Deutschland*, 12th edn (Munich, Beck, 2012), Walter Krebs, commentary on Article 19 in Ingo von Münch and Philip Kunig (eds),

that the Charter, which was first promulgated in 2000[33] and amended on the entry into force of the Treaty of Lisbon in December 2009, scarcely mentions the matter. This appears all the more puzzling when it is recalled that even before the Charter was first promulgated, the Court had already developed a wealth of case law on the fundamental rights of companies.[34] Exceptionally, Articles 42–44 of the Charter (on the rights to access to documents, to submit a complaint to the Ombudsman and to petition the European Parliament, respectively) do expressly confer rights on legal persons, but these are hardly the most important rights.[35]

Equally, there is a striking dearth of cases in which the Court has directly addressed the question as to when the Charter applies for the benefit of companies and under what conditions. This is all the more surprising given that a wealth of case law on the Charter has built up since the Treaty of Lisbon breathed binding force into it and the revised Article 6(1) TEU gave it same legal value as the Treaties; and much of this case law concerns the rights of companies. However, the Court did address these issues in *DEB*[36] and *Schecke*.[37] It is appropriate to consider the first of these cases at this juncture and the second ruling in section VI below.

In *DEB*, a German case, the question which arose was whether the 'right' to legal aid in the third paragraph of Article 47 of the Charter applies in favour of companies. As already mentioned, the ECtHR has not ruled that companies are ever entitled to legal aid, and the subsequent ruling in *Granos Organicos Nacionales* may perhaps be regarded as ruling out this possibility altogether. In assessing whether the third paragraph of Article 47 applied to legal persons, the Court set out two criteria:

— the fact that that the German version of that provision uses '*Person*' rather than '*Mensch*' *may* be an indication that it benefits legal persons;[38] and

Grundgesetz Kommentar, 6th edn (Munich, Beck, 2012); and Barbara Remmert, commentary on Article 19(3) in Theodor Maunz and Günter Dürig (eds), *Grundgesetz Kommentar* (Munich, Beck Online, 2013).

[33] [2000] OJ C364/1.

[34] See, eg, *Nold* (n 18) (rights to property and freedom to conduct a business); Case C-260/89 *ERT* [1991] ECR I-4007 [238ff] (freedom of expression); Case C-185/95 P *Baustahlgewebe v Commission* [1998] ECR I-8417 (right to fair trial within a reasonable time); and Case 374/87 *Orkem* [1989] ECR 3283 (rights of defence).

[35] Indeed, the rights under Arts 43 and 44 are not even fully enforceable: Case T-103/99 *Associazione delle cantine sociali venete v European Ombudsman and European Parliament* [2000] ECR II-4165; and Case C-261/13P *Schönberger v European Parliament* (judgment of 9 December 2014), respectively. To paraphrase George Orwell, some rights are more fundamental than others.

[36] Case C-279/09 *DEB* [2010] ECR I-13849, noted by Peter Oliver in (2011) 48 *CML Rev* 2023.

[37] *Schecke* (n 1).

[38] ibid [39]. '*Person*' refers to both natural and legal persons, whereas '*Mensch*' refers only to natural persons.

— the fact that Article 47 is in Title VI of the Charter, which contains other provisions on which legal persons can rely, *was* indeed an indication to the same effect.[39]

The first of these criteria is of somewhat limited value, as the Court itself acknowledged by saying that this 'may' be an indication as to the personal scope of the provision. When construing a provision of EU law, the Court never relies on one language version alone. In any case, some provisions of the Charter use neither of these German words. For instance, many provisions such as Articles 49(1) and 50 use the word '*niemand*' (no one), while Article 48 speaks of '*jeder Angeklagter*' (every accused). The second criterion is far more persuasive and indeed the Court attached greater weight to it.

The Court concluded that in certain circumstances, companies have a right to legal aid, thereby granting them 'more extensive protection' than the ECHR, as is expressly contemplated by Article 52(3) of the Charter.[40] At the same time, it ruled that non-profit entities enjoy broader rights in this regard than companies.[41]

Generally speaking, the Advocates General have directed equally little attention to the question of companies' fundamental rights. A particularly notable exception is the statement in Advocate General Geelhoed's Opinion in *SGL Carbon* to the effect that it is 'not possible simply to transpose the findings of the European Court of Human Rights [on natural persons] without more to legal persons and undertakings'.[42] This assertion, which was made before the Charter acquired binding force, deserves a very warm welcome, since it is not always appropriate for legal persons, especially commercial entities, to enjoy the same fundamental rights as individuals.[43]

This is clearly illustrated by *SGL Carbon* itself, which concerned the privilege against self-incrimination. Historically, this right is designed to prevent confessions being extracted by torture,[44] a concern that is not relevant to legal persons. Consequently, it is scarcely surprising that both the German Constitutional Court and the US Supreme Court have held that legal persons do not enjoy this privilege.[45] In contrast, the Court of Justice

[39] ibid [40]–[42].
[40] ibid [62].
[41] ibid.
[42] *Commission v SGL Carbon* (n 21) [63].
[43] Peter Oliver, 'How Extensive Should the Rights of Companies Be?' [2015] *ICLQ* 661 passim and *The Fundamental Rights of Companies—European and US Law Compared* (Oxford, Hart Publishing, forthcoming) passim.
[44] RH Helmholz et al, *The Privilege against Self-incrimination: Its Origins and Development* (Chicago, University of Chicago Press, 1997).
[45] See respectively BVerfGE 95, 220 (1997), paras 83–84; and *Hale v Henkel* 201 US 43, 69–70 (1906); *US v White* 322 US 694 (1944); and *Curcio v US* 354 US 118, 122 (1957).

held in *Orkem*[46] that the rights of defence precluded an undertaking from being forced to admit that it had committed an infringement of what is now Article 101 of the Treaty on the Functioning of the European Union (TFEU), but the Court found that the Commission could require an undertaking to answer factual questions and produce documents.[47] In the light of these considerations, it is not surprising that the Court in *SGL* followed Advocate General Geelhoed and resisted pressure to depart from, or reverse, its ruling in *Orkem*.[48] Surely, the caution shown by the Court is to be warmly welcomed.[49] Having said that, since the rationale for the privilege against self-incrimination is to prevent torture, it would follow that the privilege applies in full where the undertaking is a natural person.[50]

In conclusion, at the risk of pointing out the obvious, the ECHR is not primarily concerned with economic rights, whereas such rights lie at the very heart of the EU. Accordingly, in EU law, it may often be appropriate to grant 'more extensive protection' to economic actors pursuant to Article 52(3) of the Charter. Indeed, as we have just seen, that is precisely what occurred in *DEB*. Nevertheless, as already mentioned, it is of the utmost importance that the Court should proceed with great caution when considering whether to extend to economic actors (and particularly companies) existing fundamental rights case law relating to individuals.

IV. ARTICLE 8 ECHR

A. The Wording

Article 8 ECHR, which is entitled 'Right to respect for private and family life', is drafted as follows:

1. Everyone has the right to respect for his private and family life, his home and his correspondence.
2. There shall be no interference by a public authority with the exercise of this right except such as is in accordance with the law and is necessary in a democratic

[46] *Orkem* (n 34).

[47] The ECtHR has repeatedly held that, by virtue of Article 6 ECHR, individuals cannot be compelled to incriminate themselves in a criminal proceeding (eg, *Saunders v UK* (judgment of 17 December 1996)). However, there is no case law from that court as to whether companies also enjoy the privilege against self-incrimination.

[48] *Orkem* (n 34) [33ff]; see also Case C-238/99P *Limburgse Vinyl Maatschappij et al (PVC II)* [2001] ECR I-8375 [273]–[275].

[49] See Wouter Wils, 'Self-incrimination in EC Antitrust Enforcement: A Legal and Economic Analysis' (2003) 26 *World Competition* 577 and 'EU Anti-trust Enforcement Powers and Procedural Rights and Guarantees: The Interplay between EU Law, National Law, the Charter of Fundamental Rights of the EU and the European Convention on Human Rights' (2011) 34 *World Competition* 189, 206.

[50] Wils, 'Self-incrimination' (n 49). Whether unincorporated partnerships should be similarly privileged on the basis that they are no more than a group of natural persons is a nice point.

> society in the interests of national security, public safety or the economic well-being of the country, for the prevention of disorder or crime, for the protection of health or morals, or for the protection of the rights and freedoms of others.[51]

B. Private Life

The concept of 'private life'[52] is 'a broad term not susceptible to exhaustive definition' and embraces 'the right to personal development'.[53] In this sense, the concept generally comes into play with regard to aspects of human existence far removed from economic activity.[54] However, in its seminal judgment in *Niemietz v Germany*, the ECtHR stated:

> There appears ... to be no reason of principle why ... the notion of 'private life' should be taken to exclude activities of a professional or business nature since it is, after all, in the course of their working lives that the majority of people have a significant, if not the greatest, opportunity of developing relationships with the outside world. This view is supported by the fact that ... it is not always possible to distinguish clearly which of an individual's activities form part of his professional or business life and which do not ...
>
> [T]o interpret the words 'private life' and 'home' as including certain professional or business activities or premises would be consonant with the essential object and purpose of Article 8, namely to protect the individual against arbitrary interference by the public authorities.[55]

Consequently, Article 8 ECHR has been held to cover the right to work, at least in certain extreme cases. Thus, in *Sidabras v Lithuania*,[56] a statutory ban on former KGB agents taking a wide variety of jobs for a 10-year

[51] D Harris, M O'Boyle and C Warbrick, *Law of the European Convention on Human Rights*, 3rd edn (Oxford, Oxford University Press, 2014) 522ff; J Meyer-Ladewig, *Europäische Menschenrechtskonvention* (Baden-Baden, Nomos, 2011) 191ff; F Sudre, *Droit européen et international des droits de l'homme*, 11th edn (Paris, Presses Universitaires de France, 2011) 511ff; P van Dijk et al, *Theory and Practice of the European Convention on Human Rights*, 4th edn (Antwerp, Intersentia, 2006) 443ff.

[52] The anomalous use of the term 'private life' may be due to the fact that the term '*vie privée*' appears in the French version; that is the standard term for 'privacy' in French, which has no abstract noun equivalent to the English 'privacy'.

[53] *Pretty v UK* (judgment of 29 April 2002) [61]. See J Marshall, 'A Right to Personal Autonomy at the European Court of Human Rights' [2008] *European Human Rights Law Review* 337; and NA Moreham, 'The Right to Respect for Private Life in the European Convention on Human Rights: A Re-examination' [2008] *European Human Rights Law Review* 44; and the sources cited in n 51 above.

[54] See, eg, *Dudgeon v UK* (judgment of 22 October 1981) regarding sexual orientation; and *Tysiac v Poland* (judgment of 20 March 2007) concerning the denial of an abortion, where this posed a serious risk to the applicant's health.

[55] *Niemietz v Germany* (judgment of 16 February 2000) [29] and [31].

[56] *Sidabras v Lithuania* (judgment of 27 October 2004).

period beginning in 1999 was held to fall foul of Article 8 read with Article 14 ECHR, insofar as it related to employment in the private sector.[57] The contested restriction was held to have affected the applicants' ability to 'develop relationships with the outside world to a very significant degree and has created serious difficulties for them in terms of earning their living, with obvious repercussions on the enjoyment of their private lives'.[58] Moreover, the ban was disproportionate: it was impossible to ascertain any reasonable link between the jobs concerned and the legitimate aims sought by the ban on holding them.[59] This was an extreme case, and it is important not to read too much into this judgment. Indeed, the ECtHR was at pains to stress that 'the Convention does not guarantee as such the right to have access to a particular profession'[60]; and in a subsequent case it declared that 'no general right to employment or to the renewal of a fixed-term contract can be derived from Article 8'.[61] Still less could it be suggested that this case law could somehow be extended so as to create some form of freedom of enterprise.[62]

What is more, individuals acting in a professional or economic capacity enjoy the right to privacy under Article 8. This is clearly illustrated by the ruling in *Amann v Switzerland*.[63] The facts bordered on the burlesque: the applicant imported depilatory devices for sale in Switzerland; in 1981, a woman telephoned him from the Soviet Embassy in Berne to order an appliance; that telephone call was intercepted by the Federal Public Prosecutor's Office, whereupon the Swiss intelligence services carried out an investigation into the applicant and his business, and the authorities had kept a 'card' on him. Referring to the passage from *Niemietz v Germany* just cited, the ECtHR stressed that there was no reason of principle to justify excluding activities of a professional or business nature from the notion of 'private life'. To establish the existence of such an interference, the Court held, it does not matter whether the information communicated is of a sensitive

[57] The applicants had not challenged the ban as regards the public sector and the ECtHR held (at ibid [52ff]) that they could not have done so.

[58] ibid [48].

[59] ibid [51ff].

[60] ibid [52].

[61] *Fernández Martínez v Spain* (judgment of 12 June 2014) [109]. See also generally *Bigaeva v Greece* (judgment of 28 August 2009); and Rory O'Connell 'The Right to Work in the European Convention on Human Rights' [2012] *European Human Rights Law Review* 176.

[62] Insofar as such a right is covered by the ECHR at all, the relevant provision is Art 1 of Protocol 1 on the right to property. An existing professional practice or business constitutes 'possessions' within the meaning of this article: *Van Marle v The Netherlands* (judgment of 26 June 1986) and *Wendenburg v Germany* (judgment of 6 February 2003); this includes the goodwill (*Wendenburg*). But that does not extend to future earnings (*Ian Edgar (Liverpool) Ltd v UK* (judgment of 25 January 2000)), because Art 1 only confers the right to keep property, not to acquire it: *Van der Mussele v Belgium* (judgment of 23 November 1983) [48]; *Stec v UK* (judgment of 12 April 2006, GC) [53].

[63] *Amann v Switzerland* (judgment of 16 February 2000) [65].

character or whether the persons concerned have been inconvenienced in any way.[64] On this basis, it found the defendant State to be in breach of Article 8.[65]

To what extent legal persons enjoy the right to 'private life' under Article 8 is less clear. The judgment in *Niemietz v Germany* might suggest that they do, although that case concerned a natural person. However, in *Association of European Integration and Human Rights v Bulgaria*, where the applicant was a non-profit entity, the ECtHR took the opposite view.[66]

C. Family Life

Manifestly, the concept of family life has no bearing on economic actors.

D. The Home

As to the concept of the 'home', the *locus classicus* is once again *Niemietz v Germany*.[67] A police search at the Mr Niemietz's law office was held to constitute an interference with his 'home'. The ECtHR interpreted this term as extending to business premises.[68] Whilst this interpretation may seem questionable as a matter of English, the Court pointed out that it is 'fully consonant with the French text, since the French word "*domicile*" has a broader connotation than the word "home" and may extend, for example, to a professional person's office'.[69] Crucially, however, the Court also declared that in determining whether an inspection was justified under Article 8(2) ECHR, the discretion enjoyed by the Contracting Parties 'might well be more far-reaching where professional or business premises were involved than would otherwise be the case'.[70]

The concept of the 'home' was further extended in *Société Colas Est v France*.[71] Since the applicant company was suspected of involvement in a series of offences concerning public road-building contracts, anti-fraud

64 ibid.

65 ibid [70].

66 *Association of European Integration and Human Rights v Bulgaria* (judgment of 28 June 2007) [60]. Thomas Bombois *La protection des droits fondamentaux des entreprises en droit de la concurrence* (Brussels, Larcier, 2012), 28 has suggested that this ruling is hard to reconcile with the case law, which suggests that Art 8 confers on companies the right to protect their reputation (see section IX below).

67 *Niemietz v Germany* (n 21).

68 ibid [30].

69 ibid. The *Petit Robert* dictionary defines '*domicile*' as '*lieu où une personne a son principal établissement, demeure légale et officielle*'.

70 *Niemietz v Germany* (n 21) [31].

71 *Société Colas Est v France* (judgment of 16 April 2002).

inspectors carried out a number of searches at its premises. The Court held that this concept covered not only a lawyer's office (as in *Niemietz*), but also the headquarters and other premises of a company.[72] However, in *Leveau and Fillon v France*,[73] the Court drew the line at treating a pig farm as a 'home', but it failed to advance any convincing reason for distinguishing *Niemietz* and *Colas Est*, saying only that the farm could not be regarded as the farmer's business premises.

E. Correspondence

Article 8 ECHR also protects the communications of individuals acting in a professional or economic capacity[74] and of legal persons.[75] The word 'correspondence' has been construed very widely to cover forms of communication such as telephone conversations.[76]

V. ARTICLES 7 AND 8 OF THE CHARTER

A. General

Article 7 of the Charter, which bears precisely the same title as Article 8 ECHR ('Respect of private and family life'), reads as follows:

> Everyone has the right to respect for his or her private life and family life, home and communications.

Article 8 ('Protection of personal data') reads:

> 1. Everyone has the right to the protection of personal data concerning him or her.
> 2. Such data must be processed fairly for specified purposes and on the basis of the consent of the person concerned or some other legitimate basis laid down by law. Everyone has the right of access to data which has been collected concerning him or her, and the right to have it rectified.
> 3. Compliance with these rules shall be subject to control by an independent authority.

By virtue of Article 6(1) TEU and Article 52(7) of the Charter, the courts are required to take into account the official Explanations to the Charter.[77]

[72] ibid [41]; see also *Buck v Germany* (judgment of 28 April 2005) [31].
[73] *Leveau and Fillon v France* (decision of 6 September 2005).
[74] *Weber and Savaria v Germany* (decision of 29 June 2006) [77].
[75] *Association of European Integration and Human Rights v Bulgaria* (n 66) [60].
[76] *Klass v Germany* (judgment of 6 September 1978) [41]; *Malone v UK* (judgment of 2 August 1984) [64].
[77] [2007] OJ C303/17, which replaced the version drafted in 2000 (that version was never published in the Official Journal). See Jean-Paul Jacqué, 'The Explanations Relating to the Charter of Fundamental Rights of the European Union' in Steve Peers, Tamara Hervey,

According to these Explanations, Article 7 of the Charter 'corresponds' to Article 8 ECHR,[78] while Article 8 of the Charter is 'based' on Article 8 ECHR as well as on a number of other provisions and instruments, including the Council of Europe Convention of 1981 for the Protection of Individuals with regard to Automatic Processing of Personal Data and the Data Protection Directive, which introduced the latter Convention into EU law in an enhanced form. Article 52(3) of the Charter provides:

> In so far as this Charter contains rights which correspond to rights guaranteed by the Convention for the Protection of Human Rights and Fundamental Freedoms, the meaning and scope of those rights shall be the same as those laid down by the said Convention. This provision shall not prevent Union law providing more extensive protection.

Consequently, according to the Explanations, since Article 7 of the Charter 'corresponds to' Article 8 ECHR, the former provision is to be given the same meaning as the latter, subject only to the possibility of interpreting Article 7 of the Charter as granting 'more extensive protection'.

B. What is the Relationship Between Article 7 and Article 8?

To add to the confusion, it is by no means clear how Articles 7 and 8 of the Charter relate to one another. The Court of Justice has yet to grasp this nettle and has frequently referred to Articles 7 and 8 in the same breath without making any clear distinction between them.[79]

The relationship between these two provisions is an inherently fraught issue which does not permit of an easy answer. Various theories have been propounded as to the relationship between the two provisions,[80] but

Jeff Kenner and Angela Ward (eds), *The EU Charter of Fundamental Rights—A Commentary* (Oxford and Portland, Beck/Hart Publishing/Nomos, 2014) 1715; and Jacques Ziller, '*Le fabuleux destin des Explications relatives à la Charte des droits fondamentaux de l'Union européenne*' in *Chemins d'Europe—Mélanges en l'honneur de Jean-Paul Jacqué* (Paris, Dalloz, 2010) 765.

[78] The Explanations also state that the only real difference in wording, the substitution of 'correspondence' in Art 8 ECHR by 'communications' in Art 7 of the Charter, is intended to take account of developments in technology. This reflects the broad reading of the word 'correspondence' by the ECtHR (see section IV.E above).

[79] *Schecke* (n 1) [52]; *Digital Rights Ireland* (n 2) [25], [29] and [53]; *Google Spain* (n 3) [39] and [40].

[80] See in particular AG Cruz Villalòn's Opinion in *Digital Rights Ireland* (n 2) [60ff] and the speech given by Peter Hustinx on 8 September 2014 (shortly before his retirement), 'European Leadership in Privacy and Data Protection', https://secure.edps.europa.eu/EDPSWEB/edps/EDPS. See also Christopher Docksey, 'Articles 7 and 8 of the EU Charter: Two Distinct Fundamental Rights', a speech given at the conference organised by the Court of Justice on 19 September 2014 (forthcoming on the Court's website); Herke Kranenborg, commentary on Article 8 of the Charter in Peers et al (n 77) 229); and AG Juliane Kokott and Christoph Sobotta, 'The Distinction between Privacy and Data Protection in the Jurisprudence of the CJEU and the ECtHR' (2013) 3 *International Data Privacy Law* 222, 226.

a detailed consideration of this issue is beyond the scope of this chapter. Suffice it to say that, even though the Explanations describe Article 8 as being merely 'based on' on Article 8 ECHR as well as a number of other instruments, the case law of the ECtHR on the latter provision in relation to data protection retains 'all its relevance for the purpose of the interpretation of Article 8 of the Charter'.[81]

C. Does Article 7 Apply to Economic Actors?

In considering whether Article 7 of the Charter applies to economic actors, the overriding consideration is that, as we noticed earlier, this provision 'corresponds to' Article 8 ECHR.[82] As is clear from the judgment of the ECtHR in *Amann*,[83] Article 8 ECHR applies to individuals acting in a professional or economic capacity. However, as is clear from *Niemitz*, which concerned a lawyer, the discretion enjoyed by the Contracting Parties under Article 8(2) ECHR 'might well be more far-reaching where professional or business premises were involved than would otherwise be the case'.[84]

Equally, the same must surely apply to companies, insofar as they enjoy the protection of Article 8 ECHR. Consequently, nothing turns on the use of the words 'his or her' in the English version of Article 7. In any case, nothing in, say, the French and German versions indicates that this provision confers rights exclusively on natural persons. On the contrary, the German version of Article 7 of the Charter uses the word '*Person*', not '*Mensch*'; as mentioned earlier, the first of these terms covers both natural and legal persons, whereas the second refers only to individuals.

Having said that, as one would expect, it follows clearly from *Niemietz*, *Colas Est*[85] and other case law discussed in section IV above that in certain circumstances, the protection afforded by Article 7 to economic actors, and particularly companies, is more limited than that enjoyed by individuals acting in a personal capacity. Moreover, the judgment in *Schecke*, which will be considered in section VI below, has cast some doubt on the reading of Article 7 advanced here.

D. Does Article 8 Apply to Economic Actors?

According to the Explanations, Article 8 of the Charter is based on what are now Articles 39 TEU and 16 TFEU and the Data Protection Directive,[86] as

[81] AG Cruz Villalòn, fn 54 to his Opinion in *Digital Rights Ireland* (n 2).
[82] Jens Vedsted-Hansen, commentary on Article 7 of the Charter in Peers et al (n 77) 153ff.
[83] n 63 above.
[84] *Niemitz v Germany* (n 21) [31].
[85] *Colas Est* (n 71).
[86] n 4 above.

well as on Article 8 ECHR and the Council of Europe Convention of 1981 for the Protection of Individuals with regard to the Automatic Processing of Personal Data and Regulation 45/2001 on respect for data protection by EU institutions and bodies.[87] In contrast, the Explanations do not mention Directive 2002/58 of the European Parliament and the Council on privacy and electronic communication (the 'e-Privacy Directive')[88] as amended.

Apart from Article 8 ECHR, all these provisions mentioned in the Explanations are expressed to apply exclusively for the benefit of individuals. Article 8 of the Charter is drafted in almost identical terms to Article 16(1) TFEU, and neither provision contains any language indicating whether it extends to legal persons. However, Article 16(2), the legal basis for legislation on the protection of data by EU institutions and bodies and by the Member States acting within the scope of EU law, is expressly limited to the protection of individuals. In any event, the omission of the e-Privacy Directive from the Explanations on Article 8 of the Charter is significant, since this Directive protects 'the legitimate interests of subscribers who are legal persons' as well as natural persons. This omission would suggest that Article 8 of the Charter does not confer rights on companies.

On the other hand, from the reference to the Data Protection Directive, it is plain that natural persons acting in a professional or economic capacity are covered by Article 8 of the Charter: it was held in *Österreichischer Rundfunk* that natural persons acting in such a capacity fall within the scope of the Directive.[89] Indeed, Article 13(1)(d) of the Directive exempts measures taken with respect to 'breaches of ethics for regulated professions' from the obligations imposed by certain provisions of the Directive.[90]

Turning to the first test considered by the Court in *DEB*,[91] the German version of Article 8 uses the words '*Person*', which can refer both to natural and legal persons. The same applies to Article 16(1) TFEU. However, as mentioned above, this carries little weight. As to the second test in *DEB*,[92] this is not particularly helpful here: some other provisions of Title II are plainly confined to natural persons (eg, Articles 9 (the right to marry), 10 (freedom of conscience, thought and religion) and 14 (the right to education)), but others plainly do apply for the benefit of legal persons as well, especially Articles 16 (the right to conduct a business) and 17 (the right to property).

On this issue, the judgments in *Schecke* and *Digital Rights Ireland* appear to send contradictory signals. What is more, in his interim Order

[87] [2001] OJ L8/1.
[88] [2002] OJ L201/37, amended by Directive 2009/136 [2009] OJ L337/11.
[89] Case C-465/00 *Österreichischer Rundfunk* [2003] ECR I-4989 [73] and [74].
[90] See generally Case C-473/12 *Institut professionnel des agents immobiliers* (judgment of 7 November 2013).
[91] See the text accompanying n 38 above.
[92] See the text accompanying n 39 above.

in *Commission v Pilkington Group*, a case on professional secrets, the Vice-President of the Court of Justice arguably assumed that companies can rely on Article 8 of the Charter.[93] All of these rulings will be considered below.

In summary, the question as to whether Article 8 of the Charter confers rights on companies remains unclear. Surely, there can be no question of this provision applying to legal persons except perhaps in highly exceptional circumstances. Given that they cannot engage in personal relationships like human beings, their need for data protection, if any, must be very limited. Accordingly, the very idea of extending the entire body of data protection legislation to them would be misplaced.

E. The Rights to Privacy and Data Protection are not Absolute

Like nearly all the rights enshrined in the ECHR and the Charter, the rights set out in Articles 7 and 8 of the Charter are not absolute: both are subject to public interest exceptions and may yield to other fundamental rights.

That Articles 7 and 8 of the Charter are subject to various public interest exceptions is plain from their link to Article 8 ECHR, which itself contains a number of such exceptions. The Charter is drafted differently from the ECHR in that it contains a general exception clause in Article 52(1), to which in principle all the rights enshrined in the Charter are subject. In addition, Article 8(2) and (3) lays down limits to Article 8(1).[94]

A few provisions of the Charter are absolute, including Article 1 (human dignity) and Article 4 (the prohibition of torture and inhuman or degrading treatment or punishment). Admittedly, this is not clear from Article 52(1), which is expressed as being of general application. However, the absolute nature of the right to human dignity is plain from Article 1 itself, which declares this right to be inviolable.[95] As to Article 4, this repeats Article 3 ECHR word for word, which is absolute in nature,[96] and in line with the Explanations and Article 52(32) of the Charter, it follows that the same

[93] Case C-278/13P(R) *Commission v Pilkington Group* (Order of the Vice-President of 10 September 2013) [44]. The alternative reading of this passage is that the Vice-President was merely describing Pilkington's argument.

[94] Article 8 is not unique in this respect: Art 17(1) similarly contains clauses limiting the right to property. Kranenborg (n 80 above, 259ff) points out that the Charter lacks clarity as regards the relationship between Art 8(2) and (3) on the one hand and Art 52(1) on the other.

[95] See AG Wathelet in Case C-1701/13 *Huawei Technologies* (Opinion of 20 November 2014) [67]. This provision has no counterpart in the ECHR. However, human dignity is mentioned in the preamble to the (non-binding) Universal Declaration of Human Rights of 1948. In addition, the first sentence of Art 1(1) of the German Basic Law (1949) also reads: 'Human dignity is inviolable.'

[96] 'Article 3 makes no provision for exceptions and no derogation from it is permissible under Article 15 § 2 even in the event of a public emergency threatening the life of the nation': *Selmouni v France* (judgment of 28 July 1999) [95] and the sources cited there.

applies to Article 4 of the Charter.[97] By their very nature, Articles 1 and 4 apply only to natural persons.[98]

By the same token, because the rights to privacy and data protection are not absolute, they frequently have to be weighed up against other fundamental rights. The Court has held that: 'Where several rights and fundamental freedoms protected by the European Union legal order are at issue, the assessment of the possible disproportionate nature of a provision of European Union law must be carried out with a view to reconciling the requirements of the protection of those different rights and freedoms and a fair balance between them.'[99] Unfortunately, lack of space prevents us from considering the relevant case law here.[100]

VI. *SCHECKE*

The facts of *Schecke* were simple. Various measures adopted by the Council and the Commission provided for the publication of the names of recipients of subsidies under the Common Agricultural Policy, as well as of the amounts each of them received per year. These provisions were contested before the German courts by Volker und Markus Schecke GbR, a partnership, and an individual, Mr Hartmut Eifert. A reference for a preliminary ruling was made asking, inter alia, whether these provisions were valid.

The Court held that the provisions concerned were invalid as regards natural persons as being incompatible with Articles 7 and 8 of the Charter: the Council and the Commission had failed to effect the proper balance

[97] Martin Borowsky, commentary on Article 4 in Jürgen Meyer (ed), *Charta der Grundrechte der Europäischen Union*, 4th edn (Baden-Baden, Nomos, 2014) paras 1–3; Manfred Nowak and Anne Charbord, commentary on Article 4 in Peers et al (n 77) 70.

[98] In the case of Art 1, this is plain from the very word 'human' and, unsurprisingly, the German Constitutional Court has held that only natural persons can rely on the equivalent provision in the Basic Law (BVerfG 95, 220 (1997) at 242, BVerfG 118, 168 (2007) at 203). As to Art 4, the European Commission of Human Rights found in *Verein 'Kontakt-Information-Therapie' and Hagen v Austria* (decision of 12 October 1988) [1] that Art 3 ECHR is by its very nature 'not capable of being exercised by a legal person'.

[99] Case C-283/11 *Sky Österreich* (judgment of 22 January 2013) [60] and the sources cited there.

[100] Case C-275/06 *ProMusicae* [2008] ECR I-271 (privacy/data protection versus property); Case C-73/07 *Satamedia* [2008] ECR I-9831 (privacy/data protection versus freedom of expression); and Case C-70/10 *Scarlet Extended* [2011] ECR I-11959 (right to conduct a business, data protection and freedom of expression versus intellectual property). The first two cases were decided before the Charter became binding, and in *Satamedia*, the Court did not mention the Charter at all. See Guido Comparato and Hans-W Micklitz, 'Regulated Autonomy between Market Freedoms and Fundamental Rights in the Case Law of the CJEU' in Ulf Bernitz, Xavier Groussot and Felix Schulyok (eds), *General Principles of EU Law and European Private Law* (Alphen aan den Rijn, Wolters Kluwer, 2013); the case note on *ProMusicae* by Xavier Groussot (2008) 45 *CML Rev* 1745; and Peter Oliver, 'The Protection of Privacy in the Economic Sphere before the European Court of Justice' (2009) 46 *CML Rev* 1443.

between the interest of transparency enshrined in Articles 1 and 10 TEU and 15 TFEU on the one hand and the principles of privacy and data protection on the other, especially as a different type of data publication would have been less intrusive. The Court dismissed the suggestion that the applicants had consented to the publication by accepting the subsidies because they had been warned that the data in question would be published.[101]

As already mentioned, *Schecke* is one of the rare judgments in which the Court has referred specifically to the fundamental rights of legal persons. In a key passage, it stated:

> 52. [T]he right to respect for private life with regard to the processing of personal data, recognised by Articles 7 and 8 of the Charter, concerns any information relating to an identified or identifiable individual (see, in particular, European Court of Human Rights, *Amann v. Switzerland* [GC], no. 27798/95, § 65, ECHR 2000–II, and *Rotaru v. Romania* [GC], no. 28341/95, § 43, ECHR 2000–V) and the limitations which may lawfully be imposed on the right to the protection of personal data correspond to those tolerated in relation to Article 8 of the Convention.
> 53. [T]he publication required by [the contested provisions] identifies by name all beneficiaries of aid from the [Common Agricultural Policy], among whom are both natural and legal persons. Having regard to the observations in paragraph 52 above, legal persons can claim the protection of Articles 7 and 8 of the Charter in relation to such identification only in so far as the official title of the legal person identifies one or more natural persons.
> 54. That is the case with [Volker und Markus Schecke GbR]. The official title of the partnership in question directly identifies natural persons who are its partners.

Whilst it is most welcome that the Court has considered the specific status of legal persons, it is not obvious that the statement in the second sentence of paragraph 53 follows from the case law of the ECtHR cited in the previous paragraph. Nevertheless, it seems entirely logical to confine the protection of Articles 7 and 8 of the Charter to natural persons and those legal persons whose official name reveals the identity of one or more natural persons—so long as those individuals are still alive. Quite apart from that, paragraph 53 is authority for the view that, at least in some circumstances, legal persons may rely on both Article 7 and Article 8 of the Charter. Yet, as already mentioned, the very idea of Article 8 applying to legal persons except perhaps in highly exceptional circumstances is decidedly problematic.

[101] *Schecke* [61]–[63]. Article 7(a) of the Data Protection Directive (n 4) provides that data processing is lawful if consent is given 'unambiguously'. However, in *Schecke*, the Court did not rely on this Directive, or indeed any of the EU legislation discussed in section VII below, when ruling on the validity of the contested provisions.

In any event, having raised the hopes of the Schecke partnership, the Court proceeded to dash them in a later passage when it was considering the proportionality of the measures in issue:

> 87. [W]ith regard to the legal persons which [subsidies under the Common Agricultural Policy], and in so far as they may invoke the rights conferred by Articles 7 and 8 of the Charter (see paragraph 53 of the present judgment), the view must be taken that the obligation to publish which follows from the provisions of the European Union rules the validity of which has here been brought into question does not go beyond the limits imposed by compliance with the principle of proportionality. The seriousness of the breach of the right to protection of personal data manifests itself in different ways for, on the one hand, legal persons and, on the other, natural persons ... Furthermore, the obligation on the competent national authorities to examine, before the data in question are published and for each legal person which is a beneficiary of ... aid, whether the name of that person identifies natural persons would impose on those authorities an unreasonable administrative burden (see, to that effect, judgment of the European Court of Human Rights, *K.U. v. Finland*, 2 March 2009, application no 2872/02, § 48, not yet published).[102]

The upshot was that the contested provisions were held to be invalid as against Mr Eifert, but not against the Schecke partnership, even though the identities of the natural persons who were the partners were clear from the name of the partnership. This contrasts with the conclusion reached by Advocate General Sharpston in the same case, to the effect that the contested provisions (apart from one innocuous article, which was merely an enabling provision) were invalid as regards both natural and legal persons. In any case, had Volker and Markus Schecke chosen to be party to the action themselves, they would have succeeded.

VII. THE DATA PROTECTION/ RETENTION DIRECTIVES

A. The Data Protection Directive

Article 1(1) of the Data Protection Directive[103] expressly states that it only protects natural persons. As we have just observed, individuals acting in a professional or economic capacity are protected. There is little room for the view that the exclusion of legal persons from the benefits of this Directive is

[102] Ironically, in *KU v Finland* (judgment of 2 March 2009), the ECtHR did not accept the defendant's argument based on the supposedly unreasonable administrative burden of taking the steps in issue. In contrast, the Grand Chamber of the ECtHR did accept such an argument in *Stec v UK* (judgment of 12 April 2006) [57]; see the case note on *Schecke* by Michal Bobek (2011) *CML Rev* 2005.

[103] Data Protection Directive (n 4).

repugnant to Article 8 of the Charter since, according to the Explanations, the Directive is amongst the sources of inspiration for this provision.[104]

B. Regulation 45/2001

Since Directives do not bind the EU's institutions or bodies, the European Parliament and the Council enacted Regulation 45/2001 on respect for data protection by EU institutions and bodies.[105] Broadly speaking, this Regulation is modelled on the Data Protection Directive. Moreover, it is based on Article 286 EC, which was expressed to apply exclusively in favour of individuals (the second paragraph of Article 16 TFEU, which has replaced Article 286 EC, contains wording to the same effect). Unsurprisingly, then, Article 1(1) provides that this Regulation only applies for the benefit of natural persons; and, like the Data Protection Directive, the Regulation extends to individuals acting in a professional or economic capacity.[106] Finally, any attempt to argue that the exclusion of legal persons from the benefits of this Regulation runs counter to Article 8 of the Charter would seem bound to fail, given that according to the Explanations, Article 8 is partly based on the Regulation.

C. The e-Privacy Directive

According to recital 2 in the preamble, the e-Privacy Directive[107] 'seeks to ensure full respect for the rights set out in Articles 7 and 8 of [the] Charter'. The Directive 'harmonises the provisions of the Member States required to ensure an equivalent level of protection of fundamental rights and freedoms, and in particular the right to privacy, with respect to the processing of personal data in the electronic communications sector and to ensure the free movement of such data and of electronic communication equipment and services in the Community' (Article 1(1)). To this end, it 'particularises and complements' Directive 95/46 in the electronic communications sector (Article 1(2), first sentence). Its purposes are, inter alia, to ensure the security and confidentiality of electronic communications, and to regulate unsolicited communications such as 'spam'. Article 5(1) provides that Member States must ensure the confidentiality of communications by means

[104] In *Seitlinger* (n 2), the case joined with *Digital Rights Ireland* (n 2), the Austrian Constitutional Court posed a series of questions about the relationship between Art 8 of the Charter on the one hand and the Data Protection Directive and Regulation 45/2001 (n 87) on the other. For instance, how do amendments to this legislation affect the meaning of Art 8 of the Charter? These are nice questions, but the Court saw no need to answer them.

[105] n 87 above.

[106] Case C-28/08P *Commission v Bavarian Lager Co Ltd* [2010] ECR I-6055.

[107] n 88 above.

of a public communications network and publicly available electronic communications services, and of the related traffic data, and must inter alia prohibit, in principle, the storage of that data by persons other than users, without the consent of the users concerned.

Article 15(1) authorises Member States to adopt legislation to restrict the scope of certain rights enshrined in the Directive when 'such restriction constitutes a necessary, appropriate and proportionate measure within a democratic society to safeguard national security (i.e. State security), defence, public security and the prevention, investigation, detection and prosecution of criminal offences or of unauthorised use of the electronic communication system'.

In marked contrast to the Data Protection Directive and Regulation 45/2001, the e-Privacy Directive protects 'the legitimate interests of subscribers who are legal persons' as well as natural persons (Article 1(2), second sentence).[108] Unfortunately, it is by no means clear what is meant by 'legitimate interests' in this context.[109]

D. The Data Retention Directive

Directive 2006/24 of the European Parliament and the Council (hereinafter 'the Data Retention Directive')[110] imposed far-reaching obligations on providers of publicly available electronic communications services or of public communications networks to retain large quantities of electronically generated or processed data. According to its preamble, the purpose of this Directive was to harmonise the conditions under which Member States implement Article 15(1) of the e-Privacy Directive. Crucially for our purposes, Article 1(2) provides that the Directive 'shall apply to traffic and location data on both legal entities and natural persons'.

As the reader will be aware, this Directive was struck down in its entirety by the Grand Chamber in *Digital Rights Ireland*[111] as being contrary to Articles 7 and 8 of the Charter. Since this case is discussed at length elsewhere in this book,[112] it is unnecessary to set out all the issues raised in that case here.

[108] According to its terms, Art 89 of the proposed General Data Protection Regulation (n 4) would repeal Art 1(2) of the e-Privacy Directive in its entirety. Could this be an oversight as regards the second sentence? Recital 135 in the preamble to the proposed Regulation only gives reasons for the repeal of the first sentence of Art 1(2).

[109] EU legislation on privacy and data protection appears to be replete with the words 'legitimate interest', an inherently nebulous term: see also Art 7(f) of the Data Protection Directive and Art 30(2) of Regulation 1/2003 implementing Arts 81 and 82 EC [2003] OJ L1/1. See Federico Ferretti, 'Data Protection and the Legitimate Interests of Data Controllers: Much Ado about Nothing or the Winter of Rights?' (2014) 51 *CML Rev* 543.

[110] [2006] OJ L105/54.

[111] *Digital Rights Ireland* (n 2).

[112] See chs 2, 11 and 12 in this volume; see also Orla Lynskey, case note on *Digital Rights Ireland*, 51 *CML Rev* 1789.

In this context, the key point is that, despite the clear wording of Article 1(2) of the Directive, neither the Advocate General nor the Court referred to the fact that that instrument conferred rights on legal persons as well as on individuals, although of course the Directive was also annulled as regards legal persons. Nevertheless, it is worth noting the concern expressed by the Court that the Directive applied 'even to persons whose communications are subject, according to the rules of national law, to the obligation of professional secrecy'.[113]

VIII. BUSINESS AND PROFESSIONAL SECRETS

There appears to be no direct authority from the ECtHR as to whether business secrets are protected under Article 8, or indeed some other provision of the ECHR or its protocols such as Article 1 of Protocol 1 on the right to property. However, in *Van Marle v The Netherlands*,[114] it was held that goodwill (ie, the client base of an economic actor) is covered by the latter provision, and this would suggest that the list of clients is a business secret worthy of protection under some provision of the ECHR—either Article 1 of Protocol 1, if business secrets are to be regarded as property,[115] or otherwise Article 8. Morevoer, the ECtHR has held that the protection of such secrets constitutes a legitimate reason for restricting the freedom of speech pursuant to Article 10(2) ECHR, presumably under the exception relating to restrictions 'prescribed by law and ... necessary in a democratic society ... for preventing the disclosure of information received in confidence'.[116]

In contrast, EU law is replete with provisions on the protection of business secrets. Ever since the initial Treaty of Rome, the Treaties have contained a specific article on the matter, now Article 339 TFEU, which reads:

> The members of the institutions of the Community, the members of committees, and the officials and other servants of the Community shall be required, even after their duties have ceased, not to disclose information of the kind covered by the obligation of professional secrecy, in particular information about undertakings, their business relations and their cost components.[117]

[113] *Digital Rights Ireland*, para 58 of the judgment.

[114] *Van Marle v The Netherlands* (n 62).

[115] Whether business secrets should be regarded as intellectual property cannot be discussed here. For the purposes of the Agreement on Trade-Related Aspects of Intellectual Property Rights (TRIPS) [1994] OJ L336/214, they are treated as such: Arts 1(2) and 39. The Commission's proposal for a Directive of the European Parliament and the Council on trade secrets (COM(2013) 813 final) leaves this question open.

[116] *Goodwin v UK* (judgment of 26 March 1996).

[117] This article is supplemented by a large number of legislative provisions. For instance, Art 339 TFEU has been reproduced in an amended from in Art 28 of Regulation 1/2003 (n 109 above).

Two features of this provision are striking. First of all, it is expressed to cover the confidential information, inter alia, of 'undertakings' and, consequently, companies are plainly covered.[118] Second, this article is not couched in terms of rights, but in *Akzo Chemie BV v Commission* the Court held that the protection of business secrets constitutes a general principle of Community law on which undertakings can rely.[119]

A distinction is drawn, at least in competition law, between 'business secrets', which qualify for maximum protection, and other confidential information.[120] Business secrets may include the following: technical and/or financial information relating to an undertaking's know-how, methods of assessing costs, production secrets and processes, supply sources, quantities produced and sold, market shares, customer and distributor lists, marketing plans, cost and price structure, and sales strategy.[121] 'Professional secrets' in the context of competition law cover a wider category of information.[122] Regrettably, we cannot delve further into these distinctions here.

Subsequently, the Court of Justice elevated the protection of business secrets to the status of a fundamental right. In *Varec*, decided before the Charter acquired binding force, the Court ruled that the protection of business secrets falls within the protection of 'private life' in Article 8 ECHR and consequently Article 7 of the Charter—despite the absence of any authority from the ECtHR on this point.[123] The case arose out of a public procurement dispute before the Belgian Conseil d'Etat. The Court of Justice held that, pursuant to the Public Procurement Directives, the authority hearing the dispute must ensure confidentiality and business secrecy, even if that meant denying the disappointed tenderer sight of the contract concluded with its competitor.

More recently, in *Interseroh*, it was held that protection of business secrets falls under Articles 15, 16 and 17 of the Charter.[124] This case concerned EU

[118] For the purposes of Arts 101 and 102 TFEU, the concept of an 'undertaking' means 'every entity engaged in an economic activity regardless of the legal status of the entity and the way in which it is financed': Case C-41/90 *Höfner and Elser* [1991] ECR I-1979 [21]. Self-employed individuals constitute 'undertakings'.

[119] Case 53/85 *Akzo Chemie BV v Commission* [1986] ECR 1965 [28], confirmed in Case C-36/82P *SEP v Commission* [1994] ECR I-1911 [37]. Both cases concerned the treatment by the Commission of confidential documents produced by companies pursuant to Regulation 17/62 implementing what are now Arts 101 and 102 TFEU ([1962] OJ 204/62, as amended), now replaced by Regulation 1/2003 (n 109 above).

[120] Business secrets are afforded 'very special protection' (*Akzo* (n 119) [28]); see also Case T-353 *Postbank v Commission* [1996] ECR II-921 [87].

[121] Commission Notice on Rules for Access to the Commission's file in competition cases [2005] OJ C325/7, [18]. Nicholas Khan in Kerse and Khan *EU Antitrust Procedure*, 6th edn (London, Sweet & Maxwell, 2012) 224ff.

[122] Case T-198/03 *Bank Austria Creditanstalt v Commission* [2006] ECR II-1429 [71]. See also the definition of 'trade secret' in Art 2(1) of the Commission's proposal mentioned in n 115. above, which is taken from Article 39(2) of TRIPS (n 115).

[123] Case C-450/06 *Varec v Belgian State* [2008] ECR I-581 [48]–[49].

[124] Case C-1/11 *Interseroh Scrap and Metals Trading GmbH* (judgment of 29 March 2012) [43].

legislation on shipments of waste, which required dealers to disclose to their customers their source of supply so as to ensure traceability. Interseroh, the applicant company in the main case, claimed that this information was a business secret and objected to divulging it on the grounds that this would enable its customers to obtain their supplies directly from the source. The Court of Justice declined to rule on the validity of the EU legislation, since the referring court had only sought a ruling on its meaning, not its validity.[125]

An important case on interim relief is *Commission v Pilkington Group*[126] concerning the cartel in car glass to which the respondent undertaking had been party. The Commission is required to publish each of its competition decisions, including the names of the parties and the main content of the decision, while respecting the 'legitimate interests of undertakings in the protection of its business secrets'.[127] The Commission had resolved to publish a version of its decision on this cartel, which included information for which Pilkington claimed confidentiality. Pilkington had obtained an interim Order at first instance requiring the Commission to refrain from publishing that information.[128] The President of the General Court had asserted that the alleged breach of the company's rights under Article 339 TFEU and Article 8 of the Charter as well as under Article 6 ECHR and Article 47 of the Charter sufficed by themselves to establish the likelihood of serious and irreparable harm in the circumstances of the case.[129] On appeal, the Vice-President of the Court of Justice held that assertion to be erroneous: confirming earlier case law,[130] he denied the existence of a per se rule to this effect.[131] Nevertheless, he dismissed the appeal, inter alia because it

[125] The facts of this case are similar to those in Case C-453/03 *ABNA* [2005] ECR I-10423, where the manufacturers of feeding-stuffs were required to provide customers with a statement of the exact ingredients of their products, at the risk that those customers or third parties would be able to manufacture the products themselves. In the absence of any public interest grounds justifying the contested measure, it was held to be contrary to the principle of proportionality.

[126] *Commission v Pilkington Group* (n 93).

[127] Article 30 of Regulation 1/2003 (n 109); see also Art 28 of that Regulation (n 117). In this chapter, it is only possible to touch briefly on business secrets in competition law. See Bombois (n 66) 203–08; Khan (n 121 above), 224–31 and 382–83; Oliver (n 100) 1475ff; and Piet van Nuffel, 'Human Rights and Competition Law: Do Undertakings Have a "Fundamental Right" of Protection of Confidential Business Information?' in *Liber Amicorum Jacques Steenbergen* (Brussels, Larcier, 2014) 579.

[128] Case T-462/12R *Pilkington Group v Commission* (Order of 11 March 2013).

[129] ibid [44] and [45].

[130] Case C-43/98P(R) *Camar v Commission and Council* [1998] ECR I-1815 [46] and [47].

[131] Case C-278/13P(R) *Commission v Pilkington Group* [40]–[44], confirmed in Case C-389/13P(R) *European Medicines Agency v AbbVie Inc* (Order of 28 November 2013) [40]. In the latter case, the Vice-President of the Court conceded at [41] that 'the infringement of certain fundamental rights, such as the prohibition of torture and inhuman or degrading treatment or punishment, enshrined in Article 4 of the Charter, is liable, because of the very nature of the right infringed, to give rise by itself to serious and irreparable harm. Nevertheless … it is still for the party seeking an interim measure to set forth and establish the likelihood of such harm occurring in its particular case'. As we noted in section V.E above, the right enshrined in Art 4 is absolute, but those in Arts 7 and 8 are not.

would be impossible to quantify the damage which would be caused by the publication of the alleged business secrets.[132] Also worthy of note is the passage in which the Vice-President arguably stated—almost in passing—that legal persons may rely on Article 8 of the Charter, which relates to data protection.[133]

Finally, a brief consideration of the case law on requests for access to documents is in point. Regulation 1049/2001 on access to documents[134] provides for the widest possible transparency, a principle which is now reflected in Article 15(1) TFEU. However, Article 4 of the Regulation sets out a series of exceptions, including one on the 'protection of commercial interests of a natural or legal person ... unless there is an overriding public interest in disclosure', language which plainly covers the protection of business secrets. In two recent cases where parties sought access to documents which had been submitted to the Commission under the EU legislation on merger controls, the Court of Justice has given priority to this exception as well as to other exceptions in Regulation 1049/2001—albeit without referring to Articles 7 and 8 of the Charter.[135] In these judgments, the Court interpreted that Regulation in harmony with the EU merger control legislation, just as in *Bavarian Lager* it had interpreted the same Regulation in harmony with Regulation 45/2001.[136]

However, in its subsequent ruling in *Stichting Greenpeace Nederland v Commission*, the General Court failed to follow this approach.[137] Greenpeace sought access to documents which had been lodged by a number of manufacturers of plant protection products with a view to obtaining a market authorisation for them in accordance with EU legislation. The Commission divulged most of these documents, but withheld those which contained details of the production methods and the technical specifications of the active substance used; this information would have allowed competitors to manufacture these products themselves, thereby causing a considerable loss of market share to the companies which had supplied the information in the first place. Unfortunately, a number of different EU acts came into play, which inevitably led to complications. The Commission relied on the protection of business secrets, pointing out that the relevant EU legislation must be read in the light of the Charter, which protects such secrets, albeit not absolutely. Nevertheless, the General Court decided that transparency must

[132] Order in Case C-278/13P(R) [50ff].

[133] ibid [44].

[134] [2001] OJ L145/43.

[135] Case C-404/10P *Commission v Editions Odile Jacob* (judgment of 28 June 2012); and Case C-477/10 *Commission v Agrofert Holding SA* (judgment of 28 June 2012).

[136] n 87 above; similarly, see Case C-139/07 P *Commission v Technische Glaswerke Ilmenau* [2010] ECR I-5885 on State aids.

[137] Case T-545/11 *Stichting Greenpeace Nederland v Commission* (judgment of 8 October 2013). The author appeared for the Commission in this case and drafted the appeal to the Court of Justice shortly before leaving the Commission.

prevail. The ruling of the Court of Justice on the Commission's appeal[138] is likely to be of some importance—not least because similar approval schemes exist under the EU legislation on biocides, other chemicals (REACH) and genetically modified organisms.

In conclusion, despite the ruling in *Interseroh*, it is hard to see how Article 15 of the Charter can come into play here, since it provides for the right to engage in work and to pursue a 'freely chosen and accepted occupation'. On the other hand, if such secrets are indeed intellectual property,[139] then Article 17 of the Charter would appear to be applicable, and Article 16 on the right to conduct a business may well be engaged in any event.

As already mentioned, economic actors do not enjoy the full benefit of the protection afforded by Article 7 of the Charter, and a major question mark hangs over the application of Article 8 to legal persons. In contrast, there can no doubt that companies enjoy the full benefits of both Articles 16 and 17.[140] Accordingly, it seems preferable to treat business secrets as falling under one or other of the latter provisions, or perhaps both. In any event, it is submitted that whichever approach is followed should not affect the outcome of a case.

IX. RIGHT TO A REPUTATION

Individuals who have been defamed are entitled, by virtue of Article 8 ECHR, to vindicate their reputation in judicial proceedings,[141] at least where the attack on their reputation is so serious as to affect their 'personal integrity'.[142] Logically, the same should apply to businesses, since if their reputation is tarnished, they can be ruined. Although there is a dearth of direct authority on the point under Article 8 ECHR, on at least two occasions the ECtHR has acknowledged the importance of a company's reputation in relation to other articles of the Convention: *Comingersoll*,[143] where compensation was awarded for damage to the applicant company's reputation as a result of a breach of Article 6 ECHR; and *Steel and Morris v UK*,[144]

[138] Case C-673/13P *Commission v Stichting Greenpeace Nederland* (pending).

[139] See n 115 above.

[140] On Art 16, see Peter Oliver 'What Purpose Does Article 16 of the Charter Serve?' in Ulf Bernitz, Xavier Groussot and Felix Schulyok (eds), *General Principles of EU Law and European Private Law* (Alphen aan den Rijn,, Wolters Kluwer, 2013) 281 and the sources cited there.

[141] *Radio France v France* (judgment of 30 March 2004) [31]; see also *Earl and Countess Spencer v UK* (decision of the European Commission of Human Rights of 16 January 1998); *Rotaru v Romania* (judgment of 4 May 2000) [44]; *Schüssel v Austria* (decision of 21 February 2002); *Montera v Italy* (decision of 9 July 2002); *Pfeifer v Austria* (judgment of 15 February 2008).

[142] *Polanco Torres v Spain* (judgment of 21 September 2010) [40].

[143] *Comingersoll v Portugal* (n 25).

[144] *Steel and Morris v UK* (judgment of 15 February 2005) [35].

where the right of a company (*in casu* McDonald's fast food chain) to sue in defamation was held to fall within the concept of 'the protection of the reputation and the rights of others' in Article 10(2) ECHR, which sets out the exceptions to the freedom of expression enshrined in Article 10(1).[145]

Subsequently, in a case involving a journalist convicted of criminal defamation for criticising the quality of a traditional Hungarian wine produced by a particular State-owned company in outspoken terms, the Court found a breach of Article 10. Given its importance, the key passage should be quoted at length:

> [I]n addition to the public interest in open debate about business practices, there is a competing interest in protecting the commercial success and viability of companies, for the benefit of shareholders and employees, but also for the wider economic good. The State therefore enjoys a margin of appreciation as to the means it provides under domestic law to enable a company to challenge the truth, and limit the damage, of allegations which risk harming its reputation (see *Steel and Morris v. the United Kingdom*, no. 68416/01, § 94, ECHR 2005-II; *Kuliś and Różycki v. Poland*, no. 27209/03, § 35, ECHR 2009-...). However, there is a difference between the commercial reputational interests of a company and the reputation of an individual concerning his or her social status. Whereas the latter might have repercussions on one's dignity, for the Court interests of commercial reputation are devoid of that moral dimension. In the instant application, the reputational interest at stake is that of a State-owned corporation; it is thus a commercial one without relevance to moral character.[146]

This statement, which sets out the inherent differences between human beings and companies in terms somewhat redolent of the celebrated observation attributed to Lord Thurlow,[147] deserves warm applause.

In any case, these cases strongly indicate that Article 8 ECHR protects the reputation of all economic actors. If so, the same must apply to Article 7 of the Charter.

Probably the first ever action in defamation to be brought before the Court of Justice was *Ismeri Europa Srl*.[148] The Court accepted that such actions may be brought pursuant to what is now Article 340 TFEU, even where the applicant is a company, but it did not touch on the fundamental rights issue, and nor did the Advocate General.

The protection of a company's reputation has also arisen in relation to the publication of Commission's competition decisions in the Official Journal. In *Bank Austria*,[149] the Commission had fined the applicant company

[145] Confirmed in *Timpul Info-Magazin and Anghel v Moldavia* (judgment of 27 November 2011) [34].

[146] *Uj v Hungary* (judgment of 19 October 2011) [22].

[147] n 7 above and accompanying text.

[148] Case C-315/99P *Ismeri Europa Srl v Court of Auditors* [2001] ECR I-5281.

[149] n 122 above.

and several other Austrian banks for participating in a cartel. Bank Austria contested the Commission's rejection of its request that certain passages of the competition decision be expunged from the published version because they enabled its employees who had taken part in cartel meetings to be identified. Its claim was based primarily on Regulation 45/2001. However, as we noticed earlier, that Regulation only protects natural persons. Unsurprisingly, the General Court therefore held that the applicant could not rely on it.[150] We will return to this case in section XII below.

The facts of *Pergan* were more unusual.[151] There the Commission had fined the participants to a cartel in organic peroxides—except Pergan, since its infringement was time-barred. It was open to the Commission to find in the operative part of its Decision that Pergan had participated in the infringement, provided that the Commission could show a legitimate interest in doing so.[152] However, the Commission chose not to follow that course. Instead, in the body of the decision, the Commission mentioned the applicant by name and set out a detailed description of its participation in the cartel as well as the reason why the Commission had closed the file against it. Pergan had been given no opportunity to defend itself. Unsurprisingly, the General Court ruled that this was unlawful. Not only had the Commission breached the presumption of innocence enshrined in Article 48 of the Charter,[153] but it had also failed to respect the company's privacy, since the latter's 'reputation and dignity' had been tarnished.[154] Although the Court's reasoning and conclusion are undoubtedly sound, one might wonder whether the word 'dignity' is appropriate in relation to a company. This term smacks of 'human dignity' in Article 1 of the Charter, which applies only to human beings.[155]

X. INSPECTIONS

We have already considered the rulings of the ECtHR in *Niemietz*[156] and *Colas Est*.[157] Suffice it to add that in the latter case, France was held to have been in breach of Article 8 ECHR, given the lack of adequate and effective safeguards against abuse: the inspection was carried out without a judicial warrant, there was no requirement in law that a senior police officer

[150] ibid [9].
[151] Case T-474/04 *Pergan v Commission* [2007] ECR I-4225.
[152] See ibid [72], referring to Cases T–22/02 and T–23/02 *Sumitomo Chemical and Sumika Fine Chemical v Commission* [2005] ECR II–4065 [60]–[63].
[153] ibid [76]–[77].
[154] ibid. See also generally Case T-380/08 *The Netherlands v Commission* (judgment of 13 September 2013) [52].
[155] see n 98 above.
[156] see n 21 above.
[157] see n 71 above.

be present and the authorities had exclusive competence to determine the expediency, number, length and scale of inspections.[158]

Much more recently, the ECtHR delivered a noteworthy judgment in *Bernh Larsen Holding and others v Norway*.[159] The three applicant companies were independent of one another, but shared the same premises, server and email server. When auditing the accounts of these companies, the tax authorities had required them to make available a backup copy of all the data on their shared server—some 41 gigabytes. This interference with the applicants' 'home' and correspondence was held to be justified under Article 8(2) ECHR. What is particularly striking is that despite being so far-reaching, the interference was found to be proportionate, mainly because the domestic legislation contained a variety of safeguards and because failure to comply with such an order supposedly gave rise to no sanctions.[160] Interestingly, the ECtHR referred twice to its statement in *Niemietz* to the effect that the degree of enjoyed by the Contracting Parties 'might well be more far-reaching where professional or business premises were involved than would otherwise be the case'.[161] On the second occasion, the ECtHR in *Bernh Larsen* added a new twist, saying that the Contracting Parties enjoyed a wider margin of discretion when dealing with legal persons.[162] This is likely to be significant in future cases.

In contrast, the ECtHR found, albeit by a majority of only four judges to three, that Article 8 ECHR had been breached in *Delta Pekárny*.[163] The facts occurred shortly before the Czech Republic joined the EU. As the applicant company was suspected of being party to a cartel contrary to national competition law, a wide-ranging inspection was carried out at its premises by the national competition authority. Representatives of the company had been present at the inspection, the competition authority was barred from taking any originals and therefore had to resort to photocopies, and officials of that authority were bound by an obligation of confidentiality. However, these safeguards were found to be insufficient because no judicial warrant had been obtained and there was no possibility of obtaining an effective judicial review of the need for the inspection after the event; nor was there any legislative requirement that unlawfully seized documents be destroyed.[164] The ECtHR stressed that it needed to be especially vigilant where inspections are carried out without a judicial warrant, despite the broad discretion enjoyed by the Contracting States.[165]

158 *Colas Est* [49].
159 *Bernh Larsen Holding and others v Norway* (judgment of 14 March 2013).
160 ibid [162ff].
161 ibid [104], citing *Niemietz v Germany* (n 21) [31].
162 *Bernh Larsen* (n 159) [159].
163 *Delta Pekárny v Czech Republic* (judgment of 2 October 2014).
164 ibid [92].
165 ibid [83].

As is well known, the Court of Justice held in *Hoechst v Commission*[166] that Article 8 ECHR was not engaged with regard to an inspection carried out on a company's premises pursuant to Article 14 of Regulation 17/62[167] on the grounds that the 'home' in this context referred exclusively to the 'private dwellings of natural persons',[168] and in *Roquette Frères*, following the judgments in *Niemietz* and *Colas Est*, the Court reversed its position.[169] In *Roquette*, the Court therefore sought to lay down the criteria to be applied by national courts in determining whether to grant a judicial search warrant, in such a manner as to satisfy the requirements of Article 8(2) ECHR. In particular, the Court stressed that the information to be supplied by the Commission must be as detailed as reasonably possible. Article 14 of Regulation 17/62 has been reproduced in Article 20 of Regulation 1/2003,[170] albeit in a substantially amended form to reflect the judgment in *Roquette*.[171]

Finally, attention should be drawn to the important ruling in *Deutsche Bahn*.[172] The Commission had carried out three separate inspections on the premises of Deutsche Bahn and its subsidiaries. Each inspection had been preceded by a Commission decision, but no judicial warrants were obtained. Relying on Article 7 of the Charter and Article 8 ECHR, the applicants contested the legality of the three decisions because of the absence of judicial warrants. Moreover, pursuant to Article 277 TFEU, they challenged the legality of Article 20(4) of Regulation 1/2003 on the basis that it permitted inspections without such warrants. Having regard to the case law of the ECtHR,[173] the General Court rejected the contention that a judicial warrant was necessary except where there was an imminent danger of a criminal offence being committed.[174] Rather, this was merely one of several factors to be taken into account, the others being the degree of discretion

[166] Cases 46/87 and 227/88 *Hoechst v Commission* [1989] ECR 2859.

[167] n 119 above.

[168] *Hoechst v Commission* (n 166) [17]–[19].

[169] Case C-94/00 *Roquette Frères v Directeur général de la concurrence* [2002] ECR I-9011; see especially [29]. See S Douglas-Scott 'A Tale of Two Courts: Luxembourg, Strasbourg and the Growing Human Rights *Acquis*' (2006) 43 *CML Rev* 629, 649.

[170] n 109 above.

[171] Once again, it is not possible to consider the competition aspects of this topic fully within the confines of this chapter. See Khan (n 121) 144ff; Andreas Scordamaglia-Tousis, *EU Cartel Enforcement* (Alphen aan den Rijn, Wolters Kluwer, 2013) 187ff; Wouter Wils, 'Powers of Investigation and Procedural Rights and Guarantees in EU Antitrust Enforcement' (2006) 29 *World Competition* 3.

[172] Cases T-289/11, T-290/11 and T-521/11 *Deutsche Bahn v Commission* (judgment of 6 September 2013).

[173] See, eg, *Colas Est* (n 71); *Harju v Finland* (judgment of 15 February 2011) [40] and [44]; and *Heino v Finland* (judgment of 15 February 2011) [40] and [44].

[174] *Deutsche Bahn v Commission* [66]–[72]. Equally, the Court dismissed the claim of a breach of Art 47 of the Charter, which was based on the supposed inadequacy of an ex post judicial review: paras 73 to 102.

enjoyed by the authorities in deciding whether to conduct an inspection, the possible existence of safeguards and the possibility of obtaining ex post judicial review of the decision to carry out the search.[175] Following a detailed consideration of all these factors, the General Court rejected the arguments advanced by Deutsche Bahn. An appeal against this judgment is currently pending before the Court of Justice.[176]

XI. THE FREEDOM TO PURSUE A TRADE OR PROFESSION OR TO CONDUCT A BUSINESS

As we noticed earlier, it follows from the ruling in *Sidabras*[177] that in certain extreme cases, Article 8 confers on individuals the right not to be excluded from work, but this falls well short of a general right to pursue a trade or profession. Under the Charter, the relevant provision is not Article 7 or Article 8, but Article 15, which specifically provides for such a general right, and Article 16, which relates to the right to conduct a business.

XII. COMPANIES ACTING TO PROTECT THEIR STAKEHOLDERS

Companies litigating before both the Strasbourg and the Luxembourg Courts have claimed the right, and even the duty, to protect the privacy of their stakeholders.[178]

In *Bernh Larsen Holding v Norway*,[179] the ECtHR found that the applicant companies' interest in protecting the privacy of their employees and other persons working for them did not constitute a separate complaint, but only an aspect of their wider complaint under Article 8 of the Convention. The fact that no such individual person was a party to the domestic proceedings or brought an application under the Convention should not prevent the Court from taking into account such interests in its wider assessment of the merits of the application.[180]

In *Bank Austria v Commission*,[181] the General Court has proved to be less indulgent to a similar claim. As we noticed in section IX above, it held

[175] As to how ex post judicial review works in such circumstances, see Case T-296/11 *Cementos Portland Valderrivas* (judgment of 14 March 2014) [24]–[26] and [41]. That case concerned a request for information addressed to an undertaking, but the principles are essentially the same.

[176] Case C-583/13P *Deutsche Bahn v Commission.*

[177] *Sidabras v Lithuania* (n 56).

[178] On the use of the word 'stakeholder' in this context, see n 11 above.

[179] *Bernh Larsen Holding* (n 159) [90].

[180] ibid [90]. Similarly, see *Delta Pekárny v Czech Republic* (n 163) [65].

[181] Case T-198/03 *Bank Austria Creditanstalt AG v Commission* [2006] ECR II-1429 [95]–[96].

that the applicant could not rely on Regulation 45/2001. However, the point of interest to us here is that the applicant also claimed to be directly affected by the alleged breach on the basis that, under Austrian law, it was required to give legal assistance to its staff. The Court simply rejected this submission as being unsubstantiated.[182] Naturally, this leaves room for the Court to take a different position in an appropriate case in the future.

In all these cases, the individuals concerned could have brought an action, but did not.[183]

XIII. CONCLUSION

As we have observed, the privacy and data protection of economic actors have given rise to a wealth of case law, not all of which it has been possible to discuss within the confines of this chapter. Nevertheless, many of the key issues remain unsolved, namely: the relationship between Articles 7 and 8 of the Charter; the extent to which legal persons are protected by Article 7; and whether Article 8 protects legal persons. Certainly, it seems unthinkable that Article 8 of the Charter could apply generally to legal persons, since that would require the entire panoply of data protection legislation to be extended to them, and this would be wholly unwarranted.

At least, the following propositions now appear to be tolerably clear: generally speaking, natural persons acting in a professional or economic capacity enjoy the full protection of Article 7, although in certain areas such as inspections, their rights may be more limited than those of natural persons acting in a private capacity; legal persons, including companies, enjoy some rights under Article 7; and natural persons acting in a professional or economic capacity enjoy the full protection of Article 8.

The reasons for the legal uncertainties are manifold: the wording of Article 8 of the Charter and the accompanying Explanations; the nebulous concept of the 'legitimate' interests of subscribers who are legal persons in Article 1(2) of the e-Privacy Directive; the fact that most of the relevant judgments were delivered before the Charter acquired binding force with the entry into force of the Treaty of Lisbon, and therefore tend not to focus on the Charter; and the Court's apparent reluctance to address the more thorny issues.

182 ibid [96].

183 In contrast, see the situation described in n 17 above.

14

Dawn Raids in Competition Cases: Do the European Commission's Dawn Raid Procedures Stand the Test of the Charter?

HELENE ANDERSSON

I. INTRODUCTION

DURING THE YEARS that have passed since the EU Charter of Fundamental Rights (hereinafter 'the Charter') was given binding legal effect, it has gained widespread application in competition cases. Today, it is more or less standard procedure for companies targeted by the cartel investigations of the European Commission (hereinafter 'the Commission') to invoke infringement of either one or several Charter provisions. In a number of cases, companies have challenged the Commission's investigatory methods, arguing that not only do they fail to respect the right to privacy provided in Article 7 of the Charter, but also that the (lack of) judicial review of inspection decisions and measures taken by the Commission on their basis run foul of Article 47 of the Charter and the right to a fair trial enshrined therein.[1]

The Charter's binding effect is one reason why the Commission's practices are challenged so frequently nowadays. Another reason is the new and more aggressive enforcement approach adopted by the Commission. In 2004, public enforcement of the EU competition law regime underwent a drastic reform, allowing the Commission's Directorate General for Competition (DG COMP) to re-allocate its resources and focus on cartels and other hard-core infringements. As a result, the DG COMP is now perceived as an aggressive enforcer of the EU competition rules, and the fines imposed on cartel offenders keep reaching record levels.[2]

[1] See, eg, Case T-135/09 *Nexans France SAS and Nexans SA v European Commission* EU:T:2012:596; and Joined Cases T-289 and 290/11 and T-521/11 *Deutsche Bahn and others v Commission* EU:T:2013:404.

[2] See http://ec.europa.eu/competition/cartels/statistics/statistics.pdf.

Participating in cartel activity is a risky business, as anyone found guilty will have to pay hefty fines. In some jurisdictions, employees and company representatives even risk imprisonment. There may therefore be incentives to obstruct a competition authority's investigation, something which has not gone by unnoticed by the legislator. The 2004 reform included a thorough revision of the sanctions available to the Commission in the event of obstruction. As part of its more aggressive approach, the Commission has seized the opportunity and is now imposing substantial fines. The press release accompanying the announcement that the energy company E.ON had been fined €38 million for breaking a Commission seal[3] stated:

> The Commission cannot and will not tolerate attempts by companies to undermine the Commission's fight against cartels and other anti-competitive practices by threatening the integrity and effectiveness of our investigations. Companies know very well that high fines are at stake in competition cases, and some may consider illegal measures to obstruct an inquiry and so avoid a fine. This decision sends a clear message to all companies that it does not pay off to obstruct the Commission's investigation.[4]

This statement reflects the view taken not only by the Commission but also by many other competition authorities around the world. In a report to the ICN[5] Annual Conference in 2006, it was agreed that the penalties for obstruction should at least mirror, or preferably be even more severe than, the substantive offenses under investigation. Otherwise, cartel offenders would consider it worthwhile to obstruct the authorities' investigations.[6]

From this, two conclusions may be drawn: first, the success of a cartel case is dependent on the investigation running smoothly and without obstruction; and, second, the stakes have definitely been raised for those targeted by the Commission's investigations.

As companies also now risk facing severe sanctions for objecting to the Commission's investigatory methods, there is pressure on them to cooperate even where they believe that their rights are not respected by the Commission. Article 20(4) of Council Regulation 1/2003 imposes an obligation on companies to submit to the Commission's inspections. Furthermore, as EU acts enjoy the presumption of validity, their effects will be realised until such time as they are set aside.[7] Companies will have to cooperate until the Court says otherwise.

[3] A decision which was later upheld both by the General Court (see Case T-141/08 *E.ON Energie AG v European Commission* EU:T:2010:516) and the CJEU (see Case C-89/11P EU:C:2012:738).

[4] See http://europa.eu/rapid/pressReleasesAction.do?reference=IP/08/108&format=HTML &aged=0&language=EN&guiLanguage=en.

[5] The International Competition Network, a global network for competition authorities.

[6] ICN Cartels Working Group, *Obstruction of Justice in Cartel Investigations*, Report to the ICN Annual Conference 2006, available at: www.internationalcompetitionnetwork.org/uploads/library/doc350.pdf.

[7] A Türk, *Judicial Review in EU Law* (Cheltenham, Edward Elgar, 2010) 298.

For a company receiving a visit from the Commission, it may be a hard task to determine then and there whether the Commission is actually acting within its powers or not, and whether there is cause for action. Should the company object to the inspection, will it be considered to be exercising its right of defence or merely obstructing the Commission's investigation? Add to this the fact that although it is possible to challenge the inspection decision as such, the possibilities to challenge the measures taken on its basis are limited. In order for the General Court to suspend a dawn raid, one requirement is that the inspection decision is challenged. But what if there is nothing wrong the decision in itself, only the measures taken on its basis?

This raises the question whether the procedural safeguards surrounding dawn raids are adequate or if they should be struck down as incompatible with the Charter. Much indicates that the limited possibilities for review makes the procedural safeguards inadequate, and that they fail to meet the standards of the European Convention for the Protection of Human Rights and Fundamental Freedoms (ECHR) and thereby also the standards of the Charter.

Before discussing the procedural safeguards surrounding dawn raids, it is necessary to briefly present the Commission's dawn raid practices.

II. DAWN RAIDS: WHY AND WHEN?

Market-sharing and price-fixing cartels constitute the cardinal sins against Article 101 of the Treaty on the Functioning of the European Union (TFEU). Yet, or perhaps for this reason, direct evidence of cartel agreements is almost by definition hard to come by unless the cartel members have strong incentives to reveal their participation and/or the competition authority has been vested with far-reaching investigatory powers.

Today, cartel participants may indeed be inclined to reveal their behaviour as there are effective leniency programmes in place at both the EU and the national level allowing cartel participants to escape fines provided that they reveal the cartel and offer to cooperate during the investigation. This being said, the existence of effective leniency programmes does not affect the need for dawn raids.

One reason for this is that the leniency applicant is seldom able to provide enough evidence to establish the entire scope of the cartel. It may even be the case that the leniency applicant is not aware of the entire magnitude of the cartel. Perhaps it only knew of and filed for leniency regarding a national cartel for one product, while in fact the applicant was only part of a national branch of a global multi-product cartel.

Moreover, much suggests that leniency programmes would not be effective were it not for the possibility of carrying out dawn raids. In short, the theory is that leniency will work only if one cartel member either believes that the cartel risks being detected and punished without leniency or fears that at least one cartel member may hold such a belief.[8] A leniency programme may thus not become truly effective unless there is a fear of detection, and such a fear may not be achieved without efficient investigatory powers.

One of the DG COMP's most effective but also most intrusive investigatory methods is the unannounced inspection, or *dawn raid*, where the Commission officials are allowed to pay unannounced visits to companies suspected of competition law infringements and to take copies of business records and books.[9]

A dawn raid is indeed an efficient tool. As a previous official of the DG COMP has accounted for:

> It is remarkable how often the Commission has during its investigations under Article 14(3) discovered the 'smoking gun': the Cartel blueprint, the minutes of secret meetings, the detailed calculations of the quota schemes ... it has obtained documentary evidence which Justice Department attorneys would give their eye-teeth to obtain in a Sherman Act case.[10]

However it also appears that, unless the Commission already at the initial stage finds not only one smoking gun but a whole arsenal, it may have to drop the case. It is therefore crucial that the dawn raid runs smoothly and without any interruptions. In order to ensure this, there is of course a desire on the part of the enforcer that the target should not be allowed to obstruct or otherwise hinder the performance of the inspection.

Looking at the other side of the coin, the positive effects of a dawn raid are not that obvious to the company targeted by the inspection. On the contrary, a dawn raid affects both the company and its employees in a number of ways. For sure, none of these effects is positive.

Not only is the measure itself invasive, allowing the inspectors to enter and search through company premises or even the private dwellings of its employees, seal premises, take copies of documents and ask for explanations on the spot, but it will also have long-lasting negative effects on the company concerned, both in relation to the often massive negative publicity that a company will receive if it admits to being targeted by a dawn raid, and in relation to the very time-consuming internal investigations and compliance checks that usually follow on the inspection—not to mention the fact the operations of the business may be interrupted by the inspection.

[8] Wouter PJ Wils, *Efficiency and Justice in European Antitrust Enforcement* (Oxford, Hart Publishing, 2008) 419–20.

[9] Article 20 of Council Regulation (EC) No 1/2003 of 16 December 2002 on the implementation of the rules on competition laid down in Articles 81 and 82 of the Treaty [2003] OJ L1, 1–25.

[10] Speech made by Julian Joshua in 1995, available at: http://ec.europa.eu/competition/speeches/text/sp1995_044_en.html.

Add to this the fact that new technology has led the Commission to adjust its searches, making them even more intrusive. Today, information is usually being generated, stored and distributed by electronic means. This has forced competition authorities to revise their evidence searching methods and it is now standard procedure for them to make use of certain dedicated software and/or hardware, which allow them to copy, search and recover data. As the companies are bound by an obligation to cooperate, they may have to block email accounts, disconnect running computers from the network, remove and re-install hard drives from computers etc. Furthermore, if, at the end of the inspection, the Commission officials have not finished the selection of the relevant documents, they may decide to bring copies of hard drives back to Brussels for review.[11]

It is fair to assume that these practices show few similarities with the way in which dawn raids were performed only 20 years ago.

III. DAWN RAIDS FROM A FUNDAMENTAL RIGHTS PERSPECTIVE

The invasive character of a dawn raid coupled with the possibility of imposing severe sanctions may trigger a number of fundamental right concerns. Over the years, the Court of Justice of the European Union (hereinafter 'the CJEU' or 'the Court') has been given ample opportunity to determine where the line is to be drawn between the apparently diverging interests of efficient investigations and the protection of fundamental rights.

When challenging dawn raids, companies often rely on Articles 7 and 47 of the Charter and the corresponding Articles of the ECHR, that is, Articles 8 and 6.

Article 7 of the Charter establishes the right to privacy, whereas Article 47 addresses the right to an effective legal remedy and the right to the defence.

Common allegations made by companies challenging the commission's inspection decisions are, just to mention a few, that: (i) the scope of the inspection decision is too broad; (ii) the absence of a prior judicial authorisation in EU competition cases runs foul of both Articles 7 and 47 of the Charter; (iii) the measures taken by the inspectors are too intrusive; and (iv) companies are forced to incriminate themselves.

This chapter will only deal with the EU Courts' role in relation to dawn raids, without discussing the legality of any measures taken by the Commission during its inspections. The need (if any) for an ex ante review of inspection decisions will be addressed, as will the ex post control of inspection decisions and measures taken on their basis.

[11] See the Commission's Explanatory Note to an authorisation to conduct an inspection in execution of a Commission decision under Article 20(4) of Council Regulation No 1/2003, http://ec.europa.eu/competition/antitrust/legislation/explanatory_note.pdf.

IV. EX ANTE REVIEW OF INSPECTION DECISIONS

In some legal systems, such as those in Germany and Sweden, competition authorities may not carry out dawn raids without the prior approval by a court. This is not the case at the EU level.

The Commission's enforcement powers are laid down in Council Regulation 1/2003 (hereinafter 'the Regulation').[12] Article 20 empowers the Commission to conduct any inspections that are necessary for the fulfilment of its duties under the Regulation. The decision to carry out a dawn raid is made by the Commission itself.

Those critical of the EU system argue that an order where it is the investigating authority itself that decides whether it is appropriate and necessary to carry out an inspection runs foul of Article 8 ECHR and its corresponding Article 7 of the Charter establishing a right to privacy.

Article 7 of the Charter states:

> Everyone has the right to respect for his or her private and family life, home and communications.

The corresponding Article 8 ECHR reads:

> 1. Everyone has the right to respect for his private and family life, his home and his correspondence.
> 2. There shall be no interference by a public authority with the exercise of this right except such as is in accordance with the law and is necessary in a democratic society in the interests of national security, public safety or the economic well-being of the country, for the prevention of disorder or crime, for the protection of health or morals, or for the protection of the rights and freedoms of others

Reading these two provisions, one may get the impression that only natural persons are protected by the right to privacy, as the Articles contain express references to the notions of 'home' and 'family life'. However, the case law of the European Court of Human Rights (hereinafter ECtHR or 'the Strasbourg Court') establishes a broader scope of protection, also encompassing legal persons, albeit that the level of protection is not necessarily the same as for natural persons.[13]

A case from the ECtHR often cited by the critics in relation to ex ante control is *Société Colas Est*.[14]

[12] Council Regulation (EC) No 1/2003 of 16 December 2002 on the implementation of the rules on competition laid down in Articles 81 and 82 of the Treaty [2003] OJ L1, 1–25.

[13] See, eg, *Niemietz v Germany* Application No 13710/88, judgment of 16 December 1992; and *Société Colas Est and others v France* Application No 37971/97, judgment of 16 April 2002.

[14] *Colas Est* (n 13).

A. *Société Colas Est*

In this case, the French Competition Authority had conducted dawn raids at the premises of 56 companies. The dawn raids had been carried out under a statute that did not require any judicial authorisation.

During the raids, the inspectors seized various documents containing evidence of unlawful agreements relating to activities that did not appear in the list of activities concerned by the investigation. Further investigations were subsequently carried out on the basis of these documents. The companies were later found guilty of cartel participation by the Competition Authority, a decision which was upheld by the Paris Court of Appeal. However, the French Cour de Cassation quashed the decision and remitted the case to the Paris Court of Appeal.

At the retrial, the applicants contested the lawfulness of the searches and seizures carried out by the inspectors without any judicial authorisation, relying on Article 8 ECHR. This was done unsuccessfully as the Court of Appeal did not see any breach of Article 8 ECHR. The appeal to the Cour de Cassation was equally unsuccessful.[15]

This led the applicant companies to turn to Strasbourg. In their application to the Strasbourg Court, they contended that the raids were carried out without any supervision or restrictions and had infringed their right to respect for their home. They relied on Article 8 ECHR.

The Strasbourg Court observed that during the dawn raids, officials from the competition authority had inspected the applicant companies' head offices and branches in order to seize several thousand documents. It further observed that the French government had not disputed that there had been an interference with the applicants' right to privacy, although the government had argued that companies could not claim a right to privacy with as much force as an individual could in relation to his professional or business address.

The ECtHR established that there had been an interference with the applicants' right to privacy and then went on to assess whether such interference was acceptable under Article 8(2) ECHR.[16] It noted that the dawn raids were carried out simultaneously at the applicant companies' head offices and branches and that the inspectors entered these premises without judicial authorisation in order to obtain and seize numerous documents containing evidence of unlawful agreements.

It therefore appeared to the ECtHR that the operations and the manner in which they were executed constituted intrusions into the 'homes' of the applicant companies. It acknowledged that the Contracting States have a margin of appreciation in assessing the need for interference, but that such a margin goes hand in hand with European supervision. Furthermore, it

[15] ibid [21].
[16] ibid [42].

declared that the exceptions provided for in Article 8(2) should be interpreted narrowly.[17]

Here the ECtHR considered that although the scale of the operations, carried out in order to prevent the disappearance or concealment of evidence of anti-competitive practices, justified the impugned interference with the applicant companies' right to respect for their premises, the relevant legislation and practice should nevertheless afford adequate and effective safeguards against abuse.[18] The Court did not consider the safeguards surrounding the operations to be adequate.

The relevant authorities had very wide powers which, pursuant to the French law, gave them exclusive competence to determine the expediency, number, length and scale of the inspections. Moreover, the ECtHR noted that the inspections took place without any prior warrant being issued by a judge and without a senior police officer being present.

The French government had argued that the entitlement to interfere may be more far-reaching when a search is performed at the business premises of a legal person rather than at the home of an individual. Although acknowledging that this may be the case, the Strasbourg Court still considered that the operations could not be regarded as strictly proportionate to the legitimate aims pursued. In conclusion, there had been a violation of Article 8 ECHR.

The fact that the Strasbourg Court explicitly mentioned the lack of ex ante control and the absence of a senior police officer during the dawn raids could be taken to show that a system not requiring a prior judicial authorisation fails to meet the standards of the ECHR.

However, this may be reading a bit too much into this ruling. Indeed, the ECtHR did explicitly mention the lack of judicial authorisation. However, it may well be that it made an overall assessment and would have come to another conclusion had there been other safeguards available, such as the requirement of a court order to obtain a forced entry or an intense ex post review of the authorities' decisions.

In the case of *Bernh Larsen Holding*,[19] the Strasbourg Court explicitly acknowledged that other procedural safeguards may make up for the lack of prior judicial authorisation.

B. *Bernh Larsen Holding*

Bernh Larsen Holding concerns measures taken by the Norwegian tax authorities during a tax audit against Bernh Larsen Holding AS (BLH).

[17] ibid [47].

[18] ibid [48].

[19] *Bernh Larsen Holding AS and others v Norway* Application No 24117/08, judgment of 14 March 2013.

BLH shared its office space with two other companies, one of them Kver AS. Not only did the companies share their office space, they also used a common server for their respective information technology systems. Kver was the owner of the server and BLH rented server capacity.

In January 2003, the local tax authorities declared that BLH's accounts for 2001 would be audited. In March 2004, a meeting was held between the local tax office and BLH where the tax office demanded that BLH allow the auditors to make a mirror copy of the entire server. BLH refused to comply with this demand, arguing that it did not own the server and that it contained information belonging not only to BLH but also to other companies and persons. Following discussions, BLH and Kver finally agreed to hand over the previous months' backup copy of the server to the authority in a sealed envelope pending a decision on their complaint.

Having worked its way through the Norwegian system, BLH eventually turned to Strasbourg, claiming that there had been an infringement of Article 8 ECHR.

In its ruling, the Strasbourg Court explicitly acknowledged the fact that the search had not been preceded by a judicial warrant. Despite this, the Court was satisfied that:

> The interference with the applicant companies' rights to respect for correspondence and home which the contested section 4-10(1) order entailed was subject to important limitations and was accompanied by effective and adequate safeguards against abus[e].[20]

As for the nature of these procedural safeguards, the Court referred to the companies' right to complain, the fact that a copy of the backup tape was placed in a sealed envelope pending the outcome of the appeal, that the applicants were entitled to be present when the seal was broken and the files were reviewed, and that, once the files had been reviewed, they were deleted.[21]

The Court also noted the fact that the nature of the interference was not of the same seriousness and degree as is ordinarily the case for search and seizure carried out under criminal law.[22] In the case of BLH, the consequences of a tax subject's refusal to cooperate were exclusively administrative (discretionary tax assessment).[23] As the sanctions, both for failing to obey the Commission's inspection decisions and for participating in cartels, are severe, no direct parallel may be drawn between the EU system and the challenged Norwegian system.

Nevertheless, the Strasbourg Court's ruling in the *Bernh Larsen Holding* case definitely speaks in favour of an overall assessment rather than viewing a prior judicial authorisation as an absolute requirement.

[20] ibid [172].
[21] ibid [165]–[171].
[22] ibid [173].
[23] ibid [43] and [173].

In the recent case of *Delta Pekárny v Czech Republic*, the Strasbourg Court confirmed that other procedural safeguards may indeed make up for the lack of prior judicial review also when it comes to dawn raids in competition cases.

C. *Delta Pekárny*

In 2003, the Czech competition authority carried out a dawn raid at the premises of Delta Pekárny, a company within the Czech United Bakeries group. The dawn raid was not preceded by a court ruling as the Czech legislation did not require any ex ante control of dawn raid decisions. When the dawn raid was carried out, the inspectors presented Delta Pekárny with a simple authorisation (not a decision) from the competition authority indicating only that the company was suspected of infringing Article 3 § 1 of the Czech Competition Act through price fixing in the market for bakery products.[24] The authorisation contained a list of the names of the inspectors who would perform the dawn raid.[25]

During the course of the inspection, the representatives of the Czech Competition Authority soon faced difficulties. When the inspectors required to go through the mailboxes of a number of employees, some refused, while others left taking their computers with them, all claiming that the mailboxes contained personal correspondence that was out of reach for the Competition Authority. At the end of the inspection, one of the employees who had initially cooperated required the inspectors to return a number of documents that had previously been handed over to the inspectors.[26] It is fair to assume that the inspectors were not altogether satisfied with the dawn raid, and the Czech Competition Authority did later impose a CZK 300,000 fine (approximately €11,500) on Delta Pekárny for having obstructed the authority's search of the premises.

The dawn raid procedures were challenged by Delta Pekárny both in relation to the fine imposed for obstruction and during the subsequent cartel proceedings. According to Delta Pekárny, a system that did not require prior judicial authorisation by a court could not satisfy the requirements of Article 8 ECHR. The Czech courts took another view, declaring the system to meet the ECHR standard. Delta Pekárny turned to Strasbourg.

Without describing the applicable Czech legislation in detail, it should be noted that the fact that the dawn raid was not carried out on the basis of a decision, but rather on an authorisation, deprived Delta Pekárny of the right to an effective ex post judicial review of the inspection. In the case before

24 *Delta Pekárny v Czech Republic* Application No 97/11, judgment of 2 October 2014.
25 ibid [6].
26 ibid [10].

the Czech Administrative Supreme Court, the court had made an analysis based on Article 8 ECHR, but that analysis had only dealt with the powers of the inspectors once the decision to perform a dawn raid had been made. The court had not discussed the *necessity* of performing a dawn raid. Thus, the ex post judicial review had not involved an assessment of the motive behind the dawn raid or the facts or evidence that the competition authority relied upon when deciding to carry out an inspection at the premises of Delta Pekárny.[27]

The Strasbourg Court declared that, in the absence of an ex ante control and where the ex post control of the inspection did not entail an analysis of the necessity to carry out the inspection, the procedural safeguards were not considered adequate.[28]

It is clear from Delta Pekárny that the absence of an ex ante control of dawn raids is not in itself enough to strike down a system as contrary to Article 8 ECHR. Here, the Strasbourg Court looked at other procedural safeguards before declaring that the system was incompatible with the ECHR.

The Strasbourg Court thus considered that an overall assessment is required. This was also the view taken by the General Court in the *Deutsche Bahn* case, where it declared that there is no need for prior judicial authorisation provided that there are other effective safeguards in place.[29]

D. *Deutsche Bahn*

Following a number of dawn raids performed by the Commission in March and July 2011, Deutsche Bahn AG challenged the Commission's investigatory powers and inspection procedures. In a row of appeals, it opposed the Commission's decisions to carry out unannounced inspections at its premises in search of evidence of abuse of dominance.[30]

In support of its actions, the company relied on a number of pleas. According to Deutsche Bahn, the lack of prior judicial authorisation—and thereby also prior judicial review—constituted not only an infringement of the company's right to privacy (under Article 7 of the Charter), but also a breach of its right to an effective legal remedy (under Article 47 of the

[27] ibid [91].

[28] ibid [2]. The Court also stressed the fact that the Czech system did not have a system for destruction of any copies taken by the authorities. Here the ECtHR made explicit reference to the *BLH* case.

[29] Joined Cases T-289 and 290/11 and T-521/11 *Deutsche Bahn and others v Commission* EU:T:2013:404, judgment of the General Court of 6 September 2013 [66]–[78].

[30] See, eg, Joined Cases T-289 and 290/11 and T-521/11 *Deutsche Bahn and others v Commission* EU:T:2013:404, judgment of the General Court of 6 September 2013.

Charter). It also challenged the scope of the investigations, claiming that it was disproportionately wide and unspecific.

In September 2013, the General Court had its say in the matter, dismissing the applications on all grounds and fully confirming the legality of the Commission's inspection decisions. As for the requirement of a prior judicial authorisation, the General Court declared that this requirement was not absolute and that other procedural safeguards may compensate for the lack of ex ante control. It explicitly referred to the case law of the ECtHR, stating that an effective ex post control may compensate for the lack of an ex ante control.[31]

The General Court further identified five types of procedural safeguards, the first being the requirement on the part of the Commission to motivate its decision, the second the restrictions governing the inspectors during the dawn raid, the third being the fact that the Commission may not use any force during the inspection, the fourth concerning intervention by national authorities and the fifth and final being the possibility of subsequent judicial review.

The General Court regarded these safeguards to be protected in the EU system and as for the subsequent judicial review, it declared that the EU courts carry out a review in full of the inspection decisions and that the system thus complies with the Charter and the ECHR.

Deutsche Bahn appealed the General Court's ruling to the CJEU, and in February 2015 Advocate General Wahl delivered his Opinion.[32] He agreed with the General Court's findings. Referring to the ECtHR cases mentioned above, he reached the conclusion that the ECHR does not require prior judicial authorisation as long as there are other adequate procedural safeguards. As the inspection decision may be appealed to the CJEU and as the CJEU's review will not be limited to a strict legality review, he considered the EU standard to meet the ECHR standard. One interesting question raised by Advocate General Wahl is whether the Charter standard should *exceed* the ECHR standard in this area. Finding no element in either primary or secondary EU law pointing to such conclusion, he concluded that the General Court had not erred in law.[33]

Judging from the General Court's ruling and Advocate General Wahl's Opinion in *Deutsche Bahn*, there is thus no reason for concern. Is that really so?

[31] ibid [66].

[32] Opinion of AG Wahl in Case C-583/13P *Deutsche Bahn and others v European Commission* EU:C:2015:92.

[33] ibid [41] and [42].

V. THE INSPECTORS HAVE LEFT THE BUILDING: ANY CHANCE OF JUDICIAL REVIEW?

As discussed at the beginning of this chapter, dawn raids constitute a serious invasion of the integrity of targeted companies and their employees. As far as fundamental rights are concerned, it is apparent that this way of searching for evidence may interfere with a right to privacy, and companies have therefore been prone to invoke Article 8 ECHR or Article 7 of the Charter when receiving a visit from the competition authorities.

However, over the years, there is also another Article of the ECHR that has come to use in relation to dawn raids, and that is Article 6 and the right to a fair trial enshrined therein.

In the EU, the discussion is very heated at the moment. The reason for this is a line of judgments from both the ECtHR and the General Court dealing with the right to an ex post review of inspection decisions.

I will start by discussing the cases delivered by the Strasbourg Court and will then move on to a presentation of rulings from Luxembourg.

A. Dawn Raids and Judicial Review: The View of the Strasbourg Court

i. Ravon v France

It all began with a case that had nothing to do with competition law, the case of *Ravon v France*.[34] Instead of dealing with competition proceedings, this case—like so many other ECtHR cases that have been said to also apply to competition proceedings—concerned tax matters.

The French tax authorities suspected the two companies TMR International Consultant (TMR) and SCI Rue du Cherche-Midi 66 (SCI) of tax evasion. Both companies were controlled by Mr Ravon. In 2000, an investigation was launched against TMR and SCI.

During the course of this investigation, the tax authorities requested and received warrants to search the premises of the companies as well as the home of Mr Ravon. The inspections were carried out in July 2000 and documents were seized by the authorities.

Mr Ravon and his companies appealed against the inspection decisions before the 'Tribunaux de Grande Instance' of both Paris and Marseille. These two courts were also the courts that had ordered the inspections in the first place. The appeals were considered inadmissible as the courts were not empowered to review the measures taken by the tax authorities once the inspections had been effected.[35]

[34] *Ravon v France* Application No 18497/03, judgment of 21 February 2008.
[35] ibid [8]–[10].

The only route available to Mr Ravon and his companies was instead the option of a 'pourvoi de cassation' where the French Cour de Cassation may review a decision on points of law and procedure. No other judicial remedy was available to the defendants.

In the end, no criminal charges were brought against Mr Ravon or his companies, which in turn meant that it was not possible to obtain a review of the legality of the inspections. Mr Ravon and his companies argued before the ECtHR that they had been deprived of an effective judicial remedy to challenge the decisions authorising the inspections. The ECtHR ruled in favour of the applicants and concluded that the right of judicial access:

> [I]mplies with respect to premises searches, that the persons sought may obtain an effective judicial review, in fact and law, of the decision authorizing the search and, if any, of the measures taken on its basis; the remedy or remedies available must allow, in the event irregularities are uncovered, either to prevent the upcoming search or, in the event a search deemed unlawful has already taken place, to provide the relevant party with an appropriate remedy.

The court also stressed the fact that—contrary to what the government had argued—the requirement of a judicial authorisation does not compensate for the lack of an ex post review.[36] One reason for this is that, at the time of the ex ante review, the targeted company or person is not yet aware of the procedure and thus may not invoke its rights.

The ECtHR furthermore pointed to the facts that there was no obligation to inform the companies of their right to have the measures reviewed by the authorising court while the search was still conducted. Nor did the legislation allow for the companies or persons targeted to call for legal assistance or any other external contacts.

The French government had argued that there was a possibility to have an effective a posteriori review. However, the Strasbourg Court did not accept this argument, as such a review was dependent on a subsequent proceeding against the persons/companies in the underlying tax matter. In the case at hand, no criminal charges were brought against either Mr Ravon or his companies.

The ECtHR thus concluded that the applicants had not been entitled to a fair trial and an infringement of Article 6(1) ECHR was established.

Just a few months after the ruling in *Ravon*, the ECtHR received applications from three other French companies alleging that they had not been entitled to an effective review of inspections carried out at their premises. This time, the inspections had been carried out within the framework of competition cases.

[36] ibid [30].

ii. Primagaz

The French company Compagnie des gaz de pétrole primagaz (hereinafter 'Primagaz') was suspected of restrictive practices contrary to the French Commercial Code and Article 101 TFEU. In June 2005, the civil courts of Lille and Paris authorised the French Competition Authority to carry out a dawn raid at the premises of Primagaz. On 14 June 2005, the inspection was effected. Primagaz appealed the inspection decisions to the French Cour de Cassation, claiming that the decisions were contrary to Articles 6, 8 and 13 ECHR. Two years later, in November 2007, the Cour de Cassation dismissed the appeal.

Primagaz then turned to Strasbourg. Relying on the Strasbourg Court's ruling in *Ravon*, it argued that it had not been entitled to a fair trial as the only judicial remedy available was the 'pourvoi en cassation', where the Cour de Cassation may only review the legality of the decision or whether there are any procedural errors.

The French government argued that the system introduced in 2008, three years after the dawn raids were carried out, compensated for any former weaknesses in the legal system.

According to these new rules, it was now possible for companies that had appealed against an inspection decision to the Cour de Cassation prior to the new rules entered into force, and where the Cour de Cassation had dismissed such an appeal, to turn to the Court of Appeal with a new appeal. However, there was a catch. This possibility was only granted if the Competition Authority's investigation had been successful and resulted in an infringement decision. There was no possibility for a stand-alone action against the inspection decision or the measures taken on the basis of such a decision.

The government's line of argumentation was rejected by the Strasbourg Court, as it considered that in order for a company to have been ensured the right to a fair trial, this possibility should be guaranteed and thus not dependent on a decision in the underlying competition case, *and* offered within a reasonable period of time. As the Court put it:

> Or, la Cour rappelle qu'en plus d'un contrôle en fait et en droit de la régularité et du bien-fondé de la décision ayant prescrit la visite, le recours doit également fournir un redressement approprié, ce qui implique nécessairement la certitude, en pratique d'obtenir un contrôle juridictionnel effectif de la mesure litigieuse et ce, dans un délai raisonnable.[37]

Here, there was still no decision by the Competition Authority. As three years had passed since the dawn raid was carried out and the possibility of appeal was dependent on a future decision by the French Competition Authority, the Strasbourg Court established an infringement of Article 6(1) and the right to a fair trial.

[37] *Compagnie des Gaz de Pétrole Primagaz v France* Application No 29613/08, judgment of 21 December 2010 [28].

iii. Canal Plus

The French competition authority appears to have been active in 2005. Not only did it investigate the activities of Primagaz and its competitors, but in February 2005, it also decided to look into the activities of companies active in the media sector, and to pay a visit at the premises of Canal Plus and Sport+. The authority suspected them of engaging in restrictive practices and/or abusive conduct contrary to both French competition legislation and Articles 101 and 102 TFEU.

Three months later, the companies turned to the Tribunal de grande instance de Paris (which had authorised the inspections) and complained of the way in which the dawn raids had been carried out, claiming that the operations had failed to respect Articles 6, 8 and 13 ECHR. The aim was to have the report from the inspection annulled and some of the documents that had been seized returned. The companies' request was accepted in part.

However, the companies' joy over the partial success soon turned into disappointment as the French Competition Authority successfully appealed the decision to the Cour de Cassation. In its ruling the Cour de Cassation declared that the system in place did indeed respect the requirements of the ECHR.

Having exhausted all national remedies, Canal Plus and Sport+ turned to Strasbourg. In their request to the Strasbourg Court, they claimed that the French system did not allow them the right to a fair trial as the only possibility of appealing an inspection decision was through a 'pourvoi en cassation' where the review is strictly limited to procedural irregularities and points of law.

Ruling upon the matter, the Strasbourg Court commenced by reiterating its statement in *Ravon* that when it comes to searches, there must be a possibility of judicial review (covering points of law as well as fact) both of the decision authorising the search *and* of the measures taken on its basis.[38]

Using this as ground for its analysis, it then recognised that the only option available to the companies was the 'pourvoi en cassation' under which the parties could only contest the legality of the inspection decision, but would not be allowed an assessment of the underlying facts leading up to such a decision. According to the Strasbourg Court, again referring to *Ravon*, such a review could not be deemed to meet the standards of Article 6(1) ECHR.[39]

The Strasbourg Court then addressed the new rules in place which extended the possibilities of review. However, as it had concluded in *Primagaz*, these amendments were not considered sufficient as the two companies would only be able to request a review of the inspection decision if there

[38] *Société Canal Plus and others v France*, judgment of 21 December 2010 [36].
[39] ibid [36].

was an infringement decision in the underlying competition case. There was no possibility for a stand-alone action.[40]

Furthermore, as in *Primagaz*, the Strasbourg Court stressed that the possibility of review should not only be certain, but should also be timely. Just as in *Primagaz*, the companies were still awaiting the Competition Authority's final decision in the competition case. Like in *Primagaz*, the Court established an infringement of Article 6(1) ECHR.[41]

B. Dawn Raids and Judicial Review: The View of the EU Courts

The question of judicial review in relation to dawn raids has not only been a matter for the Strasbourg Court recently; the General Court has also had its say in the matter. In two judgments delivered in October 2011, it gave its view on the right to judicial review.

i. Nexans

The two companies Nexans SA and its wholly owned subsidiary Nexans France SAS are both active in the electric cable sector. The Commission suspected them of cartel activities and, in January 2009, an unannounced inspection was carried out at the premises of Nexans France. On the first day of the inspection, the inspectors declared that they wished to examine the documents and computers of three of the company's employees, Mr A, Mr B and Mr C.

Mr C turned out to be away on a business trip and had his computer with him. It was not until the third day of the inspection that the computer was brought to the office by a colleague of Mr C. Going through the computer, the inspectors recovered a number of files that had been deleted since the start of the investigation.

The inspectors decided to copy several sets of emails found in Mr A's and Mr C's computers onto data recording devices (DRDs), sealed them and had the envelopes signed by a representative of Nexans France. The envelopes were brought back to Brussels. The inspectors later also took an image-copy of the hard drive of Mr C's computer and brought it back to Brussels once the inspection was over—this despite the company explicitly asking the inspectors to go through the hard drive at its premises. The Commission officials also took formal note of the fact that Nexans France disputed the legitimacy of the procedure.

In April 2009, the companies brought action against the Commission's measures, requesting the General Court to annul the inspection decision as

[40] ibid [40].
[41] ibid [45].

well as the decision to remove copies of certain computer files and of the hard drive of Mr C's computer for review in Brussels.

Addressing the claim made by the applicants to annul the decision to bring copies of computer files to Brussels, the General Court declared that acts against which an action for annulment may be brought under Article 263 TFEU are those which produce binding legal effects capable of affecting the applicant's interests by bringing about a distinct change in his legal position.[42]

As for the copying of the computer files and the hard drive of Mr C for review in Brussels, the General Court did not regard these measures as a distinct, challengeable decision; instead, it considered theses measures as flowing from the inspection decision. The contested acts were implementing measures of an intermediate nature, designed solely to pave the way for the final decision. As the Court put it:

> It is pursuant to the decision ordering the inspection rather than pursuant to another distinct act adopted during the inspection, that those undertakings are required to allow the Commission to copy the documents at issue.[43]

The General Court also addressed the issue of documents covered by legal professional privilege (LPP), for which there is a separate procedure and where a decision by the Commission to reject a request for protection of a certain document may be challenged in a stand-alone action. However, it noted that in the present case, the applicants were not taking issue with the Commission for consulting or copying certain files, but rather for having examined them at its own premises in Brussels.

In view of the foregoing, the General Court concluded that the contested acts could not be regarded as challengeable measures and that the legality of those acts could only be examined in the context of an action challenging the final decision adopted by the Commission under Article 81(1) EC (now Article 101(1) TFEU).

Thus, what the General Court said was that in order to challenge the inspectors' decision to bring the DRDs and the copy of the hard drive back to Brussels, you will have to wait for the final decision in the underlying competition case. However, not only will you have to wait for the decision, you will also have to hope that the Commission imposes a fine so that you can challenge the measure.

Let us reiterate what the Strasbourg Court stated in *Primagaz*, where the possibilities for review were very similar to those in this case, ie, that an appeal against the inspection decision and the measures taken during such

[42] Case T-135/09 *Nexans France SAS and Nexans SA v European Commission* EU:T:2012:596 [115].

[43] ibid [121].

inspection is only possible if there is a subsequent infringement decision in the competition case. There the Strasbourg Court stated:

> Or, la Cour rappelle qu'en plus d'un contrôle en fait et en droit de la régularité et du bien-fondé de la décision ayant prescrit la visite, le recours doit également fournir un redressement approprié, ce qui implique nécessairement la certitude, en pratique d'obtenir un contrôle juridictionnel effectif de la mesure litigieuse et ce, dans un délai raisonnable.[44]

This short passage of the Strasbourg Court's ruling brings to the fore the two weaknesses in the EU system, and its application after the General Court's rulings in *Nexans* and *Prysmian*. First of all, the Strasbourg Court declared, the companies must be *guaranteed* an effective review of the measure. Second, they shall be guaranteed such a review *within a reasonable time*.

The Strasbourg Court explicitly pointed to the fact that: (i) access to legal review was uncertain as it depended not only on a decision in the competition case but also on an appeal against such; and (ii) any possibility to obtain a judicial review would by necessity be delayed by several years. In *Primagaz*, the inspections were carried out in 2005, but in 2008, there was still no decision by the French Competition Authority.

Given that the Commission's cartel investigations normally take around four years from start to finish,[45] anyone seeking to challenge the Commission's measures during a dawn raid will have to wait a considerable time, not even knowing if it will ever be able to do so. Surely, this cannot be in line with the Strasbourg Court's case law.

There is, however, one important difference between the rulings of the Strasbourg Court in *Primagaz* and *Canal Plus* as compared to the General Court's rulings in *Nexans* and *Prysmian*.[46] In the cases before the Strasbourg Court, the parties challenged the national court's decision to allow the inspection, whereas in the EU cases, it was the measures taken during the dawn raid that required review.

It could therefore be argued that the ECtHR cases are not directly applicable to the EU cases as they deal with two different parts of the process. However, in the *Ravon* case, the Strasbourg Court not only gave its view on the possibility of obtaining a review of the decision to allow for an inspection, but also as regards the measures taken by the authority during the course of such inspection. There, the Court established:

> Selon la Cour, cela implique en matière de visite domiciliaire que les personnes concernées puissent obtenir un contrôle juridictionnel effectif, en fait comme en

[44] *Compagnie des Gaz de Pétrole Primagaz v France* Application No 29613/08, judgment of 21 December 2010 [28].

[45] K Hüschelrach, U Laitenberger and F Smuda, 'Cartel Enforcement in the European Union: Determinants of the Duration of Investigations', Centrum für Europäische Wirtschaftsforschung GmbH, Discussion Paper No 12-071, 9. Available at: http://ssrn.com/abstract=2179037.

[46] Case T-140/09 *Prysmian and Prysmian Cavi e Sistemi Energia v European Commission* EU:T:2012:597.

> droit, de la régularité de la décision prescrivant la visite *ainsi que, le cas échéant, des mesures prises sur son fondemen[t]*. (Emphasis added)[47]

This statement was also reiterated by the Strasbourg Court in *Canal Plus*.[48] The right to a timely, certain and effective judicial review would thus in my view also extend to measures taken during the dawn raid. In fact, the case of *Bernh Larsen Holding* clearly speaks in favour of such a conclusion, as it dealt with intermediate measures, and intermediate measures only. There, the applicant had challenged the Norwegian tax authorities' powers to make copy images of its server. What the Strasbourg Court was requested to rule upon was the procedural safeguards surrounding such measures, not the inspection/tax audit as such.

Last but not least, it should be noted that in its ruling, the General Court referred to the possibility of bringing an action against the Commission for non-contractual liability under Article 340 TFEU. To some extent, this may indeed be a viable route. However, the damage sustained in these situations is often of a non-pecuniary nature and an action for damages would then not make good the harm sustained. In the case of *Akzo Nobel* concerning the Commission's review of certain privileged documents, the General Court decided to grant interim measures, something which can only be done if the measure in question threatens to cause *serious and irreparable* damage. According to the CJEU, damage is not irreparable if it can ultimately be subject to financial compensation.

VI. CONCLUDING REMARKS

Keeping a balance between efficient investigatory measures and fundamental rights protection is certainly not an easy task. A regime where efficiency is allowed to prevail will by necessity infringe fundamental rights, such as the right to privacy and the right to a fair trial. On the other hand, in a system where fundamental rights are considered absolute and allowed to prevail at all times, there will be no effective competition law enforcement.

However, a slight imbalance in the scales may also have undesired consequences. In order for the Commission's inspections to be truly effective and efficient, they must run smoothly. If the Commission officials are denied access to a company's premises, this may allow the company to destroy or hide evidence (although the use of so-called forensic IT has, if not eliminated, at least minimised this risk).

This has led the Commission to adopt an aggressive approach against any perceived obstruction. In the 2006 Bitumen cartel decision, Koninklijke

[47] *Ravon v France* Application No 18497/03, judgment of 21 February 2008 [28].
[48] *Société Canal Plus and others v France*, judgment of 21 December 2010 [36].

Wegenbouw Stevin (KWS) had its cartel fine increased by 10 per cent for attempts to obstruct the Commission's investigation. What the company had done was to delay the dawn raid by 47 minutes in order to wait for external counsel and, once the external counsels had arrived, it had refused access to one of the director's offices, arguing that the director in question was not responsible for any activities relating to the subject matter of the inspection decision. The General Court later upheld the Commission's decision.[49]

A system where, as in the EU, it is the competition authority that decides on dawn raids and adopts an aggressive approach against any perceived obstruction requires adequate procedural safeguards. It is clear from the case law of the Strasbourg Court that a dawn raid must be surrounded by such safeguards.

There is no absolute requirement of prior judicial authorisation; instead, there will be an overall assessment of the safeguards available in the case at hand. This is in order to determine whether other the safeguards available make up for the absence of a prior judicial authorisation. Here, the Strasbourg Court has relied on a number of different factors, including the possibility to complain, the (limited) scope of the inspection, the presence of a police officer, whether the inspectors have been specially trained for the inspection, the possibility of having a legal counsel present etc.

As for the requirement of an ex-post review, this requirement is absolute. The Strasbourg Court has on numerous occasions declared that a company must have an absolute right to a review—in law and facts—of the inspection decision as well as of *the measures taken on its basis*. Not only is this right absolute, a review must also be carried out within a reasonable time.

In the cases of both *Canal Plus* and *Primagaz*, three years had passed since the dawn raids were performed and there were still no decisions by the French Competition Authority that could be challenged. The Strasbourg Court considered this timeframe to be too long. The companies had not been granted a right to review within a reasonable time and their right to a fair trial had therefore been infringed. The average length of the Commission's cartel investigations is four years from start to finish.[50]

It is clear that the EU legal system does not meet the standards of the ECHR. There is no absolute right under EU law to get a timely review of measures taken by the authority during an inspection.

The fact that there is no effective ex post control of inspections under EU law also affects the assessment of the legitimacy of a system lacking an ex ante control. The Strasbourg Court may accept a system where the competition authority itself issues the inspection decisions provided that there are

[49] Case T-357/06 *Koninklijke Wegenbouw Stevin BV v European Commission* EU:T:2012:488 [232].

[50] Hüschelrach, Laitenberger and Smuda (n 45) 9.

other procedural safeguards that make up for such 'deficiency'. However, if there is neither an ex ante control nor an effective ex post control of the authority's actions, then it is evident that the system does not meet the requirements of the ECHR.

Let us also recall that under Article 52(3) of the Charter, the ECHR standard should be a *minimum* standard in the EU. This is something which is actually acknowledged by Advocate Generla Wahl in *Deutsche Bahn*, where he analysed the case law from the ECtHR and discussed whether Article 7 of the Charter should impose a higher standard of protection than that afforded under Article 8 ECHR.

That said, the system in place today does not even meet the minimum standard, and a revision is required in order for the system to meet the Charter standard. If there is both an effective ex ante and ex post control in place, there is also more room for the Commission and the national authorities to legitimately require full cooperation during the course of the inspection and thereby ensure a smooth operation.

15

The Charter and the EU State Aid Procedure

JOHN TEMPLE LANG*

I. INTRODUCTION

THE PROCEDURE OF the European Commission in state aid cases has traditionally been regarded as a procedure between the Commission and the Member State concerned. Other Member States, beneficiaries and potential beneficiaries of the aid, and competitors of the beneficiaries have not been regarded as parties. It is suggested here that this situation is contrary to the Charter of Fundamental Rights.

II. STATE AID PROCEDURE: AN OUTLINE

State aid procedure is based on two Regulations: Regulation 659/1999 and Regulation 734/2013.[1] In essence, the system is based on notification by the Member State of new aid measures. Aid measures may be general, applicable to a number of companies or specific, benefiting only identified companies. The Commission carries out a preliminary examination. If the Commission concludes that there are doubts about the compatibility of the aid with EU law, it begins the formal investigation procedure. The published decision to start this procedure explains the facts and the doubts,

* The author has made a complaint to the European Ombudsman about the Commission's procedure and this complaint is being investigated.

[1] The Commission published the State Aid Manual of Procedures in 2013. See L Ortiz Blanco, *EU Competition Procedure*, 3rd edn (Oxford, Oxford University Press, 2013) chs 21–27: K Bacon, *European Union Law of State Aid*, 2nd edn (Oxford, Oxford University Press, 2013): C Quigley, *EU State Law and Policy*, 2nd edn (Oxford, Hart Publishing, 2009) chs 16–17; L Hancher, T Ottervanger and PJ Slot, *EU State Aids*, 4th edn (London, Sweet & Maxwell, 2012) 17–23 and chs 25–27; M Schütte, 'Procedural Aspects of EU State Aid Law and Practice' in E Szyszczak (ed), *Research Handbook on European State Aid Law* (Cheltenham, Edward Elgar, 2011) 336–53.

and calls on the Member State *'and upon other interested parties'* to submit comments.[2] Interested parties include any undertaking whose interests might be affected by the granting of aid, in particular the beneficiary and competing undertakings (this might presumably also include suppliers, customers and technology licensors or licensees of the beneficiaries or their competitors). The Commission may request any other Member State or any undertaking or association of undertakings to provide *'all market information necessary'*, but only if the formal investigations are ineffective and only if the Member State agrees to beneficiaries being asked for information. A new aid may not be put into effect until the Commission has authorised it, or is considered to have authorised it after two months from notification.[3] New aid that is given without authorisation is repayable. Aid that is not 'new' is not repayable, but may be phased out. There is provision in the Regulations for complaints about alleged state aid. Companies that do not give the information required by the Commission may be fined, as under Regulation 1/2003.

III. FEATURES OF THE STATE AID PROCEDURE UNDER THE REGULATIONS: THE POSITION OF BENEFICIARIES AND COMPETITORS

'Interested parties' (any company whose interests might be affected by the grant of aid, in particular the beneficiary and competitors) have a right to be informed only by the decision opening the formal procedure and to know what the Commission has finally decided. The Regulations do not give interested parties any right to know what steps are being taken or what information is being obtained by the Commission or any right to comment, except on the decision to open the procedure. In the preliminary examination stage, interested parties have no rights at all, in spite of the fact that the Commission often imposes stringent conditions on the Member State, and thus indirectly on the beneficiaries, during a preliminary examination. As a result, interested parties have no right to get the information that they need to defend their interests while the procedure is going on, despite the fact that it may continue for months.

An aspect of the fact that interested parties have no statutory right to be kept informed is that the Commission regards itself as free to receive information or, under Regulation 734/2013, to seek information from private parties, but apparently does not consider that it has any legal obligations to

[2] Bacon (n 1) 442 says: '*The Member State does not … have to make its notification known to interested parties: this is the task of the Commission where it decides to open the formal investigation procedure.*'

[3] Case 120/73 *Lorenz v Germany* [1973] ECR 1471.

do so in an impartial and even-handed way.[4] Therefore, it may, and often apparently does, look for information from any party that seems likely to confirm views that have been provisionally reached by the Commission officials, without recognising any obligation to give parties with potentially opposing views a corresponding opportunity to provide information or to make comments.

These flaws in the procedure are not cured or corrected by the fact that some of the interested parties may from time to time obtain information informally, either from the Commission or from the Member State primarily involved, which may enable the interested parties to make useful comments. This happens irregularly, and interested parties cannot rely on being given such opportunities or information. They certainly cannot rely on being given, at the right time, all the information that they need or that it would be useful for them to have to defend their interests. Not only does

[4] See, however, Case T-198/01 R *Technische Glaswerke Ilmenau* [2002] ECR II-2153 [85]: '*The Commission ... may have, at least prima facie, an obligation to communicate to the recipient [of the aid] observations which it has expressly requested from a competitor.*' It is not clear whether this leads to a general duty for the Commission to treat beneficiaries and complainants impartially and thus to provide them equally with information, but that is not the Commission's practice. Beneficiaries, competitors and complainants do not have a right of access to documents: Case C-139/07 P *Technische Glaswerke Ilmenau* [2010] ECR I-5889 [61]. See Hancher, Ottervanger and Slot (n 1) 953, 984–86. But that case concerned the situation before the Charter came into force and now needs to be reconsidered for that reason. The Charter was apparently not referred to, and the company was claiming the general right of any member of the public under the freedom of information Regulation 1049/2001 rather than the right of a party to an '*effective remedy*' when its rights are in question. The Court at [61] referred to '*the existence of a general presumption that disclosure of documents on the administrative file in principle undermines protection of the objectives of investigation activities*'. However, it added that interested parties may demonstrate that a given document, disclosure of which has been requested, is not covered by that presumption or that there is a higher public interest justifying disclosure under Art 4(3) of reg 1049/2001. This '*general presumption*' seems to be little more than the Commission's convenience. In any case, it is normally not possible for a company to request '*a given document*' if it does not know what documents are on the file, and it can hardly show that a document that it has not seen is not covered by the presumption. So the exception envisaged by the Court cannot be enough to satisfy the requirements of the Charter. Bacon (n 1) 448 summarises the practice clearly: '*Third parties do not enjoy the same rights as member States in the preliminary review procedure. Rather, the right of a complainant has thus been described as the more limited right to be "associated" with the preliminary review procedure "in an adequate manner taking into account the circumstances of the case at issue". The same is true of a beneficiary, whose right is likewise only to be involved in the administrative procedure "to the extent appropriate" in the third parties as part of its duty of sound administration. But it is not under any obligation in general to give third parties an opportunity to state their views, or to conduct an exchange of views and arguments. Similarly, while in some cases the Commission might send a complainant the comments submitted by the Member State concerned, it is not bound to do so by any principle of "transparency". Nor is it, in negotiating appropriate measures in respect of existing aid, required to discuss with a complainant the appropriateness and scope of proposed commitments by the Member State. Greater protection is given, however, where following a complaint of unlawful or misused aid the Commission intends to close the case without a decision.*' In short, the Commission behaves as if it has complete discretion, with no guiding principles and no safeguards for companies' rights.

the Commission regard itself as free arbitrarily to inform some interested parties and not others, but the Member State (which apparently has no legal duty of impartiality) may choose to inform some companies and not others, depending on its view of the result that it wishes to achieve or the interests that it wishes to favour. Unofficial and informal means of correcting serious defects, inconsistently applied, are not enough to legitimate the procedure.

Interested parties cannot even rely on being given an opportunity to know about or to comment on any conditions or compensatory measures that the Commission is considering imposing, or any other modification or addition that the Commission has told the Member State to make (for example, a beneficiary may be prohibited from increasing its capacity or charging prices below those of its competitors). Nor are interested parties given any opportunity to comment or to defend their interests when the Commission intends to adopt a decision declaring the aid to be incompatible with the common market, except in the decision opening the procedure. *The Netherlands v Commission*[5] suggests that beneficiaries should be entitled to rely on the principle that any company against which an unfavourable decision may be taken must have a chance to defend its interests before the decision is adopted, but that does not seem to be the practice. A beneficiary or potential beneficiary has apparently no right to notify the Commission in order to obtain a ruling as to the lawfulness of the supposed aid.[6]

IV. NEW LIMITS ON THE COMMISSION'S POWER TO OBTAIN INFORMATION

Regulation 734/2013 provides that the Commission may *'request'* information only in a formal investigation procedure and if that procedure has been identified as being *'ineffective'*, apparently because the information provided by the Member State concerned is *'not sufficient'*. Even more surprisingly, the Commission may request information from beneficiaries only if the Member State concerned agrees to the request. The Member State has no duty to give reasons if it refuses, and a refusal could be challenged, if it could be challenged at all, only under national law.

[5] Cases C-48/90 and 66/90 *The Netherlands v Commission* [1992] ECR I-565 [50]–[51].

[6] If a supposed state aid has been notified to the Commission, the intended recipient may have a right to bring proceedings under Art 265 TFEU against the Commission for failure to decide whether the aid is lawful. Article 265 envisages a duty to adopt a decision addressed to the party claiming failure to act, and the Commission's decision is formally addressed to the Member State. However, if the recipient can show that it would be directly and individually concerned by the decision, it can bring proceedings for failure to act: Case C-68/95 *T Port* [1996] ECR I-6065 [59]; Case T-95/96 *GesTevisión Telecinco* [1998] ECR II-3407 [58]; Cases T-79/96 and others, *Camar and Tico* [2002] ECR II-2139 [72]–[84]; Case T-395/04 *Air One* [2006] ECR II-1343 [25].

These limitations seem impossible to justify, in particular because the companies usually have more relevant information than the Member State. They would enable the Member State concerned to prevent the beneficiary from giving the Commission information if it thought that the information might lead the Commission to question the need for the aid or to question the information given by it. These provisions would also enable the Member State to prevent the beneficiary from giving information that would justify the aid if the Member State's real objective were to have the aid prohibited or limited by the Commission. In short, in all cases in which there is a disagreement or a conflict of interest between the Member State aid and the beneficiary or beneficiaries, the Member State is able to control the information provided to the Commission, even when the Commission considers that the information is needed. This seems to be incompatible with the duties of cooperation of Member States under Article 4(3) of the Treaty on European Union (TEU) and appears to be illegal for that reason. It must always be wrong to give an interested party the absolute right to suppress evidence.[7]

V. EU CASE LAW ON PROCEDURAL ISSUES AND ITS LIMITATIONS

The minimal rights given by the Regulations are slightly modified by the case law of the EU courts, and the practice of the Commission in some cases is better than the bare terms of the Regulations suggest.[8] For example, it is apparently the practice to give competitors which object to a state aid an opportunity to comment before concluding, in a preliminary examination, that the measure is lawful. But the Commission is not obliged to examine objections that a complainant would certainly have made.[9]

If the Commission authorises an aid without opening a formal procedure or states that an aid is a permissible existing aid, interested parties may challenge the authorization in accordance with the *Cook* and *Matra* judgments.[10] The Commission must not reveal confidential information about companies that may be involved in the procedure, as interested parties or otherwise. The rights of interested parties to be involved in the administrative procedure depend on the circumstances of the case, the General Court said in the *NOS* case,[11] but this is so vague that it seems to be of little practical

[7] Case C-536/11 *Bundeswettbewerbsbehörde v Donau Chemie* [2013] ECR I-366 [32], [35], [38], [39].

[8] The Commission has adopted a number of Notices as guidelines to its practice. Although the Commission has sometimes argued that it is not bound to respect these Notices, the EU courts have always held that it must. See generally the *State Aid Manual of Procedure* (n 1).

[9] Case C-367/95 P *Sytraval v Commission* [1998] ECR I-1719 [60]–[61].

[10] Case C-198/91 *Cook* [1993] ECR I-2487; Case C-225/91 *Matra* [1993] ECR I-3203; Case E-1/13 *Míla v EFTA Surveillance Authority* [2014] EFTA Court Report.

[11] Joined Cases T-231/06 and T-237/06 *The Netherlands and Nederlandse omroep Stichting* [2010] ECR II-5993 [36]: See Quigley (n 1) 408–10.

importance, although involvement must be *'in an adequate manner'* (*Athinaki* judgments).[12] It has been suggested (in an Order in Case T-366/13 *France v Commission*, 29 August 2013) that the Commission's order to the Member State for repayment of aid does not have a direct *legal* effect on the beneficiary, which seems a very theoretical view.

The overriding principle seems to be that stated in the 2013 Regulation, which states that 'the provision of information by the beneficiary ... does not constitute a legal basis for bilateral negotiations between the Commission and the beneficiary'. (However, the rights of the defence are not the same as 'negotiations'.) This principle is not significantly affected by the fact that the Commission sometimes sends interested parties and the Member State concerned a draft description of the essential facts in order to confirm that it has correctly understood them. These descriptions are not draft decisions and are not intended to give the recipients an opportunity to make legal arguments.

VI. CASE LAW OF THE EUROPEAN COURT OF HUMAN RIGHTS

Because there is so much case law of the European Court of Human Rights on Article 6 of the Convention, which corresponds to Article 47 of the Charter, it is useful to refer to the judgments of the Strasbourg Court. This Court has said that 'the right to a fair trial holds so prominent a place in a democratic society that there can be no justification for interpreting Article 6(1) of the Convention restrictively'.[13]

One of the principles used by the Strasbourg Court is that of 'equality of arms'. This principle has also been recognised and accepted by the Court of Justice.[14] In essence, the principle means that in litigation, one party, normally in practice a public authority, should not be allowed to take advantage of the fact that it has a large amount of evidence that is not available to the other party and of which it could take advantage by selectively disclosing only evidence that supported its case. It has been said that the principle 'requires each party to be given a reasonable opportunity to present his case under conditions that do not place him at a substantial disadvantage vis-à-vis his opponent'.[15] Plainly, this requirement is not fulfilled when the companies have no access to the Commission's file.

[12] Cases C-521/06 P *Athinaki Techniki* [2008] ECR I-5829 and C-362/09 P *Athinaki Techniki* [2010] ECR I-13275.

[13] *Perez v France*, 2004 I, 40 EHRR 909 para 64 GC.

[14] See Ortiz Blanco (n 1) 21–23; Case C-199/11, *Otis and others* [2012] ECR I-6841. Joined Cases C-514/07 P and others, *Sweden and API* [2010] ECR I-8533 [88].

[15] *Neumeister v Austria*, A 8 (1968) 1 EHRR 91.

Another principle found in the Strasbourg case law is the right to an adversarial trial, meaning the opportunity for the parties to have knowledge of and comment on all evidence adduced or observations filed with a view to influencing the decision of the tribunal.[16] This principle apparently differs from the principle of equality of arms because it requires access to be given to all relevant material, whether the other party has access to it or not.

Both of these principles suggest that the state aid procedure is open to serious criticism under the Convention, which would mean that the same criticisms could also be made under the Charter because it must be interpreted so as to give at least as much protection for fundamental rights as is given by the Convention.

VII. COMPARISON WITH EU ANTI-SUBSIDY PROCEDURES

The objectionable nature of these features can be easily illustrated by comparing the procedure for considering state aid given by EU Member States with the procedure of the Commission for considering state aid or the equivalent given by non-EU states in anti-subsidy proceedings under Regulation 597/2009. Although the state aid procedure has been in operation since the Community Treaties came into force in 1958, the rights given to interested parties are much less, and much less clearly established, than the long-standing rights of interested parties in anti-subsidy and countervailing duty cases (astonishingly, Regulation 659/1999 was the first ever Regulation on state aid procedure). The differences are striking.[17]

In state aid cases, interested parties have no right to be informed that the Commission is investigating the supposed aid during the preliminary examination phase, although there is no time limit for the duration of that phase and no limit on what may be done during it. Interested parties have not even got a right to know whether a complaint has been made or whether the aid has been notified. In anti-subsidy cases, the Commission publishes a notice of initiation of the procedure.

In state aid cases, interested parties have no right to submit comments in the preliminary phase (and if they wished to submit comments, they would have no right to know what to comment on). In anti-subsidy cases, interested parties may submit comments as soon as the investigation has been announced. In state aid cases, they have no right to see the Commission's file, but in anti-subsidy cases, there is a right to see the file.

[16] *Vermuelen v Belgium* (1996) 1: 32 EHRR 313 para. 33GC: *Barberà messegué and Jabardo v Spain* (1988) 11 EHRR 360 [78].

[17] The first EC Regulation on anti-dumping and countervailing duties was Regulation 459/68. This Regulation has been repeatedly revised since then.

In state aid cases, interested parties have no right to be informed of the essential facts before a decision is adopted, even if the decision will clearly be contrary to their interests, and no right to be heard. (This, one would have thought, is contrary to the principle of the rights of the defence, established by the Court of Justice long ago in the *Transocean Marine Paint Association* judgment.)[18] In anti-subsidy procedures, interested parties have a right to be informed before a decision is adopted and there is a right to be heard.

There is no Hearing Officer in state aid cases, while there is a Hearing Officer in anti-subsidy procedures (and of course in other competition cases). In state aid cases, companies can now be fined for failing to provide information demanded by the Commission under Regulation 734/2013, but in anti-subsidy cases, the only sanction for failure to provided information requested is that the Commission will make use of whatever facts are available to it, even if they are known to be incomplete.

Another difference concerns the possible outcomes in the two types of cases. In anti-subsidy cases, the only foreseeable formal outcome is either a favourable decision or a countervailing duty, and the interested parties know this clearly from the beginning. In a state aid case, the Commission may impose the repayment of a large amount of aid or may impose a wide variety of different conditions, which might or might not be appropriate or proportional and on which both beneficiaries and their competitors may need to be heard in order to see if the conditions are sufficient or justified.

These procedural differences are even more striking when the consequences of adverse decisions are compared. In state aid cases, the full amount of any unlawful new aid (not merely the net economic benefit, which might be much less) is usually considered to be repayable, or the potential beneficiary may be unable to obtain any aid, whatever the consequences may be for the survival of the company. If conditions or restructuring have been imposed by the Commission, the conditions may offset or cancel out much of the benefit that the beneficiary expected to obtain. In the case of anti-subsidy duties, the only effect of an adverse decision is that duties will be imposed on imports that are designed to cancel or offset the effect of the subsidy, or to prevent the injury to the EU industry.

The procedure in anti-subsidy cases proves that there can be a satisfactory procedure on the basis of disclosure of the Commission's file. There is no reason why there could not be a similar procedure in state aid cases.

[18] Case 17/74 *Transocean Marine Paint Association v Commission* [1974] ECR 1063. In general, if a decision is of direct and individual concern to a private party under Art 265, it has a right to defend its interests before the decision is adopted: see *The Netherlands v Commission* (n 5) [50]–[51].

VIII. THE CHARTER OF FUNDAMENTAL RIGHTS

Article 47 of the Charter, which is headed 'Right to an effective remedy and to a fair trial', reads in part:

> Everyone whose rights and freedoms guaranteed by the law of the Union are violated has the right to an effective remedy before a tribunal in compliance with the conditions laid down in this Article. Everyone is entitled to a fair and public hearing within a reasonable time by an independent and impartial tribunal previously established by law.

The question arises whether, in the light of the features of the state aid procedure, beneficiaries and other interested parties have an 'effective remedy' and a 'fair hearing' if the Commission adopts decisions that are contrary to their interests.

IX. WHEN IS THERE A 'RIGHT' TO STATE AID?

The first question concerns the circumstances in which a company has a 'right' to a state aid. If the state aid measure merely gives the state authority a discretion as to whether to grant aid, there would presumably be no 'right' to the aid until there is a Member State decision to grant the aid to a given beneficiary. Until then, the companies concerned would be merely potential beneficiaries. However, it seems reasonable to say that if the Member State has enacted measures allowing aid to be given, potential beneficiaries have a right to have the lawfulness of the aid determined by the Commission so that they can apply for the aid if and when it has been determined to be lawful. Correspondingly, competitors of the potential beneficiaries have a right to have the lawfulness of the aid determined so that they can be protected against the consequences of the aid if in fact it is unlawful. The provisional nature of the interests of interested parties at a stage before the potential beneficiaries are identified or selected does not seem to prevent their interests being regarded as *'rights'* within the meaning of Article 47. It is submitted that they would certainly be *'civil rights and obligations'* under Article 6 of the European Convention on Human Rights.

If the state aid were given by way of tax exemption or relief, there would be no doubt that the companies would have a *'right'* to benefit from the exemption if the tax measure were a permissible state aid.

X. IS THERE AN 'EFFECTIVE REMEDY' FOR BENEFICIARIES OR COMPETITORS?

The second question is whether the rights of at least some interested parties to challenge the Commission's final decision in the General Court are sufficient to provide a *'fair trial'* and an *'effective'* remedy. The decision must give reasons for the conclusion reached, and it might be said that the defects in the procedure leading up to the decision are no longer relevant once the decision has been adopted. But this view does not stand up to examination. Whatever reasons may be given in a decision, if it has been adopted in violation of the rights of the defence, it should be annulled. The Commission's decision cannot consider or deal with evidence or arguments that the interested parties did not know about or never had a chance to make. The General Court certainly cannot assume that the Commission has always made such thorough enquiries that it has discovered everything that it needed to discover, and considered thoroughly and objectively every argument that might have been made if the companies had been given an opportunity to make it. Even if the EU courts were willing to consider all the evidence and arguments that could have been made to the Commission, the role of the courts under Article 263 of the Treaty on the Functioning of the European Union (TFEU) is not to retry the case on the basis of the evidence and arguments that the Commission should have considered but the parties had no chance to make. The role of the courts is to decide if the Commission's procedure was lawful and the reasons given for its conclusions were sufficient. If only a retrial with new evidence and argument can cure the defects of the administrative procedure, as seems to be the position, the remedy that the courts can give is not *'effective'* because a retrial should not be necessary. A procedure that gives only the right to make one set of submissions on the basis of a description of the Commission's views before it begins a formal investigation, and no right to submit further evidence or argument that might be relevant when further facts emerged, new assessments were developed or further arguments were made, cannot reasonably be described as a *'fair'* or satisfactory procedure. A procedure in which the Commission apparently does not regard itself as being obliged to be impartial and in which the interests of companies are defended (if at all) by a Member State which apparently has no duty of impartiality and whose own interests may not correspond to those of the companies[19] cannot be considered adequate to disclose the true situation. A procedure in which pragmatic compromises may be made between the Commission and the Member State,

[19] If aid must be repaid, it is repaid to the state. The Commission cannot assume that the state has an interest in minimising the amount to be repaid: Case T-366/00 *Scott* [2007] ECR II-797 [59]. See also Case C-290/07 P *Scott* [2010] ECR I-7763, Opinion of Advocate General Mengozzi at [55], where the fact that the recipient of aid is only an 'interested party' with no right to participate in the procedure is described as *'markedly formalistic'*. The AG also referred to the principle of good administration: [59]–[66], [73]–[77]. The Court did not refer to the Charter. Sir Jeremy Lever (op cit, 9) also points out that the Member State may not be fully informed if, eg, the aid was given by a regional or local authority. The Member State may not wish to be completely frank, even when it is fully informed. In addition, the Member State, by accepting that aid is 'new' rather than 'existing' aid, may make the recipient liable to repay the aid to the state without the recipient being consulted or informed.

in circumstances in which neither of those two parties has a duty or an interest to consult or to protect the interests of the companies concerned, cannot be considered satisfactory.

A procedure that gives interested parties no rights to be informed about the progress of the procedure, no right to know about developments on which they may wish to comment, no right to defend their interests at the appropriate times and no guarantee that they will receive the final Commission decision promptly cannot provide an 'effective remedy'. The right to a fair trial and an effective remedy must include the right to get the evidence necessary to prove one's case if the evidence exists and is identifiable. The *Laboratoires Boiron* judgment[20] confirms this. This principle applies both to challenges to the actions of the Commission in the General Court and to claims against a Member State that granted unlawful aid, under the *Francovich* principle, in the national courts.

In *Kadi*,[21] the Court of Justice said:

> [H]aving regard to the Court's case-law in other fields ... it must be held in this instance that the effectiveness of judicial review which it must be possible to apply to the lawfulness of the grounds on which ... the name of the person or entity is included in the list ... leading to the imposition on those persons of a body of restrictive measures means that the Community authority is bound to communicate those grounds to the person or entity concerned, so far as possible, either when that inclusion is decided upon or, at the very least, as swiftly as possible after that decision in order to enable those persons or entities to exercise, within the period prescribed, their right to bring an action. Observance of that obligation to communicate the grounds is necessary both to enable the persons to whom restrictive measures are addressed to defend their rights in the best possible conditions and to decide, with full knowledge of the relevant facts, whether there is any point in their applying to the Community judicature ... and to put the latter fully in a position in which it may carry out the review of the lawfulness of the Community measure in question which is its duty under the EC Treaty ... given the failure to inform them of the evidence adduced against them and having regard to the relationship ... between the rights of the defence and the right to an effective legal remedy ... their right to an effective legal remedy has also been infringed.

In cases under what are now Articles 101–02 the EU courts established that defendant companies had a right of access to the Commission's file.[22] This right is recognised by Article 27 of Regulation 1/2003 and it is now based on the Charter. The same considerations apply in state aid cases.

[20] Case C-526/04, *Laboratoires Boiron* [2006] ECR I-7529.

[21] Joined Cases C-402/05 P and C-415/05 P *Kadi and Al-Barakaat* [2008] ECR I-6351 [336]–[337], [349], [351]. See also Case C-67/13 P *Groupement des cartes bancaires* [2014] ECR I-2204 [43], [91].

[22] Joined Cases C-204/00 P and others, *Aalborg Portland* [2004] ECR I-123 [100]–[106]; Case C-109/10 P *Solvay* [2011] ECR I-10329 [51]–[70]. The Charter was referred to in both of these judgments.

The interest of the recipient of state aid is at least as vital as the interest of a defendant in a cartel case.

The Member State might challenge a Commission decision, and the company receiving the aid might do so also. But the Member State would have full access to the Commission's file, and the company would not. That would also be irrational and anomalous.

XI. THE TERMS OF COMMISSION STATE AID DECISIONS

The defects in the procedure can be seen to be even more serious when the terms of Commission decisions are considered. The decision opening the formal investigation almost never indicates the conditions that the Commission may ultimately impose. This means that unless the Commission or the Member State has chosen to give the companies concerned enough information to enable them to comment, they will have had no opportunity of any kind to criticise or object to what may be the most important elements in the final decision.

This can be seen to be particularly inappropriate because of the Commission's experience with commitment decisions under Article 9 of Regulation 1/2003, which in spite of some serious problems have proved to be a useful way of resolving difficult cases, in particular those cases in which a practical modus operandi needs to be worked out with the companies directly involved. Since the Commission can negotiate commitments, it should be willing, where appropriate, to discuss the terms of restructuring or approval of state aid with the companies involved.

XII. FUNDAMENTAL DEFECTS IN THE STATE AID PROCEDURE

In short, the state aid procedure suffers from several fundamental defects. It is entirely non-transparent: the companies cannot be sure of finding out what is being said or done. It is entirely discretionary: the Commission claims a right to make whatever enquiries it chooses and to take whatever action it wishe, without regard to any legal principles. The conduct of the Member State involved is regarded as being entirely at its discretion and not subject to constraints of any kind. The procedure entirely disregards the rights of the defence: no opportunity is guaranteed to the companies to comment on proposals that may seriously harm their interests. The procedure is inappropriate because it is regarded as primarily a dialogue or negotiation between the Commission and the Member State rather than the companies that have a direct financial or other interest of their own in the outcome. Negotiation and litigation by proxy is fundamentally bad litigation and is wholly inappropriate when the interests of the companies could be perfectly well defended by the companies themselves. Worse still, the Member State may have a conflict of interest between its presumed (but not invariable) wish to defend its own state aid measure, on the one hand, and its financial interest in minimising the cost of the aid to its budget, on the other. Companies cannot be expected to be confident when defended by such schizophrenic advocates. The procedure is bureaucratic and autocratic: Commission officials claim the power to give orders that are not subject to any supervision or control. The procedure is conducted between officials, none of whom are in necessarily direct touch with the companies directly and financially affected.

It is important to stress that no justification has been or could be suggested for withholding from the interested parties the information that is in the Commission's possession (except insofar as it may be confidential). In fact, the only explanation for the state aid procedure is that it has developed primarily for the convenience of the Commission, without regard for due process and with the assent of Member States who like the informality, secrecy and flexibility, which allows them to pursue objectives and make compromises that they might not necessarily wish to discuss or disclose openly. This convenience cannot be a sufficient justification for a failure to allow a fair trial.

State aid cases also suffer from the two basic and well-known flaws of the Commission's procedure in all competition cases, which are that the same officials write both the criticism of the practice or proposal and the decision that may prohibit it, and that the decision is formally adopted by Commissioners none of whom have seen the evidence, read the arguments or attended the hearing. These defects may not be enough by themselves to make the Commission's procedure illegal in all competition cases, but they certainly contribute still further to the likelihood that state aid procedures are contrary to both the Charter and the Convention.

XIII. CLAIMS AGAINST THE STATE IN ACCORDANCE WITH THE *FRANCOVICH* PRINCIPLE

When a competitor of a company that received an illegal aid sues the state that paid the aid for compensation in accordance with the *Francovich* principle (essentially for lost profits), the competitor will almost always require access to the Commission's file in order to have an 'effective remedy' under Article 47 of the Charter.[23] The same basic principle applies: the right to

[23] The Commission's Notice on the enforcement of state aid law by national courts [2009] OJ C85/1, 9 April, para 83 envisages claims against the state for compensation in accordance with the principle of state liability as stated in *Francovich* (n 1). The Notice envisages that the national court may ask the Commission for 'factual data, statistics, market studies and economic analysis', but it does not say that the Commission will disclose its file to the court or that it will help claimants directly. This is unfortunate, because if the Commission has

an effective remedy must include the right to get the evidence necessary to prove one's case. The right to a *'fair hearing'* must include the right to get and to use the important evidence.

If it were clearly recognised, as it is suggested here that it must be, that interested parties have a right to see the Commission's file, this would greatly increase the effectiveness of EU state aid policy, since it would facilitate claims for compensation against states that have paid illegal aid. It would create, for the first time, a financial cost for a state that grants an illegal aid. At present, there is none. It is not clear why the Commission has not understood this because state aid control is the most difficult area of EU law to enforce, and the Commission needs to use all the means of enforcement that EU law provides. The Commission therefore has a strong and clear interest in complying with its obligations under the Charter. This is one of the relatively few ways in which EU state aid policy could be made more effective.

XIV. THE RIGHT TO 'GOOD ADMINISTRATION'

The question also arises as to whether the state aid procedure is compatible with the principle of good administration under Article 41 of the Charter, which reads: '*Every person has the right to have his or her affairs handled impartially, fairly, and within a reasonable time by the institutions, bodies, offices and agencies of the Union.*' This raises several issues.

It seems that because it is stated in the Charter, the principle of good administration is a principle that has Treaty force and can override and invalidate EU secondary legislation such as the state aid Regulations.[24] In any case, the Charter clearly imposes duties on the Commission and presumably also on Member States under Article 4(3) TEU when they are (or should be) cooperating with the Commission in the implementation of EU law. These duties are legally binding and must be respected insofar as the secondary legislation allows (assuming that it is valid).

made a thorough investigation, its file can be expected to include evidence that the claimant could use to show that the aid caused loss to it and to indicate the amount of the loss, both of which are essential in state liability cases. The Commission has always been slow to encourage *Francovich* claims.

[24] Some 'General Principles' such as the principle of good administration clearly have the same status as the Treaties and can invalidate secondary legislation: J Temple Lang, 'Emerging European General Principles in Private Law' in U Bernitz, F Groussot and X Schulyok (eds), *General Principles of EU Law and European Private Law* (Alphen aan den Rijn, Wolters Kluwer, 2013) 65–117. However, Art 41 seems to give Treaty status to all the principles of 'good administration'. Handling affairs 'fairly' must mean more than handling them 'impartially', because it must include a duty to be thorough and a duty to listen. Both words must be given a meaning.

Several provisions of the Regulations may be contrary to the principle of good administration, as well as to the right to an *'effective remedy'*:

— Article 6a(2), inserted by Regulation 734/2013, insofar as it restricts the powers of the Commission to investigate facts that it considers that it needs to know. As this provision gives the Member State a veto on the Commission obtaining information, it seems to be contrary to Article 4(3) TEU and, if this is so, the question whether it is also contrary to the principle of good administration may not arise.
— Recital (4) of Regulation 734/2013 says that *'the provision of information by the beneficiary of the aid measure in question does not constitute a legal basis for bilateral negotiations between the Commission and the beneficiary in question'*. However, what is required by the Charter is not a 'negotiation', but disclosure of the evidence on which the Commission takes its decision. To describe this as 'negotiation' is seriously to misunderstand the legal position.

XV. THE COMMISSION'S OBLIGATIONS OF 'GOOD ADMINISTRATION'

The right to good administration as stated in Article 41 of the Charter includes the right to have one's case treated 'impartially, fairly', which has several consequences.

The principle, insofar as it is relevant to state aid procedure, clearly imposes several obligations on the Commission. First, it imposes a legal obligation of objectivity and impartiality. The Commission must treat both sides of a controversy (in a state aid case, typically the beneficiary and its competitors) in the same way, giving them the same information (subject to confidentiality requirements) and the same opportunities to defend their interests. The Commission must not, by asking questions to one side without sending the questions and the answers to the other side, give better opportunities to be heard to one side of the controversy than to the other.

Second, the principle imposes on the Commission a legal obligation to investigate the facts thoroughly in order to find out all that it needs to know in order to reach a correct result.[25] A superficial investigation cannot be sufficient or *'fair'*.

Third, it imposes on the Commission a legal obligation to allow and enable interested parties to make their views known, and for this purpose there

[25] The General Court has ruled that the Commission must carry out '*a diligent and impartial examination*' (*Air One* (n 6) [61]) and so must not '*prolong indefinitely*' its preliminary investigation (Cases T-228 and 233/99 *Westdeutsche Landesbank* [2003] ECR II-435 [167]).

must be a legal obligation to give the interested parties the information and evidence that they need in order to form their views and make their arguments on whatever issues are relevant.[26] The Commission (and the Member State) must not determine or limit what the interested parties may say or the questions on which they may express their views. This is particularly important insofar as the Commission is considering imposing conditions on the structure or conduct of the beneficiary.

The European Ombudsman's publication The European Code of Good Administrative Behaviour says that officials should be 'impartial, open-minded, guided by evidence and willing to hear different viewpoints'.

Fourth, the Charter imposes on the Commission a legal obligation to be consistent, and to do in one case what it does in other similar cases. It would be contrary to the principle for the Commission to give the companies full information in one case and little or no information in another. This would be illegal even if the Commission had never formally stated its policy.

Fifth, it seems reasonable to say that 'good administration' also obliges the Commission to recognise the possibility of conflicts of interest in the cases with which it is concerned and to avoid or prevent them as far as possible. This would require the Commission to recognise that the interests of the Member State granting the aid and the beneficiary may be in conflict. The Commission should be careful to avoid being misled or incompletely informed as a result of such a situation, and should not rely on information given by a party which is or may be in a conflict of interest. It would not be good administration to insist on a party being represented by someone who might have interests that are adverse to the party represented. If it is said that the Member State is not 'representing' the recipient of the aid, this merely confirms that the interests of the recipient are not being defended at all, except insofar as its interests and those of the Member State may coincide.

Sixth, Article 41 requires a result to be reached 'within a reasonable time'. This is something the Commission plainly fails to provide in many cases. If proceedings for the Commission's failure to act under Article 265 TFEU were clearly available, this could be corrected.

Seventh, Article 41 obliges the Commission to facilitate parties who wish to claim their legal rights by making evidence available. This is so in particular because national courts will ask the Commission for information when they are dealing with claims for compensation by competitors of recipients of illegal aid under the *Francovich* principle. The Commission has a

[26] This would imply reconsideration of the judgment in Case C-139/07 P *Technische Glaswerke Ilmenau* [2010] ECR I-5885 [61]. As already mentioned, that case concerned a situation that arose before the Charter came into force, and the Charter was apparently not relied on. See T Jaeger, 'A Wish-List for Commissioner Almunia' (2010) 9 *European State Aid Law Quarterly* 1–3.

duty under Article 4(3) TEU to provide readily available information to national courts when they are applying EU law and could hardly refuse to provide it.[27]

XVI. THE REGULATIONS ALLOW THE COMMISSION TO COMPLY WITH THE REQUIREMENTS OF 'GOOD ADMINISTRATION'

Although the Regulations clearly do not oblige the Commission to comply with these obligations under the Charter, it would be possible for the Commission to comply with them without infringing the Regulations, except for Article 6a(2)(b) of Regulation 734/2013. It is true that the Regulations do not regard the procedure as one in which the interested companies are parties, but as they are clearly the persons whose financial and economic positions are most directly affected by the result of the procedure, it is the interested parties that are most relevant for clarifying the obligations of the Commission under the Charter and the principle of good administration. Regulations could not deprive private parties of their rights under the Charter merely by saying that they are not the primary parties to the state aid procedure. In short, the principle of good administration requires transparency and impartiality in the procedure, and these are allowed, though not required, by the Regulations (except, once again, by Article 6a(2)(b)). It will be seen that the Commission's practice does not comply with these obligations, although it could be modified in order to do so.

If the Commission were to modify its procedure and practices to comply with these principles of good administration, the question of how far Member States are also obliged to comply with them in state aid procedures would become less important. But the Charter binds Member States when they are implementing EU law under Article 52 of the Charter. In addition, Member States have a legal duty under Article 4(3) TEU to cooperate with the Commission so as to enable it to fulfil its obligations under the Charter. Member States could not object to the Commission disclosing its file when that is required by the Charter: the Charter is also binding on them in the sphere of EU law.

XVII. THE EUROPEAN ECONOMIC AREA

The practice of the EFTA Surveillance Authority (ESA) in state aid cases under the European Economic Area Agreement seems to be essentially similar to

[27] See Case C-2/88 *Zwartveld* [1990] ECR I-3365.

the Commission's procedure under the TFEU. Strictly, the procedure of ESA and the EFTA Court are subject to the European Convention on Human Rights but not the Charter, while the procedure of the Commission is subject to both. However, this does not seem to make any significant difference, since the Charter and the Convention contain similar provisions on fair trial, and the Charter must be interpreted so as to give protection to fundamental rights at least as effective as under the Convention.[28] The Convention does not include an Article on good administration, but the analysis above of Article 41 of the Charter suggests that, as far as state aid procedure is concerned, Article 41 may not add very much to the effect of Article 47, although it undoubtedly confirms it.

It follows that the question whether the procedures in EU and European Economic Area (EEA) state aid cases are compatible with fundamental rights may arise either in the EFTA Court or in the General Court and the Court of Justice. The question might ultimately arise, of course, before the European Court of Human Rights.

There does not seem to be anything in the practice of the ESA that corresponds to Article 6(a)(2) of Regulation 734/2013. If there were, it would presumably be contrary to the duty of sincere cooperation under Article 3 EEA, which corresponds to Article 4(3) TEU, for the reasons given above.

XVIII. STRICT JUDICIAL REVIEW IS NECESSARY

It is now generally understood that the administrative stage of procedures of this kind is compatible with the Charter and the Convention only if there is sufficiently strict judicial scrutiny. This is confirmed by the judgment of the European Court of Human Rights in *Menarini Diagnostics v Italy*,[29] by the judgment of the Court of Justice in *KME*[30] and by the judgment of the EFTA Court in *Posten Norge*.[31] The case law of the European Court of Human Rights (in particular *Bryan v UK*)[32] suggests that the fairer the administrative procedure is, the less judicial scrutiny is required. However, even strict and thorough judicial review of Commission state aid decisions could not make them legal under the Charter because interested parties have no right of access to the Commission's file and therefore cannot be sure of being able to know all the relevant facts or to make the arguments that they need to

[28] Article 52 of the Charter.
[29] No 43509/08, 27 September 2011.
[30] Case C-272/09 P *KME Germany* [2011] ECR I-12789.
[31] Case E-15/10 *Posten Norge* [2012] EFTA Court Report, judgment dated 18 April 2012.
[32] *Bryan v UK* (1995), 21 EHRR 352 [45].

make.[33] It would not be enough for the Commission's file to be disclosed to the General Court, even if that were the practice.

XIX. THE LIMITED SCOPE FOR JUDICIAL REVIEW IN PRACTICE

These defects in the administrative procedure are particularly serious because the scope for effective review of the Commission's decisions by the General Court is inevitably limited. If a Commission decision orders repayment of an aid, the beneficiary may be able to obtain an Order suspending the duty to repay. But the company may have to give a bank guarantee for repayment if necessary, and will in any case have a contingent liability to repay, until the EU courts ultimately decide. If, as may be the case, the state aid was essential to keep the company in business, the Commission's decision may be fatal. If the company challenges the conditions imposed by the decision, the Court may suspend the conditions, but the uncertainty will continue until the case is finally decided by the Court. In some monitoring cases, the Commission gives orders directly or through the monitoring trustee that are not contemplated in its formal decision and on which the company has had no opportunity to comment. These orders, even if they clearly constitute decisions that could be separately challenged, cannot be suspended quickly enough to avoid serious inconvenience or loss to the companies involved.

Another limitation on the extent of judicial review should be mentioned. Although it is the Commission that orders repayment, it is the Member State that is responsible for calculating how much should be repaid and its decision can be challenged only in the national court. The General Court has not got full jurisdiction (*pleine juridiction*) to determine the amount of the refund. If the Commission has chosen to give detailed instructions about the amount to be repaid, its decision could be challenged, but that is unusual.

Whether the Commission's decision can be challenged successfully on procedural grounds in any particular case may depend on the exact facts. In a very simple case, in which all the issues were clear from the decision opening the formal investigation, the Charter might be complied with. But the more complex the case becomes, the more serious the parties' ignorance of the progress of the case becomes and the more likely it is that the procedure will become contrary to the Charter. This means that the more trouble the

[33] This is the result of the judgment of the Court of Justice in *Sytraval* (n 9), which ruled that the Commission neither needs to inform complainants in the preliminary stage nor to raise the arguments that they could be expected to make if they were informed. But the Commission has a duty to carry out a diligent and impartial examination of a complaint and this may oblige it to consider issues not expressly raised by the complainant. If a formal investigation is begun, the decision opening it gives the complainant some information.

Commission takes over a case, the more likely it is that the decision will be contrary to the Charter. This is an irrational result that the Commission would be wise to avoid. In many state aid cases, there is a failure to respect the rights of the defence of the companies, and this fact cannot be brushed aside by saying that the procedure does not concern their rights and that the only rights of defence are those of the Member State.

XX. STEPS TOWARDS A SOLUTION

The procedures in anti-subsidy cases, and those in merger cases and in commitment cases under competition Regulation 1/2003, show that it would be perfectly possible to adopt a procedure that would adequately respect and safeguard the interests of the companies primarily involved. *The Netherlands PTT* judgment[34] shows that it may be important to ensure that the interests of the companies most directly concerned are safeguarded, even in cases in which the primary parties are the Member State and the Commission. It cannot seriously be said that no better solution than Regulation 659/1999 can be imagined.

Many of the defects in the state aid procedure could be corrected by two simple but fundamental reforms. First, every document in every state aid investigation, at both the provisional investigation and the formal stage, should be open to inspection by 'interested parties', subject only to the protection of confidential information. Every written submission received and every communication from the Commission to any party should be available on the Commission's file at all stages in the procedure.

Second, the Regulation should explicitly recognise a legal obligation on both the Commission and the Member State in question to act impartially throughout the investigation and to give full and equal opportunities to make submissions to interested parties whose interests may be opposed. This may be obvious, but it clearly needs to be said formally.

Changes in Regulations 659/1999 and 734/2013 would be desirable to implement these changes fully. This presents a difficulty. There are good reasons, not always understood, for the 'Community Method' of legislating, under which only the Commission may make proposals for adoption by the Parliament and Council. But the method has one weakness. Measures that would inconvenience the Commission are less likely to be proposed. Member States that have assented to Regulation 734/2013 may not be in favour of more important changes. That is why it may be necessary, if no improvements are made, to challenge the entire state aid procedure as incompatible with the Charter and with the principle of good administration.

[34] *The Netherlands v Commission* (n 5).

But the present position is indefensible. The confidence of the business community in the Commission's state aid procedures would be greatly increased if the procedures were made transparent and impartial, and if Member States were not allowed to prevent the Commission from obtaining information that it needs. More transparent procedures should reduce substantially the number of state aid cases coming before the General Court. Of the 1,237 cases pending at the start of 2012, 152 concerned state aid.[35] During 2012, 36 new state aid cases were filed.

Reform is long overdue and it is very regrettable that the opportunity was not taken to carry it out when Regulation 734/2013 was being discussed.

XXI. WHY HAS REFORM TAKEN SO LONG?[36]

There are several reasons why criticism of state aid procedures has taken so long to develop. The first procedural Regulation was adopted only in 1999. The great majority of state aids have always been approved. Group exemptions were under consideration. The secret, flexible, pragmatic procedures suited both the Commission and the Member States, and the interests of the companies were not seen clearly. 'Modernisation' of state aid policy and practice was initiated only in 2005 and the financial crisis preoccupied everyone after that. It was due to the crisis that the Commission began frequently to impose onerous conditions. The possibility of conflicts of interest between the Member State and the beneficiaries were seen clearly only recently.[37] Before that, beneficiaries tended to assume that the state aid rules were unclear, both in law and in economics, so companies were not sure what arguments could be made even if they could exercise procedural rights. Economists were slow to analyse state aid policy seriously. It is only when EU competition law is looked at as whole that it becomes clear that the state aid rules are much less clear, much less based on economics and

[35] Annual Report of the Court of Justice. Of the 28 references on competition law under Art 267 TFEU pending in January 2014, 11 concerned state aid.

[36] A Heimler, 'European State Aid Policy in Search of a Standard: What is the Role of Economic Analysis?' in B Hawk (ed), *International Antitrust Law and Policy* (New York, Juris, 2010) 94: '*Besides an OECD roundtable on subsidies held in 2001 and two papers written a year or two earlier, one by Tim Besley and Paul Seabright and the other one by Damien Neven and Lars Hendrick Röller, there was not much else*'. F Jenny, 'Competition and State Aid Policy in the EU' (1994) *Fordham Corporate Law Institute* (B Hawk (ed)) 75–98 said (at 96) '*this apparent lack of interest in the European State aid policy is not unique to lawyers. Economists, even economists special* ized *in market mechanisms and competition, have been largely silent on the issue. This is all the more perplexing because there are hundreds of decisions taken each year by the Commission on State aids*'. It is in part because '*any sizable aid is considered to threaten or distort competition*'. '*State aid decisions … do not always appear to be grounded on a predictable economic analysis*' (at 97) and expectations of a consistent approach are not always met.

[37] It was mentioned by AG Mengozzi in Case C-290/07 P *Scott* (n 19) 55.

much more unsatisfactory procedurally than the other areas of competition policy.[38] Regulation 734/2013 introduced new express and clearly unsatisfactory limitations on the investigating powers of the Commission. The implications of the Charter have not yet been seen clearly.

The history of EC/EU state aid policy is unfortunately an example of the well-recognised phenomenon of 'regulatory capture', the tendency of regulatory authorities to get too close in their thinking and analyses to the entities that they are intended to regulate. This is particularly likely to occur when, as in the case of state aid policy, the principles on which the regulators are supposed to act were never clear. The close relationships between the Commission and the Member States have led the Commission to sympathise unduly with the political reasons for which aid is often given, and to apply inadequately whatever economic principles it should be applying. This problem is much wider than the questions of procedure discussed here, but if the procedure were more transparent, the analysis of aid cases would become clearer and more consistent with principle.

[38] J Temple Lang, 'The Evolution of EU Competition Law and Some Current Issues' in A Beck and P Sheehy Skeffington (eds), *The Impact of European Law on the Corporate World* (Dublin, Irish Centre for European Law, 2010) 87–114. J Temple Lang, 'After Forty Years: the Development of European Competition Law—Views from Fordham' in B Hawk (ed), *International Antitrust Law and Policy: Fordham Competition Law 2014* (New York, Fordham Competition Law Institute, 2015) 582–92.

Index

Statistical Modeling of Reliability Structures and Industrial Processes

This reference text introduces advanced topics in the field of reliability engineering, introduces statistical modeling techniques, and probabilistic methods for diverse applications.

It comprehensively covers important topics including consecutive-type reliability systems, coherent structures, multi-scale statistical modeling, the performance of reliability structures, big data analytics, prognostics, and health management. It covers real-life applications including optimization of telecommunication networks, complex infrared detecting systems, oil pipeline systems, and vacuum systems in accelerators or spacecraft relay stations. The text will serve as an ideal reference book for graduate students and academic researchers in the fields of industrial engineering, manufacturing science, mathematics, and statistics.

Advanced Research in Reliability and System Assurance Engineering

Series Editor
Mangey Ram, Professor, Graphic Era University, Uttarakhand, India

System Reliability Management
Solutions and Technologies
Edited by Adarsh Anand and Mangey Ram

Reliability Engineering
Methods and Applications
Edited by Mangey Ram

Reliability Management and Engineering
Challenges and Future Trends
Edited by Harish Garg and Mangey Ram

Applied Systems Analysis
Science and Art of Solving Real-Life Problems
F. P. Tarasenko

Stochastic Models in Reliability Engineering
Lirong Cui, Ilia Frenkel, and Anatoly Lisnianski

Predictive Analytics
Modeling and Optimization
Vijay Kumar and Mangey Ram

Design of Mechanical Systems Based on Statistics
A Guide to Improving Product Reliability
Seong-woo Woo

Social Networks
Modeling and Analysis
Niyati Aggrawal and Adarsh Anand

Operations Research
Methods, Techniques, and Advancements
Edited by Amit Kumar and Mangey Ram

Statistical Modeling of Reliability Structures and Industrial Processes
Edited by Ioannis S. Triantafyllou and Mangey Ram

For more information about this series, please visit: www.routledge.com/Advanced-Research-in-Reliability-and-System-Assurance-Engineering/book-series/CRCARRSAE

Statistical Modeling of Reliability Structures and Industrial Processes

Edited by
Ioannis S. Triantafyllou and Mangey Ram

CRC Press
Taylor & Francis Group
Boca Raton London

CRC Press is an imprint of the
Taylor & Francis Group, an **informa** business

First edition published 2023
by CRC Press
6000 Broken Sound Parkway NW, Suite 300, Boca Raton, FL 33487–2742

and by CRC Press
4 Park Square, Milton Park, Abingdon, Oxon, OX14 4RN

CRC Press is an imprint of Taylor & Francis Group, LLC

Library of Congress Cataloging-in-Publication Data
Names: Triantafyllou, Ioannis S., editor. | Ram, Mangey, editor.
Title: Statistical modeling of reliability structures and industrial processes / edited by Ioannis S. Triantafyllou and Mangey Ram.
Description: First edition. | Boca Raton, FL : CRC Press, 2022. | Series: Advanced research in reliability and system assurance engineering, 2767-0724 | Includes index.
Identifiers: LCCN 2022011044 (print) | LCCN 2022011045 (ebook) | ISBN 9781032066257 (hbk) | ISBN 9781032066295 (pbk) | ISBN 9781003203124 (ebk)
Subjects: LCSH: Reliability (Engineering)—Statistical methods.
Classification: LCC TA169 .S737 2022 (print) | LCC TA169 (ebook) | DDC 620/.00452—dc23/eng/20220509
LC record available at https://lccn.loc.gov/2022011044
LC ebook record available at https://lccn.loc.gov/2022011045

ISBN: 978-1-032-06625-7 (hbk)
ISBN: 978-1-032-06629-5 (pbk)
ISBN: 978-1-003-20312-4 (ebk)

DOI: 10.1201/9781003203124

Typeset in Times
by Apex CoVantage, LLC

Contents

Preface

Reliability engineering is an engineering framework that enables the definition of a complete production regime and deals with the study of the ability of the product to perform its required functions under stated conditions for a specified period. In this field, an extensive activity has been recorded for the so-called consecutive-type reliability structures, mainly due to their applications in optimization of telecommunication networks, complex infrared detecting systems. In the framework of a traditional reliability analysis, the distributional properties of the lifetime of coherent structures are under investigation, while several reliability measures and performance metrics are also considered.

On the other hand, Statistical process control is widely used to monitor the quality of the final product of a process. In any production process, no matter how carefully it is maintained, a natural variability is always present. Control charts facilitate the practitioners to identify assignable causes so that corrective actions are carried out and the process be restored to the desirable in-control state.

Throughout the lines of the present manuscript, recent advances on Statistical Modeling of reliability structures are discussed in detail. Modern and up-to-date probabilistic approaches for investigating the performance of coherent systems are also studied. In addition, new monitoring schemes are introduced and presented in detail.

In Chapter 1, an up-to-date overview of signature representations of coherent systems is presented. Recent extensions of this representation to more general cases are discussed and implemented for the computation of system's reliability and the establishment of stochastic orderings between the lifetimes of different structures.

Chapter 2 reviews the recent literature of the shock models in reliability systems. In particular, the existing results are reviewed for the applications of the shock models in reliability systems. For each type of shock model, a graphical realization for specified distributions is presented.

In Chapter 3, the problem of determining the appropriate distributional model for a given data set is discussed. A new goodness of fit exponentiality test is introduced. The proposed test offers some evidence for distinguishing between exponential and light or long-tail distributions. The test statistic is based on the principle of the so called, single big jump, while an extensive simulation procedure sheds some light on its performance.

Chapter 4 deals with the optimal redundancy allocation problems in coherent systems. Both common schemes for allocating the redundant components to the system, which are called active and standby redundancies are studied. A new concept of dependency is defined and used for establishing stochastic orderings and optimizing redundancy allocation problems.

Chapter 5 highlights unsupervised learning methodologies for large-scale, high-dimensional data, providing the potential of a unified framework that combines the knowledge retrieved from clustering and visualization. The main purpose is to uncover hidden patterns in a high-dimensional mixed dataset, which we achieve through our application in a complex, real-world dataset. The experimental analysis indicates the existence of notable information exposing the usefulness of the utilized methodological framework for similar high-dimensional real-world applications.

In Chapter 6, an extension of the well-known Moving Average control chart by combining two Moving Average schemes is presented. The proposed chart is capable to monitor shifts not only in the mean or variability of a normal process, but also in the Poisson parameter of attribute data. A comparison study reveals that the proposed scheme is a good alternative to the existing ones.

Chapter 7 focuses on the application of fractal interpolation within the reliability engineering framework. Specifically, application areas where the reliability data, such as occurrences or frequency of failures, exhibit irregular, non-smooth patterns are explored. In these cases, fractal interpolation provides an efficient way for modelling and predicting a system's functioning and reliability.

In Chapter 8, an Exponentially Weighted Moving Average chart for the lifetime of items under failure censoring reliability tests with replacement is introduced. Under the assumption that the lifetime of the items is exponentially distributed, the performance of the proposed chart is evaluated through its run length properties that are computed using Markov chain methodology.

In Chapter 9, a reliability study of the <n, f, k> systems with independent and identically distributed components is carried out. A simulation algorithm is proposed for determining the coordinates of the signature vector of the <n, f, k> systems, while several stochastic orderings among consecutive-type structures are also investigated. In addition, explicit signature-based expressions for the corresponding mean residual lifetime and the conditional mean residual lifetime of the <n, f, k> structure are provided.

In Chapter 10, some criteria used for selecting a fractional factorial design are discussed. A procedure that can be implemented for evaluating the efficacy of a design as well as for identifying fractional factorial designs with similar properties is also proposed. This procedure is based on simulations, where competitive designs are tested for their capability in correctly identifying a given true model.

In Chapter 11, a method deblurring an image using two blurred instances is presented. The cases of a blurring function, measurement errors and noise are considered. The proposed algorithm is based on Numerical Linear Algebra methods for computing the Greatest Common Divisor of polynomials. Because of the large size of the matrices representing the images, the exploitation of the special structure of the block banded matrices that are used, is of crucial importance.

Chapter 12 focuses on presenting the technology enablers and the state-of-the-art of RIS-assisted wireless systems, the need of new channel and system models as well as theoretical frameworks for their analysis and design, as well as the long-term and open research issues to be solved towards their massive deployment.

In Chapter 13, the decrease of the Totally Self-Checking Goal on Totally Self-Checking units caused by the application of low-power techniques on a safety-critical digital system is explored. Additionally, an online testing architecture is offered that adjusts the input activity, when low-power management is activated.

The chapters included in this book were all refereed and we would like to express our sincere gratitude to all reviewers for their diligent work and commitment. Generally speaking, it has been a very pleasant experience corresponding with all the authors involved. Our sincere thanks go to all the authors who have contributed to this book and provided great support and cooperation throughout the course of this project. Finally, we would like to thank the CRC Press production team for their help and patience during the preparation of this book.

October 2021, Ioannis S. Triantafyllou
Mangey Ram

Editor Biographies

Ioannis S. Triantafyllou is an assistant professor at the University of Thessaly, Greece. He received his B.S. degree in Mathematics from University of Athens, Greece, and the M.Sc. and Ph.D. degrees in Statistics from University of Piraeus, Greece. He has served as referee for more than 25 international journals. He has published over 50 peer-reviewed papers in international refereed scientific journals and edited volumes. His research interests include Applied Probability, Nonparametric Statistics, Reliability Theory and Statistical Process Control.

Mangey Ram received his Ph.D., major with Mathematics and minor in Computer Science from G. B. Pant University of Agriculture and Technology, Pantnagar, India. He is an editorial board member in many international journals. He has published over 200 research publications in national and international journals of repute. His fields of research are Reliability theory and Applied Mathematics. Currently, he is working as a Professor at Graphic Era University, Uttarakhand, India.

Contributors

Vasileios Alevizakos
National Technical University of Athens
Greece

Angeliki Alexiou
University of Piraeus
Greece
University of Thessaly
Greece

Panagiotis Anagnostou
University of Thessaly, Greece

José Luis Ayuso-Mateos
Universidad Autónoma de Madrid
Madrid, Spain

Petros Barmpas
University of Thessaly
Greece

Ivet Bayes
Centro de Investigación Biomédica en Red de Salud Mental
CIBERSAM
Spain

Jerome Bickenbach
University of Lucerne
Lucerne, Switzerland

Martin Bobak
University College London
London, UK

Alexandros-Apostolos A. Boulogeorgos
University of Piraeus
Greece

Francisco Félix Caballero
Universidad Autónoma de Madrid/ Idipaz
Madrid, Spain

Kashinath Chatterjee
Augusta University
Georgia

Somnath Chatterji
Information
Evidence and Research
World Health Organization
Geneva, Switzerland

Vasileios Chioktour
University of Thessaly
Greece

Laia Egea-Cortés
Research
Innovation and Teaching Unit. Parc Sanitari Sant Joan de Déu
Sant Boi de Llobregat, Spain

Vasileios Drakopoulos
University of Thessaly
Greece

Esther García-Esquinas
Universidad Autónoma de Madrid/ Idipaz
Madrid, Spain

Harris Evangelaras
University of Piraeus
Greece

Aleksander Galas
Jagiellonian University
Krakow, Poland

Spiros Georgakopoulos
University of Thessaly
Greece

Athanasios Kakarountas
University of Thessaly
Greece

Alex Karagrigoriou
University of the Aegean
Greece

Mohammad Khanjari Sadegh
University of Birjand
Iran

Seppo Koskinen
National Institute for Health and Welfare (THL)
Helsinki, Finland

Christos Koukouvinos
National Technical University of Athens
Greece

Ilona Koupil
Stockholm University
Stockholm, Sweden

Angeliki Lappa
National Technical University of Athens
Greece

Matilde Leonardi
Fondazione IRCCS Istituto Neurologico Carlo Besta
Milan, Italy

Polychronis Manousopoulos
Bank of Greece
Greece

Petros E. Maravelakis
University of Piraeus
Greece

Josep MariaHaro
Research
Innovation and Teaching Unit. Parc Sanitari Sant Joan de Déu
Sant Boi de Llobregat, Spain

Jorge Navarro
Universidad de Murcia

Murat Ozkut
Izmir University of Economics
Turkey

Andrzej Pająk
Jagienllonian University
Krakow, Poland

Demosthenes Panagiotakos
School of Health Science and Education
Harokopio University
Athens, Greece

Georgia Papasotiriou
National Technical University of Athens
Greece

Christos Peveretos
University of Piraeus
Greece

Vassilis P. Plagianakos
University of Thessaly
Greece

Matthew Prina
King's College London
London, UK

Martin Prince
King's College London
London, UK

Albert Sanchez-Niubo
Research
Innovation and Teaching Unit. Parc Sanitari Sant Joan de Déu
Sant Boi de Llobregat, Spain

Warren Sanderson
Wittgenstein Centre for Demography and Global Human Capital
Luxemburg, Austria

Sergei Scherbov
Wittgenstein Centre for Demography and Global Human Capital
Luxemburg, Austria

Abdonas Tamosiunas
Lithuanian University of Health Sciences
Kaunas, Lithuania

Sotiris Tasoulis
University of Thessaly
Greece

Ioannis S. Triantafyllou
University of Thessaly
Greece

Dimitrios S. Triantafyllou
Hellenic Military Academy

Ilia Vonta
National Technical University of Athens
Greece

Aristidis G. Vrahatis
University of Thessaly
Greece

1 Recent Extensions of Signature Representations

Jorge Navarro

CONTENTS

1.1 INTRODUCTION

The two main concepts in Reliability Theory are coherent systems and reliability functions. A **system** with n components (order n) can be represented as a structure (Boolean) function $\phi:\{0,1\}^n \rightarrow \{0,1\}$, where x_i represents the state of the i-th component (1 if it works and 0 if it does not work) for $i = 1, \ldots, n$ and $\phi(x_1, \ldots, x_n)$ represents the state of the system. A system is a **coherent system** if it satisfies the following properties:

(i) ϕ is increasing, that is, $\phi(x_1, \ldots, x_n) \leq \phi(y_1, \ldots, y_n)$ for all $x_i \leq y_i$;
(ii) ϕ is strictly increasing in each x_i in at least a point, that is, there exist some values $x_1, \ldots, x_{i-1}, x_{i+1}, \ldots, x_n$ such that $\phi(x_1, \ldots, x_{i-1}, 0, x_{i+1}, \ldots, x_n) < \phi(x_1, \ldots, x_{i-1}, 1, x_{i+1}, \ldots, x_n)$.

The second property means that all the components are relevant for the system. If it is replaced by (ii) $\phi(0, \ldots, 0) = 0$ and $\phi(1, \ldots, 1) = 1$, we obtain the concept of **semi-coherent system**. The basic properties of systems can be seen in the classic book by Barlow and Proschan (1975).

When we introduce the time t, the states of the components at time t determine the state of the system at that time. Hence, the component lifetimes $X_1, \ldots, X_n$ determine

DOI: 10.1201/9781003203124-1

the system lifetime T. Actually $T = X_I$ for some random variable I = 1, . . . ,n. The reliability function of the system is $R_T(t) = P(T>t)$ for $t \geq 0$. It can be proved that it is a function of the reliability functions of the components $R_i(t) = P(X_i>t)$ for i = 1, . . . ,n, that is,

$$R_T(t) = Q(R_1(t), \ldots ,R_n(t))$$

for a **distortion function** Q: $[0,1]^n \rightarrow [0,1]$. Q is a continuous and increasing function that satisfies Q(0, . . . ,0) = 0 and Q(1, . . . ,1) = 1.

The signature representation obtained in 1985 by F.J. Samaniego is a basic tool for the computation of the reliability functions of coherent systems. It proves that the system distribution is a mixture of the distributions of the ordered failure times of the components (order statistics). The vector with the weights in that mixture was called the signature vector of the system. It can be used to compute the system reliability and to compare systems with different structures just by comparing their signatures. Samaniego's representation was obtained just for systems having independent and identically distributed (i.i.d.) components with a common continuous distribution. The result can be stated as follows.

Theorem 1.1 (Samaniego, 1985): If T is the lifetime of a coherent system with i.i.d. component lifetimes having a common continuous reliability function R, then the system reliability R_T can be obtained as

$$R_T(t) = s_1 R_{1:n}(t) + \ldots + s_n R_{n:n}(t), \tag{1.1}$$

where $R_{i:n}$ is the reliability function of the i-th component failure lifetime $X_{i:n}$ (order statistic) for i = 1, . . . , n and $s_1, \ldots, s_n$ are some coefficients (weights) such that $s_i \geq 0$ and $s_1 + \ldots + s_n = 1$.

The vector $s = (s_1, \ldots, s_n)$ is called the **signature vector** of the system. These coefficients do not depend on R and can be computed as $s_i = P(T = X_{i:n})$ for i = 1, . . . ,n. It can also be computed from the structure function as

$$s_i = |A_i|/n!, \; i=1,\ldots,n, \tag{1.2}$$

where $|A_i|$ is the cardinality of the set A_i which contains all the permutations σ such that $\phi(x_1, \ldots ,x_n) = x_{i:n}$ when $x_{\sigma(1)} \leq \ldots \leq x_{\sigma(n)}$ holds.

If the conditions in Theorem 1.1 do not hold, then these weights can be different and (1.1) might not hold. For example, if we consider two i.i.d. Bernoulli distributions, that is, $P(X_i = 1) = p$ for i = 1,2, and $0<p<1$, and we consider the series system $T = \min(X_1,X_2)$, then $P(T = X_{1:2}) = 1$ and $P(T = X_{2:2}) = q^2 = (1-p)^2>0$ while the values obtained from (1.2) are $s_1 = 1$ and $s_2 = 0$ (since they just depend on the structure function).

Thus, in the general case, we can consider two signature vectors, the **probabilistic signature** $p = (p_1, \ldots ,p_n)$ defined by $p_i = P(T = X_{i:n})$ for i = 1, . . . ,n, and the **structural signature** $s = (s_1, \ldots ,s_n)$ defined by (1.2). In the Bernoulli distribution example, $p = (1,q^2)$ and $s = (1,0)$. The question is if (1.1) holds for one of these vectors when some of the conditions in Theorem 1.1 fail. This problem is examined in the next sections.

1.2 EXTENSIONS OF SAMANIEGO'S REPRESENTATION TO THE EXC CASE

The first extension was obtained in Navarro and Rychlik (2007) when the random vector $(X_1, \ldots, X_n)$ with the component lifetimes has an absolutely continuous and exchangeable joint distribution. The definition of exchangeable distributions is the following.

Definition 1.1: We say that $(X_1, \ldots, X_n)$ is exchangeable (EXC) if

$$\left(X_1,\ldots, X_n\right) =_{ST} (X_{\sigma(1)},\ldots, X_{\sigma(n)}) \tag{1.3}$$

for all permutations σ, where $=_{ST}$ denotes equality in law (distribution).

Now we can state this first extension under (1.3) as follows.

Theorem 1.2 (Navarro and Rychlik, 2007): If T is the lifetime of a coherent system with component lifetimes having a joint absolutely continuous EXC distribution, then the signature vectors p and s coincide and the system reliability can be obtained as

$$R_T\left(t\right)= p_1\, R_{1:n}\left(t\right) + \ldots + p_n\, R_{n:n}\left(t\right), \tag{1.4}$$

where $R_{i:n}$ is the reliability function of $X_{i:n}$ and $p_i = P(T = X_{i:n})$ for $i = 1, \ldots, n$ satisfy $p_1+\ldots+p_n = 1$.

Representation (1.4) for the absolutely continuous EXC case was extended in two different ways in Navarro et al. (2008). In the first one the absolutely continuous assumption is dropped out and, in this case, we have to use the structural signature vector to get (1.1). This extension can also be applied in the general i.i.d. case (without the assumption of a common continuous distribution (e.g., in the case of Bernoulli distributions). It can be stated as follows.

Theorem 1.3 (Navarro et al., 2008): If T is the lifetime of a coherent system with components having an EXC distribution, then the system reliability can be obtained as

$$R_T(t) = s_1\, R_{1:n}(t) + \ldots + s_n\, R_{n:n}(t),$$

where $R_{i:n}$ is the reliability function of $X_{i:n}$ and s_i are defined by (1.2) for $i = 1, \ldots, n$ and satisfy $s_i \geq 0$ and $s_1+\ldots+s_n = 1$.

The second one is applied to semi-coherent systems and can be used to compare systems with different numbers of components. It is stated at follows.

Theorem 1.4 (Navarro et al., 2008): If T is the lifetime of a semi-coherent system with components having an EXC distribution, then the system reliability can be obtained as

$$R_T(t) = s_1 R_{1:n}(t) + \dots + s_n R_{n:n}(t),$$

where $R_{i:n}$ is the reliability function of $X_{i:n}$ and $s_1, \dots, s_n$ are some coefficients that satisfy $s_i \geq 0$ and $s_1 + \dots + s_n = 1$.

It can be proved that these coefficients satisfy (1.2) (in dimension n) and the vector $s = (s_1, \dots, s_n)$ was called **signature of order n** of the system. Note that a coherent system of order k, can be considered as a semi-coherent system with n components for n = k+1, k+2, . . . Hence, we can compute the signatures of order k (the usual signature), k+1, k+2, . . . Actually, in Navarro et al. (2008) an explicit formula is provided to get the signature of order n+1 from the signature of order n. Even more, it can be proved that if the joint distribution of the component lifetimes is absolutely continuous, then $s_i = P(T = X_{i:n})$ for i = 1, . . . ,n (i.e., the structural signature and the probabilistic signatures of order n coincide).

For example, the first component with lifetime X_1 can be considered as a semi-coherent system of order n and if the joint distribution is EXC then its reliability can be written as

$$R_T(t) = (1/n) R_{1:n}(t) + \dots + (1/n) R_{n:n}(t),$$

That is, its signature of order n is $s = (1/n, \dots, 1/n)$. Then we can compare any coherent system with EXC component with the components (with X_1) just by comparing their signatures of order n. The same can be applied to any pair of semi-coherent systems based on these EXC components. The comparisons results can be stated as follows and extend the similar results obtained for the i.i.d. continuous case in Kochar, Mukerjee and Samaniego (1999). We consider the usual stochastic order (represented as $\leq_{ST}$), the hazard rate order (represented as $\leq_{HR}$), the mean residual life order (represented as $\leq_{MRL}$), and the likelihood ratio order (represented as $\leq_{LR}$). Their definitions and main properties can be seen in Shaked and Shanthikumar (2007).

Theorem 1.5 (Navarro et al., 2008): Let T_1 and T_2 be the lifetimes of two semi-coherent systems with component lifetimes $(X_1, \dots, X_n)$ having a common joint EXC distribution function F and let s_1 and s_2 be their respective signatures of order n.

(1) (i) If $s_1 \leq_{ST} s_2$, then $T_1 \leq_{ST} T_2$ for all EXC F.

(ii) If $s_1 \leq_{HR} s_2$, then $T_1 \leq_{HR} T_2$ for all EXC F such that

$$X_{1:n} \leq_{HR} \dots \leq_{HR} X_{n:n}. \quad (1.5)$$

(iii) If $s_1 \leq_{HR} s_2$, then $T_1 \leq_{MRL} T_2$ for all EXC F such that

$$X_{1:n} \leq_{MRL} \dots \leq_{MRL} X_{n:n}. \quad (1.6)$$

(iv) If $s_1 \leq_{LR} s_2$, then $T_1 \leq_{LR} T_2$ for all EXC abs. cont. or discrete F such that

$$X_{1:n} \leq_{LR} \ldots \leq_{LR} X_{n:n}. \tag{1.7}$$

Note that the orderings for the signatures lead to similar (distribution-free) orderings for the respective system lifetimes under some ordering conditions for the k-out-of-n systems (order statistics). In (i) we do not have this condition since they are always ST ordered (since $X_{1:n} \leq \ldots \leq X_{n:n}$ holds). If the component lifetimes are i.i.d., then conditions (1.5–1.7) hold and they can be deleted. Moreover, note that in (iii) we need the HR ordering for the signatures to get the MRL order between the system lifetimes. Here we just need the MRL orderings in (1.6) which are weaker than that in (1.5). In the i.i.d. case the result for the MRL order is not useful (since (1.5) holds and so we have the result for the HR order).

Theorem 1.5 was used to stochastically compare all the coherent systems with 1–4 EXC (or i.i.d.) components. The results can be seen in Figures 1–3 of Navarro et al. (2008). Example 5.1 that paper proves that Samaniego's representation cannot be extended to systems with independent but non-identically distributed components.

1.3 EXTENSIONS OF SAMANIEGO'S REPRESENTATION TO THE NON-EXC CASE

The first extension was obtained by Marichal, Mathonet and Waldhauser (2011). It was based on the random vector with the component states. For a fixed time $t>0$ we can define the i-th component state $S_i(t)$ as a Boolean variable such that $S_i(t) = 1$ when this component is alive at time t (that is, $\{X_i>t\}$), being $S_i(t) = 0$ when it has failed before t ($\{X_i \leq t\}$). The system state S(t) at time t (which can be seen now as a stochastic process for $t \geq 0$) can then be obtained as

$$S(t) = \phi(S_1(t), \ldots, S_n(t)),$$

where ϕ is the system structure function. Then this extension can be stated as follows.

Theorem 1.6 (Marichal, Mathonet and Waldhauser, 2011): If $n>2$, the following conditions are equivalent:

(i) Representation (1.1) with the structural signature holds for any coherent system with n components.
(ii) The vector with the component states $(S_1(t), \ldots, S_n(t))$ is EXC for any $t>0$.

The case $n = 2$ is trivial since there are only two coherent systems with two components, the series and the parallel systems and (1.1) holds for these systems in any case. These authors also provide a condition for the equality of structural and probabilistic signatures.

The condition about the components states given in (ii) above is not easy to check. The next extension provides a similar condition based on properties of the underlying copula. By using copula theory we know that the joint distribution F of the random vector with the component lifetimes $(X_1, \dots, X_n)$ can be written as

$$F(x_1, \dots, x_n) := P(X_1 \le x_1, \dots, X_n \le x_n) = C(F_1(x_1), \dots, F_n(x_n)),$$

where $F_1, \dots, F_n$ are the marginal (component) distribution functions and C is a copula function (i.e., a distribution function with uniform marginals over the interval (0,1)). If all the marginals are continuous, then C is unique (Sklar's theorem).

Then, we note that $(X_1, \dots, X_n)$ is EXC if and only if:

(i) The component lifetimes are identically distributed (i.d.) and;
(ii) The underlying copula C is EXC.

As we have mentioned above, the i.d. condition in (i) cannot be dropped out if we want to get Samaniego's representation. However, we can relax condition (ii). To this end we need the following concept.

Definition 1.2: We say that a copula C is diagonal dependent (DD for short) if

$$C(u_1, \dots, u_n) = C(u_{\sigma(1)}, \dots, u_{\sigma(n)}) \quad (1.8)$$

for all permutations σ, all $1<k<n$ and all $0<u<1$, where $u_i = u$ for $i = 1, \dots, k$ and $u_i = 1$ for $i = k+1, \dots, n$.

Note that (1.8) is trivially true for $k = n$ and for $k = 1$ (since $C(u,1 \dots ,1) = u$ and the same happen for any permutation of these values). The meaning of (1.8) is the following: for $1<k<n$, the diagonal sections of all the marginal distributions of dimension k of C coincide. For example, for $n = 3$, (1.8) is equivalent to

$$C(u,u,1) = C(u,1,u) = C(1,u,u)$$

for all $0<u<1$.

Now we can state the following theorem extracted from Navarro and Fernández-Sánchez (2020).

Theorem 1.7 (Navarro and Fernández-Sánchez, 2020): If T is the lifetime of a coherent system and the following conditions hold:

(i) The component lifetimes are identically distributed;
(ii) The survival copula of the component lifetimes is diagonal dependent;

then Samaniego's representation (1.1) holds for the structural signature of T.

The proof is based on the representation of the system reliability as a linear combination of the reliability functions of series systems and the fact that if the survival copula is DD, then the reliability functions of all the series systems with k components coincide for $1<k<n$.

This extension is not trivial. Actually, Navarro and Fernández-Sánchez (2020) proved that the set of DD copulas is dense in the set of all copulas (i.e., for any copula C we can find a 'close' DD copula). However, the set of EXC copulas is not dense in C.

Finally, the recent paper Navarro, Rychlik and Spizzichino (2020) connects these two extensions. To this end we need another concept for copulas.

Definition 1.3: Let *S* be a given subset of the interval [0, 1]. We say that a copula C is S-diagonal dependent (S-DD for short) if

$$C(u_1, \ldots, u_n) = C(u_{\sigma(1)}, \ldots, u_{\sigma(n)})$$

for all permutations σ, all $1<k<n$ and all $u \in S$, where $u_i = u$ for $i = 1, \ldots, k$ and $u_i = 1$ for $i = k+1, \ldots, n$.

Now we can state the following result.

Theorem 1.8 (Navarro, Rychlik and Spizzichino, 2020): If T is the lifetime of a coherent system with $n>2$ component lifetimes $(X_1, \ldots, X_n)$, then the following conditions are equivalent:

(i) Samaniego's representation (1.1) holds for the structural signature of T;
(ii) If $A_i = \{X_i \le t\}$ and $B_i = \{X_i > t\}$, then for any permutation σ and for $1<k<n$: $P(A_1 \cap \ldots \cap A_k \cap B_{k+1} \cap \ldots \cap B_n) = C(A_{\sigma(1)} \cap \ldots \cap A_{\sigma(k)} \cap B_{\sigma(k+1)} \cap \ldots \cap B_{\sigma(n)})$;
(iii) The random vector with the component states at time t is exchangeable for any $t>0$;
(iv) The component lifetimes are i.d. with a common distribution function F and their survival copula is S-diagonal dependent where S is the image of F.

Note that (ii) contains a new condition to get the Samaniego's representation. Also note that if F is continuous, then $S = [0,1]$ and then the survival copula should be DD.

1.4 AN EXAMPLE

Let us illustrate the theoretical results with an example. We consider the system with lifetime $T = \min(X_1, \max(X_2, X_3))$, where the component lifetimes (X_1, X_2, X_3) have a common (marginal) reliability function R and a survival copula K, that is, the joint reliability function can be written as

$$\mathbf{R}(x_1, x_2, x_3) := P(X_1>x_1, X_2>x_2, X_3>x_3) = K(R(x_1), R(x_2), R(x_3))$$

for all x_1, x_2, x_3. The system reliability R_T can be obtained as

$$R_T(t) = P(T>t) = P(X_1>t, \max(X_2,X_3)>t) = P(\min(X_1,X_2)>t \cup \min(X_1,X_3)>t)$$

And, by using the inclusion-exclusion formula, we get

$$R_T(t) = P(\min(X_1,X_2)>t) + P(\min(X_1,X_3)>t) - P(\min(X_1, X_2, X_3)>t) = q(R(t)),$$

where $q(u) = K(u,u,1)+K(u,1,u) - K(u,u,u)$ for $0 \le u \le 1$.

The system structural signature can be computed as follows. There are 3! = 6 permutations. Note that the system fails with first component failure when $X_1 \le X_2 \le X_3$ or $X_1 \le X_3 \le X_2$, that is, $s_1 = 2/6 = 1/3$. In the other cases, the system fails with the second component failure, that is, $s_2 = 2/3$. Hence $s_3 = 0$.

Similar representations can be obtained for the order statistics. For example, for the series system (first component failure) $X_{1:3} = \min(X_1,X_2,X_3)$ we have

$$R_{1:3}(t) = P(X_{1:3}>t) = P(X_1>t, X_2>t, X_3>t) = K(R(t), R(t), R(t)) = q_{1:3}(R(t)),$$

where $q_{1:3}(u) = K(u, u, u)$. Analogously for the second one (the 2-out-of-3 system) $X_{2:3}$ we get

$$R_{2:3}(t) = P(X_{2:3}>t) = q_{2:3}(R(t))$$

where $q_{2:3}(u) = K(u, u, 1) + K(u, 1, u) + K(1, u, u) - 2K(u, u, u)$. As $s_3 = 0$ we do not need the expression for the third one (the parallel system).

In particular, if the components are independent (i.e., K is the product copula), then we obtain $q(u) = 2u^2 - u^3$, $q_{1:3}(u) = u^3$ and $q_{2:3}(u) = 3u^2 - u^3$. Note that

$$q(u) = s_1\, q_{1:3}(u) + s_2\, q_{2:3}(u)$$

that is,

$$2u^2 - u^3 = (1/3)\, u^3 + (2/3)\,(3u^2 - 2u^3)$$

holds for all $0 \le u \le 1$. Hence, Samaniego's representation (1.1) holds for the i.i.d. case and any reliability function R (continuous or not).

If we choose a DD survival copula K, then this representation also holds. From Definition 1.2, K is DD if and only if

$$K(u, u, 1) = K(u, 1, u) = K(1, u, u)$$

for all $0 \le u \le 1$. In this case,

$$q(u) = 2K(u, u, 1) - K(u, u, u),$$
$$q_{1:3}(u) = K(u, u, u)$$

and

$$q_{2:3}(u) = 3K(u, u, 1) - 2K(u, u, u).$$

Therefore

$$\begin{aligned} s_1\, q_{1:3}(u) + s_2\, q_{2:3}(u) &= (1/3)\, K(u, u, u) + (2/3)\,(3K(u, u, 1) - 2\, K(u, u, u)) \\ &= 2\, K(u, u, 1) + (1/3 - 4/3)\, K(u, u, u)) \\ &= 2\, K(u, u, 1) - K(u, u, u) = q(u) \end{aligned}$$

holds for all $0 \le u \le 1$, that is, representation (1.1) holds for any reliability function R.

However, this representation is not necessarily true for non-DD copula. For example, if we choose the following Farlie-Gumbel-Morgenstern (FGM) copula

$$K(u_1, u_2, u_3) = u_1\, u_2\, u_3\, (1 + \theta\, (1 - u_2)\,(1 - u_3)),$$

for $-1 \le \theta \le 1$, then

$$\begin{aligned} q(u) &= K(u, u, 1) + K(u, 1, u) - K(u, u, u) = 2\, u^2 - K(u, u, u), \\ q_{1:3}(u) &= K(u, u, u), \\ q_{2:3}(u) &= K(u, u, 1) + K(u, 1, u) + K(1, u, u) - 2\, K(u, u, u) \\ &= 3\, u^2 + \theta\, (1 - u)^2\, u^2 - 2\, K(u, u, u) \end{aligned}$$

and if

$$g(u) = q(u) - (s_1\, q_{1:3}(u) + s_2\, q_{2:3}(u))$$

we get

$$\begin{aligned} g(u) &= 2\, u^2 - K(u, u, u) - (1/3)\, K(u, u, u) - (2/3)\,(3\, u^2 + \theta\, (1 - u)^2\, u^2 - 2\, K(u, u, u)) \\ &= (2/3)\, \theta\, (1 - u)^2\, u^2. \end{aligned}$$

Hence, representation (1.1) holds if and only if $\theta = 0$, that is, only when the components are independent. If θ is not zero, then this representation does not hold.

1.5 CONCLUSIONS

Samaniego's representation is a key point in the study of coherent systems. The system signature is a good advisor to know when the system is going to fail since it contains the probabilities of a system failure at the i-th component failure. Moreover, in the i.i.d. case, it can be used to compute the system reliability (by using well known formulas of order statistics) and to stochastically compare systems with different structures just by comparing their signature vectors (in different orderings).

This important achievement can be extended out of the i.i.d. continuous case (which is sometimes unrealistic in practice). Firstly, we need to distinguish between structural and probabilistic signatures. In several cases, these definitions (vectors) do not coincide. Secondly, we need to assume that the components are i.d. This assumption cannot be dropped out if we want to have the equality between the system reliability and Samaniego's representation. Finally, we need to assume that the underlying survival copula is EXC or at least diagonal dependent. This set is dense and so we can obtain a good approximation for any copula C. If the common distribution F is discrete, then this condition can be relaxed to get a S-DD copula where S is the image set of F.

The most important question for future research could be if this representation can be extended out of this case (i.d. components with a S-DD copula). However, Theorem 1.8 gives a negative answer to this question. In the other cases we can use approximations or (better) use the representations based on distortions which provide an exact expression for the system reliability (see, e.g., Navarro and Spizzichino, 2020). Moreover, this representation can also be used to obtain distribution-free comparisons of systems obtaining better results than that obtained with signatures (see, Navarro and del Águila, 2017, Rychlik, Navarro and Rubio, 2018, and the survey in Navarro, 2018).

1.6 ACKNOWLEDGEMENTS

JN is partially supported by Ministerio de Ciencia e Innovación of Spain under grant PID2019–103971GB-I00/AEI/10.13039/501100011033.

REFERENCES

Barlow, R. E. and Proschan, F. (1975). *Statistical Theory of Reliability and Life Testing.* International Series in Decision Processes. Holt, Rinehart and Winston, New York.

Kochar, K., Mukerjee, H. and Samaniego, F. J. (1999). The 'signature' of a coherent system and its application to comparisons among systems. *Naval Research Logistics* 46, 507–523.

Marichal, J-L., Mathonet, P. and Waldhauser, T. (2011). On signature based expressions of system reliability. *Journal of Multivariate Analysis* 102, 1410–1416.

Navarro, J. (2018). Stochastic comparisons of coherent systems. *Metrika* 81, 465–482.

Navarro, J. and del Águila, Y. (2017). Stochastic comparisons of distorted distributions, coherent systems and mixtures with ordered components. *Metrika* 80, 627–648.

Navarro, J. and Fernández-Sánchez, J. (2020). On the extension of signature-based representations for coherent systems with dependent non-exchangeable components. *Journal of Applied Probability* 57, 429–440.

Navarro, J. and Rychlik, T. (2007). Reliability and expectation bounds for coherent systems with exchangeable components. *Journal of Multivariate Analysis* 98, 102–113.

Navarro, J., Rychlik, T. and Spizzichino, F. (2020). Conditions on marginals and copula of component lifetimes for signature representation of system lifetime. *Fuzzy Sets and Systems.* Available online November 12, 2020. https://doi.org/10.1016/j.fss.2020.11.006.

Navarro, J., Samaniego, F. J., Balakrishnan, N. and Bhattacharya, D. (2008). Applications and extensions of system signatures in engineering reliability. *Naval Research and Logistics* 55, 313–327.

Navarro, J. and Spizzichino, F. (2020). Aggregation and signature based comparisons of multistate systems via decompositions of fuzzy measures. *Fuzzy Sets and Systems* 396, 115–137.

Rychlik, T., Navarro, J. and Rubio, R. (2018). Effective procedure of verifying stochastic ordering of system lifetimes. *Journal of Applied Probability* 55, 1261–1271.

Samaniego, F. J. (1985). On the IFR closure theorem. *IEEE Transactions on Reliability* 34, 69–72.

Shaked, M. and Shanthikumar, J. G. (2007). *Stochastic Orders.* Springer Series in Statistics. Springer, New York.

2 Review of Some Shock Models in Reliability Systems

Murat Ozkut

CONTENTS

2.1 INTRODUCTION

Shock models have been thoroughly investigated and have proved to be a practical tool for modeling complex reliability schemes in a random environment. The term shock is used to describe the pain that a system feels as a result of voltage spikes, temperature changes, or human operating errors. Various shock models, such as accumulated shock models, severe shock models, run shock models, delta shock models and mixed shock models, have been introduced and studied in the literature. In the extreme shock models, only the fatal shock impact is usually considered. In contrast, in cumulative shock models, the previous shock's impact is accumulated. According to the δ-shock model, the system fails when the time between two consecutive shocks falls below a fixed threshold δ.

Similarly, the system works until k consecutive shocks with critical magnitude in the run shock model. The researchers also discussed shock models with some combination of these classical types of shock. According to their suggestions, systems may fail because of extreme or cumulatively affected shocks, extreme or delta shocks, cumulative or delta shocks, and also one of these classical types of shock models

DOI: 10.1201/9781003203124-2

extreme, cumulative or delta shocks, whichever occurs first. In all these cases, authors discussed the importance of their proposed models to show the relevance to not modeled real-life problems. As a result, several academic articles on reliability shock models have been published in probability and engineering journals.

2.2 EXTREME SHOCK MODELS

Consider a system subject to random shocks at an unexpected time. The general setup in extreme shock models is a family $\{(X_k, Y_k), k \geq 0\}$ of independent and identical two-dimensional random vectors, where X_k is the magnitude of the kth shock and Y_k is the time interval between two consecutive shocks *(k-1)*th and the kth. If X_k and Y_k are independent, and if Y_k are independent and identically distributed exponential random variables, the model reduced to the homogeneous Poisson process, $k = 0,1,2,\ldots$. For the first k shocks, if the component has a probability $\bar{P}_k$ of surviving, then the component survives beyond time t can be represented as follows:

$$\bar{H}(t) = \sum_{k=0}^{\infty} \bar{P}_k \frac{e^{-\lambda t}(\lambda t)^k}{k!},\ t \geq 0 \tag{1.1}$$

for some $\lambda > 0$. For more details and properties of this model, see Esary (1957), Epstein (1958), Gaver (1963) and Esary et al. (1973). Unfortunately, this usual Poisson model is not appropriate for many real-life problems. More precisely, X_k will most probably be correlated to Y_k. Consider a stochastic input-output system. The quantity in the system increases over time. At a given time, perhaps depending on the available quantity of the system, all quantities in the system are instantly reset. For example, consider an elevator or a bus, customers arrive at a queue, and the queue's length increases over time. When the measurement reaches a specific size, all customers in the line are cleared. Shanthikumar and Sumita (1983) studied the general shock model's reliability governed by correlated pairs (X_k, Y_k) of the renewal sequence. According to this study, the system fails when the magnitude of a shock exceeds a prespecified level z. Two different models were discussed. In the first model, kth shock magnitude X_k is correlated to the length of interval since the last shock. On the other hand, in the second model, it is correlated to the length of the subsequent interval until the next shock. If $N(t)$ be the counting process associated with renewal sequence $(Y_k)_0^{\infty}$, then the distribution of the system failure time T is given by $P(T \leq t) = P(M(t) > z)$, where $M(t) = max\{X_j\}, 0 \leq j \leq N(t)$. In this study, the first two moments and the renewal process associated with T were discussed. We refer to Anderson (1987, 1988), Gut (1990) for further discussion. Gut and Hüsler (1999) studied the first passage time process $\{\tau(z), z \geq 0\}$ as $min\{n : X_n > z\}$ instead of counting process $N(t)$. The mean, variance and higher order moments of failure time $T_{\tau(z)}$ were investigated. Also, distributional results were presented. For instance, they proved that $\frac{T_{\tau(t)}}{ET_{\tau(t)}} \xrightarrow{d} \exp(1)$ as $t \to x_F$. Gut and Hüsler (2005) generalized the extreme shock models assuming that large but not fatal shocks may affect the system's tolerance to subsequent shocks. For a fixed z, a shock X_i can damage the system if it is larger than a certain boundary value $\beta_z<z$. For the magnitudes of shock $X_i<z$, the system keeps working (nonfatal shock). But if a first nonfatal shock magnitude in $[\beta_z,z]$ the maximum load limit of the system is no more than z, unlike decrease to $\alpha_z(1)\in[\beta_z,z]$. If another large shock is having a magnitude in $[\beta_z,\alpha_z(1)]$, the new threshold reduced to $\alpha_z(2)\in[\beta_z,\alpha_z(1)]$. That is, the threshold decreases until the system fails. Cirillo and Hüsler (2011) presented an alternative perspective to the extreme shock model to develop a Bayesian nonparametric approach to shock models, in the wake of some recent works like Cirillo and Hüsler (2009) by using a particular class of reinforced urn processes, as introduced by Muliere et al. (2000). Cha and Finkelstein (2011) considered the generalized extreme shock model that a failure's probability upon a shock increases with each experienced shock. In the usual extreme shock models, shocks produced from a single source affect to the system. Bozbulut and Eryilmaz (2018) extended this idea to the m possible sources. The system is assumed to be subject to shocks that may arrive from one of m potential sources. The authors of this paper imagine a military force made up of various types of guns (represent the sources) with differing capacities, and conclude that the force kills the target (describe the system) when a single gun's destruction reaches a critical amount. In this case, the lifetime T of the machine can be described as the random time spent by the military force to kill the target. Recently, the reliability and optimal replacement policies of extreme shock models have been of great interest in operational research and reliability engineering. Eryilmaz (2017a) suggested a method to measure the optimum replacement period and mean residual life of the device as described in the extreme shock model. The number of shocks that induce system failure and the time between consecutive shocks is considered to have phase-type distributions. Phase-type distributions have been commonly used in a number of areas, including reliability (Neuts and Meier, 1981). We refer to He (2014) for phase-type distributions' properties and applications. The goal of this research is to decide the best replacement period that minimizes the overall long-run average cost per unit of time. If a device or machine crashes, it is replaced by a new one, and the phase repeats. Each upgrade comes at a cost, and each loss in service comes at an additional cost. As a consequence, an engineer should try to replace the machine until it fails. As the magnitude distribution of shocks varies, Eryilmaz and Kan (2019) looked at the intense shock model. In reality, such a model is useful since a rapid change in environmental circumstances will cause a greater shock. Internal (such as wear and fatigue) and external (such as ice and wind shocks) losses to wind turbine blades were addressed by the authors. External shocks can impact various components, such as the blades of a wind turbine. A severe shock can snap a rotor, causing the wind turbine to stop and need replacement.

2.2.1 Example

Suppose that a system subjected shocks produced at random times, and the interarrival time X_i between the $(i-1)$th and i-th shock, and the magnitude of the i-th shock Y_i are assumed to be independent for all i. The system under concern fails upon the

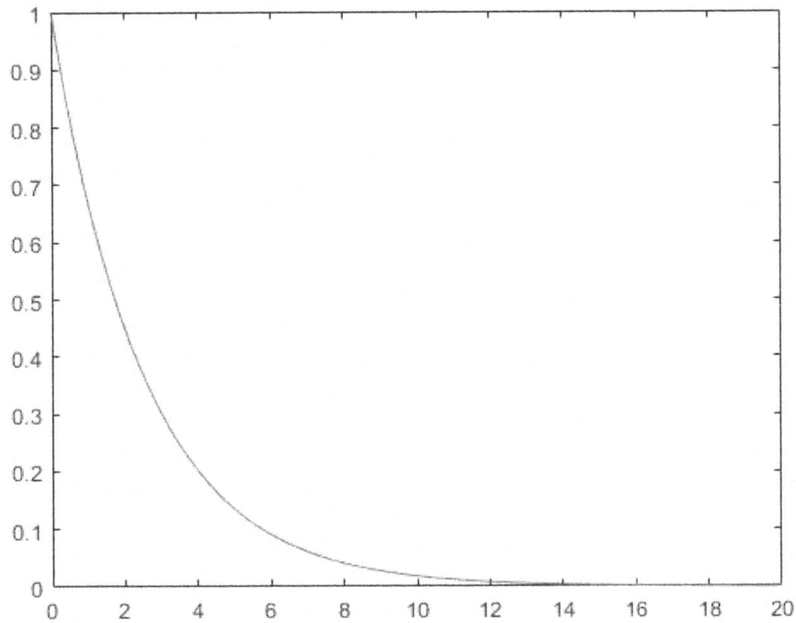

FIGURE 2.1 Survival function of the system under extreme shock model.

occurrence of extreme shock of size at least $d = 3$. Let the times between shocks produced at random times follow Exponential distribution with parameter $\lambda = 2$, and $P(Y_i > 3) = 0.2$. In Figure 2.1, we plot the survival function of the system.

2.3 CUMULATIVE SHOCK MODELS

In certain real-world systems, a single shock does not influence the system; instead, the results of multiple shocks may be cumulative. For example, earthquake losses (such as internal building cracks) are additive, and flooding of riverbeds, ocean beaches, and dams is another example. The total frequency of the shocks, rather than the highest shock value to date, defines the system's durability in these situations. Sumita and Shanhikumar (1985) investigated a class of cumulative shock models in which the system failure period T is defined as the time before the cumulative magnitude of the shocks reaches a fixed amount z for the first time.

As mentioned in the extreme shock model, the general setup in cumulative shock models is a family $\{(X_k, Y_k), k \geq 0\}$ of i.i.d two-dimensional random variables. Similarly, X_k and Y_k represent the magnitude of the kth shock and time between $(k-1)$th and kth shock, respectively. According to this model, the system fails when the cumulative shock magnitude exceeds a predefined level. More precisely, let $N(t)$ be the number of shocks in the interval $(0,t]$, and the cumulative magnitude of the shocks in *(0,t]* and the system failure time can be defined as follows

$$Z(t) = \sum_{i=0}^{N(t)} X_i \text{ and } S_z = \inf\{t : Z(t) > z\}, \tag{1.2}$$

respectively. Sumita and Shanhikumar (1985) discussed Sz's distribution, its moments, and related limit theorems under this construction. Anderson (1987, 1988) studied some limit theorems for cumulative shock models. In both of these works, the individual summands are believed to be non-negative, which is appropriate for time and shocks, but a model with (at least) positive and negative shocks may also be considered. As a result, Gut (1990) did not consider non-negativity, only the fact that the shocks' random walk has a positive drift. Some limit theorems for a system's lifetime/failure time were also presented in this analysis. Bai et al. (2006) discussed the cumulative shock process's limiting properties and generalized the classical shock model by building a cluster shock structure. Bai et al. (2014) addressed a generalized accumulated shock model and its lifetime properties. The machine is subjected to two kinds of shocks: principal shocks and secondary shocks. According to a "cluster" process, each primary shock triggers a series of secondary shocks. The shock mechanism is then a superposition of a main (shock) process and a set of adjunct (shock) processes with a cluster structure. When the superposed impact of the primary and secondary shocks reaches the threshold stage, the mechanism fails. Montoro-Cazorla and Pérez-Ocón (2015) discussed the cumulative shock models using matrix-analytic methods where shocks' arrivals are a batch Markovian arrival process. For this system, the lifetime and the number of shocks while operational are also presented. Ranjkesh et al. (2019) defined and studied a new cumulative shock model by classifying the damages inflicted by shocks based on the interarrival time between consecutive shocks. Gong et al. (2019) developed a generalized cumulative shock model considering a system subject to random shocks from various sources with different probabilities. Similar to the extreme shock models, many studies in cumulative shock models have replacement policies. Nakagawa and Kijima (1989) applied the periodic replacement with minimal repair at the failure of the cumulative damage model. Qian et al. (1999) used the cumulative damage model to backup files in a database system and obtained the optimal replacement period. Li and Xu (2006) discussed the dependence structure, incorporated the Block Imperfect Repair policy into the cumulative damage shock model. A system of components is subject to correlated shock damages and group repairs. Nakagawa (2007) summarized maintenance policies and their optimization problems for cumulative damage models. Sheu et al. (2020) recently developed a replacement policy for cumulative damage models.

2.3.1 Example

Suppose that a system subjected shocks produced at random times, and the interarrival time X_i between the *(i – 1)*th and i-th shock, and the magnitude of the i-th shock Y_i are assumed to be independent for all *i*. The system fails when the total damage

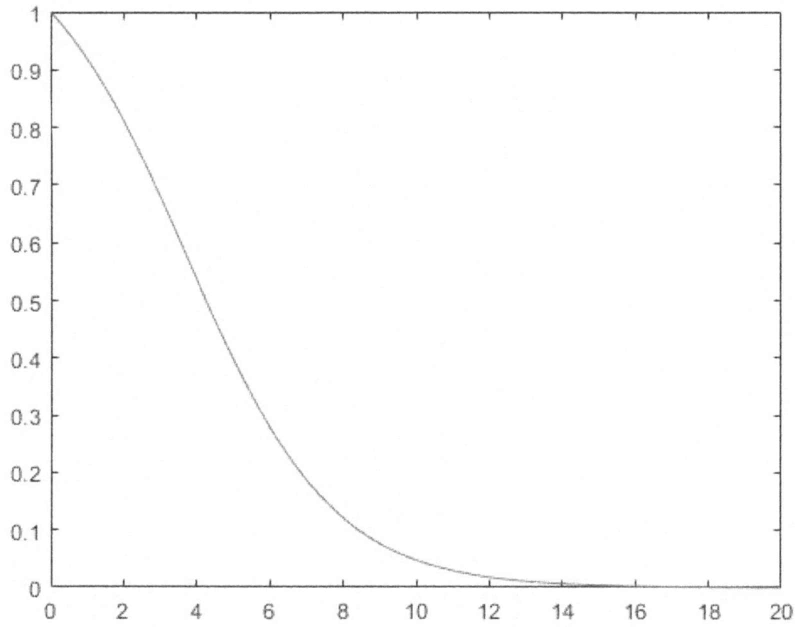

FIGURE 2.2 Survival function of the system under cumulative shock model.

has exceeded a failure level $d = 1$. Let the times between shocks produced at random times and the shock magnitude follow Exponential distribution with parameters $\lambda = 2$ and $\mu = 1$, respectively.

In Figure 2.2, we plot the survival function of the system.

2.4 δ-SHOCK MODELS

The previous models' system lifetime is defined in terms of shock magnitude. However, many appearances exist in real life where these famous structures are not applicable. Li (1984), for example, looked at traffic modeling in which pedestrians tend to cross the street when the time of two consecutive moving vehicles reaches a fixed threshold δ. In the δ-shock model, when the time between two successive shocks falls below a fixed threshold δ, the system fails. Similarly, Li et al. (1999) obtained the explicit distribution, the moment, the NBU/NWU properties of the system lifetime, and its asymptotic behavior as $\delta \to 0$. Li and Chen (2002) also discussed similar shock models. δ-shock model has a potential application in various fields such as electrical systems, earthquake modeling, inventory, insurance, and many other system reliability areas. They provide a more fair characterization over conventional shock models, especially when the shock damages are not obtainable (Li and Kong, 2007). Li and Zhao (2007) studied complex systems consisting of n i.i.d. units with a δ-shock model.

Similar to previous shock models, there is great interest in maintenance problems based on the δ–shock system. An optimal replacement policy of the repairable δ-shock system is obtained by Wang and Zhang (2001). Tang and Lam (2006) explored a geometric process maintenance issue using the δ-shock method, which Liang et al. have expanded (2011). In customer experience management, Ma and Li (2010) suggested a censored δ-shock paradigm to characterize customers' lifespan (CRM). This paradigm creates a slew of intriguing questions as well as a slew of fresh ideas. A customer's lifespan can be thought of as the sum of δ and all past trading cycles in everyday life. If the time between two consecutive trades approaches a threshold δ, a subsequent transaction from this customer will be viewed as if it were from a new customer. Eryilmaz (2012) used the idea of runs to generalize the δ-shock model. According to this model, when k consecutive interarrival periods are less than a threshold δ, the method fails. The survival function and the mean value of the system's failure time were specifically derived for exponentially spaced interarrival times. The discrete-time variant of the δ-shock model was proposed by Eryilmaz (2013). A binomial mechanism produces the shocks in this study. Interarrival times between successive shocks, more specifically, obey a geometric distribution with a mean of $1/p$.

Similarly, the life behavior of δ-shock models were studied by Eryilmaz and Bayramoglu (2014) for uniformly distributed interarrival times. For general interarrival distribution and survival functions, the first two moments of the associated lifetime random variables were investigated. Where the times between shocks adopt a uniform distribution, Pan et al. (2017) addressed parameter estimation in the censored δ-shock model. By assuming that the device is subject to two shock forms, Wang and Peng (2017) discussed generalization of the δ-shock model. Shock interarrival times $(X1, X2, \ldots)$ are independent and identically distributed with a standard continuous distribution in all of these works.

Eryilmaz (2017), on the other hand, investigated the δ-shock model under the assumption that shocks arrive through a Polya mechanism, resulting in random variable dependency. Tuncel and Eryilmaz analyze the δ-shock model under the non-identically distributed presumption of interarrival times (2018). They introduced survival function and mean time to loss expressions (MTTF). Jiang (2020) examined a multi-failure threshold generalized δ-shock model. The system fails to focus on the time intervals between two consecutive shocks that arrive according to a Poisson mechanism for the new model. The censored δ-shock model with a discrete-time shock mechanism was discussed by Bian et al. (2019). The Markov chain censored δ-shock model and the lattice renewal censored δ-shock model are also tested. Ma et al. (2019) extended the δ-shock model, suggesting that the shocks come from a discrete-time Markov chain. The device subjected to the shocks is said to malfunction in this shock model if the time interval between two successive shocks is greater than a given threshold value. In a multi-state structure, Poursaeed (2019) investigated the δ-shock model.

2.4.1 Example

Suppose that a system subjected shocks produced at random times, and the interarrival time X_i between the $(i-1)$th and i-th shock, and the magnitude of the i-th shock Y_i

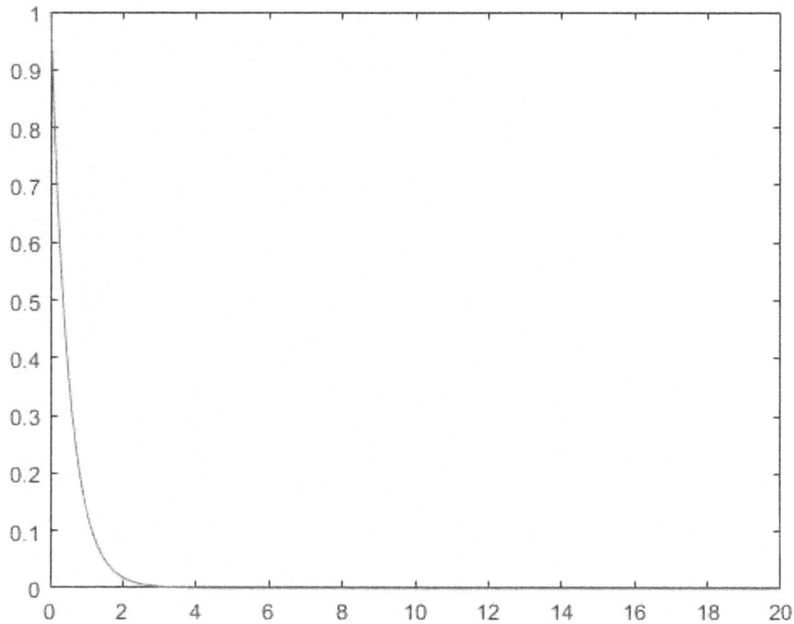

FIGURE 2.3 Survival function of the system under δ-shock model.

are assumed to be independent for all *i*. The system fails when the time between two consecutive shocks falls below a fixed threshold $\delta = 0.2$. Let the times between shocks produced at random times follow Exponential distribution with parameters $\lambda = 2$.

In Figure 2.3, we plot the survival function of the system.

2.5 RUN SHOCK MODELS

According to Mallor and Omey (2001), $(A, B), (A(1), B(1)), (A(2), B(2)), \ldots$ denote nonnegative, independent random vectors with the same joint distribution function $F(u, v) = P\{A < u, B<v\}$. For a fixed subset $R \subset [0,\infty)$ and fixed $k = 1, 2, \ldots$ the new random variable

$N(k, R) = min\{j: A(j - i) \in R, for\ i = 0, 1, \ldots, k\text{-}1\}$ counts the number of experiments until the first run of *k* consecutive *A*-values in the critical region *R* occur. This variable has a geometric distribution of order *k*. In this model, *A(i)* and *B(i)* denote the random magnitude of shocks and duration, respectively. When $k = 1$, the model reduced the idea studied by Shanthikumar and Sumita (1983) for $E(B) < \infty$. and by Anderson (1987) for $E(B) = \infty$.

This model is reduced to the Poisson shock model studied by Esary et al. (1973) since *A(i)* and *B(i)* are separate and equal exponentially distributed. By assuming that the random variable *N* has an arbitrary phase-type distribution, Yalcin et al. (2018) extended the model studied by Mallor and Omey (2001). As a result, they created a new class of shock models and developed matrix-based representations for the shock model's reliability properties. In real-world problems, the run shock concept has been commonly used. However, in some instances, a single threshold is insufficient to distinguish the magnitude of the damage sustained by the shocks.

For this reason, Gong et al. (2018) developed a generalized run shock model with two thresholds. According to this new model, a system is subject to random shocks over time. For two critical levels, $c_1 < c_2$, and given positive integers k_1 and k_2, the system is assumed to fail if at least k_1 consecutive shocks with a magnitude above c_1 or k_2 consecutive shocks magnitude above c_2 occur. Ozkut and Eryilmaz (2019) recently suggested a shock model that incorporates Marshall–Olkin and run shock models. According to the current model, a two-component structure is vulnerable to shocks from three different directions. Source 1 (2) produces a shock that only affects component 1 (2), while source 3 produces a shock that may affect all components. As a consequence, the induced shocks are categorized as either critical or non-critical. According to this model, a part fails if it is subjected to k consecutive critical shocks from the same source.

2.5.1 Example

Suppose that a system subjected shocks produced at random times, and the interarrival time X_i between the $(i-1)$th and i-th shock, and the magnitude of the i-th shock Y_i are assumed to be independent for all i. Assume that the system fails when the first run of $k = 2$ consecutive shocks that are equal to or above the critical threshold d. Let the times between shocks produced at random times follow Erlang distribution with parameters $\lambda = 1, m = 2$, and the probability that a shock exceeds the critical level is $p = 0.2$. In Figure 2.4, we plot the survival function of the system.

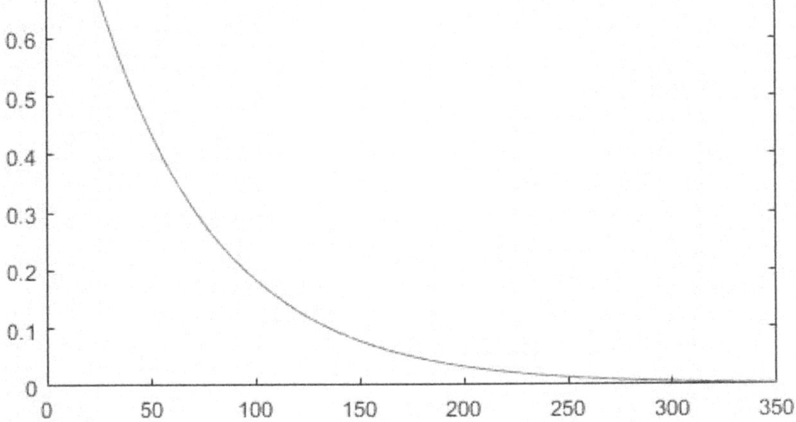

FIGURE 2.4 Survival function of the system under run shock model.

2.6 MIXED SHOCK MODELS

Several studies about the mixture of the shock models discussed above in the literature are also discussed. Gut (2001) investigated a combination of cumulative and extreme shock models, in which the system fails because of either a cumulative effect or a single large shock, depending on which occurs first. As mentioned, if X_i denotes the magnitude of the i-th shock and $S_n = \sum_{k=1}^{n} X_k$, then the first passage time for extreme shock and cumulative shock models are defined as $\tau(z) = min\{n: X_n>z\}$, $z \geq 0$, and $v(z) = min\{n: S_n>z\}$. Therefore, according to the mixed shock models defined by Gut (2001), the number of shocks at the time of failure equals $min(\tau(z),v(z))$.

Parvardeh and Balakrishnan (2015) considered two mixed shock models using delta-shock, extreme shock, and cumulative shock models. When the time between two consecutive shocks is less than a critical threshold δ, or the shock frequency is greater than another critical threshold γ, the system fails in the first model. In the second model, the mechanism fails when the time between two consecutive shocks is less than a critical threshold δ, or the total shock magnitude is greater than another critical threshold γ. Let Y_k be the time interval between the $(k\text{-}1)$th and kth shocks, and X_k be the magnitude of the kth shock. Hence, the lifetime of the system according to the first model is given by $T = \sum_{k=1}^{N} Y_k$

where $(N = n) = (Y_1 > \delta, X_1 \leq \gamma, \ldots, Y_{n-1} > \delta, X_{n-1} \leq \gamma, Y_n \leq \delta) \cup (Y_1 > \delta, X_1 \leq \gamma, \ldots, Y_{n-1} > \delta, X_{n-1} \leq \gamma, Y_n > \delta, X_n > \gamma)$. In the second model, $T = \sum_{k=1}^{N} X_k$, where

$$(N = n) = (Y_1 > \delta, Z_1 \leq \gamma, \ldots, Y_{n-1} > \delta, Z_{n-1} \leq \gamma, Y_n \leq \delta) \cup (Y_1 > \delta, Z_1 \leq \gamma, \ldots, Y_{n-1} > \delta, Z_{n-1} \leq \gamma, Y_n > \delta, Z_n > \gamma).$$

Rafiee et al. (2015) studied the hybrid shock model, which comprises three classic shock models: extreme shock model, δ-shock model, and run shock model, as opposed to the previously mentioned mixed shock models, which considered a mixture of two shock models. As a result, they established a new reliability model for devices prone to contingent competing risks due to a simplified mixed shock model. According to this new construction, the system fails when any of the three classic shocks occurs, that is, if

(i) there is a shock whose magnitude is greater than the predefined threshold (the extreme shock model),
(ii) there is a set of n consecutive shocks whose magnitudes are greater than the predefined threshold (the run shock model), or
(iii) the interarrival time between two successive shocks is less than δ (the δ-shock model). For more details about calculating the system's reliability under this type of mixed shock model, we refer to Eryilmaz and Tekin (2019).

Eryilmaz and Tekin (2019) introduced a new mixed shock model that for two settled critical values d_1 and d_2 such that $d_1 < d_2$, the system under concern fails against k consecutive occurrence shocks size at least d_1 or a single large shock of size at least d_2. More precisely, in this study, the authors combine run and extreme shock models. Besides, the reliability properties of such a system are studied for the following two cases:

i) when the interarrival time Y_i between the $(i - 1)$th and i-th shock, and the magnitude of the i-th shock X_i are independent for all i,
ii) when they are dependent for all i.

In this study, one can easily see that if $d_2 \to \infty$, then the proposed model is the same as the run shock model. Such a mixed shock model helps model various devices or systems' failure patterns. Lorvand et al. (2020a) recently suggested a modern shock model in which shocks arise according to a binomial mechanism at times $n = 1, 2, \ldots$, with interarrival times following a geometric distribution with parameter p. Each interarrival time between two consecutive shocks less than δ causes the system to transition to a lower partly operating state in this model. When k out of the interarrival times between two consecutive shocks are less than δ or the frequency of either shock is greater than the other predetermined amount γ, the system fails. Such a model creates a multi-state system having several different states. The time spent in a perfect operating environment, the probability mass functions of the system's lifespan, and the cumulative time spent in partly functional conditions are all measured in this analysis. Lorvand et al. (2020b) examined the multi-state systems life propagation behavior of a generalization of the mixed δ-shock models. According to this new model, the k out of interarrival periods between two consecutive shocks with a magnitude less than d produces a total loss. Furthermore, if the amplitude of a shock approaches another critical level, c, the system will malfunction. The lifetime survival functions, the system's time in a fully working state, and the cumulative time spent by the system in partly working states are extracted, and the first two moments are also presented, as in Lorvand et al. (2020a).

2.6.1 Example

Suppose that a system subjected shocks produced at random times, and the interarrival time X_i between the $(i - 1)$th and i-th shock, and the magnitude of the i-th shock Y_i are assumed to be independent for all i. The system fails if either a run of $k = 2$ consecutive shocks of size at least d_1 occurs or a single shock of size at least d_2 occurs, where d_1 and d_2 are two fixed thresholds such that $d_1 < d_2$. Let the times between shocks produced at random times follow Erlang distribution with parameters $\lambda = 1, m = 2$, and $P\{d_1 \le Y_i < d_2\} = 0.2$ and $P\{Y_i \ge d_2\} = 0.1$, $i = 1,2 \ldots$.

In Figure 2.5, we plot the survival function of the system.

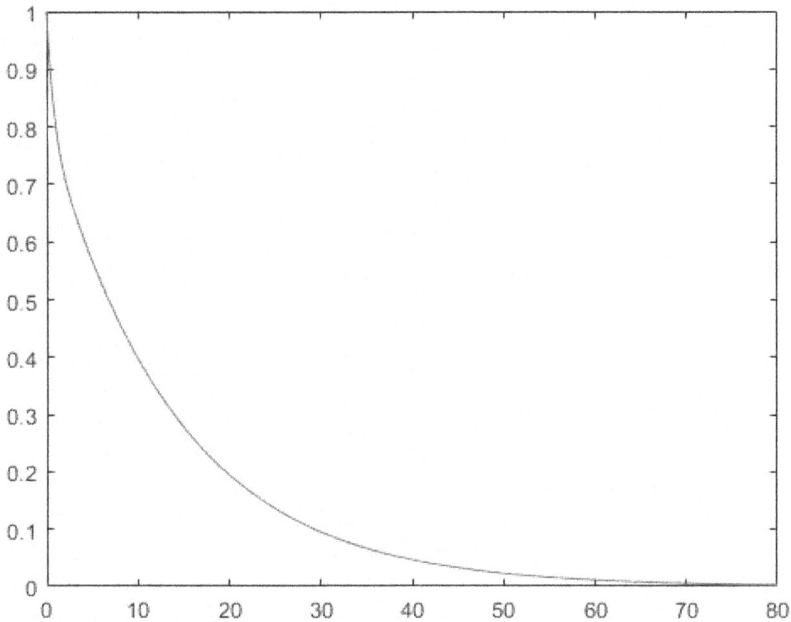

FIGURE 2.5 Survival function of the system under mixed shock model.

REFERENCES

Anderson, K.K. (1987). Limit theorems for general shock models with infinite mean inter-shock times. *Journal of Applied Probability*, 24, 449–456.

Anderson, K.K. (1988). A note on cumulative shock models. *Journal of Applied Probability*, 25, 220–223.

Bai, J.M., Li, Z.H. and Kong, X.B. (2006). Generalized shock models based on a cluster point process. *IEEE Transactions on Reliability*, 55(3), 542–550.

Bai, J.M., Zang, Z.G. and Li, Z.H. (2014). Lifetime properties of a cumulative shock model with a cluster structure. *Annals of Operations Research*, 212, 21–41.

Bian, L., Ma, M., Liu, H. and Ye, J.H. (2019). Lifetime distribution of two discrete censoreddshock models. *Communications in Statistics Theory and Methods*, 48 (14), 3451–3463.

Bozbulut, A. and Eryilmaz, S. (2018). Generalized extreme shock models and their applications. *Communications in Statistics-Simulation and Computation*, 49(1), 110–120.

Cha, J. and Finkelstein, M. (2011). On new classes of extreme shock models and some generalizations. *Journal of Applied Probability*, 48, 258–270.

Cirillo, P. and Hüsler, J. (2009). An urn-based approach to generalized extreme shock models. *Statistics and Probability Letters*, 79, 969–976.

Cirillo, P. and Hüsler, J. (2011). Extreme shock models: An alternative perspective. *Statistics and Probability Letters*, 81, 25–30.

Epstein, B. (1958). The exponential distribution and its role in life testing. *Industrial Quality Control*, 15, 2–7.

Eryilmaz, S. (2012). Generalized δ-shock model via runs. *Statistics & Probability Letters*, 82(2), 326–331.

Eryilmaz, S. (2013). On the lifetime behavior of a discrete time shock model. *Journal of Computational and Applied Mathematics*, 237(1), 384–388.

Eryilmaz, S. (2017a). Computing optimal replacement time and mean residual life in reliability shock models. *Computers and Industrial Engineering*, 103, 40–45.

Eryilmaz, S. (2017b). Delta-shock model based on Polya process and its optimal replacement policy. *European Journal of Operational Research*, 263(2), 690–697.

Eryilmaz, S. and Bayramoglu, K. (2014). Life behavior of δ-shock models for uniformly distributed interarrival times. *Statistical Papers*, 55, 841–852.

Eryilmaz, S. and Kan, C. (2019). Reliability and optimal replacement policy for an extreme shock model with a change point. *Reliability Engineering and System Safety*, 190, 106513.

Eryilmaz, S. and Tekin, M. (2019). Reliability evaluation of a system under a mixed shock model. *Journal of Computational and Applied Mathematics*, 352, 255–261.

Esary, J.D. (1957). A Stochastic theory of accident survival and fatality. Ph.D. dissertation, University of California, Berkeley.

Esary, J.D., Marshall, A.W. and Proschan, F. (1973). Shocks models and wear processes. *The Annals of Probability*, 1(17), 627–649.

Gaver, D.P. (1963). Random hazard in reliability problems. *Technometrics*, 5, 211–226.

Gong, M., Eryilmaz, S. and Xie, M. (2019). Reliability assessment of system under a generalized cumulative shock model. *Proceedings of the Institution of Mechanical Engineers, Part O: Journal of Risk and Reliability*, 234, 129–137.

Gong, M., Xie, M. and Yang, Y. (2018). Reliability assessment of system under ageneralized run shock model. *Journal of Applied Probability*, 55(4), 1249–1260.

Gut, A. (1990). Cumulative shock models. *Advances in Applied Probability*, 22, 504–507.

Gut, A. (2001). Mixed shock models. *Bernoulli*, 7, 541–555.

Gut, A. and Hüsler, J. (1999). Extreme shock models. *Extremes*, 2(3), 295–307.

Gut, A. and Hüsler, J. (2005). Realistic variation of shock models. *Statistics and Probability Letters*, 74, 187–204.

He, Q.M. (2014). *Fundamentals of Matrix-analytic Methods.* New York: Springer.

Li, H. and Xu, S.H. (2006). A multivariate cumulative damage shock model with block preventive maintenance. *Stochastic Models*, 22(2), 341–362.

Li, Z. and Kong, X. (2007). Life behavior of delta shock model. *Statistics and Probability Letters*, 77, 577–587.

Li, Z. and Zhao, P. (2007). Reliability analysis on the-shock model of complex systems. *IEEE Transactions on Reliability*, 56 (2), 340–348.

Li, Z.H. (1984). Some distributions related to Poisson processes and their application in solving the problem of traffic jam. *Journal of Lanzhou University (Natural Sciences)*, 20, 127–136.

Li, Z.H. and Chen, F. (2002). The distribution of dual delta-shock model and its properties, *Proceeding of the 6th Conference of China Society for Industrial and Applied Mathematics*, 258–263.

Li, Z.H., Huang, B.S. and Wang, G.J. (1999). Life distribution and its properties of shock models under random shocks. *Journal of Lanzhou University*, 35(4), 1–7.

Liang, X.L., Lam, Y. and Li, Z.H. (2011). Optimal replacement policy for a general geometric process model with δ-shock. *International Journal of Systems Science*, 42(12), 2021–2034.

Lorvand, H., Nematollahi, A.R. and Poursaeed, M.H. (2020a). Assessment of a generalized discrete time mixed delta-shock model for the multi-state systems. *Journal of Computational and Applied Mathematics*, 366, 112415.

Lorvand, H., Poursaeed, M.H. and Nematollahi, A.R. (2020b). On the life distribution behavior of the generalized mixed delta-shock models for the multi-state systems. *Iranian Journal of Science and Technology Transaction A-Science*, 44(3), 839–850.

Ma, M., Bian, L.N., Liu, H. and Ye, J.H. (2019). Lifetime behavior of discrete Markov chain censored delta shock model. *Communications in Statistics: Theory and Methods.* doi: 10.1080/03610926.2019.1650184.

Ma, M. and Li, Z. (1010). Life behavior of censored -shock model. *Indian Journal of Pure and Applied Mathematics*, 41, 401–420.

Mallor, F. and Omey, E. (2001). Shocks, runs and random sums. *Journal of Applied Probability*, 38(2), 438–448.

Montoro-Cazorla, D. and Pérez-Ocón, R. (2015). A reliability system under cumulative shocks governed by a BMAP. *Applied Mathematical Model*, 39(23), 7620–7629.

Muliere, P., Secchi, P. and Walker, S.G. (2000). Urn schemes and reinforced random walks. *Stochastic Processes and Their Applications*, 88, 59–78.

Nakagawa, T. (2007). *Shock and Damage Model in Reliability Theory.* London: Springer Verlag.

Nakagawa, T. and Kijima, M. (1989). Replacement policies for a cumulative damage model with minimal repair at failure. *IEEE Transactions on Reliability*, 13, 581–584.

Neuts, M.F. and Meier, K.S. (1981). On the use of phase-type distributions in reliability modeling of systems with two components. *OR Spektrum*, 2, 227–234.

Ozkut, M. and Eryilmaz, S. (2019). Reliability analysis under Marshall–Olkin run shock model. *The Journal of Computational and Applied Mathematics*, 349, 52–59.

Pan, B.J., Ming, M. and Wen, Y.Y. (2017). Parameter estimation of the censored δ-shock model on uniform interval. *Communications in Statistics: Theory and Methods*, 46, 6936–6946.

Parvardeh, A. and Balakrishnan, N. (2015). On mixed delta-shock models. *Statistics and Probability Letters*, 102, 51–60.

Poursaeed, M.H. (2019). On d-shock model in a multi-state system. *Communications in Statistics–Theory and Methods.* doi:10.1080/03610926.2019.1565784.

Qian, C., Nakamura, S. and Nakagawa, T. (1999). Cumulative damage model with two kinds of shocks and its application to the backup policy. *Journal of the Operations Research Society of Japan*, 42(4), 501–511.

Rafiee, K., Feng, Q. and Coit, D.W. (2015). Condition-based maintenance for repairable deteriorating systems subject to a generalized mixed shock model. *IEEE Transactions on Reliability*, 64(4), 1164–1174.

Ranjkesh, S.H., Hamadania, A.Z. and Mahmoodi, S. (2019). A new cumulative shock model with damage and inter-arrival time dependency. *Reliability Engineering and System Safety*, 192, 106047.

Shanthikumar, J.G. and Sumita, U. (1983). General shock models associated with correlated renewal sequences. *Journal of Applied Probability*, 20, 600–614.

Sheu, S.H., Liu, T.H., Zhang, Z.G. and Tsai, H.N. (2020). Optimum replacement policy for cumulative damage models based on multi-attributes. *Computers and Industrial Engineering*, 139, 106206.

Tang, Y.Y. and Lam, Y. (2006). A delta-shock maintenance model for a deteriorating system. *European Journal of Operational Research*, 168, 541–556.

Tuncel, A. and Eryilmaz, S. (2018). System reliability under delta shock model. *Communications in Statistics: Theory and Methods*, 47 (19), 4872–4880.

Wang, G.J. and Peng, R. (2017). A generalized δ-shock model with two types of shocks. *International Journal of System Science: Operations and Logistics*, 4(4), 372–383.

Wang, G.J. and Zhang, Y.L. (2001). Delta-shock model and its optimal replacement policy. *Journal of Southeast University*, 31, 121–124.

Yalcin, F., Eryilmaz, S. and Bozbulut, A.R. (2018). A generalized class of correlated run shock models. *Dependence Model*, 6, 131–138.

3 Goodness of Fit Exponentiality Test against Light and Heavy Tail Alternatives

Alex Karagrigoriou, Georgia Papasotiriou and Ilia Vonta

CONTENTS

3.1 INTRODUCTION

In all scientific fields, the problem of determining the appropriate distribution or the appropriate model for a given data set is extremely important for reducing the possibility of erroneous inference. Additional issues are raised in biomedicine and in reliability theory where the existence of censoring schemes makes the determination of the proper distribution or model a rather challenging problem. An important aspect is how to check validity of a specific model assumption.

Some of the most popular continuous distributions in biomedicine, engineering, survival analysis and reliability are the exponential, lognormal, Gamma, Inverse Gaussian, Weibull, Pareto, and Positive Stable distributions. The family of the two-parameter Inverse Gaussian distribution is one of the basic models for describing positively skewed data which arise in a variety of fields of applied research as cardiology, hydrology, demography, linguistics, employment service, etc. (see for instance Chhikara and Folks, 1977).

In this work we focus on exponentiality tests. For testing exponentiality we can use probability plots, quantile versus quantile plot (qq plot) and percent

DOI: 10.1201/9781003203124-3

versus percent plot (pp plot) (see Wilk and Gnanadesikan, 1968). In addition, an entire class of goodness of fit (gof) tests are based on measures of divergence or distance between two probability distributions and they have a long history going back more than a century to the work of Pearson in multinomial distributions (see e.g., Cressie and Read, 1984; Mattheou et al., 2009; Vonta et al., 2012). Classical are also the tests of Kolmogorov-Smirnov and Cramér-von Mises which are based on the empirical distribution function. Other tests include the Gini statistic (Gail and Gastwirth, 1978), the test of Cox and Oakes (1984), the Klar's test (2001) (based upon the integrated distribution function), the L-test of Henze and Meintanis (2002a) (based upon empirical Laplace transform), the W-tests of Henze and Meintanis (2002b) (based upon empirical characteristic function) and the test of Baratpour and Rad (2012) (based on the cumulative residual entropy). For an extended review on exponentiality tests the interested reader is referred to Henze and Meintanis (2005).

In the present work we combine all the above issues under a single umbrella and present an exponentiality test. Using a specific property, we focus on hypothesis testing for distinguishing between exponential, light-tailed and heavy-tailed distributions. Note that log-concavity is associated with light-tail distributions while log-convexity with heavy-tailed ones (see An, 1998). Log-concavity is a widely studied topic with substantial literature (see e.g., Gupta and Balakrishnan, 2012) which is mainly due to the fact that log-concavity provides desirable estimation properties (see Walther, 2009; Dümbgen and Rufibach, 2009). For instance, under log-concavity, the maximum likelihood estimator is unique. This work is filling up the gap in the literature regarding the verification of the log-concavity property. At the same time it is vital in reliability, in engineering and in stochastic modeling as it was mentioned earlier, to distinguish between an exponential distribution, a light-tailed one or a heavy tail one. In this work we propose a goodness of fit exponentiality test to be used for distinguishing between exponential and light or long-tail distributions. The test statistic is based on the principle of the so called, single big jump. The details of the formulation of the test are provided in Section 3.2. An extended simulated study which shows the performance of the proposed test statistic is given in Section 3.3. Some concluding remarks are provided in Section 3.4.

3.2 THE THEORETICAL BACKGROUND

An important class of heavy-tailed distributions is the subexponential class which for two independent random variables X and Y with common cumulative distribution function (cdf) F, is defined by the property

$$P\left(X+Y>d\right)\sim 2F(d)$$

Note that all subexponential distributions are long-tailed, but the reverse is not necessarily true. The intuition underlying this definition is the principle of a single big jump (Foss et al., 2007): the summation $X + Y$ is large if one of X, Y is large, whereas the other remains typical. This observation implies that

$$R = \frac{|X - Y|}{X + Y} \tag{3.1}$$

is close to 1. On the other hand, if the two variables contribute equally to their summation, then R will be close to 0 and a light-tail is likely.

It should be pointed out that for a sequence of random variables $X_1, \ldots, X_n$, with $X_{(n)} = \max(X_1, \ldots, X_n)$, the above property can be written as follows:

$$P(X_1 + X_2 + \ldots + X_n > d) \sim P(X_{(n)} > d)$$

It was recently shown (Lehtomaa, 2015) that these properties of R hold in greater generality and that asymptotic properties of the corresponding conditional random variable

$$C_d = R \mid X + Y > d \tag{3.2}$$

provides a sharp borderline between log-convexity and log-concavity. Then, the expectation of the C_d in (3.2) which is given by,

$$E(C_d) \equiv h(d) = E\left[\frac{|X - Y|}{X + Y} \middle| X + Y > d\right] \tag{3.3}$$

can be considered as a generalization of the above with a similar interpretation: being close to 0 for large d if the two variables contribute equally to the summation and close to 1 for large d if one of the variables is of the same magnitude as the summation.

Asmussen and Lehtomaa (2017) proved that for log-concave distributions we have

$$\limsup_{d \to \infty} h(d) \leq \frac{1}{2} \tag{3.4}$$

while for log-convex distributions we have

$$\liminf_{d \to \infty} h(d) \geq \frac{1}{2}. \tag{3.5}$$

Asmussen and Lehtomaa (2017) used the empirical counterpart of (3.3) for a graphical analysis. In this work we are analyzing fully the behavior of the empirical counterpart of (3.3) and use it for constructing a goodness of fit exponentiality test against heavy- and/or light-tailed alternatives.

3.3 THE EXPONENTIALITY TEST

Consider a two-dimensional sequence of random variables $X_1, \dots, X_n$ and $Y_1, \dots, Y_n$. The empirical counterpart of (3.3) is defined to be the test statistic given by

$$T(d,n) = \frac{\sum_{i=1}^{n} R_i 1(X_i + Y_i > d)}{\sum_{i=1}^{n} 1(X_i + Y_i > d)} \tag{3.6}$$

where

$$R_i = \frac{|X_i - Y_i|}{X_i + Y_i}, \; i = 1, \dots, n \tag{3.7}$$

and $1(A)$ is the indicator of A.

Remark. The test statistic (3.6) requires as input a two-dimensional sequence of random variables. For the case of independent and identically distributed (i.i.d.) random variables $Z_1, \dots, Z_{2n}$ one could use, without loss of generality, any pairing of the variables involved. For instance, one could take $X_i = Z_{2i-1}$ and $Y_i = Z_{2i}$.

Figures 3.1 – 3.2 clearly show that the test statistic given in (3.6) takes values around 0.5 for the exponential distribution while for light-tail distributions like the Weibull with shape parameter equal to 1.5 (and scale parameter 1) is less than 0.5. For heavy-tailed distributions like the Weibull with shape parameter equal to 0.5 (and scale parameter 1) the test statistic is greater than 0.5 (see Figure 3.3). Observe that the results hold true for various values of the index *d*. In this particular case we have used different *d* values equal to four different percentiles of the associated distribution under the null, namely the *80th (q80)*, *85th (q85)*, *90th (q90)* and *95th (q95)* percentile. Although the shape of the distribution and therefore the variability differs, the mean appears to stay stable in the sense that it is always greater than *0.5* for heavy tails and smaller than *0.5* for light tails. Finally note that the parameter values used in Figures 3.1–3.3 do not affect the position of the associated distribution.

The position of the exponential distribution in Figure 3.1 is the same irrespectively of the value of the parameter (here is taken to be equal to *1*). The same holds for the shape parameter of the Weibull distribution (both light and heavy-tailed) in Figures 3.2 and 3.3 (keeping the scale parameter fixed and equal to *1* since the distribution is scale invariant).

All the above considerations lead to the use of the test statistic given in (3.6) for testing exponentiality against light or heavy tailed alternatives. In fact, in terms of *h(d)* the hypothesis problem is stated as follows:

$$\mathrm{H}_0 : h(d) = \frac{1}{2} \quad vs. \quad \mathrm{H}_1 : h(d) < \frac{1}{2} \tag{3.8}$$

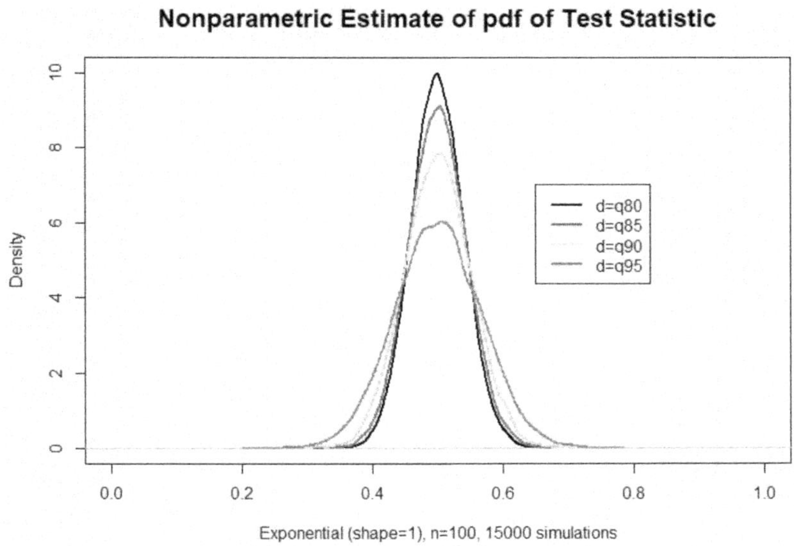

FIGURE 3.1 Exponential distribution—Shape of the test statistic for different *d* values.

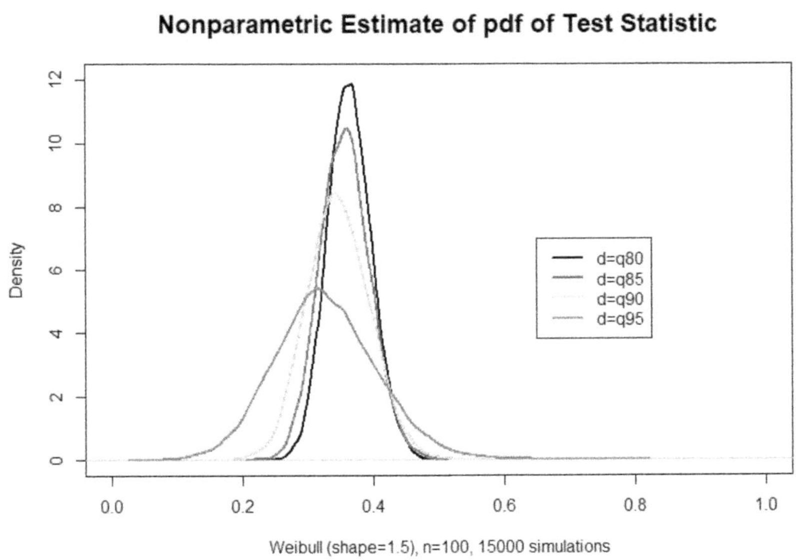

FIGURE 3.2 Weibull with light tail (shape = 1.5) – $n = 100$.

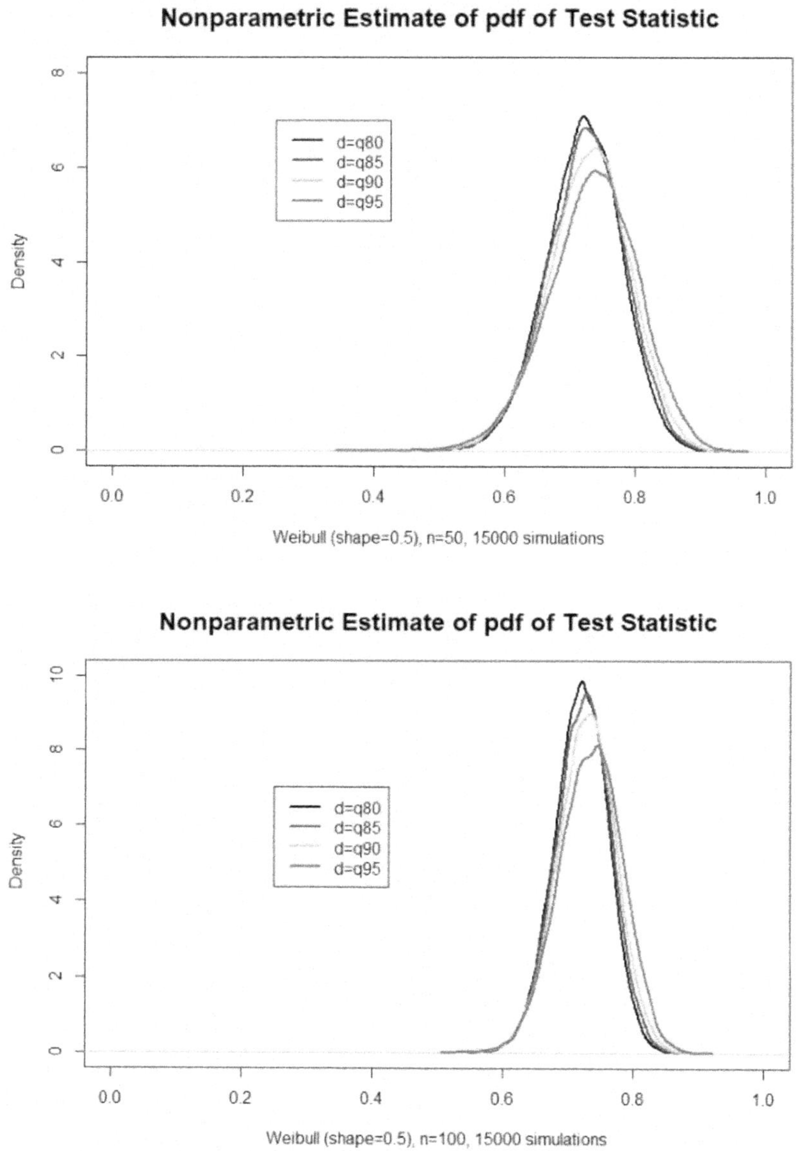

FIGURE 3.3 Weibull with heavy tail (shape = 0.5) – n = *50* (left) and n = *100* (right).

for the case of log-concavity where the exponential distribution is investigated against light-tailed alternatives and

$$\mathrm{H}_0 : h(d) = \frac{1}{2} \quad vs. \quad \mathrm{H}_1 : h(d) > \frac{1}{2} \tag{3.9}$$

for the case of log-convexity where the exponential distribution is investigated against heavy-tailed alternatives.

Although the tests given in (3.8) and (3.9) are sufficient to cover all practical purposes, it should be noted that a two-sided test is also possible to be investigated for the case of no-exponential alternatives:

$$H_0 : h(d) = \frac{1}{2} \quad vs. \quad H_1 : \left| h(d) - \frac{1}{2} \right| > 0$$

3.3.1 Properties of the Test Statistic

One of the most important issues for the test statistic proposed in (3.6) is that its asymptotic mean as well as its asymptotic variance are possible to be obtained for any value of *d*.

In fact, it can be shown that under exponentiality the asymptotic mean is always equal to ½ irrespectively of the value of *d* (see Figure 3.1). Furthermore, this is true for any finite sample size (values of n as small as 30 have been used). In regard to the variance it can be shown (see Figures 3.1–3.3) that the variability depends on *d* and for typical sample sizes ($n = 30$ to $n = 500$) ranges from *0.047* (for *d* equal to the *80th* percentile of the exponential distribution) to *0.077* for *d* equal to the *95th* percentile. For values of *d* equal to the *85th* and *90th* percentiles of the exponential distribution (i.e., under the null), the asymptotic standard deviation is equal to *0.051* and *0.060* respectively. Note that the corresponding asymptotic variances for the above four values of *d* are approaching, as expected, the value of 0 since asymptotically the test statistic is exactly equal to ½ under the assumption of exponentiality. Based on the above discussion the following claim appears to be true for typical sample sizes:

$$Z = \frac{T(d,n) - 0.5}{sd(d)} \overset{approx.}{\sim} N(0,1) \qquad (3.10)$$

where *sd(d)* stands for the standard deviation of the test statistic under exponentiality for typical sample sizes, associated with the value of the index *d*. Hence, as expected, by using the asymptotic mean and variance, the standardized test statistic is asymptotically standard Normal as shown in Figure 3.4.

Although we could rely on the standardized test statistic for the goodness of fit with the typical critical points (e.g., *1.645* for $a = 5\%$ and *1.28* for $a = 10\%$) one may prefer to obtain the unstandardized critical points and use them together with the original test statistic. The approach appears to be ideal since the critical points are independent of the sample size which makes the proposed methodology attractive for practitioners.

Table 3.1 gives both the upper and the lower unstandardized critical points appropriate for hypotheses against both light and heavy tailed alternatives. Indeed, for the standardized critical points, we reject exponentiality in favor of a heavy-tail alternative (see (3.9)) at a *5%* level if

$$Z = \frac{T(d,n) - 0.5}{sd(d)} > 1.645$$

and in favor of a light-tail alternative (see (3.8)) if

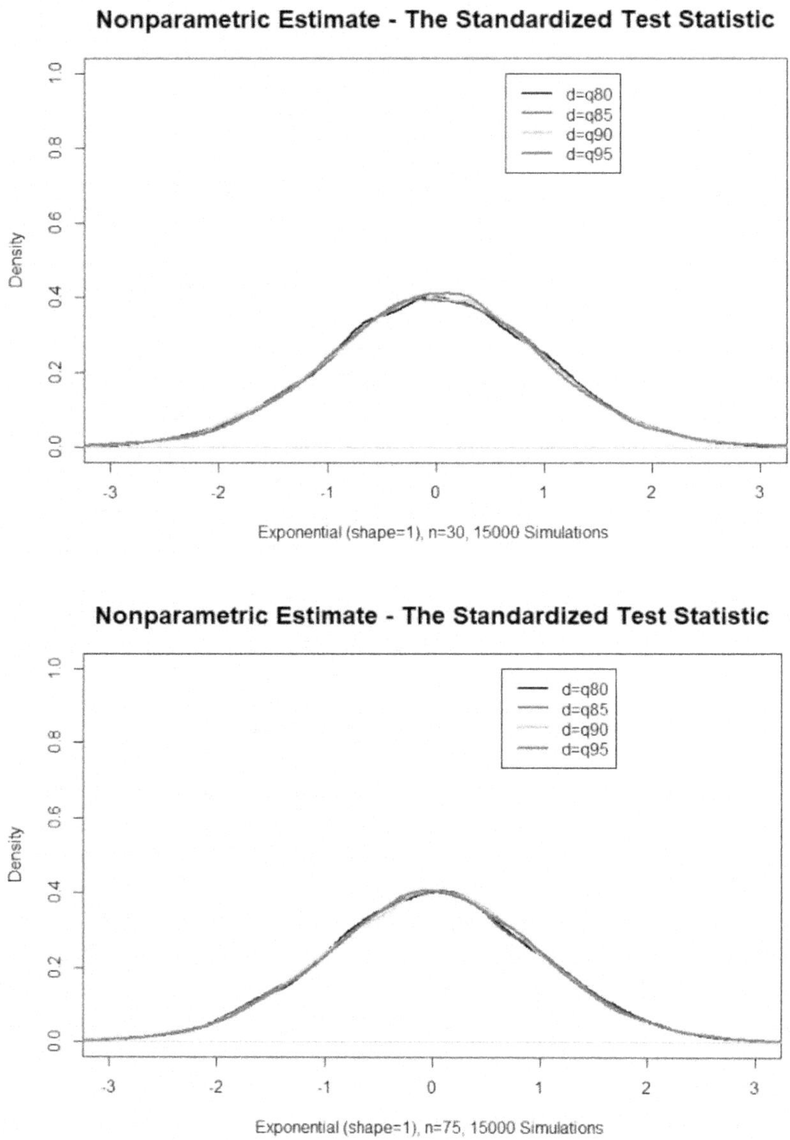

FIGURE 3.4 Standardized Test Statistic n = *30* (left) and n = *75* (right).

TABLE 3.1
Critical Points for the Exponentiality Gof Test

α	d = q95	d = q90	stand. point
		HEAVY TAIL	
5%	*1.645*0.077+0.5* = ***0.626665***	*1.645*0.060+0.5* = ***0.5987***	*1.645*
10%	*1.28*0.077+0.5* = ***0.5986***	*1.28*0.060+0.5* = ***0.5768***	*1.28*
		LIGHT TAIL	
5%	*−1.645*0.077+0.5* = ***0.373335***	*−1.645*0.060+0.5* = ***0.4013***	*−1.645*
10%	*−1.28*0.077+0.5* = ***0.4014***	*−1.28*0.060+0.5* = ***0.4232***	*−1.28*

$$Z = \frac{T(d,n)-0.5}{sd(d)} < -1.645$$

The corresponding values for a *10%* significance level are *1.28* and *−1.28*.

Combining the above standardized critical points together with the asymptotic mean (*0.5* irrespectively of d) and the asymptotic standard deviation (which depends on d) we obtain the unstandardized values given below (for specific d values see Table 3.1):

$$T(d,n) > 0.5 + z_{\alpha} sd(d) \tag{3.11}$$

for heavy tails and for light tails

$$T(d,n) < 0.5 + z_{1-\alpha} sd(d) \tag{3.12}$$

Note that for the two-sided test a non-exponential alternative is accepted if

$$|T(d,n)| > 0.5 + z_{\alpha/2} sd(d).$$

For comparative reasons Table 3.2 provides both the unstandardized critical points together with the exact critical points. The values refer to the upper points (heavy-tailed distributions) but the lower points (light-tailed distributions) are also available (not shown). The results in Table 3.2 show that the critical points proposed for practical purposes for all sample sizes (shown in Table 3.1 and also in boldface in Table 3.2) are close to the average of the exact critical points for sample sizes ranging from $n = 30$ to $n = 500$. Indeed, for $d = q95$, the critical point for any sample size for $a = 5\%$ is equal to *0.626665* which is in the middle between the value *0.5473111* (exact critical point for $n = 500$) to *0.7066978* (exact critical point for $n = 30$). The appropriateness of the proposed test statistic with the critical points as in Table 3.1 which depend only on the value of d and not on the sample size will be shown through a series of simulations for both the size and the power in the following section.

TABLE 3.2
Critical Points for the Exponentiality Gof Test (heavy tail)

		$\alpha = 5\%$	
n	**d = q95**	**d = q90**	**stand. point**
unstand.	***0.626665***	***0.5987***	
500	*0.5473111*	*0.5367998*	
100	*0.6081175*	*0.5836378*	
75	*0.6258382*	*0.59744*	1.645
50	*0.6544912*	*0.6182006*	
30	*0.7066798*	*0.6537647*	
		$\alpha = 10\%$	
unstand.	***0.5986***	***0.5768***	
500	*0.5372985*	*0.5290265*	
100	*0.5849879*	*0.565686*	
75	*0.5974592*	*0.575677*	*1.28*
50	*0.6195537*	*0.5921176*	
30	*0.659948*	*0.6195243*	

TABLE 3.3
Size for the Exponentiality Gof Test

	n	**30**	**50**	**75**	**100**	**200**
q95	***10%***	*0.099*	*0.101*	*0.102*	*0.102*	*0.099*
q95	*5%*	***0.052***	***0.054***	***0.052***	***0.052***	***0.051***
q90	***10%***	*0.100*	*0.104*	*0.103*	*0.104*	*0.101*
q90	*5%*	***0.052***	***0.051***	***0.050***	***0.053***	***0.051***
q85	***10%***	*0.102*	*0.103*	*0.104*	*0.103*	*0.100*
q85	*5%*	***0.052***	***0.049***	***0.053***	***0.053***	***0.050***
q80	***10%***	*0.100*	*0.104*	*0.105*	*0.102*	*0.101*
q80	*5%*	***0.053***	***0.049***	***0.051***	***0.054***	***0.052***

3.4 THE SIZE AND POWER EVALUATION

The performance of the proposed exponentiality test has been examined in terms of the size of the test. For this purpose *20,000* simulations were performed for various sample sizes ranging from $n = 30$ to $n = 200$ and for d equal to the *80th, 85th, 90th* and *95th* percentiles of the exponential distribution. Recall that the distribution is scale invariant and therefore the value of the parameter chosen is irrelevant. The results for size $\alpha = 5\%$ and $\alpha = 10\%$ are given in Table 3.3.

For the power of the test we examine both light and heavy alternatives. First, we focus on the Weibull distribution with a scale parameter that moves away from the exponential to either direction. Values less than 1 are referring to heavy tail alternatives (Table 3.4) while values larger that 1 to light tail alternatives (Table 3.5). The power increases as we move further away giving respectable results even for alternatives extremely close to the exponential distribution (null hypothesis). Tables 3.6 and 3.7 provide the powers when the focus is on Gamma and lognormal alternatives. The cases considered move again away from the exponential distribution to either direction. More specifically, the power performance is investigated for various values of (a) the scale parameter in the case of the Gamma distribution (light tails for values larger than 1 and heavy tails for values less than 1) and (b) the logarithm of the standard deviation in the case of the lognormal distribution (light tails for values smaller than 1 and heavy tails for values larger than 1). As expected, the results in all alternative scenarios are very similar due to the fact that the proposed test statistic given in (3.6), is asymptotically normal irrespectively of the underlying distribution. The only difference is that the density of the test statistic under exponentiality is centered *at 0.5* while under all other distributions, its center is either larger or smaller than 0.5 depending on whether we are dealing with a heavy or a light tail (e.g., see Figures 3.1 – 3.3).

TABLE 3.4
Power for the Exponentiality Gof Test—Heavy Tail Alternatives (*q90, q95*)

20,000 samples	30	50	75	100	200
		95th percentile			
Wei 0.9	0.262 0.236	0.195 0.175	0.157 0.125	0.125 0.088	0.051 0.031
Wei 0.8	0.433 0.364	0.405 0.323	0.389 0.283	0.365 0.250	0.325 0.175
Wei 0.7	0.631 0.539	0.667 0.548	0.706 0.558	0.719 0.551	0.804 0.590
Wei 0.6	0.814 0.729	0.877 0.783	0.920 0.827	0.950 0.854	0.991 0.943
Wei 0.5	0.933 0.884	0.975 0.933	0.993 0.967	0.999 0.990	1.000 0.998
Wei 0.4	0.983 0.970	0.997 0.987	1.000 0.999	1.000 1.000	1.000 1.000
Wei 0.3	0.998 0.997	1.000 1.000	1.000 1.000	1.000 1.000	1.000 1.000
Wei 0.2	1.000 1.000	1.000 1.000	1.000 1.000	1.000 1.000	1.000 1.000
		90th percentile			
Wei 0.9	0.345 0.319	0.309 0.265	0.263 0.220	0.225 0.185	0.150 0.102
Wei 0.8	0.528 0.480	0.534 0.453	0.546 0.441	0.548 0.428	0.559 0.393
Wei 0.7	0.716 0.642	0.778 0.686	0.819 0.719	0.849 0.734	0.925 0.830
Wei 0.6	0.872 0.813	0.924 0.874	0.960 0.913	0.981 0.948	0.999 0.989
Wei 0.5	0.960 0.928	0.988 0.971	0.998 0.990	1.000 0.998	1.000 1.000
Wei 0.4	0.992 0.985	0.998 0.990	1.000 1.000	1.000 1.000	1.000 1.000
Wei 0.3	0.999 0.998	1.000 1.000	1.000 1.000	1.000 1.000	1.000 1.000
Wei 0.2	1.000 1.000	1.000 1.000	1.000 1.000	1.000 1.000	1.000 1.000

TABLE 3.5

Power for the Exponentiality Gof Test—Light Tail Alternatives (*q90, q95*)

20,000 samples	30	50	75	100	200
			95th percentile		
Wei 1.9	0.945 0.672	0.983 0.809	0.994 0.893	0.998 0.934	1.000 0.984
Wei 1.8	0.921 0.681	0.964 0.810	0.990 0.880	0.996 0.920	1.000 0.980
Wei 1.7	0.880 0.688	0.936 0.790	0.967 0.850	0.982 0.883	0.998 0.954
Wei 1.6	0.824 0.663	0.884 0.747	0.923 0.801	0.950 0.827	0.989 0.906
Wei 1.5	0.743 0.626	0.798 0.675	0.840 0.714	0.876 0.737	0.945 0.813
Wei 1.4	0.645 0.555	0.676 0.575	0.706 0.597	0.731 0.602	0.811 0.634
Wei 1.3	0.512 0.463	0.515 0.455	0.518 0.438	0.517 0.428	0.527 0.385
Wei 1.2	0.381 0.358	0.343 0.314	0.306 0.272	0.283 0.246	0.208 0.155
			90th percentile		
Wei 1.9	0.965 0.699	0.991 0.842	0.998 0.923	1.000 0.956	1.000 0.994
Wei 1.8	0.948 0.721	0.983 0.848	0.997 0.917	0.998 0.951	1.000 0.991
Wei 1.7	0.920 0.732	0.934 0.812	0.986 0.901	0.994 0.932	1.000 0.983
Wei 1.6	0.878 0.720	0.944 0.831	0.963 0.868	0.981 0.898	0.998 0.963
Wei 1.5	0.817 0.685	0.874 0.755	0.913 0.808	0.944 0.837	0.987 0.915
Wei 1.4	0.727 0.626	0.781 0.675	0.823 0.709	0.855 0.735	0.932 0.808
Wei 1.3	0.612 0.542	0.639 0.563	0.663 0.575	0.688 0.584	0.755 0.611
Wei 1.2	0.473 0.444	0.465 0.423	0.451 0.406	0.449 0.389	0.431 0.333

TABLE 3.6

Power for the Exponentiality Gof Test—Light Tail Alternatives (*q90, q95*)

20,000 samples	30	50	75	100	200
			95th percentile		
Gamma 1.6	0.429 0.288	0.398 0.229	0.377 0.185	0.361 0.146	0.303 0.067
Gamma 1.8	0.571 0.381	0.582 0.346	0.605 0.309	0.611 0.281	0.661 0.206
Gamma 2.0	0.707 0.502	0.755 0.489	0.796 0.477	0.833 0.483	0.911 0.470
LN 0.8	0.305 0.157	0.254 0.103	0.207 0.051	0.177 0.031	0.092 0.031
LN 0.6	0.809 0.503	0.874 0.505	0.919 0.500	0.949 0.495	0.989 0.487
LN 0.4	1.000 0.800	1.000 0.882	1.000 0.932	1.000 0.957	1.000 0.993
			90th percentile		
Gamma 1.6	0.581 0.443	0.592 0.420	0.616 0.399	0.628 0.383	0.676 0.333
Gamma 1.8	0.718 0.565	0.767 0.582	0.817 0.598	0.847 0.603	0.930 0.650
Gamma 2.0	0.836 0.693	0.894 0.734	0.938 0.781	0.963 0.813	1.000 0.893
LN 0.8	0.433 0.247	0.408 0.186	0.394 0.138	0.376 0.101	0.330 0.035
LN 0.6	0.894 0.623	0.945 0.655	0.976 0.688	0.987 0.718	0.991 0.788
LN 0.4	1.000 0.841	1.000 0.925	1.000 0.965	1.000 0.983	1.000 0.999

TABLE 3.7
Power for the Exponentiality Gof Test—Heavy Tail Alternatives (*q90, q95*)

20,000 samples	30	50	75	100	200
		95th percentile			
Gamma 0.8	0.326 0.311	0.274 0.254	0.232 0.209	0.191 0.165	0.110 0.085
Gamma 0.6	0.510 0.423	0.512 0.441	0.509 0.436	0.517 0.430	0.514 0.386
Gamma 0.4	0.582 0.393	0.672 0.507	0.718 0.581	0.753 0.620	0.831 0.678
LN 1.2	0.329 0.315	0.286 0.259	0.234 0.212	0.196 0.177	0.117 0.096
LN 1.4	0.600 0.536	0.626 0.550	0.649 0.553	0.671 0.557	0.732 0.578
LN 1.6	0.793 0.727	0.851 0.779	0.903 0.827	0.931 0.859	0.983 0.934
		90th percentile			
Gamma 0.8	0.393 0.373	0.360 0.335	0.334 0.299	0.298 0.260	0.231 0.185
Gamma 0.6	0.564 0.469	0.584 0.507	0.599 0.517	0.620 0.526	0.657 0.522
Gamma 0.4	0.611 0.413	0.710 0.536	0.723 0.622	0.803 0.667	0.886 0.750
LN 1.2	0.452 0.449	0.436 0.431	0.414 0.409	0.395 0.393	0.355 0.346
LN 1.4	0.714 0.679	0.764 0.725	0.810 0.763	0.844 0.793	0.922 0.875
LN 1.6	0.868 0.830	0.924 0.888	0.962 0.935	0.981 0.960	0.999 0.994

3.5 CONCLUDING REMARKS

In this work a goodness of fit test is proposed which compares the exponential distribution against heavy or light-tailed alternatives. The performance of the test is evaluated via simulations that show great results making the test an important tool for practical purposes in reliability theory whenever the underlying distribution needs to be established for inferential purposes.

REFERENCES

An MY (1998) Logconcavity versus logconvexity: A complete characterization. *The Journal of Economic Theory*, 80, 350–369.

Asmussen S and Lehtomaa J (2017) Distinguishing log-concavity from heavy tails. *Risks*, 5, 10.

Baratpour S and Rad AH (2012) Testing goodness-of-fit for exponential distribution based on cumulative residual entropy. *Communications in Statistics—Theory and Methods*, 41(8), 1387–1396.

Chhikara RS and Folks JL (1977) The inverse Gaussian distribution as a lifetime model. *Technometrics*, 19, 461–468.

Cox DR and Oakes D (1984) *Analysis of survival data*. Chapman and Hall, New York.

Cressie N and Read TRC (1984) Multinomial goodness-of-fit tests. *Journal of the Royal Statistical Society*, 5, 440–454.

Dümbgen L and Rufibach K (2009) Maximum likelihood estimation of a log-concave density and its distribution function: Basic properties and uniform consistency. *Bernoulli*, 15, 40–68.

Foss S, Konstantopoulos T and Zachary S (2007) Discrete and continuous time modulated random walks with heavy-tailed increments. *Journal of Theoretical Probability*, 20(3), 581–612.

Gail MH and Gastwirth JL (1978) A scale-free goodness-of-fit test for the exponential distribution based on the Gini statistic. *Journal of the Royal Statistical Society: Series B*, 40, 350–357.

Gupta RC and Balakrishnan N (2012) Log-concavity and monotonicity of hazard and reversed hazard functions of univariate and multivariate skew-normal distributions. *Metrika*, 75, 181–191.

Henze N and Meintanis SG (2002a) Tests of fit for exponentiality based on the empirical Laplace transform. *Statistics*, 36, 147–161.

Henze N and Meintanis SG (2002b) Omnibus tests for exponentiality based on the empirical characteristic function. *Preprint Nr. 02/3*, Faculty of Mathematics, University of Karlsruhe, Germany.

Henze N and Meintanis SG (2005) Recent and classical tests for exponentiality: A partial review with comparisons. *Metrika*, 61, 29–45.

Klar B (2001) Goodness-of-fit tests for the exponential and the normal distribution based on the integrated distribution function. *Annals of the Institute of Statistical Mathematics*, 53, 338–353.

Lehtomaa J (2015) Limiting behaviour of constrained sums of two variables and the principle of a single big jump. *Statistics & Probability Letters*, 107, 157–163.

Mattheou K, Lee S and Karagrigoriou A (2009) A model selection criterion based on the BHHJ measure of divergence. *The Journal of Statistical Planning and Inference*, 139, 128–135.

Vonta F, Mattheou K and Karagrigoriou A (2012) On properties of the (Φ,α)-power divergence family with applications in goodness of fit tests. *Methodology and Computing in Applied Probability*, 14, 335–356.

Walther G (2009) Inference and modeling with log-concave distributions. *Statistical Science*, 24, 319–327.

Wilk MB and Gnanadesikan R (1968) Probability plotting methods for the analysis of data. *Biometrika*, 55(1), 1–17.

4 Some Topics on Optimal Redundancy Allocation Problems in Coherent Systems

Mohammad Khanjari Sadegh

CONTENTS

4.1 INTRODUCTION

Consider a system consisting of n components in which all components and the system are in working or failed state. The state of the system is completely determined by the states of the components. Let $\phi(x_1, \ldots, x_n)$ denote the state of the system and x_i denotes the state of the i-th component for $i = 1, \ldots, n(x_i = 1$ means that the i-th component is working and $x_i = 0$ that it is not). ϕ is called the system structure function. The system is coherent if ϕ be increasing, that is, when the state of a component is improved, the state of the system cannot be worse, and every component be relevant for the system, that is, ϕ is strictly increasing in each variable in at least a point. For details on coherent systems refer to Barlow and Proschan (1975).

In a fixed point of time consider a coherent system with n components and structure ϕ and let

$$h(\mathbf{p}) = E[\phi(\mathbf{X})] = P(\phi(\mathbf{X}) = 1)$$

be the reliability function of the system in which $\mathbf{X} = (X_1, \ldots, X_n)$, $\mathbf{p} = (p_1, \ldots, p_n)$ and $p_i = P(X_i = 1)$ is the reliability of i-th component.

DOI: 10.1201/9781003203124-4

In during of the time the system lifetime is usually denoted by $T = \phi(T_1, \ldots, T_n)$ where T_i is the lifetime of i-th component and note that here ϕ refers to the system structure only and is not binary. We assume that the system components are independent, that is X_i's or T_i's are independent random variables. Also assume that T_i's are nonnegative and absolutely continuous. We denote by $F_i(t) = P(T_i \le t)$, $\bar{F}_i(t) = 1 - F_i(t)$, $f_i(t)$, $h_i(t) = f_i(t)/\bar{F}_i(t)$ and $r_i(t) = f_i(t)/F_i(t)$ the distribution, reliability, density, hazard rate and reversed hazard rate functions of T_i, respectively. The reliability function of the system at time t is denoted by

$$\bar{F}_T(t) = P(T > t) = h(\mathbf{p}_t) = h(p_1(t), \ldots, p_n(t))$$

where $p_i(t) = \bar{F}_i(t) = P(T_i > t)$.

The use of redundancy mechanisms is an important and effective way to improve the performance of the system. Two common schemes for allocating the redundant components to the system, are called *active* and *standby* redundancies. In the former, the redundant components are put in parallel to the original components of the system, while in later, they start working immediately after component failures. In fact, the use of redundancy means that, the improvement of system performance via the improving of its components. It is therefore important to study the effect of improving system components in improvement of the whole system.

Suppose m is the number of redundant components and r_i is the number of redundant components added to the i-th original system component. Then the vector $\mathbf{r} = (r1, \ldots, rn)$ where $\sum_1^n r_i = m$ is called an allocation. The relevant and essential problem related to the redundancy in systems is how to find the optimal allocation strategy such that the performance of the system be optimal in the sense of some stochastic orders. In this chapter the usual stochastic order is mainly considered and therefore we want to find the optimal allocation strategy such that the system reliability be maximized.

We recall the two stochastic orders that will be used in the sequel. A random variable X is said to be less than Y in usual stochastic order and denoted by $X \le_{st} Y$, if $\bar{F}X(t) \le \bar{F}Y(t)$ for all t. Also X is said to be less than Y in hazard rate order and denoted by $X \le_{hr} Y$, if $h_X(t) \ge h_Y(t)$ for all t. It is known that $X \le_{hr} Y$ implies $X \le_{st} Y$. For a comprehensive coverage of the various notions of stochastic orderings and their applications see Shaked and Shanthikumar (2007).

Although the redundancy allocation to original system components is a common technique to improve system reliability but, allocation of redundant components is not an easy task and must be considered properly with respect to environmental working conditions and possible restrictions such as cost, volume and weight. Therefore, the problem of finding optimal allocations is of great importance.

In last three decades the redundancy allocation problem has been widely studied by many authors. The most existing studies are usually concerned to particular structures such as series, parallel and k-out-of- n systems or coherent systems with $m = 1$ redundant component. See for examples Boland et al. (1992), Kotz et al. (2003), Hu and Wang (2009), Belzunce et al. (2011, 2013) and Jeddi and Doostparast (2016, 2020).

It seems that this subject was considered first by Boland et al. (1988). They considered a series system with n independent and identically distributed (i.i.d.) components having common lifetime distribution F and m i.i.d. active redundant components with common lifetime distribution G and showed that the strategy of balanced allocation, that is the allocation with $\left|r_i - r_j\right| \leq 1$, for all $i \neq j$ is optimal and maximizes the system reliability. Obviously the balanced allocation is not unique unless m/n be an integer. In this case the only balanced allocation is the equal allocation $\mathbf{r}^* = (m/n, \ldots, m/n)$. In view of the hazard rate order, Singh and Singh (1997) showed that the balanced allocation optimizes the failure rate of the system if $F = G$, that is the system failure rate is minimized. Misra et al. (2009) obtained a stronger result and showed that if lnG/lnF is an increasing function then the balanced allocation is optimal and minimizes the failure rate of the system.

In view of some other stochastic orders Zhao et al. (2017) considered the optimal allocation policy in a series system with $m = 1$ redundancy. Jeddi and Doostparast (2016, 2020) considered the optimal allocation of redundancies in series and parallel systems with dependent components when $m \leq 2$. Zhuang and Li (2015) considered k-out-of-n systems with independent components and m i.i.d. redundant components. Fang and Li (2016, 2020) considered the optimal allocation in active redundancy for some coherent systems containing symmetric components.

There are connections between the optimal redundancy allocation problems and components importance in coherent systems. We study these connections and introduce a new measure of component importance which is useful to obtain the optimal redundancy allocation.

In some practical applications in statistics and particularly in system reliability studies, the independence assumption is not valid and realistic. Because of some environmental factors like temperature, pressure and loading, the component lifetimes of a system may not be independent and exhibit some dependency. So the failure of one component results in increased load on each of the other surviving components. For more information see Barlow and Proschan (1975) and Lai and Xie (2006). Therefore the effect of dependence between lifetimes of the system components on the reliability and the mean time to failure (MTTF) of the system should be considered. We want to know that if the degree of dependency (correlation) between system component lifetimes in some sense is increased (decreased), whether the system reliability of the system will be increased (decreased) or not. Obviously it depends on the structure of the system and we show at least in series and parallel systems that the reliability of these systems have quite different behaviors.

The rest of this chapter is organized as follows. In Section 2 a coherent system with independent components is considered and the effect of improvement of one and two components of the system-on-system reliability is discussed. Also the effect of the reduction of $h_i(t)$, the hazard rate function of i-th component lifetime on $h_T(t)$, the hazard rate function of the system lifetime is also studied. Although an increasing in reliability of any system component causes an increasing on system reliability but it is known in general that the reduction in $h_i(t)$ does not necessarily imply a reduction in $h_T(t)$. We show that the reductions in $h_T(t)$ and $h_i(t)$ are the same, if and only if the i-th component be in series with the other system components. Using this a characterization for the series systems is given. Similar results for the effect of reversed hazard rate of components on the reversed hazard rate of the system are also obtained. In Section 3 we define a new measure of component importance which is an extension of the well-known Birnbaum measure of importance. It is useful in both active and standby redundancies problems in coherent systems with $m = 1$ redundant component. Using it an algorithm is proposed to find the optimal allocation when $m > 1$. It is assumed that all original and redundant components are independent and not necessarily identical.

Finally in Section 4 redundancy allocation problem in series and parallel systems with dependent components is studied. It is shown that the reliability of these systems have quite different behavior when the rate of dependence between system component lifetimes is varied. For this we first define a new concept of dependency and call it diagonally dependence and then use it for stochastic ordering and redundancy allocation problems in series and parallel systems. We also verify that how the diagonally dependence provides more weak conditions for some well-known results in optimal redundancy allocation problems of series and parallel systems with dependent components.

4.2 THE EFFECT OF SYSTEM COMPONENT IMPROVEMENT ON SYSTEM RELIABILITY

In this section, we consider a coherent system with n independent components and study the effect of improve of components on the system reliability. For the sake of completeness we first give the effect of improving one component on the system reliability, a result obtained by Xie and Shen (1989).

Lemma 4.1. Let Δ_i denote the increase of system reliability due to the increasing of i-th component reliability as much as δ_i. Then

$$\Delta_i = \delta_i I_B(i) \tag{4.1}$$

where

$$I_B(i) = P\left(\varphi(1_i,\mathbf{X}) - \varphi(0_i,\mathbf{X}) = 1\right) = h(1_i,\mathbf{p}) - h(0_i,\mathbf{p}) = \frac{\partial h(\mathbf{p})}{\partial p_i}$$

is the well-known Birnbaum importance measure of the i-th component. Also

$$(\cdot_i,\mathbf{X}) = (X_1,\ldots,X_{i-1},\cdot,X_{i+1},\ldots,X_n)$$

and

$$(\cdot_i,\mathbf{p}) = (p_1,\ldots,p_{i-1},\cdot,p_{i+1},\ldots,p_n).$$

Based on the above result we will introduce in the next section, a new measure of component importance which is useful to find optimal allocation in coherent system with one redundant component.

We now extend the above lemma when two components i and j are improved.

Lemma 4.2. Let Δ_{ij} denote the increase of system reliability due to the increasing of i-th and jth component reliabilities as much as δ_i and δ_j, respectively. Then

$$\Delta_{ij} = \delta_{ij}\frac{\partial^2 h(\mathbf{p})}{\partial p_i \partial p_j} + \delta_i \frac{\partial h(0_j,\mathbf{p})}{\partial p_i} + \delta_j \frac{\partial h(0_i,\mathbf{p})}{\partial p_j} \tag{4.2}$$

where $\delta_{ij} = (p_i + \delta_i)(p_j + \delta_j) - p_i p_j$.

Proof. If we use double pivotal decomposition as

$$\varphi(\mathbf{X}) = X_i X_j \varphi(1_i,1_j,\mathbf{X}) + X_i(1-X_j)\varphi(1_i,0_j,\mathbf{X}) + (1-X_i)X_j\varphi(0_i,1_j,\mathbf{X}) + (1-X_i)(1-X_j)\varphi(0_i,0_j,\mathbf{X})$$

we then have

$$h(\mathbf{p}) = p_i p_j h(1_i,1_j,\mathbf{p}) + p_i(1-p_j)h(1_i,0_j,\mathbf{p}) + (1-p_i)p_j h(0_i,1_j,\mathbf{p}) + (1-p_i)(1-p_j)h(0_i,0_j,\mathbf{p}).$$

In view of the given formula for $I_B(i)$ and noting to

$$\Delta_{ij} = h(p_i + \delta_i, p_j + \delta_j, \mathbf{p}) - h(\mathbf{p})$$

the proof of the lemma follows.

Remark 4.1. Obviously $\Delta_{ij} \geq 0$ as the system is coherent but the first term in Equation (4.2) may be negative. Also note that when $\delta_j = 0$ it can be shown that (4.2) reduces to (4.1).

We now consider the relationship between component failure rates and system failure rate. Let $T = \varphi(T_1, \ldots, T_n)$ denote the lifetime of a coherent system with structure φ where the component lifetimes, T_i's, are independent and absolutely continuous random variables. It is known that

$$\bar{F}_T(t) = P(T > t) = h(\bar{F}_1(t), \ldots, \bar{F}_n(t)) = h(\bar{\mathbf{F}}(t)) = h(\mathbf{p})\,|_{\mathbf{p}=\bar{\mathbf{F}}(t)}$$

where $\bar{F}_i(t) = P(T_i > t)$. Note that as the system components are independent h is a multilinear function. It means h is linear in each argument. Let $h_i(t)$ be the failure rate function of component i and $h_T(t)$ the failure rate function of the system. By the chain rule for differentiation we have

$$h_T(t) = \sum_{i=1}^{n} h_i(t) \frac{\bar{F}_i(t) \frac{\partial h(\mathbf{p})}{\partial p_i}\Big|_{\mathbf{p}=\bar{\mathbf{F}}(t)}}{h(\bar{F}_1(t), \ldots, \bar{F}_n(t))}. \tag{4.3}$$

See for example Esary and Proschan (1963).

Now assume that T_i' is an improved lifetime for component i in the sense of $h_i'(t) \leq h_i(t)$ for all $t \geq 0$, that is $T_i \leq_{hr} T_i'$.

If $T' = \varphi(T_1,\ldots,T_{i-1},T_i',T_{i+1},\ldots,T_n)$ then in general $T \leq_{hr} T'$ does not hold true except for series systems. See for example Boland et al. (1994). As we have already seen, if $T_i \leq_{st} T_i'$ then $T \leq_{st} T'$ but this is not true in general for hazard rate order. In other words a reduction in the failure rate of component i does not necessarily imply a reduction in the system failure rate. Here we have the following result.

Lemma 4.3. The reduction in the failure rate function of component i implies the same reduction in the system failure rate if and only if the component i is in series with the remaining components.

Proof. The Equation (4.3) can be written as

$$h_T(t) = \sum_{i=1}^{n} h_i(t) c_i(t)$$

where $c_i(t) = \dfrac{\bar{F}_i(t) \dfrac{\partial h(\mathbf{p})}{\partial p_i}\Big|_{\mathbf{p}=\bar{\mathbf{F}}(t)}}{h\left(\bar{F}_1(t),\ldots,\bar{F}_n(t)\right)}$. It is easy to show that the component i is in series with the other components if and only if $c_i(t) = 1$. This completes the proof of the lemma.

Remark 4.2. Similar to Equation (4.3), we have the following expression for $r_T(t)$, the reversed hazard rate function of the system:

$$r_T(t) = \sum_{i=1}^{n} r_i(t) \frac{F_i(t) \dfrac{\partial h(\mathbf{p})}{\partial p_i}\Big|_{\mathbf{p}=\bar{\mathbf{F}}(t)}}{1 - h\left(\bar{F}_1(t),\ldots,\bar{F}_n(t)\right)} \tag{4.4}$$

where $r_i(t)$ is the reversed hazard rate of component i.

Regarding the Equation (4.4) we have the following result.

Lemma 4.4. The reduction in the reversed hazard rate function of component i implies the same reduction in the reversed hazard rate of the system if and only if the component i is in parallel with the remaining components.

Proof. The proof is similar to that of Lemma 4.3.

Remark 4.3. From Lemmas 4.3 and 4.4 we have a simple characterization for series and parallel systems, respectively. If the reduction in failure rate (reversed failure rate) of each component implies the same reduction in the failure rate (reversed failure rate) of the system then system is series (parallel). It is known that in a series system $h_T(t) = \sum_1^n h_i(t)$ and in a parallel system $r_T(t) = \sum_1^n r_i(t)$. See for example Barlow and Proschan (1975).

4.3 A NEW MEASURE OF COMPONENT IMPORTANCE USEFUL IN ACTIVE AND STANDBY REDUNDANCIES

In this section using the Equation (4.1) we introduce a new measure of component importance which is helpful to find the best allocation when there is only $m = 1$ redundant component. It makes ready the required conditions to obtain optimal redundancy allocation when $m > 1$. For this a general algorithm is also proposed.

We now return to the Equation (4.1) and consider three special cases as follows.

Case 1. If $\delta_i = \delta$, $i = 1, \ldots, n$, that is the improvement of all components be the same, then from (4.1) we see that in view of the Birnbaum measure of importance, improvement of the most important component causes the largest increasing in system reliability. In other words the Birnbaum measure of importance is crucial to find the best component in order to increase the system reliability. This is not case if $\delta_i \neq \delta$ and therefore a new measure of importance is needed. One may use $\Delta_i = \delta_i I_B(i)$ as the new measure of importance for component *i*. But it is not applicable in redundancy allocation problem as Δ_i depends on the arbitrary value δ_i whereas in redundancy problem δ_i depends on the redundant component. It is explained in the following case.

Case 2. Suppose we want to allocate an active redundancy component with reliability p to a single system component. We assume that it is independent of all original system components. The question is how to find the optimal allocation. If we allocate it to the component *i* then p_i will be increased to $1-(1-p_i)(1-p)=1-q_iq$ and therefore $\delta_i = 1-q_iq-p_i = q_i - q_iq = q_ip$. Hence $\Delta_i = q_ipI_B(i)$. Based on this we now introduce our new measure of importance for component *i* as follow

$$I_{\text{AR}}(i) = (1-p_i)I_B(i). \tag{4.5}$$

AR in $I_{\text{AR}}(i)$ refers to active redundancy. It is a generalization of $I_B(i)$ as it depends to p_i the reliability of component *i* but $I_B(i)$ does not. Hence the optimal allocation is the component that has the largest $I_{\text{AR}}(.)$.

Case 3. In this case we want to allocate one independent standby component with reliability p and lifetime S to a single system component and find the optimal allocation. If we allocate it to the component *i* with lifetime T_i then p_i will be increased to $p_i * p$. By $p_i * p$ we mean $\bar{F}_i * \bar{F}(t) = P(T_i + S > t)$, the convolution of $\bar{F}_i$ and $\bar{F}$, the reliability functions of T_i and S, respectively. Therefore

$$\delta_i = p_i * p - p_i = P(T_i + S > t) - P(T_i > t)$$

and our new measure of importance for component *i* is

$$I_{\text{SR}}(i) = (p_i * p - p_i)I_B(i). \tag{4.6}$$

SR in $I_{\text{SR}}(i)$ refers to standby redundancy. Hence in this case the optimal allocation is the component that has the largest $I_{\text{SR}}(.)$.

Remark 4.4. If the system components are identical, that is $p_1 = \cdots = p_n$ we then in both cases 2 and 3 have, $\delta_1 = \cdots = \delta_n$ and therefore in order to find the optimal allocations, $I_{\text{AR}}(i)$ and $I_{\text{SR}}(i)$ will be equivalently reduced to $I_B(i)$. Also note that in case 3, $I_{\text{SR}}(i)$ depends on the lifetime distributions of original and spare components. In other words it is a dynamic measure whereas in case 2 this is not case for $I_{\text{AR}}(i)$. To obtain $I_B(i)$ in case 3, p_i should be replaced by $p_i(t) = P(T_i > t) = \bar{F}_i(t)$.

We now ready to propose our general algorithm to obtain the optimal allocation in active and standby redundancy problems of a coherent system consisting of n independent components equipped with m independent redundant components.

Assume that all original and spare components are also independent. We want to find the optimal allocation in the sense of usual stochastic order.

We also assume that the functional form of the system reliability function $h(\mathbf{p}) = h(p_1, \ldots, p_n)$, is known. Without loss of generality we assume that $p_1' \geq \cdots \geq p_m'$ where p_j' is the reliability of the jth redundant component. Note that if we want to allocate the redundant component j to the original component i in fact $\Delta_i = p_j'(1-p_i)I_B(i)$ must have the largest value and since $p_1' \geq \cdots \geq p_m'$ therefore the redundant components should be added to the system components consecutively, first the redundant component 1 and then the redundant component 2, etc. Therefore it is enough in each stage, that we first find the original component with largest value of $I_{\text{AR}}(i) = (1-p_i)I_B(i)$ and then add the current redundant component to it. In other words the measure of $I_{\text{AR}}(i) = (1-p_i)I_B(i)$ is crucial to find the optimal allocation.

Now based on the measure of $I_{\text{AR}}(i)$ we propose the following algorithm to find the optimal allocation in case of active redundancy.

An algorithm for optimal allocation in active redundancy

Input: $p_1, \ldots, p_n, m, p_1' \geq \cdots \geq p_m'$ and $h(p_1, \ldots, p_n)$.

Output: The optimal allocation $\mathbf{r}^* = (r_1, \ldots, r_n)$.

Step 0. Put $I = 1$ and $r_i = 0$ and $q_j' = 1 - p_j'$ for $i = 1, \ldots, n$ and $j = 1, \ldots, m$.

Step 1. Compute $I_B(i) = \dfrac{\partial h(\mathbf{p})}{\partial p_i}$, $q_i = 1 - p_i$, and $I_{\text{AR}}(i) = q_i I_B(i)$ for $i = 1, \ldots, n$.

Step 2. Determine the i^* such that

$$I_{\text{AR}}(i^*) = max\{I_{\text{AR}}(i), i = 1, \ldots, n\}.$$

Step 3. Put $r_{i^*} = r_{i^*} + 1$ and $p_{i^*} = 1 - q_I' q_{i^*}$ and update the value of system reliability function $h(p_1, \ldots, p_n)$.

Step 4. If $I = m$, Stop. Otherwise put $I = I + 1$ and Go to Step 1.

To illustrate how the above algorithm works see the following example.

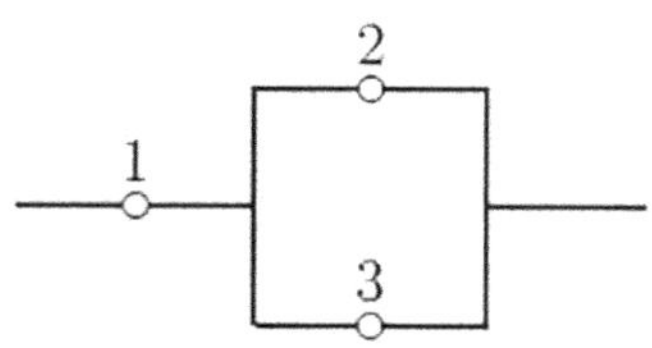

Example 1. Consider the following series-parallel system.

Suppose $p_1 = 0.4$, $p_2 = 0.8$ and $p_3 = 0.3$ Also let $m = 4$ and for simplicity suppose $p_1' = \cdots = p_4' = 0.5$. We follow the above algorithm step by step to find the optimal allocation such that the reliability of the system be maximized. It is known that for this system we have

$$h(p_1, p_2, p_3) = p_1p_2 + p_1p_3 - p_1p_2p_3 = 0.404.$$

Therefore $I_B(1) = p_2 + p_3 - p_2p_3 = 0.86$, $I_B(2) = p_1 - p_1p_3 = 0.28$ and $I_B(3) = p_1 - p_1p_2 = 0.08$. Also $I_{AR}(1) = q_1I_B(1) = 0.516$ and similarly $I_{AR}(2) = 0.056 = I_{AR}(3)$. We get $i^* = 1$. That is the first redundant component should be added to component 1. Hence $r_1 = 1$ and $p_1 = 1-0.5\times0.6 = 0.7$. Using this new value of p_1 we update $h(p_1, p_2, p_3)$ and start the second repetition. We now have $I_B(1) = 0.86$, $I_B(2) = 0.49$ and $I_B(3) = 0.14$. Also $I_{AR}(1) = q_1I_B(1) = 0.258$, $I_{AR}(2) = 0.098 = I_{AR}(3)$. Therefore $i^* = 1$ and hence $r_1 = 2$ and $p_1 = 1-qp_1 = 1-0.5\times0.3 = 0.85$. That is the second redundant component should be again added to component 1. Similarly in third repetition we obtain $i^* = 1$, $r_1 = 3$ and $p_1 = 1 - 0.5 \times 0.15 = 0.925$ and finally in last repetition have $I_{AR}(1) = 0.0645$, $I_{AR}(2) = I_{AR}(3) = 0.1295$. Therefore $i^* = 2$ or 3. That is two allocations $\mathbf{r}^*_1 = (3, 1, 0)$ and $\mathbf{r}^*_2 = (3, 0, 1)$ are both optimal. We note that although the optimal allocation is not unique but one can simply verify that both of $\mathbf{r}^*_1$ and $\mathbf{r}^*_2$ lead to the unique maximum value of $h(p_1, p_2, p_3)$ which is equal to 0.86025. This holds true in general.

Remark 4.5. One can simply obtain an algorithm to find the optimal allocation in case of standby redundancy if $I_{AR}(i)$ be replaced by $I_{SR}(i)$ in the above algorithm. As mentioned before we note that $I_{SR}(i)$ is a time dependent measure and the lifetime distributions of original and redundant components are needed.

4.4 REDUNDANCY ALLOCATION PROBLEM IN SE- RIES AND PARALLEL SYSTEMS WITH DEPENDENT COMPONENTS

The redundancy allocation problem for the systems with dependent components has not been extensively studied. For some recent works on redundancy problems in series and parallel systems with dependent components see for example Jeddi and Doostparast (2016, 2020). They considered the redundancy allocation problems in both series and parallel systems with dependent components without any assumption on the dependency structure among the component lifetimes. On the best of our knowledge Kotz et al. (2003) have done the first work on this subject. They investigated the increase in MTTF of parallel two components systems when the component lifetimes are positive (negative) dependent.

In this section we define a new concept of dependence and call it diagonally dependence. When the marginal distributions of the component lifetimes are fixed, we show that if the joint distribution of the component lifetimes of a series (parallel) system becomes more positive diagonally dependent (PDD), the reliability and the MTTF of the system will become more (less). As some examples, different bivariate distributions that can be used in the modeling of dependent components are discussed. A minor mistake result given in Kotz et al. (2003) is also mentioned. At the end of this section an open problem is stated. Finally the redundancy allocation problems in series and parallel systems with dependent components are considered. Under the more weak conditions, positive (negative) diagonally dependent, PDD (NDD), we show that the most existing recent results also hold true.

Diagonally Dependence

We define a new concept of dependence and call it diagonally dependence and discuss its properties in stochastic orderings of series and parallel systems with dependent components. Also its particular applications in redundancy allocation problems of those systems are given.

Lehmann (1966) defined a random vector (X_1, X_2) is positive (negative) quadrant dependent(PQD(NQD)), if for all x_1, x_2

$$P(X_1 > x_1, X_2 > x_2) \geq (\leq) P(X_1 > x_1) P(X_2 > x_2)$$

which is equivalent to

$$P(X_1 \leq x_1, X_2 \leq x_2) \geq (\leq) P(X_1 \leq x_1) P(X_2 \leq x_2).$$

He showed that it is also equivalent to $Cov(a(X_1), b(X_2)) \geq (\leq) 0$ for every pair of real increasing functions a and b.

Hoeffding (1940) showed that

$$Cov(X_1, X_2) = \int_{-\infty}^{\infty}\int_{-\infty}^{\infty}\left[F(x_1, x_2) - F_1(x_1)F_2(x_2)\right]dx_1dx_2$$

$$= \int_{-\infty}^{\infty}\int_{-\infty}^{\infty}\left[\bar{F}(x_1, x_2) - \bar{F}_1(x_1)\bar{F}_2(x_2)\right]dx_1dx_2$$

where

$F(x_1, x_2) = P(X_1 \leq x_1, X_2 \leq x_2)$ and $\bar{F}(x_1, x_2) = P(X_1 > x_1, X_2 > x_2)$ are joint distribution and reliability functions of (X_1, X_2), respectively.

Remark 4.6. From the above equation we see that if (X_1, X_2) is PQD(NQD) then $\rho(X_1, X_2) \geq (\leq) 0$, as the integrand in $Cov(X_1, X_2)$ is nonnegative (non-positive). Because of this we see that in all PQD or NQD bivariate distributions, such as the well-known bivariate normal distribution, $\rho = 0$ is equivalent to independence. Note that if (X_1, X_2) is PQD or NQD then $\rho(X_1, X_2) = 0$ immediately implies the integrand in $Cov(X_1, X_2)$ is 0, that is X_1 and X_2 are independent.

Usually $F(x_1, x_2) = F_\theta(x_1, x_2)$ where θ is called the dependence parameter. Therefore $\rho = Corr(X_1, X_2) = \rho(\theta)$. Using θ we can simply measure and also change the degree of correlation between X_1 and X_2. In order to compare the systems containing dependent components with those of containing independent components, we assume that when the degree of correlation between component lifetimes changed their marginal distributions will not be changed and are fixed. That is $F_1(x_1)$ and $F_2(x_2)$ do not depend on θ. From above equation if $F_\theta(x_1, x_2)$ is increasing (decreasing) in θ then $\rho(\theta)$ is also increasing (decreasing) in θ. Also we will see that the reliability and MTTF of the series (parallel) system is increasing (decreasing) in θ as we know in a two components series system that

$$P(T_s > t) = P(min(X_1, X_2) > t) = P(X_1 > t, X_2 > 2) = \bar{F}_\theta(t, t)$$

and $MTTF(T_s) = E_\theta(T_s) = \int_0^\infty P(T_s > t)dt$.

Also in a two components parallel system we have

$$P(T_p > t) = P(max(X_1, X_2) > t) = 1 - P(X_1 \leq t, X_2 \leq t) = 1 - F_\theta(t, t).$$

Therefore we see that if the dependence parameter θ be such that $F_\theta(x_1, x_2)$ is a monotone function of θ then the reliability of a two components series system and that of a parallel system have quite different behaviors.

We now give our definition of diagonally dependence and then consider its applications in stochastic orderings of series and parallel systems.

Definition 4.1. We call a random vector (X_1, X_2) is positive (negative) diagonally dependent PDD(NDD), if for all t

$$P(X_1 \le t, X_2 \le t) \ge (\le) P(X_1 \le t) P(X_2 \le t).$$

If the equality holds, we say X_1 and X_2 are diagonally independent.

We will see that the PQD(NQD) assumption, used in some existing results in literature, can simply replaced by the weaker assumption PDD(NDD).

We know that $X_1 + X_2 = min(X_1, X_2) + max(X_1, X_2) = T_s + T_p$. Hence $E(X_1) + E(X_2) = E(T_s) + E(T_p)$. Therefore the sum of MTTF of the series and parallel systems are fixed, as we assumed that the marginal distributions of X_1 and X_2 are fixed. Hence under any dependence structure between X_1 and X_2, if $E(T_s)$ increases (decreases), then $E(T_p)$ decreases (increases). Also it shows that the variations in $E(T_s)$ and $E(T_p)$ are 0 sum.

Kotz et al. (2003) showed that if $F\ (x_1, x_2)$ is PQD(NQD), $F_1 = F_2 = F$ and $EX1 = EX2 = \mu$ then $E(T_p) \le (\ge) 2\mu - \int_0^\infty \bar{F}^2(t)dt$. Navarro and Lai (2007) extended their result and showed that if $F\ (x_1, x_2)$ is PQD(NQD) then $E(T_p) \le (\ge) E(X_1) + E(X_2) - \int_0^\infty \bar{F}_1(t)\bar{F}_2(t)dt$ and $E(T_s) \ge (\le) \int_0^\infty \bar{F}_1(t)\bar{F}_2(t)dt$. In other words we have $E^{(PQ)}(T_p) \le E^I(T_p) \le E^{(NQ)}(T_p)$ and $E^{(NQ)}(T_s) \le E^I(T_s) \le E^{(PQ)}(T_s)$ where $E^I(T_p)$ and $E^I(T_s)$ are the MTTF of the parallel and series systems with independent components. In part (a) of Proposition (2.1) in Navarro and Lai (2007), it is claimed in mistake, that if the above inequality reduces to equality, then the components are independent. We show in the sequel that the components are not necessarily independent but are diagonally independent. They also showed a more general result as follow:

$$T_p^{(PQ)} \le_{st} T_p^I \le_{st} T_p^{(NQ)} \text{ and } T_s^{(NQ)} \le_{st} T_s^I \le_{st} T_s^{(PQ)}$$

where $\le_{st}$ refers to the usual stochastic ordering. Note that under the PQD assumption we have:

$$E^{(PQ)}(T_p) = \int P(T_p > t)dt = E(X_1) + E(X_2)$$
$$- \int \bar{F}(t,t)dt \le E(X_1) + E(X_2) - \int \bar{F}_1(t)\bar{F}_2(t)dt = E^I(T_p)$$

Now if equality holds we have

$$\int \bar{F}(t,t)dt = \int \bar{F}_1(t)\bar{F}_2(t)dt$$

it implies that $\bar{F}(t, t) = \bar{F}^1(t)\bar{F}^2(t)$, as (X_1, X_2) is PQD. That is the component lifetimes are diagonally independent.

Remark 4.7. It is easy to see that in both above mentioned results of Kotz et al. (2003) and Navarro and Lai (2007), the strong assumption PQD(NQD) can be replaced by the weaker assumption PDD(NDD). Note that for series and parallel systems with $n > 2$ components, we can define the concepts of Positive Lower Diagonally Dependence (PLDD) and Positive Upper Diagonally Dependence (PUDD) which are weaker dependence notions than those well-known concepts PLOD and PUOD.

The following lemmas provide some useful results for the sequel.

Lemma 4.5. Let $F_\theta(x_1, x_2)$ be a joint distribution function which is strictly increasing in θ and its marginals, $F_1(x_1)$ and $F_2(x_2)$, do not depend on θ. Then, regardless to (X_1, X_2) be PQD(NQD), $\rho(\theta) = Corr(X_1, X_2)$ is increasing in θ if and only if $T_s = min(X_1, X_2)(T_p = max(X_1, X_2)$ is stochastically increasing (decreasing) in θ.

Lemma 4.6. Let $F(x, y)$ be an arbitrary joint distribution function with F_1 and F_2 as its marginals. Then

$$\begin{aligned} F^*(x,y) &= F(x,y) \qquad \text{if } x \neq y \\ &= F_1(x)F_2(y) \ \ \text{if } x = y \end{aligned}$$

is a joint distribution function in which $F_1^* = F_1$ and $F_2^* = F_2$, that is

F^* is a diagonally independent joint distribution.

Definition 4.2 (More Quadrant Dependent). $F(x_1, x_2)$ is said to be more quadrant dependent than $F^*(x_1, x_2)$ if $F(x_1, x_2) \geq F^*(x_1, x_2)$ or equivalently $\bar{F}(x_1, x_2) \geq \bar{F}^*(x_1, x_2)$ for all x_1, x_2. We assume that the marginal distributions of $F(x_1, x_2)$ and $\bar{F}^*(x_1, x_2)$ are common.

Obviously we have $T_p \leq_{st} T_p^*$, $T_s \geq_{st} T_s^*$ and $\rho(X_1, X_2) \geq \rho^*(X_1, X_2)$.

Also it is clear that a bivariate PQD distribution is always more quadrant dependent than a NQD distribution.

Let F and F^* be two joint distributions. Lai and Lin (2014), defined two new dependence orderings as follows.

F is more diagonal dependent than F^* if $F(t, t) \geq F^*(t, t)$ or equivalently $\bar{F}(t, t) \geq \bar{F}^*(t, t)$ for all t.

They also called F is more correlated than F^* if $\rho \geq \rho^*$. It is clear that more quadrant dependent implies both more diagonal dependent and more correlated. They showed that if F is more diagonal dependent than F^* then $E(T_s) \geq E^*(T_s)$ and $E(T_p) \leq E^*(T_p)$ which is a stronger result than that of Kotz et al. (2003). A stronger result than above is $T_s \geq_{st} T_s^*$ and $T_p \leq_{st} T_p^*$.

Example 2.

1. (Gumbel's Type I Distribution)
   $\bar{F}_\theta(x_1, x_2) = \bar{F}_1(x_1)\left[\bar{F}_2(x_2)\right]^{1-\theta ln\bar{F}_1(x_1)} = \bar{F}_2(x_2)\left[\bar{F}_1(x_1)\right]^{1-\theta ln\bar{F}_2(x_2)}$, $x1, x2 > 0$,
   $0 \leq \theta \leq 1$ which is a NQD distribution. Therefore $\rho(\theta) = \rho_\theta(X_1, X_2)$
   0 is decreasing in θ and $T_s(T_p)$ is stochastically decreasing (increasing) in θ.
2. (F-G-M Distribution)

$F_\alpha(x_1,x_2)=F_1(x_1)F_2(x_2)[1+\alpha\bar{F}_1(x_1)\bar{F}_2(x_2)], x_1,x_2>0,-1\le\alpha\le 1$ which is a PQD(NQD) distribution if $\alpha > 0(\alpha < 0)$. Therefore $\rho(\alpha) = \rho_\alpha(X_1, X_2)$ is increasing in α and $T_s(T_p)$ is stochastically increasing (decreasing) in α.

3. (Lomax Distribution)

   $\bar{F}_k\ (x_1,x_2)=(1+x_1+x_2+kx_1x_2)^{-\alpha}, x_1,x_2>0,\alpha>0,0\le k\le\alpha+1$ which is a PQD(NQD) distribution for $0\le k<1\ \left(1<k\le\alpha+1\right)$ $\alpha + 1$). Therefore $\rho(k) = \rho_k(X_1, X_2)$ is decreasing in k and $T_s(T_p)$ is stochastically decreasing (increasing) in k. If $k = 0$ Clayton family of distributions can be found.

4. (Gumbel Type B extreme value Distribution)

   $\bar{F}_r(x_1,x_2)=exp\left[\left(ln\bar{F}_1(x_1)\right)^r+\left(ln\bar{F}_2(x_2)\right)^r\right]^{1/r}, x_1,x_2>0,\ r\ge 1$) which is a PQD distribution. Therefore $\rho\left(r\right)=\rho_r\left(X_1,X_2\right)\ge 0$ is increasing in r and $T_s(T_p)$ is stochastically increasing (decreasing) in r.

5. (A-M-H Distribution)

   $F_\theta\left(x_1,x_2\right)=\dfrac{F_1\left(x_1\right)F_2\left(x_2\right)}{1-\theta F_1\left(x_1\right)F_2\left(x_2\right)}$ $x_1, x_2 > 0$, $0 \le \theta \le 1$ which is again a PQD distribution. Therefore $\rho(\theta)=\rho_\theta(X_1,X_2)\ge 0$ is increasing in θ and $T_s(T_p)$ is stochastically increasing (decreasing) in θ.

6. (Regression Family of Distributions)

   $F_\theta(x_1,x_2)=\theta min(F_1(x_1),F_2(x_2))+(1-\theta)F_1(x_1)F_2(x_2), x_1,x_2>0,0\le\theta\le 1$. This family of distributions belongs to PQD distributions, $\rho(\theta)=\rho_\theta(X_1,X_2)\ge 0$ is increasing in θ and $T_s(T_p)$ is stochastically increasing (decreasing) in θ.

Remark 4.8. In all above examples (in both cases when F_θ is PQD or NQD), we see that when $\rho(\theta) = \rho_\theta(X_1, X_2)$ increases (decreases) then $T_{(1)}(T_{(2)})$ is stochastically increasing (decreasing). Whether this holds in general? In other words if $\rho(\theta) = \rho_\theta(X_1, X_2)$ is increasing (decreasing) then under what conditions $F_\theta(x_1, x_2)$ is monotone?

We have seen that when the diagonally dependence between X_1 and X_2 increases (decreases), the MTTF or even the reliability of the series (parallel) system increases. Whether this holds for other systems for example in a k-out-of-n system, what is the value of k_0 in which when the diagonally dependence between $X_1, \ldots, X_n$ increases, the system reliability for $k\le k_0(k>k_0)$ increases (decreases)? The interested reader may consider these as open problems. Recall that a k-out-of-n system works if at least k out of its n components work. Special cases of these systems are series and parallel systems when $k = n$ and $k = 1$, respectively.

Remark 4.9. As we have seen the strong assumptions PQD(NQD) and PUOD(PLOD) which are used in some existing literature results, for example Kotz et al. (2003), Navarro and Lai (2007) and Jeddi and Doostparast (2016, 2020), can simply be replaced by the weaker conditions PDD(NDD) and PUDD(PLDD), respectively. Our new concept of dependence, diagonally dependence is not only useful in study of the effect of dependence on reliability and mean time to failure of the series and parallel systems but also in the optimal redundancy allocation problems of these systems.

REFERENCES

Barlow, R. E. and Proschan, F. (1975). *Statistical Theory of Reliability and Life Testing*. Holt, Rinehart and Winston, New York.

Belzunce, F., Martinez-Puertas, H. and Ruiz, J. M. (2011). On optimal allocation of redundant components for series and parallel systems of two dependent components. *Journal of Statistical Planning and Inference*, **141**, 3094–3104.

Belzunce, F., Martinez-Puertas, H. and Ruiz, J. M. (2013). On allocation of redundant components for systems with dependent components. *European Journal of Operational Research*, **230**, 573–580.

Boland, P. J., El-Neweihi, E. and Proschan, F. (1988). Active redundancy allocation in coherent systems. *Probability in the Engineering and Informational Sciences*, **2**, 343–353.

Boland, P. J., EI-Neweihi, E. and Proschan, F. (1992). Stochastic order for redundancy allocations in series and parallel systems. *Advances in Applied Probability*, **24**, 161–171.

Boland, P. J., EI-Neweihi, E. and Proschan, F. (1994). Applications of the hazard rate ordering in reliability and order statistics. *Journal of Applied Probability*, **31, 1**, 180–192.

Esary, J. D. and Proschan, F. (1963). Relationship between system failure rate and component failure rates. *Technometrics*, **5, 2**, 183–189.

Fang, R. and Li, X. (2016). On allocating one active redundancy to coherent systems with dependent and heterogeneous components' lifetimes. *Naval Research Logistics*, **63**, 335–345.

Fang, R. and Li, X. (2020). Active redundancy allocation for coherent systems with independent and heterogeneous components. *Probability in the Engineering and Informational Sciences*, **34, 1**, 72–91.

Hoeffding, W. (1940). Masstabinvariante Korrelationstheorie. *Schriften des Mathematischen Instituts und des Instituts fur Angewandte Mathematik der Universit at Berlin*, **5**, 181–233.

Hu, T. and Wang, Y. (2009). Optimal allocation of active redundancies in r-out-of-n systems. *Journal of Statistical Planning and Inference*, **139**, 3733–3737.

Jeddi, H. and Doostparast, M. (2016). Optimal redundancy allocation problems in engineering systems with dependent component lifetime. *Applied Stochastic Models in Business and Industry*, **32**, 199–208.

Jeddi, H. and Doostparast, M. (2020). Allocation of redundancies in systems: A general dependency-base framework. *Annals of Operations Research*. https://doi.org/10.1007/s10479020-03795-2

Kotz, S., Lai, C. D. and Xie, M. (2003). On the effect of redundancy for systems with dependent components. *IIE Transactions*, **35**, 1103–1110.

Lai, C. D. and Lin, G. D. (2014). Mean time to failure of systems with dependent components. *Applied Mathematics and Computation*, **246**, 103–111.

Lai, C. D. and Xie, M. (2006). *Stochastic Ageing and Dependence for Reliability*. Springer.

Lehmann, E. L. (1966). Some concepts of dependence. *The Annals of Mathematical Statistics*, **37**, 1137–1153.

Misra, N., Dhariyal, I. D. and Gupta, N. (2009). Optimal allocation of active spares in series systems and comparison of component and system redundancies. *Journal of Applied Probability*, **46**, 19–34.

Navarro, J. and Lai, C. D. (2007). Ordering properties of systems with two dependent components. *Communications in Statistics-Theory and Methods*, **36**, 645–655.

Shaked, M. and Shanthikumar, G. (2007). *Stochastic Orders*. Springer.

Singh, H. and Singh, R. S. (1997). Note: Optimal allocation of resources to nodes of series systems with respect to failure-rate ordering. *Naval Research Logistics*, **44**, 147–152.

Xie, M. and Shen, K. (1989). The increase of reliability of k-out-of-n systems through improving a component. *Reliability Engineering & System Safety*, **26, 3**, 189–195.

Zhao, P., Zhang, Y. and Chen, J. (2017). Optimal allocation policy of one redundancy in a n-component series system. *European Journal of Operational Research*, **257, 2**, 656–668.

Zhuang, J. and Li, X. (2015). Allocating redundancies to k-out-of-n systems with independent and heterogeneous components. *Communications in Statistics—Theory and Methods*, **44**, 5109–5119.

5 Unsupervised Learning for Large Scale Data

The ATHLOS Project

Petros Barmpas, Sotiris Tasoulis, Aristidis G. Vrahatis, Panagiotis Anagnostou, Spiros Georgakopoulos, Matthew Prina, José Luis Ayuso-Mateos, Jerome Bickenbach, Ivet Bayes, Martin Bobaki, Francisco Félix Caballero, Somnath Chatterji, Laia Egea-Cortés, Esther García-Esquinas, Matilde Leonardi, Seppo Koskinen, Ilona Koupil, Andrzej Pająk, Martin Prince, Warren Sanderson, Sergei Scherbov, Abdonas Tamosiunas, Aleksander Galas, Josep MariaHaro, Albert Sanchez-Niubo, Vassilis P. Plagianakos, and Demosthenes Panagiotakos

CONTENTS

DOI: 10.1201/9781003203124-5

5.1 INTRODUCTION

In recent years, the embracement of technology in various domains has experienced remarkable growth, and as a result, the data generation has increased significantly and is expected to multiply in the near future (Alharthi, Krotov and Bowman 2017; Gupta and Rani 2019; Gu et al. 2017). Simultaneously, utilizing the innovations in the collection, recording, and storage, huge databases are being constructed, including various data types from different sources (Roh, Heo and Whang 2019; Plageras et al. 2018; Wang, Ng and Brook 2020). However, along with the vast increase in size, it is not easy to simultaneously produce and categorize them, thus leading to heterogeneity phenomena. Therefore, advanced processing techniques that allow the management of such data become necessary, aiming to retrieve patterns, reduce dimensionality and at the same time automate the processing (Hsu and Glass 2018; Usama et al. 2019; Wang et al. 2019). This development constantly reinforces the "Big Data" term, enabling the research community to enhance insight, decision-making, and process automation while simultaneously necessitating cost-effective, novel means of information processing (Sagiroglu and Sinanc 2013). The arising Big Data characteristics though may weaken prediction accuracy and pattern discovery by imposing noise through measurement errors and false correlations (Fan, Han and Liu 2014).

Diverse dimensionalities and heterogeneous structure are two key features that intensify large-scaled data complexity. When we consider massive heterogeneous data (Zhu et al. 2018), the features may represent different types of information of the same individual (Fan and Fan 2008). These issues become significant challenges when trying to enable data aggregation (Fan and Fan 2008; Fan, Guo and Hao 2012; Li et al. 2016).

In an early stage of data centralized information systems, the focus is on finding the best feature values to represent each observation (Tufekci 2014; Keyes and Westreich 2019). This type of sample feature representation inherently treats each individual as an independent entity without considering their social connections. In a dynamic world, the features used to represent the individuals and the social ties used to represent their connections may also evolve concerning temporal, spatial, and other factors. Such complexity is becoming part of Big Data applications' reality, introducing significant computational challenges for data analytics (Jin et al. 2015; Marx 2013).

Nevertheless, techniques and methods that fall into the category of unsupervised learning have shown encouraging results and are able to overcome some of the difficulties of vast, heterogeneous data (Casolla et al. 2019; Hameed et al. 2018; Ma et al. 2017; Xiang et al. 2018). In this study, we focus on the area of unsupervised learning, presenting a complete methodological procedure that utilizes recent advances in the field. We begin with a review of state of the art methods for clustering and dimensionality reduction and conclude with their utilization in a real world dataset, characterized by the aforementioned challenges. The organization of this paper is as follows. Chapter 3 presents the basic principles and characteristics of unsupervised learning and introduces some indicative techniques for two subcategories, dimensional reduction, and clustering respectively. Chapter 4 presents the methodology followed for the experimental procedure, in an attempt to extract knowledge from the data set at hand, that of the ATHLOS Cohort. Finally, in Chapter 5, we conclude with a discussion upon the results and potential perspectives.

5.2 UNSUPERVISED LEARNING METHODS AS AN APPROACH FOR KNOWLEDGE EXTRACTION

The term "Big Data" is often defined in terms of volume, variety, and velocity or "3Vs" (Laney and others 2001; Kitchin and McArdle 2016). The term refers to bulk data sets that must be computed to disclose patterns and correlations. Therefore, Big Data is much more than simple data: these are statistical methods, machine learning, algorithms, complex visualizations, databases, and information infrastructures that make possible the refinement, organization, and realization of data. It is now widespread that big data comes from combining four elements, whose joint appearance represents an unprecedented combination. First, the data must be large (Volume) to a degree that until recently was unthinkable. The second characteristic is diversity or variety. Stored data can be unstructured or structured texts, images, signals, numeric values based on points, metadata. The third property of big data refers to velocity, i.e., the speed of analytical processing. The last element of big data is the accuracy or uncertainty of the data.

Unsupervised learning is one of the main categories of Machine Learning, along with supervised and reinforcement learning (Hinton, Sejnowski et al. 1999), and hybrid methods like semi-supervised learning (Zhu and Goldberg 2009; X. J. Zhu 2005). Unsupervised learning can be divided into three main application fields (Ghahramani 2003). The first one concerns data samples segmentation by some shared attributes, next is the outlier detection (Both can be attributed to Clustering methods (Jiang and An 2008; Chawla and Gionis 2013)), while the last is dataset simplification by aggregating variables with similar attributes, a procedure known as Dimensionality Reduction accompanied with Feature Selection (Wei and Billings 2006; Masaeli, Fung and Dy 2010; Mladenić 2005). In summary, Unsupervised Learning aims to study the intrinsic structure of the data to find patterns that should not be considered plain, unstructured noise (Ghahramani 2003).

Each of the subcategories has the potential to extract helpful information regarding a dataset. However, the combination of them has been previously shown to produce encouraging results (Diaz-Papkovich, Anderson-Trocmé and Gravel 2019; Allaoui, Kherfi and Cheriet 2020; Hozumi et al. 2021). In what follows, we highlight some of most representative techniques from each subcategory that we also utilize on our experimental analysis. Our aim is to incorporate both well-established and recent state-of-the-art and popular methods.

5.2.1 Dimensionality Reduction for Pattern Discovery through Visualization

Biomedical and health technologies are constantly evolving generating ultra-high dimensional data since we have several features for each record. Sampling techniques aim to reduce the dataset's size but still do not offer a solution for high-dimensional datasets. In such cases, Dimensionality Reduction precedes Clustering procedures as a preprocessing step (Kaski 1998; Yan et al. 2006). Dimensionality Reduction (DR) aims to solve the Curse of Dimensionality (Bellman 1957) depicting that when the dimensionality increases, the volume of the space increases at such a rate that the dataset becomes sparse, opposing statistical methods. The goal is to find low-dimensional representations of the data that retain their fundamental properties, typically in two or three dimensions (Ghodsi 2006; Sorzano, Vargas and Montano 2014). As such this process is also essential for data visualization in lower dimensions (Xia et al. 2017). Visualization tools can assist in identifying the data structure while plotting the data in two dimensions allows researchers to pinpoint any remaining technical variability source between samples, which should be removed by normalization (Rostom et al. 2017).

Meanwhile, well-established visualization techniques that have proven effective for small or intermediate size data face a significant challenge when applied to big and high dimensional data. Visualizing high-dimensional data could allow the discovery of hidden relationships between the hidden variables and numeric values (Xia et al. 2017). Although there is remarkable progress in this field, identifying an extremely low-dimensional representation of large-scale and high-dimensional data remains a major challenge. Dimensionality reduction techniques able to handle large data are presented below, either traditional, established methods or state-of-the-art approaches specifically designed for Big Data scenarios.

Principal component analysis (PCA) is probably one of the most popular multivariate statistical techniques used by almost all disciplines. It is also likely the oldest multi-variable technique. Its origins date back to Pearson (Pearson 1901). PCA is a statistical process that uses a rectangular transformation to convert a set of observations of possible associated variables (entities each receiving different numeric values) into a set of values of linearly unrelated variables called main variables. This transformation is defined so that the first principal component has the highest possible variance (i.e., gives the highest volatility to the data), and each subsequent one has the next highest variance, subject to the constraint that it is rectangular with the previous components. By visualizing the two main components, the user can apprehend some of the topologies that the data have while also being assured that most of the relevant information is still preserved. PCA, though, is mainly able to produce acceptable results in linear datasets (Shah et al. 2013). For this reason, a large number of non-linear dimensionality reduction techniques have been created to preserve the topology of the dataset better. In what follows, we present some state-of-the-art tools that have seen adoption in recent years.

Van der Maaten and Hinton proposed t-distributed stochastic neighborhood embedding (t-SNE) in 2008. Until recently, it was considered to have vast applicability and great accuracy (Kobak and Berens 2019; Rauber et al. 2016). This technique is an extension of the SNE as proposed by Hinton and Roweis in 2003 (Hinton and Roweis, Stochastic neighbor embedding 2003), which is a technique that minimizes the Kullback-Leibler (Kullback 1997) deviation of the scaled similarities among pairs of points both in high and low dimensional spaces. SNE uses a Gaussian kernel to compute similarities in a high and low dimensional space. The t-Distributed Stochastic Neighborhood Embedding improves SNE by using a t-Distribution as a kernel in low dimensional space. Because of the heavy-tailed t-distribution, t-SNE maintains local neighborhoods of the data better and penalizes wrong embeddings of dissimilar points (Maaten and Hinton 2008). This property makes it especially suitable to represent clustered data and complex structures in a few dimensions. The minimization of the Kullback-Leibler divergence with respect to the points is performed using gradient descent.

Uniform Manifold Approximation and Projection (UMAP) (McInnes, Healy and Melville 2018) is a new multi-dimensional learning technique for non-linear manifolds. The UMAP algorithm is competitive with t-SNE in terms of visualization quality and, according to the authors, maintains a more comprehensive structure with superior runtime performance. Furthermore, UMAP has no computational restrictions on the embedding dimension, making it viable as a general-purpose dimension reduction technique for machine learning. What characterizes UMAP is that it uses local approximations of the dataset and then links them with fuzzy unions to construct simplicial sets representing the high-dimensional data's topological geometry.

LargeVis (Tang et al. 2016) is another novel visualization technique. Many recent approaches like the t-SNE, as mentioned above, construct a K-nearest neighbor graph and then project the graph into the 2-d space. LargeVis follows a similar procedure. First, LargeVis produces an accurately approximated K-nearest neighbor graph from the data and then layouts the graph in the low-dimensional space but, in contrast, uses an efficient algorithm for K-nearest neighbor graph construction and a principled probabilistic model for graph visualization. The whole procedure thus could scale to millions of high-dimensional data points. According to the authors, LargeVis outperforms state-of-the-art methods in both efficiency and effectiveness.

5.2.2 Unsupervised Learning through Clustering

Broadly defined clustering aims to identify subgroups (clusters) in the data that are distinguished by an appropriate measure of similarity (or regularity), without any previous knowledge about the assignment of observations to clusters or even the presence of clusters (Everitt et al. 2011). The main goal is to group sets of objects so that samples in the same group are more similar to each other than samples in different groups. Clustering is among the most used exploratory data analysis techniques (Berkhin 2006; Gan, Ma and Wu 2020; Jajuga, Sokolowski and Bock 2012). The recent explosion of data availability leads to an ever-growing tendency to "let the data speak" (Cios, Pedrycz and Swiniarski 1998). However, the properties of novel data sources and the increasing size, dimensionality, and speed at which data are captured pose challenges for established methods. Applications for cluster analysis include gene sequence analysis, market research, and object recognition. In general, clustering techniques aimed at big data can be categorized into single-machine and distributed clustering algorithms (Shirkhorshidi et al. 2014).

Partitioning clustering algorithms aim to divide the space that the data points lie on into sub-spaces that each contains a set of data points, according to a pre-specified number. Their simplicity and performance have attracted the research community's interest even in recent years proposing sophisticated variations and big data capable versions (Sreedhar, Kasiviswanath and Reddy 2017). One significant advantage of such approaches is that every set of data points has a distinct center (representative) As a result, a new point can be efficiently assigned to the appropriate set after the fact. Usually, Partitioning methods (*K*-means, PAM clustering) are most suitable for finding spherical or convex clusters, meaning they work well only for compact and well-separated clusters. Moreover, they can be severely affected by the presence of noise and outliers in the data. For such cases, density-based approaches are usually employed (Gao et al. 2016; Hahsler et al. 2017); however, they typically fall short in the presence of vast amounts of high dimensional data. The computational and memory requirements in Big Data scenarios are prohibitive for density-based algorithms. Simultaneously, we lose the ability to extract representatives that allow a straightforward procedure of allocating new samples into clusters.

K-means (Forgy 1965) algorithm is an iterative algorithm that tries to partition a dataset in *K* pre-defined discrete non-overlapping clusters where each data point belongs to only one group. *K*-means is a simple algorithm that has been used in a variety of fields. The goal is to make the data points belonging to the same cluster as similar as possible while keeping the clusters as distant from each other as possible. For a set of samples $\left(x1, x2, \ldots, xn\right)$ in the d-dimensional space, cluster the dataset into clusters $C = \left\{C1, C2, \ldots, Ck\right\}$ by minimizing the within-cluster sum of squares or variance according to the following objective:

$$\arg\min_{\mathbf{C}} \sum_{i=1}^{k} \sum_{\mathbf{x} \in C_i} \| \mathbf{x} - \mu_i \|^2 = \arg\min_{\mathbf{C}} \sum_{i=1}^{k} \left|C_i\right| \operatorname{Var} C_i ,$$

where μ_i is the mean of points in the i-th cluster C_i. The algorithm assigns data points to a cluster in such a way that the total sum of the squared distances among the data points and their cluster's centroid (mean value of the data points that belong to a cluster) is minimized. The less variation there is within groups, the more similar data points are within each cluster.

Hierarchical clustering constructs hierarchies of clusters in a top-down (agglomerative) or bottom-up (divisive) fashion. The former starts from n clusters, where n stands for the number of data points, each containing a single data point and iteratively merging the clusters satisfying certain closeness measures. Divisive algorithms follow a reverse approach, starting with a single cluster containing all the data points and iteratively split existing clusters into subsets. Hierarchical clustering algorithms have been shown to result in high-quality partitions, especially for applications involving clustering text collections. Nonetheless, their high computational requirements usually prevent their usage in big data scenarios. However, more recent advancements in both agglomerative (Murtagh and Legendre 2014; Zhang, Zhao and Wang 2013) and divisive strategies (Sharma, López and Tsunoda 2017; Tasoulis et al. 2014) have exposed their broad applicability and robustness. In particular, when divisive clustering is combined with dimensionality reduction (Hofmeyr, Clustering by minimum cut hyperplanes 2016; Pavlidis, Hofmeyr and Tasoulis 2016), we can still get methods capable of indexing large data collection that allow fast sample allocation due to their tree structure.

The Normalized Cut Divisive Clustering (Ncutdc) (Hofmeyr 2016) algorithm is a computationally efficient divisive clustering algorithm relying on hyperplane separators. It generates a binary partitioning tree by recursively partitioning a dataset using a hierarchical collection of hyperplanes with low normalized cut measured across them. As in the minimum density hyperplane case, the projection pursuit problem is formulated as a minimization problem. The normalized cut (NCut) (Shi and Malik 2000) associated with a partition of X into clusters $C1,...,Ck$ is expressed as,

$$\mathrm{NCut}\left(\mathcal{C}_1,\ldots,\mathcal{C}_k\right)=\sum_{m=1}^{k}\frac{\mathrm{Cut}\left(\mathcal{C}_m,\mathcal{X}\setminus\mathcal{C}_m\right)}{\mathrm{volume}\left(\mathcal{C}_m\right)}$$

By minimizing the normalized cut, this leads to solutions for which $Cut\left(Cm,X\setminus Cm\right)$ is small and volume $\left(Cm\right)$ is large, for all m. Since volume $\left(\mathcal{C}_m\right)=\mathrm{Cut}\left(\mathcal{C}_m,\mathcal{X}\setminus\mathcal{C}_m\right)+\sum_{i,j:\mathbf{x}_i,\mathbf{x}_j\in\mathcal{C}_m}\mathrm{similarity}\left(x_i,x_j\right)$, where the last term is the total internal similarity of points in $\mathcal{C}_m$, this implies that the similarity within clusters is high whereas the similarity between clusters is low. Similarities are defined as a notion of the distances between pairs of points, i.e., similarity $\mathrm{similarity}\left(x_i,x_j\right)=\mathrm{k}\left(\|x_i-x_j\|\right)$, where $k:\mathbb{R}^+\rightarrow\mathbb{R}^+$ is a decreasing function. However, the NCut problem is NP-hard, and, instead, a continuous relaxation of the problem known as spectral clustering (Shi and Malik 2000; Von Luxburg 2007) is considered. This leads to a reduction in complexity, but this method remains applicable only to moderate size situations.

The Genie (Gagolewski, Bartoszuk and Cena 2016) algorithm is an alternative for the more classical, single-linkage criteria hierarchical clustering. The algorithm aims to offset the disadvantages of the single linkage scheme, that is, sensitivity to outliers, the creation of very skewed dendrograms, and consequently not reflecting the actual underlying data structure unless there are well-separated clusters. Simultaneously, to retain the single-linkage's simplicity and efficiency, the following linkage criterion, referred to as the Genie algorithm, was created. Let F be a fixed inequity measure (e.g., the Gini-index) and $g\in\left(0,1\right]$ be some threshold. At step j: If $\mathrm{F}\left(c_{(n-j)},\ldots,c_{(1)}\right)\leq g, c_i=\left|C_i^{(j)}\right|$, apply the original single linkage criterion:

$$\arg\min_{(u,v),u<v}\left(\min_{\mathbf{a}\in C_u^{(j)},\mathbf{b}\in C_v^{(j)}}\mathrm{D}\left(\mathbf{a},\mathbf{b}\right)\right),$$

else if $\mathrm{F}\left(c_{(n-j)},\ldots,c_{(1)}\right)>g$, restrict the search domain only to pairs of clusters such that one of them is the smallest:

$$\arg\min_{(u,v),u<v,}\left(\min_{\mathbf{a}\in C_u^{(j)},\mathbf{b}\in C_v^{(j)}}\mathrm{D}\left(\mathbf{a},\mathbf{b}\right)\right)$$

$$\left|C_u^{(j)}\right|=\min_i\left|C_i^{(j)}\right| \text{ or}$$

$$\left|C_v^{(j)}\right|=\min_i\left|C_i^{(j)}\right|$$

This modification prevents extreme increases of the chosen inequity measure and forces early merges of small clusters with others.

Finally, in density-based clustering, a cluster is a set of data objects spread in the data space over a contiguous region of high density of objects. Density-based clusters are separated from each other by contiguous regions of low density of objects. Data objects located in low-density regions are typically considered noise or outliers. Density-based clustering algorithms are able to discover arbitrary-shaped clusters, but usually suffer from increased computational costs, preventing them to be scalable. DensityPeaks (Rodriguez and Laio 2014) algorithm is a novel density-based approach. Similar to the K-medoids method, it has its basis only in the distance between data points. Like DBSCAN (Hahsler et al. 2017) and the mean-shift process, it can detect non-spherical clusters and automatically find the correct number of clusters. As in the mean-shift method, the cluster centers are defined as local maxima in the density of data points. However, unlike the mean-shift method, this procedure does not require embedding the data in a vector space and maximizing explicitly the density field for each data point. The algorithm assumes that cluster centers are surrounded by regions with lower local density and are relatively far away from higher local density points. For each data point, the algorithm computes two measures: its local density and its distance from samples of higher density. Both these measures depend exclusively on the intervals between data points, which are considered to satisfy the triangular inequality.

5.3 EXPERIMENTAL ANALYSIS

To the best of the writer's knowledge, there is no singular unsupervised methodology that is able to extract all the available information from any dataset (Adam et al. 2019). In many cases, methods from different fields are combined, resulting in more sophisticated techniques with benefits from all the components. This section presents some combinatorial methodologies and an example of such schemes in a Big Data scenario. More precisely, we will implement a complete unsupervised learning methodology for the ATHLOS cohort dataset while also utilizing very recent techniques for variable exploration.

5.3.1 DATA SPECIFICATION AND PRE-PROCESSING

ATHLOS (Ageing Trajectories of Health: Longitudinal Opportunities and Synergies) is a project funded by the European Union's Horizon 2020 Research and Innovation Program, which aims to interpret aging's impact on health better. The ATHLOS project provides a harmonized dataset (Sanchez-Niubo et al. 2019), built upon several longitudinal studies and originated from five continents. More specifically, it contains samples coming from more than 355,000 individuals who participated in 17 general population longitudinal studies in 38 countries. Based on the WHO healthy aging framework, researchers from the ATHLOS consortium reviewed measures of functional ability in the aging cohorts and identified 47 items related to health, physical, and cognitive functioning. The consortium harmonized these 47 items into binary variables and used item-response theory modeling to generate a common measure for healthy aging across cohorts.

In this paper, we used 15 of these studies, namely the 10/66 Dementia Research Group Population-Based Cohort Study (Prina et al. 2017), the Australian Longitudinal Study of Aging (ALSA) (Luszcz et al. 2016), the Collaborative Research on Ageing in Europe (COURAGE) (Leonardi et al. 2014), the ELSA (Steptoe et al. 2013), the study on Cardiovascular Health, Nutrition and Frailty in Older Adults in Spain (ENRICA) (Rodríguez-Artalejo et al. 2011), the Health, Alcohol and Psychosocial factors in Eastern Europe Study (HAPIEE) (Peasey et al. 2006), the Health 2000/2011 Survey (Koskinen 2018), the HRS (Sonnega et al. 2014), the JSTAR (Ichimura, Shimizutani and Hashimoto 2009), the KLOSA (Park et al. 2007), the MHAS (Wong, Michaels-Obregon and Palloni 2017), the SAGE (Kowal et al. 2012), SHARE (Börsch-Supan et al. 2013), the Irish Longitudinal Study of Ageing (TILDA) (Whelan and Savva 2013) and the Longitudinal Aging Study in India (LASI) (Arokiasamy et al. 2012). The 15 general population longitudinal studies utilized in this work consist of 990,000 samples in total, characterized by 184 variables. The version used here is a preprocessed dataset where a selection of variables has been removed along with several samples. The resulting data matrix constituted by 770,764 samples and 107 variables has been imputed using the Vtreat (Zumel and Mount 2016) imputation method in order to populate the missing values in a meaningful manner. As a result 458 dummy variables has been created constituting the final data dimensionality.

Due to the high number of variables in this study we do not procced to a detailed presentation of each one of them for brevity reasons. As a result, a brief description of the main groups of variables follows with the reader prompted to read more into the supplementary material provided online[1] To begin with, there were indexing variables regarding the studies, cohorts, dates, and samples removed from our analytical procedures. Next, there were general information and quantitative laboratory measures of an individual about their physical characteristics like age, sex, Cholesterol and Triglycerides, blood pressure, and more. Also, there were critical variables regarding someone's damaging habits like smoking and alcohol consumption and frequency. Moreover, included were variables resulting from questionnaires and individuals' answers. Those variables include any pre-existing conditions or accidents that an individual may have like falls, asthma, strokes, and more, followed by demographic variables regarding one's socioeconomic status, employment status, education, wealth, etc. In addition, there were variables derived from an individual's answers about their social position regarding children, political and religious activity, and contacts with relatives and friends. Last but not least, there were variables regarding the physical activity of the correspondents, like the number and intensity of exercises.

5.3.2 Data Visualization for Pattern Recognition

To this end, we employ a series of dimensionality reduction algorithms for embedding the ATHLOS dataset in two dimensions. All methodologies are implemented using the R-project open-source environment for statistical computing, and experiments were conducted for each algorithm to tune its hyper-parameters. In what follows,

[1] https://github.com/athlosproject/athlos-project.github.io

we provide the details of each implementation tested, referring to the corresponding R packages when possible. For PCA, we employed the implementation found in the "dimRed" package (Kraemer, Reichstein and Mahecha 2018). The fast "Rtsne" implementation for tSNE (Krijthe 2015) was used, and the two main hyper-parameters were set as follows, "perplexity" at a range of 30 to 800 and "theta" at a range of 0.1 to 1. The "uwot" implementation of the UMAP algorithm (McInnes, Healy and Melville 2018) is used, and the two main hyper-parameters were examined, "cluster neighbors" at a range from 15 to 100 and "minimum distance" at a range from 0.01 to 0.15. Finally, the "largeVis" implementation of the LargeVis algorithm (Elberg 2020) was used, and the hyper-parameters, "Kapa" and "max iterations," were set at a range from 10 to 200 and from 10 to 50 accordingly.

In Figure 4.1, we observe the resulting visualization for all methods across the samples. It is evident that PCA tends to produce a more coherent representation without however distinguishing any particular clusters. The advantage of this technique, however, is that the coordinates have a strict and valuable definition. UMAP and LargeVis seem to produce very similar results creating several very distinct clusters. tSNE also created groups that were, however, larger, taking into account their in-between cluster distances. As depicted in Figure 4.1, the non-linear dimensionality reduction techniques, in this case, tend to separate more clearly groups of individuals that lie more closely in the intrinsic dimensionality manifold.

5.3.3 Clustering for Verification

The next step of our analysis is to determine the existence of clusters that could be verified through visualization. As a first step, we looked at the clustering tendency of the dataset. That is whether the data contain any inherent grouping structure. For this purpose, we calculated the well-known "Hopkins" statistic (Lawson and Jurs 1990), for which values close to 1 indicate a clusterable dataset. In our case, using the "clusterland" R package (YiLan and RuTong 2015), the corresponding calculated value is *83%*, suggesting a high degree of clusterability. Subsequently, for brevity and the sake of the reader's convenience, we choose to determine a representative number of clusters to accompany visualizations instead of providing extensive parameter analysis, which would hinder visual interpretation. Apparently, this task is not trivial, and there are over thirty different approaches in the literature regarding this exact case. After both heuristic experiments and counseling the results provided by the "factoextra" R package (Kassambara, Mundt and others 2017), we propose that any number between *4* to *12* clusters is an appropriate choice. Consequently, we proceed to the clustering step. For the Kmeans algorithm, we chose the memory efficient implementation found in (Emerson and Kane 2020), optimized for large scale applications. For the Genie algorithm, the corresponding R package "genie" (Gagolewski, Bartoszuk and Cena 2016) was used. For the Ncutdc algorithm, the implementation found in the authors 's "PPCI" (Hofmeyr and Pavlidis, PPCI: an R Package for Cluster Identification using Projection Pursuit 2019) package was used. Lastly, any attempt to use popular density-based approaches in the original dimension space, unfortunately, failed due to the dataset's scale. In particular, we employed the recent implementation of the DensityPeaks algorithm found in (Pedersen, Hughes and Qiu 2017) but hardware requirements exceeded 1TB of RAM usage. Thus, we chose to firstly reduce the number of dimensions down to 50 with the PCA method in order to be able to run all the algorithms in a reasonable amount of time. Afterward, we extracted a uniformly random subsample of the dataset of 20000 samples. The DensityPeaks algorithm lacks the ability to tune the parameters "rho" and "delta" that affect the number of retrieved clusters. Instead, provided is a graphical tool with which the user can manually set the respective values through a scatter plot's visual investigation. In our tests, we set these as the mean values across the parameters calculated for all samples.

Cluster memberships depicted in Figure 4.1 arise from the application of bigKmeans, Genie, DensityPeaks and Ncutdc clustering algorithms on the ATHLOS dataset in the 50-d dimensional space, with k = 10. It is observed that there is a clear correlation between the embeddings in the two-dimensional space and the clusters assigned by bigKmeans. Also, the Ncutdc algorithm produces very distinct clusters, similar to bigKmeans, with minor tangling, as it is the case of Genie. Lastly, for DensityPeaks, a large number of data points appear to be mixed regarding the allocated cluster and the corresponding location within the embedding. Thus, this result further verifies that the visualizations were representative and that there are groups of individuals with some distinct characteristics. However, which variables are the

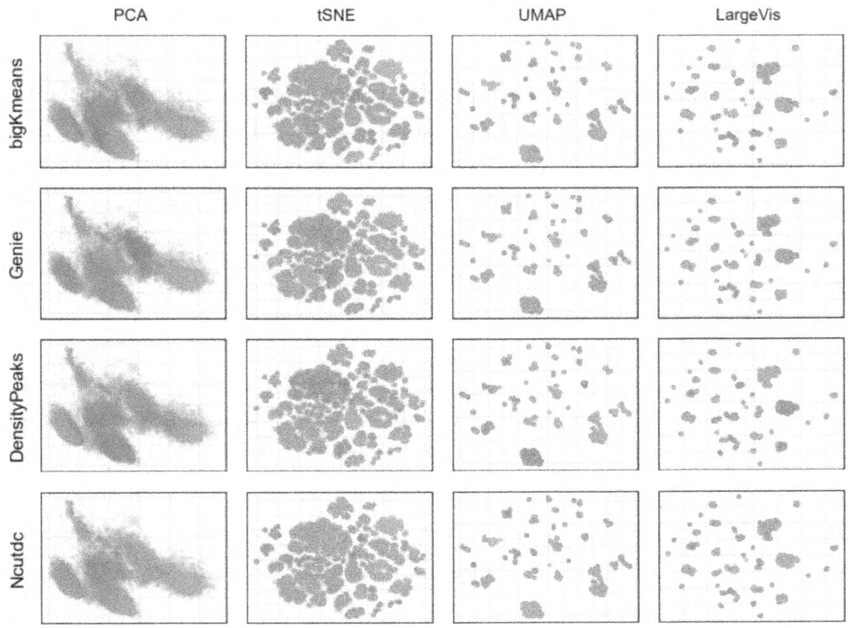

FIGURE 5.1 2D visualization of PCA, tSNE, UMAP and LargeVis embeddings (column-wise) on the ATHLOS dataset clustered with "bigKmeans," "Genie," "DensityPeaks," and "Ncutdc" clustering algorithms (row-wise) accordingly. Circular points represent each sample of data colored by the corresponding cluster ID resulting from the respective clustering algorithms.

dominant separation attributes is not easy to interpret only with statistical measures or exhaustive search for each feature in every cluster.

To numerically validate the clustering result of the aforementioned algorithms, we employ an implementation of the Silhouette index (Rousseeuw 1987) Dunn index (Bezdek and Pal 1995) and Separation index specifically designed for Large-scale data provided by the "fpc" R package (Hennig 2020). Silhouette is a method of interpretation and validation of consistency within a cluster. The silhouette index compares how similar an object is to its group compared to other clusters. The notion of silhouette index is given as:

$$s(i) = \frac{b(i) - a(i)}{\max\{a(i), b(i)\}}$$

where $a(i)$ is the mean distance between the i-th point from the points of the same cluster, or similarity score, and $b(i)$ is the mean distance between the i-th point and every other point that is not of the same cluster, or dissimilarity score. The silhouette has a range of *−1* to *+1*, where a high value indicates that the object is well matched to its cluster and poorly matched to neighboring clusters. The Dunn index is defined as:

$$DI_m = \frac{\min \delta(C_i, C_j)}{\max \Delta_k}$$

and depicts the ratio of the smallest distance between observations not in the same cluster with $\min \delta(C_i, C_j)$, to the largest intra-cluster distance with $\max \Delta_k$ and has a value between zero and infinity. One downside with this metric is the computational cost associated as the number of clusters and the dimensionality increases. The Separation Index is defined based on the distances for every data point to the closest neighbor not in the same group. The separation index then depicts the mean of the smallest proportion of these distances. Separation index takes into account a portion p, of objects in every cluster that are closest to another group. For every sample $x_i \in C_j, i = 1, \ldots, n, j \in \{1, \ldots, K\}$ let $d_{j:i} = \min_{y \notin C_j} d(x_i, y)$. Let$d_{j:(i)} \leq \cdots \leq d_{j:(n_j)}$ be the values of $d_{j:i}$ for $x_i \in C_j$ ordered in an increasing manner, and let $\lfloor pn_j \rfloor$ be the largest integer $\leq pn_j$. Then the p-separation index is given by:

$$I_{p-sep}(C) = \frac{1}{\sum_{j=1}^{K} \lfloor pn_j \rfloor} \sum_{j=1}^{K} \sum_{i=1}^{\lfloor pn_j \rfloor} d_{j:(i)}$$

This allows formalizing separation less sensitive to a single or a few ambiguous points. Considering the results of the aforementioned metrics presented in Table 5.1, it is verified that "DensityPeaks" do not separate clusters as effectively as the other three methods with "Ncustdc" achieving the highest scores.

In an attempt to extract knowledge based on the identified patterns, the 2d embedding of the tSNE method was colored according to some categorical variables of

TABLE 5.1
Internal Validation Metrics for the Clustering Algorithms.

	Silhouette	Dunn	Separation
BigKmeans	0.1265699	0.738058	8.343318
Genie	0.04942602	0.7035942	6.956037
DensityPeaks	−0.1252029	0.4331565	8.033905
Ncutdc	**0.1301279**	**0.7423549**	**8.436816**

Larger values depict greater similarities within the same cluster, while the clusters been more separate.

TABLE 5.2
Internal Validation Metrics for the Most Separated Features.

	Silhouette	Dunn	Separation
Cardiovascular_History	0.2239903	1.2507654	1.1195133
Angina_History	0.2198167	1.2698951	1.2975713
Respiratory_History	0.2059388	1.3212471	1.0268838
Hypertension_History	0.1861763	1.2968042	0.9150790
Frequent_Contacts	0.1800876	1.2259719	0.1931220
Group_Sports	0.1533813	1.2334624	4.9907552

Larger values depict greater similarities within the samples of with the same value for that particular feature, while the samples not in the same category been more separate.

interest (see Figure 4.2). The variables were selected according to the following scheme. For every categorical variable, we calculated the Silhouette (Rousseeuw 1987), Dunn (Bezdek and Pal 1995) and Separation (Hennig 2020) indexes for the 2d embeddings, considering the variables as a typical clustering results. Then, we chose six variables that presented the highest separability according to these metrics. There are apparent correlations with some of the variables and the resulting clumps in the visualization, implying that individuals have some distinct characteristics. We interestingly observe that we are able to identify separable regions characterized by particular levels of the categorical variables, potentially leading to straight forward cluster characterization.

In more detail, the features depicted in Table 5.2 are the following: Cardiovascular_History: Is a binary variable and refers to the history of stroke or myocardial infarction (heart attack) of an individual. Angina_History: Is a binary variable and refers to the "h_angina" variable of the original dataset that depicts whether or not an individual had a history of angina. Respiratory_History: Refers to the categorical "h_respiratory" variable of the original dataset that depicts one's history of chronic respiratory diseases such asthma, CPD, COPD, bronchitis, etc. This variable is then transformed

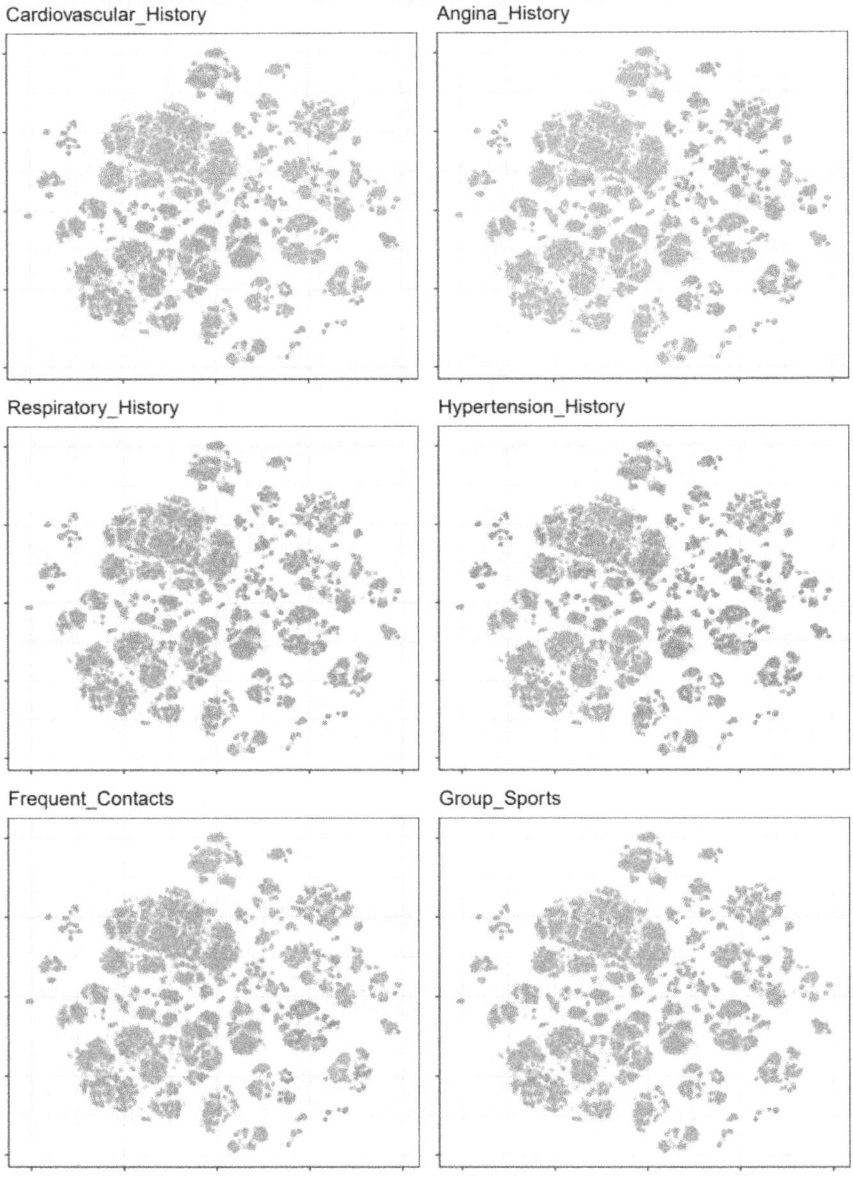

FIGURE 5.2 Visualizations of the 2d embedded dataset using t-SNE with respect to a selection of variables found in the ATHLOS dataset. Each subplot corresponds to different variables, while different colors correspond to different values for every variable.

with the "Vtreat" package to an encoding that expresses the within-group deviation of the outcome conditioned on each categorical level in the original data and thus, amend the high cardinality of the variable. Hypertension_History: Refers to the categorical "h_hypertension" variable of the original dataset that depicts one's history of hypertension for an individual. This variable is then transformed with the "Vtreat"

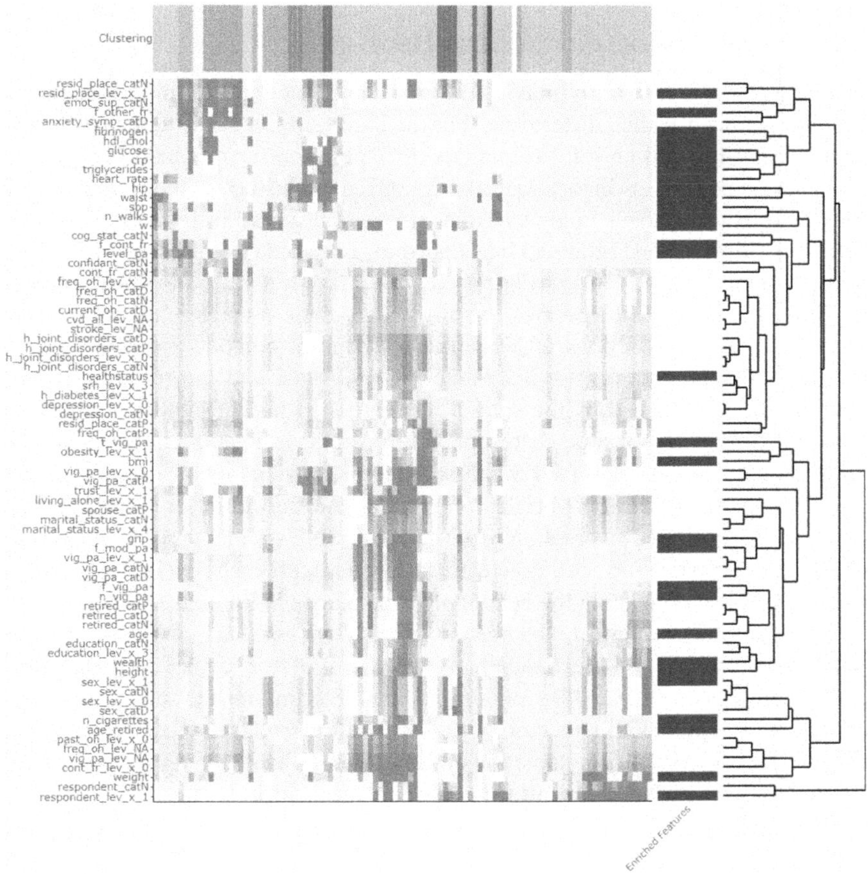

FIGURE 5.3 Heatmap Visualization of the Athlos dataset. Depicted are the Variables in every row, colored according to their respective value, with red depicting a larger value. The columns represent 100 bins of samples and are arranged according to their 1d-tSNE embedding. Also, the "Clustering" bar depict the cluster assignment of the DBSCAN algorithm run in the 2d-tsne embedding of the dataset. The "Enriched_Features" bar depicts the additional variables returned by the 1d-tsne-heatmap function where in blue color are the variables of interest as an input for the function and with white color are the additional variables returned for the "enrich" parameter equal to 5.

package to an encoding that expresses the within-group deviation of the outcome conditioned on each categorical level in the original data and thus, amend the high cardinality of the variable. Frequent_Contacts: Is a binary variable and refers to the "cont_fr" variable of the original dataset that depicts if an individual has frequent contacts with friends/neighbors. Group_Sports: Is a binary variable and refers to the "sport" variable of the original dataset that depicts if an individual participates currently in group sport activities.

5.3.4 Variable Importance through Heatmaps

Motivated by the previous sections' findings, we introduce an additional step to visualize the regions' variable differences. For the final step, we chose to include a novel method so far utilized only for Genomics in Gene Expression (Linderman, Rachh, et al. 2019). The process incorporates both tSNE and clustering in order to produce a Heatmap that visualizes many variables (instead of genes) of interest at the same time. To build the t-SNE Heatmap introduced in (Linderman, Rachh, et al. 2019), we initially compute t-SNE embeddings of the Variables of interest into one dimension. This implementation incorporates the FIt-SNE (Linderman, Rachh, et al. 2017), which is scalable to millions of Variables in terms of computational time. Then, the 1D t-SNE embeddings are discretized in 100 bins, and the representation of each variable is produced by the sum of its expression in the samples contained in each bin, while each variable corresponds to a vector in R^100. Hierarchical clustering upon the aforementioned vectors produces even more meaningful results. Subsequently, for some set of variables of interest, the algorithm "enriches" the variables that have a similar expression pattern in the t-SNE (see Figure 4.3). Afterward, these vectors are transformed into Heatmap format, with each row being a variable and each column a bin using the heatmaply R package (Galili et al. 2018).

This is possible because it has been previously shown that t-SNE preserves the cluster structure of well-clustered data regardless of the embedding dimension (Linderman, Rachh, et al. 2019), and thus 1D t-SNEs contains the same information as 2D t-SNEs. The resulting vectors visualized in the produced Heatmap presented in Figure 4.3 provides a clear depiction of the variables' behavior among the clusters, with hundreds of variables visualized at the same time.

5.4 CONCLUSIONS

This study provided insight into recent Unsupervised Learning methods and their popular implementations through their application on a complex real-world dataset. As shown, based on these methods, we were able to provide a comprehensive example of knowledge extraction and pattern recognition analysis. In addition, we utilized a promising novel unsupervised learning approach from the Gene Expression field to provide helpful information of Variable expression for the ATHLOS cohort dataset, exposing the method's usefulness in similar Big Data tasks. In addition, further investigation regarding recently published ensemble schemas in combination with voting theory could be utilized to enhance the clustering procedure. Another possible path for further development could be to compare the methods of this study in labeled datasets to measure their separation ability in a supervised manner.

5.5 ACKNOWLEDGEMENTS

This work is supported by the ATHLOS (Aging Trajectories of Health: Longitudinal Opportunities and Synergies) project, funded by the European Union's Horizon 2020 Research and Innovation Program under grant agreement number 635316.

REFERENCES

Adam, Stavros P., Stamatios-Aggelos N. Alexandropoulos, Panos M. Pardalos, and Michael N. Vrahatis. 2019. "No free lunch theorem: A review." *Approximation and Optimization* (Springer): 57–82.

Alharthi, Abdulkhaliq, Vlad Krotov, and Michael Bowman. 2017. "Addressing barriers to big data." *Business Horizons* (Elsevier) 60: 285–292.

Allaoui, Mebarka, Mohammed Lamine Kherfi, and Abdelhakim Cheriet. 2020. "Considerably improving clustering algorithms using UMAP dimensionality reduction technique: A comparative study." *International Conference on Image and Signal Processing*, 317–325.

Arokiasamy, P., David Bloom, Jinkook Lee, Kevin Feeney, and Marija Ozolins. 2012. "Longitudinal aging study in India: Vision, design, implementation, and preliminary findings." In *Aging in Asia: Findings from new and emerging data initiatives*. National Academies Press (US).

Bellman, Richard. 1957. "Dynamic programming, princeton univ." *Prese} Princeton, 19S7.*

Berkhin, Pavel. 2006. "A survey of clustering data mining techniques." In *Grouping multidimensional data*, 25–71. Springer.

Bezdek, James C., and Nikhil R. Pal. 1995. "Cluster validation with generalized Dunn's indices." *Proceedings 1995 Second New Zealand International Two-Stream Conference on Artificial Neural Networks and Expert Systems*, 190–193.

Börsch-Supan, Axel, Martina Brandt, Christian Hunkler, Thorsten Kneip, Julie Korbmacher, Frederic Malter, Barbara Schaan, Stephanie Stuck, and Sabrina Zuber. 2013. "Data resource profile: The Survey of Health, Ageing and Retirement in Europe (SHARE)." *International Journal of Epidemiology* (Oxford University Press) 42: 992–1001.

Casolla, Giampaolo, Salvatore Cuomo, Vincenzo Schiano Di Cola, and Francesco Piccialli. 2019. "Exploring unsupervised learning techniques for the Internet of Things." *IEEE Transactions on Industrial Informatics* (IEEE) 16: 2621–2628.

Chawla, Sanjay, and Aristides Gionis. 2013. "k-means-: A unified approach to clustering and outlier detection." *Proceedings of the 2013 SIAM International Conference on Data Mining*. 189–197.

Cios, Krzysztof J., Witold Pedrycz, and Roman W. Swiniarski. 1998. "Data mining and knowledge discovery." In *Data mining methods for knowledge discovery*, 1–26. Springer.

Diaz-Papkovich, Alex, Luke Anderson-Trocmé, and Simon Gravel. 2019. "UMAP reveals cryptic population structure and phenotype heterogeneity in large genomic cohorts." *PLoS Genetics* (Public Library of Science) 15: e1008432.

Elberg, Amos B. 2020. "largeVis: High-quality visualizations of large, high-dimensional datasets." https://github.com/elbamos/largeVis.

Emerson, John W., and Michael J. Kane. 2020. "biganalytics: Utilities for 'big.matrix' objects from package 'bigmemory.' " https://CRAN.R-project.org/package = biganalytics.

Everitt, Brian S., Sabine Landau, Morven Leese, and Daniel Stahl. 2011. *Cluster analysis.* John Wiley & Sons.

Fan, Jianqing, and Yingying Fan. 2008. "High dimensional classification using features annealed independence rules." *Annals of Statistics* (NIH Public Access) 36: 2605.

Fan, Jianqing, Fang Han, and Han Liu. 2014. "Challenges of big data analysis." *National Science Review* (Oxford University Press) 1: 293–314.

Fan, Jianqing, Shaojun Guo, and Ning Hao. 2012. "Variance estimation using refitted cross-validation in ultrahigh dimensional regression." *Journal of the Royal Statistical Society: Series B (Statistical Methodology)* (Wiley Online Library) 74: 37–65.

Forgy, Edward W. 1965. "Cluster analysis of multivariate data: Efficiency versus interpretability of classifications." *Biometrics* 21: 768–769.

Gagolewski, Marek, Maciej Bartoszuk, and Anna Cena. 2016. "Genie: A new, fast, and outlier-resistant hierarchical clustering algorithm." *Information Sciences* 363: 8–23. doi:10.1016/j.ins.2016.05.003.

Galili, Tal, Alan O'Callaghan, Jonathan Sidi, and Carson Sievert. 2018. "heatmaply: An R package for creating interactive cluster heatmaps for online publishing." *Bioinformatics* (Oxford University Press) 34: 1600–1602.

Gan, Guojun, Chaoqun Ma, and Jianhong Wu. 2020. *Data clustering: Theory, algorithms, and applications.* SIAM.

Gao, Jing, Liang Zhao, Zhikui Chen, Peng Li, Han Xu, and Yueming Hu. 2016. "ICFS: An improved fast search and find of density peaks clustering algorithm." *2016 IEEE 14th Intl Conf on Dependable, Autonomic and Secure Computing, 14th Intl Conf on Pervasive Intelligence and Computing, 2nd Intl Conf on Big Data Intelligence and Computing and Cyber Science and Technology Congress (DASC/PiCom/DataCom/CyberSciTech)*, 537–543.

Ghahramani, Zoubin. 2003. "Unsupervised learning." *Summer School on Machine Learning*, 72–112.

Ghodsi, Ali. 2006. "Dimensionality reduction a short tutorial." *Department of Statistics and Actuarial Science, Univ. of Waterloo, Ontario, Canada* 37: 2006.

Gu, Dongxiao, Jingjing Li, Xingguo Li, and Changyong Liang. 2017. "Visualizing the knowledge structure and evolution of big data research in healthcare informatics." *International Journal of Medical Informatics* (Elsevier) 98: 22–32.

Gupta, Deepak, and Rinkle Rani. 2019. "A study of big data evolution and research challenges." *Journal of Information Science* (SAGE Publications Sage UK: London, England) 45: 322–340.

Hahsler, Michael, Matthew Piekenbrock, S. Arya, and D. Mount. 2017. "dbscan: Density based clustering of applications with noise (DBSCAN) and related algorithms." *R Package Version* 1–0.

Hameed, Pathima Nusrath, Karin Verspoor, Snezana Kusljic, and Saman Halgamuge. 2018. "A two-tiered unsupervised clustering approach for drug repositioning through heterogeneous data integration." *BMC Bioinformatics* (Springer) 19: 129.

Hennig, Christian. 2020. "fpc: Flexible procedures for clustering." https://CRAN.R-project.org/package = fpc.

Hinton, Geoffrey E., and Sam T. Roweis. 2003. "Stochastic neighbor embedding." *Advances in Neural Information Processing Systems*, 857–864.

Hinton, Geoffrey E., Terrence Joseph Sejnowski, Tomaso A. Poggio, and others. 1999. *Unsupervised learning: Foundations of neural computation.* MIT Press.

Hofmeyr, David P. 2016. "Clustering by minimum cut hyperplanes." *IEEE Transactions on Pattern Analysis and Machine Intelligence* (IEEE) 39: 1547–1560.

Hofmeyr, David P., and Nicos G. Pavlidis. 2019. "PPCI: An R package for cluster identification using projection pursuit." *The R Journal.* doi:10.32614/RJ-2019-046.

Hozumi, Yuta, Rui Wang, Changchuan Yin, and Guo-Wei Wei. 2021. "UMAP-assisted K-means clustering of large-scale SARS-CoV-2 mutation datasets." *Computers in Biology and Medicine* (Elsevier) 104264.

Hsu, Wei-Ning, and James Glass. 2018. "Extracting domain invariant features by unsupervised learning for robust automatic speech recognition." *2018 IEEE International Conference on Acoustics, Speech and Signal Processing (ICASSP)*, 5614–5618.

Ichimura, Hidehiko, Satoshi Shimizutani, and Hideki Hashimoto. 2009. "JSTAR first results 2009 report." *Tech. rep.*, Research Institute of Economy, Trade and Industry (RIETI).

Jajuga, Krzystof, Andrzej Sokolowski, and Hans-Hermann Bock. 2012. *Classification, clustering, and data analysis: Recent advances and applications.* Springer Science & Business Media.

Jiang, Sheng-yi, and Qing-bo An. 2008. "Clustering-based outlier detection method." *2008 Fifth International Conference on Fuzzy Systems and Knowledge Discovery*, 429–433.

Jin, Xiaolong, Benjamin W. Wah, Xueqi Cheng, and Yuanzhuo Wang. 2015. "Significance and challenges of big data research." *Big Data Research* (Elsevier) 2: 59–64.

Kaski, Samuel. 1998. "Dimensionality reduction by random mapping: Fast similarity computation for clustering." *1998 IEEE International Joint Conference on Neural Networks Proceedings. IEEE World Congress on Computational Intelligence (Cat. No. 98CH36227)*, 413–418.

Kassambara, Alboukadel, Fabian Mundt, and others. 2017. "Factoextra: Extract and visualize the results of multivariate data analyses." *R Package Version* 1: 337–354.

Keyes, Katherine M., and Daniel Westreich. 2019. "UK Biobank, big data, and the consequences of non-representativeness." *Lancet (London, England)* (NIH Public Access) 393: 1297.

Kitchin, Rob, and Gavin McArdle. 2016. "What makes big data, big data? Exploring the ontological characteristics of 26 datasets." *Big Data & Society* (SAGE Publications Sage UK: London, England) 3: 2053951716631130.

Kobak, Dmitry, and Philipp Berens. 2019. "The art of using t-SNE for single-cell transcriptomics." *Nature Communications* (Nature Publishing Group) 10: 1–14.

Koskinen, S. 2018. "Health 2000 and 2011 surveys—THL Biobank. National Institute for Health and Welfare." *Health 2000 and 2011 Surveys—THL Biobank. National Institute for Health and Welfare.* https://thl.fi/en/web/thl-biobank/for-researchers/sample-collections/health-2000-and-2011-surveys

Kowal, Paul, Somnath Chatterji, Nirmala Naidoo, Richard Biritwum, Wu Fan, Ruy Lopez Ridaura, Tamara Maximova, et al. 2012. "Data resource profile: The World Health Organization Study on global AGEing and adult health (SAGE)." *International Journal of Epidemiology* (Oxford University Press) 41: 1639–1649.

Kraemer, Guido, Markus Reichstein, and Miguel D. Mahecha. 2018. "dimRed and coRanking—Unifying dimensionality reduction in R." *R Journal* (R Foundation) 10: 342–358.

Krijthe, Jesse H. 2015. "Rtsne: T-distributed stochastic neighbor embedding using Barnes-Hut implementation." *R Package Version 0.13.* https://github.com/jkrijthe/Rtsne.

Kullback, Solomon. 1997. *Information theory and statistics.* Courier Corporation.

Laney, Doug, and others. 2001. "3D data management: Controlling data volume, velocity and variety." *META Group Research Note* (Stanford) 6: 1.

Lawson, Richard G., and Peter C. Jurs. 1990. "New index for clustering tendency and its application to chemical problems." *Journal of Chemical Information and Computer Sciences* (ACS Publications) 30: 36–41.

Leonardi, Matilde, Somnath Chatterji, Seppo Koskinen, Jose Luis Ayuso-Mateos, Josep Maria Haro, Giovanni Frisoni, Lucilla Frattura, et al. 2014. "Determinants of health and disability in ageing population: The COURAGE in Europe Project (collaborative research on ageing in Europe)." *Clinical Psychology & Psychotherapy* (Wiley Online Library) 21: 193–198.

Li, Miaomiao, Xinwang Liu, Lei Wang, Yong Dou, Jianping Yin, and En Zhu. 2016. "Multiple kernel clustering with local kernel alignment maximization." https://ro.uow.edu.au/cgi/viewcontent.cgi?article = 7525&context = eispapers

Linderman, George C., Manas Rachh, Jeremy G. Hoskins, Stefan Steinerberger, and Yuval Kluger. 2017. "Efficient algorithms for t-distributed stochastic neighborhood embedding." *arXiv preprint arXiv:1712.09005.*

Linderman, George C., Manas Rachh, Jeremy G. Hoskins, Stefan Steinerberger, and Yuval Kluger. 2019. "Fast interpolation-based t-SNE for improved visualization of single-cell RNA-seq data." *Nature Methods* (Nature Publishing Group) 16: 243–245.

Luszcz, Mary A., Lynne C. Giles, Kaarin J. Anstey, Kathryn C. Browne-Yung, Ruth A. Walker, and Tim D. Windsor. 2016. "Cohort profile: The Australian longitudinal study of ageing (ALSA)." *International Journal of Epidemiology* (Oxford University Press) 45: 1054–1063.

Ma, Fenglong, Chuishi Meng, Houping Xiao, Qi Li, Jing Gao, Lu Su, and Aidong Zhang. 2017. "Unsupervised discovery of drug side-effects from heterogeneous data sources." *Proceedings of the 23rd ACM SIGKDD International Conference on Knowledge Discovery and Data Mining*, 967–976.

Maaten, Laurens van der, and Geoffrey Hinton. 2008. "Visualizing data using t-SNE." *Journal of Machine Learning Research* 9: 2579–2605.

Marx, Vivien. 2013. "The big challenges of big data." *Nature* (Nature Publishing Group) 498: 255–260.

Masaeli, Mahdokht, Glenn Fung, and Jennifer G. Dy. 2010. "From transformation-based dimensionality reduction to feature selection." *ICML.* https://ece.northeastern.edu/fac-ece/jdy/papers/333-masaeli-icml10.pdf

McInnes, Leland, John Healy, and James Melville. 2018. "Umap: Uniform manifold approximation and projection for dimension reduction." *arXiv preprint arXiv:1802.03426.*

Mladenić, Dunja. 2005. "Feature selection for dimensionality reduction." *International Statistical and Optimization Perspectives Workshop "Subspace, Latent Structure and Feature Selection,"* 84–102.

Murtagh, Fionn, and Pierre Legendre. 2014. "Ward's hierarchical agglomerative clustering method: Which algorithms implement Ward's criterion?" *Journal of Classification* (Springer) 31: 274–295.

Park, Joon Hyuk, Soo Lim, J. Lim, K. Kim, M. Han, In Young Yoon, J. Kim, et al. 2007. "An overview of the Korean longitudinal study on health and aging." *Psychiatry Investigation* (Young Cho Chung) 4: 84.

Pavlidis, Nicos G., David P. Hofmeyr, and Sotiris K. Tasoulis. 2016. "Minimum density hyperplanes." *The Journal of Machine Learning Research* (JMLR. org) 17: 5414–5446.

Pearson, Karl. 1901. "LIII. On lines and planes of closest fit to systems of points in space." *The London, Edinburgh, and Dublin Philosophical Magazine and Journal of Science* (Taylor & Francis) 2: 559–572.

Peasey, Anne, Martin Bobak, Ruzena Kubinova, Sofia Malyutina, Andrzej Pajak, Abdonas Tamosiunas, Hynek Pikhart, Amanda Nicholson, and Michael Marmot. 2006. "Determinants of cardiovascular disease and other non-communicable diseases in Central and Eastern Europe: Rationale and design of the HAPIEE study." *BMC Public Health* (Springer) 6: 255.

Pedersen, Thomas Lin, Sean Hughes, and Xiaojie Qiu. 2017. "densityClust: Clustering by fast search and find of density peaks." https://CRAN.R-project.org/package = densityClust.

Plageras, Andreas P., Kostas E. Psannis, Christos Stergiou, Haoxiang Wang, and Brij B. Gupta. 2018. "Efficient IoT-based sensor BIG Data collection—processing and analysis in smart buildings." *Future Generation Computer Systems* (Elsevier) 82: 349–357.

Prina, A. Matthew, Daisy Acosta, Isaac Acosta, Mariella Guerra, Yueqin Huang, A. T. Jotheeswaran, Ivonne Z. Jimenez-Velazquez, et al. 2017. "Cohort profile: The 10/66 study." *International Journal of Epidemiology* (Oxford University Press) 46: 406–406i.

Rauber, Paulo E., Alexandre X. Falcão, Alexandru C. Telea, and others. 2016. "Visualizing time-dependent data using dynamic t-SNE." https://people.irisa.fr/Guillaume.Gravier/ADM/articles2019/rauber-16.pdf

Rodriguez, Alex, and Alessandro Laio. 2014. "Clustering by fast search and find of density peaks." *Science* (American Association for the Advancement of Science) 344: 1492–1496.

Rodríguez-Artalejo, Fernando, Auxiliadora Graciani, Pilar Guallar-Castillón, Luz M. León-Muñoz, M. Clemencia Zuluaga, Esther López-García, Juan Luis Gutiérrez-Fisac, et al. 2011. "Rationale and methods of the study on nutrition and cardiovascular risk in Spain (ENRICA)." *Revista Española de Cardiología (English Edition)* (Elsevier) 64: 876–882.

Roh, Yuji, Geon Heo, and Steven Euijong Whang. 2019. "A survey on data collection for machine learning: A big data-ai integration perspective." *IEEE Transactions on Knowledge and Data Engineering* (IEEE) 33(4): 1328–1347.

Rostom, Raghd, Valentine Svensson, Sarah A. Teichmann, and Gozde Kar. 2017. "Computational approaches for interpreting scRNA-seq data." *FEBS Letters* (Wiley Online Library) 591: 2213–2225.

Rousseeuw, Peter J. 1987. "Silhouettes: A graphical aid to the interpretation and validation of cluster analysis." *Journal of Computational and Applied Mathematics* (Elsevier) 20: 53–65.

Sagiroglu, Seref, and Duygu Sinanc. 2013. "Big data: A review." *2013 International Conference on Collaboration Technologies and Systems (CTS)*, 42–47.

Sanchez-Niubo, Albert, Laia Egea-Cortés, Beatriz Olaya, Francisco Félix Caballero, Jose L. Ayuso-Mateos, Matthew Prina, Martin Bobak, et al. 2019. "Cohort profile: The ageing trajectories of health—longitudinal opportunities and synergies (ATHLOS) project." *International Journal of Epidemiology* (Oxford University Press) 48: 1052–1053i.

Shah, Jamal Hussain, Muhammad Sharif, Mudassar Raza, and Aisha Azeem. 2013. "A survey: Linear and nonlinear PCA based face recognition techniques." *The International Arab Journal of Information Technology* 10: 536–545.

Sharma, Alok, Yosvany López, and Tatsuhiko Tsunoda. 2017. "Divisive hierarchical maximum likelihood clustering." *BMC Bioinformatics* (BioMed Central) 18: 546.

Shi, Jianbo, and Jitendra Malik. 2000. "Normalized cuts and image segmentation." *IEEE Transactions on Pattern Analysis and Machine Intelligence* (IEEE) 22: 888–905.

Shirkhorshidi, Ali Seyed, Saeed Aghabozorgi, Teh Ying Wah, and Tutut Herawan. 2014. "Big data clustering: A review." *International Conference on Computational Science and Its Applications*, 707–720.

Sonnega, Amanda, Jessica D. Faul, Mary Beth Ofstedal, Kenneth M. Langa, John W. R. Phillips, and David R. Weir. 2014. "Cohort profile: The health and retirement study (HRS)." *International Journal of Epidemiology* (Oxford University Press) 43: 576–585.

Sorzano, Carlos Oscar Sánchez, Javier Vargas, and A. Pascual Montano. 2014. "A survey of dimensionality reduction techniques." *arXiv preprint arXiv:1403.2877.*

Sreedhar, Chowdam, Nagulapally Kasiviswanath, and Pakanti Chenna Reddy. 2017. "Clustering large datasets using K-means modified inter and intra clustering (KM-I2C) in Hadoop." *Journal of Big Data* (Springer) 4: 27.

Steptoe, Andrew, Elizabeth Breeze, James Banks, and James Nazroo. 2013. "Cohort profile: The English longitudinal study of ageing." *International Journal of Epidemiology* (Oxford University Press) 42: 1640–1648.

Tang, Jian, Jingzhou Liu, Ming Zhang, and Qiaozhu Mei. 2016. "Visualizing large-scale and high-dimensional data." *Proceedings of the 25th International Conference on World Wide Web*, 287–297.

Tasoulis, S., L. Cheng, N. Välimäki, N. J. Croucher, S. R. Harris, W. P. Hanage, T. Roos, and J. Corander. 2014. "Random projection based clustering for population genomics." *2014 IEEE International Conference on Big Data (Big Data)*, 675–682. doi:10.1109/BigData.2014.7004291.

Tufekci, Zeynep. 2014. "Big questions for social media big data: Representativeness, validity and other methodological pitfalls." *Proceedings of the International AAAI Conference on Web and Social Media* 8: 505–514.

Usama, Muhammad, Junaid Qadir, Aunn Raza, Hunain Arif, Kok-Lim Alvin Yau, Yehia Elkhatib, Amir Hussain, and Ala Al-Fuqaha. 2019. "Unsupervised machine learning for networking: Techniques, applications and research challenges." *IEEE Access* (IEEE) 7: 65579–65615.

Von Luxburg, Ulrike. 2007. "A tutorial on spectral clustering." *Statistics and Computing* (Springer) 17: 395–416.

Wang, C. Jason, Chun Y. Ng, and Robert H. Brook. 2020. "Response to COVID-19 in Taiwan: Big data analytics, new technology, and proactive testing." *JAMA* (American Medical Association) 323: 1341–1342.

Wang, Shiping, Jinyu Cai, Qihao Lin, and Wenzhong Guo. 2019. "An overview of unsupervised deep feature representation for text categorization." *IEEE Transactions on Computational Social Systems* (IEEE) 6: 504–517.

Wei, Hua-Liang, and Stephen A. Billings. 2006. "Feature subset selection and ranking for data dimensionality reduction." *IEEE Transactions on Pattern Analysis and Machine Intelligence* (IEEE) 29: 162–166.

Whelan, Brendan J., and George M. Savva. 2013. "Design and methodology of the Irish longitudinal study on ageing." *Journal of the American Geriatrics Society* (Wiley Online Library) 61: S265–S268.

Wong, Rebeca, Alejandra Michaels-Obregon, and Alberto Palloni. 2017. "Cohort profile: The Mexican health and aging study (MHAS)." *International Journal of Epidemiology* (Oxford University Press) 46: e2–e2.

Xia, Jiazhi, Fenjin Ye, Wei Chen, Yusi Wang, Weifeng Chen, Yuxin Ma, and Anthony K. H. Tung. 2017. "LDSScanner: Exploratory analysis of low-dimensional structures in high-dimensional datasets." *IEEE Transactions on Visualization and Computer Graphics* (IEEE) 24: 236–245.

Xiang, Lingyun, Guohan Zhao, Qian Li, Wei Hao, and Feng Li. 2018. "TUMK-ELM: A fast unsupervised heterogeneous data learning approach." *IEEE Access* (IEEE) 6: 35305–35315.

Yan, Jun, Benyu Zhang, Ning Liu, Shuicheng Yan, Qiansheng Cheng, Weiguo Fan, Qiang Yang, Wensi Xi, and Zheng Chen. 2006. "Effective and efficient dimensionality reduction for large-scale and streaming data preprocessing." *IEEE Transactions on Knowledge and Data Engineering* (IEEE) 18: 320–333.

YiLan, Luo, and Zeng RuTong. 2015. "clustertend: Check the clustering tendency." https://CRAN.R-project.org/package = clustertend.

Zhang, Wei, Deli Zhao, and Xiaogang Wang. 2013. "Agglomerative clustering via maximum incremental path integral." *Pattern Recognition* (Elsevier) 46: 3056–3065.

Zhu, Chengzhang, Longbing Cao, Qiang Liu, Jianping Yin, and Vipin Kumar. 2018. "Heterogeneous metric learning of categorical data with hierarchical couplings." *IEEE Transactions on Knowledge and Data Engineering* (IEEE) 30: 1254–1267.

Zhu, Xiaojin Jerry. 2005. *Semi-supervised learning literature survey.* University of Wisconsin-Madison Department of Computer Sciences.

Zhu, Xiaojin, and Andrew B. Goldberg. 2009. "Introduction to semi-supervised learning." *Synthesis Lectures on Artificial Intelligence and Machine Learning* (Morgan & Claypool Publishers) 3: 1–130.

Zumel, Nina, and John Mount. 2016. "vtreat: A data. Frame processor for predictive modeling." *arXiv preprint arXiv:1611.09477.*

6 Monitoring Process Location and Dispersion Using the Double Moving Average Control Chart

Vasileios Alevizakos, Kashinath Chatterjee, Christos Koukouvinos and Angeliki Lappa

CONTENTS

6.1 INTRODUCTION

Control charts constitute a very important tool of Statistical Process Control (SPC) and they are used for on-line monitoring of processes within a certain level of variation. When a process contains only common causes of variation is considered to be in-control (IC), but when it also contains assignable causes of variation, then, the process is declared as out-of-control (OOC) and one should take corrective actions

DOI: 10.1201/9781003203124-6

to identify and eliminate these causes. Shewhart (1926, 1927) first introduced the control charting technique. The control charts are classified into two types; the variable control charts and the attribute control charts. The variable control charts are used for monitoring quality characteristics of interest that can be measured on a numerical scale. The Shewhart $\overline{X}$, R, S and S^2 charts are used to monitor the mean and variability of variables (Montgomery 2013). On the other hand, attribute control charts are used for monitoring quality characteristics that cannot be measured numerically, such as the number of nonconformities in a production unit and the fraction of nonconforming. The most well-known Shewhart control charts for monitoring Poisson distributed data are the *c*- and *u*-charts. The Shewhart control charts are known to be very effective in detecting large shifts, but, unfortunately, they are insensitive for small to moderate shifts. For this reason, Page (1954) introduced the cumulative sum (CUSUM) chart and Roberts (1959, 1966) developed the exponentially weighted moving average (EWMA) and moving average (MA) charts. Unlike, the Shewhart-type charts, these charts are memory-type because they use both the past and current information.

The properties and design of control charts for monitoring the process mean have been investigated by many authors, such as Crowder (1987, 1989), Lucas and Saccucci (1990), Klein (1996), Steiner (1999), Wong et al. (2004), Woodall and Mahmoud (2005), Hsu et al. (2007) and Hawkins and Wu (2014). Moreover, several modifications of the Shewhart, CUSUM, EWMA and MA charts have been proposed in order to improve their detection ability in a specific range of shifts. Lucas (1982) developed a combined Shewhart-CUSUM chart, while Shamma and Shamma (1991, 1992) proposed a double EWMA (DEWMA) chart for monitoring shifts in the process mean by combining two EWMA charts. Zhang and Chen (2005) studied in more detail the properties of the DEWMA chart. Abbas et al. (2013a) introduced a mixed EWMA-CUSUM (MEC) chart and Abbas et al. (2013c) proposed the progressive mean (PM) chart, where, unlike the MA chart, the value of span is not fixed. Khoo and Wong (2008) developed the double MA (DMA) chart to improve the performance of the MA chart for small to moderate shifts in the process mean. Unfortunately, the computed variance of the DMA statistic was not correct. Alevizakos et al. (2020) computed the correct variance of the DMA statistic and they also studied the performance of the DMA chart for monitoring shifts in the process mean.

Except for the control charts for the process mean, several authors have investigated control charting techniques for the process dispersion. It should be noted that in most online processes, it is essential to monitor shifts in the process dispersion rather than the process mean, since an increase in the process dispersion results in a decrease in the process capability. Khoo (2005), Acosta-Mejia and Pignatiello (2008) and Zhang (2014) studied Shewhart-type charts for process dispersion. Castagliola (2005) and Castagliola et al. (2009) used a three-parameter logarithmic transformation to derive the S^2-EWMA and CUSUM-S^2 charts, respectively. Abbas et al. (2013b) developed a MEC scheme for monitoring shifts in the process dispersion, named as CS-EWMA chart. Adeoti and Olaomi (2016) and Koukouvinos and

Lappa (2019) studied the MA chart for monitoring the process dispersion (MAS). Other dispersion control charts can be found in the works of Crowder and Hamilton (1992), Maravelakis and Castagliola (2009), Castagliola et al. (2010) and Abbas et al. (2014). Recently, motivated by the works of Khoo and Wong (2008) and Adeoti and Olaomi (2016), Adeoti et al. (2019) proposed a DMA control chart for monitoring the process variability. However, the computed variance of the charting statistic and, consequently, the control limits of that chart were not correctly developed. Based on the work of Alevizakos et al. (2020), where the correct variance of the DMA statistic is given, the performance of the DMA chart for process dispersion is presented in Section 6.4.

Many control charts have also been developed based on the Poisson distribution. Lucas (1985) studied the structure of the CUSUM chart for monitoring Poisson data. Gan (1990) proposed three modified EWMA charts for monitoring Poisson processes where the charting statistics are rounded to an integer value. White et al. (1997) compared the c-chart with the PCUSUM chart and they showed that the latter chart is more effective. Borror et al. (1998) developed the EWMA chart for Poisson data (PEWMA) and they found it more sensitive than the c-chart and Gan's modified EWMA charts. Khoo (2004) presented the Poisson MA (PMA) chart. Other control charts based on the Poisson distribution can be found in the works of Mei et al. (2011), Jiang et al. (2011), Shu et al. (2012) and Paulino et al. (2016). A comparison study among the most widely used Poisson control charts is presented in Alevizakos and Koukouvinos (2020b).

In the present chapter, we study the design and the properties of three DMA control charts for monitoring the process location and dispersion parameters of a normal process, as well as the Poisson mean of attribute data. Particularly, taking into consideration the work of Alevizakos et al. (2020), we also develop the DMA charts for monitoring the process dispersion (referred as DMAS chart) and Poisson data (named as PDMA chart) by using the correct variance of the DMA statistic. We also compare the DMA schemes with other existing schemes. Furthermore, three illustrative examples based on real data are provided to implement the application of DMA charts.

The rest of this chapter is organized as follows. In Section 6.2, the definition of a DMA sequence and its properties are presented. In Section 6.3, we study the DMA chart for monitoring the process location parameter, i.e., the sample mean $\bar{X}$, of a normal process (DMA-$\bar{X}$) while in Section 6.4, we investigate the DMA chart for monitoring the sample standard deviation (DMAS). In Section 6.5, the use of the DMA for monitoring the Poisson process mean is presented. Three illustrative examples are provided to show the implementation of the DMA charts in Section 6.6. Finally, some concluding remarks are made in Section 6.7.

6.2 PROPERTIES OF THE DMA SEQUENCES

Let X_i, $i = 1, 2, \ldots$ be a sequence of independently and identically distributed (i.i.d.) random variables following any continuous or discrete distribution and let $w \in \mathbb{N}^*$

be a constant. From the sequence of random variables X_i, we define the sequence of moving averages MA_i using the formula

$$MA_i = \begin{cases} \dfrac{\sum_{j=1}^{i} X_j}{i} & ,i < w, \\ \dfrac{\sum_{j=i-w+1}^{i} X_j}{w} & ,i \geq w, \end{cases} \tag{6.1}$$

while the sequence of double moving averages DMA_i is defined as

$$DMA_i = \begin{cases} \dfrac{\sum_{j=1}^{i} MA_j}{i} & ,i < w, \\ \dfrac{\sum_{j=i-w+1}^{i} MA_j}{w} & ,i \geq w. \end{cases} \tag{6.2}$$

The difference between the MA_i and DMA_i is that the latter one is based on more random variables X_i than the MA_i. More specifically, the MA_i is a linear combination of i random variables for $i < w$ and w random variables for $i \geq w$ where, in both cases, the weights of them are equally. On the other hand, the DMA_i is a linear combination of i non-equally weighted random variables for $i < 2w - 1$ and $2w - 1$ random variables for $i \geq 2w - 1$ where the $(1/w)100\%$ of the weight is placed on the middle random variable and the remaining weight is placed on the other $2w - 2$ random variables. For example, suppose $w = 3$. Then $MA_1 = X_1$, $MA_2 = \frac{1}{2}X_1 + \frac{1}{2}X_2$ and $MA_i = \frac{1}{w}X_{i-2} + \frac{1}{w}X_{i-1} + \frac{1}{w}X_i$ for $i \geq 3$. On the other side, $DMA_1 = X_1$, $DMA_2 = \frac{3}{4}X_1 + \frac{1}{4}X_2$, $DMA_3 = \frac{11}{18}X_1 + \frac{5}{18}X_2 + \frac{1}{9}X_3$, $DMA_4 = \frac{5}{18}X_1 + \frac{7}{18}X_2 + \frac{2}{9}X_3 + \frac{1}{9}X_4$ and $DMA_i = \frac{1}{9}X_{i-4} + \frac{2}{9}X_{i-3} + \frac{1}{3}X_{i-2} + \frac{2}{9}X_{i-1} + \frac{1}{9}X_i$ for $i \geq 5$.

Assume that $E(X_i) = \mu$ and $Var(X_i) = \sigma^2$ are the expected value and variance of the random variables $X_1, X_2, \ldots$ Using Eq. 6.1, it is easy to compute that $E(MA_i) = \mu$ and the variance of MA_i is given by

$$Var(MA_i) = \begin{cases} \dfrac{\sigma^2}{i} & ,\text{for } i < w, \\ \dfrac{\sigma^2}{w} & ,\text{for } i \geq w, \end{cases} \tag{6.3}$$

On the other hand, using Eq. 6.2, it can be shown that $E(DMA_i) = \mu$ while the variance of DMA_i is given by

$$Var(DMA_i)=\begin{cases}\dfrac{\sigma^2}{i^2}\left[\sum_{j=1}^{t}\dfrac{1}{j}+2\sum_{j_1=1}^{i-1}\sum_{j_2=j_1+1}^{t}\dfrac{1}{j_2}\right] &, i<w, \quad (6.4)\\ \left(\dfrac{\sigma^2}{w^2}\right)\left[\sum_{j_1=i-w+1}^{w-1}\dfrac{1}{j_1}+\sum_{i-w+1\le j_{11}<j_{12}\le w-1}\dfrac{2}{j_{12}}+\sum_{j_1=i-w+1}^{w-1}\sum_{j_2=w}^{i}\dfrac{2(j_1-j_2+w)}{j_{1w}}\right.\\ \left.+\dfrac{i-w+1}{w}+\sum_{w\le j_{21}<j_{22}\le i}\dfrac{2(j_{21}-j_{22}+w)}{w^2}\right] &, w\le i<2w-1, \quad (6.5)\\ \dfrac{\sigma^2}{w^2}\left[1+\sum_{i-w+1\le j_1<j_2\le i}\dfrac{2(j_1-j_2+w)}{w^2}\right] &, i\ge 2w-1, \quad (6.6)\end{cases}$$

The proofs for the expected value and variance of the DMA_i can be seen analytically in Alevizakos et al. (2020). As Eq. 6.4 to 6.6 are complex, we provide the $Var(DMA_i)$ values in units of σ^2, for different values of i and w in Table 6.1.

It should be noted that when $w = 1$, the sequences $MA_1, MA_2, \ldots$ and $DMA_1, DMA_2, \ldots$ are a copy of the initial sequences $X_1, X_2, \ldots$

TABLE 6.1

The Variance of DMA_i (in units of variance) for Different Values of i and w

w = 2		w = 3		w = 4		w = 5		w = 8		w = 10	
i	**Var**	**i**	**Var**	**i**	**Var**	**i**	**Var**	**i**	**Var**	**i**	**Var**
1	1.0000	1	1.0000	1	1.0000	1	1.0000	1	1.0000	1	1.0000
2	0.6250	2	0.6250	2	0.6250	2	0.6250	2	0.6250	2	0.6250
≥ 3	0.3749	3	0.4630	3	0.4630	3	0.4630	3	0.4630	3	0.4630
		4	0.2901	4	0.3698	4	0.3698	4	0.3698	4	0.3698
		≥ 5	0.2346	5	0.2474	5	0.3087	5	0.3087	5	0.3087
				6	0.1927	6	0.2175	6	0.2653	6	0.2653
				≥ 7	0.1719	7	0.1705	7	0.2328	7	0.2328
						8	0.1460	8	0.2075	8	0.2075
						≥ 9	0.1360	9	0.1608	9	0.1873
								10	0.1323	10	0.1707
								11	0.1130	11	0.1373
								12	0.0999	12	0.1158
								13	0.0913	13	0.1004
								14	0.0862	14	0.0890
								≥ 15	0.0840	15	0.0806
										16	0.0746
										17	0.0706
										18	0.0681
										≥ 19	0.0670

6.3 DMA CONTROL CHART FOR PROCESS LOCATION

6.3.1 The Structure of DMA-$\overline{X}$ Control Chart

Let X_{ij}, with $i = 1, 2, \ldots, m$ and $j = 1, 2, \ldots, n$ be the jth observation in the i-th sample of size $n \geq 1$ and assume that $X_{ij} \overset{iid}{\sim} N\left(\mu_0, \sigma_0^2\right)$, where μ_0 and σ_0, are the IC values of the process mean and standard deviation, respectively. The sample mean $\overline{X}_i$ of the i-th sample is

$$\overline{X}_i = \frac{1}{n}\sum_{j=1}^{n} X_{ij}. \tag{6.7}$$

Assuming that the process variance is IC and remains unchanged, the DMA-$\overline{X}$ control chart is constructed by plotting the statistics DMA_i, given by Eq. 6.2, versus the sample number i. Note that the random variable X_j is substituted with the sample mean $\overline{X}_j$ in Eq. 6.1 and σ^2 with σ_0^2/n in Eq. 6.3 to 6.6. Thus, the upper and lower control limits (*UCL* and *LCL*, respectively) and the centerline (*CL*) of the DMA-$\overline{X}$ chart are defined as

$$UCL_i/LCL_i = \mu_0 \pm L\sqrt{Var\left(DMA_i\right)}, CL = \mu_0, \tag{6.8}$$

where $L > 0$ is the control chart multiplier. For $w = 2$, the control limits are computed based on variance Eq. 6.4 and 6.6. The process is considered to be IC if $LCL_i < DMA_i < UCL_i$; otherwise, if $DMA_i \leq LCL_i$ or $DMA_i \geq UCL_i$, the process is declared as OOC and a shift in the process mean has occurred. The DMA-$\overline{X}$ chart reduces to the Shewhart-$\overline{X}$ chart for $w = 1$. On the other side, when the value of w is not fixed, then the statistics MA_i and DMA_i are cumulative averages over the i. In this case, we have the progressive mean (PM) and double progressive mean (DPM) statistics instead of the MA and the DMA statistics, respectively. The corresponding PM and DPM control charts for monitoring shifts in the process mean have been studied by Abbas et al. (2013c), Abbas et al. (2019) and Riaz et al. (2021), respectively.

6.3.2 Performance Analysis and Comparison Study

The performance of a control chart is usually measured in terms of the average run-length (ARL) which is defined as the expected number of charting statistics that must be plotted on a control chart until an OOC signal is detected (Montgomery 2013). In an IC state, the ARL (regarded as ARL_0) should be large to avoid any false alarms. On the other hand, in an OOC state, the ARL (regarded as ARL_1) should be small to detect the shift very quickly. Moreover, other characteristics of the run-length distribution, such as the standard deviation (SDRL) and percentile points, are used in order to obtain more information about the run-length distribution. In this study, we use only the ARL measure, as the IC SDRL ($SDRL_0$) values of the DMA-$\overline{X}$ charts are approximately equal to the corresponding ARL_0 values.

The ARL values of the DMA-$\overline{X}$ chart are calculated performing Monte Carlo simulations in R software with 10,000 repetitions. Without loss of generality, we consider $\mu_0 = 0$, $\sigma_0 = 1$ and $n = 1$ (individual measurements) and 5 (subgrouped data) while the pre-specified value of ARL_0 is set equal to 370. The shift δ in the IC process mean is in terms of the process standard deviation, i.e., $\delta = \sqrt{n}\frac{\mu_1 - \mu_0}{\sigma_0}$, where μ_1 is the OOC value of μ. The considered shifts are δ= 0.20, 0.40, 0.60, 0.80, 1.00, 1.25, 1.50, 2.00, 3.00.

Table 6.2 presents the ARL of the DMA-$\overline{X}$ chart for w = 2, 3, 4 and 5. Moreover, the ARL values of the Shewhart-$\overline{X}$, MA-$\overline{X}$, EWMA-$\overline{X}$ and CUSUM-$\overline{X}$ charts are also provided for comparison reasons. We note that the CUSUM-$\overline{X}$ charts have optimally been designed to detect shifts of δ= 0.20, 0.80 and 1.50. From Table 6.2, we observe that the performance of the DMA-$\overline{X}$ chart improves as the value of w increases. On other words, the DMA-$\overline{X}$ chart with $w = 5$ is more effective than other DMA-$\overline{X}$ charts with a smaller value of w. Moreover, the performance of the DMA-$\overline{X}$ chart improves as the value of n increases. The same applies for the MA-$\overline{X}$ chart. However, the range of shifts where the DMA-$\overline{X}$ chart outperforms the MA-$\overline{X}$ chart decreases as the value of w or n increases. For example, in the case of $n = 1$ ($n = 5$) and $w = 2$, the DMA-$\overline{X}$ chart is more effective than the MA-$\overline{X}$ chart for $\delta \leq 2.00$ ($\delta \leq 0.80$) while the for rest range of shifts, the two charts are comparable. On the other side, when $w = 5$, the DMA-$\overline{X}$ chart is more sensitive than the MA-$\overline{X}$ chart for $\delta \leq 1.00$ ($\delta \leq 0.40$) while for the rest range of shifts, the MA-$\overline{X}$ chart performs a slightly better. Finally, it should be noted that both the DMA-$\overline{X}$ and MA-$\overline{X}$ charts have better detection ability than the Shewhart-$\overline{X}$ chart, especially for small to moderate shifts.

A performance comparison study between the DMA-$\overline{X}$ and EWMA-$\overline{X}$ charts indicates that in the case of $n = 1$, the EWMA-$\overline{X}$ chart with $\lambda = 0.05$ is more effective for $\delta \leq 0.80$ while the DMA-$\overline{X}$ chart with $w = 5$ performs similarly with the best-performing EWMA-$\overline{X}$ chart for the rest range of shifts. In the case of $n = 5$, the EWMA-$\overline{X}$ chart with $\lambda = 0.05$ is more sensitive than the DMA-$\overline{X}$ charts for $\delta \leq 0.40$ while for the rest range of shifts, the DMA-$\overline{X}$ chart performs a slightly better for moderate shifts and similarly for large shifts.

Comparing the DMA-$\overline{X}$ chart with the CUSUM-$\overline{X}$ chart, it can be noted that when $n = 1$, the CUSUM-$\overline{X}$ chart optimally designed to detect a shift of δ= 0.20 outperforms the DMA-$\overline{X}$ chart for $\delta \leq 0.60$ while for the rest range of shifts, the DMA-$\overline{X}$ chart is more sensitive. The superiority of the DMA-$\overline{X}$ chart against the CUSUM-$\overline{X}$ chart increases as the shift δ, where the CUSUM-$\overline{X}$ chart is optimally designed to detect, increases. For example, the DMA-$\overline{X}$ chart with $w = 5$ has better detection ability than the CUSUM-$\overline{X}$ chart optimally designed to detect a shift of δ= 1.50 over the entire range of shifts. Similar results are observed for $n = 5$.

Consequently, we observe that the sample size n affects the performance of the competing charts. More specifically, the superiority of the DMA-$\overline{X}$ chart against the MA-$\overline{X}$ chart for small to moderate shifts increases as the value of n decreases, while the DMA-$\overline{X}$ chart is more effective than the EWMA-$\overline{X}$ and CUSUM-$\overline{X}$ charts in a wider range of moderate to large shifts for large values of n.

TABLE 6.2
ARL Values of Shewhart- $\overline{X}$, DMA- $\overline{X}$, MA- $\overline{X}$, EWMA- $\overline{X}$ and CUSUM- $\overline{X}$ Control Charts

		Shewhart- $\overline{X}$	DMA- $\overline{X}$				MA- $\overline{X}$				EWMA- $\overline{X}$			CUSUM- $\overline{X}$		
		w = 1	2	3	4	5	2	3	4	5	λ = 0.05	0.25	0.50	δ = 0.2	0.8	1.5
n	δ	L = 3.000	2.951	2.864	2.780	2.709	2.981	2.950	2.917	2.880	2.492	2.898	2.978	h = 13.4749	5.7033	3.3412
1	0.00	369.2	371.5	370.3	369.6	369.7	369.2	369.8	370.5	370.2	370.4	370.2	370.2	370.5	370.0	370.6
	0.20	306.1	250.2	218.0	198.9	186.0	267.0	244.7	222.4	205.0	99.1	176.5	237.5	98.3	145.2	202.8
	0.40	197.0	119.4	90.5	75.3	65.5	141.2	109.4	92.0	79.3	36.6	63.1	105.7	43.1	47.2	78.4
	0.60	118.6	57.7	40.8	33.6	29.6	70.3	51.1	42.3	35.3	20.8	28.2	48.6	27.4	22.6	33.6
	0.80	70.5	29.7	21.6	18.1	15.9	37.7	26.4	21.5	18.7	14.2	15.8	26.0	19.8	14.1	17.5
	1.00	44.0	17.4	12.9	10.9	10.2	21.7	15.4	12.6	10.9	10.8	10.3	15.1	15.7	10.2	10.9
	1.25	24.6	9.7	7.7	7.1	7.0	12.2	8.8	7.3	6.7	8.2	6.9	9.1	12.5	7.5	7.1
	1.50	14.8	6.3	5.4	5.1	5.2	7.4	5.7	4.9	4.6	6.7	5.2	6.0	10.3	5.9	5.2
	2.00	6.3	3.4	3.3	3.3	3.3	3.5	3.1	2.8	2.8	5.0	3.5	3.4	7.7	4.2	3.4
	3.00	2.0	1.7	1.7	1.6	1.6	1.6	1.6	1.6	1.5	3.3	2.2	1.9	5.2	2.8	2.1
5	0.00	370.5	370.7	370.3	370.9	369.1	370.5	370.0	370.4	370.8	370.3	370.5	370.2	370.6	370.4	370.1
	0.20	177.7	100.8	75.4	60.9	53.5	119.3	91.3	76.8	64.4	31.0	50.8	89.0	37.8	38.4	63.9
	0.40	55.5	22.9	16.5	14.0	12.8	29.1	20.6	16.5	14.3	12.3	12.8	19.7	17.6	11.8	13.5
	0.60	20.4	8.4	6.7	6.2	6.1	10.0	7.3	6.3	5.8	7.6	6.1	7.7	11.5	6.9	6.2
	0.80	8.8	4.2	3.9	3.9	3.9	4.6	3.8	3.5	3.3	5.6	4.0	4.2	8.6	4.8	4.0
	1.00	4.5	2.8	2.7	2.7	2.7	2.8	2.5	2.4	2.3	4.5	3.0	2.8	6.9	3.8	2.9
	1.25	2.4	1.9	1.9	1.8	1.8	1.8	1.7	1.7	1.7	3.6	2.4	2.0	5.6	3.0	2.3
	1.50	1.5	1.4	1.4	1.4	1.3	1.4	1.4	1.4	1.3	3.0	2.0	1.6	4.7	2.5	1.9
	2.00	1.1	1.1	1.1	1.0	1.0	1.1	1.1	1.1	1.1	2.3	1.5	1.2	3.6	2.0	1.4
	3.00	1.0	1.0	1.0	1.0	1.0	1.0	1.0	1.0	1.0	1.9	1.0	1.0	2.6	1.3	1.0

6.4 DMA CONTROL CHART FOR PROCESS DISPERSION

6.4.1 The Structure of DMAS Control Chart

In the current section, we describe the construction of the DMA chart for monitoring process dispersion, referred as DMAS control chart. Let X_{ij} be a random sample of size n taken over m subgroups, where $i = 1, \ldots, m$ and $j = 1, \ldots, n$. The samples are assumed to be independent with size n and taken from a process following a $N(\mu_0, \rho\sigma_0)$ distribution. The process is considered to be IC if $\rho = 1.00$; otherwise, if $\rho \neq 1.00$, the process is said to be OOC. We are interested in monitoring a shift in the process dispersion, from an IC value σ_0^2 to an OOC value $\sigma_1^2 = (\rho\sigma_0)^2$, where $\rho \neq 1.00$, by maintaining the process mean μ_0 unchanged. Moreover, let

$$S_i = \sqrt{\frac{1}{n-1}\sum_{j=1}^{n}\left(X_{ij} - \overline{X}_i\right)^2}, \quad i = 1, \ldots, m \tag{6.9}$$

be the sample standard deviation, where $\overline{X}_i$ is given by Eq. 6.7. The mean and the variance of the S_i are $E(S_i) = c_4\sigma$ and $Var(S_i) = \sigma^2(1 - c_4^2)$, respectively, where

$c_4 = \sqrt{\frac{2}{n-2}}\frac{\Gamma\left(\frac{n}{2}\right)}{\Gamma\left(\frac{n-1}{2}\right)}$ is a constant that depends only on the sample size n.

The MAi statistic using the Si is defined as follows

$$MA_i = \begin{cases} \dfrac{\sum_{j=1}^{i} S_j}{i}, & i < w, \\ \dfrac{\sum_{j=i-w+1}^{i} S_j}{w}, & i \geq w, \end{cases} \tag{6.10}$$

while the DMA_i statistic is defined using Eq. 6.2. It is easy to see that, the mean and the variance of the MA_i statistic are given, respectively, by $E(MA_i) = c_4\sigma$, and

$Var(MA_i) = \begin{cases} \dfrac{\sigma^2(1-c_4^2)}{i}, & i < w, \\ \dfrac{\sigma^2(1-c_4^2)}{w}, & i \geq w, \end{cases}$. Furthermore, the mean and the variance

of the DMA_i statistic are defined, respectively, as

$$E(DMA_i) = c_4\sigma, \tag{6.11}$$

and

$$Var(DMA_i)=\begin{cases}\dfrac{\sigma^2\left(1-c_4^2\right)}{i^2}\left[\sum_{j=1}^{i}\dfrac{1}{j}+2\sum_{1\le j_1<j_2\le i}\dfrac{1}{j_2}\right], i<w, & (6.12)\\ \dfrac{\sigma^2\left(1-c_4^2\right)}{w^2}\left[\sum_{j_1=i-w+1}^{w-1}\dfrac{1}{j_1}+\sum_{i-w+1\le j_{11}<j_{12}\le w-1}\dfrac{2}{j_{12}}+\sum_{j_1=i-w+1}^{w-1}\sum_{j_2=w}^{i}\dfrac{2\left(j_1-j_2+w\right)}{j_{1w}}\right.\\ \left.+\dfrac{i-w+1}{w}+\sum_{w\le j_{21}<j_{22}\le i}\dfrac{2\left(j_{21}-j_{22}+w\right)}{w^2}\right], w\le i<2w-1, & (6.13)\\ \dfrac{\sigma^2\left(1-c_4^2\right)}{w^2}\left[1+\sum_{i-w+1\le j_1<j_2\le i}\dfrac{2\left(j_1-j_2+w\right)}{w^2}\right], i\ge 2w-1. & (6.14)\end{cases}$$

Therefore, the control limits of the DMAS chart are given by

$$UCL_i \,/\, LCL_i = E(DMA_i)\pm L\sqrt{Var(DMA_i)}, CL = c_4\sigma, \tag{6.15}$$

where $L > 0$ is the control chart multiplier. It is to be noted, that if $LCL_i < 0$, then we replace the LCL by zero. The DMAS chart raises an OOC signal when $DMA_i \le LCL_i$ or $DMA_i \ge UCL_i$; otherwise the process is considered to be IC.

6.4.2 Performance Analysis and Comparison Study

Similarly, we only apply the ARL performance measure, to evaluate the efficiency of the DMAS. It is to be noted that, when the process variability is IC, a large value of ARL_0 is preferred. Nevertheless, when the process is OOC, i.e., the variability shifts from σ_0 to $\sigma_1 = \rho\sigma_0$ (where $\rho \ne 1.00$), a small ARL_1 is desired.

A Monte Carlo simulation algorithm with 10,000 repetitions is developed in R software to calculate the ARL values of the DMAS chart. In order to study the performance of the DMAS chart, we consider that the underlying process for the IC condition follows the normal distribution with $\mu_0 = 0$ and $\sigma_0 = 1$, while the OOC process is normally distributed with $\mu_1 = 0$ and $\sigma_1 = \rho\sigma_0$, where $\rho \ne 1.00$. The considered shifts in the process dispersion are ρ = 0.50, 0.60, 0.70, 0.80, 0.90, 1.00, 1.10, 1.20, 1.30, 1.40, 1.50, 2.00, 2.50 and 3.00. Here, $\rho > 1.00$ represents upward shifts, $\rho < 1.00$ corresponds to downward shifts, while $\rho = 1.00$ is the IC state. The pre-specified value of ARL_0 is set equal to 200 and in order to study the effect of the sample size on the performance of the DMAS chart, we choose n = 5, 7 and 9. Table 6.3 presents the ARL values of the DMAS chart with span w = 2, 3, 4 and 5.

From Table 6.3, we observe that, for fixed values of ρ and n, the ARL_1 decreases with an increase in the value of the span w. It should be noted that the DMAS chart with a small value of w is ARL-biased for small downward shifts, i.e., the ARL_1 values are larger than the ARL_0. Moreover, for a fixed value of n, the L value decreases as w increases; downward shifts of smaller magnitude are detected more quickly as w increases; and the DMAS chart has better detection ability for small upward

TABLE 6.3
ARL Values of the DMAS Chart

	$n = 5$				$n = 7$				$n = 9$			
	$w = 2$	3	4	5	2	3	4	5	2	3	4	5
ρ	**$L = 2.754$**	**2.643**	**2.553**	**2.472**	**2.742**	**2.642**	**2.552**	**2.474**	**2.739**	**2.643**	**2.554**	**2.472**
0.50	11.6	5.5	5.1	5.1	4.3	3.6	3.6	3.5	2.9	2.8	2.8	2.6
0.60	32.3	10.8	8.0	7.3	9.6	5.7	5.2	5.2	5.3	4.1	4.1	4.1
0.70	95.8	27.5	17.3	13.7	27.4	12.5	9.4	8.5	14.2	8.0	6.8	6.5
0.80	285.9	85.8	50.6	37.3	93.1	38.9	26.1	20.7	49.3	24.4	17.6	14.7
0.90	553.1	260.7	175.0	133.2	297.3	153.9	108.4	86.0	195.9	108.5	78.3	62.8
1.00	200.3	200.8	200.8	201.00	200.3	200.6	200.6	200.2	200.2	200.2	200.2	200.2
1.10	56.6	55.1	54.9	54.1	48.6	46.3	45.1	43.6	42.7	39.9	38.2	36.2
1.20	22.4	21.2	20.7	20.4	17.3	16.0	15.4	14.9	14.0	12.9	12.4	12.0
1.30	11.9	11.2	11.1	11.0	8.7	8.3	8.1	8.1	6.9	6.6	6.5	6.5
1.40	7.4	7.2	7.2	7.3	5.4	5.3	5.4	5.5	4.3	4.3	4.3	4.4
1.50	5.3	5.2	5.4	5.4	3.9	3.9	4.0	4.1	3.1	3.2	3.3	3.3
2.00	2.2	2.2	2.3	2.3	1.7	1.7	1.7	1.7	1.4	1.4	1.4	1.4
2.50	1.5	1.5	1.5	1.5	1.2	1.2	1.2	1.2	1.1	1.1	1.1	1.1
3.00	1.3	1.3	1.3	1.2	1.1	1.1	1.1	1.1	1.0	1.0	1.0	1.0

shifts rather than small downward shifts. Furthermore, larger values of w are recommended for identifying shifts of size $\rho < 1.50$, whereas smaller values of w are preferred for larger shifts ($1.50 \le \rho \le 2.00$). In case of $\rho \ge 2.00$, similar performance is noticed for all w values. Finally, for fixed values of w and ρ, the ARL_1 decreases as the sample number n is getting higher, i.e., the sensitivity of the DMAS chart increases as the sample size n becomes larger.

Furthermore, we compare the performance of the DMAS chart with the S, MAS, S^2-EWMA, CUSUM-S^2 and CS-EWMA charts in terms of the ARL measure. The ARL_0 value of the competing control charts is set at 200 and the sample size n is equal to 5. Tables 6.4 and 6.5 present the performance of the S, MAS ($w = 2, 3, 4, 5$), S^2-EWMA ($\lambda = 0.05, 0.10, 0.25, 0.50, 0.75$), CUSUM-$S^2$ ($K = 0.10, 0.25, 0.50, 0.75, 1.00$) and CS-EWMA ($\lambda = 0.05, 0.10, 0.25, 0.50$, $K_q = 0.10, 0.25, 0.50, 0.75, 1.00$) charts, where w, λ, K and K_q are the design parameters of the competing control charts.

It should be mentioned that, for the S chart, only the upward shifts are taken into consideration, since $LCL = 0$ for $n = 5$. From Tables 6.3 and 6.4, we observe that the DMAS chart is more sensitive than the S chart in detecting small and moderate shifts, while for shifts of size $\rho > 2.00$, both charts perform similarly.

The comparison of the DMAS chart with the MAS chart indicates that the first chart outperforms the latter in detecting downward shifts. Moreover, the DMAS chart has better detection ability than the MAS chart for small to moderate upward shifts ($\rho < 1.50$), while for shifts of size $1.50 \le \rho \le 2.00$, the MAS chart seems to perform better. For larger upward shifts ($\rho > 2.00$), it is observed similar performance for both charts.

In addition, comparing the DMAS chart with the S^2-EWMA chart, reveals that the latter chart with $\lambda < 0.50$ gives smaller ARL_1 values for both downward and upward shifts in the process dispersion. However, it is to be noted that, for $\lambda \ge 0.50$ and $w \ge 4$, the DMAS chart has better detection ability for $\rho \le 1.30$. For moderate upward shifts, both charts display similar performance, whereas for larger upward shifts, the DMAS chart seems to be more efficient.

Generally, the CUSUM-S^2 chart is more sensitive in detecting downward shifts. However, as $K \ge 0.75$ and the span w increases, the DMAS chart gives better ARL performance. Additionally, for small upward shifts, where $\rho \le 1.20$, the CUSUM-S^2 performs better than the DMAS chart. Nevertheless, for $\rho > 1.20$, a DMAS chart with $w \ge 3$ is more sensitive in detecting moderate and large shifts in the process dispersion. Tables 6.3 and 6.5 indicate that for small downward shifts, the CS-EWMA has smaller ARL_1 values, whereas for larger downward shifts, such as $\rho < 0.70$, the DMAS chart seems to perform better. In addition, both charts have similar performance for $\rho = 1.10$, when $w = 2 - 5$ and $K_q = 0.10$. It is to be mentioned that the DMAS chart is more sensitive in identifying shifts of size $\rho \ge 1.20$, compared with the CS-EWMA chart.

TABLE 6.4
ARL Values of the S, MAS, S^2-EWMA and CUSUM-S^2 Control Charts

	S	MAS				S^2-EWMA					CUSUM-S^2				
		w = 2	3	4	5	λ = 0.05	0.10	0.25	0.50	0.75	K = 0.10	0.25	0.50	0.75	1.00
ρ	L = 2.895	2.792	2.738	2.696	2.659	2.269	2.452	2.621	2.639	2.632	H = 10.530	6.476	3.855	2.620	1.906
0.50	-	33.7	8.1	5.3	4.6	9.3	6.9	5.5	7.7	360.0	9.1	6.5	5.2	5.1	6.1
0.60	-	100.3	20.7	11.3	8.4	11.7	8.9	8.0	16.8	1987.4	11.4	8.5	7.3	8.3	13.3
0.70	-	271.0	59.6	30.1	20.4	16.2	13.0	14.5	48.9	6262.7	15.6	12.2	12.4	18.4	43.0
0.80	-	675.2	171.2	91.4	61.6	26.2	23.8	37.0	167.5	6999.7	24.4	21.7	29.8	60.5	170.7
0.90	-	749.5	398.0	260.8	198.1	63.8	70.5	135.4	471.8	1267.2	54.9	64.1	116.5	227.7	476.7
1.00	200.7	199.2	200.0	200.0	200.0	201.5	200.1	200.1	201.5	199.3	201.8	198.4	201.2	203.3	201.4
1.10	65.2	58.1	55.5	54.5	53.8	32.5	42.1	48.9	51.7	56.4	52.7	51.0	53.5	54.1	54.6
1.20	28.7	23.3	21.6	20.6	20.1	11.8	15.3	18.0	19.9	23.0	24.9	20.8	20.1	20.6	21.5
1.30	15.0	12.2	11.2	10.7	10.3	7.0	8.7	9.7	10.6	12.0	16.4	12.6	11.2	11.0	11.3
1.40	9.2	7.5	7.0	6.7	6.5	5.0	6.0	6.4	6.7	7.5	12.3	9.2	7.6	7.1	7.1
1.50	6.3	5.3	5.0	4.8	4.7	4.0	4.7	4.8	4.8	5.2	10.0	7.3	5.8	5.3	5.1
2.00	2.2	2.1	2.0	2.0	2.0	2.1	2.4	2.3	2.5	2.1	5.5	3.9	2.9	2.4	2.2
2.50	1.5	1.4	1.4	1.4	1.4	1.6	1.8	1.6	1.5	1.5	4.1	2.8	2.1	1.7	1.6
3.00	1.3	1.2	1.2	1.2	1.2	1.3	1.5	1.4	1.3	1.2	3.3	2.4	1.7	1.4	1.3

TABLE 6.5
ARL Values of the CS-EWMA Chart

	λ = 0.05					**0.10**				
	Kq = 0.10	**0.25**	**0.50**	**0.75**	**1.00**	**0.10**	**0.25**	**0.50**	**0.75**	**1.00**
δ	**Hq = 62.60**	**47.06**	**29.50**	**18.15**	**10.62**	**48.10**	**35.50**	**22.27**	**14.10**	**8.81**
0.50	23.2	20.6	17.5	15.1	13.3	17.7	15.4	12.8	11.0	9.7
0.60	26.7	23.8	20.3	17.8	15.8	20.6	17.9	15.0	13.0	11.6
0.70	32.3	29.0	25.0	22.2	20.0	25.3	22.2	18.7	16.5	15.1
0.80	43.1	39.1	34.3	31.1	28.9	34.8	30.7	26.7	24.4	23.2
0.90	73.8	68.8	63.9	61.8	61.2	63.8	58.9	55.7	55.8	57.7
1.00	201.0	200.2	201.8	201.7	200.3	199.7	200.8	201.2	199.4	200.6
1.10	52.6	46.9	41.1	37.8	36.0	55.6	50.1	46.0	44.3	44.1
1.20	31.7	27.3	22.1	18.6	16.2	30.5	26.3	22.0	19.6	18.1
1.30	24.7	21.2	16.9	13.8	11.5	22.5	19.1	15.5	13.3	11.8
1.40	21.1	18.0	14.3	11.5	9.4	18.6	15.7	12.6	10.6	9.2
1.50	18.7	16.1	12.7	10.2	8.2	16.2	13.7	10.9	9.1	7.7
2.00	13.5	11.6	9.1	7.2	5.7	11.1	9.4	7.4	6.0	5.0
2.50	11.4	9.7	7.7	6.1	4.8	9.1	7.8	6.1	5.0	4.1
3.00	10.2	8.7	6.9	5.4	4.3	8.1	6.9	5.4	4.4	3.6

	λ = 0.25					**0.50**				
	Kq = 0.10	**0.25**	**0.50**	**0.75**	**1.00**	**0.10**	**0.25**	**0.50**	**0.75**	**1.00**
δ	**Hq = 31.31**	**21.88**	**13.50**	**8.85**	**5.80**	**20.10**	**13.25**	**7.99**	**5.27**	**3.57**
0.50	13.1	10.7	8.6	7.4	6.6	10.8	8.3	6.4	5.6	5.2
0.60	15.6	12.8	10.3	9.0	8.2	13.3	10.2	8.1	7.3	7.1
0.70	20.1	16.5	13.6	12.3	11.7	17.6	13.9	11.6	11.3	12.2
0.80	29.3	24.8	21.7	21.2	21.9	26.7	22.2	21.1	24.0	30.6
0.90	58.7	54.2	55.7	62.8	71.8	56.3	54.3	65.8	86.5	113.9
1.00	200.2	200.9	200.3	200.1	200.7	200.5	201.6	197.5	200.1	198.8
1.10	56.8	51.3	49.5	50.6	51.7	55.4	50.7	51.5	53.5	54.6
1.20	29.2	24.4	21.0	19.8	19.4	27.5	22.6	20.3	20.0	20.1
1.30	20.2	16.5	13.5	12.1	11.3	18.5	14.6	12.1	11.3	11.0
1.40	15.9	12.9	10.3	9.0	8.1	14.2	11.0	8.8	7.9	7.4
1.50	13.4	10.8	8.6	7.3	6.5	11.7	9.0	7.0	6.1	5.6
2.00	8.4	6.8	5.3	4.4	3.8	6.9	5.2	4.0	3.3	2.9
2.50	6.8	5.5	4.3	3.5	3.0	5.3	4.0	3.1	2.5	2.2
3.00	5.9	4.8	3.7	3.1	2.5	4.5	3.5	2.6	2.2	1.9

6.5 DMA CONTROL CHART FOR POISSON DATA

6.5.1 The Structure of PDMA Control Chart

The Poisson distribution is a discrete probability distribution used to monitor attribute data, such as the number of nonconformities in a production unit, the number of events occurred in a fixed time, etc. Let X_i, $i = 1, 2, \ldots$ be independent random variables from a Poisson distribution with parameter μ. The process is considered to be IC if $\mu = \mu_0$; otherwise, the process is declared as OOC and then, $\mu = \mu_1 \neq \mu_0$. The probability density function (pdf) of X is given by

$$f(x;\mu) = \frac{e^{-\mu}\mu^{x}}{x!}, x = 0,1,2,\ldots, \tag{6.16}$$

where $\mu > 0$ is the Poisson parameter. The mean and the variance of X are $E(X) = Var(X) = \mu$. The MA_i and DMA_i statistics for Poisson data (regarded as PMA_i and $PDMA_i$, respectively) are defined using Eq. 6.1 and 6.2, while their variance are computed by Eq. 6.3 and 6.4–6.6 where σ^2 is substituted with μ_0. Thus, the control limits of the PDMA chart are defined as

$$UCL_i \,/\, LCL_i = \mu_0 \pm L\sqrt{Var(PDMA_i)}, CL = \mu_0, \tag{6.17}$$

We notice that if the computed value of LCL is negative, then we set it equal to zero. The PDMA chart raises an OOC signal when $DMA_i \leq LCL_i$ or $DMA_i \geq UCL_i$. The PDMA chart reduces to the c-chart for $w = 1$ while another special case is studied next.

6.5.2 Performance Analysis and Comparison Study

In order to study the performance of the proposed chart, without loss of generality, we consider $\mu_0 = 4$, 6, 8, 10, 12 and 16 while the pre-specified value of ARL_0 is chosen equal to 200. We note that this value cannot be achieved with accuracy because the Poisson distribution is discrete. Thus, the computed ARL_0 values range from 182.9–230.6. When the process is IC, then $\mu = \mu_0$, but when a shift has occurred, then $\mu_1 = \mu_0 + \delta\sqrt{\mu_0}$ with $\delta \neq 0.00$. Table 6.6 presents the performance of the PDMA chart with $w = 2$, 3, 4 and 5. The "N/A" that appears in this table (and other tables hereafter) corresponds to ARL_1 values that are not applicable because the corresponding values of μ_1 are negative. From this table, we observe the following:

1. As the value of span w increases, the value of L decreases in order to obtain the pre-specified value of ARL_0.
2. A PDMA chart with a small value of w is ARL-biased for small downward shifts, as the ARL_1 values are larger than the corresponding ARL_0 values. More specifically, for $\mu_0 = 4$ and 6, the PDMA charts with $w = 2$ and 3 are ARL-biased for $\delta = -0.25$, while for larger values of μ_0, only the PDMA chart with $w = 2$ is ARL-biased.

TABLE 6.6
ARL Values of the PDMA Chart

	$\mu_0 = 4$				$\mu_0 = 6$				$\mu_0 = 8$			
	w = 2	3	4	5	2	3	4	5	2	3	4	5
δ	L = 2.855	2.640	2.556	2.491	2.790	2.625	2.580	2.479	2.743	2.670	2.559	2.490
-3.00	N/A	N/A	N/A	N/A	N/A	N/A	N/A	N/A	N/A	N/A	N/A	N/A
-2.50	N/A	N/A	N/A	N/A	N/A	N/A	N/A	N/A	1.7	1.7	1.7	1.7
-2.00	N/A	N/A	N/A	N/A	2.9	2.8	2.7	2.6	2.9	2.8	2.7	2.7
-1.75	3.8	3.6	3.6	3.2	3.9	3.5	3.5	3.4	4.0	3.5	3.5	3.5
-1.50	7.0	4.6	4.5	4.5	6.2	4.6	4.5	4.5	6.4	4.6	4.5	4.5
-1.25	15.2	7.3	6.0	6.0	11.6	7.0	6.2	6.0	11.8	6.8	6.1	6.0
-1.00	39.8	14.2	9.7	8.9	25.6	12.5	9.7	8.8	25.4	11.6	9.7	8.8
-0.75	113.5	35.6	19.4	16.2	63.1	28.1	19.0	15.7	61.6	24.7	19.0	15.7
-0.50	319.7	105.7	52.0	41.2	166.4	77.0	49.2	37.6	163.6	64.1	48.9	36.7
-0.25	442.0	300.3	160.3	135.7	314.6	212.3	152.1	120.0	340.1	172.6	150.9	116.9
0.00	184.1	218.8	182.9	192.8	189.7	208.0	198.0	190.1	228.2	190.7	212.3	196.8
0.25	67.0	72.0	63.7	64.0	72.7	74.8	70.6	67.1	87.2	73.2	76.1	70.3
0.50	30.4	29.6	26.1	25.2	32.2	30.2	27.9	26.3	37.3	30.0	29.6	27.0
0.75	16.2	15.3	13.7	13.1	16.9	15.5	14.1	13.5	18.8	15.3	14.6	13.8
1.00	9.9	9.3	8.7	8.5	10.1	9.2	8.8	8.6	11.0	9.1	8.8	8.7
1.25	6.7	6.4	6.2	6.1	6.7	6.3	6.2	6.2	7.0	6.2	6.1	6.1
1.50	5.0	4.8	4.8	4.7	4.9	4.7	4.7	4.8	5.1	4.7	4.7	4.8
1.75	3.9	3.8	3.9	3.8	3.8	3.7	3.8	3.9	3.8	3.7	3.8	3.9
2.00	3.2	3.1	3.2	3.1	3.1	3.1	3.2	3.2	3.1	3.1	3.1	3.2
2.50	2.3	2.3	2.4	2.2	2.2	2.3	2.3	2.3	2.2	2.3	2.3	2.3
3.00	1.8	1.8	1.9	1.7	1.7	1.8	1.8	1.8	1.7	1.8	1.7	1.7

	$\mu_0 = 10$				$\mu_0 = 12$				$\mu_0 = 16$			
	w = 2	3	4	5	2	3	4	5	2	3	4	5
δ	**L = 2.715**	**2.615**	**2.527**	**2.470**	**2.715**	**2.650**	**2.564**	**2.474**	**2.760**	**2.640**	**2.560**	**2.468**
-3.00	1.1	1.1	1.0	1.0	1.2	1.2	1.1	1.1	1.4	1.2	1.2	1.1
-2.50	1.8	1.8	1.5	1.4	1.8	1.9	1.6	1.6	2.0	1.8	1.8	1.6
-2.00	2.9	2.8	2.6	2.5	2.9	2.9	2.7	2.6	3.0	2.8	2.8	2.6
-1.75	3.9	3.5	3.3	3.3	3.9	3.6	3.5	3.4	4.0	3.5	3.5	3.4
-1.50	6.0	4.6	4.3	4.4	5.8	4.7	4.5	4.5	6.0	4.6	4.5	4.4
-1.25	10.4	6.7	6.0	5.9	9.8	6.9	6.1	5.9	10.3	6.8	6.1	6.0
-1.00	20.9	11.4	9.3	8.7	19.4	11.8	9.4	8.8	19.6	11.3	9.3	8.7
-0.75	48.3	23.7	17.7	15.5	43.5	24.5	17.3	15.5	43.5	22.9	17.1	15.1
-0.50	121.8	61.1	43.7	36.6	108.9	62.4	42.3	36.3	106.2	56.4	40.1	34.2
-0.25	263.3	165.8	129.8	114.5	236.4	174.5	123.8	112.5	246.0	157.4	118.8	106.1
0.00	211.9	202.4	200.3	208.1	204.1	216.2	191.2	203.8	230.6	212.2	194.2	201.3
0.25	84.8	78.2	73.8	72.6	87.0	84.8	75.0	75.1	97.5	85.2	77.2	75.3
0.50	37.3	31.4	28.4	27.5	37.4	32.8	28.5	27.2	41.0	33.1	29.0	27.2
0.75	18.5	15.5	14.0	13.5	19.0	16.6	14.4	13.8	20.4	16.3	14.5	13.7
1.00	10.7	9.2	8.6	8.5	10.9	9.6	8.7	8.6	11.6	9.5	8.8	8.5
1.25	7.1	6.3	6.0	6.1	6.9	6.3	6.0	6.0	7.3	6.3	6.1	6.0
1.50	5.0	4.7	4.5	4.6	5.0	4.8	4.6	4.6	5.1	4.6	4.6	4.6
1.75	3.8	3.7	3.6	3.7	3.8	3.8	3.7	3.7	3.9	3.7	3.7	3.7
2.00	3.0	3.0	3.0	3.0	3.0	3.1	3.0	3.1	3.1	3.0	3.1	3.0
2.50	2.2	2.2	2.2	2.1	2.2	2.3	2.2	2.2	2.2	2.2	2.2	2.1
3.00	1.7	1.8	1.6	1.6	1.7	1.7	1.7	1.6	1.7	1.7	1.7	1.6

3. The performance of the PDMA chart is better, especially for small to moderate shifts, as the value of w increases. On the other hand, for large upward shifts ($\delta \geq 2.00$), the performance is approximately similar independently the value of w, whereas for large downward shifts ($\delta \leq -2.00$), when it is possible, a PDMA chart with a large value of w has better detection ability.
4. The PDMA chart detects small to moderate upward shifts more quickly than the corresponding downward shifts and vice versa for large shifts. This range of shifts becomes narrower as the value of w increases.

It is of interest to study the performance of the PDMA chart for the case where the value of w is not fixed. In this case, the PDMA chart reduces to the Poisson DPM (PDPM) chart. The variance of the PDPM statistic is given by Eq. 6.4 and the control limits and the centerline of the PDPM chart are defined as

$$UCL_i \,/\, LCL_i = \mu_0 \pm L \frac{1}{tf(t)} \sqrt{\mu_0 \left[\sum_{j=1}^{t} \frac{1}{j} + 2 \sum_{j_1=1}^{t-1} \sum_{j_2=j_1+1}^{t} \frac{1}{j_2} \right]}, CL = \mu_0, \qquad (6.18)$$

where $f(t)$ is an arbitrary function of t which achieves narrower control limits for large values of t. In this study, we use $f(t) = t^{0.2}$ among a variety of values as this choice optimizes the properties of the run-length distribution. It is worth mentioning that Alevizakos and Koukouvinos (2020a) first introduced the PDPM chart but, unfortunately, the variance of the PDPM statistic that they used was not correct.

Performing numerical simulations, we evaluate the performance of the PDPM chart. The results are presented in Table 6.7 where the SDRL values are also shown. From this table, we conclude that the PDPM chart is more effective than the PDMA chart for the entire range of shifts. However, this superiority is accompanied with a large value of $SDRL_0$.

In the following lines, we compare the PDMA chart with the c-chart, PMA, PEWMA and PCUSUM charts. The ARL_0 of the competing control charts is set approximately equal to 200. Table 6.8 shows the ARL values of the PEWMA and PMA control charts for $\mu_0 = 4$, 8 and 12. We notice that in some cases, the ARL_0 values of the PMA charts are not so close to the pre-specified value. Comparing Tables 6.6 and 6.8, we conclude that PDMA chart is more effective than the PMA chart in detecting small to moderate shifts while the latter chart performs a slightly better in large shifts. The range of shifts where the PDMA chart is more sensitive than the PMA chart decreases as the value of w increases. For example, when $\mu_0 = 8$, the PDMA chart outperforms the PMA chart in detecting shifts of $-2.00 \leq \delta \leq 1.75$ when $w = 2$ and $-1.25 \leq \delta \leq 1.00$ when $w = 5$.

Moreover, from the same table, it can be seen that the PDMA chart with $w = 4$ or 5 has a slightly better detection ability than the PEWMA chart with $\lambda = 0.25$ or 0.50 in detecting moderate to large downward shifts and large upward shifts. For the rest range of shifts, the PEWMA chart with $\lambda = 0.05$ is more effective than the PDMA chart. Additionally, it should be noted that the PDMA chart even with $w = 2$ is more effective than the c-chart (PEWMA chart with $\lambda = 1.00$) for the entire range of shifts.

TABLE 6.7
ARL and SDRL Values for the PDPM Chart

	$\mu_0 = 4$, L = 1.283		$\mu_0 = 6$, L = 1.276		$\mu_0 = 8$, L = 1.285		$\mu_0 = 10$, L = 1.285		$\mu_0 = 12$, L = 1.275		$\mu_0 = 16$, L = 1.277	
δ	ARL	SDRL	ARL	SDRL	ARL	SDRL	ARL	SDRL	ARL	SDRL	ARL	SDRL
-3.00	N/A	N/A	N/A	N/A	N/A	N/A	1.0	0.1	1.0	0.1	1.0	0.1
-2.50	N/A	N/A	N/A	N/A	1.0	0.1	1.0	0.1	1.0	0.2	1.1	0.2
-2.00	N/A	N/A	1.1	0.3	1.1	0.4	1.4	0.7	1.2	0.5	1.2	0.5
-1.75	1.1	0.4	1.3	0.6	1.3	0.6	1.4	0.7	1.4	0.7	1.4	0.8
-1.50	1.4	0.8	1.6	0.9	1.6	1.0	1.7	1.1	1.6	1.1	1.7	1.1
-1.25	1.9	1.4	2.1	1.5	2.1	1.6	2.2	1.7	2.1	1.7	2.2	1.7
-1.00	2.7	2.4	2.9	2.5	2.9	2.7	3.1	2.7	3.0	2.8	3.1	2.8
-0.75	4.4	4.4	4.5	4.6	4.5	4.7	4.7	4.8	4.6	4.8	4.7	4.9
-0.50	7.9	9.5	8.1	9.7	8.1	9.9	8.3	10.0	8.2	10.0	8.4	10.2
-0.25	19.7	30.8	19.9	30.9	19.8	31.3	20.4	31.7	19.8	31.1	20.4	31.9
0.00	200.6	891.6	200.4	897.2	201.7	902.5	200.9	873.4	199.8	890.6	200.1	874.0
0.25	21.4	34.4	21.3	34.0	21.0	33.8	21.5	34.1	20.8	33.4	21.1	33.4
0.50	9.4	12.2	9.3	11.9	9.1	11.8	9.2	11.7	9.0	11.5	9.1	11.5
0.75	5.5	6.5	5.5	6.3	5.3	6.1	5.4	6.1	5.3	6.0	5.3	6.0
1.00	3.8	4.1	3.7	3.9	3.6	3.8	3.7	3.8	3.6	3.7	3.6	3.7
1.25	2.8	2.8	2.8	2.7	2.7	2.6	2.8	2.6	2.6	2.5	2.7	2.5
1.50	2.3	2.1	2.2	1.9	2.1	1.9	2.2	1.9	2.1	1.8	2.1	1.8
1.75	1.9	1.6	1.9	1.5	1.8	1.4	1.8	1.4	1.8	1.4	1.8	1.3
2.00	1.6	1.2	1.6	1.1	1.6	1.1	1.6	1.1	1.5	1.0	1.5	1.0
2.50	1.3	0.8	1.3	0.7	1.3	0.7	1.3	0.7	1.3	0.6	1.3	0.6
3.00	1.2	0.5	1.2	0.5	1.1	0.5	1.2	0.5	1.1	0.4	1.1	0.4

TABLE 6.8
ARL Values of the PEWMA and PMA Charts

	PEWMA											
	$\mu_0 = 4$				$\mu_0 = 8$				$\mu_0 = 12$			
	$\lambda = 0.05$	0.25	0.50	1.00	0.05	0.25	0.50	1.00	0.05	0.25	0.50	1.00
δ	L = 2.220	2.690	2.854	2.500	2.218	2.692	2.823	2.860	2.216	2.687	2.812	2.830
-3.00	N/A	N/A	N/A	N/A	N/A	N/A	N/A	N/A	3.0	2.0	1.8	1.3
-2.50	N/A	N/A	N/A	N/A	3.5	2.2	2.1	N/A	3.5	2.3	2.2	2.9
-2.00	N/A	N/A	N/A	N/A	3.5	2.2	2.1	N/A	4.4	3.1	3.0	8.5
-1.75	5.0	3.5	4.3	N/A	5.0	3.6	4.0	N/A	5.0	3.6	4.0	15.4
-1.50	5.8	4.6	7.2	N/A	5.9	4.6	5.9	N/A	5.9	4.6	5.7	28.9
-1.25	7.1	6.3	14.7	N/A	7.2	6.2	9.9	N/A	7.2	6.1	9.0	56.4
-1.00	9.2	9.7	39.4	N/A	9.3	9.3	19.8	N/A	9.3	9.2	16.9	109.8
-0.75	13.2	18.8	130.7	N/A	13.2	16.8	47.4	N/A	13.2	16.2	37.4	205.9
-0.50	22.3	50.2	490.1	N/A	22.2	40.4	135.2	N/A	22.2	37.9	99.3	311.9
-0.25	58.7	182.9	614.8	N/A	57.7	134.3	308.4	N/A	56.5	121.6	237.7	268.4
0.00	200.8	200.3	200.3	121.9	200.1	200.2	200.8	268.1	200.6	200.3	200.7	152.6
0.25	51.9	59.5	66.9	79.1	52.7	64.6	73.9	120.2	53.5	67.3	77.9	78.3
0.50	21.7	23.5	29.1	31.8	21.8	24.8	31.3	60.8	21.9	25.3	32.6	40.8
0.75	13.3	12.6	15.5	18.7	13.2	12.9	16.1	33.3	13.3	13.3	16.9	23.8
1.00	9.6	8.3	9.6	12.1	9.5	8.3	9.7	20.1	9.5	8.3	9.9	14.8
1.25	7.4	6.0	6.6	8.2	7.4	5.9	6.5	12.5	7.3	5.9	6.6	9.6
1.50	6.1	4.7	4.9	5.9	6.1	4.6	4.9	8.7	6.1	4.6	4.9	6.7
1.75	5.2	3.9	3.9	4.4	5.2	4.0	3.8	6.2	5.2	3.8	3.8	4.9
2.00	4.6	3.3	3.2	3.5	4.5	3.2	3.1	4.6	4.5	3.2	3.1	3.7
2.50	3.7	2.6	2.4	2.4	3.7	2.5	2.3	3.0	3.6	2.5	2.3	2.4
3.00	3.1	2.1	1.9	1.8	3.1	2.1	1.9	2.1	3.1	2.1	1.8	1.8

	PMA											
	w = 2	3	4	5	2	3	4	5	2	3	4	5
δ	L = 2.815	2.830	2.600	2.610	2.750	2.660	2.655	2.660	2.660	2.670	2.670	2.668
-3.00	N/A	N/A	N/A	N/A	N/A	N/A	N/A	N/A	1.2	1.2	1.2	1.2
-2.50	N/A	N/A	N/A	N/A	1.7	1.6	1.6	1.6	1.8	1.7	1.7	1.7
-2.00	N/A	N/A	N/A	N/A	3.3	2.4	2.3	2.3	2.9	2.6	2.5	2.5
-1.75	4.3	2.8	2.8	2.8	5.5	3.2	3.0	2.9	4.3	3.4	3.1	3.1
-1.50	10.1	5.4	4.0	3.8	10.3	5.0	4.2	3.9	7.1	5.0	4.2	4.0
-1.25	24.3	10.6	6.4	5.5	21.6	8.6	6.8	5.6	12.9	8.1	6.3	5.8
-1.00	61.5	25.1	12.0	9.4	49.9	17.0	12.4	9.4	26.1	15.3	10.8	9.5
-0.75	159.9	67.7	27.8	19.9	122.5	39.9	27.6	18.5	56.9	33.7	22.2	18.7
-0.50	350.6	189.9	76.4	52.8	291.5	103.2	74.6	45.9	130.8	84.5	54.8	45.4
-0.25	322.0	372.4	201.4	149.8	452.4	240.5	208.1	131.0	231.9	199.7	144.8	130.3
0.00	132.9	197.9	165.5	158.6	243.0	203.7	220.7	173.1	179.4	202.9	181.6	190.2
0.25	54.6	69.3	60.4	58.3	96.4	79.6	81.5	66.3	81.3	85.3	76.2	75.1
0.50	26.3	30.0	25.3	24.0	42.5	33.3	31.8	26.6	37.0	35.3	30.1	28.5
0.75	14.7	15.5	13.4	12.7	21.5	16.6	15.5	13.3	19.6	17.6	15.2	14.3
1.00	9.1	9.4	8.2	7.8	12.4	9.5	8.9	8.0	11.2	9.9	8.8	8.4
1.25	6.2	6.3	5.6	5.4	7.7	6.2	5.9	5.4	7.2	6.4	5.8	5.6
1.50	4.5	4.7	4.2	4.1	5.5	4.5	4.3	4.1	5.1	4.6	4.3	4.2
1.75	3.5	3.6	3.3	3.2	4.0	3.4	3.3	3.2	3.8	3.5	3.3	3.3
2.00	2.9	2.9	2.7	2.7	3.1	2.7	2.7	2.6	3.0	2.8	2.7	2.7
2.50	2.1	2.2	2.0	2.0	2.2	2.0	2.0	2.0	2.1	2.0	2.0	2.0
3.00	1.7	1.7	1.6	1.6	1.6	1.6	1.6	1.6	1.6	1.6	1.6	1.6

TABLE 6.9
ARL Values of One-Sided PCUSUM Charts

	Upper-Sided				Lower-Sided		
μ_0	**4**	**8**	**12**		**4**	**8**	**12**
μ_1	**5.77**	**10.75**	**15**		**3**	**6.4**	**10**
δ	$h = 9$	**11.5**	**15**	δ	**10.5**	**13.5**	**17.1429**
0.00	203.7	203.6	200.5	-3.00	NA	NA	2.2
0.25	51.5	54.1	51.3	-2.50	NA	2.9	2.8
0.50	21.2	21.8	20.7	-2.00	NA	3.4	3.5
0.75	12.1	12.0	11.8	-1.75	4.2	3.9	4.1
1.00	8.2	8.0	7.9	-1.50	4.9	4.6	4.8
1.25	6.2	5.9	5.9	-1.25	6.0	5.7	6.0
1.50	5.0	4.8	4.8	-1.00	7.8	7.5	7.8
1.75	4.2	4.0	4.0	-0.75	11.2	10.9	11.1
2.00	3.6	3.4	3.4	-0.50	19.2	18.9	19.0
2.50	2.9	2.7	2.7	-0.25	47.7	47.6	46.2
3.00	2.4	2.3	2.3	0.00	215.5	200.8	203.2

The ARL values of one-sided PCUSUM schemes are presented in Table 6.9 where μ_1 represents the shift that the PCUSUM chart is optimally designed to detect. The upper-sided PCUSUM charts are optimal designed to detect a shift of $\delta = 0.75 - 1.00$ while the lower-sided a shift of $\delta = 0.50 - 0.60$. From Tables 6.6 and 6.9, we observe that the PDMA chart is more effective in detecting shifts of $|\delta| \geq 1.50$ while the PCUSUM chart outperforms the PDMA chart for small to moderate shifts.

6.6 ILLUSTRATIVE EXAMPLES

6.6.1 Flow Width in a Hard-Bake Process

In this example, we use the flow width measurements (in microns) on a semiconductor manufacturing process, provided by Montgomery (2013). The dataset consists of 45 samples, each of size $n = 5$ and is presented in Table 6.10. The first 25 samples represent the Phase I where the IC values of mean and standard deviation are $\mu_0 = 1.5056$ and $\sigma_0 = 0.1394$. The last 20 samples represent the Phase II. Setting an $ARL_0 = 370$ and $w = 5$, we construct the DMA-$\overline{X}$ control chart with $L = 2.709$ and the MA-$\overline{X}$ control chart with $L = 2.880$. The charting statistics of the two charts are also presented in Table 6.10, and the control charts are displayed in Figure 6.1 and Figure 6.2. From these figures, we observe that the DMA-$\overline{X}$ chart detects the shift at the last sample while the MA-$\overline{X}$ chart cannot detect the shift.

TABLE 6.10
Flow Width Measurements Data and Charting Statistics

i	X_1	X_2	X_3	X_4	X_5	$\overline{X}_i$	MA_i	DMA_i
1	1.3235	1.4128	1.6744	1.4573	1.6914	1.5119	1.5119	1.5119
2	1.4314	1.3592	1.6075	1.4666	1.6109	1.4951	1.5035	1.5077
3	1.4284	1.4871	1.4932	1.4324	1.5674	1.4817	1.4962	1.5039
4	1.5028	1.6352	1.3841	1.2831	1.5507	1.4712	1.4900	1.5004
5	1.5604	1.2735	1.5265	1.4363	1.6441	1.4882	1.4896	1.4982
6	1.5955	1.5451	1.3574	1.3281	1.4198	1.4492	1.4771	1.4913
7	1.6274	1.5064	1.8366	1.4177	1.5144	1.5805	1.4942	1.4894
8	1.4190	1.4303	1.6637	1.6067	1.5519	1.5343	1.5047	1.4911
9	1.3884	1.7277	1.5355	1.5176	1.3688	1.5076	1.5120	1.4955
10	1.4039	1.6697	1.5089	1.4627	1.5220	1.5134	1.5170	1.5010
11	1.4158	1.7667	1.4278	1.5928	1.4181	1.5242	1.5320	1.5120
12	1.5821	1.3355	1.5777	1.3908	1.7559	1.5284	1.5216	1.5174
13	1.2856	1.4106	1.4447	1.6398	1.1928	1.3947	1.4937	1.5152
14	1.4951	1.4036	1.5893	1.6458	1.4969	1.5261	1.4974	1.5123
15	1.3589	1.2863	1.5996	1.2497	1.5471	1.4083	1.4763	1.5042
16	1.5747	1.5301	1.5171	1.1839	1.8662	1.5344	1.4784	1.4935
17	1.3680	1.7269	1.3957	1.5014	1.4449	1.4874	1.4702	1.4832
18	1.4163	1.3864	1.3057	1.6210	1.5573	1.4573	1.4827	1.4810
19	1.5796	1.4185	1.6541	1.5116	1.7247	1.5777	1.4930	1.4801
20	1.7106	1.4412	1.2361	1.3820	1.7601	1.5060	1.5126	1.4874
21	1.4371	1.5051	1.3485	1.5670	1.4880	1.4691	1.4995	1.4916
22	1.4738	1.5936	1.6583	1.4973	1.4720	1.5390	1.5098	1.4995
23	1.5917	1.4333	1.5551	1.5295	1.6866	1.5592	1.5302	1.5090
24	1.6399	1.5243	1.5705	1.5563	1.5530	1.5688	1.5284	1.5161
25	1.5797	1.3663	1.6240	1.3732	1.6887	1.5264	1.5325	1.5201
26	1.4483	1.5458	1.4538	1.4303	1.6206	1.4998	1.5386	1.5279
27	1.5435	1.6899	1.5830	1.3358	1.4187	1.5142	1.5337	1.5327
28	1.5175	1.3446	1.4723	1.6657	1.6661	1.5332	1.5285	1.5323
29	1.5454	1.0931	1.4072	1.5039	1.5264	1.4152	1.4978	1.5262
30	1.4418	1.5059	1.5124	1.4620	1.6263	1.5097	1.4944	1.5186
31	1.4301	1.2725	1.5945	1.5397	1.5252	1.4724	1.4889	1.5087
32	1.4981	1.4506	1.6174	1.5837	1.4962	1.5292	1.4919	1.5003
33	1.3009	1.5060	1.6231	1.5831	1.6454	1.5317	1.4916	1.4929
34	1.4132	1.4603	1.5808	1.7111	1.7313	1.5793	1.5245	1.4983
35	1.3817	1.3135	1.4953	1.4894	1.4596	1.4279	1.5081	1.5010
36	1.5765	1.7014	1.4026	1.2773	1.4541	1.4824	1.5101	1.5052
37	1.4936	1.4373	1.5139	1.4808	1.5293	1.4910	1.5025	1.5074
38	1.5729	1.6738	1.5048	1.5651	1.7473	1.6128	1.5187	1.5128
39	1.8089	1.5513	1.8250	1.4389	1.6558	1.6560	1.5340	1.5147
40	1.6236	1.5393	1.6738	1.8698	1.5036	1.6420	1.5768	1.5284
41	1.4120	1.7931	1.7345	1.6391	1.7791	1.6716	1.6147	1.5493
42	1.7372	1.5663	1.4910	1.7809	1.5504	1.6252	1.6415	1.5771
43	1.5971	1.7394	1.6832	1.6677	1.7974	1.6970	1.6584	1.6051
44	1.4295	1.6536	1.9134	1.7272	1.4370	1.6321	1.6536	1.6290
45	1.6217	1.8220	1.7915	1.6744	1.9404	1.7700	1.6792	1.6495

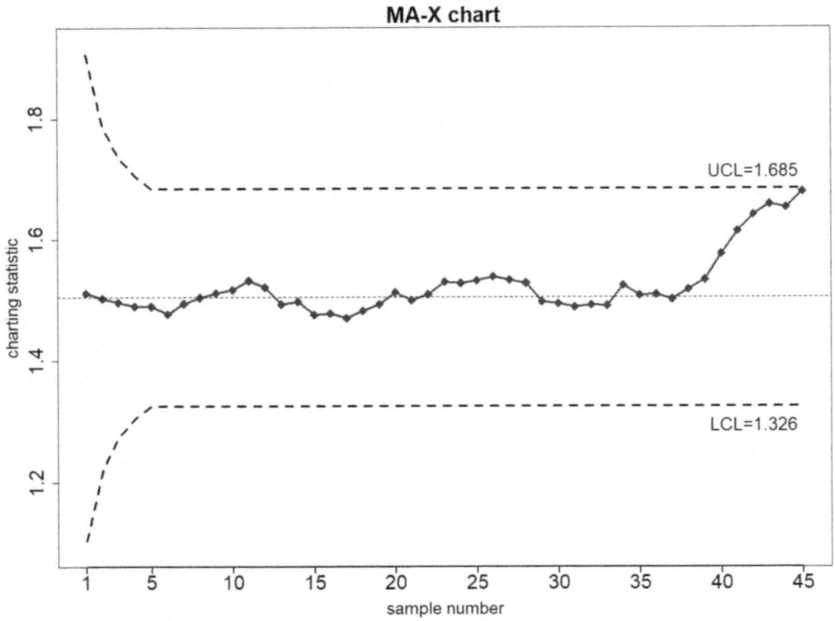

FIGURE 6.1 The MA-$\overline{X}$ control chart for flow width in the hard-bake process.

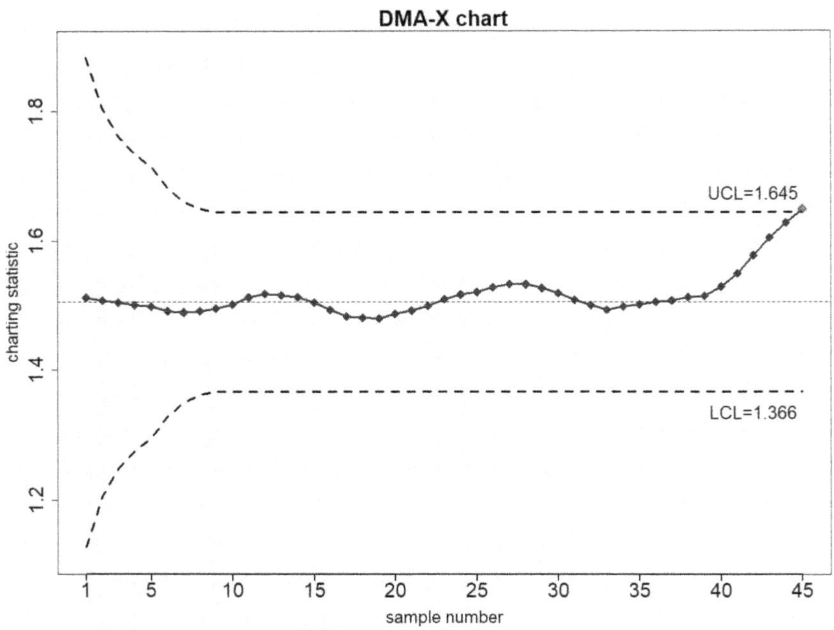

FIGURE 6.2 The DMA-$\overline{X}$ control chart for flow width in the hard-bake process.

6.6.2 Fill Volume of Soft-Drink Beverage Bottles

In the current example, we use a dataset about the fill volume of soft-drink beverage bottles presented in Huang et al. (2014). The manager of a beverage company in northern Taiwan is interested in understanding the fill volume of their own company's products. The dataset, that was taken from a manufacturing process, consists of 25 samples of n = 5 and is displayed in Table 6.11. The estimated values of the process mean and standard deviation are 601.320 and 7.093, respectively. Setting an ARL0 = 200 and w = 4, we construct the DMAS control chart with L = 2.553 and the MAS control chart with L = 2.696. The charting statistics of the two charts are also listed in Table 6.11 and the control charts are provided in Figure 6.3 and Figure 6.4. From these figures, we observe that the DMAS chart raises an OOC signal at the 12th sample while the MAS chart fails to detect any shift in the process variance.

TABLE 6.11
Fill Volume of Soft-Drink Beverage Bottles and Charting Statistics

i	X_1	X_2	X_3	X_4	X_5	S_i	MA_i	DMA_i
1	580	599	597	598	604	9.127	9.127	9.127
2	598	590	605	591	600	6.301	7.714	8.420
3	610	602	607	603	600	4.037	6.488	7.776
4	594	604	592	594	608	7.127	6.648	7.494
5	602	594	607	599	592	6.058	5.881	6.683
6	596	590	600	598	607	6.181	5.851	6.217
7	601	594	591	594	600	4.301	5.917	6.074
8	599	603	602	601	592	4.393	5.233	5.720
9	597	602	594	601	602	3.564	4.610	5.403
10	606	599	601	603	600	2.775	3.758	4.893
11	605	609	610	608	603	2.915	3.412	4.253
12	594	611	605	598	606	6.760	4.004	3.946
13	601	615	589	614	598	11.059	5.877	4.263
14	594	606	603	618	600	8.899	7.409	5.175
15	607	590	603	599	604	6.580	8.325	6.404
16	602	594	598	606	608	5.727	8.066	7.419
17	594	601	608	593	597	6.107	6.829	7.657
18	597	610	621	604	587	12.872	7.822	7.760
19	605	610	598	614	604	6.099	7.702	7.605
20	596	602	601	602	598	2.683	6.941	7.323
21	608	600	602	612	581	11.950	8.401	7.716
22	605	610	605	604	590	7.530	7.066	7.527
23	601	596	594	608	592	6.419	7.145	7.388
24	606	626	594	611	605	11.632	9.383	7.999
25	613	600	602	606	611	5.595	7.794	7.847

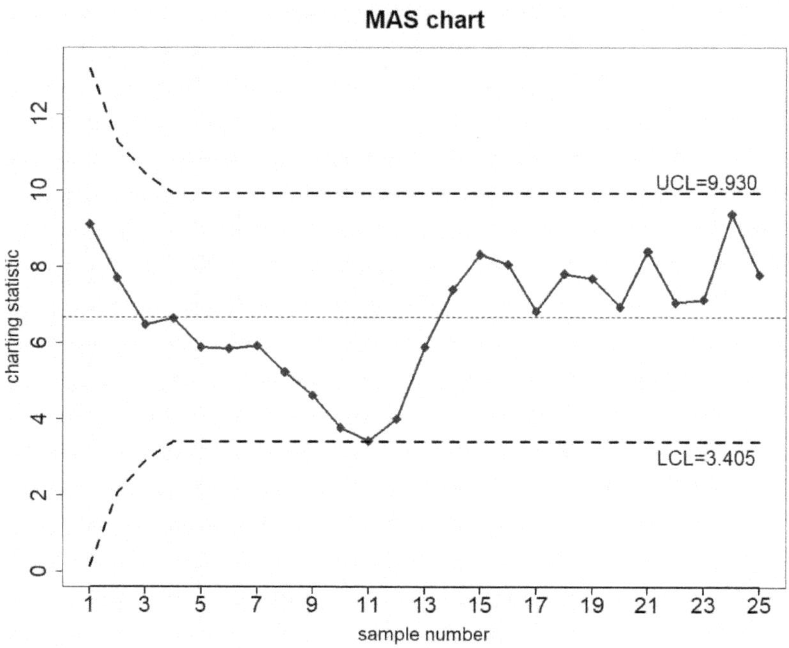

FIGURE 6.3 The MAS control chart for fill volume of soft-drink beverage bottles.

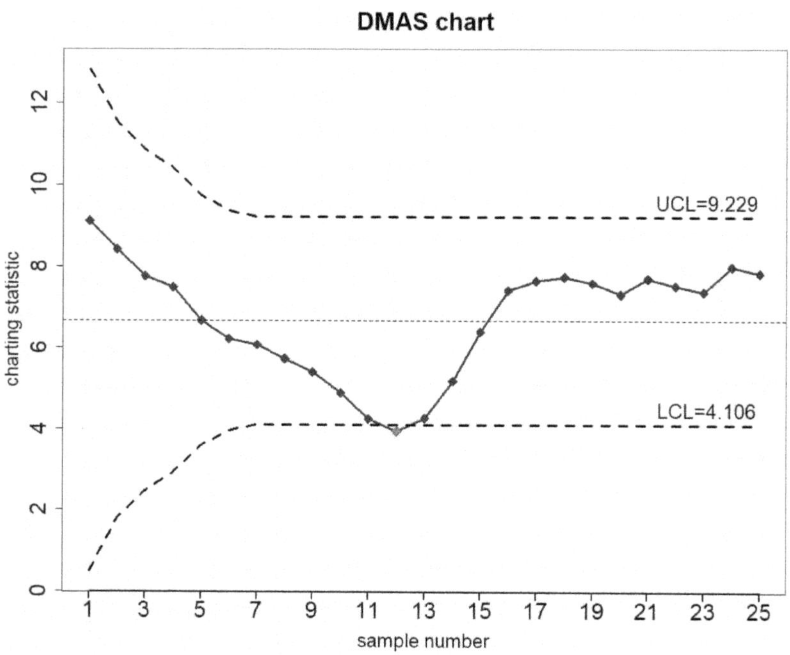

FIGURE 6.4 The DMAS control chart for fill volume of soft-drink beverage bottles.

6.6.3 Male Thyroid Cancer Surveillance in New Mexico

We use the dataset on the annual incidence of male thyroid cancer per 100,000 persons in New Mexico between 1973 and 2006. The data have also been studied by Mei et al. (2011) and Shu et al. (2012) and are presented in Table 6.12. The dataset consists of 34 observations where the first 16 (period from 1973 to 1988) represent the phase I observations. The annual incidence rate is estimated to be $\mu_0 = 2$ incidents of male thyroid cancer per 100,000 persons. Furthermore, it is known that the annual incidence rate has increased since 1989. The main objective is to detect the upward shift as soon as possible in order to take actions to identify the cause of this deterioration. We construct the PMA chart with $w = 3$ and $L = 2.850$ and the PDMA chart with $w = 3$ and $L = 2.640$. This choice of design parameters gives ARL_0 values equal to 155.7 for the PMA chart and 197.9 for the PDMA chart. The two control charts are displayed in Figure 6.5 and Figure 6.6 and their charting statistics are also shown in Table 6.12. The PMA chart gives an OOC signal in the year 2000 and the PDMA chart in the year 1999.

TABLE 6.12
Data on the Incidence of Male Thyroid Cancer in New Mexico and Charting Statistics

i	X_i	MA_i	DMA_i	*i*	X_i	MA_i	DMA_i
1973	2	2.000	2.000	1990	4	3.000	2.444
1974	2	2.000	2.000	1991	2	3.000	2.778
1975	4	2.667	2.222	1992	3	3.000	3.000
1976	4	3.333	2.667	1993	4	3.000	3.000
1977	2	3.333	3.111	1994	2	3.000	3.000
1978	2	2.667	3.111	1995	3	3.000	3.000
1979	2	2.000	2.667	1996	4	3.000	3.000
1980	2	2.000	2.222	1997	4	3.667	3.222
1981	2	2.000	2.000	1998	4	4.000	3.556
1982	3	2.333	2.111	1999	4	4.000	3.889
1983	2	2.333	2.222	2000	5	4.333	4.111
1984	2	2.333	2.333	2001	5	4.667	4.333
1985	2	2.000	2.222	2002	7	5.667	4.889
1986	2	2.000	2.111	2003	5	5.667	5.333
1987	2	2.000	2.000	2004	7	6.333	5.889
1988	2	2.000	2.000	2005	6	6.000	6.000
1989	3	2.333	2.111	2006	5	6.000	6.111

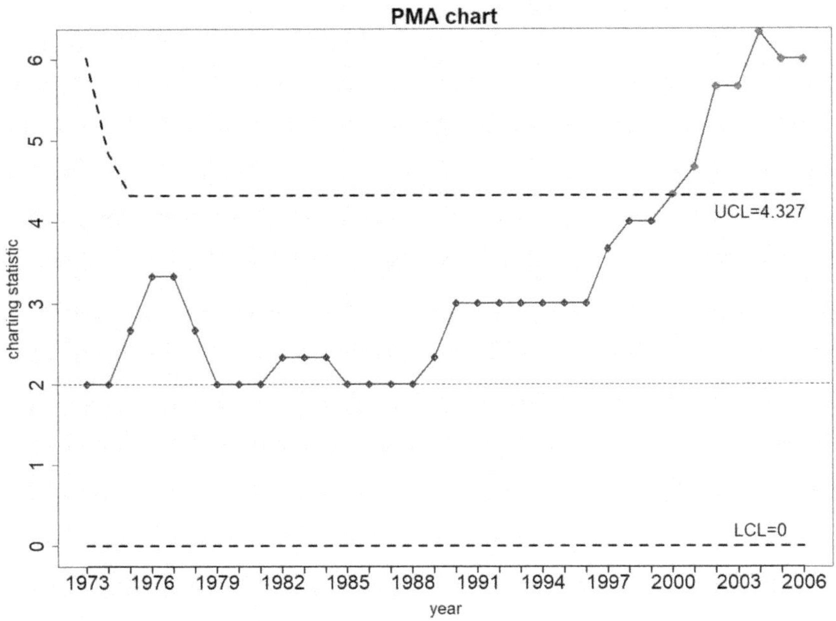

FIGURE 6.5 The PMA control chart for the annual incidence of male thyroid cancer in New Mexico.

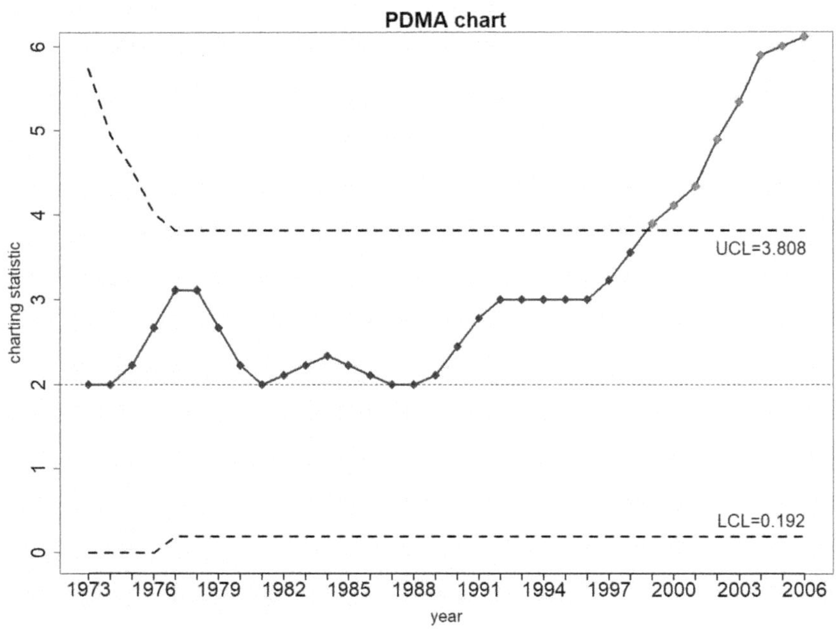

FIGURE 6.6 The PDMA control chart for the annual incidence of male thyroid cancer in New Mexico.

6.7 CONCLUSIONS

This chapter presented three DMA control charts for monitoring shifts in the process mean or dispersion of normally distributed data, as well as in the Poisson parameter of attribute data. The DMA scheme is an extension of the well-known MA scheme by imitating exactly the DEWMA technique. Performing Monte Carlo simulations, we computed the ARL of the DMA charts for different values of the design parameter w. Generally, it is found that a DMA chart with a large value of w has better detection ability than other DMA charts with a small value of w. In the cases of monitoring shifts in the process dispersion or Poisson mean, the DMA chart with a small value of w is ARL-biased for small downward shifts, especially when the sample size or the IC Poisson mean is small. We also compared its performance with other existing control charts.

The comparison study of control charts designed for monitoring the process location indicated that the DMA-$\overline{X}$ chart is more effective than the Shewhart-$\overline{X}$ chart over the entire range of shifts while it outperforms the MA-$\overline{X}$ chart for small to moderate shifts. The superiority of the DMA-$\overline{X}$ against the MA-$\overline{X}$ chart decreases as the value of w or n increases. Moreover, in the case of individual measurements (n = 1), the DMA-$\overline{X}$ chart is less effective than the EWMA-$\overline{X}$ and CUSUM-$\overline{X}$ charts for small to moderate shifts and vice versa for large shifts, while in the case of subgrouped data, the DMA-$\overline{X}$ chart is superior to the EWMA-$\overline{X}$ and CUSUM-$\overline{X}$ charts in a wider range of shifts.

In addition, we compared control charts for process dispersion for a fixed value of sample size (n = 5). The DMAS chart is found to be more sensitive than the S chart, especially for small to moderate upward shifts while it has better detection ability than the MAS chart for downward and small to moderate upward shifts. Additionally, the DMAS chart performs a slightly better or similarly with the S^2-EWMA and CUSUM-S^2 charts for large shifts and vice versa for small to moderate shifts. Finally, comparing with the CS-EWMA chart, the DMAS chart is found to be more sensitive for upward and large downward shifts.

As mentioned, the DMA scheme was also designed for monitoring shifts in the Poisson process mean. Its statistical performance was compared with the c-chart, PMA, PEWMA and PCUSUM charts. The results showed that the PDMA chart is more effective than PMA chart for small to moderate shifts and vice versa for large shifts while it outperforms the c-chart for the entire range of shifts. Furthermore, the PDMA chart is a good alternative to the PEWMA and PCUSUM charts in detecting moderate to large shifts.

In terms of future research, the DMA scheme could be investigated for joint monitoring of process mean and dispersion, as well as for monitoring attribute data following a binomial or COM-Poisson distribution.

REFERENCES

Abbas, N., H.Z. Nazir, N. Akhtar, M. Riaz, and M. Abid. 2019. An enhanced approach for the progressive mean control charts. *Quality and Reliability Engineering International* 35: 1046–1060.

Abbas, N., M. Riaz, and R.J.M.M. Does. 2013a. Mixed exponentially weighted moving average-cumulative sum charts for process monitoring. *Quality and Reliability Engineering International* 29: 345–356.

Abbas, N., M. Riaz, and R.J.M.M. Does. 2013b. CS-EWMA chart for monitoring process dispersion. *Quality and Reliability Engineering International* 29: 653–663.

Abbas, N., M. Riaz, and R.J.M.M. Does. 2014. Memory-type control charts for monitoring the process dispersion. *Quality and Reliability Engineering International* 30: 623–632.

Abbas, N., R.F. Zafar, M. Riaz, and Z. Hussain. 2013c. Progressive mean control chart for monitoring process location parameter. *Quality and Reliability Engineering International* 29: 357–367.

Acosta-Mejia, C.A., and J.J. Pignatiello. 2008. Modified *R* charts for improved performance. *Quality Engineering* 20: 361–369.

Adeoti, O.A., A.A. Akomolafe, and F.B. Adebola. 2019. Monitoring process variability using double moving average control chart. *Industrial Engineering & Management Systems* 18: 210–221.

Adeoti, O.A., and J.O. Olaomi. 2016. A moving average *S* control chart for monitoring process variability. *Quality Engineering* 28: 212–219.

Alevizakos, V., K. Chatterjee, C. Koukouvinos, and A. Lappa. 2020. A double moving average control chart: Discussion. *Communications in Statistics—Simulation and Computation* doi:10.1080/03610918.2020.1788591.

Alevizakos, V., and C. Koukouvinos. 2020a. A double progressive mean control chart for monitoring Poisson observations. *Journal of Computational and Applied Mathematics* 373: 112232.

Alevizakos, V., and C. Koukouvinos. 2020b. A comparative study on Poisson control charts. *Quality Technology & Quantitative Management* 17: 354–382.

Borror, C.M., C.W. Champ, and S.E. Rigdon. 1998. Poisson EWMA control charts. *Journal of Quality Technology* 30: 352–361.

Castagliola, P. 2005. A new S^2-EWMA control chart for monitoring process variance. *Quality and Reliability Engineering International* 21: 781–794.

Castagliola, P., G. Celano, and S. Fichera. 2009. A new CUSUM-S^2 control chart for monitoring the process variance. *Journal of Quality in Maintenance Engineering* 15: 344–357.

Castagliola, P., G. Celano, and S. Fichera. 2010. A Johnson's type transformation EWMA-S^2 control chart. *International Journal of Quality Engineering and Technology* 1: 253–275.

Crowder, S.V. 1987. A simple method for studying run-length distributions of exponentially weighted moving average charts. *Technometrics* 29: 401–407.

Crowder, S.V. 1989. Design of exponentially weighted moving average schemes. *Journal of Quality Technology* 21: 155–162.

Crowder, S.V., and M.D. Hamilton. 1992. An EWMA for monitoring a process standard deviation. *Journal of Quality Technology* 24: 12–21.

Gan, F.F. 1990. Monitoring Poisson observations using modified exponentially weighted moving average control charts. *Communications in Statistics—Simulation and Computation* 19: 103–124.

Hawkins, D.M., and Q. Wu. 2014. The CUSUM and the EWMA head-to-head. *Quality Engineering* 26: 215–222.

Hsu, B.M., P.J. Lai, M.H. Shu, and Y.Y. Hung. 2007. A comparative study of the monitoring performance for weighted control charts. *Journal of Statistics and Management Systems* 12: 207–228.

Huang, C.J., S.H. Tai, and S.L. Lu. 2014. Measuring the performance improvement of a double generally weighted moving average control chart. *Expert Systems with Applications* 41: 3313–3322.

Jiang, W., L. Shu, and K.L. Tsui. 2011. Weighted CUSUM Control charts for monitoring Poisson processes with varying sample sizes. *Journal of Quality Technology* 43: 346–362.
Khoo, M.B.C. 2004. Poisson moving average versus c chart for nonconformities. *Quality Engineering* 16: 525–534.
Khoo, M.B.C. 2005. A modified *S* chart for the process variance. *Quality Engineering* 17: 567–577.
Khoo, M.B.C., and V.H. Wong. 2008. A double moving average control chart. *Communications in Statistics—Simulation and Computation* 37: 1696–1708.
Klein, M. 1996. Composite Shewhart-EWMA statistical control schemes. *IIE Transactions* 28: 475–481.
Koukouvinos, C., and A. Lappa. 2019. A moving average control chart using a robust scale estimator for process dispersion. *Quality and Reliability Engineering International* 35: 2462–2493.
Lucas, J.M. 1982. Combined Shewhart-CUSUM quality control schemes. *Journal of Quality Technology* 14: 51–59.
Lucas, J.M. 1985. Counted data CUSUM's. *Technometrics* 27: 129–144.
Lucas, J.M., and M.S. Saccucci. 1990. Exponentially weighted moving average control schemes: Properties and enhancements. *Technometrics* 32: 1–12.
Maravelakis, P.E., and P. Castagliola. 2009. An EWMA chart for monitoring the process standard deviation when parameters are estimated. *Computational Statistics and Data Analysis* 53: 2653–2664.
Mei, Y.J., S.W. Han, and K.L. Tsui. 2011. Early detection of a change in Poisson rate after accounting for population size effects. *Statistica Sinica* 21: 597–624.
Montgomery, D.C. 2013. *Introduction to Statistical Quality Control*. 7th ed. New York, NY: Wiley.
Page, E.S. 1954. Continuous inspection schemes. *Biometrika* 41: 100–115.
Paulino, S., M.C. Morais, and S. Knoth. 2016. An ARL-unbiased c-chart. *Quality and Reliability Engineering International* 32: 2847–2858.
Riaz, M., M. Abid, Z. Abbas, and H.Z. Nazir. 2021. An enhanced approach for the progressive mean control charts: A discussion and comparative analysis. *Quality and Reliability Engineering International* 37: 1–9.
Roberts, S.W. 1959. Control chart tests based on geometric moving averages. *Technometrics* 1: 239–250.
Roberts, S.W. 1966. A comparison of some control chart procedures. *Technometrics* 8: 411–430.
Shamma, Amin R.W., and A.K. Shamma. 1991. A double exponentially weighted moving average control procedure with variable sampling intervals, *Communication in Statistics: Simulation & Comnputation* 20: 511–528.
Shamma, S.E., and A.K. Shamma. 1992. Development and evaluation of control charts using double exponentially weighted moving averages. *International Journal of Quality & Reliability Management* 9: 18–25.
Shewhart, W.A. 1926. Quality control charts. *Bell System Technical Journal* 5: 593–603.
Shewhart, W.A. 1927. Quality control. *Bell Systems Technical Journal* 6: 722–735.
Shu, L., W. Jiang, and Z. Wu. 2012. Exponentially weighted moving average control charts for monitoring increases in Poisson rate. *IIE Transactions* 44: 711–723.
Steiner, S.H. 1999. EWMA control charts with time-varying control limits and fast initial response. *Journal of Quality Technology* 31: 75–86.
White, C.H., J.B. Keats, and J. Stanley. 1997. Poisson CUSUM versus c chart for defect data. *Quality Engineering* 9: 673–679.
Wong, H.B., F.F. Gan, and T.C. Chang. 2004. Designs of moving average control chart. *Journal of Statistical Computation and Simulation* 74: 47–62.

Woodall, W.H., and M.A. Mahmoud. 2005. The inertial properties of quality control charts. *Technometrics* 47: 425–436.

Zhang, G. 2014. Improved *R* and *s* control charts for monitoring the process variance. *Journal of Applied Statistics* 41: 1260–1273.

Zhang, L., and G. Chen. 2005. An extended EWMA mean chart. *Quality Technology & Quantitative Management* 2: 39–52.

7 On the Application of Fractal Interpolation Functions within the Reliability Engineering Framework

Polychronis Manousopoulos and Vasileios Drakopoulos

CONTENTS

7.1 INTRODUCTION

Reliability engineering provides a framework for modelling, monitoring and optimizing the ability of a system or component to function as required, usually within a predetermined time interval and under specific functional and cost conditions. It is useful in a diversity of areas, including, for example, financial, military and production systems, where the ability to predict or prevent a failure is important; see e.g., [1–3] for an overview.

Fractal interpolation, as defined in [4], provides an efficient way of interpolating data that exhibit an irregular and non-smooth structure, possibly presenting details at different scales or some degree of self-similarity. In contrast to traditional interpolation techniques which use smooth functions such as polynomials and produce smooth interpolants, fractal interpolation based on the theory of iterated function

DOI: 10.1201/9781003203124-7

systems [5] is successful, for example, in modelling projections of physical objects such as coastlines and plants, or experimental data of non-integral dimension.

In this chapter, we focus on the application of fractal interpolation within the reliability engineering framework. Specifically, we explore application areas where the reliability data, such as occurrences or frequency of failures, exhibit irregular, non-smooth patterns. In these cases, fractal interpolation provides an efficient way for modelling and predicting a system's functioning and reliability.

7.2 ITERATED FUNCTION SYSTEM

Let (X,ρ) be a complete metric space, e.g., $(A \subseteq \mathbb{R}^n, \|\cdot\|)$. A function $f : X \to X$ is called a *Lipschitz function*, if there exists $k \in \mathbb{R}$ such that $\rho(f(x), f(y)) \le k\,\rho(x,y)$ for all $x, y \in X$; obviously, it is $k \ge 0$. If $k < 1$, then the function f is called a *contraction* with respective *contractivity factor* k. Let $\mathcal{H}(X)$ denote the set of non-empty, compact subsets of X. The metric space $(\mathcal{H}(X), h)$, where h is an appropriate metric such as the Hausdorff metric, is often called the "space of fractals," but it is noted that not every member of $\mathcal{H}(X)$ is necessarily a fractal.

An *iterated function system* (*IFS*) is the collection of a complete metric space (X,ρ) together with a finite set of continuous mappings $w_n : X \to X, n = 1,2,\ldots,N$. An IFS is often denoted as $\{X; w_n, n = 1,2,\ldots,N\}$. If all mappings w_n are contractions with respective contractivity factors $s_n, n = 1,2,\ldots,N$, then the IFS is called *hyperbolic* with contractivity factor $s = \max_{n=1,\ldots,N} s_n$. Let $W : \mathcal{H}(X) \to \mathcal{H}(X)$ be a mapping defined as $W(B) = \bigcup_{n=1}^{N} w_n(B)$, where $B \in \mathcal{H}(X)$ and $w_n(B) = \{w_n(b), b \in B\}$. The *attractor* of a hyperbolic IFS is the unique set $\mathcal{A} \in \mathcal{H}(X)$ for which it is $\mathcal{A} = W(\mathcal{A}) = \lim_{n\to\infty} W^n(B)$ for every $B \in \mathcal{H}(X)$, where W^n denotes the n-fold composition $W \circ W \circ \cdots \circ W$. In other words, the attractor $\mathcal{A}$ is the unique fixed point of W and every set $B \in \mathcal{H}(X)$ converges to it under successive applications of W. The second property justifies the use of the term attractor and provides the basis for the computational construction of the attractor of a given IFS, namely using the *deterministic iteration algorithm* or the *random iteration algorithm* (see e.g., [5]).

7.3 FRACTAL INTERPOLATION FUNCTIONS ON $\mathbb{R}^2$

Let Δ_1 be a partition of the real compact interval $I = [a,b]$, i.e., $\Delta_1 = \{u_0, u_1, \ldots, u_M\}$ where $a = u_0 < u_1 < \cdots < u_M = b$. The set of *data points* is represented as $P = \{(u_m, v_m) \in I \times \mathbb{R}, m = 0,1,\ldots,M\}$. Let Δ_2 be another partition of $I = [a,b]$, i.e., $\Delta_2 = \{x_0, x_1, \ldots, x_N\}$ where $a = x_0 < x_1 < \cdots < x_N = b$, such that Δ_1 is a refinement of Δ_2. The set of *interpolation points* is represented as $Q = \{(x_i, y_i) \in I \times \mathbb{R}, i = 0,1,\ldots,N \le M\}$ and it is a subset of the data points, i.e., $Q \subseteq P$. The subintervals of Δ_2, i.e., $[x_i, x_{i+1}]$, $i = 0,1,\ldots,N-1$, are called *interpolation intervals*; the abscissas x_i of the interpolation points may be chosen equidistantly or not. The set of data points within the nth interpolation interval $I_n = [x_{n-1}, x_n], n = 1,2,\ldots,N$, is represented as $P_n = \{(u_m, v_m) : x_{n-1} \le u_m \le x_n\}$; obviously, it is $P = \bigcup_{n=1}^{N} P_n$.

An *affine transformation* is defined as the composition of a linear transformation and a translation. Let $\{\mathbb{R}^2; w_n, n = 1,2,\ldots,N\}$ be an *iterated function system* (*IFS*) with affine transformations

$$w_n \begin{bmatrix} x \\ y \end{bmatrix} = \begin{bmatrix} a_n & 0 \\ c_n & s_n \end{bmatrix} \begin{bmatrix} x \\ y \end{bmatrix} + \begin{bmatrix} d_n \\ e_n \end{bmatrix}$$

constrained to satisfy

$$w_n \begin{bmatrix} x_0 \\ y_0 \end{bmatrix} = \begin{bmatrix} x_{n-1} \\ y_{n-1} \end{bmatrix} \text{ and } w_n \begin{bmatrix} x_N \\ y_N \end{bmatrix} = \begin{bmatrix} x_n \\ y_n \end{bmatrix}$$

for every $n = 1,2,\ldots,N$, i.e., the interval I is mapped by each affine transformation w_n to its corresponding interpolation interval. Solving these constraint equations leads to

$$a_n = \frac{x_n - x_{n-1}}{x_N - x_0},\ d_n = \frac{x_N x_{n-1} - x_0 x_n}{x_N - x_0}$$

$$c_n = \frac{y_n - y_{n-1}}{x_N - x_0} - s_n \frac{y_N - y_0}{x_N - x_0},\ e_n = \frac{x_N y_{n-1} - x_0 y_n}{x_N - x_0} - s_n \frac{x_N y_0 - x_0 y_N}{x_N - x_0} \ //$$

i.e., the real numbers a_n, c_n, d_n, e_n are uniquely determined by the interpolation points, while the real numbers s_n are *free parameters* of the transformations constrained to satisfy $|s_n| < 1, n = 1,2,\ldots,N$, in order to guarantee that the resulting IFS is *hyperbolic* with respect to an appropriate metric. The transformations w_n are *shear* transformations. In other words, they map line segments parallel to the y-axis to line segments also parallel to the y-axis contracted by a factor $|s_n|$. For this reason, the parameters s_n are called *vertical scaling factors* or *contractivity factors* of the transformations w_n.

The attractor of the aforementioned IFS, i.e., the unique set $G = \bigcup_{n=1}^{N} w_n(G)$, is the graph of a continuous function $f : [x_0, x_N] \to \mathbb{R}$ that passes through all interpolation points $(x_i, y_i), i = 0,1,\ldots,N$. This function is called *fractal interpolation function* (*FIF*) corresponding to these points. It is a *self-affine* function since each affine transformation w_n maps the entire graph of the function to its section within the corresponding interpolation interval. An example of a fractal interpolation function is depicted in Figure 7.1, where a set of 10 interpolation points is used along with vertical scaling factors $s_n = 0.3$, $n = 1,\ldots,10$. We note that even from a simple set of few points a complicated interpolant is generated.

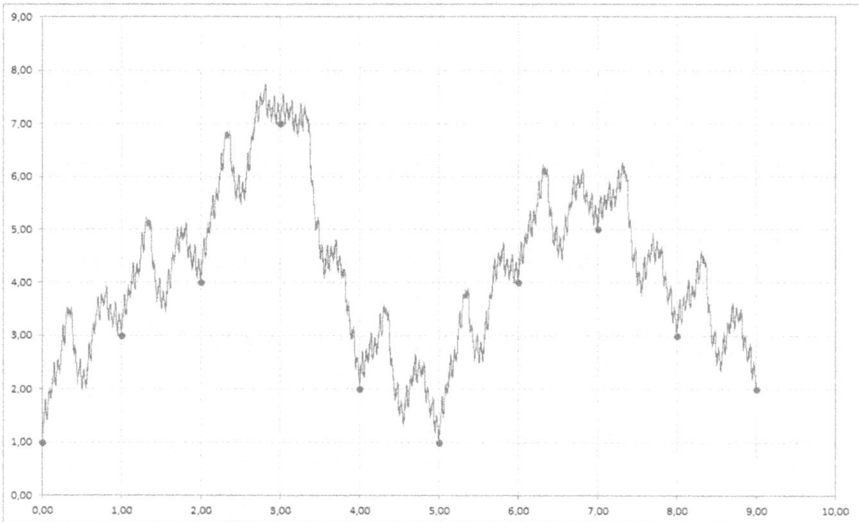

FIGURE 7.1 A fractal interpolation function constructed using the set of interpolation points $Q = \{(0,1),(1,3),(2,4),(3,7),(4,2),(5,1),(6,4),(7,5),(8,3),(9,2)\}$ and the vertical scaling factors $s_n = 0.3,\ n = 1,\ldots,10$.

The *remaining data points* $P \setminus Q$ are *approximated* by the fractal interpolation function, since it does not necessarily pass through them. In order to optimize the closeness of fit, various methods have been proposed in the literature for determining the vertical scaling factors, the only free parameters for a given set P. In most of the cases, the vertical scaling factors are calculated so as to minimize an error measure. This is commonly the squared error between the ordinates of the original and the reconstructed points $\sum_{m=0}^{M} \left(v_m - G\left[u_m\right]\right)^2$, where $G\left[u_m\right]$ is the attractor ordinate at abscissa u_m, or the Hausdorff distance $h(P,G)$. For example, in [6] an algebraic and a geometric method is proposed for minimizing the squared error; the first one provides analytical calculation of the factors, while the second one exploits geometric properties of the data. In [7, 8] the use of bounding volumes, namely bounding rectangles and convex hulls, of data points subsets is suggested; in both cases the target is optimizing the fit of original and transformed bounding volumes instead of individual points. Alternative methods include, for example, the use of fractal dimension [9], where the target is the preservation of the fractal dimension of the data points and not the minimization of an error measure; the use of wavelets is proposed in [10], where the target is the detection of self-affinity and the related vertical scaling factors in the continuous wavelet transform of the data. An example is presented in Figure 7.2, where a set of 37 data points is interpolated by a fractal interpolation function using every 3rd points as interpolation points, i.e., 13 points in total; the vertical scaling factors are calculated by the analytic algorithm of [6]. We note that despite the use of only approximately 1/3 of the data points and the simple,

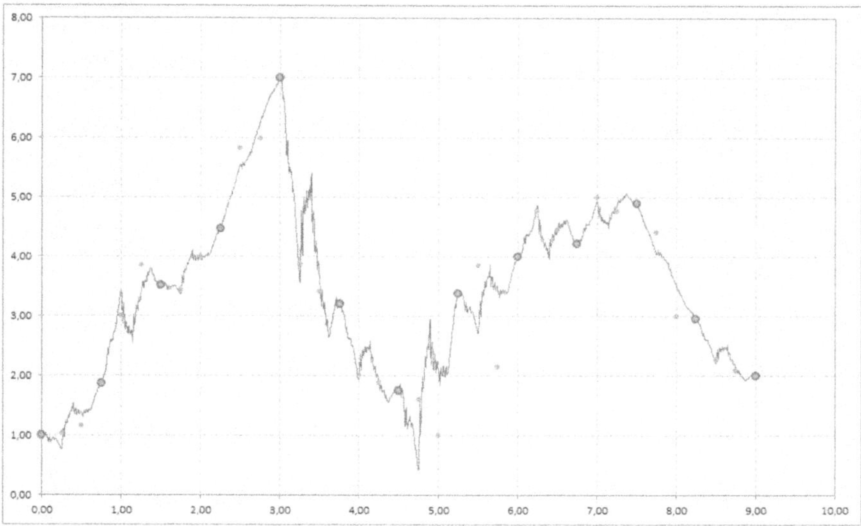

FIGURE 7.2 A fractal interpolation function constructed using a set of 13 interpolation points (red) selected from a set of 37 data points (green). The vertical scaling factors have been calculated by the analytic algorithm of [6].

symmetric definition of the interpolation intervals, the resulting interpolant approximates rather well the remaining data points.

Obviously, one could use all data points as interpolation points thus assuring that the resulting fractal interpolation function passes through all of them. While this may initially seem attractive, it is not always desirable in practice. A proper selection of interpolation points, in addition to the calculation of the vertical scaling factors as previously described, will result in a fractal interpolation function that achieves adequate goodness of fit, while offering a considerable compression ratio and avoiding overfitting. The selection of the interpolation points can be done either symmetrically, i.e., choosing every i-th data point as interpolation point, or algorithmically in order to minimize some error measure, see e.g., [6].

7.4 RECURRENT FRACTAL INTERPOLATION FUNCTIONS ON $\mathbb{R}^2$

The recurrent fractal interpolation functions are a generalization of the fractal interpolation functions defined in the previous section by extending the property of self-affinity. Initially, the partitions Δ_1 and Δ_2, the set P of data points and its subsets P_n, the set Q of interpolation points and the interpolation intervals I_n are defined exactly as in the previous section. Additionally, each interpolation interval is associated with a pair of data points called *address points*. Specifically, each interpolation interval $I_n = \left[x_{n-1}, x_n\right], n = 1,2,\ldots,N$ is associated with the distinct data points $\left(x'_{n,1}, y'_{n,1}\right)$, $\left(x'_{n,2}, y'_{n,2}\right) \in P$, i.e., $\left(x'_{n,k}, y'_{n,k}\right) = \left(u_{m_k}, v_{m_k}\right)$ for $k = 1,2$

and some $m_k \in \{0,1,\ldots,M\}$. Each pair of address points defines the corresponding *address interval* $\left[x'_{n,1}, x'_{n,2}\right]$, where $x'_{n,1} < x'_{n,2}$ by definition. The address points are not necessarily unique among interpolation intervals, i.e., a data point may be used in the definition of more than one address interval. Moreover, every address interval should have strictly greater length than its corresponding interpolation interval, i.e., $\left(x'_{n,2} - x'_{n,1}\right) > \left(x_n - x_{n-1}\right)$, for all $n = 1,2,\ldots,N$. The set of data points within the nth address interval $I'_n = \left[x'_{n,1}, x'_{n,2}\right], n = 1,2,\ldots,N$, is represented as $A_n = \left\{\left(u_m, v_m\right) : x'_{n,1} \le u_m \le x'_{n,2}\right\}$.

Let $\left\{\mathbb{R}^2; w_n, n = 1,2,\ldots,N\right\}$ be an iterated function system (IFS) with affine transformations

$$w_n = \begin{bmatrix} x \\ y \end{bmatrix} = \begin{bmatrix} a_n & 0 \\ c_n & s_n \end{bmatrix} \begin{bmatrix} x \\ y \end{bmatrix} + \begin{bmatrix} d_n \\ e_n \end{bmatrix}$$

constrained to satisfy

$$w_n \begin{bmatrix} x'_{n,1} \\ y'_{n,1} \end{bmatrix} = \begin{bmatrix} x_{n-1} \\ y_{n-1} \end{bmatrix} \text{ and } w_n \begin{bmatrix} x'_{n,2} \\ y'_{n,2} \end{bmatrix} = \begin{bmatrix} x_n \\ y_n \end{bmatrix}$$

For every $n = 1,2,\ldots,N$, i.e., each address interval is mapped to its corresponding interpolation interval. Solving these constraint equations leads to

$$a_n = \frac{x_n - x_{n-1}}{x'_{n,2} - x'_{n,1}}, d_n = \frac{x'_{n,2} x_{n-1} - x'_{n,1} x_n}{x'_{n,2} - x'_{n,1}}$$

$$c_n = \frac{y_n - y_{n-1}}{x'_{n,2} - x'_{n,1}} - s_n \frac{y'_{n,2} - y'_{n,1}}{x'_{n,2} - x'_{n,1}},\ e_n = \frac{x'_{n,2} y_{n-1} - x'_{n,1} y_n}{x'_{n,2} - x'_{n,1}} - s_n \frac{x'_{n,2} y'_{n,1} - x'_{n,1} y'_{n,2}}{x'_{n,2} - x'_{n,1}}$$

i.e., the real numbers a_n, c_n, d_n, e_n are uniquely determined by the interpolation points and the address points, while the real numbers s_n are free parameters of the transformations constrained to satisfy $\left|s_n\right| < 1, n = 1,2,\ldots,N$, in order to guarantee that the resulting IFS is hyperbolic with respect to an appropriate metric. As previously, the transformations w_n are shear transformations and the parameters s_n are called vertical scaling factors or contractivity factors of the transformations w_n.

The attractor of the aforementioned IFS, i.e., the unique set $G = \bigcup_{n=1}^{N} w_n(G)$, is the graph of a continuous function $f : \left[x_0, x_N\right] \to \mathbb{R}$ that passes through all interpolation points $\left(x_i, y_i\right), i = 0,1,\ldots,N$. This function is called *recurrent fractal interpolation function* (*RFIF*) corresponding to these points. It is a *piecewise self-affine* function since each affine transformation w_n maps the part of the graph of the function within the corresponding address interval to its section within the corresponding interpolation interval. An example of a recurrent fractal interpolation

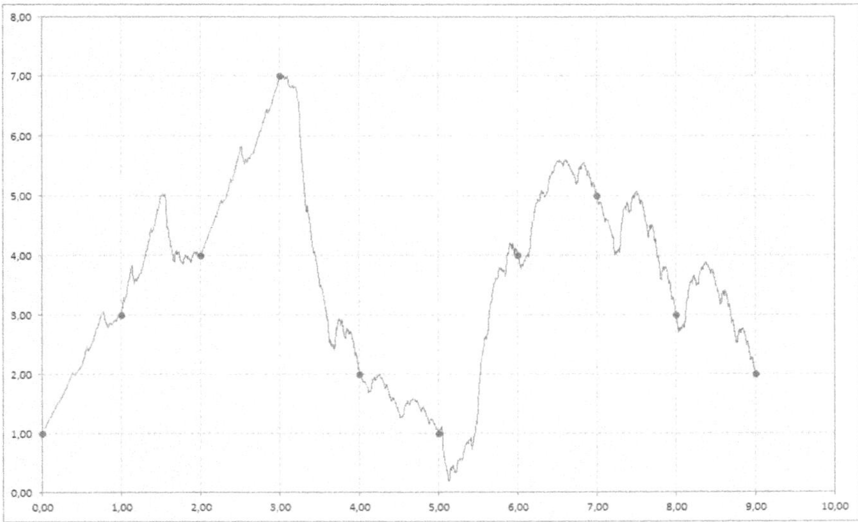

FIGURE 7.3 A recurrent fractal interpolation function constructed using the set of interpolation points Q of Figure 7.1. The address intervals are $\{[Q^0,Q^2],$ $[Q^1,Q^5],[Q^0,Q^3],[Q^2,Q^7],[Q^7,Q^9],[Q^3,Q^8],[Q^5,Q^8],[Q^4,Q^9],[Q^5,Q^9]\}$, where Q^i denotes the i-th interpolation point, and the vertical scaling factors are $s_n = 0.3, n = 1,\ldots,10$.

function is depicted in Figure 7.3, where the set of interpolation points of Figure 7.1 is used, while the address intervals are distinct and the vertical scaling factors are $s_n = 0.3$, $n = 1,\ldots,10$. We note that even though the same vertical scaling factors as in Figure 7.1 have been used, the resulting interpolant is smoother. This is due to the fact that each address intervals contains fewer interpolation points than the whole function, thus resulting in smaller variation within the respective interpolation interval to which it is mapped.

The *remaining data points* $P \setminus Q$ are *approximated* by the recurrent fractal interpolation function, since it does not necessarily pass through them. In order to optimize the closeness of fit, the vertical scaling factors are determined by methods similar to those described in the previous section for the fractal interpolation functions. Usually, the vertical scaling factors are calculated so as to minimize an error measure, using algebraic and geometric methods [6], or bounding volumes [7, 8]. Alternative methods include, for example, the use of fractal dimension [9], or wavelets [10]. The remarks made in the previous section about the selection of the interpolation points apply here as well. An example is presented in Figure 7.4, where the set of data points and interpolation points of Figure 7.2 is used, the address intervals are of variable length and the vertical scaling factors are calculated by the analytic algorithm of [6]. We note that the recurrent interpolant approximates even better the remaining data points. This is achieved by allowing partial, piecewise self-affinity

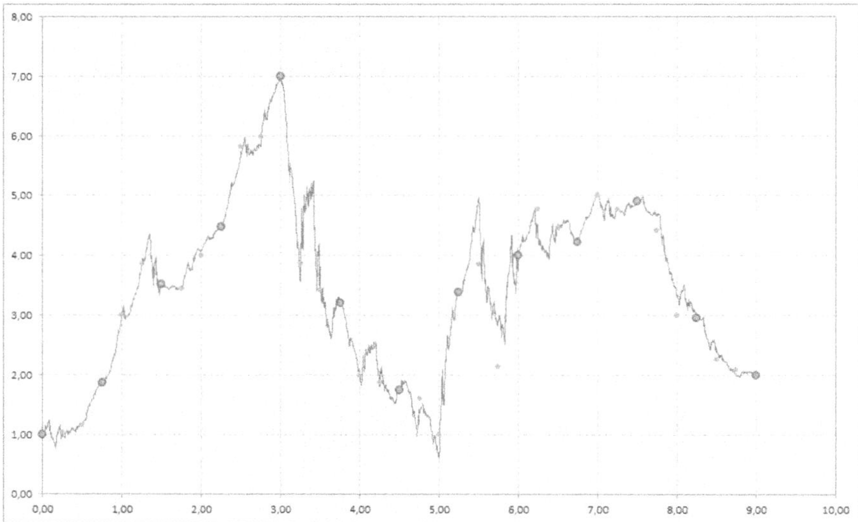

FIGURE 7.4 A recurrent fractal interpolation function constructed using the interpolation points (red) and data points (green) of Figure 7.2. The address intervals are $\left[P^{18},P^{36}\right]$, $\left[P^{0},P^{15}\right]$, $\left[P^{9},P^{18}\right]$, $\left[P^{0},P^{30}\right]$, $\left[P^{0},P^{36}\right]$, $\left[P^{0},P^{33}\right]$, $\left[P^{0},P^{18}\right]$, $\left[P^{6},P^{24}\right]$, $\left[P^{3},P^{36}\right]$, $\left[P^{9},P^{18}\right]$, $\left[P^{3},P^{27}\right]$, $\left[P^{18},P^{36}\right]$, where P^{i} denotes the i-th data point, while the vertical scaling factors have been calculated by the analytic algorithm of [6].

and not only total self-affinity, as is the case for the fractal interpolation function of Figure 7.2.

7.5 RELIABILITY DATA MODELLING

Within the reliability engineering framework, one usually deals with datasets that describe the operation or the failures of a system or a component. Two main tasks have to be accomplished with these datasets, namely modelling and prediction. The former includes the application of a mathematical model to the dataset, aiming mainly at gaining insight into the dataset's properties and structure. The latter includes estimating values beyond the dataset's time span, aiming mainly at predicting and thus preventing future failures. These two tasks are covered in the current and the next section.

In this section, we focus on the area of software reliability engineering which, as the term implies, examines the case of software systems, see e.g., [11] for an overview. Specifically, two tests are performed which include the application of fractal interpolation to the modelling of software reliability data.

The first test is based on the well-known Musa's dataset of software failures [12], which has been extensively studied in the literature, see e.g., [13–15]. Specifically, the dataset represents the failures for the system T1 of the Rome Air Development

TABLE 7.1
The Absolute and Cumulative Number of Weekly Detected Failures for the System T1

Week	Number of Detected Failures	Cumulative Number of Detected Failures
1	2	2
2	0	2
3	0	2
4	1	3
5	1	4
6	2	6
7	1	7
8	9	16
9	13	29
10	2	31
11	11	42
12	2	44
13	11	55
14	14	69
15	18	87
16	12	99
17	12	111
18	15	126
19	6	132
20	3	135
21	1	136

Center (RADC), which was used for a real-time command and control application. The software is reported to consist of approximately 21.700 object instructions, while its testing phase lasted 21 weeks. The dataset contains the absolute and cumulative number of weekly detected failures and is presented in Table 7.1.

We have modelled the absolute number of detected failures with the recurrent fractal interpolation function presented in Figure 7.5. The set of data points corresponds to the absolute number of weekly failures, while every second data point is used as interpolation point, i.e., half of the data points are approximately used. The address intervals have been chosen with variable length, while the vertical scaling factors have been calculated with the analytic algorithm. We observe that the dataset possesses non-smooth structure with significant variance which the fractal interpolant is able to successfully model. It is worth noting that although half of the data points are used, the fluctuations of the dataset are correctly captured; on the contrary, a typical, smooth interpolant, like a cubic spline for example, would not adequately model the entire dataset using the same set of interpolation points.

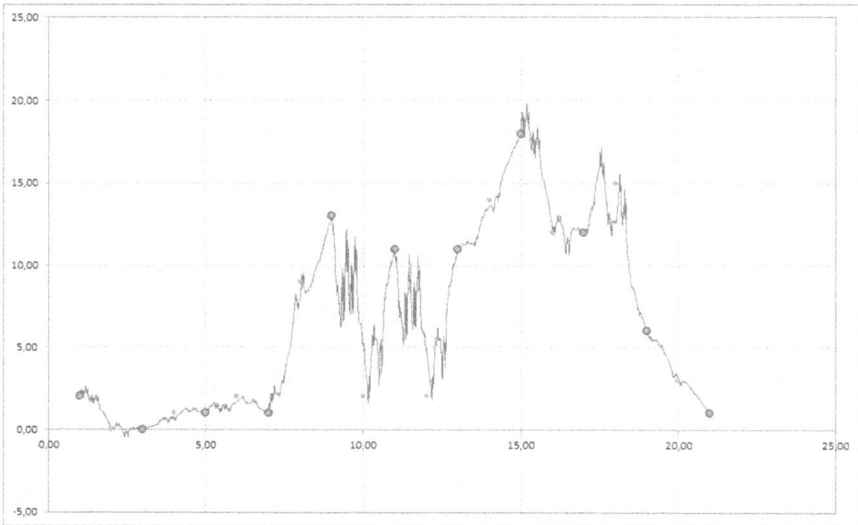

FIGURE 7.5 A dataset of software failures modelled by a recurrent fractal interpolation function; every 2nd data point (green) is used as interpolation point (red), the address intervals are $[P^8, P^{20}]$, $[P^2, P^{20}]$, $[P^6, P^{20}]$, $[P^{14}, P^{20}]$, $[P^6, P^{20}]$, $[P^6, P^{20}]$, $[P^{12}, P^{20}]$, $[P^{10}, P^{20}]$, $[P^{12}, P^{20}]$, $[P^{14}, P^{20}]$, where P^i denotes the i-th data point, while the vertical scaling factors have been calculated by the analytic algorithm of [6].

The second test is based on a larger dataset of software failures. Specifically, the dataset represents the failures for system P1; it is reported in [16] and examined in [14], while it spans a period of 86 months. The dataset contains the absolute and cumulative number of monthly detected failures and is presented in Table 7.2.

We have modelled the absolute number of detected failures with the recurrent fractal interpolation function presented in Figure 7.6. The set of data points corresponds to the absolute number of monthly failures, while every second data point is used as interpolation point. The address intervals have been chosen with fixed length, each containing 11 consecutive data points. For each interpolation interval, the corresponding address interval is chosen between all possible candidates by minimizing the Hausdorff distance between the original and mapped data points, i.e., $A_n = \arg\left\{ \min_{A \in A(P,l)} h\left(P_n, w_n\left(A\right)\right) \right\}$, $n = 1, 2, \ldots, N$, where $A\left(p, l\right)$ denotes the set of subsets of P spanning l consecutive data points. The vertical scaling factors have been calculated with the analytic algorithm. We observe that the dataset possesses significant variance and non-smooth structure, which is more complicated than that of the first dataset. The constructed fractal interpolant is able to successfully model this dataset as well, despite using approximately half of the data points; the fluctuations of the dataset are adequately captured.

TABLE 7.2
The Absolute and Cumulative Number of Weekly Detected Failures for the System P1

Months	Number of Detected Failures	Cumulative Number of Detected Failures	Months	Number of Detected Failures	Cumulative Number of Detected Failures
1	2	2	44	79	1365
2	0	2	45	183	1548
3	0	2	46	129	1677
4	1	3	47	176	1853
5	2	5	48	106	1959
6	2	7	49	62	2021
7	3	10	50	49	2070
8	12	22	51	99	2169
9	8	30	52	43	2212
10	2	32	53	47	2259
11	11	43	54	174	2433
12	2	45	55	179	2612
13	0	45	56	229	2841
14	1	46	57	65	2906
15	0	46	58	66	2972
16	6	52	59	40	3012
17	4	56	60	54	3066
18	0	56	61	31	3097
19	5	61	62	103	3200
20	3	64	63	63	3263
21	2	66	64	107	3370
22	2	68	65	59	3429
23	6	74	66	69	3498
24	7	81	67	78	3576
25	5	86	68	62	3638
26	20	106	69	97	3735
27	34	140	70	58	3793
28	46	186	71	65	3858
29	21	207	72	53	3911
30	55	262	73	139	4050
31	61	323	74	60	4110
32	58	381	75	50	4160
33	60	441	76	70	4230
34	60	501	77	31	4261
35	109	610	78	44	4305
36	76	686	79	63	4368
37	110	796	80	36	4404
38	86	882	81	38	4442

(Continued)

TABLE 7.2 (Continued)

Months	Number of Detected Failures	Cumulative Number of Detected Failures	Months	Number of Detected Failures	Cumulative Number of Detected Failures
39	73	955	82	28	4470
40	63	1018	83	18	4488
41	36	1054	84	17	4505
42	120	1174	85	25	4530
43	112	1286	86	8	4538

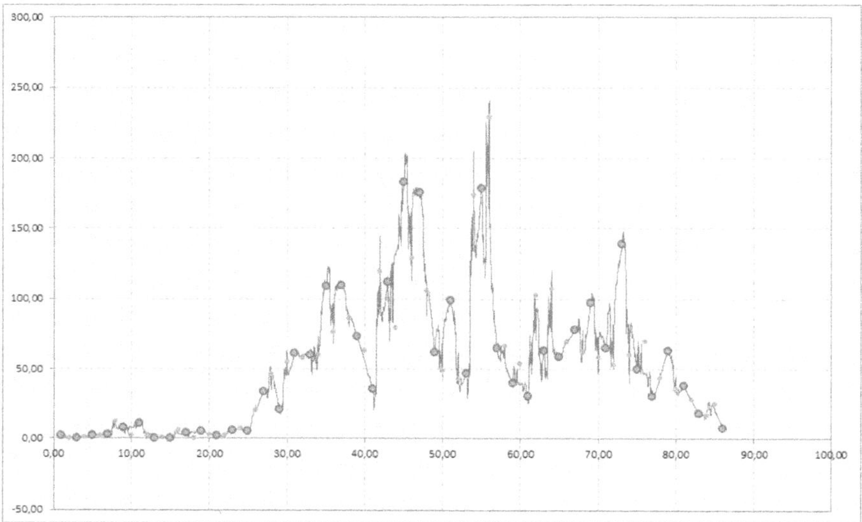

FIGURE 7.6 A dataset of software failures modelled by a recurrent fractal interpolation function; every 2nd data point (green) is used as interpolation point (red), the address intervals have fixed span of 11 data points optimally chosen using the Hausdorff distance as error measure, while the vertical scaling factors have been calculated by the analytic algorithm of [6].

7.6 RELIABILITY DATA PREDICTION

In this section, we examine the prediction of software reliability data using fractal interpolation. In other words, our aim is estimating future reliability values, i.e., values beyond the dataset's time span. The test is based on a software reliability dataset and is performed as follows. Initially, the dataset is split into two subsets, namely a training subset and a testing subset; the former chronologically precedes the latter. A fractal interpolation function is constructed for the training subset and its fractal dimension is calculated. Then the training subset is augmented by adding one or more interpolation points beyond the subset's time span; these extrapolated values are calculated as a function of the l last (in time order) values of the training subset. Then, a new fractal interpolation function is used to model the augmented training subset. The vertical scaling factors are calculated so as to preserve the fractal dimension of the original fractal interpolant. Finally, the predicted values within the new interpolation intervals are compared to the respective values of the testing subset in order to estimate the prediction accuracy. The above procedure is repeated for various different splits of the dataset into training and testing subsets. A constraint to the minimum and maximum number of elements of the training subset is also applied, in order to define a meaningful testing range. The described test is summarized as follows:

1. Let D[1..K] be the dataset, each point denoted as $D[i]=(D[i].x, D[i].y)$, $i=1,2,\ldots,K$.
2. Define the testing range indices K_{min}, K_{max}, where $1<K_{min}<K_{max}<K$, the prediction horizon in periods h and the number of last points l for calculating the new interpolation points.
3. Define the parametrization for generating a fractal interpolation function, i.e., the interpolation interval length and the algorithm for calculating the vertical scaling factors, collectively denoted as P_f.
4. *For* $k=K_{min}$ *to* K_{max}
   4.1. Set the training subset $TR_k=D[k_0..k]$, where $1\le k_0<k$.
   4.2. Set the testing subset $TS_k=D[k+1..K]$
   4.3. Generate the fractal interpolation function $FIF(TR_k,\ P_f)\equiv f_k$ for the training subset TR_k and calculate its fractal dimension D.
   4.4. Generate the interpolation point(s) to add to the training subset as $trp_{k,j}=\left(D[k].x+j\delta_x, Y\left(\{D[i].y\}_{i=k-l+1}^{k}, j\right)\right)$, for $j=1,\ldots,h$, where δ_x denotes the period length.
   4.5. Set the augmented training subset $TR_k^{'}=TR_k\cup\{trp_{k,j}\}$.
   4.6. Generate the fractal interpolation function $FIF(TR_k^{'},\ P_f)\equiv f_k^{'}$ for the augmented training subset $TR_k^{'}$. The vertical scaling factors are calculated such that the fractal dimension of $f_k^{'}$ is $D'=D$.
   4.7. Calculate the prediction error for each point $TS_k[i]$ of the testing subset within the prediction horizon in comparison to the respective estimated point, i.e., $E\left(TS_k[i].y, f_k^{'}(TS_k[i].x)\right)$, where $E(\cdot)$ denotes the error function.

In step 1 of the algorithm, the reliability dataset D is provided. Generally, $D[i].x$ is the time or index of the measurement and $D[i].y$ is the measured reliability value, e.g., the number of system failures. In steps 2 and 3, the parameterization of the algorithm is defined. In step 4, successive prediction tests are performed. In step 4.3, the fractal dimension is calculated as $D=1+\left(\log\sum_{n=1}^{N}|s_n|/\log N\right)$, assuming equidistant interpolation points (see [5]). In step 4.4, it assumed that the dataset has constant period length, i.e., $\delta_x = D[k].x - D[k-1].x$ and it is $(D[i].x - D[i-1].x) = (D[j].x - D[j-1].x)$, for all $i, j \in \{2,\ldots,K\}$ with $i \neq j$; it is possible to extend this to variable period length datasets. In step 4.5, we refer only to interpolation points; the data points within the new interpolation intervals are irrelevant since they are not used in any calculation (as mentioned, the vertical scaling factors are otherwise determined). In step 4.6, the new vertical scaling factors are calculated based on the formula used in step 4.3. For example, in the case of one interpolation interval, in order to have $D' = D$ we may set $|s_{N+1}| = (N+1)^{D-1} - \sum_{n=1}^{N} |s_n|$. In step 4.7, the prediction error can be calculated as (a function of) the absolute error $|TS_k[i].y - f_k(TS_k[i].x)|$, i.e., as (a function of) the difference between the original and reconstructed ordinates. We note that $f_k(TS_k[i].x)$ cannot be calculated analytically, since there does not exist an analytic formula for a fractal interpolation function; it is estimated, to any desirable degree of accuracy, by the closest attractor point.

In Figure 7.7, results of this test are presented. Specifically, the testing algorithm has been executed for the second dataset of the previous section. The testing range is defined by $K_{min} = 60$ and $K_{max} = 80$. Each training subset is defined by $k_0 = k - 30$. The prediction horizon is to $h = 3$ periods ($=$ months), i.e., 3 additional interpolation points have been added to the augmented training subset; each extrapolated value has been calculated using the values of the last $l = 30$ training data points. For the

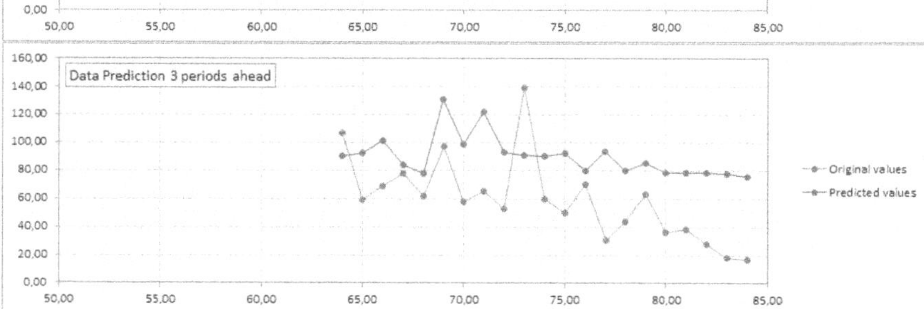

FIGURE 7.7 Comparison of original values (blue) and predicted values (red) of a dataset of software failures, modelled by a fractal interpolation function (details in the text). The predictions in the upper part of the figure are made 1 period beyond the end of the training subset, while the predictions in the lower part of the figure are made 3 periods beyond the end of the training subset.

construction of each fractal interpolation function, every second training data point is used as interpolation point. The vertical scaling factors of the original fractal interpolation functions (step 4.3) have been calculated with the analytic algorithm; their average fractal dimension has been calculated to be $D = 1.2189$. The figure shows the original and predicted values 1 and 3 periods ahead respectively, i.e., the prediction was made 1 or 3 periods beyond the time span of the training subset. We note that in both cases the predictions closely follow the dataset and its fluctuations, implying that the fractal interpolants have properly modelled the underlying dataset.

7.7 CONCLUSIONS

In this chapter, we have examined the application of fractal interpolation to the field of reliability engineering. We have seen that indeed there exist areas in this field, where the reliability data to be modelled or predicted possess a non-smooth structure with significant fluctuations, thus rendering fractal interpolation a reasonable methodology to choose. Specifically, we have tested the use of (recurrent) fractal interpolation functions to both modelling and predicting software reliability data, namely datasets of periodic software system failures. The results indicate that fractal interpolation is useful in this application, being able to encapsulate the intrinsic non-smooth nature of these datasets. The constructed (recurrent) fractal interpolation functions have been successful in both modelling and predicting the tested datasets; in other words, they have exhibited both in-sample and out-of-sample satisfactory performance. Further work will focus on creating a generic, systematic framework for modelling and predicting reliability data based on a fractal interpolation methodology.

REFERENCES

[1] A. Birolini. *Reliability Engineering: Theory and Practice* (8th ed.). Springer-Verlag, 2017.
[2] H. Pham (ed.). *Handbook of Reliability Engineering*. Springer-Verlag, 2003.
[3] I. Vonta and M. Ram (eds.). *Reliability Engineering: Theory and Applications*. CRC Press. 2019.
[4] M. F. Barnsley. Fractal functions and interpolation. *Constructive Approximation*, 2:303–329, 1986.
[5] M. F. Barnsley. *Fractals Everywhere* (3rd ed.). Dover Publications, Inc., 2012.
[6] D. S. Mazel and M. H. Hayes. Using iterated function systems to model discrete sequences. *IEEE Transactions on Signal Processing*, 40(7):1724–1734, 1992.
[7] P. Manousopoulos, V. Drakopoulos and T. Theoharis. Parameter identification of 1D fractal interpolation functions using bounding volumes. *Journal of Computational and Applied Mathematics*, 233(4):1063–1082, 2009.
[8] P. Manousopoulos, V. Drakopoulos and T. Theoharis. Parameter identification of 1D recurrent fractal interpolation functions with applications to imaging and signal processing. *Journal of Mathematical Imaging and Vision*, 40:162–170, 2011.
[9] S. Uemura, M. Haseyama and H. Kitajima. Efficient contour shape description by using fractal interpolation functions. *IEEE Proceedings of International Conference on Image Processing*, 485–488, 2002.
[10] R. Brinks. A hybrid algorithm for the solution of the inverse problem in fractal interpolation. *Fractals*, 13(3):215–226, 2005.

[11] M. R. Lyu. Software reliability engineering: A roadmap. *IEEE Proceedings of Future of Software Engineering*, 153–170, 2007.
[12] A. Iannino and J. D. Musa. Software reliability. *Advances in Computers*, 30:85–170, 1990.
[13] N. Davies, J. M. Marriott, D. W. Wightman and A. Bendell. The Musa data revisited: Alternative methods and structure in software reliability modelling and analysis. *Achieving Safety and Reliability with Computer Systems*, 118–130, 1987.
[14] C. Y. Huang and T. Y. Hung. Software reliability analysis and assessment using queueing models with multiple change-points. *Computers and Mathematics with Applications*, 60:2015–2030, 2010.
[15] N. Ullah, M. Morisio and A. Vetro. A comparative analysis of software reliability growth models using defects data of closed and open source software. *IEEE Proceedings of 35th Annual Software Engineering Workshop*, 187–192, 2012.
[16] K. Z. Yang. An infinite server queueing model for software readiness assessment and related performance measures, PhD Dissertation, Department of Electrical Engineering and Computer Science, Syracuse University, Syracuse, NY, 1996.

8 The EWMA Control Chart for Lifetime Monitoring with Failure censoring Reliability Tests and Replacement

Petros E. Maravelakis

CONTENTS

8.1 INTRODUCTION

Statistical Process Monitoring (SPM) is a collection of methods to monitor a process aiming at the continuous improvement of its quality. Control charts is the method mainly used to achieve the above-mentioned goal. They are able to detect both small and large shifts in a process. Shewhart control charts are used to detect large shifts whereas Cumulative Sum (CUSUM) charts and Exponentially Weighted Moving Average charts (EWMA) are used to detect small to moderate shifts in a process (see for example Montgomery (2013)).

A control chart plots on the horizontal axis the sample number or the time that a sample from the process was drawn and on the vertical axis a statistic of the characteristic (or characteristics) measured for each sample or for the time of the horizontal axis. The successive points are connected using a straight line showing the process output in terms of the measured characteristic(s) in time or in successive samples. The chart is also accompanied by the control limits (upper (UCL) and lower (LCL)) and the center line (CL). A process is considered to be in control when the line

DOI: 10.1201/9781003203124-8

connecting the sequence of points does not cross UCL or LCL. If a point plots above UCL or below LCL then the process is considered to be out of control. In such a case, management has to take on corrective actions in order to reassure that the process will return to the in-control state.

Control charts have been used to monitor a variety of processes in diverse fields such us industry, health care and reliability. A main target in reliability is the monitoring of the lifetime of products. The lifetime is most of the times modelled using a continuous non-negative distribution like the exponential, the lognormal or the weibull. A lot of authors have used control charts to monitor the lifetime of products (see for example Arif et al. (2016), Aslam and Jun (2015), Aslam, Khan and Jun (2016), Batson et al. (2006), Faraz et al. (2015), Raza et al. (2015, 2016), Steiner (1999), Steiner and Jock Mackay (2000), Tsai and Lin (2009), Xu and Jeske (2018), Zhang and Chen (2004) and Zhang, Tsung and Xiang (2016)).

Life testing is time consuming and because of this fact researchers have used a variety of techniques to conduct the test in reduced time. The most known techniques are failure censoring (type II censoring), time censoring (type I censoring), progressive censoring and truncated life testing. In type II censoring, the products are simultaneously tested and the test stops when a specific number of failures is observed (see for example Rasay and Arshad (2020)). In type I censoring, the test ends when the available time for the test has ended (see for example Xu and Jeske (2018)). In Aslam and Jun (2015) and Aslam, Khan and Jun (2016) truncated life testing is applied. Triantafyllou (2021) proposed a non-parametric Shewhart control chart based on progressive censoring.

It must be stressed that censoring is usually used in lifetime testing due to the increased time of the duration of a test. The censoring schemes are either with or without replacement. There are a lot of papers that studied the without replacement policy (see for example Dickinson et al. (2014), Xu and Jeske (2018)) but few papers for the with replacement case.

The aim of this paper is to propose an EWMA control chart to monitor the lifetime of products assumed to follow an exponential distribution. The chart is designed for the case of type II censoring. It is assumed that n items are tested at the same time (the test starts simultaneously for all the items) and the test ends when the *sth* failure is observed. It is further assumed that when the failure of an item occurs the item is immediately replaced by a new one, therefore the total number of items under inspection is equal to n throughout the test. Rasay and Arshad (2020) proposed a Shewhart for this case.

The remaining of the paper is organized as follows. In Section 8.2, the proposed EWMA control chart is presented. In Section 8.3, the Run Length properties of the proposed chart are given using the Markov Chain approach. Section 8.4, presents the performance of the proposed EWMA control chart and it also compares this chart to the Shewhart chart of Rasay and Arshad (2020). An example of the use of the chart is given in Section 8.5, followed by the conclusions.

8.2 THE PROPOSED EWMA CHART

In this section is presented the proposed EWMA control chart for lifetime monitoring under failure censoring reliability tests with replacement (for general information concerning the EWMA chart see for example Lucas and Saccucci (1990)). Let us define by Y_i the lifetime of items $i = 1, 2, \dots$ that is exponentially distributed with failure rate $1/r$, for some $r > 0$. Therefore, the probability density function of Y is given by

$$f_Y\left(y|r\right)=\begin{cases}\frac{e^{-y/r}}{r}, & \text{if } y\geq 0\\ 0, & \text{if } y<0\end{cases} \tag{8.1}$$

The main goal here is to monitor the mean of Y and since $E(Y) = r$ the aim is to monitor r, that is the mean lifetime.

It has to be stressed that the exponential distribution is the proper model used when the failure rate is constant which is the result of a Poisson process. The mean time to failure is given by r. Several applications of the exponential distribution for lifetime data have been proposed in the literature (see, e.g. Li et al. (2021), Nasar et al. (2021), Fan and Wang (2021)). It is demonstrated that a variety of processes are properly modelled using the exponential distribution. For a detailed list see O'Connor and Kleyner (2012).

In order to perform a life testing initially there is the need to select a random sample of n items from the process. All of these items are used in the test and every time an item fails in the test, it is immediately replaced by a new one. Under this perspective the sample size remains constant and equal to n. An assumption here is that the time needed for each replacement is approximately equal to zero.

The assumption of zero time for replacement is actually imposed to make the calculations easier to interpret since the time needed for the control chart to signal is attributed to internal characteristics of the process only. In real-world applications this assumption holds in automated processes where the replacement of a failured item takes place in almost zero time because the operator does not have to do actually anything. The case of different assumptions for the time needed to replace an item that has failed is presented in Stapelberg (2009). There are several choices in this case for example to assume a constant replacement time or to assume that this time is distributed with a proper model taking into account the possible different replacement strategies, the available personnel to perform the replacement etc.

Let us define by N_t the number of items that fail in time t from the beginning of the test, then N_t follows the Poisson distribution with parameter nt/r.

Therefore, the probability to observe s failed items in time t is equal to

$$P\left(N_t=s\right)=\frac{e^{-nt/r}\left(nt/r\right)^s}{s!}, s=0,1,2,\dots \tag{8.2}$$

where $s = 0, 1, 2, \dots$

Let us now define by V_s the elapsed time until the *sth* failure in a life test. It is well known that the time between events in a Poisson process follows an exponential distribution. It is also known that the exponential distribution with parameter $1/r$ is equal to the gamma distribution with parameters $(1, 1/r)$. Therefore, the time until the observation of the *sth* failure is gamma distributed with shape parameter s and scale parameter n/r_0 where $1/r_0$ is the target value of the failure rate. Keeping in mind the relationship between the gamma and the chi-square distribution it is obvious that $2n\frac{1}{r_0}V_s$ is chi-square distributed with $2s$ degrees of freedom.

Let $V_s^i, i = 1,2,...,$ be the lifetime of product items, from the start of a test till the *sth* failure, of the sample *i* comprising of *n* items. Let Z_1, Z_2, . . . be the EWMA sequence obtained from $2n\frac{1}{r_0}V_s^1, 2n\frac{1}{r_0}V_s^2,...,$ i.e., for $i \in \{1, 2, . . .\}$

$$Z_i = (1-\lambda)Z_{i-1} + \lambda\left(2n\frac{1}{r_0}V_s^i\right) \tag{8.3}$$

where $Z_0 = 2s$ and $\lambda \in (0,1]$ is a smoothing constant. If the observations V_s^i are independent random variables and since $2n\frac{1}{r_0}V_s^i$ is chi-square distributed with $2s$ degrees of freedom the variance of Z_i is equal to

$$Var(Z_i) = 4s\frac{\lambda}{2-\lambda}[1-(1-\lambda)^{2i}]. \tag{8.4}$$

The control limits of the proposed EWMA chart are equal to

$$LCL = 2s - 2K\sqrt{s\frac{\lambda}{2-\lambda}[1-(1-\lambda)^{2i}]}, \tag{8.5}$$

$$UCL = 2s + 2K\sqrt{s\frac{\lambda}{2-\lambda}[1-(1-\lambda)^{2i}]}, \tag{8.6}$$

where $K > 0$ is a constant. If the control chart has been running for some time then the control limits converge to the following values

$$LCL = 2s - 2K\sqrt{s\frac{\lambda}{2-\lambda}}, \tag{8.7}$$

$$UCL = 2s + 2K\sqrt{s\frac{\lambda}{2-\lambda}}, \tag{8.8}$$

Note that the control limits given in (8.5) and (8.6) should be used when the number of the plotted observations is small.

8.3 RUN LENGTH PROPERTIES OF THE PROPOSED CHART

The Run Length properties of the proposed EWMA chart are computed through the Markov chain approach of Brook and Evans (1972). Initially, the interval [*LCL*, *UCL*] is divided into $2m + 1$ subintervals

$$(H_j - \Delta, H_j + \Delta], j \in \{-m,...,0,...,+m\}$$

where

$$\Delta = \frac{UCL - LCL}{2(2m+1)}$$

and

$$H_j = \frac{LCL + UCL}{2} + 2j\Delta$$

is the center of each subinterval. Each subinterval $(H_j - \Delta, H_j + \Delta]$, $j \in \{-m, \ldots, 0, \ldots, +m\}$, represents a transient state of a Markov chain. If $V_s^i \in (H_j - \Delta, H_j + \Delta]$ then the Markov chain is in transient state $j \in \{-m, ..., 0, ..., +m\}$ for sample i. If $Z_i \notin (H_j - \Delta, H_j + \Delta]$ then the Markov chain reached the absorbing state. It is assumed that H_j is the representative value of state $j \in \{-m, \ldots, 0, \ldots, +m\}$. Let $\mathbf{Q}$ be the $(2m + 1, 2m + 1)$ submatrix of probabilities $Q_{j,k}$ corresponding to the $2m + 1$ transient states defined above, i.e.

$$\mathbf{Q} = \begin{pmatrix} Q_{-m,-m} & \cdots & Q_{-m,-1} & Q_{-m,0} & Q_{-m,+1} & \cdots & Q_{-m,+m} \\ \vdots & \vdots & \vdots & \vdots & \vdots & \vdots & \vdots \\ Q_{-1,-m} & \cdots & Q_{-1,-1} & Q_{-1,0} & Q_{-1,+1} & \cdots & Q_{-1,+m} \\ Q_{0,-m} & \cdots & Q_{0,-1} & Q_{0,0} & Q_{0,+1} & \cdots & Q_{0,+m} \\ Q_{+1,-m} & \cdots & Q_{+1,-1} & Q_{+1,0} & Q_{+1,+1} & \cdots & Q_{+1,+m} \\ \vdots & \vdots & \vdots & \vdots & \vdots & \vdots & \vdots \\ Q_{+m,-m} & \cdots & Q_{+m,-1} & Q_{+m,0} & Q_{+m,+1} & \cdots & Q_{+m,+m} \end{pmatrix}$$

By definition, it holds that $Q_{j,k} = P\,(Z_i \in (H_k - \Delta, H_k + \Delta] | Z_{i-1} = H_j)$ or, equivalently, $Q_{j,k} = P\,(Z_i \le H_k + \Delta | Z_{i-1} = H_j) - P\,(Z_i \le H_k - \Delta | Z_{i-1} = H_j)$. Replacing $Z_i = (1 - \lambda)Z_{i-1} + \lambda V_s^i$, $Z_{i-1} = H_j$ and solving for $2n\frac{1}{r_0}V_s^i$ gives

$$\begin{aligned} Q_{j,k} &= P\left(2n\frac{1}{r_0}V_s^i \le 2n\frac{H_k + \Delta - (1-\lambda)H_j}{r_0\lambda}\right) - P\left(2n\frac{1}{r_0}V_s^i \le 2n\frac{H_k - \Delta - (1-\lambda)H_j}{r_0\lambda}\right) \\ &= F_{\chi^2}\left(2n\frac{H_k + \Delta - (1-\lambda)H_j}{r_0\lambda} \,|\, 2s\right) - F_{\chi^2}\left(2n\frac{H_k - \Delta - (1-\lambda)H_j}{r_0\lambda} \,|\, 2s\right), \end{aligned}$$

where $F_\chi 2\,(\ldots|2s)$ is the chi square c.d.f. (cumulative distribution function) with $2s$ degrees of freedom, that is

$$F_{\chi^2}\left(y|2s\right) = \frac{1}{\Gamma(s)}\gamma\left(s, \frac{y}{2}\right), y \ge 0,$$

$\Gamma(.)$ is the gamma function and $\gamma(.,.)$ is the incomplete gamma function.

Let $\mathbf{q} = (q_{-m}, \ldots, q_0, \ldots, q_m)^T$ be the $(2m+1, 1)$ vector of initial probabilities whose elements correspond to the $2m + 1$ transient states, where

$$q_j = \begin{cases} 0 \text{ if } Z_0 \notin (H_j - \Delta, H_j + \Delta] \\ 1 \text{ if } Z_0 \in (H_j - \Delta, H_j + \Delta] \end{cases}.$$

The Run Length properties of the proposed EWMA chart can now be effectively computed as long as the number $2m + 1$ of subintervals in matrix $\mathbf{Q}$ is sufficiently large (for all the computations in this paper we use $m = 200$, that is $2m + 1 = 401$).

Apparently, the Run Length (RL) of the proposed EWMA chart is a *Discrete PHase-type* (or DPH) random variable of parameters ($\mathbf{Q}$, $\mathbf{q}$), see for instance Latouche and Ramaswami (1999) or Latouche and Ramaswami (1999), therefore the p.d.f. (probability density function) $f_{RL}(\pounds)$ and the c.d.f. $F_{RL}(\pounds)$ of the RL are respectively equal to

$$f_{RL}(\pounds) = \mathrm{q}^T \mathrm{Q}^{\pounds-1} r, F_{RL}(\pounds) = 1 - \mathrm{q}^T \mathrm{Q}^{\pounds} 1,$$

where $\mathbf{r} = \mathbf{1}\ \mathbf{Q1}$ with $\mathbf{1} = (1, 1, \ldots, 1)^T$ and the mean (ARL), the second non-central moment $E2RL = E(RL^2)$ and standard-deviation ($SDRL$) of the RL are respectively equal to

$$ARL = \nu_1$$

$$E2RL = \nu_1 + \nu_2$$

$$SDRL = \sqrt{E2RL - ARL^2},$$

where ν_1 and ν_2 are the first and second factorial moments of RL, i.e.

$$\nu_1 = \mathbf{q}^T (\mathbf{I} - \mathbf{Q})^{-1} \mathbf{1},$$

$$\nu_2 = 2\mathbf{q}^T (\mathbf{I} - \mathbf{Q})^{-2} \mathbf{Q1}.$$

8.4 PERFORMANCE OF THE PROPOSED EWMA CONTROL CHART

A control chart's performance is evaluated through the properties of its RL distribution. The number of points (samples or observations) needed for the statistic plotted in a control chart to cross the control limits is one observation of the RL distribution. When a process is in-control, the mean and the standard deviation of the RL distribution are denoted as ARL_0 and $SDRL_0$ respectively. On the other hand, when a process is out-of-control, the mean and the standard deviation of the RL distribution are denoted as ARL_1 and $SDRL_1$ respectively. The ARL optimal chart among several competitors for a specific shift is the one that has the smaller ARL_1 value for this specific shift, when all the charts have the same ARL_0 value. The ARL is usually computed under the assumption that the plotted statistic starts at the specified initial value. This actually means that either the process does not shift or if we assume that the process shifts this occurs before monitoring initiates.

TABLE 8.1
Performance of the Proposed EWMA Chart when $ARL_0 = 250$

	$\lambda = 0.05$						$\lambda = 0.10$					
	s = 1		s = 2		s = 3		s = 1		s = 2		s = 3	
Shift	**ARL**	**SDRL**	**ARL**	**SDRL**	**ARL**	**SDRL**	**ARL**	**SDRL**	**ARL**	**SDRL**	**ARL**	**SDRL**
0.4	18.81	4.53	11.71	2.15	9.15	1.47	28.40	12.17	11.83	2.95	8.52	1.74
0.6	36.57	17.36	20.48	7.34	15.38	4.74	122.59	101.14	26.31	13.84	16.56	6.98
0.8	130.31	105.89	62.51	43.19	43.30	26.71	1064	1050	145.43	129.32	71.73	57.94
1	250.00	242.27	250.00	240.36	250.00	239.69	250.00	247.52	250.00	245.91	250.00	245.05
1.2	63.21	55.95	45.09	36.77	35.91	27.42	62.21	58.07	44.18	39.20	35.36	30.04
1.4	29.22	23.04	19.67	13.47	15.50	9.63	28.69	24.78	18.65	14.48	14.44	10.32
1.6	18.43	13.40	12.38	7.65	9.82	5.46	17.71	14.30	11.36	7.99	8.83	5.63
1.8	13.46	9.28	9.08	5.28	7.25	3.78	12.69	9.74	8.17	5.38	6.40	3.79
2.0	10.65	7.09	7.22	4.04	5.79	2.91	9.91	7.33	6.42	4.04	5.06	2.86
2.2	8.86	5.77	6.04	3.30	4.86	2.38	8.17	5.87	5.33	3.25	4.23	2.31
2.4	7.63	4.88	5.21	2.80	4.22	2.03	6.99	4.92	4.58	2.73	3.65	1.95
2.6	6.73	4.25	4.61	2.45	3.74	1.78	6.14	4.24	4.05	2.37	3.24	1.70
2.8	6.04	3.76	4.15	2.19	3.38	1.60	5.49	3.75	3.64	2.10	2.92	1.51
3.0	5.50	3.42	3.79	1.98	3.09	1.45	4.99	3.37	3.32	1.89	2.68	1.37

(Continued)

TABLE 8.1 (Continued)

	$\lambda = 0.15$						$\lambda = 0.20$					
	s = 1		s = 2		s = 3		s = 1		s = 2		s = 3	
Shift	**ARL**	**SDRL**	**ARL**	**SDRL**	**ARL**	**SDRL**	**ARL**	**SDRL**	**ARL**	**SDRL**	**ARL**	**SDRL**
0.4	1472	1447	15.22	5.58	9.05	2.36	556521494	556521685	35.63	23.81	11.12	3.98
0.6	102732	102728	61.10	47.70	22.73	13.14	119145	119160	684.51	670.02	47.80	37.70
0.8	2738	2742	806.81	794.10	182.78	170.62	2178	2180	4698.65	4700.09	831.39	821.32
1	250.00	248.18	250.00	247.62	250.00	247.09	250.00	248.54	250.00	248.17	250.00	247.93
1.2	66.97	64.00	46.17	42.58	36.45	32.58	71.31	69.04	49.52	46.72	38.65	35.61
1.4	30.73	27.77	19.12	8.62	14.45	11.20	32.82	30.48	20.24	17.60	14.98	12.28
1.6	18.58	15.89	11.34	5.69	8.59	5.96	19.61	17.41	11.73	9.42	8.67	6.41
1.8	13.08	10.67	8.01	5.69	6.11	3.93	13.62	11.60	8.13	6.12	6.07	4.15
2.0	10.07	7.92	6.22	4.21	4.79	2.92	10.37	8.52	6.24	4.46	4.70	3.04
2.2	8.22	6.27	5.12	3.34	3.97	2.33	8.38	6.69	5.09	3.50	3.87	2.39
2.4	6.97	5.19	4.38	2.78	3.42	1.95	7.06	5.50	4.32	2.88	3.32	1.98
2.6	6.08	4.44	3.85	2.39	3.03	1.68	6.13	4.67	3.79	2.46	2.93	1.70
2.8	5.42	3.90	3.46	2.10	2.73	1.49	5.44	4.07	3.39	2.15	2.64	1.50
3.0	4.91	3.48	3.15	1.89	2.50	1.34	4.91	3.62	3.08	1.92	2.41	1.34

TABLE 8.2
Performance of the Proposed EWMA Chart when $ARL_0 = 500$

	$\lambda = 0.05$						$\lambda = 0.10$					
	s = 1		s = 2		s = 3		s = 1		s = 2		s = 3	
Shift	**ARL**	**SDRL**	**ARL**	**SDRL**	**ARL**	**SDRL**	**ARL**	**SDRL**	**ARL**	**SDRL**	**ARL**	**SDRL**
0.4	24.13	5.95	13.96	2.51	10.69	1.66	83.37	57.48	15.48	4.14	10.30	2.13
0.6	54.11	28.39	25.69	9.36	18.55	5.67	2145.48	2113.81	44.49	27.74	22.33	10.24
0.8	310.09	276.64	97.89	72.69	60.40	39.25	10936.16	10942.70	545.35	524.45	154.37	136.72
1	500.00	492.29	500.00	489.41	500.00	488.26	500.00	496.48	500.00	495.50	500.00	494.72
1.2	86.91	77.19	58.53	47.88	45.33	34.65	97.21	91.68	62.63	56.31	47.57	41.00
1.4	36.61	28.59	23.57	15.89	18.24	11.10	39.60	34.46	23.58	18.39	17.53	12.54
1.6	22.21	15.82	14.41	8.67	11.29	6.09	22.89	18.48	13.67	9.55	10.31	6.49
1.8	15.88	10.66	10.42	5.87	8.24	4.16	15.80	12.03	9.59	6.21	7.32	4.26
2.0	12.41	8.02	8.22	4.45	6.54	3.17	12.04	8.79	7.42	4.58	5.73	3.17
2.2	10.23	6.45	6.82	3.60	5.45	2.58	9.77	6.90	6.09	3.63	4.74	2.53
2.4	8.74	5.42	5.86	3.05	4.71	2.19	8.25	5.70	5.20	3.03	4.07	2.12
2.6	7.67	4.69	5.17	2.65	4.16	1.92	7.18	4.86	4.56	2.61	3.59	1.84
2.8	6.85	4.16	4.63	2.36	3.74	1.71	6.37	4.26	4.08	2.30	3.23	1.63
3.0	6.21	3.75	4.21	2.14	3.42	1.56	5.75	3.80	3.71	2.07	2.94	1.47

(Continued)

TABLE 8.2 (Continued)

	$\lambda = 0.15$						$\lambda = 0.20$					
	s = 1		s = 2		s = 3		s = 1		s = 2		s = 3	
Shift	**ARL**	**SDRL**	**ARL**	**SDRL**	**ARL**	**SDRL**	**ARL**	**SDRL**	**ARL**	**SDRL**	**ARL**	**SDRL**
0.4	$58 * 10^9$	$58 * 10^9$	28.26	14.49	12.04	3.50	$47 * 10^8$	$47 * 10^8$	880.81	862.55	19.14	9.31
0.6	1209848	1209882	388.86	370.21	43.96	31.14	476481	476495	308858	308841	264.60	251.00
0.8	7540	7543	12595	12590	969.60	954.51	5745	5746	15793	15797	13323	13317
1	500.00	497.56	500.00	497.01	500.00	496.67	500.00	498.18	500.00	497.75	500.00	497.51
1.2	108.74	104.99	70.39	65.92	52.59	47.84	118.35	115.60	78.11	74.73	58.53	54.87
1.4	44.02	40.30	25.51	21.51	18.34	14.40	48.29	45.44	27.86	24.66	19.72	16.48
1.6	24.72	21.36	14.16	10.83	10.31	7.17	26.72	24.04	14.98	12.19	10.67	7.97
1.8	16.62	13.64	9.64	6.84	7.14	4.55	17.64	15.20	9.45	7.54	7.20	4.94
2.0	12.42	9.77	7.32	4.92	5.49	3.31	12.98	10.76	7.42	5.32	5.46	3.51
2.2	9.92	7.55	5.94	3.83	4.50	2.60	10.24	8.22	5.95	4.08	4.43	2.72
2.4	8.29	6.14	5.03	3.14	3.85	2.16	8.47	6.62	4.99	3.31	3.76	2.23
2.6	7.14	5.18	4.38	2.68	3.38	1.85	7.25	5.53	4.32	2.79	3.28	1.89
2.8	6.31	4.49	3.91	2.34	3.03	1.63	6.36	4.76	3.84	2.42	2.94	1.65
3.0	5.66	3.98	3.54	2.09	2.76	1.46	5.68	4.19	3.46	2.14	2.67	1.47

TABLE 8.3
Performance of the Proposed EWMA Chart when $ARL_0 = 750$

	$\lambda = 0.05$						$\lambda = 0.10$					
	s = 1		s = 2		s = 3		s = 1		s = 2		s = 3	
Shift	**ARL**	**SDRL**	**ARL**	**SDRL**	**ARL**	**SDRL**	**ARL**	**SDRL**	**ARL**	**SDRL**	**ARL**	**SDRL**
0.4	28.27	7.24	15.40	2.75	11.62	1.77	391.88	357.84	18.44	5.31	11.55	2.43
0.6	72.53	41.83	29.39	10.94	20.59	6.32	59766	59729	68.50	48.61	27.34	13.48
0.8	645.76	606.37	133.49	104.45	74.56	50.48	22177	22186	1643	1619	280.37	260.32
1	750.00	741.86	750.00	738.94	750.00	737.58	750.00	745.89	750.00	745.03	750.00	744.38
1.2	106.37	95.05	68.34	56.25	51.82	39.82	126.56	120.27	77.89	70.77	57.21	49.87
1.4	42.06	32.82	26.13	17.53	19.95	12.04	47.67	41.83	27.16	21.33	19.67	14.13
1.6	24.83	17.54	15.69	9.32	12.18	6.47	26.43	21.44	15.24	10.64	11.27	7.07
1.8	17.51	11.60	11.24	6.24	8.82	4.38	17.82	13.57	10.51	6.77	7.91	4.56
2.0	13.56	8.63	8.82	4.69	6.97	3.32	13.39	9.73	8.06	4.93	6.14	3.36
2.2	11.12	6.89	7.29	3.78	5.60	2.69	10.75	7.55	6.57	3.88	5.06	2.67
2.4	9.46	5.76	6.25	3.19	4.99	2.28	9.02	6.18	5.58	3.21	4.33	2.23
2.6	8.27	4.97	5.49	2.77	4.40	1.99	7.80	5.24	4.88	2.75	3.81	1.93
2.8	7.37	4.40	4.92	2.47	3.96	1.78	6.90	4.57	4.35	2.42	3.41	1.70
3.0	6.67	3.95	4.47	2.23	3.60	1.62	6.20	4.06	3.94	2.17	3.11	1.54

(Continued)

TABLE 8.3 (Continued)

	$\lambda = 0.15$						$\lambda = 0.20$					
	s = 1		s = 2		s = = 3		s = 1		s = 2		s = 3	
Shift	**ARL**	**SDRL**	**ARL**	**SDRL**	**ARL**	**SDRL**	**ARL**	**SDRL**	**ARL**	**SDRL**	**ARL**	**SDRL**
0.4	$21 * 10^{10}$	$21 * 10^{10}$	52.29	35.15	14.55	4.67	$15 * 10^{9}$	$15 * 10^{9}$	129883	129861	31.64	19.67
0.6	2807145	2807179	2540	2518	77.42	62.36	1048525	1048540	$26 * 10^{6}$	$26 * 10^{6}$	1373	1358
0.8	13489	13492	42546	42552	3658	3642	10045	10047	28786	28790	54747	54749
1	750.00	747.27	750.00	746.67	750.00	746.36	750.00	748.01	750.00	747.54	750.00	747.29
1.2	144.58	140.42	90.44	85.50	65.81	60.57	159.50	156.51	102.22	98.54	74.93	70.94
1.4	54.25	50.11	30.15	25.71	21.12	16.76	60.55	57.44	33.55	30.04	23.15	19.59
1.6	29.10	25.35	16.05	12.36	11.45	7.99	31.96	29.03	17.23	14.16	12.00	9.05
1.8	19.01	15.70	10.69	7.59	7.79	4.96	20.46	17.78	11.13	8.50	7.92	5.45
2.0	13.95	11.01	8.01	5.37	5.93	3.55	14.74	12.31	8.17	5.88	5.92	3.81
2.2	11.00	8.38	6.44	4.13	4.83	2.77	11.46	9.24	6.48	4.45	4.76	2.92
2.4	9.11	6.74	5.41	3.37	4.10	2.28	9.37	7.35	5.39	3.57	4.01	2.37
2.6	7.80	5.64	4.70	2.85	3.59	1.95	7.95	6.09	4.64	2.99	3.49	2.01
2.8	6.84	4.86	4.17	2.48	3.21	1.71	6.93	5.20	4.10	2.58	3.11	1.75
3.0	6.11	4.28	3.76	2.21	2.92	1.53	6.16	4.54	3.69	2.27	2.82	1.55

In order to comment on the performance of the proposed EWMA chart we present in Tables 8.1, 8.2 and 8.3 the *ARL* profile of the chart for different shifts. Specifically, for $n = 5$ we have computed the *ARL* and *SDRL* values when $s = 1, 2, 3$ and $\lambda = 0.05$, 0.1, 0.15, 0.2. The shift is defined as the fraction $\frac{r_1}{r_0}$ where r_0 is the in-control lifetime and r_1 is the out-of-control lifetime (similar definition is given for example in Rasay and Arshad (2020)). When the shift is equal to 1 the process is in control, for values less than unity there is a decrease in the lifetime and for values greater than unity there is an increase in the lifetime. The performance of the chart is evaluated for $ARL_0 = 250, 500, 750$ using the Markov chain theory developed in Section 8.3.

From the results we conclude that for $s = 3$ we have the smallest ARL_1 value for almost all the shifts among the different s values assumed, for the schemes with the same ARL_0. This result can be attributed to the fact that an increased value of s changes the shape of the distribution a fact that leads to faster detection of the out-of-control situations. As the value of s increases we expect to have better results keeping in mind though that we have to wait until s failures occur. Moreover, $\lambda = 0.05$ gives the smallest ARL_1 values for the same s and shift values. As λ increases there is an increasing bias effect on the ARL_1 values for the downward shifts (the ARL_1 values are larger than the ARL_0 values for specific shifts). For $\lambda = 0.05$ and $s = 3$ the bias effect is diminished.

In Table 8.4, we present the results of the *ARL* comparison for the proposed EWMA chart (for $\lambda = 0.05$) and the Shewhart chart proposed by Rasay and Arshad (2020). Results are given for $ARL_0 = 200$ and $ARL_0 = 370$ for $s = 1, 2, 3$ and shifts ranging from 0.4 to 2.8. For all the considered cases the EWMA chart has smaller ARL_1 values for both upward and downward shifts and the results are much better for $s = 1$ in relation to the Shewhart chart.

8.5 AN EXAMPLE

In this section we present a simulated application of the proposed methodology in the development of compact fluorescent lamps (CFL). An industry produces the globe screw-in CFL lamps of 16 watts, with $r_0 = 10000$ hours as the mean lifetime. When the process is in-control 60 samples, of size $n = 5$ each, are collected and the lifetime of each CFL is measured in hours. Then, another 60 samples are collected when the process has an upward shift. This production process is monitored in the case of $s = 1, 2, 3$. In the case $s = 1$, each observation recorded is the time in hours that the first failure occurs in the sample. In the cases $s = 2$ ($s = 3$) each observation recorded is the time in hours that the second (third) failure occurs in the sample. The observations are multiplied by $2n\frac{1}{r_0}$ and the statistic in (8.3) is computed along with the control limits (8.5) and (8.6). The EWMA control charts for $\lambda = 0.05$ and $s = 1, 2, 3$ are given in Figure 8.1, Figure 8.2 and Figure 8.3, respectively. It is noted that the control limits of the charts are computed so that $ARL_0 = 200$ and $ARL_0 = 370$ in the top and the bottom of each figure, respectively.

TABLE 8.4
A Comparison of the Proposed EWMA Chart to the Shewhart Chart

	ARL = 200						ARL = 370					
	s = 1		s = 2		s = 3		s = 1		s = 2		s = 3	
Shift	Shewhart	EWMA	Shewhart	EWMA	Shewhart	EWMA	Shewhart	EWMA	Shewhart	EWMA	Shewhart	EWMA
0.4	160.29	17.40	68.75	11.03	34.18	8.67	296.29	21.60	124.78	12.96	59.83	10.02
0.6	237.57	32.76	148.30	19.01	98.25	14.42	440.96	45.08	272.28	23.29	177.34	17.13
0.8	271.51	105.03	235.18	54.83	202.02	39.03	513.35	203.09	440.15	79.78	374.20	52.12
1	200.00	200.00	200.00	200.00	200.00	200.00	370.00	370.00	370.00	370.00	370.00	370.00
1.2	112.74	57.25	98.86	41.41	88.89	33.22	192.66	75.43	166.47	52.27	148.00	41.01
1.4	63.96	27.20	48.17	18.50	38.72	14.65	101.12	33.15	74.28	21.81	58.65	17.03
1.6	39.67	17.36	26.89	11.74	20.20	9.35	59.03	20.47	38.85	13.51	28.59	10.65
1.8	26.86	12.75	16.99	8.66	12.28	6.93	38.14	14.78	23.37	9.83	16.52	7.81
2.0	19.51	10.13	11.80	6.91	8.34	5.55	26.71	11.61	15.62	7.78	10.79	6.21
2.2	14.97	8.46	8.79	5.78	6.15	4.67	19.90	9.61	11.28	6.48	7.70	5.20
2.4	11.99	7.29	6.90	5.01	4.81	4.05	15.55	8.24	8.64	5.58	5.86	4.49
2.6	9.92	6.44	5.65	4.44	3.93	3.60	12.61	7.24	6.92	4.93	4.70	3.98
2.8	8.43	5.79	4.77	4.00	3.33	3.26	10.53	6.49	5.74	4.43	3.91	3.59

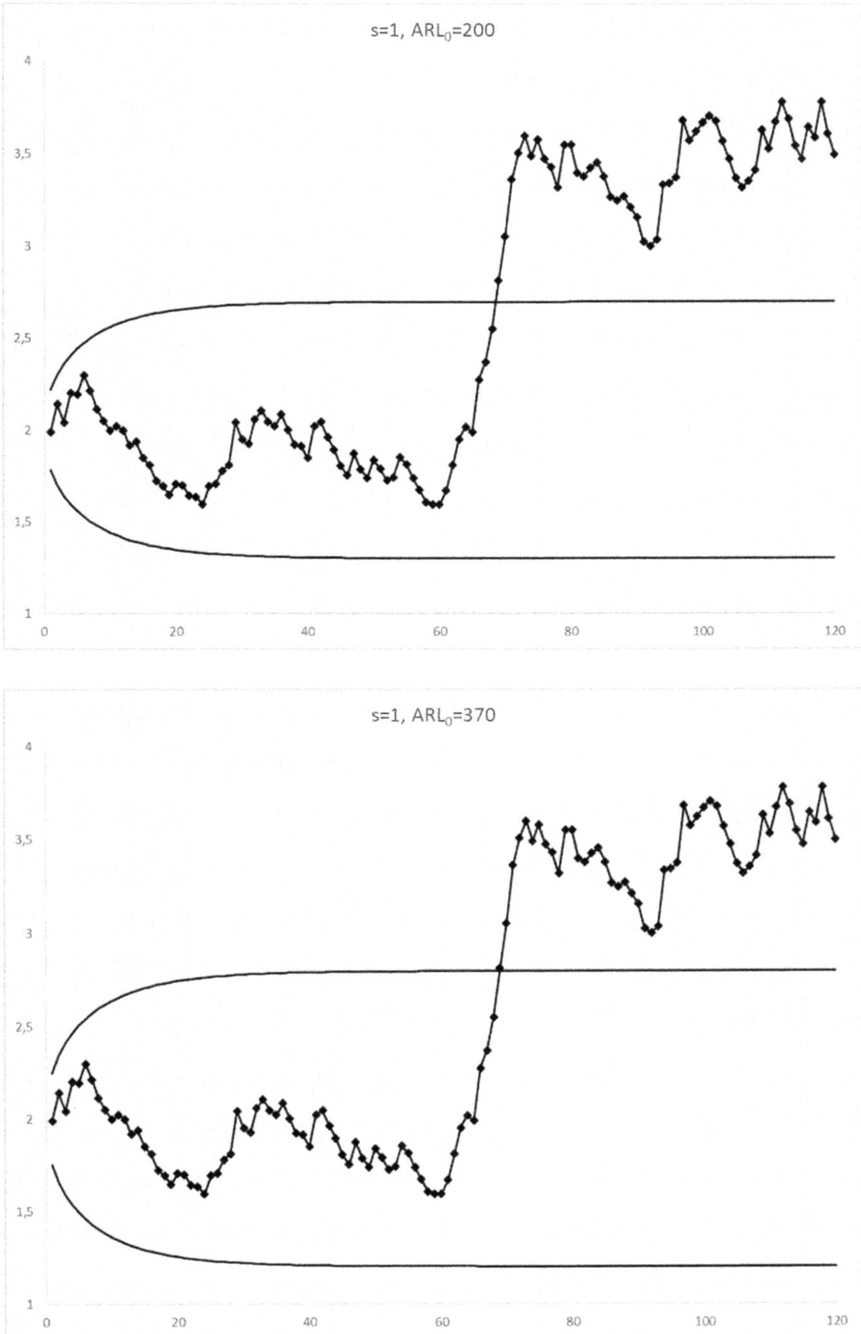

FIGURE 8.1 EWMA chart when s = 1 and ARLo = 200 (top), ARLo = 370 (bottom)

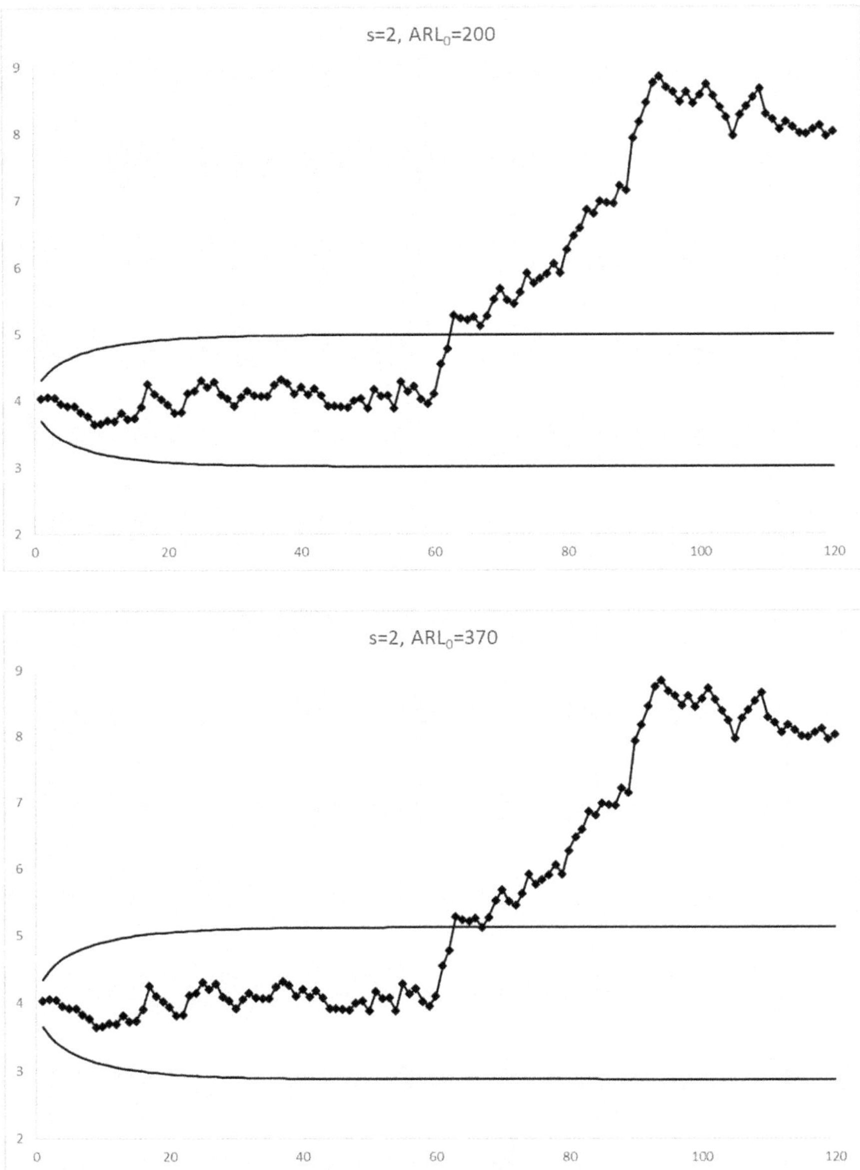

FIGURE 8.2 EWMA chart when s = 2 and ARLo = 200 (top), ARLo = 370 (bottom)

From the figures we observe that the control limits of the charts for $ARL_0 = 370$ are larger than the control limits for $ARL_0 = 200$ as expected. This fact leads to faster detection of the out-of-control situation when $ARL_0 = 200$ but if the process is in control we expect to have more false alarms. In Figure 8.1 we see that both control charts detect the out-of-control situation in sample number 69. Note that faster detection

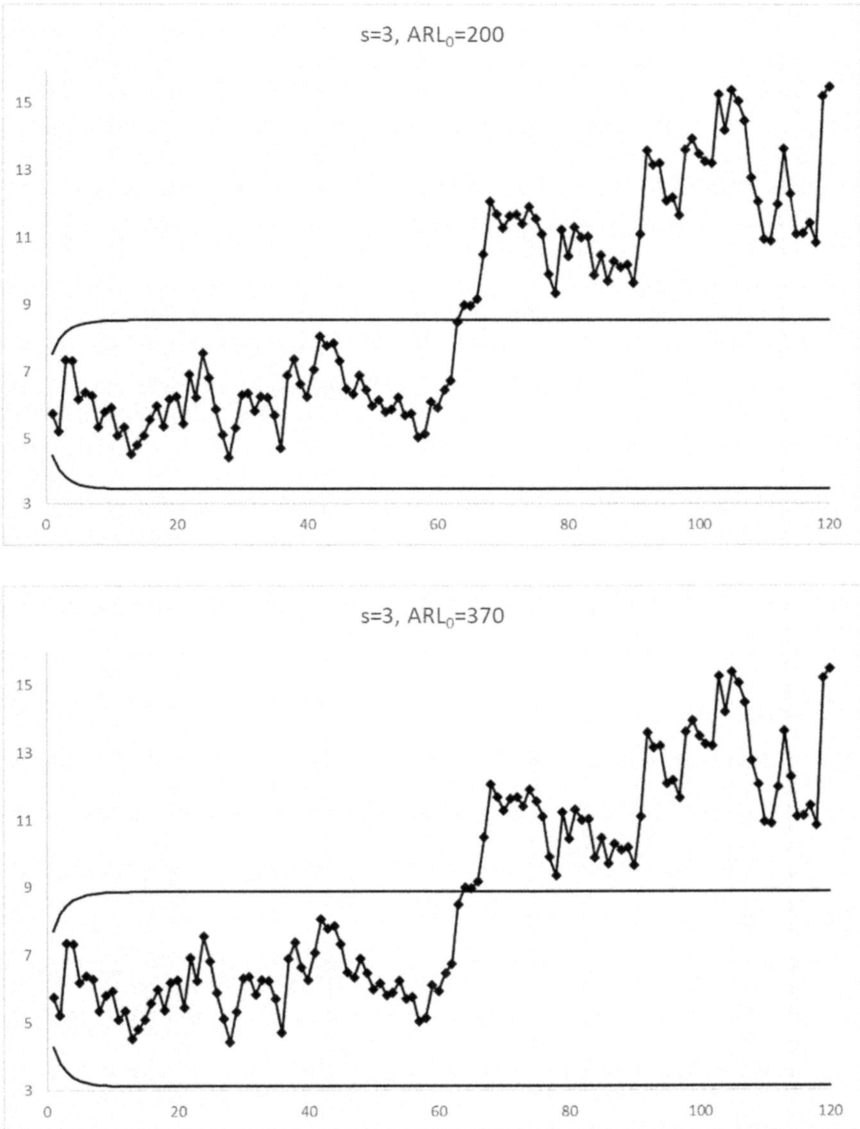

FIGURE 8.3 EWMA chart when s = 3 and ARLo = 200 (top), ARLo = 370 (bottom)

would be possible if the inertia problem did not occur in this case. For example the charts in Figure 8.2 are able to give a signal in sample point 63 since this problem did not occur. The same result is deduced and from Figure 8.3 that gives a signal in sample point 64.

8.6 CONCLUSIONS

In this paper we presented an EWMA control chart for monitoring the lifetime of products that is assumed to be exponentially distributed. The proposed chart is developed under type II censoring and it is further assumed that n items are tested at the same time and the test ends as soon as the *rth* failure occurs. A failured item is immediately replaced by a new one, so that the total number of items under inspection is equal to n throughout the test. We presented the statistic plotted and the control limits of the chart as well as the theory for the computation of the *RL* properties of the chart. We computed the *ARL* and *SDRL* values of the proposed chart for several different combinations of its parameters and we compared the performance of the chart to an alternative one. The results revealed the properties of the proposed chart and its superiority against the already established Shewhart chart for the problem under study. We also concluded that increased s values significantly improve the ability of the chart to detect an out-of-control situation.

The case of non-constant failure rate is the next step in this research field. Specifically, other distributional models like the Weibull maybe considered in such a case since it is a rather flexible choice. Our expectations is that with such a model we will be able to check the effect of non-constant failure on the performance of the chart as well as the parameters effect since we will be able to use a two and a three parameter case of this distribution.

REFERENCES

Arif, O.H., Aslam, M. and Jun, C.-H. (2016). EWMA np control chart for the Weibull distribution. *Journal of Testing and Evaluation* 45: 1022–1028.

Aslam, M. and Jun, C.H. (2015). Attribute control charts for the Weibull distribution under truncated life tests. *Quality Engineering* 27: 283–288.

Aslam, M., Khan, N. and Jun, C.H. (2016). A control chart for time truncated life tests using Pareto distribution of second kind. *Journal of Statistical Computation and Simulation* 86: 2113–2122.

Batson, R.G., Jeong, Y., Fonseca, D.J. and Ray, P.S. (2006). Control charts for monitoring field failure data. *Quality and Reliability Engineering International* 22: 733–755.

Brook, D. and Evans, D.A. (1972). An approach to the probability distribution of CUSUM run length. *Biometrika* 59: 539–549.

Dickinson, R.M., Olteanu Roberts, D.A., Driscoll, A.R., Woodall, W.H. and Vining, G.G. (2014). CUSUM charts for monitoring the characteristic life of censored Weibull lifetimes. *Journal of Quality Technology* 46: 340–358.

Fan, T.-H. and Wang, Y.-F. (2021). Comparison of optimal accelerated life tests with competing risks model under exponential distribution. *Quality and Reliability Engineering International* 37: 902–919.

Faraz, A., Saniga, E.M. and Heuchenne, C. (2015). Shewhart control charts for monitoring reliability with Weibull lifetimes. *Quality and Reliability Engineering International* 31: 1565–1574.

Latouche, G. and Ramaswami, V. (1999). *Introduction to Matrix Analytic Methods in Stochastic Modelling*. ASA, SIAM.

Li, Q., Mukherjee, A., Song, Z. and Zhang, J. (2021). Phase-II monitoring of exponentially distributed process based on type-II censored data for a possible shift in location—scale. *Journal of Computational and Applied Mathematics* 389: 113315.

Lucas, J.M. and Saccucci, M.S. (1990). Exponentially weighted moving average control schemes: Properties and enhancements. *Technometrics* 32: 1–12.

Montgomery, D.C. (2013). *Introduction to Statistical Quality Control.* Wiley.

Nassar, M., Okasha, H. and Albassam, M. (2021). E-Bayesian estimation and associated properties of simple stepstress model for exponential distribution based on type-II censoring. *Quality and Reliability Engineering International* 37: 997–1016.

Neuts, M.F. (1981). *Matrix-Geometric Solutions in Stochastic Models: An Algorithmic Approach.* Dover Publications Inc.

O'Connor, P.D.T. and Kleyner, A. (2012). *Practical Reliability Engineering, 5th ed.* Wiley.

Rasay, H. and Arshad, H. (2020). Designing variable control charts under failure censoring reliability tests with replacement. *Transactions of the Institute of Measurement and Control* 42: 3002–3011.

Raza, S.M.M., Riaz, M. and Ali, S. (2015). On the performance of EWMA and DEWMA control charts for censored data. *Journal of the Chinese Institute of Engineers, Transactions of the Chinese Institute of Engineers, Series A* 38: 714–722.

Raza, S.M.M., Riaz, M. and Ali, S. (2016). EWMA control chart for poisson-exponential lifetime distribution under type I censoring. *Quality and Reliability Engineering International* 32: 995–1005.

Stapelberg, R.F. (2009). *Handbook of Reliability, Availability, Maintainability and Safety in Engineering Design.* Springer-Verlag.

Steiner, S.H. (1999). EWMA control charts with time-varying control limits and fast initial response. *Journal of Quality Technology* 31: 75–86.

Steiner, S.H. and Jock Mackay, R. (2000). Monitoring processes with highly censored data. *Journal of Quality Technology* 32: 199–208.

Triantafyllou, I.S. (2021). Wilcoxon-type rank-sum control charts based on progressively censored reference data. *Communications in Statistics—Theory and Methods* 50: 311–328.

Tsai, T.-R. and Lin, C.-C. (2009). The design of EWMA control chart for average with type-I censored data. *International Journal of Quality and Reliability Management* 26: 397–405.

Xu, S. and Jeske, D.R. (2018). Weighted EWMA charts for monitoring type I censored Weibull lifetimes. *Journal of Quality Technology* 50: 220–230.

Zhang, L. and Chen, G. (2004). EWMA charts for monitoring the mean of censored Weibull lifetimes. *Journal of Quality Technology* 36: 321–328.

Zhang, C., Tsung, F. and Xiang, D. (2016). Monitoring censored lifetime data with a weighted-likelihood scheme. *Naval Research Logistics* 63: 631–646.

9 On the Lifetime of <*n*, *f*, *k*> Reliability Systems

Ioannis S. Triantafyllou

CONTENTS

9.1 INTRODUCTION

In the field of Reliability Modeling, an intriguing goal calls for the design of appropriate structures, which cover real-life applications adequately and match suitably to existing devices and contrivances. A discrete group of reliability models, which seems to reel in the scientists during the last decades, is the family of consecutive-type systems. Due to the abundance of their applications in Engineering, the so-called consecutive-type structures comprise an engrossing scope of research quest.

The general framework of constructing a consecutive-type system requires n linearly or circularly ordered components. The resulting system stops its operation, whenever a pre-specified consecutive-type condition (or more than one condition) is fulfilled. The potential and time placement of the failure rule's activation for each structure, are strongly related to its reliability characteristics, such as the reliability function, mean residual lifetime or the signature vector.

Following the abovementioned infrastructure, several systems have been proposed in the literature. For example, a consecutive–k–out–of–n: F system consists of n linearly ordered components and stops its operation if and only if at least k consecutive units break down (see, e.g., Derman *et al.* (1982), Triantafyllou and Koutras (2008a) or Triantafyllou and Koutras (2008b)). Moreover, the so-called the

DOI: 10.1201/9781003203124-9

m–consecutive– k–out–of–n: F system seems to be a direct generalization of the traditional m–out–of–n: F system and the consecutive–k–out–of–n: F structure; it consists of n linearly ordered components such that the system stops its operation if and only if there are at least m non-overlapping runs of k consecutive failed units (see, e.g., Griffith (1986) or Eryilmaz *et al.* (2011)). An additional modification of the common consecutive–k–out–of–n: F system is known as r–within–consecutive k–out–of–n: F structure. The aforementioned system was introduced by Tong (1985) and fails if and only if there exist k consecutive components which include among them, at least r failed units (see also Griffith (1986) or Triantafyllou and Koutras (2011)). It is evident that plenty variations of the above structures have been suggested in order to accommodate more flexible operation principles. For some recent contributions on the field of consecutive-type structures, the interested reader is referred to Dafnis *et al.* (2019), Kumar and Ram (2018, 2019), Triantafyllou (2020a) or Kumar *et al.* (2019).

On the other hand, several real-life applications involve two different criteria which can lead to the failure of the corresponding device. In order to cover the abovementioned application field, a variety of reliability structures have been proposed and studied in the literature. For instance, the (n, f, k) structure proposed by Chang *et al.* (1999), fails if, and only if, there exist at least f failed units or at least k consecutive failed units. Several reliability characteristics of the so-called (n, f, k) systems are studied in detail by Zuo *et al.* (2000) or Triantafyllou and Koutras (2014). Among others, the $< n, f, k >$ structure (see, e.g., Cui *et al.* (2006) or Triantafyllou (2020b)), the constrained (k, d)–out–of–n: F system (see, e.g., Eryilmaz and Zuo (2010) or Triantafyllou (2020c)) and the $((n_1, n_2, ..., n_N), f, k)$ structure involving N modules (see, e.g., Cui and Xie (2005) or Eryilmaz and Tuncel (2015)) could be reported as indicative paradigms of consecutive-type reliability systems with two failure criteria. For a detailed and up-to-date survey on the consecutive-type systems, we refer to the detailed reviews offered by Chao *et al.* (1995) or Triantafyllou (2015) and the well-documented monographs devised by Chang *et al.* (2000), Kuo and Zuo (2003) or Kumar *et al.* (2019). A survey of reliability approaches in various fields of Engineering and Physical Sciences is also provided by Ram (2013).

Throughout the lines of the present chapter, the reliability characteristics of the r–within–consecutive k–out–of–n: F structure are investigated. In Section 2, an algorithmic procedure for evaluating the coordinates of the signature vector of the aforementioned reliability structures is discussed, while s numerical experimentation is carried out for several choices of the design parameters. In Section 3, we present signature-based expressions for the reliability function, the mean residual lifetime and the conditional mean residual lifetime of the r–within–consecutive k–out–of–n: F systems. Several numerical results, which are produced by the aid of the proposed algorithmic procedure, are also displayed and discussed in some detail. Section 4 provides signature-based comparisons of the underlying r–within–consecutive k–out–of–n: F structure versus several well-known members of the class of consecutive-type systems. Finally, the Discussion section summarizes the outcomes provided in the present manuscript, while some interesting conclusions drawn in previous sections are highlighted.

9.2 THE SIGNATURE VECTOR OF THE *R*-WITHIN-CONSECUTIVE-*K*-OUT-OF-*N*: *F* STRUCTURE

In this section, we develop the step-by-step algorithmic approach for computing the coordinates of the signature of the *r*–within–consecutive *k*–out–of–*n*: *F* structures with independent and identically distributed components. Let us first denote by T the lifetime of a reliability structure consisting of n components with respective lifetimes $T_1, T_2, ..., T_n$. Under the assumption that lifetimes $T_1, T_2, ..., T_n$ are independent and identically distributed (*i.i.d.* hereafter), the signature vector of the *r*–within–consecutive *k*–out–of–*n*: *F* structure is given as $(s_1(r,k,n), s_2(r,k,n), ..., s_n(r,k,n))$ with

$$s_i(r,k,n) = P(T = T_{i:n}), i = 1,2,...,n, \tag{9.1}$$

where $T_{1:n} \leq T_{2:n} \leq ... \leq T_{n:n}$ express the respective ordered random lifetimes. In other words, the probability $s_i(r,k,n), i = 1,2,...,n$ is defined as the ratio $A_i / n!$, where A_i indicates the number of those permutations of the components' lifetimes of the structure, for which the *i–th* component failure leads to the stoppage of the reliability system. It is well-known that the signature of a coherent system is strongly related to some important reliability characteristics (see, e.g., Samaniego (1985, 2007)) and that turns it to a useful tool for evaluating the structure's performance.

We next describe the algorithmic process for computing the coordinates of the signature vector of the *r*–within–consecutive *k*–out–of–*n*: *F* system.

Step 0. Define the vector $\mathbf{w} = (w_1, w_2, ..., w_n)$ with initial values $w_i = 0,\ i = 1,2,...,n$.

Step 1. Generate a random sample of size *n* from an arbitrary continuous distribution *F*. The resulting sample indicates the components' lifetimes of the underlying *r*–within–consecutive *k*–out–of–*n*: *F* structure.

Step 2. Determine the input parameters of the algorithm, namely the design parameters r, k, where $1 \leq r \leq k \leq n$.

Step 3. Define the random variable *W* as the chronologically ordered lifetime that results in the stoppage of the *r*–within–consecutive *k*–out–of–*n*: *F* model. The random quantity *W* ranges from 1 to *n* in according to which unit arises to be the destructive one for the functioning of the reliability system.

Step 4. Find out the value of *W* for the particular sample of order *n* which has been produced in Step 1. Each time the random variable *W* takes on a specific value *i* ($i = 1,2,...,n$), the respective coordinate of vector $\mathbf{w}$ increases appropriately, namely the quantity a_i becomes $a_i + 1$.

All steps 1–4 are supposed to be repeated *m* times and the probability that the *r*–within–consecutive *k*–out–of–*n*: *F* model fails at the chronologically i-th ordered unit failure is equal to a_i divided by *m*, namely $s_i(r,k,n) = a_i / m, i = 1,2,...,n$. It goes without saying that the amount of repetitions is suggested to be as large as possible.

We first apply the abovementioned algorithmic procedure for the special case $r = 2$, namely for the 2–within–consecutive *k*–out–of–*n*: *F* system. Despite the fact that for this case, Triantafyllou and Koutras (2011) offered a recursive scheme for computing the corresponding signature, we next proceed to calculate the signature of the 2–within–consecutive k–out–of–n: F system by the aid of the proposed simulation in order to verify its validity. Please note that for the simulation study

TABLE 9.1
Exact and Simulation-Based Signatures of the 2–within–consecutive k–out–of–n: F Structure

n	k	i = 1	i = 2	i = 3	i = 4	i = 5	i = 6	i = 7	i = 8	i = 9	i = 10
2	2	0	1								
		0	1								
3	2	0	0.669	0.331							
			0.667	0.333							
	3	0	1	0							
			1	0							
4	2	0	0.499	0.501	0						
		0	0.500	0.500	0						
	3	0	0.834	0.166	0						
		0	0.833	0.167	0						
5	2	0	0.401	0.501	0.098	0					
		0	0.400	0.500	0.100	0					
	3	0	0.697	0.303	0	0					
		0	0.700	0.300	0	0					
6	2	0	0.334	0.466	0.200	0	0				
		0	0.333	0.467	0.200	0	0				
	3	0	0.602	0.398	0	0	0				
		0	0.600	0.400	0	0	0				
7	2	0	0.288	0.429	0.258	0.025	0	0			
		0	0.286	0.428	0.257	0.029	0	0			
	3	0	0.523	0.448	0.029	0	0	0			
		0	0.524	0.448	0.028	0	0	0			
8	2	0	0.249	0.392	0.289	0.070	0	0	0		
		0	0.250	0.393	0.286	0.071	0	0	0		
	3	0	0.467	0.462	0.071	0	0	0	0		
		0	0.464	0.464	0.071	0	0	0	0		
9	2	0	0.220	0.358	0.031	0.112	0.009	0	0	0	
		0	0.222	0.360	0.030	0.111	0.007	0	0	0	
	3	0	0.419	0.464	0.117	0	0	0	0	0	
		0	0.417	0.464	0.119	0	0	0	0	0	
10	2	0	0.199	0.332	0.300	0.144	0.025	0	0	0	0
		0	0.200	0.333	0.300	0.143	0.024	0	0	0	0
	3	0	0.380	0.455	0.161	0.004	0	0	0	0	0
		0	0.378	0.456	0.162	0.004	0	0	0	0	0

Each cell contains the simulation-based signature (upper entry) and the exact signature (lower entry)

carried out throughout the lines of the present manuscript, the MATLAB package has been used, while 10.000 replications have been accomplished for producing each numerical result. To sum up, we decided first to implement the above algorithm in cases where the numerical results were already known (by applying an alternative approach), so the correctness of the proposed method to be numerically confirmed. Table 9.1 displays the signature vector of the corresponding 2–within–consecutive k–out–of–n: F model for different values of its design parameters. Both exact and simulation-based results are presented in each cell of the following table. More precisely, the upper entries have been calculated by the aid of the proposed algorithm, while the lower entries depict the exact values of the respective signature vector. Since we examine the same cases as those considered by Triantafyllou and Koutras (2011), the lower entries of all cells in Table 9.1, have been reproduced from their Table I (p. 318).

Based on Table 9.1, one may readily deduce that the simulation-based outcomes are very close to the exact results in all cases considered. For instance, let us suppose that a 2–within–consecutive 3–out–of–7: F structure has been implemented. Under the aforementioned model, the exact non-zero signatures, namely the 2nd, 3rd and 4th coordinate of the respective vector equal to 52.4%, 44.8%, and 2.8% correspondingly, while the simulation-based probability values which have been produced by the aid of the proposed procedure are 52.3%, 44.8%, and 2.9% respectively.

We next apply the algorithmic process for calculating the signatures of additional members of the family of r–within–consecutive k–out–of–n: F models for several designs. We now extend our computations for larger values of parameter r, namely for $r > 2$. More precisely, Table 9.2 presents the numerical outcomes for the signature vector of the r–within–consecutive k–out–of–n: F systems for $r = 3$, $k > r$ and $n = 5,6, \ldots ,10$.

For illustration purposes, let us consider the 3–within–consecutive 5–out–of–7: F model, namely the design parameters are defined as $r = 3, k = 5, n = 7$. The resulting system breaks down at the 3rd ordered failure unit with probability 62.626%, at the 4th ordered component lifetime with probability 34.526%, while its 5th failed component leads to the failure of the whole structure with probability 2.848%.

In addition, Table 9.2 can be proved useful for reaching some interesting conclusions about the impact of the design parameters k, n over the performance of the corresponding model. More precisely, Figure 9.1 depicts the signatures of 3–within–consecutive 4–out–of–n: F systems for $n = 5,6, \ldots, 10$.

As it is easily observed, the larger the parameter n, the longer the life expectancy of the corresponding structure becomes. On the other hand, Figure 9.2 reveals the influence of parameter k over the signatures of the r–within–consecutive k–out–of–n: F models. More specifically, we next consider all possible cases of 3–within–consecutive k–out–of–9: F designs and the resulting graphical representation of the corresponding signatures is given in the following figure.

Based on Figure 9.2, we readily observe that as parameter k increases, the failure of the resulting structure tends to take place sooner. In other words, it is preferable for the practitioner to design the suitable 3–within–consecutive k–out–of–n: F system for its application, by determining the value of parameter k as smaller as possible.

TABLE 9.2
The Signatures of the 3–within–consecutive *k*–out–of–*n*: *F* Systems under Several Designs

n	k	i = 1	i = 2	i = 3	i = 4	i = 5	i = 6	i = 7	i = 8	i = 9	i = 10
5	4	0	0	0.69866	0.30134	0	0	0			
6	4	0	0	0.50008	0.43184	0.06808	0				
	5	0	0	0.80184	0.19816	0	0				
7	4	0	0	0.37040	0.45962	0.16998	0	0			
	5	0	0	0.62626	0.34526	0.02848	0	0			
	6	0	0	0.85830	0.14170	0	0	0			
8	4	0	0	0.29118	0.42376	0.28506	0	0	0		
	5	0	0	0.40338	0.43568	0.16094	0	0	0		
	6	0	0	0.71216	0.27348	0.01436	0	0	0		
	7	0	0	0.89350	0.10650	0	0	0	0		
9	4	0	0	0.22416	0.38844	0.34040	0.04700	0	0	0	
	5	0	0	0.40338	0.43568	0.16094	0	0	0	0	
	6	0	0	0.59602	0.35532	0.04866	0	0	0	0	
	7	0	0	0.77340	0.21888	0.00772	0	0	0	0	
	8	0	0	0.91760	0.08240	0	0	0	0	0	
10	4	0	0	0.18110	0.34090	0.36002	0.11284	0.00514	0	0	0
	5	0	0	0.33362	0.42572	0.24066	0	0	0	0	0
	6	0	0	0.50138	0.40322	0.09540	0	0	0	0	0
	7	0	0	0.66754	0.30414	0.02832	0	0	0	0	0
	8	0	0	0.81876	0.17704	0.00420	0	0	0	0	0
	9	0	0	0.93268	0.06732	0	0	0	0	0	0

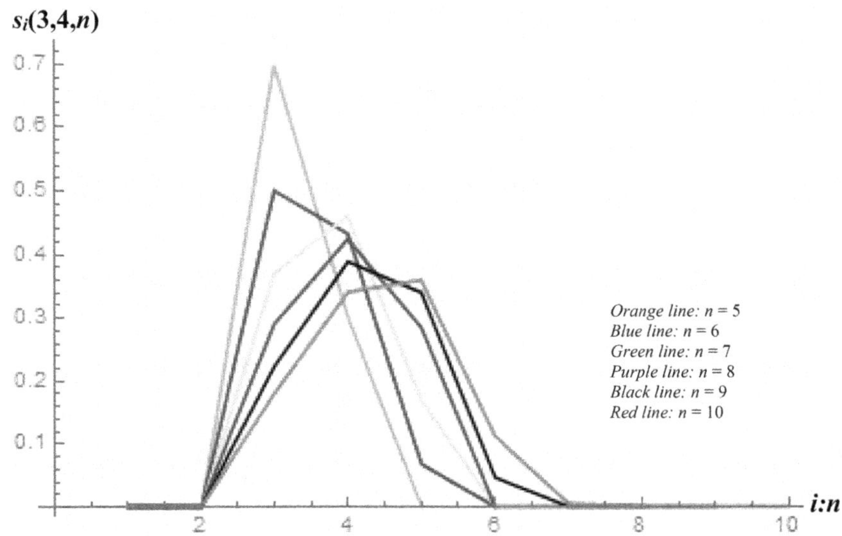

FIGURE 9.1 The signatures of 3–within–consecutive 4–out–of–*n*: *F* models.

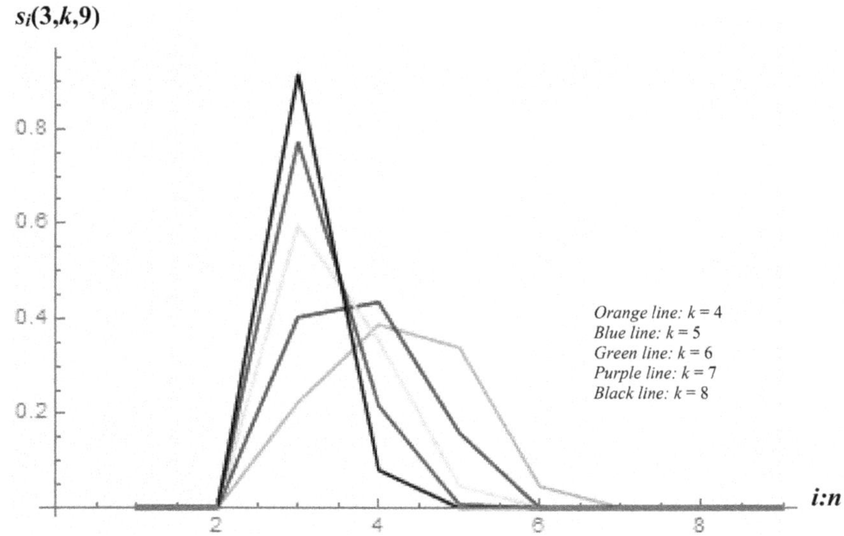

FIGURE 9.2 The signatures of 3–within–consecutive k–out–of–9: F models.

Furthermore, Table 9.3 presents the numerical outcomes for the signature vector of the r–within–consecutive k–out–of–n: F systems for $r = 4$, $k > r$ and $n = 6$, 7, . . . ,10.

For illustration purposes, let us consider the 4–within–consecutive 6–out–of–9: F model, namely the design parameters are defined as $r = 4, k = 6, n = 9$. The resulting system breaks down at the 4th ordered failure unit with probability 35.942%, at the 5th ordered component lifetime with probability 45.18%, while its 6th and 7th failed component leads to the failure of the whole structure with probability 17.646% and 1.232% respectively.

In addition, Table 9.3 can be proved useful for reaching some interesting conclusions about the influence of the design parameters k, n over the performance of the corresponding model. More precisely, Figure 9.3 depicts the signatures of 4–within–consecutive 6–out–of–n: F systems for $n = 7, 8, 9, 10$.

As it is easily observed, the larger the parameter n, the longer the operation expectancy of the respective system tends to be. On the other hand, Figure 4 reveals the impact of parameter k over the signatures of the r–within–consecutive k–out–of–n: F structures. More specifically, we next consider all possible cases of 4–within–consecutive k–out–of–9: F models and the resulting graphical depiction of the corresponding signatures is given below.

Based on Figure 9.4, we conclude that as parameter k increases, the failure of the resulting structure tends to take place sooner. In other words, it is preferable for the practitioner to design the suitable 4–within–consecutive k–out–of–n: F system for its application, by determining the value of parameter k as smaller as possible.

TABLE 9.3
The Signatures of the 4–within–consecutive *k*–out–of–*n*: *F* Systems under Several Designs

n	k	i = 1	i = 2	i = 3	i = 4	i = 5	i = 6	i = 7	i = 8	i = 9	i = 10
6	5	0	0	0	0.60040	0.39960	0				
7	5	0	0	0	0.36966	0.48324	0.14710	0			
	6	0	0	0	0.71518	0.28482	0	0			
8	5	0	0	0	0.24276	0.43702	0.28396	0.03626	0		
	6	0	0	0	0.49318	0.43508	0.07174	0	0		
	7	0	0	0	0.78612	0.21388	0	0	0		
9	5	0	0	0	0.16892		0.35692	0.11706	0	0	
	6	0	0	0	0.35942	0.45180	0.17646	0.01232	0	0	
	8	0	0	0	0.59590	0.36520	0.03890	0	0	0	
	8	0	0	0	0.83208		0	0	0	0	
10	5	0	0	0	0.11792	0.28950	0.35432	0.23826	0	0	0
	6	0	0	0	0.26186	0.42074	0.26926	0.04814	0	0	0
	7	0	0	0	0.45284	0.42760	0.11450	0.00506	0	0	0
	8	0	0	0	0.66352	0.31262	0.02386	0	0	0	0
	9	0	0	0	0.86710	0.13290	0	0	0	0	0

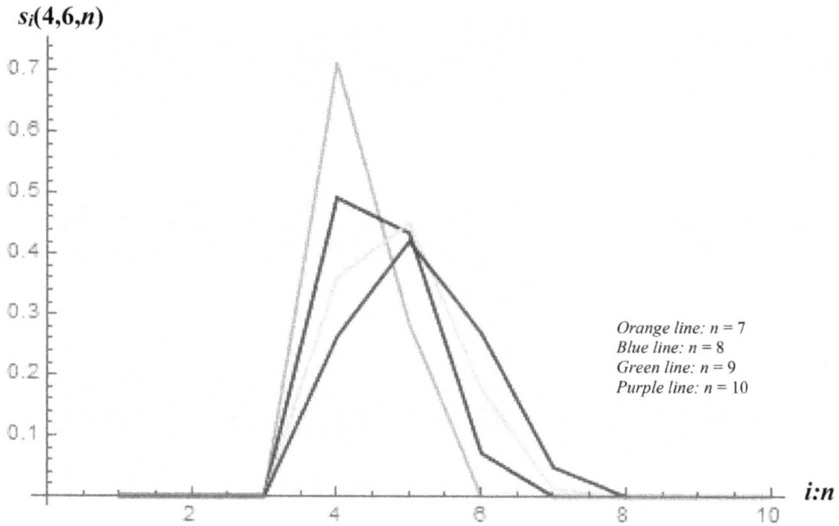

FIGURE 9.3 The signatures of 4–within–consecutive 6–out–of–*n*: *F* models.

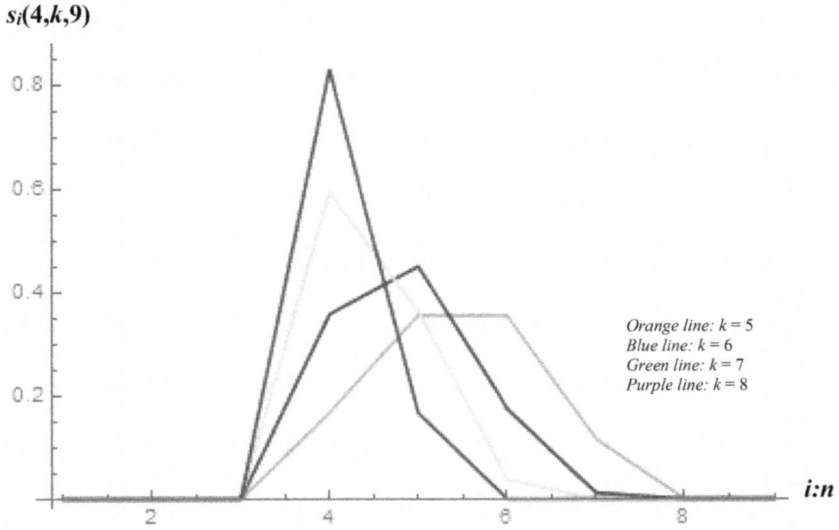

FIGURE 9.4 The signatures of 4–within–consecutive *k*–out–of–9: *F* models.

9.3 FURTHER RELIABILITY CHARACTERISTICS OF THE *R*-WITHIN-CONSECUTIVE-*K*-OUT-OF-*N*: *F* STRUCTURE

The signature vector of a reliability structure is strongly connected to several well-known performance characteristics, a fact turning it to a crucial tool for investigating coherent structures. For instance, the reliability polynomial of a system can be readily expressed by the aid of its signature, while stochastic relationships between structures' lifetimes can be also studied by comparing the corresponding signatures (see e.g., Samaniego (1985), Koutras *et al.* (2016) or Kochar *et al.* (1999)).

Let us next consider the *r*–within–consecutive *k*–out–of–*n*: *F* structure consisting of *i.i.d.* components with common reliability *p*. Then, the reliability polynomial of the abovementioned system can be expressed in terms of its signature as follows (see e.g., Samaniego (2007))

$$R(p)=\sum_{j=1}^{n}\left(\sum_{i=n-j+1}^{n} s_i(r,k,n)\right)\binom{n}{j}p^j(1-p)^{n-j}. \tag{9.2}$$

Combining equation (2) and the algorithmic procedure presented previously, we may reach closed formulae for the reliability polynomial of any member of the family of *r*–within–consecutive *k*–out–of–*n*: *F* models. Table 9.4 displays the reliability polynomial of *r*–within–consecutive *k*–out–of–*n*: *F* structures of order $n = 9$ or 10 for different values of the remaining design parameters.

In order to investigate the impact of the design parameter *k* over the performance of the resulting structure, we next depict the reliability polynomials of *r*–within–consecutive *k*–out–of–*n*: *F* structures consisting of $n = 10$ *i.i.d.* components under

TABLE 9.4
Reliability Polynomial of *r*–within–consecutive *k*–out–of–*n*: *F* Structures for Different Values of n, r, k

n	r	k	Reliability polynomial
9	3	4	$5.922p^4 + 19.2024p^5 - 70.859p^6 + 74.1427p^7 - 33.1279p^8 + 5.71984p^9$
	3	5	$20.2784p^5 - 30.9977p^6 + 7.3224p^7 + 6.23448p^8 - 1.83764p^9$
	3	6	$6.13116p^5 + 9.40968p^6 - 29.016p^7 + 14.2783p^8 + 0.19864p^9$
	3	7	$0.97272p^5 + 15.1435p^6 - 15.2669p^7 - 9.78768p^8 + 9.93832p^9$
	3	8	$6.9216p^6 + 15.2352p^7 - 42.2352p^8 + 21.0784p^9$
	4	5	$9.83304p^3 + 0.72342p^4 - 46.3957p^5 + 65.6897p^6 - 37.4227p^7 + 9.74484p^8 - 1.17236p^9$
	4	6	$1.03488p^3 + 17.577p^4 - 22.6951p^5 - 21.6871p^6 + 45.9389p^7 - 21.1302p^8 + 1.96168p^9$
	4	7	$4.9014p^4 + 26.4096p^5 - 70.6524p^6 + 40.4856p^7 + 9.8406p^8 - 9.9848p^9$
	4	8	$21.1579p^5 - 0.63168p^6 - 89.0525p^7 + 104.368p^8 - 34.8421p^9$
10	3	4	$10.794p^4 - 23.3755p^5 + 65.0622p^6 - 138.554p^7 + 144.217p^8 - 70.4432p^9 + 13.3463p^{10}$
	3	5	$50.5386p^6 - 122.189p^7 + 108.335p^8 - 42.2576p^9 + 6.573p^{10}$
	3	6	$20.034p^6 - 20.3016p^7 - 14.2992p^8 + 19.3672p^9 - 3.8004p^{10}$
	3	7	$5.9472p^6 + 16.1064p^7 - 39.0024p^8 + 15.8968p^9 + 2.052p^{10}$

3	**8**	$0.882p^6 + 18.2208p^7 - 14.9544p^8 - 18.2816p^9 + 15.1332p^{10}$
3	**9**	$8.0784p^7 + 20.7468p^8 - 55.7648p^9 + 27.9216p^{10}$
4	**5**	$50.0346p^4 - 150.877p^5 + 189.105p^6 - 128.338p^7 + 53.6382p^8 - 14.504p^9 + 1.94124p^{10}$
4	**6**	$10.1094p^4 + 19.3284p^5 - 93.2736p^6 + 97.6224p^7 - 33.1506p^8 - 0.77p^9 + 1.134p^{10}$
4	**7**	$1.0626p^4 + 23.7535p^5 - 19.803p^6 - 59.5752p^7 + 89.0694p^8 - 35.3444p^9 + 1.83708p^{10}$
4	**8**	$6.01272p^5 + 40.5972p^6 - 102.516p^7 + 48.8376p^8 + 27.4204p^9 - 19.3519p^{10}$
4	**9**	$27.909p^6 + 8.364p^7 - 147.546p^8 + 168.364p^9 - 56.091p^{10}$

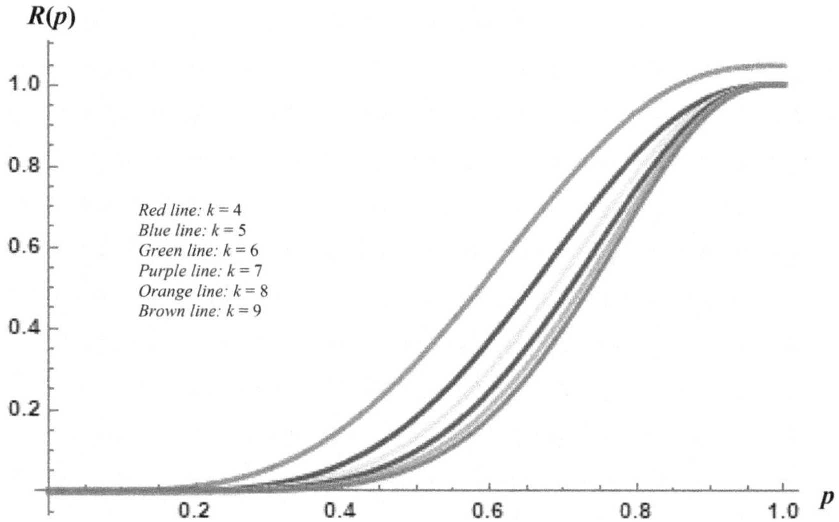

FIGURE 9.5 The reliability polynomials of 3–within–consecutive k–out–of–10: F models.

the pre-specified design parameter $r = 3$ versus the common reliability of its components p. Indeed, Figure 9.5 shows off the influence of the design parameter k on the reliability of the resulting system.

More precisely, six different designs appear at Figure 9.5, namely the 3–within–consecutive k–out–of–10: F structures under the choices $k_= 4$ (Red line), $k_= 5$ (Blue line), $k_= 6$ (Green line), $k_= 7$ (Purple line), $k_= 8$ (Orange line) and $k_= 9$ (Brown line). It is evident that the reliability polynomial under the design parameter $k = 4$ (Red color line) exceeds the remaining polynomials displayed in Figure 9.5. In other words, based on the above figure, it is easily deduced that the reliability of the 3–within–consecutive k–out–of–10: F structure decreases as the design parameter k increases. Similar conclusions could be reached by looking at the reliability polynomials of the structures of order $n = 9$ which are displayed at Table 9.4.

We next study the residual lifetime of the r–within–consecutive k–out–of–n: F structure consisting of n *i.i.d.* components. More precisely, signature-based formulae for the *mean residual lifetime* (*MRL*, hereafter) and the conditional mean residual lifetime (*CMRL*, hereafter) of the r–within–consecutive k–out–of–n: F model are discussed, while for illustration purposes an application is also presented.

The *MRL* function of the r–within–consecutive k–out–of–n: F structure can be expressed as

$$m_{r,k,n}(t) = E(T - t | T > t) = \frac{1}{P(T > t)} \int_t^{\infty} P(T > x)dx, \tag{9.3}$$

where T corresponds to the structure's lifetime.

In other words, the *MRL* function denotes actually the expected (additional) survival time of the underlying structure of age *t*. Since the system's reliability can be viewed as a mixture of the reliabilities of *i*–out–of–*n*: *F* structures (see Samaniego (1985)), we deduce that

$$P(T > t) = \sum_{i=1}^{n} s_i(r,k,n)P(T_{i:n} > t). \tag{9.4}$$

Combining formulae (2) and (3), we may express the *MRL* function as

$$m_{r,k,n}(t) = \frac{\sum_{i=1}^{n} s_i(r,k,n)P(T_{i:n} > t)m_{i:n}(t)}{\sum_{i=1}^{n} s_i(r,k,n)P(T_{i:n} > t)}, \tag{9.5}$$

where $m_{i:n}(t)$ corresponds to the *MRL* function of an *i*-out-of-*n*: *F* model consisting of components with *i.i.d.* lifetimes $T_1, T_2, ..., T_i$ ($1 \le i \le n$) and can be written as

$$m_{i:n}(t) = \frac{1}{P(T_{i:n} > t)} \int_t^{\infty} P(T_{i:n} > x)dx. \tag{9.6}$$

Since the components are assumed to be *i.i.d.*, it is known that the probability appeared in the above integral, can be determined as (see e.g., David and Nagaraja (2003))

$$P(T_{i:n} > t) = 1 - \sum_{j=n-i+1}^{n} (-1)^{j-n+i-1} \binom{j-1}{n-i} \binom{n}{j} P(T_{1:j} \le t),$$

where

$$P(T_{1:j} \le t) = 1 - P(T_1 > t, ..., T_j > t) = 1 - \bar{F}_j(t, ..., t),$$

while $\bar{F}_j(t_1, ..., t_j) = P(T_1 > t_1, ..., T_j > t_j)$ corresponds to the joint survival function of lifetimes $T_1, T_2, ..., T_j$ picked out from the *i.i.d.* random lifetimes $T_1, T_2, ..., T_n$. Therefore, under the *i.i.d.* assumption the following holds true

$$P(T_{i:n} > t) = 1 - \sum_{j=n-i+1}^{n} (-1)^{j-n+i-1} \binom{j-1}{n-i} \binom{n}{j} (1 - \bar{F}_j(t, ..., t)). \tag{9.7}$$

On the other hand, the so-called conditional mean residual lifetime (*CMRL*), namely the average value of lifetime $T - t$ under the restriction that $T_{z:n} > t$ corresponds to the expected remaining lifetime of a structure of age *t* given that, at least $n - z + 1$ components of the structure are still working at that time $(1 \le z \le n)$. Consequently, the *CMRL* function of the *r*–within–consecutive *k*–out–of–*n*: *F* structure is given as

$$m_{r,k,n}(t;z) = E(T-t \mid T_{z:n} > t) = \int_0^{\infty} P(T > t+x \mid T_{z:n} > t)dx. \tag{9.8}$$

Since

$$P(T > s \mid T_{z:n} > t) = \sum_{i=1}^{n} s_i(r,k,n) P(T_{i:n} > s \mid T_{z:n} > t), \text{ for } t < s$$

it is straightforward that the *CMRL* function can be computed as

$$m_{r,k,n}(t;z) = \sum_{i=1}^{n} s_i(r,k,n) \int_0^{\infty} P(T_{i:n} > t+x \mid T_{z:n} > t)dx$$

$$= \frac{1}{P(T_{z:n} > t)} \sum_{i=1}^{n} s_i(r,k,n) \int_0^{\infty} P(T_{i:n} > t+x, T_{z:n} > t)dx \tag{9.9}$$

A similar argumentation for the determination of *MRL* and *CMRL* functions of other reliability models has been followed by Triantafyllou and Koutras (2014), Eryilmaz *et al.* (2011) and Triantafyllou (2020c).

For illustration purposes, we next implement the above expressions under the Pareto model. More precisely, we assume that the random vector $(T_1, T_2, \ldots, T_n)$ follows a *multivariate Pareto* distribution, namely

$$\bar{F}_n(t_1,\ldots,t_n) = \left(\sum_{i=1}^{n} t_i - n + 1 \right)^{-a}, \quad t_i > 1, \text{ for } i = 1,2,\ldots,n$$

where a is a positive parameter. Under the Pareto distribution, we have

$$\bar{F}_j(t,t,\ldots,t) = \left(j(t-1)+1 \right)^{-a}, \quad t > 1,$$

while the corresponding *MRL* function of an i-out-of-n: F model can now be expressed as

$$m_{i:n}(t) = \frac{\int_t^{\infty} [1 - \sum_{j=n-i+1}^{n} (-1)^{j-n+i-1} \binom{j-1}{n-i} \binom{n}{j} (1-(j(x-1)+1)^{-a})]dx}{1 - \sum_{j=n-i+1}^{n} (-1)^{j-n+i-1} \binom{j-1}{n-i} \binom{n}{j} (1-(j(t-1)+1)^{-a})}.$$

Consequently, the *MRL* and the *CMRL* function of the r–within–consecutive k–out–of–n: F model can now be viewed as

$$m_{r,k,n}(t) = \frac{\sum_{i=1}^{n} s_i(r,k,n)(1 - \sum_{j=n-i+1}^{n} (-1)^{j-n+i-1} \binom{j-1}{n-i} \binom{n}{j} \left(1-(j(t-1)+1)^{-a}\right)) m_{i:n}(t)}{\sum_{i=1}^{n} s_i(r,k,n)(1 - \sum_{j=n-i+1}^{n} (-1)^{j-n+i-1} \binom{j-1}{n-i} \binom{n}{j} \left(1-(j(t-1)+1)^{-a}\right))}$$

and

$$E(T_{r,k,n} - t \mid T_{1:n} > t) = \frac{1+n(t-1)}{a-1} \sum_{i=1}^{n} s_i(r,k,n) \sum_{j=0}^{i-1} \sum_{l=0}^{j} (-1)^l \binom{n}{j} \binom{j}{l} \frac{1}{n-j+l}, a > 1$$

respectively. Table 9.5 presents the *MRL* and *CMRL* values of the *r*–within–consecutive *k*–out–of–*n*: *F* structure for different values of the design parameters r, n, k, a and $t > 0$.

Based on the above numerical results, we may reach some interesting conclusions. More precisely, the *MRL* function of the *r*–within–consecutive *k*–out–of–*n*: *F* structure, under the multivariate Pareto model with parameter *a*, seems to:

- drop off in regard to *n* (for a fixed group of the remaining design parameters t, r, k, a)
- increase in regard to *r* (for a fixed group of the remaining design parameters t, n, k, a)
- increase in regard to *t* (for a fixed group of the remaining design parameters n, r, k, a)
- drop off in regard to *k* (for a fixed group of the remaining design parameters t, r, n, a)
- drop off in regard to *a* (for a fixed group of the remaining design parameters t, r, k, n).

TABLE 9.5
The *MRL* and *CMRL* of the *r*–within–consecutive *k*–out–of–*n*: *F* Model under the Multivariate Pareto Model

			a = 1.2		a = 1.8		a = 2.4		a = 3	
n	(r, k)	t	MRL	CMRL	MRL	CMRL	MRL	CMRL	MRL	CMRL
6	(3, 4)	2	7.9058	28.6071	1.91571	7.15178	1.07267	4.08673	0.740779	2.86071
		3	12.8201	53.1275	3.14708	13.2819	1.77835	7.58965	1.2362	5.31275
		4	17.7896	77.6479	4.39072	19.412	2.48984	11.0926	1.73481	7.76479
		5	22.774	102.168	5.63752	25.5421	3.20275	14.5955	2.23416	10.2168
		6	27.7645	126.689	6.8856	31.6722	3.91622	18.0984	2.73379	12.6689
		7	32.7581	151.209	8.13432	37.8023	4.62997	21.6013	3.23354	15.1209
		8	37.7535	175.73	9.38341	43.9324	5.34388	25.1042	3.73337	17.573
		9	42.7501	200.25	10.6327	50.0625	6.05788	28.6071	4.23324	20.025
		10	47.7474	224.77	11.8822	56.1926	6.77194	32.11	4.73315	22.477
6	(3,5)	2	7.37351	23.8952	1.78967	5.9738	1.00264	3.4136	2.07215	2.38952
		3	12.307	44.3768	3.02466	11.0942	1.7095	6.33954	4.96993	4.43768
		4	17.2834	64.8584	4.26946	16.2146	2.42126	9.26549	8.73908	6.48584
		5	22.2713	85.34	5.51682	21.335	3.13427	12.1914	13.2579	8.534
		6	27.2639	105.822	6.76522	26.4554	3.84779	15.1174	18.45	10.5822

(Continued)

TABLE 9.5 (Continued)

			a = 1.2		a = 1.8		a = 2.4		a = 3	
n	(r, k)	t	MRL	CMRL	MRL	CMRL	MRL	CMRL	MRL	CMRL
		7	32.259	126.303	8.01415	31.5758	4.56156	18.0433	24.2613	12.6303
		8	37.2555	146.785	9.26338	36.6962	5.27548	20.9693	30.6503	14.6785
		9	42.2528	167.266	10.5128	41.8166	5.98949	23.8952	37.5841	16.7266
		10	47.2507	187.748	11.7624	46.937	6.70357	26.8211	45.0352	18.7748
6	(4,5)	2	8.96488	40.243	2.13917	10.0607	1.18343	5.749	0.809355	4.0243
		3	13.7817	74.737	3.34749	18.6843	1.87703	10.6767	1.29697	7.4737
		4	18.715	109.231	4.58283	27.3078	2.58422	15.6044	1.79281	10.9231
		5	23.6805	143.725	5.85236	35.9313	3.29493	20.5321	2.29073	14.3725
		6	28.6594	178.219	7.07083	44.5548	4.00706	25.4599	2.78948	17.8219
		7	33.6452	212.713	8.3178	53.1783	4.71991	30.3153	3.28865	21.2713
		8	38.635	247.207	9.56562	61.8018	5.43316	35.3153	3.78806	24.7207
		9	43.6273	281.701	10.014	70.4252	6.14667	40.243	4.28761	28.1701
		10	48.6213	316.195	12.0627	79.0488	6.86036	45.1707	4.78727	31.6195
7	(3,4)	2	7.51198	28.9434	1.81981	7.23584	1.01796	4.13476	0.701869	2.89434
		3	12.4364	54.2688	3.05258	13.5672	1.72361	7.75268	1.19663	5.42688
		4	17.4095	79.5942	4.29658	19.8986	2.43494	11.3706	1.69485	7.95942
		5	22.3957	104.92	5.54352	26.2299	3.14773	14.9885	2.19396	10.492
		6	27.3872	130.245	6.79168	32.5613	3.86111	18.6064	2.69343	13.0245
		7	32.3816	155.571	8.04044	38.8926	4.57479	22.2244	3.19307	15.5571
		8	37.3775	180.896	9.28955	45.224	5.28865	25.8423	3.69281	18.0896
		9	42.3745	206.221	10.5359	41.5553	6.00261	29.4602	4.19262	20.6221
		10	47.3721	231.547	11.7884	57.8867	6.71664	33.0781	4.69247	23.1547
7	(3,5)	2	7.11198	24.4981	1.72957	6.12452	0.970326	3.49973	0.670584	2.44981
		3	12.0572	45.9339	2.96726	11.4835	1.67856	6.56199	1.16701	4.59339
		4	17.0378	67.3697	4.21301	16.8424	2.39079	9.62425	1.66582	6.73697
		5	22.028	88.8056	5.46086	22.2014	3.10405	12.6865	2.16523	8.88056
		6	27.022	110.241	6.70957	27.5603	3.81772	15.7488	2.66488	11.0241
		7	32.018	131.677	7.9587	32.9193	4.53159	18.811	3.16464	13.1677
		8	37.0151	153.113	9.20808	38.2783	5.24558	21.8733	3.66448	15.3113
		9	42.0129	174.549	10.4576	43.6372	5.95965	24.9356	4.16435	17.4549
		10	47.0112	195.985	11.7072	48.9962	6.67376	27.9978	4.66425	19.5985
7	(4,5)	2	8.56974	41.7275	2.05123	10.4319	1.13798	5.96107	0.780286	4.17275
		3	13.4186	78.239	3.26763	19.5598	1.83609	11.177	1.27101	7.8239
		4	18.3643	114.751	4.5061	28.6876	2.54496	16.3929	1.768	11.4751
		5	23.3364	151.262	5.75012	37.8155	3.25654	21.6089	2.26653	15.1262
		6	28.3194	187.774	6.99657	46.9434	3.96921	26.8248	2.76565	18.7774
		7	33.3079	224.285	8.2442	56.0713	4.68242	32.0407	3.26507	22.4285
		8	38.2997	260.797	9.4925	65.1992	5.39594	37.2567	3.76466	26.0797
		9	43.2935	297.308	10.7412	74.3271	6.10965	42.4726	4.26435	29.7308
		10	48.2887	333.82	11.9902	83.455	6.82349	47.6886	4.76411	33.382

In addition, Table 9.5 reveals that, under multivariate Pareto model with parameter a, the *CMRL* function of the r–within–consecutive k–out–of–n: F system seems to:

- increase in regard to n (for a fixed group of the remaining design parameters t,r,k,a)
- increase in regard to r (for a fixed group of the remaining design parameters t,n,k,a)
- increase in regard to t (for a fixed group of the remaining design parameters n,r,k,a)
- drop off in regard to k (for a fixed group of the remaining design parameters t,r,n,a)
- drop off in regard to a (for a fixed group of the remaining design parameters t,r,k,n).

9.4 SIGNATURE-BASED COMPARISONS AMONG CONSECUTIVE-TYPE SYSTEMS

In this section, we shall illustrate how the signature vectors can be exploited for comparing the lifetimes of well-known reliability structures. We shall focus on results pertaining to the usual stochastic order. More precisely, if T_1 and T_2 denote the lifetimes of two systems with cumulative distribution functions F_1 and F_2, respectively, then T_1 will be said to be stochastically smaller than T_2 in the usual stochastic order (denoted by $T_1 \leq_{st} T_2$) if the following inequality holds true

$$P(T_1 > t) \leq P(T_2 > t), \quad t \in (-\infty, +\infty).$$

Generally speaking, $T_1 \leq_{st} T_2$ if and only if T_1 is less likely than T_2 to take on values beyond t. Kochar *et al.* (1999) offered a sufficient condition for the signature-based stochastic ordering of structures' lifetimes. More specifically, denoting by $s_{1j}(n)$, $s_{2j}(n)$, $j = 1,2,...,n$ the signature coordinates of two reliability systems, they proved that if

$$\sum_{j=i}^{n} s_{1j}(n) \leq \sum_{j=i}^{n} s_{2j}(n) \tag{9.10}$$

for all $i = 1,2,...,n$, then $T_1 \leq_{st} T_2$. It is noteworthy that the aforementioned ordering attribute has been extended by Navarro *et al.* (2005) to coherent structures with (possibly) dependent units. Taking into advantage the numerical experimentation, which has been carried out previously, we next compare the r–within–consecutive k–out–of–n: F system versus several well-known consecutive-type structures. More precisely, we first consider six different reliability systems of order n = 8 and we then compare stochastically their lifetimes by the aid of (9). Table 9.6 presents the stochastic orderings among the following structures

TABLE 9.6
Stochastic Orderings among Consecutive-Type Structures of Order $n = 8$

	3-within-consecutive-4-out-of-8: *F*	consecutive-3-out-of-8: *F*	2-consecutive-2-out-of-8: *F*	(8,3,2) system	<8,3,2> system	3-out-of-8: *F*
3-within-consecutive-4-out-of-8: *F*	$=_{st}$	$\leq_{st}$	$\leq_{st}$	$\geq_{st}$	$\geq_{st}$	$\geq_{st}$
consecutive-3-out-of-8: *F*		$=_{st}$	--	$\geq_{st}$	$\geq_{st}$	$\geq_{st}$
2-consecutive-2-out-of-8: *F*			$=_{st}$	$\geq_{st}$	$\geq_{st}$	$\geq_{st}$
(8,3,2) system				$=_{st}$	$\leq_{st}$	$\leq_{st}$
<8,3,2> system					$=_{st}$	$\geq_{st}$
3-out-of-8: *F*						$=_{st}$

- the 3–within–consecutive 4–out–of–8: *F* system
- the consecutive 3–out–of–8: *F* system (see, e.g., Derman *et al.* (1982))
- the 2- consecutive 2–out–of–8: *F* system (see, e.g., Eryilmaz *et al.* (2011))
- the (8,3,2) system (see, e.g., Triantafyllou and Koutras (2014))
- the <8,3,2> system (see, e.g., Triantafyllou (2020b))
- the 3–out–of–8: *F* system.

By recalling (9) we managed to establish several stochastic relationships between the consecutive-type structures, which have been considered. Based on Table 9.6, it is straightforward that, among the underlying structures, the 2- consecutive 2–out–of–8: *F* system and the consecutive 3–out–of–8: *F* system seem to perform better than the remaining competitors. On the other hand, the (8,3,2) system and the 3–out–of–8 structure are stochastically worse than the remaining competitive models.

9.5 DISCUSSION

In the present chapter, the *r*–within–consecutive *k*–out–of–*n*: *F* system with independent and identically distributed components ordered in a line has been studied. An algorithmic procedure for computing the signature vector of the *r*–within–consecutive *k*–out–of–*n*: *F* model has been presented in detail. An extensive numerical experimentation carried out, offers to the reader the signatures of several members of the aforementioned class under specified designs. In addition, a signature-based reliability analysis of the performance of the *r*–within–consecutive *k*–out–of–*n*: *F* structures is accomplished. More precisely, the reliability function, the mean residual lifetime and the conditional mean residual lifetime of these consecutive-type systems are studied in some detail, while several numerical and graphical results reveal the impact of the design parameters over their performance. It is concluded that the r–within–consecutive k–out–of–n: F system exhibits better performance for larger values of the design parameter r and n, while it seems that its competency weakens as the parameter k increases. Furthermore, the r–within–consecutive k–out–of–n: F system is stochastically compared to several consecutive-type reliability models of the same order and has been proved to be quite competitive. Finally, the reliability study of structures with two common failure criteria which have not yet been fully covered, could be an interesting topic for future research.

REFERENCES

Chang, J. G., Cui, L. & Hwang, F. K. (1999). Reliabilities for (n, f, k) systems, *Statistics & Probability Letters*, **43(3)**, 237–242.

Chang, J. G., Cui, L. & Hwang, F. K. (2000). *Reliabilities of consecutive-k systems*, Kluwer Academic Publishers, The Netherlands.

Chao, M. T., Fu, J. C. & Koutras, M. V. (1995). Survey of reliability studies of consecutive-k-out-of-n: F & related systems, *IEEE Transactions on Reliability*, **44(1)**, 120–127.

Cui, L., Kuo, W., Li, J. & Xie, M. (2006). On the dual reliability systems of (n, f, k) and $< n, f, k >$, *Statistics & Probability Letters*, **76(11)**, 1081–1088.

Cui, L. & Xie, M. (2005). On a generalized k-out-of-n system and its reliability, *International Journal of Systems Science*, **36**, 267–274.

Dafnis, S. D., Makri, F. S. & Philippou, A. N. (2019). The reliability of a generalized consecutive system, *Applied Mathematics and Computation*, **359**, 186–193.

David, H. A. & Nagaraja, H. N. (2003). *Order statistics*, John Wiley & Sons, NY.

Derman, C., Lieberman, G. J. & Ross, S. M. (1982). On the consecutive-k-out-of-n: F system, *IEEE Transactions on Reliability*, **31(1)**, 57–63.

Eryilmaz, S., Koutras, M. V. & Triantafyllou, I. S. (2011). Signature based analysis of m-consecutive k-out-of-n: F systems with exchangeable components, *Naval Research Logistics*, **58(4)**, 344–354.

Eryilmaz, S. & Tuncel, A. (2015). Computing the signature of a generalized k-out-of-n system, *IEEE Transactions on Reliability*, **64**, 766–771.

Eryilmaz, S. & Zuo, M. J. (2010). Constrained (k,d)-out-of-n systems, *International Journal of Systems Science*, **41(3)**, 679–685.

Griffith, W. S. (1986). On consecutive–k–out–of–n: Failure systems and their generalizations, In: Basu, A. P. (ed.) *Reliability and Quality Control*, Elsevier, Amsterdam, 157–165.

Kochar, S., Mukerjee, H. & Samaniego, F. J. (1999). The signature of a coherent system and its application to comparison among systems, *Naval Research Logistics*, **46(5)**, 507–523.

Koutras, M. V., Triantafyllou, I. S. & Eryilmaz, S. (2016). Stochastic comparisons between lifetimes of reliability systems with exchangeable components, *Methodology and Computing in Applied Probability*, **18**, 1081–1095.

Kumar, A. & Ram, M. (2018). Signature reliability of *k-out-of-n* sliding window system, In: Ram, M. (ed.) *Modeling and Simulation Based Analysis in Reliability Engineering,* CRC Press: Taylor & Francis Group, Boca Raton, pp. 233–247.

Kumar, A. & Ram, M. (2019). Signature of linear consecutive *k-out-of-n* systems, In: Ram, M. & Dohi, T. (eds.) *Systems Engineering: Reliability Analysis Using k-out-of-n Structures*, CRC Press: Taylor & Francis Group, Boca Raton, pp. 207–216.

Kumar, A., Singh, S. B. & Ram, M. (2019). Reliability appraisal for consecutive-k-out-f-n: F system of non-identical components with intuitionistic fuzzy set, *International Journal of Operation Research*, **36**, 362–374.

Kuo, W. & Zuo, M. J. (2003). *Optimal Reliability Modeling: Principles and Applications*, John Wiley & Sons, Hoboken, NJ.

Navarro, J., Ruiz, J. M. & Sandoval, C. J. (2005). A note on comparisons among coherent systems with dependent components using signatures, *Statistics and Probability Letters*, **72**, 179–185.

Ram, M. (2013). On system reliability approaches: A brief survey, *International Journal of System Assurance Engineering and Management*, **4**(2), 101–117.

Samaniego, F. J. (1985). On closure of the *IFR* class under formation of coherent systems, *IEEE Transactions on Reliability*, **34(1)**, 69–72.

Samaniego, F. J. (2007). *System Signatures and Their Applications in Engineering Reliability*, Springer, NY.

Tong, Y. L. (1985). A rearrangement inequality for the longest run, with an application to network reliability, *Journal of Applied Probability*, **22**, 386–393.

Triantafyllou, I. S. (2015). Consecutive-type reliability systems: An overview and some applications, *Journal of Quality and Reliability Engineering*, **2015**, Article ID 212303, 20 pages.

Triantafyllou, I. S. (2020a). On consecutive k_1 and k_2-out-of-n: F reliability systems, *Mathematics*, **8**, 630.

Triantafyllou, I. S. (2020b). Reliability study of <$n,f,2$> systems: A generating function approach, *International Journal of Mathematical, Engineering and Management Sciences, accepted for publication.*

Triantafyllou, I. S. (2020c). On the lifetime and signature of the constrained (k,d) out-of-n: F reliability systems, *International Journal of Mathematical, Engineering and Management Sciences, accepted for publication.*

Triantafyllou, I. S. & Koutras, M. V. (2008a). On the signature of coherent systems and applications for consecutive–k–out–of–n: F systems, In: Bedford, T., Quigley, J., Walls, L., Alkali, B., Daneshkhah, A. & Hardman, G. (eds.) *Advances in Mathematical Modeling for Reliability*. IOS Press, Amsterdam, pp. 119–128.

Triantafyllou, I. S. & Koutras, M. V. (2008b). On the signature of coherent systems and applications, *Probability in the Engineering and Informational Science*, **22(1)**, 19–35.

Triantafyllou, I. S. & Koutras, M. V. (2011). Signature and *IFR* preservation of 2-within-consecutive k-out-of-n: F systems, *IEEE Transactions on Reliability*, **60(1)**, 315–322.

Triantafyllou, I. S. & Koutras, M. V. (2014). Reliability properties of (n, f, k) systems, *IEEE Transactions on Reliability*, **63(1)**, 357–366.

Zuo, M. J., Lin, D. & Wu, Y. (2000). Reliability evaluation of combined k–out–of–n:F, consecutive–k–out–of–n:F and linear connected–(r,s)–out–of– (m,n): F system structures, *IEEE Transactions on Reliability*, **49**, 99–104.

10 A Technique for Identifying Groups of Fractional Factorial Designs with Similar Properties

Harry Evangelaras and Christos Peveretos

CONTENTS

10.1 INTRODUCTION

In most experimental situations and at the beginning of the experimentation process, usually many factors are considered for having a significant influence on the process that is investigated. The effects of these potential active factors are explored using a carefully designed screening experiment. Therefore, screening designs are widely used to identify which factors have a significant influence on the response of interest, see Wu and Hamada (2009) and Goos and Jones (2011). The design matrix has in general n rows and k columns. Factors are assigned to the columns of the design and each row of the design shows a specific combination of the levels of the factors also known as treatment or run. The active factors are then further studied, in a second phase of experimentation. Screening designs must be carefully chosen by the experimenter, aiming at:

i. reducing the experimentation cost by controlling the number of experiments that must be conducted and
ii. providing efficient estimations of the factorial effects of interest.

DOI: 10.1201/9781003203124-10

The main design principle for the efficient use of screening designs is the "effect sparsity" principle, as introduced by Box and Meyer (1986). Box and Meyer observed that, when many factors are examined in an experiment, usually only few of them have a significant effect on the response of interest. Under this principle, one can carefully design an economical experiment that would be able to identify this small set of the active factors. For reducing the experimental cost, the factors are usually tested in two levels and the designs used belong to the class of the two-level screening designs. The factors that are identified active, can then be further studied in a second experimentation phase, using another experimental design, which can be designed, for instance, to accommodate factors in more than two levels.

Most of the times, the main interest of the experimenter who uses a two-level screening design relies on the estimation of the main effects of the factors. Using standard regression techniques (for a nice overview on regression one may refer to Montgomery, Peck and Vining (2012)), a first order model of the form

$$Y = b_0 + \sum_{i=1}^{k} b_i x_i + \varepsilon$$

is fitted to the data and active main effects are identified. Under this first order model, the most efficient designs that can be used belong to the class of the two-level Orthogonal Arrays, $OA(n, k, 2, t)$, since their use provide uncorrelated estimates of the parameters of the given model. An orthogonal array $OA(n, k, 2, t)$ is an $n \times k$ matrix with n rows and k columns consisting of 2 distinct symbols arranged in such a way that, for each selection of t columns of the matrix, all 2^t distinct row-vectors appear the same number of times. For a complete overview on orthogonal arrays see Hedayat, Sloane and Stufken (1999).

Orthogonal arrays can be considered as fractional factor designs, where n is the number of experimental runs, k is the number of the two-level factors that are examined, and t is the strength of the array, which can be used to reveal the aliasing of effects. For example, in an array with strength $t = 2$ then main effects are not aliased with each other but are aliased with two-factor interactions. Therefore, orthogonal arrays with strength 2, are fractional factorial designs with resolution *III* and offer uncorrelated estimates of the parameters in the first-order model, but not in models that interactions of factors are also considered. When the two-factor interactions are also of interest, an orthogonal array with strength $t = 4$ can be used, since such an array corresponds to a fractional factorial design with resolution *V*, and therefore main effects and two-factor interactions are free of aliasing. We note that the use of an orthogonal array with a large strength, requires many runs (actually, many more than the runs of an orthogonal array of strength 2, for a given number of factors, k) and therefore deviates from the main requirements of a screening design. Wang and Wu (1995) showed that most orthogonal arrays with strength $t = 2$ possess a "hidden projection property" under which, a collection of effects (main or/and interactions) can be efficiently estimated with their use. Under this property, a second order model of the form

$$Y = b_0 + \sum_{i=1}^{k} b_i x_i + \sum_{i=1}^{k-1} \sum_{j=i+1}^{k} b_{ij} x_i x_j + \varepsilon \tag{10.1}$$

TABLE 10.1
Number of Non-Isomorphic Two-Level Orthogonal Arrays for Various *n* and *k*

n	k			
	3	**4**	**5**	**6**
12	2	1	2	2
16	3	5	11	27
20	3	3	11	75
24	4	10	63	1350
28	4	7	127	17826
32	5	19	491	266632

is usually adopted for the analysis and the efficiency of the estimation of its parameters is quantified using the popular D–efficiency criterion that is based on the determinant of the information matrix of the model used.

To summarize, the class of two-level orthogonal arrays of strength $t = 2$ offers excellent designs for running a screening experiment. An additional advantage that the two-level orthogonal arrays possess, is that they exist for any run size n that is a multiple of 4. Therefore, one can look for an economical and efficient design for conducting a screening experiment in the class of two-level orthogonal arrays. Notably, one can construct many two-level orthogonal arrays, given the number of runs n and the number of factors k. Therefore, for a given number of runs n and of factors k, there may be many competitive designs to choose of. Some of them may share the same properties and so can be considered equivalent, but there may be designs that are superior to others. Two n x k orthogonal arrays are said to be "isomorphic" if one can be obtained from the other by a sequence of row permutations, column permutations and permutations of symbols in any of the k columns. Otherwise, they are called "non-isomorphic." Isomorphic arrays share the same design properties and so, they are regarded as equivalent. A common technique for identifying the superior design with n runs and k columns is the identification of the list of the non-isomorphic n x k orthogonal arrays and then, the evaluation of them using some criteria. Table 10.1, shows the number of non-isomorphic two-level orthogonal arrays for various n and k, as found by Evangelaras, Koukouvinos and Lappas (2007). We note that the full list of orthogonal arrays for larger values of n is unknown, due to the large complexity of the construction procedure. For an up-to-date information on non-isomorphic orthogonal arrays, we refer to www.pietereendebak.nl/oapackage/series.html (Schoen, Eendebak and Nguyen 2010).

In the next section we review the most popular criteria that are used to evaluate orthogonal arrays and cater for the proper selection of a superior design.

10.2 WELL-KNOWN DESIGN SELECTION CRITERIA

Many of the design selection criteria that have been proposed in the literature consider capturing the aliasing structures of a design. A key design principle that enhances the use of such criteria is the "effect hierarchy principle." Under this principle, effects of lower order are likely to be significant in an experiment. Therefore, for running an experiment, it seems wise to select a design that minimizes the aliasing between the effects of lower orders (usually main effects and two factor interactions).

Deng and Tang (1999) defined the *J* characteristics of a two-level orthogonal array as quantities that can be used to extensively study the aliasing structure of these designs. In detail, a two-level orthogonal array $D=\left(d_{ij}\right)$ with $n = 4z$ runs and k columns is regarded as a set of k column vectors with elements -1 and +1, $D=\left\{\boldsymbol{d}_1,\boldsymbol{d}_2,\ldots,\boldsymbol{d}_k\right\}$. For each subset S of m design columns $S=\left\{\boldsymbol{d}_{j_1},\boldsymbol{d}_{j_2},\ldots,\boldsymbol{d}_{j_m}\right\}$, $1 \le m \le k$, the quantity

$$J_m\left(S\right)=J_m\left(\boldsymbol{d}_{j_1},\boldsymbol{d}_{j_2},\ldots,\boldsymbol{d}_{j_m}\right)=\left|\sum_{i=1}^{n} d_{ij_1}\cdot d_{ij_2}\cdots d_{ij_m}\right|$$

is the *J* characteristic of the specific set of columns *S*. Clearly, the product of the symbols of the *m* columns from each subset *S* essentially corresponds to an *m*-order interaction of factors and therefore, the value of $J_m\left(S\right)$ shows the degree of aliasing between the specific *m*-order interaction and the grand mean. Equivalently, this value also shows the degree of aliasing between a main effect of a factor in *S* and the $(m-1)$-order interaction of the remaining factors in *S*, and so on. Obviously $0 \le J_m\left(S\right) \le n$, with the maximum value of *n* achieved when the corresponding effects are fully aliased. The minimum value of zero is achieved when the corresponding effects are orthogonal and therefore free of aliasing. Note that the orthogonal arrays with strength $t \ge 2$ have $J_1\left(S\right)=J_2\left(S\right)=0$, since the main effects are orthogonal to each other.

The values of the *J* characteristics are the cornerstone of the design aberration criteria. For two-level orthogonal arrays, Deng and Tang (1999, 2002) proved that these values are a multiple of 4 and the whole information regarding the aliasing structure of a design *D* can be summarized in the so-called Confounding Frequency Vector (CFV) of *D*. In detail, let $f_{m,j}$ be the frequency that each subset *S* of $m > 2$ design columns gives $J_m\left(S\right)=4\left(z+1-j\right)$, for $j=1,2,\ldots z+1$. The CFV of *D* is defined to be the following vector with $(k-2)(z+1)$ elements:

$$CFV=\left[f_{3,1},f_{3,2},\ldots,f_{3,z+1}\right];\left[f_{4,1},f_{4,2},\ldots,f_{4,z+1}\right];\ldots;\left[f_{k,1},f_{k,2},\ldots,f_{k,z+1}\right].$$

This vector provides essential information on how the factorial effects are confounded and can be used to distinguish between competitive designs. Let two non-isomorphic designs *D*1 and *D*2 with *n* runs and *k* two-level columns and let $f_i\left(D1\right)$ and $f_i\left(D2\right)$ be the i-th entry in their CFVs, $i=1,2,\ldots\left(k-2\right)\left(z+1\right)$. If *c* is the smallest integer such $f_c\left(D1\right)\neq f_c\left(D2\right)$ and $f_c\left(D1\right)<f_c\left(D2\right)$ we say that *D*1 has less generalized aberration than *D*2 and therefore is preferable over *D*2. As an example, in the Table 10.2 we list the CFVs of the eleven non-isomorphic orthogonal arrays with 20 runs and five columns.

Clearly, using this criterion, design 20.5.11 is the one that has less generalized aberration than the others. This design is the generalized minimum aberration

TABLE 10.2
The CFVs of the 11 Non-Isomorphic *OA*(20,5,2,2)

Array	CFV
20.5.1	[0, 0, 2, 0, 8, 0]; [0, 0, 1, 0, 4, 0]; [0, 0, 0, 1, 0, 0]
20.5.2	[0, 0, 2, 0, 8, 0]; [0, 0, 1, 0, 4, 0]; [0, 0, 0, 0, 0, 1]
20.5.3	[0, 0, 2, 0, 8, 0]; [0, 0, 1, 0, 4, 0]; [0, 0, 0, 1, 0, 0]
20.5.4	[0, 0, 0, 0, 10, 0]; [0, 0, 1, 0, 4, 0]; [0, 0, 0, 0, 0, 1]
20.5.5	[0, 0, 0, 0, 10, 0]; [0, 0, 1, 0, 4, 0]; [0, 0, 0, 1, 0, 0]
20.5.6	[0, 0, 1, 0, 9, 0]; [0, 0, 1, 0, 4, 0]; [0, 0, 0, 0, 0, 1]
20.5.7	[0, 0, 1, 0, 9, 0]; [0, 0, 0, 0, 5, 0]; [0, 0, 0, 1, 0, 0]
20.5.8	[0, 0, 1, 0, 9, 0]; [0, 0, 0, 0, 5, 0]; [0, 0, 0, 0, 0, 1]
20.5.9	[0, 0, 2, 0, 8, 0]; [0, 0, 0, 0, 5, 0]; [0, 0, 0, 0, 0, 1]
20.5.10	[0, 0, 0, 0, 10, 0]; [0, 0, 0, 0, 5, 0]; [0, 0, 0, 1, 0, 0]
20.5.11	[0, 0, 0, 0, 10, 0]; [0, 0, 0, 0, 5, 0]; [0, 0, 0, 0, 0, 1]

design in the class of all two-level designs with 20 runs and 5 columns since there does not exist another design with 20 runs and 5 columns with less generalized aberration than 20.5.11.

Tang and Deng (1999) exploited the J characteristics of a two-level design to propose a related criterion, called Minimum G_2 – Aberration (see also Tang 2001). For $1 \le m \le k$, all the $J_m(S)$ values of a design D with n runs and k columns are summarized in a single value,

$$A_m^g = \frac{1}{n^2}\sum J_m^2(S)$$

and then, the k values $A_1^g, A_2^g, \ldots A_k^g$ are summarized in the vector $GWP(D) = [A_1^g, A_2^g, \ldots A_k^g]$ that is called the Generalized Wordlength Pattern of D. Using this criterion, minimum G_2 – Aberration designs are those that sequentially minimize the values $A_1^g, A_2^g, \ldots A_k^g$ of $GWP(D)$. Note again that the orthogonal arrays with strength $t \ge 2$ have $A_1^g = A_2^g = 0$, since $J_1(S) = J_2(S) = 0$. For example, in Table 10.3 we list the *GWP*s of the eleven non-isomorphic orthogonal arrays with 20 runs and 5 columns.

This criterion still highlights the design 20.5.11 as the one that has less generalized aberration than the others. So, 20.5.11 is the minimum G_2 – aberration design in the class of all two-level designs with 20 runs and 5 columns.

Another popular criterion that is frequently applied is the D – efficiency criterion, which is used to measure the overall efficiency for estimating a collection of factorial effects using a design D. If the model of interest has the form

$$Y = b_0 + \sum_{i=1}^{p} b_i x_i + \varepsilon$$

the D – efficiency value is calculated using the formula

TABLE 10.3
The *GWPs* of the 11 Non-Isomorphic *OA*(20,5,2,2)

Array	GWP
20.5.1	[0, 0, 1.04, 0.52, 0.16]
20.5.2	[0, 0, 1.04, 0.52, 0]
20.5.3	[0, 0, 1.04, 0.52, 0.16]
20.5.4	[0, 0, 0.40, 0.52, 0]
20.5.5	[0, 0, 0.40, 0.52, 0.16]
20.5.6	[0, 0, 0.72, 0.52, 0]
20.5.7	[0, 0, 0.72, 0.20, 0.16]
20.5.8	[0, 0, 0.72, 0.20, 0]
20.5.9	[0, 0, 1.04, 0.20, 0]
20.5.10	[0, 0, 0.40, 0.20, 0.16]
20.5.11	[0, 0, 0.40, 0.20, 0]

$$\left|X^T X\right|^{\frac{1}{p+1}}$$

where $X = \left[\frac{1}{\|1\|}, \frac{\boldsymbol{x}_1}{\|\boldsymbol{x}_1\|}, \ldots, \frac{\boldsymbol{x}_p}{\|\boldsymbol{x}_p\|}\right]$ is the corresponding normalized model matrix. Under the effect hierarchy principle, k out of the p parameters correspond to the k main effects of the factors (that are often of primary interest) and the remaining $p - k$ parameters correspond to some or even all two-factor interactions (if they are of interest). It is obvious that a design with a high value of D–efficiency allows the estimation of the parameters of the given model of interest with high efficiency. The design with n runs and k columns that gives the highest value for a given model is the D–optimal design and hence, is preferred. Clearly, the value of D–efficiency ranges between 0 and 1. The maximum value of 1 is attained when the information matrix of the given model is diagonal and hence, the estimates of all parameters are uncorrelated.

Clearly, the D–efficiency criterion is model based and its value—given a design—can be significantly altered if a different model is considered. Therefore, a thorough design evaluation using this criterion is computer intensive, since a D–efficiency value should be calculated for all possible models and then, a comparison of these values for different designs should be performed. For example, when investigating the main effects and the two-factor interactions of 5 factors and under the hierarchy principle that requires the estimation of at least the 5 main effects, all models that consist of the 5 main effects and i two-factor interactions, $0 \le i \le 10$, are $\binom{10}{i}$ and so, a full evaluation requires the calculation of 1024 values from a given design. To overcome such cumbersome calculations, the evaluation is usually conducted by considering the D–efficiency value of the full second order model of the form (10.1),

TABLE 10.4
The *D*–Efficiency of the Model (2.1) for the 11 Non-Isomorphic *OA*(20,5,2,2)

Array	*D*–efficiency
20.5.1	0
20.5.2	0
20.5.3	0
20.5.4	0.75
20.5.5	0
20.5.6	0
20.5.7	0
20.5.8	0.75
20.5.9	0
20.5.10	0.86
20.5.11	0.87

since a high value of the *D*–efficiency of this model guarantees an efficient estimation of the parameters of any of its sub-models. Table 10.4 shows the *D*–efficiency of the model (10.1) for the 11 non-isomorphic *OA*(20,5,2,2).

With respect to the *D*–efficiency criterion, and under the model (10.1) that consists of all the main effects and the two-factor interactions, the design 20.5.11 is the best with a value of *D*–efficiency equal to 0.87. We note that only four out of the eleven non-isomorphic *OA*(20,5,2,2) can adequately estimate the 16 parameters of model (10.1). However, if the model of interest is changed, the behavior of the designs that are tested may be different. To illustrate this fact, we list in Table 10.5 the *D*–efficiencies of the eleven arrays for the model

$$Y = b_0 + \sum_{i=1}^{5} b_i x_i + b_{12}x_1x_2 + b_{15}x_1x_5 + b_{23}x_2x_3 + b_{34}x_3x_4 + b_{45}x_4x_5 + \varepsilon$$

which possesses a "cyclic" structure with respect to the interactions that are accommodated.

As Table 10.5 shows, the parameters of this new model can be efficiently estimated by 10 out of the 11 designs and 7 of them provide a *D*–efficiency value that exceeds 0.8.

As mentioned in the introduction, the main interest in the beginning of an experimental process is the quick identification of the (potentially few) active factorial effects using an economical but efficient screening design. In the next section, we propose a procedure that can be used to evaluate competitive designs. This procedure aims to evaluate the ability of a design to correctly identify the few active effects that significantly affect the process of interest.

TABLE 10.5
The *D*–Efficiency of the New Model for the 11 Non-Isomorphic *OA*(20,5,2,2)

Array	*D*–efficiency
20.5.1	0.738
20.5.2	0
20.5.3	0.739
20.5.4	0.853
20.5.5	0.852
20.5.6	0.780
20.5.7	0.840
20.5.8	0.806
20.5.9	0.815
20.5.10	0.917
20.5.11	0.917

10.3 DESIGN EVALUATION VIA SIMULATIONS

A method that can be used to evaluate a given design with n runs and k columns for its ability to correctly identify active factorial effects, is to simulate the responses from its n runs using a given "true" model and then check if the true model can be fully and correctly identified using standard regression techniques. The design can be evaluated using a large number r of iterations and keep track of the number of times the true model has been identified in these r iterations.

In detail, for implementing the procedure for a given design D, a true model consisting of p factorial effects and with p predefined parameters b_i, $i = 1,2,\ldots,p$ of the form

$$Y = b_0 + \sum_{i=1}^{p} b_i x_i + \varepsilon$$

is considered and simulated responses are obtained using the runs of D, the true model, and a vector of simulated independent and normally distributed errors $\boldsymbol{\varepsilon}$, with zero mean and a variance σ^2. The magnitude of the predefined parameters can be selected relatively to the error variance. Since it is desirable to highlight designs that can identify small to moderate effects, it is recommended to use magnitudes up to 3σ.

If there are many competitive designs to evaluate, this procedure can be applied to each of them to find superior designs by comparing the number of times each design succeeds in identifying the true model. An issue that must be considered, is the assignment of the factors to the columns of the design, since there may be certain assignments of factors to the columns of the design that could give better results than other assignments. For example, when dealing with a five-factor case, if the true model contains three main effects and an interaction, it is evident that the selection of the three columns of the design that will cater for the active main effects will play an important role in the resulting correct identifications. To eliminate such discrepancies, we first define the structure of the true model with respect to the number of the active main effects and interactions it would contain, and then we evaluate all possible true models that have such a structure, using the described procedure. Therefore, for every design tested, a vector $\mathbf{d}_{\mathrm{m}}(D)$ of size m is obtained which contains the number of true identifications in the r iterations for each one of the m models that are considered in total. Since m may be quite large in most cases, the values of $\mathbf{d}_{\mathrm{m}}(D)$ can be summarized using a smaller vector $\mathbf{v}_D$ having values that efficiently describe the distribution of the values of $\mathbf{d}_{\mathrm{m}}(D)$, such as the average, quartiles, minimum and maximum, etc. All the vectors $\mathbf{v}_D$ obtained from each competitive design can by further exploited using clustering methods to form groups of designs with similar properties and furthermore, to highlight efficient and economical designs. Another but less important issue that must be considered is the search space for the potentially active effects. In most situations, higher order interactions are assumed inactive and so, the search for active effects is usually restricted to the set of the main effects and the two-factor interactions. The following algorithm summarizes the steps of the procedure.

Step 1. Define the list of competitive designs.
Step 2. Define the structure of the true model and the space of the potentially active effects.
Step 3. Define the number of iterations r and the magnitude of the true effects.
Step 4. Pick a design D from the list of Step 1 and produce data for every true model that have the structure of Step 2, according to the settings of Step 3.
Step 5. Apply regression techniques to analyze the simulated data of Step 4 for every model considered. Define the vector $\mathbf{d}_{\mathrm{m}}(D)$ from the correct identifications.
Step 6. Repeat Steps 4 and 5 for every design in the list of Step 1.
Step 7. Summarize each $\mathbf{d}_{\mathrm{m}}(D)$ with $\mathbf{v}_D$, using values that efficiently describe the distribution of the values of $\mathbf{d}_{\mathrm{m}}(D)$.
Step 8. Apply clustering procedures to create clusters of designs with similar properties, using the values of $\mathbf{v}_D$.

To illustrate the procedure, we evaluate the four orthogonal arrays 20.5.4, 20.5.8, 20.5.10, and 20.5.11 with 20 runs and 5 columns that can efficiently estimate the parameters of the complete second order model (10.1), under a true model that consists of any three effects (either main effects or two-factor interactions). For every design, we will conduct $r = 10000$ iterations for each of the $m = 455$ models that have the predefined structure. First, we produce 10000 vectors of normal errors having mean zero and variance $\sigma^2 = 1$ and, for every model, we simulate response vectors from each design and for each iteration using $b_i = 3\sigma$. We used standard regression techniques to analyze the data and we studied the set of all main effects and two-factor interactions, assuming that higher order interactions are inactive. We have chosen to control the experimental error rate for the case of no active effects at about

FIGURE 10.1 TK

TABLE 10.6
The Vector v_D of the Selected 4 Non-Isomorphic $OA(20,5,2,2)$ Using $b_i = 3\sigma$

D	v_D = [min, Q1, Q2, Q3, max, average]
20.5.4	[4045, 5465, 8296, 8474.5, 9646, 7315.2]
20.5.8	[5102, 5527, 8254, 8513, 9664, 7370.3]
20.5.10	[9455, 9484, 9494, 9504, 9531, 9493.8]
20.5.11	[9542, 9558, 9565, 9573, 9592, 9565.7]

TABLE 10.7
The Vector v_D of the Selected 4 Non-Isomorphic $OA(20,5,2,2)$ $b_i = 1.5\sigma$

D	v_D = [min, Q1, Q2, Q3, max, average]
20.5.4	[0, 0, 574, 1093.5, 3740, 696.3]
20.5.8	[0, 0, 685, 1209, 3669, 741.9]
20.5.10	[2428, 2731.5, 2820, 2929.5, 3186, 2831]
20.5.11	[2943, 3117, 3178, 3238, 3397, 3178.2]

5%. The distribution of the values in the vector $\mathbf{d}_{455}(D)$ for every design tested is shown in the following boxplots.

To summarize these values with the vector $\mathbf{v}_D$, we use the average, minimum, maximum, 1st quartile, median and 3rd quartile of the values of $\mathbf{d}_{455}(D)$. Table 10.6 shows the values of the vector $\mathbf{v}_D$ for the four designs being tested.

Table 10.7 shows the values of the vector $\mathbf{v}_D$ for the four designs being tested using the same settings as described, but with $b_i = 1.5\sigma$.

These values show that designs 20.5.10 and 20.5.11 are superior to 20.5.4 and 20.5.8 for identifying any three active effects. In the next section, we will evaluate all non-isomorphic designs with $n \leq 32$ runs and with 5 and 6 factors following the algorithm described above under several "true" model set-ups. Using clustering techniques, we will form groups of designs with similar properties and highlight superior designs.

10.4 RESULTS

In this section we explore the non-isomorphic orthogonal arrays $OA(n, k, 2, t)$, which can be used to study $5 \leq k \leq 6$ factors with $20 \leq n \leq 32$ experimental runs, under several true model conditions. Higher order interactions of factors are assumed inactive so the search for active effects is restricted to the set of the main effects and the two-factor interactions. For reducing the computational cost, we have chosen to compare only the orthogonal arrays that can estimate the parameters of the model (10.1) with high D–efficiency and search for active effects using standard regression techniques with a controlled experimental error rate for the case of no active effects at about 5%. For every design, we conducted $r = 10000$ iterations, in the same fashion described in the illustration of the previous section. For each model structure we checked two different magnitudes of effects, namely 3σ and 1.5σ.

After the simulation process, the arrays tested have been assigned to homogenous clusters, using their $\mathbf{v}_D$ vectors. In each such vector, we record the average, minimum, maximum, 1st quartile, median and 3rd quartile of the values of $\mathbf{d}_{\mathrm{m}}(D)$. For selecting the appropriate number of clusters, the NbClust library in R combined with a variety of indexes as presented by Charrad et al. (2014) can be used. Obviously, the number of clusters and the cluster membership can be significantly altered if one uses different methods. For our illustration, we used the Euclidean distance and the agglomeration method proposed by Ward, which minimizes the total within-cluster variance.

In detail, for the five-factor case, we considered 4 designs with 20 runs (out of the 11), 27 designs with 24 runs (out of the 63), 35 designs with 28 runs (out of the 127) and 46 designs with 32 runs (out of the 491). All these designs can estimate the full model (10.1) with high D–efficiency so, it is expected that they will not have huge differences when model identification is of interest. We evaluated four different "true" model structure scenarios: a three-term model consisting of any three effects, a four-term model consisting of any four effects, a four-term model with at least two main effects and a five-term model with at least three main effects. The findings are summarized in Table 10.8 where, for each "true" model structure and for each magnitude of active effects used, we show how many designs for each run-order belong to the best cluster.

Overall, and with respect to the four model structures studied, the clustering procedure we applied shows that there are designs with 24 runs that behave equally well with designs with 28 or 32 runs, when the correct identification of the few active effects is of interest. Therefore, if the cost of experimentation is also important along with the correct identification of the active parameters, our procedure can provide us with good designs of various run sizes. However, the variety on run sizes is more obvious as the magnitude of the active effects enlarges.

For the six-factor case, we considered 47 designs with 24 runs (out of the 1350), 73 designs with 28 runs (out of the 17826) and 57 designs with 32 runs (out of

TABLE 10.8
Number of *n*-Run Designs in the Best Cluster, $20 \leq n \leq 32$

Model Structure	1.5σ Magnitude	3σ Magnitude
Three-term model:	20-run designs: 0	20-run designs: 02
any three effects	24-run designs: 01	24-run designs: 23
	28-run designs: 35	28-run designs: 35
	32-run designs: 46	32-run designs: 46
Four-term model:	20-run designs: 0	20-run designs: 0
any four effects	24-run designs: 0	24-run designs: 23
	28-run designs: 05	28-run designs: 19
	32-run designs: 46	32-run designs: 06
Four-term model:	20-run designs: 0	20-run designs: 02
at least two main effects	24-run designs: 0	24-run designs: 23
	28-run designs: 16	28-run designs: 35
	32-run designs: 46	32-run designs: 46
Five-term model:	20-run designs: 0	20-run designs: 02
at least three main effects	24-run designs: 0	24-run designs: 23
	28-run designs: 05	28-run designs: 35
	32-run designs: 46	32-run designs: 46

TABLE 10.9
Number of *n*-Run Designs in the Best Cluster, $24 \leq n \leq 32$

Model Structure	1.5σ Magnitude	3σ Magnitude
Four-term model:	24-run designs: 0	24-run designs: 0
at least three main effects	28-run designs: 0	28-run designs: 73
	32-run designs: 57	32-run designs: 57
Five-term model:	24-run designs: 0	24-run designs: 0
at least three main effects	28-run designs: 0	28-run designs: 73
	32-run designs: 57	32-run designs: 57

the 266632). We evaluated two different "true" model structure scenarios: a four-term model with at least three main effects and a five-term model with at least three main effects but with a smaller simulation study which consisted of r = 1000 iterations, due to the complexity of the calculations. The findings are summarized in Table 10.9 where, for each "true" model structure and for each magnitude of active effects used, we show how many designs for each run-order belong to the best cluster.

In this case, when the magnitude of the active effects is 1.5σ, all the 32-run designs tested are equally efficient in identifying the true active set of effects. This is also true and for all 28-run designs tested, as the magnitude of effects raises to 3σ.

10.5 CONCLUSIONS AND FURTHER CONSIDERATIONS

In this chapter, we propose a method that can be used to identify groups of two-level designs with respect to the correct identification of active factorial effects. The method consists of two stages. First, a simulation study is conducted, where responses are simulated using the design matrix, a given true model structure and independent identically distributed. normal errors. Using regression techniques, the times that the true model is correctly identified are recorded, and a vector $\mathbf{v}_D$ that summarizes the distribution of correct identifications, is appended to each design. In the second step, competitive designs are clustered using their $\mathbf{v}_D$ vectors.

The procedure is computationally expensive, especially when many designs are investigated under several true model structures and effect magnitudes. Moreover, the computational cost is also affected by the number of the iterations in the simulation as well as by the number of factorial effects that could be potentially active and should be considered. Finally, for the clustering stage, several methods can be applied simultaneously, and their results should be efficiently filtered to conclude the best partition. However, our proposed algorithm can be efficiently implemented in R as well as in other environments, exploiting various model structures, different model selection techniques and clustering techniques.

The procedure can be applied to any fractional factorial design, not only to two-level orthogonal arrays. When the "best" cluster contains designs with various run-orders, one may select an economical design with respect to run size, to conduct the experiment.

REFERENCES

G. E. P. Box and R. D. Meyer, An analysis for unreplicated fractional factorials, *Technometrics*, **28** (1986), 11–18.

M. Charrad, N. Ghazzali, V. Boiteau and A. Niknafs, NbClust: An R package for determining the relevant number of clusters in a data set, *Journal of Statistical Software*, **61** (2014), 1–36.

L.-Y. Deng and B. Tang, Generalized resolution and minimum aberration criteria for Plackett-Burman and other nonregular factorial designs, *Statistica Sinica*, **9** (1999), 1071–1082.

L.-Y. Deng and B. Tang, Design selection and classification for Hadamard matrices using generalized minimum aberration criteria, *Technometrics*, **44** (2002), 173–184.

H. Evangelaras, C. Koukouvinos and E. Lappas, Further contributions to nonisomorphic two level orthogonal arrays, *Journal of Statistical Planning and Inference*, **137** (2007), 2080–2086.

P. Goos and B. Jones, *Optimal Design of Experiments: A Case Study Approach*, Wiley, Chichester, 2011.

A. S. Hedayat, N. J. A. Sloane and J. Stufken, *Orthogonal Arrays: Theory and Applications*, Springer-Verlag, New York, 1999.

D. C. Montgomery, E. A. Peck and G. G. Vining, *Introduction to Linear Regression Analysis*, 5th ed., J. Wiley and Sons, New York, 2012.

E. D. Schoen, P. T., Eendebak and M. V. M. Nguyen, Complete enumeration of pure-level and mixed-level orthogonal arrays, *Journal of Combinatorial Designs*, **18** (2010), 123–140.

B. Tang, Theory of *J*-characteristics for fractional factorial designs and projection justification of minimum G_2-aberration, *Biometrika*, **88** (2001), 401–407.

B. Tang and L.-Y. Deng, Minimum G_2-aberration for nonregular fractional factorial designs, *The Annals of Statistics*, **27** (1999), 1914–1926.

J. C. Wang and C. F. J. Wu, A hidden projection property of Plackett-Burman and related designs, *Statistica Sinica*, **5** (1995), 235–250.

C. F. J. Wu and M. Hamada, *Experiments: Planning, Analysis, and Parameter Design Optimization*, 2nd ed., Wiley, New York, 2009.

11 Structured Matrix Factorization Approach for Image Deblurring

Dimitrios S. Triantafyllou

CONTENTS

11.1 INTRODUCTION

Image restoration seems to be useful in various real-life applications, such as the medical imaging, magnetic resonance imaging, computational tomography, satellite imaging and consequently it has attracted a lot of research interest (see e.g., [1–7]). Throughout the lines of the present chapter, the reconstruction of an image from two blurred instances of the same picture through structured matrix factorization is presented. Numerical Linear Algebra methods for the computation of the Greatest Common Divisor (GCD) of two univariate polynomials through matrix factorization are also utilized.

An image is represented with a limited number of digits according to the RGB or Grayscale intensity of its pixels on red, green and blue or on black and white scales respectively. Defocussing the camera's lens, the different wavelengths of the light, motion, the weather, a glass between the theme or the camera's lens correspond to crucial factors (among others) that can affect the image resulting in a blurred recorded picture. There are several types of noise such as, gaussian, salt and pepper, shot, quantization, film grain or anisotropic noise. Measurement errors also corrupt the image information. The percentage of the information that we can recover in

DOI: 10.1201/9781003203124-11

the reconstructed image depends on the existing noise and blur process. The main scope of this study is the construction of efficient and reliable algorithms in order to recover as much information as possible, deblurring and denoising two blurred instances of the same initial clean image using blind deconvolution methods. The cases of added noise and measurement errors are presented in detail, while efficient algorithms using matrices of special structure are also proposed.

Since images have often thousand or millions of pixels, the size of the matrices representing them are of huge size. Thus, the computational complexity of the methods, which are implemented for reconstructing the image is of great importance. Appropriate modifications of classical procedures applied to structured matrices aim at reducing per one order the required computational complexity of the methods, by taking advantage of their special block form.

More precisely, a modification of the structured Sylvester matrix is applied in order to compute the Greatest Common Divisor (GCD) of two univariate polynomials efficiently. In case that the added noise is large, the computation of Approximate GCD (AGCD) seems to be more suitable. Due to their stability and complexity, the proposed methodological tools lead to efficient procedures for computing the initial sharp image.

The rest of the present chapter is organized as follows. In Section 2, the motivation of the problem is presented in some detail. In Section 3, the required mathematical tools for represnting a single picture, the corresponding blurring function, the added noise and measurement errors are developed. The upper triangularization, the right nullspace computation of a matrix and the computation of the GCD of polynomials are breifly presented. In Section 4, the restoration of the initial clean image P having two blurred instances of P is built up. Finally, Section 5 summarizes the outcomes of the proposed methodology, while some concluding remarks are also deduced.

11.2 MOTIVATION OF THE PROBLEM

Let P be the initial sharp image, thus the picture that we see with no blur, F the point spread function, E the measurement errors, thus the approximation of the sharp image P using limited number of digits, N a white additive Gaussian noise and B the final recorded image icluding all the previous blur. The general model, representing the most complicated case, is the following [3]

$$B = (P + E) * F + N,$$

where * denotes the convolution of matrices.

The methods developed below, can handle efficiently all the combinations of blur, noise and/or measurement errors. In case that there is no spread function but only noise is added to the initial sharp image, the proposed methods are more sensitive and an inner tolerance ε_t (any computed number which is less in absolute value than ε_t will be zeroed) of the same order of the added noise has to be used in order to deblur the image. Since the order of the added noise is not known, the selection of the most suitable inner tolerance is a hard task and many experiments have to be made in order to compute efficiently the GCD or the approximate GCD, increasing the computational complexity. Alternativelly, the procedures presented in [8–10] can be used in order to denoise the image.

According to the kind of arithmetic that is used, we next categorize the algorithms to three different families: Numerical, Symbolical and Hybrid one. The first category utilizes floating point arithmetic. It is faster than the other two, but rounding off errors, catastrophic cancellation of significant digits during the numerical computations may result in significant errors and consequently incorrect results. The use of a small tolerance ε_t of the order of the added noise/measurement errors, zeroing all entries which are less than tol, improves the stability of the algorithms., improves the stability of the algorithms. The second one, which is called Symbolical category, guarantees the stability of the methods with no rounding off errors, but it increases significantly the required time, since all the computations are performed symbolically. Because of the large size of the initial matrices and the high computational complexity of the methods, the exclusive use of symbolic arithmetic is not recommended. The third category combines above-mentioned arithmetics, numerical and symbolical in a hybrid way evaluating the computations in floating point arithmetic, in case that the procedures are stable and in symbolical arithmetic, when it is possible the computations to cause serious rounding off errors.

According to the used transformations, the algorithms can be categorized as follows.

- Non orthogonal
- Orthogonal

The first category of algorithms utilizes non orthogonal transformations and has been proved to be faster than the second one. Nevertheless, it is more sensitive to perturbations and rounding off errors. The second category uses orthogonal transformations and it seems to be more stable. However, the required complexity is quite higher.

According to the nature of the computations, we combine the previous categories of algorithms in an efficient way, in order to construct stable and fast procedures restoring the initial image. analyzed leading to useful conclusions.

11.3 MATHEMATICAL TOOLS

In this section, the required mathematical tools for deblurring and denoising an image are presented in some detail. Firstly, the representation of a digital image and a blurring function is analyzed as well the blurring of an image. Next, Numerical Linear Algebra methods such as matrix triangularization for the computation of the Greatest Common Divisor (GCD) of polynomials are also presented.

11.3.1 Digital Image and Blurring Function Representation

The *2D*-matrix representation of an $m \times n$ grayscale digital image *P* is the following.

$$P = \begin{bmatrix} p_{1,1} & p_{1,2} & p_{1,3} & \cdots & p_{1,n} \\ p_{2,1} & p_{2,2} & p_{2,3} & \cdots & p_{2,n} \\ \vdots & \vdots & \vdots & \cdots & \vdots \\ \vdots & \vdots & \vdots & \cdots & \vdots \\ p_{m,1} & p_{m,2} & p_{m,3} & \cdots & p_{m,n} \end{bmatrix} \tag{11.1}$$

where $p_{i,j}$ is an integer corresponding to the colour values of the position of the *(i,j)*-th pixel of the image. In case of coloured images three similar matrices should be considered, namely one matrix for each one of the colours Red, Green and Blue (RGB). The entries of matrix P are integer-valued inside the range *[0,255]* uint8 entries (unsigned, integer, 8-bits entries) where *0* corresponds to black and *255* to white or *[0,65535]* uint16 entries (unsigned, integer, 16-bits entries)where *0* corresponds to black and *65535* to white. In a double precision representation, the values are in the range *0*, corresponding to black, to *1*, corresponding to white [4].

Equivalently, the image can be represented as a vector,

$$P = \begin{bmatrix} p_1 & p_2 & p_3 & \cdots & p_{m \cdot n} \end{bmatrix} \tag{11.2}$$

or as a polynomial of two variables ($2D$ polynomial, hereafter),

$$p(x,y) = \sum_{i=1}^{m} \sum_{j=1}^{n} P_{i,j} \cdot x^i \cdot y^j \tag{11.3}$$

or as a univariate polynomial,

$$p(x) = \sum_{i=1}^{m \cdot n} P_i \cdot x^i \tag{11.4}$$

The blurring function, Measurement Errors and Noise are then presented respectively. For example, let us consider the following 3×3 blurring function:

$$F = \begin{bmatrix} 0.05 & 0.1 & 0.05 \\ 0.1 & 0.4 & 0.1 \\ 0.05 & 0.1 & 0.05 \end{bmatrix}.$$

Its vector representation can be viewed as

$$F = \begin{bmatrix} 0.05 & 0.1 & 0.05 & 0.1 & 0.4 & 0.1 & 0.05 & 0.1 & 0.05 \end{bmatrix}.$$

while its *2D* polynomial representation is given by

$$f(x,y) = 0.05 + 0.1 \cdot x + 0.05 \cdot x^2 + 0.1 \cdot y + 0.4 \cdot y \cdot x$$
$$+ 0.1 \cdot y \cdot x^2 + 0.05 \cdot y^2 + 0.1 \cdot y^2 \cdot x + 0.05 \cdot y^2 \cdot x^2$$

whereas the *1D* is

$$f(x) = 0.05 + 0.1 \cdot x + 0.05 \cdot x^2 + 0.1 \cdot x^3 + 0.4 \cdot x^4 + 0.1x^5 + 0.05 \cdot x^6 + 0.1 \cdot x^7 + 0.05 \cdot x^8$$

Throughout the lines of the present work, we will handle grayscale images and use the *2D* matrix or *1D* polynomial representation of the clean and blurred image, measurement errors and noise.

11.3.2 Blurring an Image

In the sequel, the blurring of an image by the aid of appropriate mathematical modeling is described in some detail, in order to imlement it for the reconstruction of the image. Let P be an image of dimensions $m \times n$ ($n>m$) and F an $r \times r$ point spread function ($m>r$).

In mathematical terms, the blurred image B is obtained through the operation of convolution between the point spread function F and the image P: $B = P*F$, where B is an $(m+r)\times(n+r)$ matrix while

$$B(i,j) = \sum_{k=1}^{r} \sum_{l=1}^{r} P(i-k, j-l) \cdot F(k,l). \tag{11.5}$$

In *1D* polynomial representation, the convolution is evaluated through polynomial multiplication as follows

$$b(x) = p(x) \cdot f(x) \tag{11.6}$$

In Figure 11.1 an initial clean image and its convolution with a point spread function are presented.

If there are measurement errors and noise, then the corresponding formula is given as follows

$$b(x) = (p(x) + e(x)) \cdot f(x) + n(x) \ \ or\, B = (P+E) * F + N \tag{11.7}$$

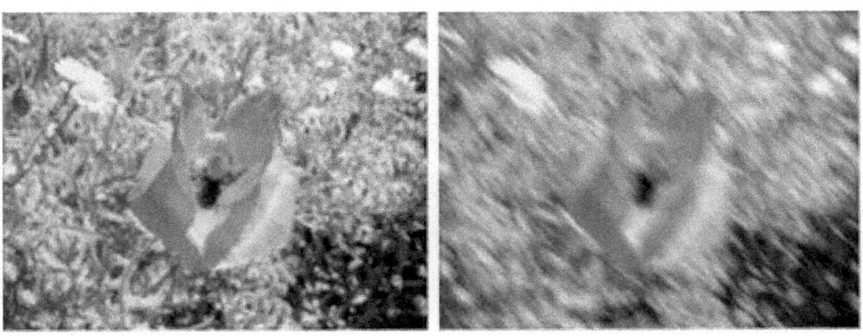

FIGURE 11.1 Initial clean and blurred image.

where *e(x)* (or E) are the measurement errors, *f(x)* (or F) correspond to the point spread function and *n(x)* (or N) expresses the added noise in *1D* polynomial (*2D* matrix) representation.

11.3.3 Matrix Factorization

In the sequel, efficient algorithms for matrix triangularization and computation of matrix right nullspace are presented in some detail. Let A be an $m \times n$ matrix. There are several procedures for computing its upper triangularization. In this section, two of them are discussed: the first one utilizes non-orthogonal transformations, known as LU factorization with partial pivoting (gaussian elimination), while the second procedure calls for orthogonal transformations, known as QR factorization [11, 12].

In both methods mentioned above, the resultant matrix $\tilde{A}$ is an upper triangular of size $m \times n$. In Figure 11.2, the upper triangularization, namely U, of all possible cases in terms of the size of matrix A is presented.

Generally speaking, matrix A can be factorized as follows

$$\prod \cdot A = L \cdot U,$$

where $\prod$ is a permutation matrix, L is lower triangular matrix having units accross its main diagonal, while U is an upper triangular matrix. Below, the LU factorization algorithm of a matrix is briefly presented.

LU factorization with partial pivoting [11–13]
Input: Matrix A.
Output: The computed upper triangularization of A.
for $k = 1 : n-1$
find row $r : |a_{rk}| = max_{k \le i \le n} |a_{i,k}|$
Interchange row k, r.
$a_{ik} \leftarrow m_{ik} = -\dfrac{a_{ik}}{a_{kk}}, = k+1 : n$
$a_{ij} \leftarrow a_{ij} + m_{ik} \cdot a_{kj},\ i = k+1 : n,\ j = k+1 : n$

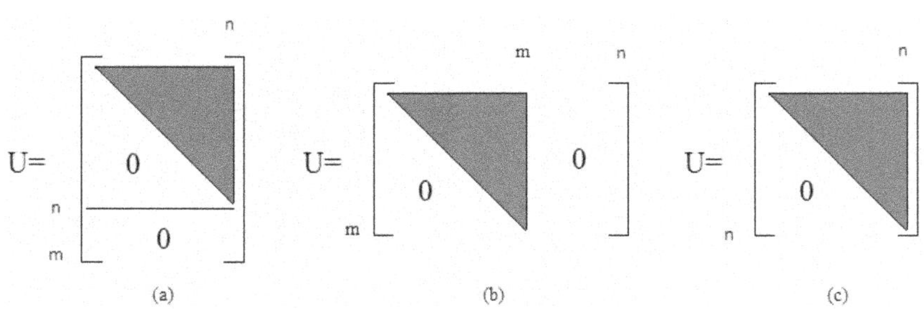

FIGURE 11.2 (a) $m > n$ (b) $m < n$ (c) $m = n$.

Complexity

The required complexity for the LU factorization of an $m \times n$ matrix ($m > n$) is $O(\frac{n^2}{2}\left(m - \frac{n}{3}\right))$ flops.

Error Analysis

The computed LU factorization is the factorization of a slightly perturbed matrix $A+E$, where the error E is bounded as follows.

$$\|E\|_\infty \le n^2 \rho u \|A\|_\infty ,$$

where ρ is the growth factor. The LU factorization with partial pivoting is stable in practise [11].

Another method triangularizing a matrix is the QR factorization which uses orthogonal transformations and is more stable than LU but it requires the double floating point operations. Below, the main strictire of the so-called QR factorization of matrix A is described in some detail.

QR factorization [11–13]

Input: Matrix A.

Output: The computed upper triangularization of A.

$Q = I_m$

for $k = 1{:}min(m\text{-}1,n)$

$[u,\sigma] = house1(A_{k:n,k})$

$Q_{1:n,k:n} = housmulp(Q_{1:n,k:n}, u)$

$A_{k,k} = \sigma$

$A_{k+1:n,k} = u_{2:n-k+1}$

$v_k = u_1$

$\beta = 2/(u^T u)$

$s = \beta \cdot \sum_{j=k+1}^{n} u_{1:n-k+1}^T \cdot A_{k:n,j}$

$A_{k:n,j} = A_{k:n,j} - s \cdot u_{1:n-k+1}, j = k+1, \ldots, n$

end

Note that function housmulp computes the product $H_i \cdot B$ of a matrix B with the Housholder matrix H_i. The so-called housnulp algorithm is given below.

housmulp Algorithm [11]

$$[m,n] = \text{size}(A)$$

$$\beta = \frac{2}{u^T \cdot u}$$

$$s = \beta \cdot sum_{i=1}^{m} u_{1:n} \cdot A_{i,1:n}$$

$$A_{i,1:n} = A_{i,1:n} - sum \cdot u_{1:n}^{T}, i = 1, \ldots, m$$

Kindly mention that algorithm House1 computes the vector u which is used for the construction of the Householder matrix. The so-called House1 algorithm is given below.

House1 Algorithm [11]

$$m = max|x|$$

$$u = \frac{x}{m}$$

$$\sigma = sign(u_1) \cdot \sum_{i=1} nu_i^2$$

$$u_1 = u_1 + \sigma$$

$$\sigma = -m \cdot \sigma$$

Complexity

The required complexity for the QR factorization of an $m \times n$ matrix (*m*>*n*) is $n^2\left(m - \frac{n}{3}\right)$ flops.

Error Analysis

The computed QR factorization is the exact factorization of a slightly perturbed matrix $A + E$: $A + E = \hat{Q}\hat{R}$, where the error matrix *E* is bounded as follows.

$$\|E\|_F \leq \phi(n)\mu\|A\|_F$$

where $\phi(n)$ is a slowly growing function of n and μ is the machine precision [11].

More details about the accuracy of LU and QR factorization can be found in [13, 14].

Another crucial method for factorization of a matrix is the so-called Singular Value Decomposition (SVD). Generally speaking, let us consider a matrix $A \in \mathbb{R}^{m \times n}$. Then there exist orthogonal matrices $U \in \mathbb{R}^{m \times n}$, $V \in \mathbb{R}^{m \times n}$ and a diagonal matrix $\Sigma_1 \in \mathbb{R}^{m \times n}$ such that

$$U^T A V = \Sigma = \begin{bmatrix} \Sigma_1 & 0 \\ 0 & 0 \end{bmatrix},$$

where the diagonal entries of Σ_1 are the singular values of A and the columns of V corresponding to the zero singular values of A form a base M for the right nullspace of A (see [11, 12] for details).

11.3.4 GCD of Two Polynomials

Consider two polynomials

$$a(s) = s^n + a_{n-1}s^{n-1} + \ldots + a_1 s + a_0$$

$$b(s) = b_n s^n + b_{n-1}s^{n-1} + \ldots + b_1 s + b_0$$

with $\vartheta\{a(s)\} = \vartheta\{b(s)\}$, representing two blurred instances of the same initial image. The GCD of polynomials is the kernel of deblurring the image (see subsection 11.4 below). In several works appeared in the literature (see, e.g., [5, 6]), several methods computing the GCD of polynomials through Discrete Fourier Transformations (DFT) have been introduced, whereas in [15, 16] the DFTs are approximately computed. In this subsection, an approach based on the $2(n+1)\times 2(n+1)$ Sylvester matrix [17] of $a(s), b(s)$ is discussed. More specifically, we assume that matrix S is of the following form.

$$S(a,b) = \begin{bmatrix} a_n & a_{n-1} & a_{n-2} & \cdots & \cdots & \cdots & \cdots & a_0 & 0 & \cdots & \cdots & 0 & 0 \\ 0 & a_n & a_{n-1} & a_{n-2} & \cdots & \cdots & \cdots & \cdots & a_0 & 0 & \cdots & 0 & 0 \\ . & . & . & \cdots & \cdots & \cdots & \cdots & \cdots & . & \cdots & \cdots & . & . \\ 0 & 0 & 0 & \cdots & a_n & a_{n-1} & . & . & . & . & \cdots & a_1 & a_0 \\ - & - & - & - & - & - & - & - & - & - & - & - & - \\ b_n & b_{n-1} & b_{n-2} & \cdots & \cdots & b_0 & 0 & \cdots & \cdots & \cdots & \cdots & 0 & 0 \\ 0 & b_n & b_{n-1} & \cdots & \cdots & \cdots & b_0 & 0 & \cdots & \cdots & \cdots & 0 & 0 \\ . & . & . & \cdots & \cdots & \cdots & \cdots & \cdots & \cdots & \cdots & \cdots & . & . \\ 0 & 0 & 0 & \cdots & \cdots & \cdots & \cdots & b_n & b_{n-1} & \cdots & \cdots & b_1 & b_0 \end{bmatrix}$$

Theorem 1. *[17, 18]*

Let $S(a,b)$ be the resultant matrix of a pair of polynomials $(a(s), b(s))$, ρ = rank$(S(a,b))$ and let S_1 (a,b) denote the upper triangular form of $S(a,b)$ obtained by applying the LU factorization with partial pivoting or the QR factorization to, i.e.

$$S_1(a,b) = \begin{bmatrix} x & x & \cdots & \cdots & x & \cdots & \cdots & x \\ 0 & x & \cdots & \cdots & x & \cdots & \cdots & x \\ \vdots & . & \cdots & \cdots & . & \cdots & \cdots & \vdots \\ 0 & 0 & \cdots & \cdots & x & \cdots & \cdots & x \\ 0 & 0 & \cdots & \cdots & 0 & \cdots & \cdots & 0 \\ . & . & \cdots & \cdots & . & \cdots & \cdots & . \\ 0 & 0 & \cdots & \cdots & 0 & \cdots & \cdots & 0 \end{bmatrix}$$

where the x leading element of each nonzero row is also nonzero. Then,

- the degree of GCD of $a(s), b(s)$ is equal to the rank ρ of $S(a,b)$
- the nonzero elements of the last nonzero row of S_1 (a,b) define the coefficients of GCD in reverse order.

We modify the above classical Sylvester matrix as follows.

$$S^*(a,b) = \begin{bmatrix} a_n & a_{n-1} & a_{n-2} & a_{n-3} & \cdots & a_0 & 0 & 0 & \cdots & 0 \\ b_n & b_{n-1} & b_{n-2} & b_{n-3} & \cdots & b_0 & 0 & 0 & \cdots & 0 \\ 0 & a_n & a_{n-1} & a_{n-2} & \cdots & a_1 & a_0 & 0 & \cdots & 0 \\ 0 & b_n & b_{n-1} & b_{n-2} & \cdots & b_1 & b_0 & 0 & \cdots & 0 \\ 0 & 0 & a_n & a_{n-1} & \cdots & a_2 & a_1 & a_0 & \cdots & 0 \\ 0 & 0 & b_n & b_{n-1} & \cdots & b_2 & b_1 & b_0 & \cdots & 0 \\ . & . & . & . & \cdots & . & . & . & \cdots & 0 \\ 0 & 0 & 0 & 0 & \cdots & 0 & a_n & a_{n-1} & \cdots & a_0 \\ 0 & 0 & 0 & 0 & \cdots & 0 & b_n & b_{n-1} & \cdots & b_0 \end{bmatrix}$$

The modified Sylvester matrix has n same blocks of dimension $2 \times (n+1)$. Theorem 1 holds for the modified matrix S^* too.

The following algorithm is a modification of the classical procedure computing the exact GCD of two polynomials, taking into advantage the special form of the modified Sylvester matrix and reducing per one order the required complexity.

Algorithm MSGCD (Modified Sylvester GCD) [3, 19]

1. Construct the matrix S^* of two polynomials.
2. Perform the fast upper triangularization of S^* presented in [19] using LU or QR factorization.
3. GCD = the last non zero row of the resultant upper triangular matrix.

The MSGCD algorithm is evaluated numerically. The computational complexity for an $2n \times 2n$ modified Sylvester matrix is $O(3n^2)$ flops applying appropriately modified LU and $O(6n^2)$ flops applying QR factorization factorization. Note that its complexity is one order less than the corresponding one of the classical procedures. Due to the errors through the computations in floating point arithmetic, it is possible that some neglible entries (eg. of order of 10^{-12}) may appear after the real last non-zero row which simply represents the coefficients of the exact GCD. In such a case, the degree and the coefficients of the computed GCD are not accurate. Thus, the implementation of an inner tolerance ϵ_t at the end of every iteration of LU or QR factorization is needed. The abobe-mentioned quantity is a small bound utilized for zeroing any entry that is in absolute value less than ϵ_t. Note that the order of ϵ_t is not constant, while different ϵ_t s can lead to different GCDs. This is the main problem of evaluating numerically the algorithms. On the other hand, the symbolical implementation of the procedures is not always efficient, since the required time is significantly high. Thus, the combination of the numerical and symbolical arithmetic in a hybrid way leads to fast and stable algorithms.

Because of rounding off errors such as catastrophic cancellation of significant digits and the perturbation of the initial data caused by measurement errors and mainly by the added noise, the computed GCD of the polynomials may differ from the exact one, even if a tolerance $\in_t$ is used. In order to handle even better such cases, the computation of the approximate GCD of polynomials is preferred in practice. The computation of the approximate GCD of polynomials can be achieved by relaxing the exact conditions for computing the exact GCD. More precisely, the computation of the "near null space" [20, 21] through the Singular Value Decomposition (SVD) is computed. Thus, in cases that the added noise perturbs significantly the initial data, the computation of the approximate GCD produces more realistic results than the corresponding outcomes of the exact one presented previously. The following algorithm computes the approximate GCD.

Algorithm MAGCD [3, 19]

1. Define a threshold $t > 0$.

   Apply the SVD algorithm to S^* using the modified QR factorization [3, 19] for the first phase of SVD.

   Define a basis M for the right "near nullspace" of the Sylvester matrix S^* as follows:

   $S^* = U\Sigma V^T$. The columns of V corresponding to the smaller than t singular values, define the right "near null space" of S^*.

2. Define symbilically the Matrix Pencil $Z(s) = s \cdot M_1 - M_2$,where M_1 and M_2 are the matrices obtained from M by deleting the last and the first row of M respectively.

3. Form the polynomial matrix $Z(s)$ with elements all nonzero determinants of maximal order.

   Specify the matrix B containing the coefficients of the polynomials of $Z(s)$.

4. Find the SVD of B: $B = \tilde{U} \cdot \tilde{\Sigma} \tilde{V}^T$.

To sum up, the approximate GCD coincides with the largest singular value column of $\tilde{V}$.

The MAGCD algorithm is implemented in a hybrid way. The numerical part of MAGCD requires $O(n^3)$ flops, which is one order less than the corresponding complexity of the classical method.

11.4 IMAGE RECOVERY USING TWO BLURRED INSTANCES

Let P be an initial $m \times n$ image, while F_1, F_2 correspond to two blurring functions of smaller than the initial image dimensions, say $r \times r$. These two functions are applied through convolution on P and result in two blurred instances B_1 and B_2 of P, having dimensions equal to $(m+r)\times(n+r)$. Given the two blurred instances B_1 and B_2, the aim is to restore the initial clean image P. In the *1D* polynomial representation, e.g., $b_1(x) = f_1(x)\cdot p(x)$, $b_2(x) = f_2(x)\cdot p(x)$, $b_1(x)b_2(x)$ correspond to the two blurred instances of the initial clean image $p(x)$ while $f_1(x), f_2(x)$ are the blurring functions. Obviously, $p(x) = GCD(b1(x), b2(x))$. Note, that the dimensions of the above-mentioned blurring functions, are not necessarily equal. However, throughout the lines of the present manuscript we consider, for simplicity reasons, the case of equal dimensions. In [6] and [5] the following algorithm in *2D* matrix–polynomial level has been proposed.

Algorithm 1:

1. Read the $2D$ matrices B_1 and B_2 of the two blurred instances.
2. Find the $2D$ polynomials of images B_1 and B_2, namely $b_1(x,y)$ and $b_2(x,y)$ using equation (3).
3. Calculate the *2D* polynomial of initial image P, namely $p(x,y)$, as:
   $p(x,y) = GCD(b_1(x,y), b_2(x,y))$

Polynomial p is the representative polynomial of the initial image. The above algorithm requires the computation of the GCD of two $2D$ polynomials. In [6] and [5] a DFT based algorithm is applied for this computation. If the minimal number of floating point multiplications required for computing the exact DFT of block length N, is denoted by $M_{DFT}(N)$, then the following theorem holds true.

Theorem 2

For a given $N = \prod_{i=1}^{m} p_i^{e_i}$, *where* $p_i, i = 1,\ldots,m$ *are distinct primes and* $e_i, i = 1,\ldots,m$ *are positive integers, it follows:*

$$M_{DFT}(N) = 2\cdot N - \sum_{i_1=0}^{e_1}\sum_{i_2=0}^{e_2}\cdots\sum_{i_m=0}^{e_m}\phi\left(GCD\left(\prod_{i=1}^{m} p_j^{i_i}, 4\right)\right)\cdot 1 +$$

$$\sum_{d_1 \mid \frac{\phi\left(p_1^{i_1}\right)}{\phi\left(GCD\left(p_1^{i_1},4\right)\right)}} \sum_{d_2 \mid \frac{\phi\left(p_2^{i_2}\right)}{\phi\left(GCD\left(p_2^{i_2},4\right)\right)}} \cdots \sum_{d_m \mid \frac{\phi\left(p_m^{i_m}\right)}{\phi\left(GCD\left(p_m^{i_m},4\right)\right)}} \frac{\prod_{k=1}^{m}\phi(d_k)}{\phi\left(LCM\left(d_1, d_2,\ldots,d_m\right)\right)},$$

TABLE 11.1
Floating–Point Multiplications Required for the Exact Computation of the *DFT*

N	2	3	4	5	6	8	12	16	24	32	48	64	128	256
$M_{DFT}(N)$	0	1	0	4	2	2	4	10	12	32	38	84	198	438

where $\phi(\cdot)$ is the Euler's totient function, *G1.CD(.,.)* denotes the greatest common divisor, and *LCM(.,.)* is the least common multiple [22].

Table 11.1 illustrates the number of floating–point multiplications required for the exact computation of the *DFT* for a few selected block lengths.

At this point, a modification of Algorithm A_1 is presented, in order to use the 1*D* polynomial form. The modified algorithm takes advantage of the super fast 1*D* polynomial *MSGCD* algorithm, which does not use *DFT* operation.

Algorithm MA_1 **(Modified** A_1**):**

1. Read the *2D* matrices QF_1 and QF_2 of the two blurred instances.
2. Find the *1D* polynomials of images QF_1 and QF_2 namely $qf_1(x)$ and $qf_2(x)$ using equation (11.4)
3. Calculate the *1D* polynomial of initial image *Q*, namely *q*, as:
   $q(x) = MSGCD(qf_1(x),qf_2(x))$ or $q(x) = MAGCD(qf_1(x),qf_2(x))$

A tolerance ϵ_t of the order of the added noise/measurement errors is often a good choice. Numerical experiments show that the MSGCD algorithm gives accurate results for added noise of order $O(10{-}^{3})$, whereas MAGCD for adde noise up to $O(10^{1})$.

Next, Algorithm MA_1 is illustrated through an example.

Example 1:

Let us consider that we are given the two blurred instances of Figure 11.3. Actually, the left part of Figure 11.2 was produced by applying the 5×5 gaussian blurring function

$$F_1 = \begin{bmatrix} 0.0392 & 0.0398 & 0.0400 & 0.0398 & 0.0392 \\ 0.0398 & 0.0404 & 0.0406 & 0.0404 & 0.0398 \\ 0.0400 & 0.0406 & 0.0408 & 0.0406 & 0.0400 \\ 0.0398 & 0.0404 & 0.0406 & 0.0404 & 0.0398 \\ 0.0392 & 0.0398 & 0.0400 & 0.0398 & 0.0392 \end{bmatrix}$$

on the clean image, and the right part, by applying the 7×7 gaussian blurring function

$$F_2 = \begin{bmatrix} 0.0194 & 0.0199 & 0.0202 & 0.0203 & 0.0202 & 0.0199 & 0.0194 \\ 0.0199 & 0.0204 & 0.0207 & 0.0208 & 0.0207 & 0.0204 & 0.0199 \\ 0.0202 & 0.0207 & 0.0210 & 0.0211 & 0.0210 & 0.0207 & 0.0202 \\ 0.0203 & 0.0208 & 0.0211 & 0.0212 & 0.0211 & 0.0208 & 0.0203 \\ 0.0202 & 0.0207 & 0.0210 & 0.0211 & 0.0210 & 0.0207 & 0.0202 \\ 0.0199 & 0.0204 & 0.0207 & 0.0208 & 0.0207 & 0.0204 & 0.0199 \\ 0.0194 & 0.0199 & 0.0202 & 0.0203 & 0.0202 & 0.0199 & 0.0194 \end{bmatrix}$$

on the same image. F_1 and F_2 are unknown.

Performing the *1D*-polynomial MSGCD algorithm (see subsection 11.3) on the resulting *1D* polynomials of the two previous blurred instances, an *1D* polynomial corresponding to the Figure 11.4 is readily deduced.

Note that the dimensions of the resulting image should be smaller than the dimensions of the two blurred images when full convolution is applied. More precisely, the left part of Figure 11.3 is a 68×68 pixels image and the right part is a 70×70 pixels image. The restored image contains 64×64 pixels. This is absolutely reasonable as the first filter is of dimensions 5×5 and the second filter is of dimensions 7×7. This implies that the first filter increases the number of columns and rows of the image by 4, while the second filter by 6. This is observed since the highest degree of the polynomial representation of the filters is 4 and 6 respectively. In addition, for the above-mentioned example we recover the exact initial image for $\epsilon_t = 10^{-11}$.

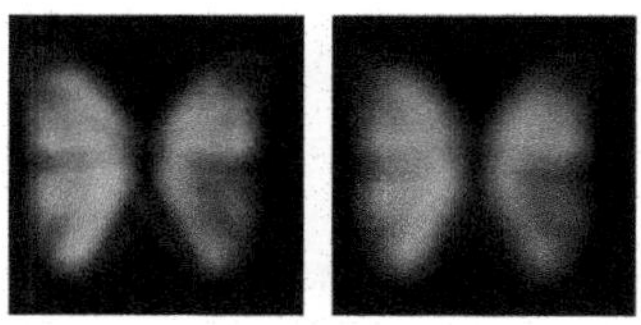

FIGURE 11.3 Two given blurred instances of the same image for Example 1.

FIGURE 11.4 Restored image of Example 1.

11.5 CONCLUSIONS

In this study, the issue of reconstructing a blurred image having two blurred instances of the same initial clean image is discussed. The proposed methods are based on structured matrix factorization, on Numerical Linear Algebra techniques and the algorithms are implemented numerically or in a hybrid way, in order to assure the desired level of stability. The computation of the exact GCD of the blurred instances leads to significantly faster algorithms, computing efficiently the initial deblurred image, when the added noise is not of high order. In case of a higher added noise the computation of the approximate GCD instead of the exact one seems to be preferable. The measurement errors do not affect the procedures as much as the noise does. The proposed algorithms have been applied to appropriately modified structured matrices and managed to reduce per one order the required complexity of the methods without reducing their stability.

REFERENCES

[1] Ke Chen, Introduction to variational image-processing models and applications, *International Journal of Computer Mathematics*, vol. 90:1 (2013), pp. 1–8.

[2] N. Chumchob, Ke Chen and C. Brito-Loeza, A new variational model for removal of combined additive and multiplicative noise and a fast algorithm for its numerical approximation, *International Journal of Computer Mathematics*, vol. 90:1 (2013), pp. 140–161.

[3] A. Danelakis, M. Mitrouli and D. Triantafyllou, Blind image deconvolution using a banded matrix method, *Numerical Algorithms*, vol. 64 (2013), pp. 43–72.

[4] P.C. Hansen, J.G. Nagy and D.P. O' Leary, *Deblurring Images Matrices, Spectra and Filtering*, SIAM, Philadelphia, 2006.

[5] A.R. Heindl, *Fourier Transform, Polynomial GCD, and Image Restoration*, Master Thesis for Clemson University, Department of Mathematical Sciences, 2005.

[6] S. Unnikrishna Pillai and Ben Liang, Blind image deconvolution using a robust GCD approach, *IEEE Transactions on Image Processing*, vol. 8 (1999), pp. 295–301.

[7] F. Wang and Michael K. Ng, A fast minimization method for blur and multiplicative noise removal, *International Journal of Computer Mathematics*, vol. 90:1 (2013), pp. 48–61.

[8] A. Foi, V. Katkovnik and K. Egiazarian, Pointwise shape—adaptive DCT for high—quality deblocking of compressed color images, *IEEE Transactions on Image Processing*, vol. 16 (2007), pp. 1057–7149.

[9] A. Beck and Y.C. Eldar, Regularization in regression with bounded noise: A chebyshev center approach, *SIAM Journal on Matrix Analysis and Applications*, vol. 29 (2007), pp. 606–625.

[10] P. Chatterjee, Denoising using the K-SVD method, *Image Processing and Reconstruction* (2007), pp. 1–12.

[11] B.N. Datta, *Numerical Linear Algebra and Applications*, SIAM, Second Edition, Philadephia, 2010.

[12] G.H. Golub and C.F. Van Loan, *Matrix Computations*, The Johns Hopkins University Press, Third Edition, Baltimore and London, 1996.

[13] N.J. Higham, *Accuracy and Stability of Numerical Algorithms*, SIAM, Philadephia, 1996.

[14] J.H. Wilkinson, *The Algebraic Eigenvalue Problem*, Oxford University Press Inc., New York, 1968.
[15] W.M. Gentleman and G. Sande, Fast Fourier transforms-for fun and profit, *Proceedings AFIPS*, vol. 29 (1966), pp. 563–578.
[16] C.J. Schatzman, Accuracy of the discrete Fourier transform and the fast fourier transform., *SIAM Journal on Scientific Computing*, vol. 17 (1996), pp. 1150–1166.
[17] S. Barnett, Greatest common divisor from generalized sylvester resultant matrices, *Linear and Multilinear Algebra*, vol. 8 (1980), pp. 271–279.
[18] N. Karcanias, M. Mitrouli and S. Fatouros, A resultant based computation of the Greatest Common divisor of two polynomials, in *Proceedings of 11th IEEE Mediteranean Conference on Control and Automation*, Rodos Palace Hotel, MED'03, June 18–20, 2003, Rhodes, Greece.
[19] D. Triantafyllou and M. Mitrouli, On rank and null space computation of the generalized Sylvester matrix, *Numerical Algorithms*, vol. 54 (2009), pp. 297–324.
[20] N. Karcanias, M. Mitrouli and D. Triantafyllou, Matrix pencil methodologies for computing the greatest common divisor of polynomials: Hybrid algorithms and their performance, *International Journal of Control*, vol. 79 (2006), pp. 1447–1461.
[21] Nelson C. Dorny, *A Vector Space Approach to Models and Optimization*, John Wiley and Sons, New York, 1975.
[22] M.T. Heideman and C.S. Burrus, On the number of multiplications necessary to compute a length-2n DFT, *IEEE Transactions on Acoustics Speech and Signal Processing*, vol. 34 (1986), pp. 91–95.

12 Reconfigurable Intelligent Surfaces for Exploitation of the Randomness of Wireless Environments

Alexandros-Apostolos A. Boulogeorgos and Angeliki Alexiou

CONTENTS

12.1 INTRODUCTION

The evolution of the wireless world towards the beyond fifth generation (B5G) era comes with higher reliability, data-rates and traffic demands, which is driven by innovative applications, such as unmanned mobility, three-dimensional media, augmented and virtual reality that are expected to play a key role in Industry 4.0. Technological advances, such as massive multiple-input multiple-output (MaMIMO), full-duplexing (FD), and high-frequency communications, have been advocated, due to their increased hardware cost, power-consumption, as well as their need to operate in unfavorable electromagnetic wave propagation environment, where they have to deal with a number of medium particularities.

As a remedy, the exploitation of the implicit randomness of the propagation environment through reconfigurable intelligent surfaces (RIS), in order to improve the quality of service (QoS) and experience (QoE), attracts the eyes of both academia

DOI: 10.1201/9781003203124-12

and industry. RISs are able to transform wireless systems into smart platforms capable of sensing the environment and of applying customized transformations to the radio waves. The RIS-assisted smart environments have the potential to provide B5G wireless networks with uninterrupted wireless connectivity, and with the capability of transmitting data without generating new signals but recycling existing radio waves.

Motivated by the advances in this area, this chapter focuses on presenting the technology enablers and the state-of-the-art of RIS-assisted wireless systems, the need of new channel and system models as well as theoretical frameworks for their analysis and design, as well as the long-term and open research issues to be solved towards their massive deployment.

The rest of this chapter is organized as follows: Section 12.2 is dedicated to the presentation of the concept of smart radio environments (SREs) by explaining the structure and functionalities of its main pillar, namely RIS, and identifying its main application scenarios. Next, Section 12.3 reviews the technical literature and reveals research gaps concerning channel modeling. Building upon the findings of Section 12.3, Section 12.4 presents research directions and summarizes this chapter.

12.2 RECONFIGURABLE INTELLIGENT SURFACES AS SMART RADIO ENVIRONMENTS ENABLERS

This section focuses on presenting and explaining the concept of SREs as well as its main enabler, i.e., RIS. In this sense, Section x.2.1 is devoted to the presentation of the RIS operation principles, structure and functionalities, while Section x.2.2 documents the application scenarios of RIS that can be identified in the technical literature.

12.2.1 RIS Definition and Operation

The key idea of SREs is to exploit the randomness of the propagation environment by making it programmable. Towards this direction, it is expected to use as key enabler novel structures, called RIS, which are capable of changing their electromagnetic properties in order to adapt to the propagation conditions. As illustrated in Figure 12.1, an RIS is a meta-surface (i.e., a composite material) that usually consists of a two-dimensional (2D) array of meta-atom. Note that the metasurface is characterized as 2D, because its thickness is less than $\lambda/5$, where λ stands for the transmission wavelength (Liaskos et al., Sept. 2018).

Meta-atoms* are in general passive elements of small electrical size (in the order of $\lambda/10 - \lambda/5$) and they can be categorized into static and dynamic ones. In static meta-atoms, their current patterns can be fully defined by their structure. As a consequence, they are not reconfigurable. On the other hand, dynamic meta-atoms can be controlled by a diode array (Tan, Sun, Jornet, & Pados, May 2016; Tan, Sun,

* The prefix meta is a Greek word "beyond." In the context of meta-atoms, it refers to a three-dimensional (3D) and 2D structures that exhibits some kind of exotic properties that are not posed by natural materials.

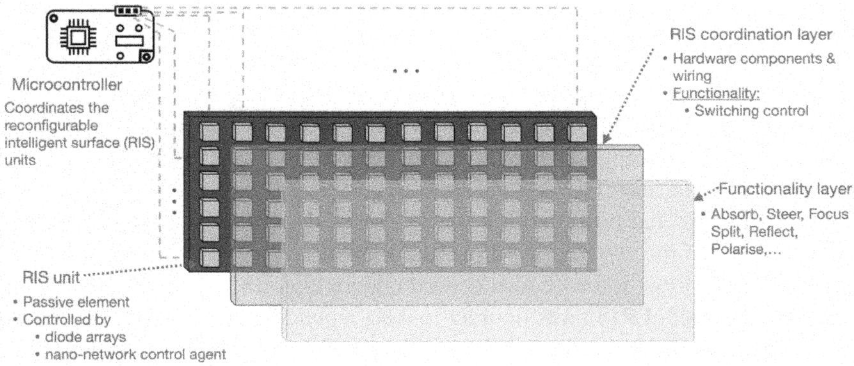

FIGURE 12.1 RIS structure and functionalities.

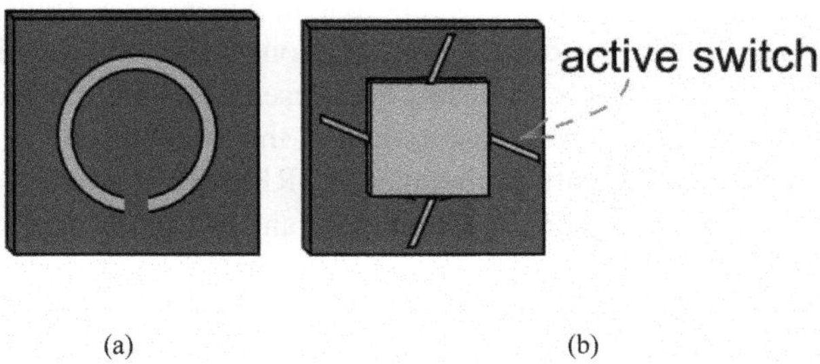

FIGURE 12.2 Indicative examples of static (a) and dynamic meta-atoms.

Koutsonikolas, & Jornet, Apr. 2018; Li et al., Mar. 2019) or a nano-network agent (Liu, Sternbach, & Basov, Nov. 2016; McGahan et al., Jan. 2017; Liaskos et al., Fourthquarter 2015). As a result, they can dynamically change their current pattern and thus their electromagnetic properties. Two indicative examples of static and dynamic meta-atoms are depicted in Figure 12.2 (Singh & Zheludev, Sept. 2014; He, Sun, & Zhou, July 2019).

To ensure collaboration between the meta-atoms an inexpensive microcontroller is used. The microcontroller optimizes the electromagnetic behavior of each meta-atom in order to allow the RIS to perform functionalities like *beam absorption*, *steering*, *refraction*, *focusing*, *splitting*, *polarization manipulation*, *collimation*, *analog processing*, etc. Based on the selected functionality, different parameters need to be known to the microcontroller. For example, for beam steering, the transmitter's and receiver's positions as well as the operation frequency need to be prior-communicated to the microcontroller. On the other hand, for beam focusing, except from the operation frequency, transmitter's and receiver's positions, the incident beam footprint as well as the beamwidth of the reflected one should be prior-determined. Finally, for absorption, no parameter concerning the incident wave need to be fed to the microcontroller.

12.2.2 Application Scenarios

From a communications point of view, due to their low-implementation and operation cost as well as the unpresented features that they bring, RISs can find several applications. In Figure 12.3, eight (8) of the most prominent applications are identified, namely: (i) signal modulation; (ii) blockage avoidance; (iii) multi-hoping; (iv) wireless power transfer; (v) physical layer security; (vi) interference coordination; (vii) broadcasting; and (viii) multiple access. Next, the aforementioned applications are discussed and the key role of RIS is highlighted.

Signal modulation: the core idea behind employing RIS as a signal modulator is to activate a subset of RIS units in order to steer a pencil-beam towards the receiver, while exploiting the indices of the activated units to implicitly convey the RIS's information. In more detail, the transmitter slits the message to be transmitted into two groups. The first group contains $\log_2(K)$ bits, where K is the number of the RIS's subsets, while the second group has a length of $\log_2(M)$ bits, with M being the modulation order. The transmitter uses the first beam to steer its beam towards the corresponding RIS subset, while the second one to generate the transmitted signal. On the other side, the receiver detects the direction of the received signal (i.e., the identifier (ID) of the RIS subset that has been used) and the received signal that belongs to the second group. Next, it reproduces the transmitted signal. This concept is also called reflection pattern modulation (RPM) (Lin et al., Aug. 2020) and has its routes to index modulation (IM) (Basar, Jan. 2020) that was introduced for MaMIMO systems.

Blockage avoidance: One of the most attractive applications of RIS is blockage avoidance by creating alternative communication paths between the transmitter and receiver; thus, enhancing the wireless system's reliability. As documented in (Ntontin et al., March 2021), (Boulogeorgos & Alexiou, Performance Analysis of Reconfigurable Intelligent Surface-Assisted Wireless Systems and Comparison With Relaying, May 2020) and (Boulogeorgos & Alexiou, Sept. 2020), the use of RIS for blockage avoidance can significantly enhance the received signal-to-noise ratio as well as improve the system's outage and ergodic capacity performance; especially, in high-frequency communications, where the penetration loss is extremely high (Papasotirou, Boulogeorgos, Stratakou, & Alexiou, Sept. 2020; Boulogeorgos, Goudos, & Alexiou, Users Association in Ultra Dense THz Networks, Aug. 2018).

Multi-hopping: Several researchers consider RISs the relay's descendants, since they are an attractive approach for coverage expansion (Boulogeorgos & Alexiou, Coverage Analysis of Reconfigurable Intelligent Surface Assisted THz Wireless Systems, Jan. 2021). Motivated by this, a great amount of effort was put on comparing the technical characteristics of the two technologies as well as the performance of the corresponding systems (Boulogeorgos & Alexiou, Performance Analysis of Reconfigurable Intelligent Surface-Assisted Wireless Systems and Comparison With Relaying, May 2020). Towards this direction, Table 12.1 presents a brief comparison between RIS, amplify-and-forward (AF), decode-and-forward (DF), and FD relaying. From this table, it becomes evident that RIS-based solution have lower hardware cost as well as power consumption, due to lack of radio frequency (RF) chains, compared to the corresponding relaying ones (Di Renzo et al., June 2020). On the other

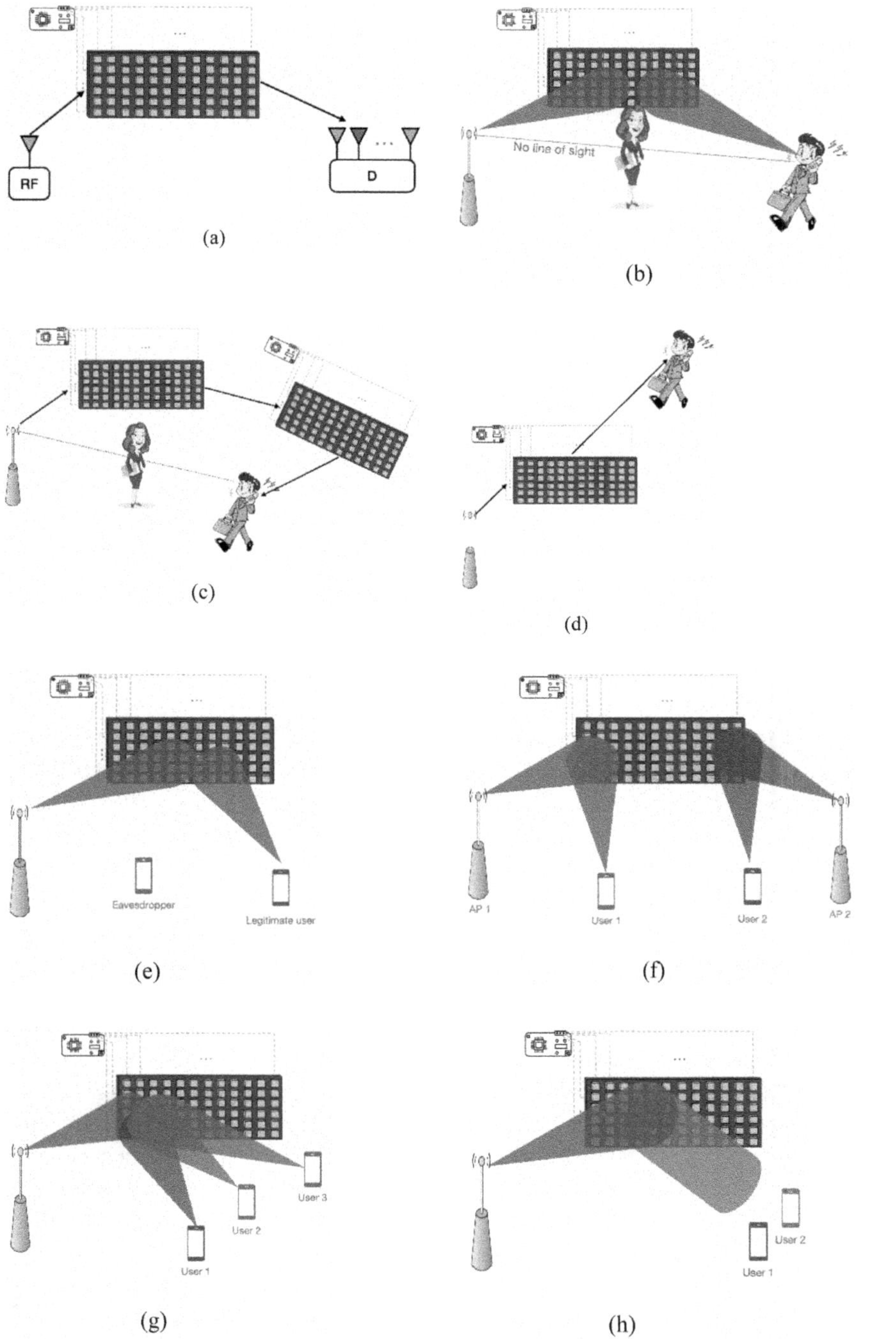

FIGURE 12.3 RIS-related application scenarios: (a) signal modulation, (b) blockage avoidance, (c) multi-hopping, (d) wireless power transfer, (e) physical layer security, (f) interference coordination, (g) broadcasting, and (h) multiple access.

TABLE 12.1
RIS and Relaying Comparison

	RIS	AF	DF	FD
Contains RF chains?	No	Yes	Yes	Yes
Has signal processing capabilities?	Analog	Analog	Analog & Digital	Analog & Digital
Add extra noise to the received signal?	No	Yes	Yes	Yes
Support FD links?	Yes	No	No	Yes
Hardware cost	Low	Medium	High	Very high
Power consumption	Low	Medium	High	Very high

hand and in contrary to AF and DF relays, RIS offers FD capabilities, which enables significant spectral efficiency improvements (Atapattu et al., Oct. 2020). Similarly to AF relaying and in contrary to DF and FD ones, RIS's have only analog signal processing capabilities.

From performance point of view, there are several contributions that report outage, error and capacity comparisons between RIS and relay-assisted wireless systems. For example, in (Basar et al., Aug. 2019), the authors present a central limit theorem (CLT) based error rate approximation, assuming that source (S)–RIS and RIS–destination (D) channels are independent Rayleigh distributed ones. Similarly, in (Jung, Saad, Jang, Kong, & Choi, Dec. 2019), again, by applying the CLT, the authors provided an outage probability approximation for large RIS structures. Finally, in (Boulogeorgos & Alexiou, Performance Analysis of Reconfigurable Intelligent Surface-Assisted Wireless Systems and Comparison With Relaying, May 2020), the authors provided closed-form expressions for the outage probability, error rate, ergodic capacity, diversity order and gain for RIS and AF relay assisted systems, assuming S-RIS and RIS-D channels to be identical, independent and Rayleigh distributed.

Indicative results that highlight the outage probability, symbol error rate (SER), and ergodic capacity performance of RIS-assisted wireless systems are depicted in **Figure 12.4**. In more detail, **Figure 12.4**.a illustrates the outage probability as a function of the ratio between the transmission signal-to-noise-ratio (SNR) to the SNR threshold (ρ_s/ρ_{th}), for different number of RIS units (N). As a benchmark, the outage probability of the corresponding AF relaying systems is plotted. From this figure, we observe that, for a fixed N, as ρ_s/ρ_{th} increases, the outage probability decreases. Likewise, it becomes appartent that RIS-aided wireless systems outperforms the corresponding AF ones, in terms of outage probability, since for the same ρ_s/ρ_{th}, the RIS-aided wireless system with N = 1, achieves lower outage probability compared to the corresponding AF one. Moreover, as N increases, the outage performance improves. For example, for ρ_s/ρ_{th} = 20 dB, the outage probability decreases for more than 100 times, as N increases form 1 to 2.

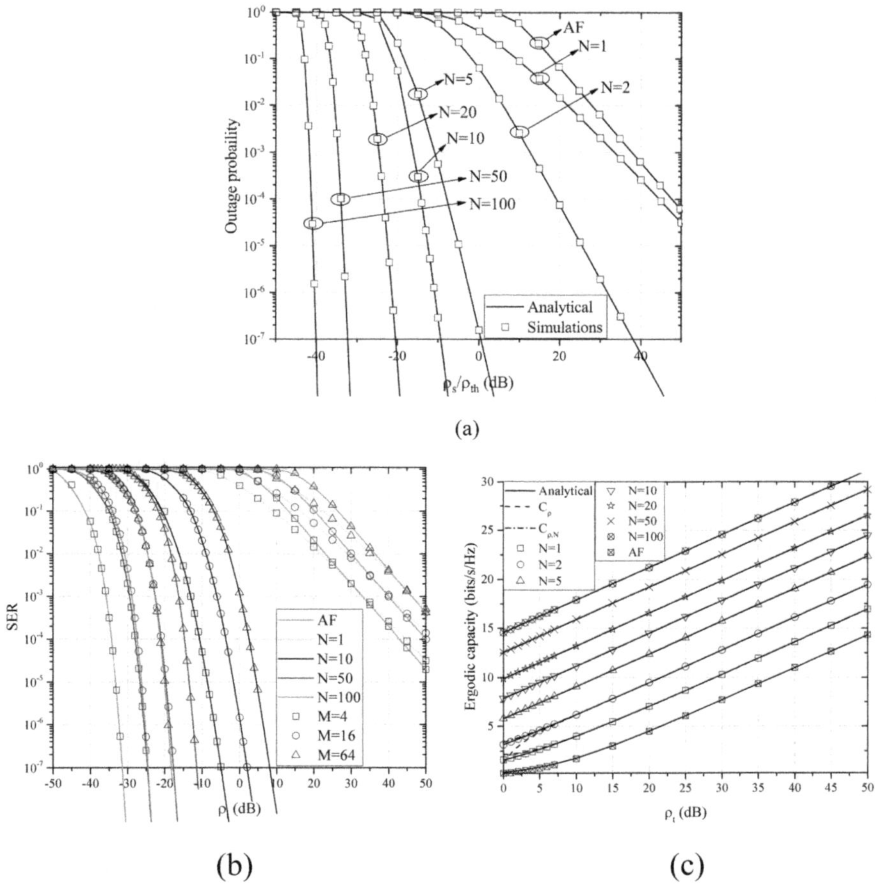

FIGURE 12.4 Performance comparison of RIS and relay-assisted wireless systems.

Similarly, **Figure 12.4**.b depicts the SER as a function of the transmission SNR for different number of N and M-ary quadrature amplitude modulation (QAM) schemes. Of note, QAM is one of the most commonly used constellation in wireless communications; thus, it is included in most wireless standards, such as long-term evolution (LTE), wireless fidelity (WiFi), etc. Again, the error performance of the corresponding AF system is given. From this figure, it becomes apparent that for fixed M and N, as the transmission SNR increases, the SER decreases. For example, for N = 10 and M = 64, the SER decreases for more than 7 orders of magnitude, as the transmission SNR changes from -10 to 10 dB. Interestingly, we observe that only for N = 1, in the high SNR regime, the AF system outperforms the RIS in terms of SER. Additionally, for given N and transmission SNR, as M increases, the SER also increases, while, for fixed M and transmission SNR, as N increases, the SER decreases. Finally, to sum up, from this figure, it becomes apparent that in order to increase the wireless systems performance, we have three choices: (i) increase the transmission SNR, (ii) increase N, and (iii) decrease M.

Figure 12.4.c illustrates ergodic capacity as a function of the transmission SNR for different values of N. For the sake of comparison, the ergodic capacity of the corresponding AF system is also presented. As expected, for a given N, as the transmission SNR increases, the ergodic capacity also increases. For example, for N = 10, the ergodic capacity doubles as the transmission SNR increases for 5 dB. From this figure, it also becomes evident that for a fixed transmission SNR, RIS systems achieve higher ergodic capacity than the corresponding AF one. Finally, for a given transmission SNR, as N increases, the diversity gain and order increases; thus, the ergodic capacity also increases.

Wireless power transfer: Another application, in which RIS may find application, is wireless power transfer (WPT) (Zhao, Wang, & Wang, Apr. 2020). RISs are able to address the distance limitation of conventional wireless power transfer systems by enabling coverage expansion (Yang, Yuan, Fang, & Liang, Feb. 2021). Motivated by this, recently, several researchers turned their attention to this subject. In more detail, in (Gong, Yang, Xing, An, & Hanzo, Dec. 2020), the authors optimized the beamforming and phase shift vectors of an RIS-assisted MIMO simultaneous wireless information and power transfer (SWIPT) system for Internet of Things (IoT) networks, while, in (Mohjazi et al., July 2020), the analytical framework for the statistical analysis of the battery recharging time RIS-assisted WPT system was provided. Both contributions agree that RIS is a key component to enable long-range WPT.

Physical layer security: In contrast to conventional encryption-based security methods, physical layer security (PLS) has been recognized as an attractive alternative (Karas, Boulogeorgos, & Karagiannidis, Oct. 2016). PLS is based on the exploitation of the channel and transceivers' hardware particularities in order to achieve higher capacity in the AP-legitimate user channel than in the AP-eavesdropper one (Karas, Boulogeorgos, Karagiannidis, & Nallanathan, Physical Layer Security in the Presence of Interference, Aug. 2017; Boulogeorgos, Karas, & Karagiannidis, How Much Does I/Q Imbalance Affect Secrecy Capacity?, Apr. 2016). Two approaches are usually employed. The first one assumes that the legitimate user is much closer to the AP than the eavesdropper; as a consequence, it experiences lower pathloss and thus higher capacity. The second one creates artificial noise and utilizes beamforming in order to increase the AP-legitimate user channel capacity, while reducing the one of the AP-eavesdropper channel. The first approach can be employed in a limited number of network topologies, while the second one is against the "green philosophy" (Gursoy, Apr. 2012).

To overcome these limitations, recently published research papers investigated the secrecy performance of RIS-assisted wireless systems. For example, in (Tsiftsis, Valagiannopoulos, Liu, Boulogeorgos, & Miridakis, Feb. 2021), the authors proposed the use of RIS in order to surpass the distance limitation without employing an artificial noise scheme. In more detail, they used the RIS in order to manipulate the wireless environment in a way, in which the AP transmitted power to be collected to the legitimate UE, while the power leakage towards the eavesdropper is quite low. This approach is expected to open the road to novel RIS-assisted PLS approaches.

Interference coordination: is an important task in wireless networks that allow them to provide access to a large number of wireless devices (Boulogeorgos, Interference mitigation techniques in modern wireless communication systems, 2016). Most interference coordination techniques are based on designing appropriate transmission schemes and codes as well as interference cancellation approaches that enables the orthogonalization of transmission signals. In other words, conventional interference coordination is based on manipulating the inputs or/and the outputs of the communication network. However, as depicted in Figure 12.3.f, by enabling spatial coordination and creating a beneficial wireless environment, RISs provide extra degrees of freedom that boost the massive connectivity capabilities of wireless networks (Chen et al., Dec. 2020).

Broadcasting: another important RIS usage is to broadcast information in multiple users that are located outside the AP transmission range. As described in (Boulogeorgos & Alexiou, Coverage Analysis of Reconfigurable Intelligent Surface Assisted THz Wireless Systems, Jan. 2021) as well as (Xu, Liang, Yang, & Zhao, Dec. 2020) and depicted in Figure 12.3.g, in this case, the AP employs high-directional transmissions towards the RIS, which uses beam splitting to broadcast the incident signal in a number of users. For this scenario, the AP and users positions should be known to the RIS in order to select the appropriate phase shifts.

Multiple access: non-orthogonal multiple access (NOMA) has been employed in several RIS-assisted wireless systems to simultaneously support more than one users. For instance, in (Yang, Xu, Liang, & Di Renzo, Jan. 2021), a downlink RIS-assisted NOMA scenario was studied, while, in (Zuo, Liu, & Al-Dhahir, Dec. 2020), a RIS-assisted cooperative NOMA was investigated. Finally, a similar approach called layered-division-multiplexing (LDM) was employed in (An, Shi, & Zhou, June 2020). In LDM, the AP simultaneously transmits non-orthogonal unicast and broadcast messages to multiple users, which have different quality of service (QoS) requirements, through an RIS.

12.3 CHANNEL MODELLING IN RIS-ASSISTED WIRELESS SYSTEMS

Outdoor RIS-assisted wireless systems: Scanning the technical literature, several contributions can be identified that study the performance of RIS-assisted wireless systems under different conditions as well as channel models and quantify a variety of key performance indicators. In more detail, in (Basar et al., Aug. 2019) and in (Najafi, Schmauss, & Schober, May 2020), the authors assumed an additive white Gaussian channel (AWGN) and extracted the bit error rate (BER) of the RIS-assisted wireless systems. Likewise, in (Ntontin et al., Mar. 2021), an AWGN was assumed and the end-to-end average received power as well as the SNR at the destination were presented.

The aforementioned contributions refer to backhauling scenarios in outdoor environments in which there is no direct link between the source (S) and the destination (D). In this case, the source of randomness is the noise induced by the receiver's RF chain. As a consequence, the received signal can be expressed as

$$y = h_l s + n \tag{12.1}$$

where s and n respectively stand for the transmission signal and the AWGN, while h_l denotes the channel coefficient that can be obtained as

$$h_l = \sqrt{L_1 G L_2} \tag{12.2}$$

with L_1 and L_2 being respectively the path-gain of the S-RIS and RIS-D links and G representing the RIS gain. According to (Tang et al., Jan. 2021), in RF and microwave links, the path-gain of the S-RIS and RIS-D links can be written as

$$L_1 = \frac{G_s \lambda^2}{(4\pi)^2 d_1^2} \mathrm{U}(\theta_s, \phi_s) \tag{12.3}$$

and

$$L_2 = \frac{G_d \lambda^2}{(4\pi)^2 d_2^2} \mathrm{U}(\theta_r, \phi_r) \tag{12.4}$$

where λ is the transmission wavelength, G_s and G_d are respectively the S and D antenna gains, while d_1 and d_2 are respectively the S-RIS and RIS-DI distance. Moreover, as depicted in Figure 12.5, θ_s and ϕ_s are respectively the elevation and azimuth angle of the center of the RIS to the S, while θ_r and ϕ_r respectively denote the elevation and azimuth angle of the center of the RIS to the D. Additionally,

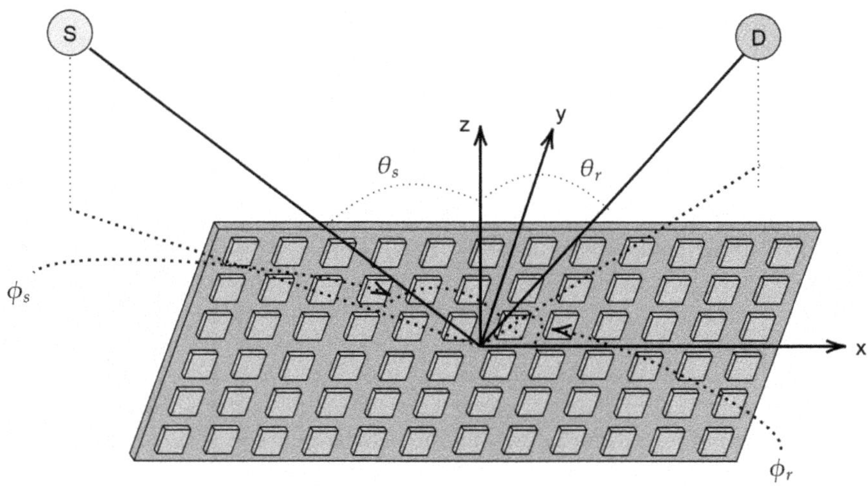

FIGURE 12.5 RIS-assisted wireless system without direct link between S and D.

U(θ, ϕ) stands for the RIS element normalized power radiation pattern. Of note, the range of L_1, L_2 and thus y in (x.1), (x.3), and (x.4) depend on the transmission frequency, distances, antenna technology, materials, and designs, transmission power, and D's electronics. As a consequence, their tightly connected to the application and technology; thus, it is very difficult or even impossible to determine their limits. On the other hand, G_s and G_d are expected to be in the order of [0, 60 dBi]. Finally, G can be obtained as

$$G = 4M^2N^2 d_x d_y \left|\Gamma\right|^2 \gamma_1\gamma_2 \tag{12.5}$$

where

$$\gamma_1 = \left| \frac{\operatorname{sinc}\left(\frac{M\pi}{\lambda}\left(\sin(\theta_s)\cos(\phi_s)+\sin(\theta_r)\cos(\phi_r)-\sin(\theta_t)\cos(\phi_t)-\sin(\theta_o)\cos(\phi_o)\right)d_x\right)}{\operatorname{sinc}\left(\frac{\pi}{\lambda}\left(\sin(\theta_s)\cos(\phi_s)+\sin(\theta_r)\cos(\phi_r)-\sin(\theta_t)\cos(\phi_t)-\sin(\theta_o)\cos(\phi_o)\right)d_x\right)} \right|^2 \tag{12.6}$$

and

$$\gamma_2 = \left| \frac{\operatorname{sinc}\left(\frac{N\pi}{\lambda}\left(\sin(\theta_s)\cos(\phi_s)+\sin(\theta_r)\cos(\phi_r)-\sin(\theta_t)\cos(\phi_t)-\sin(\theta_o)\cos(\phi_o)\right)d_x\right)}{\operatorname{sinc}\left(\frac{\pi}{\lambda}\left(\sin(\theta_s)\cos(\phi_s)+\sin(\theta_r)\cos(\phi_r)-\sin(\theta_t)\cos(\phi_t)-\sin(\theta_o)\cos(\phi_o)\right)d_x\right)} \right|^2 \tag{12.7}$$

Of note, in (12.5)–(12.7), M and N represents the number of RIS elements at the horizontal and vertical direction, respectively, d_x and d_y respectively stand for the spatial periodicity of the horizontal and vertical RIS elements, and (θ_o, ϕ_o) is the desired beam steering direction. Finally, |Γ| represents the amplitude of the RIS element reflection coefficient. In practice, |Γ| is in the range of [0, 1], while M and N are expected to be in the range of [1, 1024]. Moreover, d_x and d_y ranges from λ/10 to λ/4, while γ_1 and γ_2 are in the range of [0, 1]. As a consequence, G/λ^2 is in the range of [0, 50 dBi].

In higher frequency communications, such as millimeter wave and THz ones, the atmospheric conditions should be taken also into account (Boulogeorgos & Alexiou, Coverage Analysis of Reconfigurable Intelligent Surface Assisted THz Wireless Systems, Jan. 2021). In this direction, the received signal should be modeled as

$$y_h = h_a h_l s + n \tag{12.8}$$

where h_a stands for the environmental related channel coefficient and can be obtained as

$$h_a = \exp\left(-\frac{1}{2}\kappa(f)(d_1+d_2)\right) \tag{12.9}$$

with κ(f) being the frequency (f) dependent atmospheric coefficient that can be evaluated as in (Boulogeorgos & Alexiou, Coverage Analysis of Reconfigurable Intelligent Surface Assisted THz Wireless Systems, Jan. 2021).

Finally, in RIS-assisted optical wireless communications (OWCs) two approaches have been followed. The first one treats the RIS as a reflecting mirror (Najafi, Schmauss, & Schober, May 2020) and creates an equivalent model that capture the atmospheric loss, turbullence as well as the geometric and misalignment losses (GML). In this case, the received signal can be obtained as

$$y_s = h_o s + n \tag{12.10}$$

where h_o stands for the channel gain and can be expressed as

$$h_o = \eta h_{al} h_t h_g \tag{12.11}$$

In (12.11), η stands for the receiver's photodetectors responsivity, h_{al} is the end-to-end atmospheric loss, h_t is the turbulence induced fading, and h_g denotes the GML coefficient. The end-to-end atmospheric loss is deterministic and captures the path loss due to absorption and scattering losses as well as the path gain due to the optical RIS (ORIS); thus, it can be obtained as

$$h_{al} = \zeta 10^{\kappa \frac{d_1 + d_2}{2}} \tag{12.12}$$

where ζ is in the range of [0.7, 1] and denotes the ORIS reflection efficiency, while κ is the weather-dependent attenuation coefficient of the FSO link.

Moreover, the GML coefficient is a random process with probability density function (PDF) that can be obtained as

$$f_{h_g}(x) = \frac{\sqrt{\rho}}{\sqrt{\pi} A_o} \left(\frac{x}{A_o} \right)^{\rho - 1} \left(\ln \left(\frac{A_o}{x} \right) \right)^{-1/2}, 0 \le x \le A_o \tag{12.13}$$

where

$$\rho = \frac{t}{4\sigma_t^2} \tag{12.14}$$

and A_o the maximum fraction of optical power captured by the PD lens.
In (x.14),

$$t = \frac{A_o}{\pi} \tag{12.15}$$

and

$$\sigma_t^2 = \frac{\sin^2(\theta_s + \theta_r)}{\cos^2(\theta_s)} \sigma_r^2 \tag{12.16}$$

with σ_r being the standard deviation of the spatial jitter.

Finally, the turbulence coefficient follows log-normal (LN) or gamma-gamma (GG) distribution with PDFs that can be expressed as (Najafi, Schmauss, & Schober, May 2020)

$$f_{h_t}(x) = \begin{cases} \frac{1}{\sqrt{8\pi\sigma^2}x}\exp\left(-\frac{\left(\ln(x)+2\sigma^2\right)^2}{8\sigma^2}\right), & \text{LN} \\ \frac{2(\alpha\beta x)^{\frac{\alpha+\beta}{2}}}{\Gamma(\alpha)\Gamma(\beta)x}\mathrm{K}_{\alpha\text{-}\beta}\left(2\sqrt{\alpha\beta x}\right), & \text{GG} \end{cases} \tag{12.17}$$

where

$$\sigma^2 \approx \frac{\sigma_R^2}{4} \tag{12.18}$$

with

$$\sigma_R^2 = 1.23C_n^2\left(\frac{2\pi}{\lambda}\right)^{7/6}\left(d_1+d_2\right)^{11/6} \tag{12.19}$$

In (12.19), C_n is the squared index of refraction structure parameter. Likewise, in (x.17),

$$\alpha = \left(\exp\left(\frac{0.49\sigma_R^2}{\left(1+1.11\sigma_R^{12/5}\right)^{7/6}}\right)-1\right)^{-1} \tag{12.20}$$

and

$$\beta = \left(\exp\left(\frac{0.51\sigma_R^2}{\left(1+0.69\sigma_R^{12/5}\right)^{5/6}}\right)-1\right)^{-1} \tag{12.21}$$

Finally, $K_n(.)$ stands for the modified Bessel of the second kind.

Indoor RIS-assisted wireless systems: The most indicative contributions of modeling the stochastic nature of the end-to-end indoor wireless channels in RIS-assisted system are (Boulogeorgos & Alexiou, Coverage Analysis of Reconfigurable Intelligent Surface Assisted THz Wireless Systems, Jan. 2021) and (Boulogeorgos & Alexiou, Performance Analysis of Reconfigurable Intelligent Surface-Assisted Wireless Systems and Comparison With Relaying, May 2020). In the first contribution, the authors assumed a broadcasting scenario, in which an access point servers M mobile user equioments that belong in a signle cluster through an RIS. The position of each user is unknown to the RIS. On the other hand, the cluster center and radius is known. By assuming that the users are uniformly located within a circle of specific radius, the authors proved that the coverage probability can be obtained as

$$P_c = \begin{cases} 1, & p_{th} < \left(h_{nu}^{l}\right)^2 \left(\dfrac{2}{k(f)(d+r_{th})} - 1\right)^2 P_{AP} \\ \dfrac{1}{2} - \dfrac{1}{\pi} \dfrac{\left(d - \dfrac{2h_{nu}^{l}}{\kappa(f)\left(\sqrt{\dfrac{P_{th}}{P_{AP}}} + h_{nu}^{l}\right)}\right)\sqrt{r_{th}^2 - \left(d - \dfrac{2h_{nu}^{l}}{\kappa(f)\left(\sqrt{\dfrac{P_{th}}{P_{AP}}} + h_{nu}^{l}\right)}\right)}}{r_{th}^2} \\ -2\sin^{-1}\left(\dfrac{d - \dfrac{2h_{nu}^{l}}{\kappa(f)\left(\sqrt{\dfrac{P_{th}}{P_{AP}}} + h_{nu}^{l}\right)}}{r_{th}}\right) \\ \left(h_{nu}^{l}\right)^2 \left(\dfrac{2}{\kappa(f)(d+r_{th})} - 1\right)^2 \\ \qquad P_{AP} \le P_{th} \le \left(h_{nu}^{l}\right)^2 \left(\dfrac{2}{\kappa(f)(d-r_{th})} - 1\right)^2 P_{AP} \\ 0, & P_{th} \ge \left(h_{nu}^{l}\right)^2 \left(h_{nu}^{l}\right)^2 \left(\dfrac{2}{\kappa(f)(d-r_{th})} - 1\right)^2 P_{AP} \end{cases} \tag{12.22}$$

where P_{AP} and P_{th} are respectively the access point transmission power and the receiver's power threshold, h_{n_u}^l is the end-to-end channel coefficient due to free space loss, d is the euclidean distance between the center of the RIS and the center of the cluster, and r_{th} is the radius of the maximum path-gain region. Next, by setting

$$\tau = \frac{2h_{n_u}^{l}}{\kappa(f)\left(\sqrt{\dfrac{P_{th}}{P_{AP}}} + h_{n_u}^{l}\right)} \tag{12.23}$$

(12.22) can be rewritten in a more compact form as

$$P_c = \begin{cases} 1, & d + r_{rh} \le \tau \\ \frac{1}{2} - \frac{1}{\pi} \frac{(d-\tau)\sqrt{r_{th}^2 - (d-\tau)^2}}{r_{th}^2} - 2\sin^{-1}\left(\frac{d-\tau}{r_{th}}\right) & d - r_{th} \le \tau \le d + r_{th} \\ 0, & \tau > d - r_{rh} \end{cases} \quad (12.23)$$

To quantify the coverage performance of the RIS-assisted broadcasting system, we consider the following insightful scenario. The relative humity, atmospheric pressure, and temperature are set to 50%, 101325 Pa, and 296°K, respectively. The access point antenna has 50 dBi gain and the transmission frequency is 100 GHz. Moreover, $\varphi_s = \pi$, $\varphi_r = 0$ and $\theta_s = \theta_r = \pi/4$. As illustrated in Figure 12.6, for fixed RIS zize and d, as P_{AP}/P_{th} increases, the coverage probability increases. Moreover, for given d and P_{AP}/P_{th}, as the RIS size increases, the coverage probability increases. Additionally, we observe that for fixed RIS size and P_{AP}/P_{th}, as d increases, the coverage probability decreases. Finally, as can be also observed in (12.21), there exists a P_{AP}/P_{th}, beyond which the coverage probability becomes equal to 1.

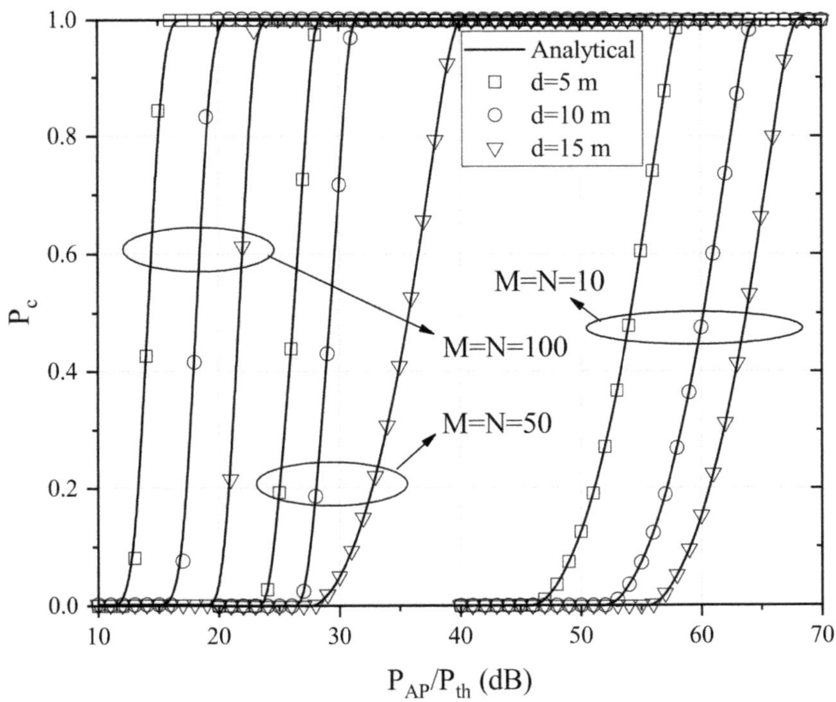

FIGURE 12.6 P_c vs P_{AP}/P_{th} for different RIS sizes and d.

In (Boulogeorgos & Alexiou, Performance Analysis of Reconfigurable Intelligent Surface-Assisted Wireless Systems and Comparison With Relaying, May 2020), the authors assumed that that the link between S and the i-th RIS element as well as the one between the i-th RIS element and D can be modeled as independent and identical Rayleigh distributed random processes. Moreover, the RIS has full channel state information and selects the optimum phase shifts. As a result, the received signal can be obtained as

$$r = As + n \tag{12.22}$$

where

$$A = \sum_{i=1}^{M \times N} |h_i||g_i| \tag{12.23}$$

and h_i, g_i being the channel coefficients of the S to the i-th RIS element and the i-th RIS element to D links, respectively.

To characterize A, the authors provided a theorem that return its PDF and cumulative density function (CDF), which can respectively expressed as

$$f_A(x) = \frac{x^a}{b^{a+1}\Gamma(a+1)} \exp\left(-\frac{x}{b}\right) \tag{12.24}$$

and

$$F_A(x) = \frac{\gamma\left(1+a, \frac{x}{b}\right)}{\Gamma(a+1)} \tag{12.25}$$

where

$$a = \frac{k_1^2}{k_2} - 1 \tag{12.26}$$

and

$$b = \frac{k_2}{k_1} \tag{12.27}$$

with

$$k_1 = \frac{MN\pi}{2} \tag{12.28}$$

and

$$k_2 = 4MN\left(1 - \frac{\pi^2}{16}\right) \tag{12.29}$$

The aforementioned expressions provided the necessary theoretical tools for the analysis, performance evaluation and optimization of RIS assisted systems. Based on this theorem, the authors in (Boulogeorgos & Alexiou, Performance Analysis of Reconfigurable Intelligent Surface-Assisted Wireless Systems and Comparison With Relaying, May 2020), extracted the RIS-assisted system outage probability, error rate, diversity gain and order, average SNR, and ergodic capacity. Moreover, building upon them, in (Boulogeorgos & Alexiou, How Much do Hardware Imperfections Affect the Performance of Reconfigurable Intelligent Surface-Assisted Systems?, Aug. 2020), the impact of hardware imperfections in RIS assisted wireless system was quantified. Finally, in (Yang et al., Oct. 2020), the secreacy performance of RIS-assisted wireless systems were evaluated.

12.4 RESEARCH DIRECTIONS & CONCLUSIONS

Although an important amount of research effort was put on designing, analyzing, optimizing and developing RISs and RIS-assisted wireless systems and networks, there are still several open research questions that need to be addressed. Aspired by this, this section takes a fresh look and reports main research directions in a number of different domains, i.e., materials, modeling, theoretical analysis, as well as system and network optimization.

Materials, RIS design and development: Recently several in-lab RIS designs were presented and measured. For example, in (Kaina, Dupre, Lerosey, & Fink, Oct. 2014), a RIS, consisting of 102 elements spaced by half a wavelength ($\lambda/2$) and operating in 2.47 GHz, was presented. In this design, the RIS elements operate as binary reflectors; thus, the RIS can only provide steering and focusing capabilities. Moreover, it could support transmissions of bandwidth no more than 100 MHz. Similarly, in (Yang et al., Oct. 2016), the authors designed and tested a large RIS ($>20\ \lambda$) that consisted of 5 identical sub-metasurfaces and operated at 11.1 GHz. Each one of the sub-metasurface consisted of 320 active binary meta-atoms (i.e., they could be either ON or OFF) and could be independently controlled. Thus, the RIS could support polarization, steering, focusing, and splitting capabilities. Additionally, in (Akbari, Samadi, Sebak, & Denidni, Apr. 2019), a broadband RIS capable of providing steering, focusing, and polarization at the 4.8–22.8 GHz band was reported, while, in (Ding et al., Nov. 2015), an ultra-thin metasurface that consists of two types of static meta-atoms and is capable of providing reflection and transmission capabilities in the 8–11 GHz band was documented.

In the industrial world, NTT DOCOMO and Metawave provided the world's first meta-structure reflect-array technology demonstration in the 28 GHz band in November 2018. The meta-structure reflect-array type RIS, which is depicted in Figure 12.7.a, was able to achieve a data rate of 560 Mbps, which was about 10 times higher than the one achieved in its absence. Of note, the aforementioned RIS had reflection and beam shaping capabilities (Businesswire, 2018). Finally, in January 2020, NTT DOCOMO presented the first transparent RIS, which is illustrated in Figure 12.7.b, and operates in 28 GHz (NTT DOCOMO, 2020), while a transparent metasurface lense operating in the same frequency band was preseted

(a)

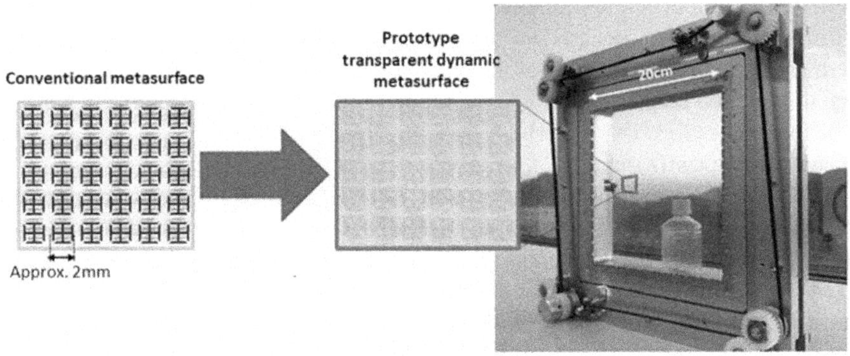

(b)

FIGURE 12.7 RIS's industrial implementations.

by NTT DOCOMO and AGC in January 2021 (NTT DOCOMO, 2021). These RISs allow wave manipulation, while maintaining window's transparency. They support full reflection and transition, beam splitting as well as focusing functionalities.

Despite the high technology readiness level of RIS technology, there are several open research directions that can be followed. In more detail, from the literature review it becomes evident that there are no RIS implementations in the sub-THz and THz bands. This is because, in these bands, the wave has a semi-optical behavior. As a result, the designs cannot straightforwardly scale. Moreover, in this band, it worth designing and developing graphene based RISs, which are expected to experience lower losses, have larger meta-atoms density and thus achieve higher efficiency. Finally, to the best of the author's knowledge, no RISs that consist of heterogeneous meta-atom types have been presented in the open literature. Such structures could be able to apply a different number of functionalities and support broadband transmissions.

Modeling and theoretical analysis: From the electromagnetic point of view, several models that are based on the conventional Maxwell theory or transmission line theory were presented (see e.g., (Simovski & Tretyakov, 2020) and reference therein). However, the interface between electromagnetic and signal processing models have not yet been created. Such an interface would provide the appropriate tool to analyze and optimize the performance of communication and localization systems as well as open the door in understanding the impact of hardware parameters in the KPIs.

Moreover, it is important to note that RIS-assisted wireless systems require the development of a new beyond Shannon and Wiener information theoretic framework. In particular, Shannon's and Wiener's theories are based on the assumption that the communication channel cannot be manipulated by external interventions. However, RIS's are capable of sensing the wireless medium and changing it in order to create a favorable electromagnetic environment. This contrasts the main assumption of both Shannon's and Wiener's principles and calls for a new information theoretic framework. This framework should define the performance envelop of RIS assisted system by taking into account the RIS functionalities, characteristics, and capabilities.

System and network optimization: RIS assisted systems create a space of formulating and solving a number of new optimization problems that concerns the minimization of energy consumption or the maximization of energy/spectral efficiency by choosing RIS optimal placement (Ntontin et al., Mar. 2021) or suitable source's and RIS's beamforming codebooks and phase shifting vectors (Wu & Zhang, Nov. 2019). An important constraint for such systems is the overhead send to the RIS. In face of this constraint, the use of artificial intelligence (AI) approaches seems an attractive solution.

Finally, mobility management in RIS assisted wireless systems is also an open issue. To support mobility management, the RIS needs to predict the mobile user's future position and pre-adjust its element parameters in order to be able to follow it. To predict the future position of the user, several researchers have turned their eyes into creating mobility patterns based on machine learning approaches (see e.g., (Taha, Zhang, Mismar, & Alkhateed, Feb. 2020)).

To sum up, this chapter revised the technology enablers of SRE, namely RIS, and discussed the state-of-the-art related to them. The discussion revealed the need to create new types of RIS that can support broadband transmission as well as a number of different electromagnetic functionalities, while being transparent. For RIS-assisted systems, new channel and system models as well as the interface between the electromagnetic theory and signal processing was deemed a necessity to be developed. Building upon this interface as well as the observation that the Shannon's and Wiener's information theory fundamental assumptions do not hold in RIS-assisted systems, we identified the need to develop a novel information theoretic framework for their analysis and optimization, as well as new KPIs.

REFERENCES

Akbari, M., Samadi, F., Sebak, A.-R., & Denidni, T. A. (Apr. 2019). Superbroadband Diffuse Wave Scattering Based on Coding Metasurfaces: Polarization Conversion Metasurfaces. *IEEE Antennas and Propagation Magazine*, 40–52.

An, Q., Shi, Y., & Zhou, Y. (June 2020). Reconfigurable Intelligent Surface Assisted Non-Orthogonal Unicast and Broadcast Transmission. *IEEE 91st Vehicular Technology Conference (VTC2020-Spring)* (pp. 1–5). Antwerp, Belgium: IEEE.

Atapattu, S., Fan, R., Dharmawansa, P., Wang, G., Evans, J., & Tsiftsis, T. A. (Oct. 2020). Reconfigurable Intelligent Surface Assisted Two–Way Communications: Performance Analysis and Optimization. *IEEE Transactions on Communications*, 6552–6567.

Basar, E. (Jan. 2020). Reconfigurable Intelligent Surface-Based Index Modulation: A New Beyond MIMO Paradigm for 6G. *ArXiV*, 1–10.

Basar, E., Di Renzo, M., De Rosny, J., Debbah, M., Alouini, M.-S., & Zhang, R. (Aug. 2019). Wireless Communications Through Reconfigurable Intelligent Surfaces. *IEEE Access*, 116753–116773.

Boulogeorgos, A.-A. A. (Nov. 2016). Interference Mitigation Techniques in Modern Wireless Communication Systems. *PhD Thesis*. Thessaloniki, Greece: Department of Electrical and Computer Engineering, Aristotle University of Thessaloniki.

Boulogeorgos, A.-A. A., & Alexiou, A. (Jan. 2021). Coverage Analysis of Reconfigurable Intelligent Surface Assisted THz Wireless Systems. *IEEE Open Journal of Vehicular Technology*, 94–110.

Boulogeorgos, A.-A. A., & Alexiou, A. (May 2020). Performance Analysis of Reconfigurable Intelligent Surface-Assisted Wireless Systems and Comparison with Relaying. *IEEE Access*, 94463–94483.

Boulogeorgos, A.-A. A., & Alexiou, A. (Aug. 2020). How Much Do Hardware Imperfections Affect the Performance of Reconfigurable Intelligent Surface-Assisted Systems? *IEEE Open Journal of the Communications Society*, 1185–1195.

Boulogeorgos, A.-A. A., & Alexiou, A. (Sept. 2020). Ergodic Capacity Analysis of Reconfigurable Intelligent Surface Assisted Wireless Systems. *IEEE 3rd 5G World Forum (5GWF)* (pp. 395–400). Bangalore, India: IEEE.

Boulogeorgos, A.-A. A., Goudos, S. K., & Alexiou, A. (Aug. 2018). Users Association in Ultra Dense THz Networks. *IEEE 19th International Workshop on Signal Processing Advances in Wireless Communications (SPAWC)* (pp. 1–5). Kalamata, Greece: IEEE.

Boulogeorgos, A.-A. A., Karas, D. S., & Karagiannidis, G. K. (Apr. 2016). How Much Does I/Q Imbalance Affect Secrecy Capacity? *IEEE Communications Letters*, 1305–1308.

Businesswire. (Apr. 12, 2018). Retrieved from NTT DOCOMO and Metawave Announce Successful Demonstration of 28GHz-Band 5G Using World's First Meta-Structure Technology: www.businesswire.com/news/home/20181204005253/en/NTT-DOCOMO-and-Metawave-Announce-Successful-Demonstration-of-28GHz-Band-5G-Using-Worlds-First-Meta-Structure-Technology

Chen, Y., Ai, B., Zhang, H., Niu, Y., Song, L., Han, Z., & Vincent Poor, H. (Dec. 2020). Reconfigurable Intelligent Surface Assisted Device-to-Device Communications. *IEEE Transactions on Wireless Communications*, 20: 2792-2804

Ding, X., Yu, H., Zhang, S., Wu, Y., Zhang, K., & Wu, Q. (Nov. 2015). Ultrathin Metasurface for Controlling Electromagnetic Wave with Broad Bandwidth. *IEEE Transactions on Magnetics*, 1–4.

Di Renzo, M., Ntontin, K., Song, J., Danufane, F. H., Qian, X., Lazarakis, F., . . . Shamai, S. (June 2020). Reconfigurable Intelligent Surfaces vs. Relaying: Differences, Similarities, and Performance Comparison. *IEEE Open Journal of the Communications Society*, 798–807.

Gong, S., Yang, Z., Xing, C., An, J., & Hanzo, L. (Dec. 2020). Beamforming Optimization for Intelligent Reflecting Surface Aided SWIPT IoT Networks Relying on Discrete Phase Shifts. *IEEE Internet of Things Journal*, 8585–8602.

Gursoy, M. C. (Apr. 2012). Secure Communication in the Low-SNR Regime. *IEEE Transactions on Communications*, 1114–1123.

He, Q., Sun, S., & Zhou, L. (July 2019). Tunable/Reconfigurable Metasurfaces: Physics and Applications. *Research*, 16.

Jung, M., Saad, W., Jang, Y., Kong, G., & Choi, S. (Dec. 2019). Reliability Analysis of Large Intelligent Surfaces (LISs): Rate Distribution and Outage Probability. *IEEE Wireless Communications Letters*, 1662–1666.

Kaina, N., Dupre, M., Lerosey, G., & Fink, M. (Oct. 2014). Shaping Complex Microwave Fields in Reverberating Media with Binary Tunable Metasurfaces. *Scientific Reports*, 6693.

Karas, D. S., Boulogeorgos, A.-A. A., & Karagiannidis, G. K. (Oct. 2016). Physical Layer Security with Uncertainty on the Location of the Eavesdropper. *IEEE Wireless Communications Letters*, 540–543.

Karas, D. S., Boulogeorgos, A.-A. A., Karagiannidis, G. K., & Nallanathan, A. (Aug. 2017). Physical Layer Security in the Presence of Interference. *IEEE Wireless Communications Letters*, 802–805.

Li, L., Ruan, H., Liu, C., Li, Y., Shuang, Y., Alu, A., . . . Cui, T. J. (Mar. 2019). Machine-learning Reprogrammable Metasurface Imager. *Nature Communications*, 1–8.

Liaskos, C., Nie, S., Tsioliaridou, A., Pitsillides, A., Ioannidis, S., & Akyildiz, I. (Sept. 2018). A New Wireless Communication Paradigm through Software-Controlled Metasurfaces. *IEEE Communications Magazine*, 162–169.

Liaskos, C., Tsiolaridou, A., Pitsillides, A., Akyildiz, I. F., Kantartzis, N. V., Lalas, A. X., . . . Soukoulis, C. M. (Fourthquarter 2015). Design and Development of Software Defined Metamaterials for Nanonetworks. *IEEE Circuits and Systems Magazine*, 12–25.

Lin, S., Zheng, B., Alexandropoulos, G. C., Wen, M., Di Renzo, M., & Chen, F. (Aug. 2020). Reconfigurable Intelligent Surfaces with Reflection Pattern Modulation: Beamforming Design and Performance Analysis. *ArXiV*, 1–31.

Liu, M., Sternbach, A. J., & Basov, D. N. (Nov. 2016). Nanoscale Electrodynamics of Strongly Correlated Quantum Materials. *Reports on Progress in Physics.*

McGahan, C., Gamage, S., Liang, J., Cross, B., Marvel, R. E., Haglund, R. F., & Abate, Y. (Jan. 2017). Geometric Constraints on Phase Coexistence in Vanadium Dioxide Single Crystals. *Nanotechnology*, 9.

Mohjazi, L., Muhaidat, S., Abbasi, Q. H., Imran, M. A., Dobre, O. A., & Di Renzo, M. (July 2020). Battery Recharging Time Models for Reconfigurable Intelligent Surface-Assisted Wireless Power Transfer Systems. *ArXiV*, 1–11.

Najafi, M., Schmauss, B., & Schober, R. (May 2020). Intelligent Reconfigurable Reflecting Surfaces for Free Space Optical Communications. *ArXiV*, 1–31.

Ntontin, K., Boulogeorgos, A.-A. A., Selimis, D. G., Lazaridis, F. I., Alexiou, A., & Chatzinotas, S. (Mar. 2021). Reconfigurable Intelligent Surface Optimal Placement in Millimeter-Wave Networks. *IEEE Open Journal of the Communications Society*, 704–718.

NTT DOCOMO. (Jan. 17, 2020). *DOCOMO Conducts World's First Successful Trial of Transparent Dynamic Metasurface*. Retrieved from NTT docomo: www.nttdocomo.co.jp/english/info/media_center/pr/2020/0117_00.html

NTT DOCOMO. (Jan. 26, 2021). Retrieved from DOCOMO and AGC Use Metasurface Lens to Enhance Radio Signal Reception Indoors: www.nttdocomo.co.jp/english/info/media_center/pr/2021/0126_00.html

Papasotirou, E. N., Boulogeorgos, A.-A. A., Stratakou, A., & Alexiou, A. (Sept. 2020). Performance Evaluation of Reconfigurable Intelligent Surface Assisted D-band Wireless Communication. *IEEE 3rd 5G World Forum (5GWF)* (pp. 360–365). Bangalore, India: IEEE.

Simovski, C., & Tretyakov, A. (2020). *An Introduction to Metamaterials and Nanophotonics*. Cambridge, UK: Cambridge University Press.

Singh, R., & Zheludev, N. (Sept. 2014). Superconductor photonics. *Nature Photonics*, 679–680.

Taha, A., Zhang, Y., Mismar, F. B., & Alkhateed, A. (Feb. 2020). Deep Reinforcement Learning for Intelligent Reflecting Surfaces: Towards Standalone Operation. *ArXiV*, 1–6.

Tan, X., Sun, Z., Jornet, J. M., & Pados, D. (May 2016). Increasing Indoor Spectrum Sharing Capacity Using Smart Reflect-array. *IEEE International Conference on Communications (ICC)*. Kuala Lumpur, Malaysia: IEEE.

Tan, X., Sun, Z., Koutsonikolas, D., & Jornet, J. M. (Apr. 2018). Enabling Indoor Mobile Millimeter-wave Networks Based on Smart Reflect-arrays. *IEEE Conference on Computer Communications (INFOCOM)* (pp. 270–278). Honolulu, HI, USA: IEEE.

Tang, W., Chen, M. Z., Chen, X., Dai, J. Y., Han, Y., Di Renzo, M., . . . Cui, T. J. (Jan. 2021). Wireless Communications with Reconfigurable Intelligent Surface: Path Loss Modeling and Experimental Measurement. *IEEE Transactions on Wireless Communications*, 421–439.

Tsiftsis, T. A., Valagiannopoulos, C., Liu, H., Boulogeorgos, A.-A. A., & Miridakis, N. I. (Feb. 2021). Metasurface-Coated Devices: A New Paradigm for Energy-Efficient and Secure 6G Communications. *ArXiV*, 1–8.

Wu, Q., & Zhang, R. (Nov. 2019). Intelligent Reflecting Surface Enhanced Wireless Network via Joint Active and Passive Beamforming. *IEEE Transactions on Wireless Communications*, 5394–5409.

Xu, X., Liang, Y.-C., Yang, G., & Zhao, L. (Dec. 2020). Reconfigurable Intelligent Surface Empowered Symbiotic Radio over Broadcasting Signals. *IEEE Global Communications Conference (GLOBECOM)* (pp. 1–6). Taipei, Taiwan: IEEE.

Yang, G., Xu, X., Liang, Y.-C., & Di Renzo, M. (Jan. 2021). Reconfigurable Intelligent Surface Assisted Non-Orthogonal Multiple Access. *IEEE Transactions on Wireless Communications*, 3137–3151.

Yang, H., Cao, X., Yang, F., Gao, J., Xu, S., Li, M., . . . Li, S. (Oct. 2016). A Programmable Metasurface with Dynamic Polarization, Scattering and Focusing Control. *Scientific Reports*, 35692.

Yang, H., Yuan, X., Fang, J., & Liang, Y.-C. (Feb. 2021). Reconfigurable Intelligent Surface Aided Constant-Envelope Wireless Power Transfer. *IEEE Transactions on Signal Processing*, 1347–1361.

Yang, L., Yang, J., Xie, W., Hasna, M. O., Tsiftsis, T., & Di Renzo, M. (Oct. 2020). Secrecy Performance Analysis of RIS-Aided Wireless Communication Systems. *IEEE Transactions on Vehicular Technology*, 12296–12300.

Zhao, L., Wang, Z., & Wang, X. (Apr. 2020). Wireless Power Transfer Empowered by Reconfigurable Intelligent Surfaces. *IEEE Systems Journal*, 1–4.

Zuo, J., Liu, Y., & Al-Dhahir, N. (Dec. 2020). Reconfigurable Intelligent Surface Assisted Cooperative Non-orthogonal Multiple Access Systems. *ArXiV*, 1–30.

13 Degradation of Reliability of Digital Electronic Equipment Over Time and Redundant Hardware-based Solutions

Athanasios Kakarountas and Vasileios Chioktour

CONTENTS

13.1 INTRODUCTION

A discontinuity of nowadays technology in low-power and high-performance portable computing is present when it comes to meet safe-operation demanding applications. The safety of these systems operation under hostile environments is achieved by introducing redundant hardware. Thus, with respect to the required level of safety, the safe system can even present three times the initial area cost and power dissipation of the non-safe system. The latter increases the requirements designs of small size and low-power [1, 2] in order to introduce to the market portable devices targeting safety-critical applications.

A variety of techniques to achieve design for testability have been proposed. The most common technique is the utilization of off-line Built-In Self-Test (BIST) units. These units are used either after manufacturing to verify functionality, or before operation after power up of the system. They are considered as diagnostic tools to detect

DOI: 10.1201/9781003203124-13

permanent errors due to faults belonging to a targeted fault model (e.g., stuck-at fault model). Their functionality is based on the application of test vectors to the input of the system under test and then comparison of the output with the expected one. Any deviation from the expected output detects a fault occurrence, which may be revealed after several test vectors are applied. In case the system is checked successfully without the detection of a fault, then the BIST unit is deactivated and the system starts its operation without being interrupted by the BIST unit until power goes off. More information on offline BIST units and techniques can be found in [3, 4].

In contrast, online BIST is achieved using dedicated hardware that allows error detection in due time. This approach requires the interruption of the system periodically by the BIST unit and set it under a test mode. This is achieved by storing the state of the system in memory, and during the test mode, test vectors (stored or generated by the BIST units) are applied to the inputs of the system. Then, the output of the system under test is read and compared to the expected one, which is also stored in the BIST unit's memory. The test mode is terminated if no erroneous output is detected after a short period of time, and the system is recovered to the previous state, before test mode was applied, by fetching previous values from memory. Usually a system is entering the test mode during idle operation, that is no operation of the microprocessor, or during low-power mode (which is in many applications similar to sleep or hibernate mode).

A special category of online BIST units is that of concurrent online testing, which is performed exploiting the inputs of the system as test vectors and testing is performed concurrently. The methods that are still used in this field have been introduced several decades ago contrary to applications' technological needs that target the modern multimedia and portable telecommunication market. These methods are based on the use of multi-channeled architectures of unreliable components [5] to continuously monitor the operation of the system.

The introduction of special encoding schemes to detect and correct errors has enabled the reduction of the requirements in terms of area and power. In any case, the approach of concurrent testing introduces a higher implementation cost than a system not embedding such special hardware, and the encoding scheme should be selected wisely. Since reliability and the self-testing property of the system is of utmost importance, a metric to evaluate the new structures is required. Lo and Fujiwara have introduced a probabilistic measure for self-checking (SC) circuits in [6]. This paper presents the effect of the known low-power methods, targeting minimization of bit activity in a circuit, on the TSCG(t) of a Self-Checking (SC) circuit and proposes an architecture to achieve the targeted TSCG(t).

13.2 RELIABILITY OF SELF-CHECKING CIRCUITS

The typical fault model widely used is based on the single fault occurrence, and hereinafter the stuck-at (s-a) fault model is considered, that is s-a-0 and s-a-1 cases. According to this fault model, faults occur one at a time, and the time interval between the occurrences of any two faults is sufficiently extended so that all input code words are applied to the circuit. The information bits derived from the data bits and the encoding bits are referred hereinafter as code word. In [6] a complete probabilistic measure is proposed for the SC circuits, which is analogous to the reliability of fault-tolerant systems. The probability to achieve TSC Goal in a circuit is defined as follows:

$$TSCG(t) = P\{\text{TSC goal is guaranteed at cycle } t\} = R(t)+S(t) \tag{13.1}$$

where R(t) represents the conditional probability that the circuit guarantees the TSC goal when the circuit is fault-free at cycle t, and S(t) is the conditional probability that a circuit guarantees the TSC goal when faults occur before or on cycle t. The term S(t) is calculated by adding all the probabilities that the circuit is fault-secure and/or self-testing with respect to the first fault and the probabilities that a fault is detected before a second one occurs. The term R(t) is the qualitative representation of the reliability of a circuit and it is relative to the constant failure rates. The term R(t) tends to value '0' as time reaches the Mean Time Before Failure (MTBF), as calculated by the manufacturer. Although, R(t) is characterized by the manufacturing process, in contrast S(t) is characterized by the number of test vectors applied to a system in a given time period, to ensure TSC property. Thus, the less test vectors applied in time, the less S(t) may contribute to TSCG. Due to the characteristic behavior of R(t) and S(t), the TSCG(t) is ranging in [0,1].

Formal Low-Power technique: The most common and broadly met technique used to dynamically manage power is the reduction of the activity on the units' inputs. A plethora of methods have been proposed on this technique, but the main discipline is the introduction of local control signals to manipulate the functionality of the circuit. Global signals like clock or reset can be gated by a local control signal and their propagation in the rest of the system can be dynamically controlled. Another method is the re-scheduling of the tasks to be executed (e.g., algorithm transformation) in order to reduce the activity on large global buses. More information about the latter techniques can be found in [1, 2].

13.3 THE IMPACT ON TSCG(T)

In Figure 13.1 a typical structure of a TSC checker tree that checks for fault occurrence in Units A and B is illustrated. Applying any technique to minimize the units' output activity, and consequently reduce power dissipation, will reduce the frequency of the test vector's bits activity. This results in turn to a constant test vector applied to the TSC checker inputs for a long period. Though the checker tree is considered to be TSC, this property can be maintained only if the input of the TSC circuit presents a certain activity, otherwise a fault may be masked (that is the fault remains undetectable before a second fault occurs). Unfolding the equation of the TSCG to its terms R(t) and S(t), the effect of the input activity can be better presented.

The S(t) term can be analyzed into two terms S1(t) and S2(t),

$$S(t)=S1(t)+S2(t) \tag{13.2}$$

The term S1(t) represents the conditional probability to detect the fault generating the erroneous output using one test vector, while S2(t) represents the conditional

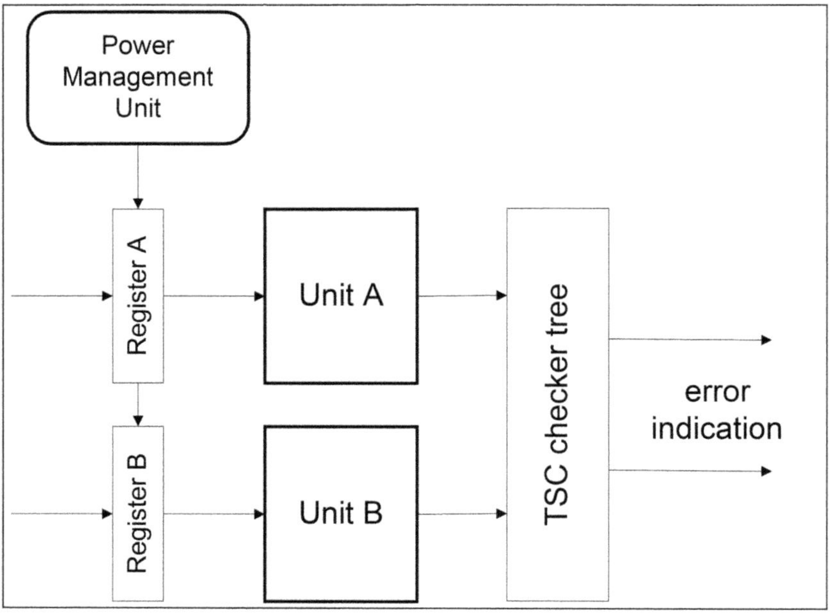

FIGURE 13.1 Formal architecture of an online testable system with a dynamic power management unit

probability to detect it using a combination of two vectors. There is no need to consider faults requiring more than two test vectors in sequence, since there is the need to detect a fault at first occurrence in due time. The last-mentioned term S2(t) is not contributing to the TSCG(t) when the input of the circuit is 'locked' to one state due to the application of a low-power technique. Furthermore, S1(t) is contributing to the TSCG(t) in a smaller degree due to the fact that only the possibilities to detect a fault with one input test vector (the 'locked' vector of the input) are participating to the calculation of S1(t).

$$S1(t) = \sum_{i=1}^{M}\sum_{j=1}^{t}\lambda_i \alpha^{t-j_b j}\left(\sum_{k=j}^{t}\frac{Q_i^{k-j}T_i b^{k-j}}{\alpha^{k-j}} + \frac{Q_i^{t-j+1}b^{t-j}}{\alpha^{t-j}}\right)$$

$$= \sum_{i=1}^{M}\lambda_i \left(\begin{array}{l} \dfrac{\alpha^{t+1}bT_i + b^{t+2}\left(Q_i - Q_i^{t+1}\right) - \alpha b^{t+1}\left(1 - Q_i^{t+1}\right)}{(\alpha - b)(\alpha - bQ_i)} \\ + \dfrac{b^t\left(Q_i - Q_i^{t+1}\right)}{T_i} \end{array}\right) \quad (13.3)$$

where T_i is the probability that error f_i can be detected at each cycle, and $Q_i^{k-j}T_i$ represents the probability that f_i is detected at the kth cycle given that $Q_i = 1-T_i$, $\alpha = e^{-\lambda i}, b = exp\left(-\sum_{r=1}^{N}\lambda_r\right)$.

$$S2(t)=\sum_{i=1}^{P}\sum_{j=1}^{t}\lambda_i\alpha^{t-j}b^j\left(\sum_{k=j+1}^{t}(k-j)\frac{T_i^2Q_i^{k-j-1}b^{k-j}}{\alpha^{k-j}}+\frac{b^{t-j}\left(Q_i^{t-j+1}+(t-j+1)T_iQ_j^t\right)}{\alpha^{t-j}}\right)$$

$$=\sum_{i=1}^{P}\lambda_i\left(\frac{\alpha^{t+1}b^2-\alpha b^{t+2}Q_i^t+tb^{t+3}Q_i^{t+1}}{(\alpha-b)(\alpha-bQ_i)^2}+\frac{tT_ib^{t+1}Q_i^t-b^{t+1}}{\alpha-b}\right.$$

$$\left.+\frac{\alpha b^{t+1}Q_i^t-b^{t+2}Q_i^{t+2}}{(\alpha-bQ_i)^2}+\frac{b^t(1+Q_i-Q_i^t-Q_i^{t+1}-tT_iQ_i^t}{T_i}\right)\ (1.4) \qquad (13.4)$$

The term R(t) remains unaffected, due to the fact that it is referring to the fault-free state of the circuit. Thus, to keep the TSCG(t) of a circuit in high levels its input bits must present a certain activity. In addition, a system that includes TSC checkers must maintain the TSCG(t) in high levels. Assuming exponential failure law, the reliability (at time instance t) of a circuit composed by N logic gates (can be expanded to components for systems) is given by

$$R(t)=\exp\left(-\sum_{i=1}^{N}\lambda_i t\right) \qquad (13.5)$$

where λ_i is the constant failure rate of gate (component) i. The exponential failure law is realistic for electronic components, since they are affected by effects like electromigration, thermal noise, which have an accumulative behavior that is better described by an exponential decrease. The above mentioned may be better understood with the following example.

EXAMPLE 1. Figure13.2 shows the TSC dual-rail checker. In Table 13.1, we summarize the T_is of this circuit for all the possible stuck-at-0 (s-a-0) and stuck-at-1

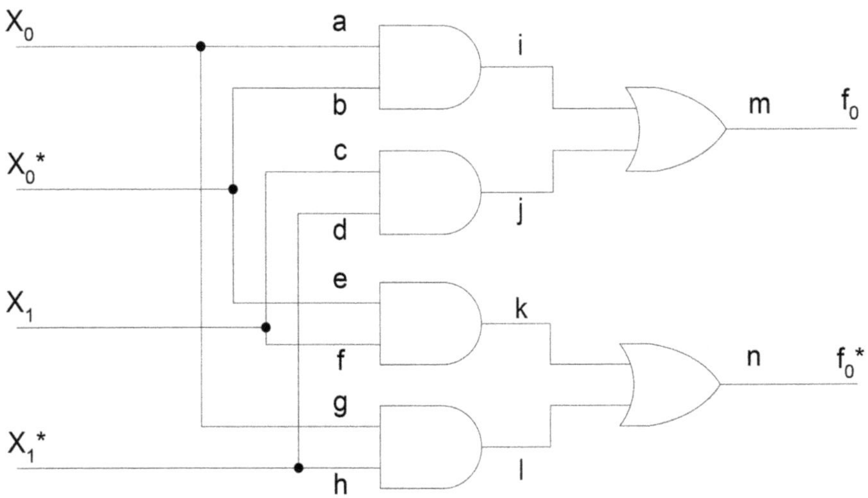

FIGURE 13.2 A Dual-Rail Totally-Self Checking Checker.

TABLE 13.1
The Tis of the Dual-Rail TSC Checker's Nodes

i	f_i	$\{x_0, x_0^*, x_1, x_1^*\}$	T_i	i	f_i	$\{x_0, x_0^*, x_1, x_1^*\}$	T_i
1	a s-a-0	1001	0.25	2	a s-a-1	0101	0.25
3	b s-a-0	1001	0.25	4	b s-a-1	1010	0.25
5	c s-a-0	0110	0.25	6	c s-a-1	1010	0.25
7	d s-a-0	0110	0.25	8	d s-a-1	0101	0.25
9	e s-a-0	1010	0.25	10	e s-a-1	0110	0.25
11	f s-a-0	1010	0.25	12	f s-a-1	1001	0.25
13	g s-a-0	0101	0.25	14	g s-a-1	1001	0.25
15	h s-a-0	0101	0.25	16	h s-a-1	0110	0.25
17	i s-a-0	1001	0.25	18	i s-a-1	0101,1010	0.50
19	j s-a-0	0110	0.25	20	j s-a-1	0101,1010	0.50
21	k s-a-0	1010	0.25	22	k s-a-1	0110,1001	0.50
23	l s-a-0	0101	0.25	24	l s-a-1	0110,1001	0.50
25	m s-a-0	0110,1001	0.50	26	m s-a-1	0101,1010	0.50
27	n s-a-0	0101,1010	0.50	28	n s-a-1	0110,1001	0.50

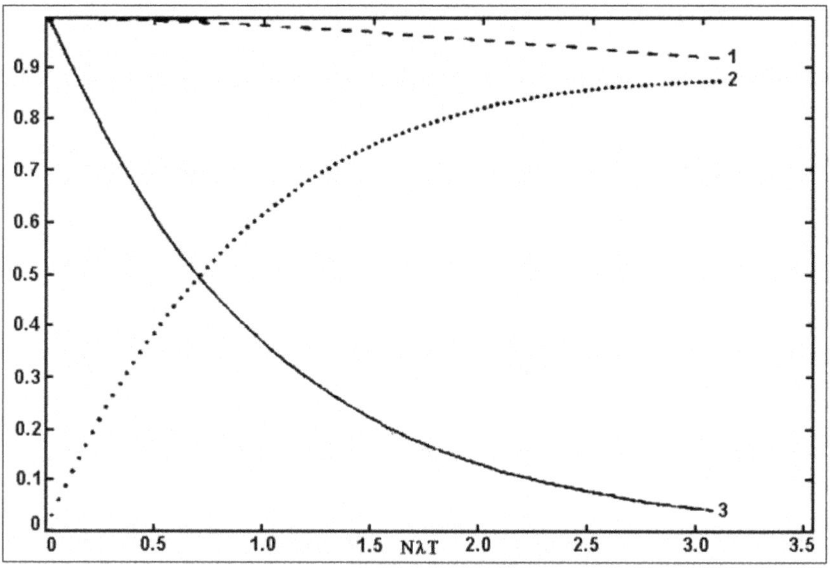

FIGURE 13.3 The calculation of TSCG(t), S(t) and R(t) in time.

(s-a-1) faults. There are 28 possible faults in total: 20 of them are detected by one code word input, i.e., $T_i = 0.25$, and eight of them are detected by two code word inputs, i.e., $T_i = 0.5$. Therefore, N = 28, M = 28 and P = 0. Assuming identical failure rate, $\lambda_i = \lambda$ for all i, the reliability R(t), TSCG(t) and S(t) of this gate level TSC two-rail checker are plotted in Figure 13.3.

13.4 STATIC CONFRONTATION OF THE TSC PROPERTY DEGRADATION

In the past a novel architecture was proposed by the authors to preserve the level of the TSCG(t) [7]. The main target of the architecture is to use time-slots and perform automated testing during idle state of units with reduced activity due to the application of a low-power technique. The inputs (T) of these units (usually) follow the same encoding of their output (T'). Thus, feeding the units' inputs T instead of their outputs T' to the TSC checker tree the required activity to the SC circuit is achieved. In Figure 13.4 the proposed architecture is illustrated. The main target of the proposed architecture is to increase the term S2(t) when the input activity is decreased due to a low power technique application. This is achieved by contributing with an extra S2'(t) which is derived from the by-pass technique. Thus, the new input T of the TSC circuit preserves the level of the TSCG(t), due to the fact that T_i, that corresponds to the sum of the arrival rates of all second tests of error f_i, is no more equal to zero. This is valid, due to the fact that $T_{i,1}$ and $T_{i,2}$, the sum of the arrival rates of all first and second tests respectively, are equal when a low-power technique is applied.

An extra advantage of this architecture is the low area overhead that is introduced. The area overhead due to the addition of a 2-to-1 multiplexer isn't significant although the critical path is slightly increased. This architecture can guarantee the level of the TSCG(t) assuming that the new inputs T of the TSC checker tree are not also subject to a low-power technique. Thus, exploration of every input T must be performed before selecting it as an alternative input for the TSC checker tree.

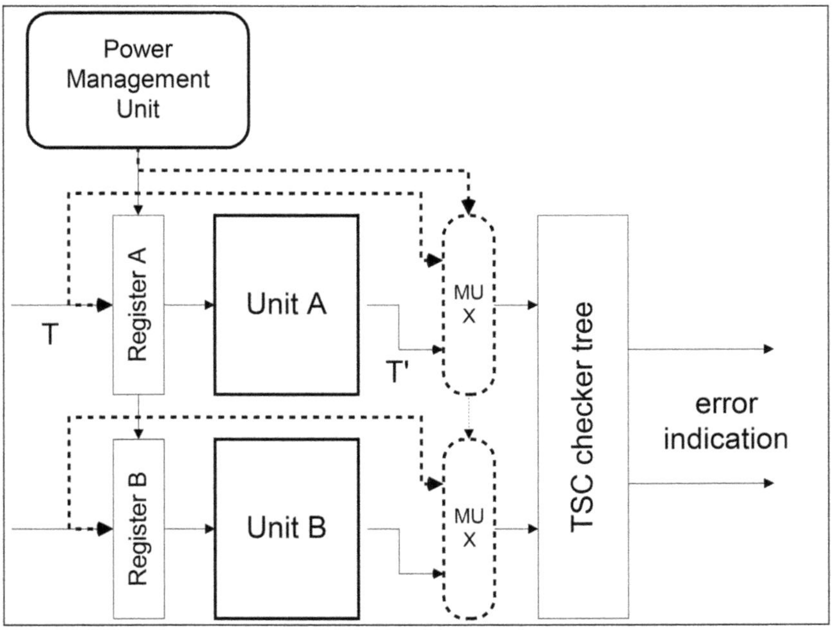

FIGURE 13.4 The proposed architecture with by-pass and input re-use technique.

The EDA (Electronic Design Automation) tools (e.g., Synopsys Design Compiler, Formality, TestMAX DFT [8]) that are used to implement the targeted algorithm can be used to extract this information. An analytical investigation of the Control Data Flow Graph (CDFG) of the system and comparison to the dynamic power management algorithm provides all the required information. In the case that no input T is appropriate for the proposed architecture, a hybrid of the proposed architecture and the Built-In Self Test technique can be used. This architecture is illustrated on Figure 13.5. An Automatic Test Pattern Generator (ATPG) unit is used to generate the required vectors. Thus, an on-line BIST mode is activated and any error will produce erroneous output (error indication). A Linear-Feedback Shift Register (LFSR) can be used as the ATPG unit. This hybrid architecture presents an extra area overhead due to the insertion of the ATPG unit while the TSC checker tree must be actually duplicated to check in addition the ATPG unit.

The effect of the degradation of the TSCG(t) due to the application of low-power techniques was investigated for the two-rail checker (TRC), which is a commonly used TSC checker. In Figure 13.6 the TSCG(t) is illustrated before and after this technique's application. This checker presents the R(t) and S(t) (curves 2 and 3 respectively) and their sum results TSCG(t) (curve 1), as they can be calculated from equations (13.1), (13.2) and (13.3). Applying a low-power technique, there is no effect on the R(t) term. However, the S(t) degrades, as it is illustrated in Figure 13.6 (curve 4), due to the reasons described in Section 13.3. Thus, a new degraded TSCG'(t) is resulted as shown in curve 5. Using the proposed architecture, the level of TSCG(t) is

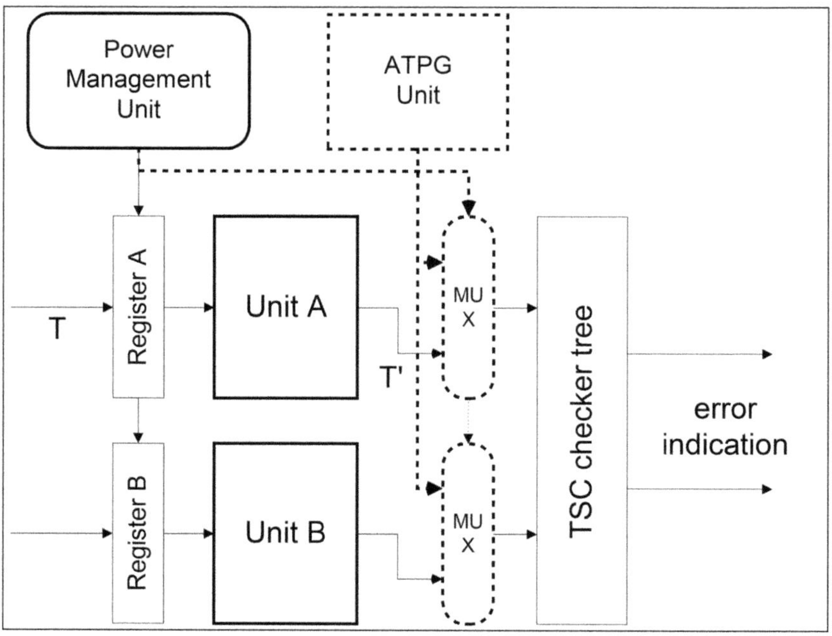

FIGURE 13.5 The proposed architecture with the use of the ATPG unit.

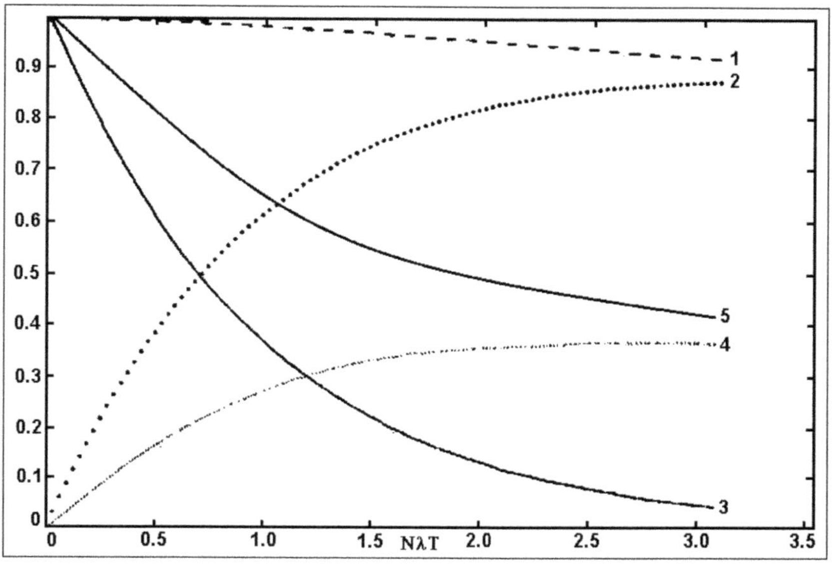

FIGURE 13.6 The degrading effect of the activity reduction on the input of a two-rail checker.

preserved to the initial value. The power dissipation of the unit under dynamic power management is kept low, while power dissipation on the TSC checker is reduced to the lowest possible.

Due to the nature of the technique there is no qualitative measure available to show the order of magnitude of the introduced power dissipation penalty. In fact, it is highly dependent of the unit's function and the length of the TSC checkers inputs. Thus, this technique is advisable and efficient for application in high levels of the design flow.

In order to show the efficiency of this technique, it was applied on a processing core that was developed in the bounds of the CoSafe design approach. The core was designed so that it can be embedded in systems targeting safety-critical applications. A significant design constraint of the core was the requirement for low-power dissipation [9], without violating the safety levels of its operation.

In Table 13.2 below, the characteristics of the core are offered, while in Table 13.3 below the area and power penalty are showed, normalized to the initial design. The enhancement of the TSCG(t) is also showed in Table 13.3. The benefits of the proposed implementation have been identified as the decay of degradation of the reliability of the digital circuit. However, the drawback of the proposed work is the fact that the test vectors are applied sequentially, as stored in memory. This approach poses a considerable risk, since there is statistically significant probability to mask an error, if the appropriate test vector is not applied in due time. Additionally, no statistical analysis is performed, during design, on the applied test vectors, since the generation of the test vectors set is independent from the application of the actual input during normal operation.

TABLE 13.2
The Main Characteristics of the Cosafe Processing Core

Feature	Measure
Core	8-bit Data Bus, 16-bit Address Bus, 256 Direct Address Peripherals, Built-In Signature Analysis, Watchdog, Wallace Multiplier, Barrel Shifter
Area	38,000eq. gates (27 mm^2, AMS 0,6um)
Power consumption	7.5 mW/MHz (upper bound)

TABLE 13.3
Effects of the Technique's Application

	Power	Area	TSCG(t)
Initial	100%	100%	0.55
After technique's application	102.8%	101%	0.98

13.5 DYNAMIC CONFRONTATION OF THE TSC PROPERTY DEGRADATION

A novel architecture for dynamic confrontation of the TSC property degradation over time is proposed in this subsection. It is based on the previously mentioned architecture, embedding a more sophisticated mechanism for the automatic test-vector generation. The new mechanism is comprised by k ATPG circuits, which generate k clusters of test-vectors. The k clusters were resulted by the application of a k-Means algorithm on the digital system during design phase, at the generation of the minimized test-vectors set to achieve the highest fault coverage.

During the operation of the proposed implementation, the actual inputs are analyzed by the k-Means component and are included to one of the k clusters. For performance reasons, high-speed counters [10] are used to count the appearance of an input belonging to the corresponding cluster. Then a comparison of the counters' values is performed, and the counter of the minimum value is selected. Thus, the cluster of the least appeared inputs is selected and the appropriate ATPG is selected to stimulate the circuit under test during its idle state.

This approach allows dynamic selection of the test-vectors subset confronting not only the degradation of the TSC property over time, but also address the high probability for masking of a fault in due time. This approach successfully considers the dynamic nature of the inputs and addresses the drawback of the previously mentioned implementation. Although the benefits are significant, there is in contrast an increase in integration area, which, however, is affordable for safety-critical applications.

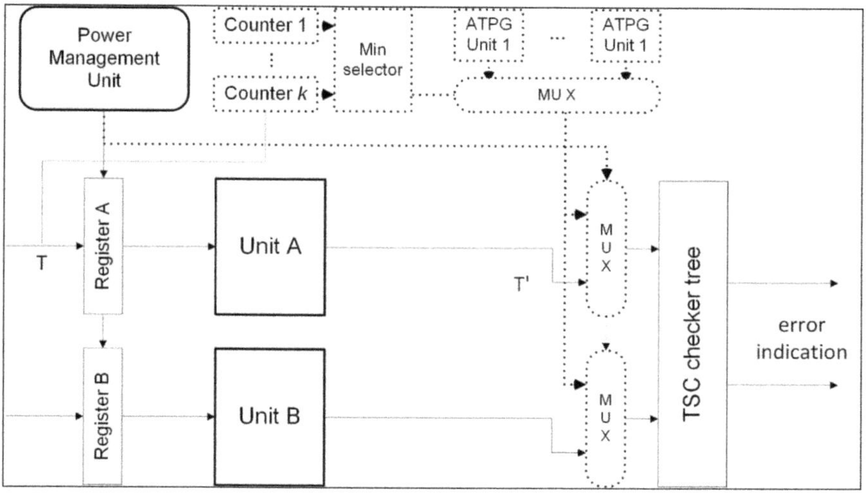

FIGURE 13.7 Dynamic selection of test vectors set to confront degrading effect due to late appearance of the appropriate test vector.

13.6 CONCLUSIONS

It has been illustrated that the application of low-power techniques on safety-critical systems that embed concurrent online BIST techniques degrades its testability. An example that exhibits the effect of low-activity on a network of TSC checkers was presented. The terms of TSCG(t) have proven to be sensitive to minimization of the activity of the inputs. Thus, extra consideration has be paid to the design of extra mechanisms that maintain the TSCG(t) of critical units in acceptable levels. An architecture that confronts TSCG(t) degradation due to low-power modes imposed to the system has been proposed and the typical Two-Rail Checker was used as an example.

REFERENCES

[1] Raghunathan, A., Jha, N.K., and Dey, S., *High-Level Power Analysis and Optimization*, Kluwer Academic Publishers, New York, 1998.

[2] Chandrakasan, A., and Brodersen, R.W., *Low Power Digital CMOS Design*, Kluwer Academic Publishers, Boston, USA, 1995.

[3] Abramovici, M., Breuer, M.A., and Friedman, A.D., *Digital Systems Testing and Testable Design*, IEEE Press, New York, 1992.

[4] Bushnell, M.L., and Agrawal, V.D., *Essentials of Electronic Testing for Digital, Memory and Mixed-signal VLSI Circuits*, Kluwer Academic Publishers, Boston, MA, 2001, 2nd printing.

[5] Pradhan, D.K., *Fault-Tolerant Computer System Design*, Prentice-Hall, Upper Saddle River, NJ, 1996.

[6] Lo, J.-C., and Fujiwara, E., "Probability to Achieve TSC Goal," *IEEE Transactions on Computers*, vol. 45, no. 4, pp. 450–460, April 1996.
[7] Soudris, D., Piguet, C., and Goutis, C.E. (eds.), *Designing CMOS Circuits for Low Power*, Springer Publishing Company, Incorporated, Boston, MA, 2002.
[8] Zorian, A., Shanyour, B., and Vaseekar, M., "Machine Learning-Based DFT Recommendation System for ATPG QOR," in *Proceedings of 2019 IEEE International Test Conference (ITC)*, IEEE, 2019.
[9] Kakarountas, A.P., Papadomanolakis, K.S., Spiliotopoulos, V., Nikolaidis, S., and Goutis, C.E., "Designing a Low Power Fault-Tolerant Microcontroller for Medicine Infusion Devices," in *Proceedings of DATE2002*, IEEE, Paris, March 2002.
[10] Kakarountas, A.P., Theodoridis, G., Papadomanolakis, K.S., and Goutis, C.E., "A Novel High-speed Counter with Counting Rate Independent of the Counter's Length," *Proceedings of the 10th IEEE International Conference on Electronics, Circuits and Systems*, vol. 3, pp. 1164–1167, 2003.

Index

For Product Safety Concerns and Information please contact our EU representative GPSR@taylorandfrancis.com
Taylor & Francis Verlag GmbH, Kaufingerstraße 24, 80331 München, Germany

www.ingramcontent.com/pod-product-compliance
Ingram Content Group UK Ltd.
Pitfield, Milton Keynes, MK11 3LW, UK
UKHW020158200926
475702UK00004B/518
* 9 7 8 1 0 3 2 0 6 6 2 5 7 *